W9-BYL-454

REA's Test Prep Books Are The Best!

(a sample of the <u>hundreds of letters</u> REA receives each year)

" I did well because of your wonderful prep books... I just wanted to thank you for helping me prepare for these tests. "

Student, San Diego, CA

" My students report your chapters of review as the most valuable single resource they used for review and preparation. "

Teacher, American Fork, UT

" Your book was such a better value and was so much more complete than anything your competition has produced (and I have them all!). "

Teacher, Virginia Beach, VA

" Compared to the other books that my fellow students had, your book was the most useful in helping me get a great score. "

Student, North Hollywood, CA

" Your book was responsible for my success on the exam, which helped me get into the college of my choice... I will look for REA the next time I need help. "

Student, Chesterfield, MO

" Just a short note to say thanks for the great support your book gave me in helping me pass the test... I'm on my way to a B.S. degree because of you! "

Student, Orlando, FL

(more on next page)

(continued from front page)

" I just wanted to thank you for helping me get a great score
on the AP U.S. History exam... Thank you for making great test preps! "
Student, Los Angeles, CA

" Your *Fundamentals of Engineering Exam* book was the absolute best
preparation I could have had for the exam, and it is one of the major
reasons I did so well and passed the FE on my first try. "
Student, Sweetwater, TN

" I used your book to prepare for the test and found that the advice and the
sample tests were highly relevant... Without using any other material, I earned
very high scores and will be going to the graduate school of my choice. "
Student, New Orleans, LA

" What I found in your book was a wealth of information sufficient to shore up
my basic skills in math and verbal... The section on analytical ability was
excellent. The practice tests were challenging and the answer explanations most
helpful. It certainly is the *Best Test Prep for the GRE*! "
Student, Pullman, WA

" I really appreciate the help from your excellent book. Please keep up
the great work. "
Student, Albuquerque, NM

" I am writing to thank you for your test preparation... your book helped me
immeasurably and I have nothing but praise for your *GRE* preparation."
Student, Benton Harbor, MI

(more on back page)

U.S. History
for *Builder*
Standardized Tests

By the Staff of
Research & Education Association

Research & Education Association
Visit our website at
www.rea.com

Research & Education Association
61 Ethel Road West
Piscataway, New Jersey 08854
E-mail: info@rea.com

U.S. HISTORY BUILDER
for Standardized Tests

Copyright © 2007, 2002, 2000, 1998, 1995 by Research & Education Association, Inc. All rights reserved. No part of this book may be reproduced in any form without permission of the publisher.

Printed in the United States of America

Library of Congress Control Number 2006937337

International Standard Book Number 0-87891-961-9

REA® is a registered trademark of Research & Education Association, Inc.

CONTENTS

ACKNOWLEDGMENTS

We would like to thank Paul R. Babbitt, Ph.D., for compiling and editing the manuscript; John Chilton, Ph.D., for his technical editing of the manuscript; Adriane Ruggiero, M.A., and Miriam Greenblatt, M.S., for their editorial contributions to the manuscript. In addition, we would like to thank Larry B. Kling, Vice President, Editorial, for his editorial direction; Pam Weston, Vice President, Publishing, for setting the quality standards for production integrity and managing the publication to completion; Christine Saul, Senior Graphic Designer, for our cover design; Molly Solanki, Associate Editor, for coordinating revisions; and Rachel DiMatteo, Graphic Designer, for typesetting revisions.

CHAPTER 1

About the U.S. History Builder

ABOUT RESEARCH & EDUCATION ASSOCIATION

REA is an organization of educators, scientists, and engineers specializing in various academic fields. REA was founded in 1959 for the purpose of disseminating the most recently developed scientific information to groups in industry, government, high schools, and universities. Since then, REA has become a successful and highly respected publisher of study aids, test preparation books, handbooks, and reference works.

REA's Test Preparation series extensively prepares students and professionals for the Graduate Record Examination (GRE), Graduate Management Admission Test (GMAT), SAT®, Medical College Admission Test (MCAT), and Advanced Placement exams.

REA's publications and educational materials are highly regarded for their significant contribution to the quest for excellence that characterizes today's educational goals. We continually receive an unprecedented amount of praise from professionals, instructors, librarians, parents, and students for our published books. Our authors are as diverse as the subjects and fields represented in the books we publish. They are well-known in their respective fields and serve on the faculties of prestigious high schools, colleges, and universities throughout the United States and Canada.

Today REA's wide-ranging catalog is a leading resource for teachers, students, and professionals.

We invite you to visit us at *www.rea.com* to find out how "REA is making the world smarter."

ABOUT THIS BOOK

REA's staff of authors and educators has prepared material, exercises, and tests compatible with each of the major standardized exams, including the Advanced Placement (AP®) United States History, SAT® Subject Test in United States History, Praxis™ Specialty Area Test in Social Studies, CLEP® General Examination in Social Sciences and History, GED, and the two CLEP® subject exams in U.S History. The types of questions represented on these exams have been analyzed in order to produce the most comprehensive preparatory material possible. You will find review material, helpful strategies, and exercises geared to your level of studying. This book will teach as well as review and refresh your knowledge of U.S. history needed to score high on standardized tests.

HOW TO USE THIS BOOK

If you are preparing to take the AP® United States History, GED, or the SAT® Subject Test in United States History, or one of the Praxis® or CLEP® exams, you will be taking a test that requires an excellent knowledge of U.S. history. This book comprises a comprehensive U.S. history review that can be tailored to your specific test preparation needs.

Locate your test on the chart shown on pages 4 and 5, and then find the corresponding sections recommended for study. REA suggests that you study the indicated material thoroughly as a review for your exam.

CROSS-REFERENCING CHART

	1500–1763 Chapter 2 Pages 9–58	1763–1787 Chapter 3 Pages 59–100	1787–1789 Chapter 4 Pages 101–128	1789–1824 Chapter 5 Pages 129–181	1824–1850 Chapter 6 Pages 182–246	1850–1861 Chapter 7 Pages 247–285	1861–1877 Chapter 8 Pages 287–335
AP United States History	X	X	X	X	X	X	X
CLEP General Exam Social Sciences & History	X	X	X	X	X	X	X
CLEP U.S. History I	X	X	X	X	X	X	X
CLEP U.S. History II						X	X
GED	X	X	X	X	X	X	X
Praxis Specialty Area Test: Social Studies	X	X	X	X	X	X	X
SAT United States History	X	X	X	X	X	X	X

CROSS-REFERENCING CHART

	1877–1912 Chapter 9 Pages 337–416	1912–1920 Chapter 10 Pages 417–463	1920–1929 Chapter 11 Pages 465–502	1929–1941 Chapter 12 Pages 503–553	1941–1960 Chapter 13 Pages 555–609	1960–1972 Chapter 14 Pages 611–648	1972–2001 Chapter 15 Pages 649–690
AP United States History	X	X	X	X	X	X	X
CLEP General Exam Social Sciences & History	X	X	X	X	X	X	X
CLEP U.S. History I	X	X	X	X			
CLEP U.S. History II	X	X	X	X	X	X	X
GED	X	X	X	X	X	X	X
Praxis Specialty Area Test: Social Studies	X	X	X	X	X	X	X
SAT: United States History	X	X	X	X	X	X	X

This book will help you prepare for your exam because it includes different types of questions and drills that are representative of what appears on each exam. The book also includes diagnostic tests so that you can determine your strengths and weaknesses within a specific subject. The explanations are clear and comprehensive, explaining why the answer is correct. REA's U.S. History Builder gives you practice within a wide range of categories and question types.

1500-1763: The Colonial Period prepares students for questions on the AP United States History, GED, CLEP General, CLEP United States History I, Praxis Specialty Area, and SAT: United States History exams. It includes a comprehensive review of the exploration by Europeans of the New World, and the establishment and development of colonies in North America.

1763-1787: The American Revolution prepares students for questions on the AP United States History, CLEP General, CLEP United States History I, GED, Praxis Specialty Area, and SAT: United States History exams. The events of this period, including the acts of the British Parliament which led the colonies to revolution, the war for independence, and the creation of new governments are fully covered.

1787-1789: The United States Constitution helps students prepare for questions on the AP United States History, CLEP General, CLEP United States History I, GED, Praxis Specialty Area, and SAT: United States History exams. It reviews the development and ratification of the Constitution, as well as providing an outline of the Articles of the Constitution.

1789-1824: The New Nation discusses events under the new Constitution, from the presidency of George Washington through the Monroe administration, including the Louisiana Purchase and the War of 1812. Students should study this chapter to prepare for the AP United States History, CLEP General, CLEP United States History I, GED, Praxis Specialty Area, and SAT: United States History exams.

1824-1850: Jacksonian Democracy and Westward Expansion will prepare students for questions on the AP United States History, CLEP General, CLEP United States History I, GED, Praxis Specialty Area, and SAT: United States History exams. This chapter reviews democracy under the Jackson administration, the diverging life in the Southern states, westward expansion, and the war with Mexico under the Polk administration.

1850-1861: Sectional Conflict reviews the development of the rift between the Northern and Southern states which led to the secession of Southern states. Students should study this chapter to prepare for questions on the AP United States History, CLEP General, CLEP United States History I, GED, Praxis Specialty Area, and SAT: United States History exams.

1861-1877: The Civil War and Reconstruction will prepare students to answer questions on the AP United States History, CLEP General, CLEP United States History I and II, GED, Praxis Specialty Area, and SAT: United States History exams. The chapter reviews the events of the Civil War from the outbreak of hostilities to Reconstruction under the Johnson and Grant administrations, through the Compromise of 1877.

1877-1912: Industrialism and the Progressive Era reviews the events of the period, including technological and social developments, their role in the changing economy, and America's increasing political and financial involvement on the international level. Students should study this chapter to answer questions on the AP United States History, CLEP General, CLEP United States History II, GED, Praxis Specialty Area, and SAT: United States History exams.

1912-1920: Wilson and World War I will prepare students to answer questions on the AP United States History, CLEP General, CLEP United States History II, GED, Praxis Specialty Area, and SAT: United States History exams. This chapter reviews the events of these years, including the Wilson administrations, the events leading to America's involvement in World War I, and the aftermath of the war.

1920-1929: The Roaring Twenties and Economic Collapse reviews the social conflicts of the 1920s and the economic events leading to the stock market crash of 1929. Students should study this chapter to prepare for questions on the AP United States History, CLEP General, CLEP United States History II, GED, Praxis Specialty Area, and SAT: United States History exams.

1929-1941: The Great Depression and the New Deal will prepare students to answer questions on the AP United States History, CLEP General, CLEP United States History II, GED, Praxis Specialty Area, and SAT: United States History exams. This chapter provides a comprehensive review of the causes of the Great Depression, and recovery under the first and second New Deals as America became involved in the events of World War II.

1941-1960: World War II and the Postwar Era reviews American history in this period—including United States participation in World War II, the anticommunism of the 1950s and the Cold War, the war in Korea, and the beginnings of the civil rights movement in this country. Students should study this chapter to prepare for questions on the AP United States History, CLEP General, CLEP United States History II, GED, Praxis Specialty Area, and SAT: United States History exams.

1960-1972: The New Frontier, Vietnam and Social Upheaval will prepare students for questions on the AP United States History, CLEP General, CLEP United States History II, GED, Praxis Specialty Area, and SAT: United States History exams. It thoroughly reviews the events of the Kennedy administration, the progress of civil rights in the 1960s and the "New Left," and American involvement in Vietnam.

1972-2001: Watergate and the New Conservatism reviews the Watergate scandal under the Nixon administration, America's continuing involvement in Vietnam, events of the Carter administration (including the Iranian hostage crisis and the Camp David Accords), domestic and foreign policy issues during the Reagan, Bush, and Clinton administrations, the early days of the second Bush administration (after one of the tightest elections in American history), and the collapse of Communism. This chapter should be studied by students preparing to take the AP United States History, CLEP General, CLEP United States History II, GED, Praxis Specialty Area, and SAT: United States History exams.

Finally, before getting started, here are a few guidelines:

➤ Study full chapters. If you think after a few minutes that the chapter appears easy, continue studying. Many chapters (like the tests themselves) become more difficult as they continue.

➤ Use this guide as a supplement to the review materials provided by the test administrators.

➤ Take the diagnostic test before each review chapter, even if you feel confident that you already know the material well enough to skip a particular chapter. Taking the diagnostic test will put your mind at ease: you will discover either that you absolutely know the material or that you need to review. This will eliminate the panic you might otherwise experience during the test upon discovering that you have forgotten how to approach a certain type of question.

As you prepare for a standardized test in U.S. history, you will want to review the various historical periods and events. The more familiar you are with these periods and events, the better you will do on your test. Our U.S. history review represents the various historical periods and events that appear on standardized U.S. history tests or those tests with U.S. history sections.

Along with knowledge of these historical periods and events, how quickly and accurately you answer history questions will have an effect on your success. All tests have time limits, so the more questions you can answer correctly in the given period of time, the better off you will be. Our suggestion is that you first take each diagnostic test, make sure to complete the drills as you review for extra practice, and to take the Mini Tests when you feel confident with the material. Pay special attention to both the time it takes to complete the diagnostic tests and Mini Tests, and the number of correct answers you achieve.

The glossary at the end of each chapter will also refresh your memory after you have completed the reviews and drills. Important terms, events, and groups are clearly defined to enhance your study regimen.

CHAPTER 2

1500–1763
THE COLONIAL PERIOD

➤ Diagnostic Test
➤ 1500–1763 Review & Drills
➤ Glossary

1500-1763
DIAGNOSTIC TEST

1. (A) (B) (C) (D) (E)		19. (A) (B) (C) (D) (E)
2. (A) (B) (C) (D) (E)		20. (A) (B) (C) (D) (E)
3. (A) (B) (C) (D) (E)		21. (A) (B) (C) (D) (E)
4. (A) (B) (C) (D) (E)		22. (A) (B) (C) (D) (E)
5. (A) (B) (C) (D) (E)		23. (A) (B) (C) (D) (E)
6. (A) (B) (C) (D) (E)		24. (A) (B) (C) (D) (E)
7. (A) (B) (C) (D) (E)		25. (A) (B) (C) (D) (E)
8. (A) (B) (C) (D) (E)		26. (A) (B) (C) (D) (E)
9. (A) (B) (C) (D) (E)		27. (A) (B) (C) (D) (E)
10. (A) (B) (C) (D) (E)		28. (A) (B) (C) (D) (E)
11. (A) (B) (C) (D) (E)		29. (A) (B) (C) (D) (E)
12. (A) (B) (C) (D) (E)		30. (A) (B) (C) (D) (E)
13. (A) (B) (C) (D) (E)		31. (A) (B) (C) (D) (E)
14. (A) (B) (C) (D) (E)		32. (A) (B) (C) (D) (E)
15. (A) (B) (C) (D) (E)		33. (A) (B) (C) (D) (E)
16. (A) (B) (C) (D) (E)		34. (A) (B) (C) (D) (E)
17. (A) (B) (C) (D) (E)		35. (A) (B) (C) (D) (E)
18. (A) (B) (C) (D) (E)		

1500–1763
DIAGNOSTIC TEST

This diagnostic test is designed to help you determine your strengths and weaknesses in your knowledge of the Colonial Period (1500-1763). Follow the directions for each part and check your answers.

Study this chapter for the following tests:
AP U.S. History, CLEP General, CLEP United States History I,
GED, Praxis Specialty Area, SAT: United States History

---

35 Questions

DIRECTIONS: Choose the correct answer for each of the following questions. Fill in each answer on the answer sheet.

1. All of the following were early explorers of North America EXCEPT

   (A) Francisco Coronado.   (B) Robert La Salle.

   (C) Samuel de Champlain.   (D) Francisco Pizarro.

   (E) Jacques Marquette.

2. Which of the following was NOT involved in the "triangular trade" of the colonial period?

   (A) Rum   (B) Molasses

   (C) Cotton   (D) Slaves

   (E) Tobacco

3. Colonial law generally defined slaves as chattels. This meant that they were considered

   (A) human beings with limited rights.

   (B) servants who served for a limited period of time.

   (C) slaves who received freedom upon the death of their masters.

   (D) pieces of property with no rights.

   (E) employees who received pay for their work.

4. Which of the following correctly describes the Puritans?

    (A) Their primary goal was to find gold.

    (B) They established the Virginia Colony.

    (C) They established an economy based on tobacco.

    (D) They wanted to build a society based upon biblical teachings.

    (E) They established religious toleration. *Roger Williams*

5. The French and Indian War took place during

    (A) 1740–1748.   (B) 1754–1763.

    (C) 1689–1699.   (D) 1702–1713.

    (E) 1776–1783.

6. The leading scientist in colonial America was

    (A) John Peter Zenger.   (B) Jonathan Edwards.

    (C) William Byrd.   (D) Benjamin Franklin.

    (E) George Whitefield.

7. Historians believe the British trade regulations during the colonial period

    (A) were bad for all the American colonies.

    (B) favored the Southern colonies over the Northern colonies.

    (C) provided both advantages and disadvantages for the American colonies.

    (D) encouraged the development of colonial industry.

    (E) favored the Northern colonies over the Southern colonies.

8. Which of the following statements best describes the ethnic makeup of colonial America?

    (A) French Huguenots settled heavily in New England.

    (B) Germans concentrated in Pennsylvania.

    (C) The Scots- (or Scotch-) Irish moved into the southern tidewater area.

    (D) Maryland was largely a Dutch-dominated colony.

    (E) Spanish and Portuguese Jews settled in the Appalachian backcountry.

9. The rights to "life, liberty, and property" are associated with which political philosopher?

    (A) Roger Williams   (B) Benjamin Franklin

(C)   John Winthrop   • (D)   John Locke
                                                Enlightenment

(E)   Francis Drake

10.   The immediate issue in dispute in Bacon's Rebellion was

   (A)   the jailing of individuals or seizure of their property for failure to pay taxes during a time of economic hardship.

 • (B)   the under-representation of the backcountry in Virginia's legislature.

   (C)   the refusal of large planters to honor the terms of their contracts with former indentured servants.

   (D)   the perceived failure of Virginia's governor to protect the colony's frontier area from the depredations of raiding Indians.

   (E)   the colonial governor's manipulation of tobacco prices for the benefit of himself and a small clique of his friends.

11.   The main reason for the British colonial authorities' preference for royal colonies over those with other types of government was

 • (A)   the desire to exercise closer control over the colonies.

   (B)   the desire to prevent corruption within colonial governments.

   (C)   the desire to assure that the rights of the colonists were not infringed by greedy proprietors.

   (D)   the need to reduce the size of the colonial bureaucracy.

   (E)   the desire to increase colonial prosperity.

12.   The first religious development to have an impact throughout colonial America was

   (A)   the establishment of religious toleration in Maryland.

   (B)   the spread of Quaker ideas from Pennsylvania.

   (C)   the Half-Way Covenant.

   (D)   the Parsons' Cause.   *Anglican Church*

 • (E)   the Great Awakening.

13.   All of the following helped shape the development of colonial American agriculture EXCEPT

   (A)   availability of land.

 • (B)   abundance of capital.

   (C)   limitations of climate and land.

(D) shortage of labor.

(E) European demand for agricultural products.

14. In which of the following colonies was the economy in the eighteenth century dependent on the cultivation of rice and indigo?

(A) Pennsylvania

(B) Maryland

(C) Virginia

(D) North Carolina

(E) South Carolina

15. The Great Awakening of the mid-eighteenth century refers to

(A) a series of religious revivals that swept through the English colonies spreading evangelistic fervor and challenging the control of traditional clerics over their congregations.

(B) the intellectual revolution which served as a precursor to the Enlightenment and challenged orthodox religion's claims to knowledge of humankind and the universe.

(C) the beginnings of the Industrial Revolution in England and its New World colonies.

(D) the growing realization among English colonists that independence from England was only a matter of time and was the key to their future success.

(E) the sudden awareness among North American Indians that their only chance for survival against the rapidly growing number of European colonists was to fight them before the Europeans grew any stronger.

16. The Albany Congress of 1754 was convened for the major purpose of

(A) adding New York to the Dominion of New England.

(B) getting the colonies to form a "grand council" to coordinate their western expansion and their common defense against Indians.

(C) uniting the colonies under a "grand council" to resist British economic sanctions and coordinate activities against British tax officials.

(D) cooperating with the French in their efforts to rid western New York and southern Canada of raiding Indian tribes.

(E) writing a proclamation to be sent to King George in protest of the Stamp Act.

17. The first successful English colony in North America was located in

    (A) Roanoke, Virginia.   (B) Plymouth, Massachusetts.

    ·(C) Jamestown, Virginia.   (D) Salem, Massachusetts.

    (E) Manhattan, New York.

18. Which of the following is NOT true of English colonial families in mid-eighteenth century America?

    (A) Physical punishment was the normal method of enforcing unquestioned obedience from children.

    (B) Women lost virtually all of their legal rights as individuals once they married.

    (C) Most families bore children who lived long enough to bear children of their own.

    (D) Women, while subservient to their husbands, set the moral standards by which children were raised and decided how the children would be educated and trained. *NoT YeT "Republican Mother"*

    (E) More than 90 percent of families lived in rural areas at about this time.

19. A major impact of the French and Indian War on the attitudes of Americans was

    (A) it led many Americans to question the superiority of English colonial rule and to support French colonial rule.

    (B) it convinced most Americans to avoid further exploration and settlement of the Ohio and Mississippi valleys until after the American Revolution.

    (C) it bound the American colonists more tightly to England than ever before and made most of them realize they needed English protection from foreign powers such as the French.

    (D) it led many colonists who had previously supported independence from England to call for moderation because they feared that the huge British military presence in the colonies (brought over from England to fight the French) could now be turned on rebellious colonists.

    ·(E) with the threat of the French now gone from their borders, many colonists now felt that English protection was unnecessary and they felt free to take a more independent stand toward Britain than they had taken previously.

18 + 33
Clarify Women's
RMoMB + Re ES

20. All of the following contributed to the success and stability of the New England colonies, and the bare survival of the Chesapeake Bay colonies EXCEPT

    (A) New England colonists tended to arrive in family units while the vast majority of Chesapeake Bay colonists were young single males who arrived as indentured servants.

    (B) the Chesapeake Bay region had a much higher death rate among its colonists than did the New England region.

    (C) women were treated more as equals in the New England colonies than they were in the Chesapeake Bay region, making it more difficult to attract women to Chesapeake Bay.

    (D) the ratio of males to females in Chesapeake Bay was much more imbalanced than in New England, making it more difficult for males in Chesapeake Bay to find wives and start families.

    (E) the population increased faster in New England, avowing for the development of stable communities, than it did in the Chesapeake Bay region.

21. The Mayflower Compact of 1620 established

    (A) a land of religious freedom.   (B)   the colony of Massachusetts.

    (C) a royal colony.   • (D)   Plymouth Colony.

    (E) the colony of Rhode Island.

22. On the eve of Columbus' first arrival in 1492, the native Indian population of the Western Hemisphere was estimated at

    (A) 1–5 million.   (B)   10–20 million.

    (C) 25–40 million.   (D)   50–60 million.

    (E) 80–100 million.

23. Columbus undertook his 1492 voyage to the Americas to

    (A) Christianize the Indian population.

    (B) prove that the Earth was round.

    (C) discover new worlds.

    (D) test the geographic theories of Ptolemy.

    (E) secure wealth and power for himself and the Spanish throne.

24. Jamestown survived as the first permanent English settlement in America because

    (A) the settlers followed the example of Roanoke.

    • (B) of the emergence of tobacco as a cash crop.

    (C) of the religious convictions of its first settlers.

    (D) of the mild climate of Virginia.

    (E) of its use of Indian slaves as a labor force.
    → new enslaved

25. Roger Williams is best known in American history as

    (A) advocating the uniting of church and state into a theocracy.

    • (B) an early champion of religious freedom.

    (C) the chief justice at the Salem witch trials.

    (D) the founder of New Hampshire.

    (E) the first royal governor of Massachusetts.

26. Indentured servants in colonial America experienced

    (A) great upward economic mobility.

    (B) political power.

    (C) racial harmony with black slaves.

    (D) a high standard of living.

    • (E) low social status.

27. During the seventeenth century, black slaves in the Southern colonies

    (A) came directly from West Africa.   *Triangle Trade*

    . (B) grew slowly as a labor force.

    (C) were treated the same as slaves in the British West Indies.

    (D) were allowed to set their children free.

    (E) lived mostly in urban areas.

28. Which of the following statements is NOT true of colonial Pennsylvania?

    • (A) Only Quakers could own land in the colony.   *Toleration*

    (B) Delaware was at first a part of the colony of Pennsylvania.

    (C) German immigrants in the eighteenth century found Pennsylvania attractive.

(D) William Penn was able to maintain peaceful relations with the Indians.

(E) Grain was an important export of the colony.

29. William Penn's plans for a Quaker colony in Pennsylvania included all of the following EXCEPT

(A) establishing peaceful relations with the Indians.

(B) allowing for religious freedom.

•(C) establishing a democracy.

(D) the making of an economic profit.

(E) establishing a colony loyal to Great Britain.

30. At the close of the Seven Years' War in 1763, France ceded to Great Britain

(A) the French West Indies.   (B) Florida.

•(C) Canada.   (D) the African slave trade.

(E) the Louisiana Territory.

31. The eighteenth century population in British North America

•(A) nearly doubled every 25 years.

(B) become increasingly more homogeneous.

(C) had a life expectancy of 45 years for males.

(D) was clustered inside the new cities of the colonies.

(E) was comprised of less than 2 percent African-Americans.

32. In seventeenth century New England, married women were denied the right to

(A) vote for elected officials.

(B) divorce their husbands.

(C) arrange marriages for their children.

(D) own property.

(E) all of the above.

33. Colonies such as the Carolinas were known as "restoration colonies" because

•(A) their creation was mainly due to the restoration of the Stuarts to the English throne.

(B)   they were created as places to send criminals to restore them to civilized behavior and give them a chance to lead decent, honest lives.

(C)   their creation was mainly due to an effort by the English government to restore a balance of power in the New World between the thriving English colonies in New England and the less successful English colonies in the South.

(D)   their creation was mainly due to the restoration of the power of English Parliament over the king.

(E)   their creation was an attempt to restore the supremacy of the Anglican church in the colonies.

34.   By 1760, the biggest problem with the economy of the English colonies was

(A)   smuggling.

(B)   a trade surplus so large that England was threatening to confiscate American assets to help balance the English economy.

(C)   a lack of demand for the vast quantities of high-quality American manufactured goods now being produced, leading to high unemployment in the American colonies.

(D)   a huge balance-of-trade deficit that threatened the solvency of the colonial economy.

(E)   a lack of adequate deep-water ports to provide loading and unloading facilities for the large number of ships now trying to bring goods to or carry goods from the colonies.

35.   The Dominion of New England was established by the English government in 1686 to

(A)   increase the power of the Puritans.

(B)   end the Glorious Revolution and restore James II to the English throne.

(C)   stimulate trade among the fledgling New England colonies.

(D)   increase the effectiveness of the various New England legislatures.

(E)   increase the authority of the English government over the New England colonies.

1500–1763
DIAGNOSTIC TEST

ANSWER KEY

1.	(D)	8.	(B)	15.	(A)	22.	(E)	29.	(C)
2.	(C)	9.	(D)	16.	(B)	23.	(E)	30.	(C)
3.	(D)	10.	(D)	17.	(C)	24.	(B)	31.	(A)
4.	(D)	11.	(A)	18.	(D)	25.	(B)	32.	(A)
5.	(B)	12.	(E)	19.	(E)	26.	(E)	33.	(A)
6.	(D)	13.	(B)	20.	(C)	27.	(B)	34.	(D)
7.	(C)	14.	(E)	21.	(D)	28.	(A)	35.	(E)

DETAILED EXPLANATIONS
OF ANSWERS

1.   **(D)**   Francisco Pizzaro explored Peru while Francisco Coronado traveled through the area of Texas, Oklahoma, and Kansas. Robert La Salle and Jacques Marquette pursued the Mississippi River, and Samuel de Champlain explored the New England coast, Lake Champlain, and the Great Lakes.

2.   **(C)**   Cotton did not become a major product until the invention of the cotton gin in the 1790s. Sugar or molasses was purchased in the West Indies and taken to New England where it was manufactured into rum. The rum was then traded in Africa for slaves. In other forms of the triangular trade, tobacco was a major product.

3.   **(D)**   "Chattel" was the legal term for a piece of property. Black slaves were not considered human beings and therefore had no rights, nor were they employees. Servants who served for a limited period of time were called indentured servants. Individual masters might grant slaves freedom in their wills, but this happened infrequently.

4.   **(D)**   The Puritans, who established the Massachusetts Bay Colony, sought to build a society based upon the will of God as revealed in the Bible according to their understanding. Rather than establishing religious toleration, they allowed only their Congregational Church free exercise of religion. It was the founders of the Virginia Colony who sought gold and later established tobacco as the basis of their economy.

5.   **(B)**   The French and Indian War was the culmination of a series of wars between France and England: King William's War (1689–1697), Queen Anne's War (1700–1713), King George's War (1740–1748), and the French and Indian War (1754–1763). The American Revolution took place between 1776 and 1783.

6.   **(D)**   Benjamin Franklin made important discoveries regarding electricity. John Peter Zenger was a newspaper editor involved in a 1735 libel case. Jonathan Edwards was the New England preacher who probably started the Great Awakening. William Byrd was one of the leading Virginia planters of the early eighteenth century. George Whitefield was a British itinerant evangelist who preached throughout the American colonies during the Great Awakening.

7.   **(C)**   The British trade regulations provided both advantages and disadvantages for the American colonies. For example, while guaranteeing access to the British market, they prevented access to the markets of other countries. Individual laws often favored certain colonies over others, but as a whole they did

not favor one section of the American colonies.

8.   **(B)**   The Germans, known as the Pennsylvania Dutch, settled heavily in Pennsylvania. The French Huguenots could be found in New York and South Carolina. The Scots-Irish settled the frontier areas of the middle and southern colonies. The Dutch were concentrated in New York, although the English were the dominant ethnic group even in that colony. Spanish and Portuguese Jews could be found in the urban areas of New York, Rhode Island, and South Carolina.

9.   **(D)**   John Locke wrote that all people were entitled to the natural rights of "life, liberty, and property" in his *Second Treatise on Government.* This work, written in 1688, was influential in American political thought. Roger Williams founded the colony of Rhode Island, after he and his followers were expelled from the Massachusetts Bay Colony for religious reasons. Benjamin Franklin was a leading figure in the American enlightenment. John Winthrop was an important leader of the Puritan colony of Massachusetts. Francis Drake was an explorer for the English who sailed around the world.

10.   **(D)**   Bacon's followers were disgruntled at what they saw as the governor's refusal to protect their frontier area from Indian raids. The jailing of individuals or seizure of their property for failure to pay taxes during a time of economic hardship (A) was the source of Massachusetts' 1786 Shays' Rebellion. The under-representation of the backcountry areas in colonial legislatures (B) was an ongoing source of irritation in the colonial South. The mistreatment of former indentured servants by large planters (C) and the favoritism of Virginia's Governor Berkeley to his clique of friends—though he almost certainly could not have manipulated tobacco prices himself (E)—may have been underlying causes but were not the immediate issue in dispute in Bacon's Rebellion.

11.   **(A)**   The British preferred royal colonies for the greater control these gave them over colonial affairs. Within the eighteenth century, British system corruption (B) and bureaucracy (D) were unavoidable regardless of the particular arrangement, and the rights (C) and prosperity (E) of the colonists were very much secondary considerations to the British authorities.

12.   **(E)**   The Great Awakening was the first religious development to have an impact throughout colonial America. Toleration in Maryland (A) and Quakerism in Pennsylvania (B) showed little tendency to spread to other colonies. The Half-Way Covenant (C) was a late seventeenth–century religious compromise involving only colonial New England. The Parsons' Cause (D) involved Anglican Church establishment.

13.   **(B)**   Though land was abundant (A), capital (B) and labor (D) were scarce in early America. Limitations of climate and land (C) prevented New England from developing the staple-crop agriculture in demand in Europe (E).

14.　**(E)**　The colonial economy of South Carolina, unlike those of any of the more northerly colonies, was dependent on the cultivation of rice and indigo, the latter a plant used to make blue dye. Maryland (B), Virginia (C), and North Carolina (D) were primarily tobacco-growing colonies, while Pennsylvania (A) produced grain.

15.　**(A)**　The Great Awakening was a series of religious awakenings, or rebirths, centered primarily in New England but spread throughout the colonies which changed the lives of English colonists. It challenged the old hierarchical religious order in which ordained clergy were deferred to and were believed to have knowledge based on extensive formal learning that the average member of a congregation lacked. It brought a much broader sense of community to colonists making them aware of others with similar questions and beliefs who lived outside their village or town. In many ways, it was the first of a series of events that helped to forge distinctively American regional identities, separate from their European heritage, among the North American colonists.

16.　**(B)**　After the defeat of George Washington's Virginian forces at Fort Necessity by the French, it became clear that the colonies were too weak to individually tackle either the French or their various Indian allies. Benjamin Franklin perceived that united action by the colonies was the only hope of providing for their security. He called together the Albany Congress to discuss plans to enlist the aid of the various Iroquois tribes in colonial defense and to coordinate defense plans among the English colonies. It also called for the establishment of a "grand council" with representatives from each of the colonies to enact taxes and coordinate colonial economic activity. The plan is notable because it was the first plan calling for the individual colonies to act as a single, united entity. While the plan was visionary and ultimately necessary, the colonial legislatures ultimately rejected it.

17.　**(C)**　While the Roanoke Colony (1587) actually preceded the Jamestown Colony (1607), the Roanoke Colony was not successful. A supply ship sent to Roanoke in 1590 could find no survivors at the colony. The word "croatoan," which referred to a nearby island, carved into a tree was the only clue left behind. No other sign of the colonists was ever found.

18.　**(D)**　All of the other choices are true. Physical punishment was the norm for disciplining children, as most religions preached the "spare the rod, spoil the child" philosophy. Children were treated as miniature adults and were expected to conform to adult standards of behavior. Behavioral standards were strict and punishments were severe, for both adults and children, when those standards were broken.

Women were limited in their legal rights to own property and engage in commerce even when single. Once they married they lost whatever legal rights they had. They could no longer own property, earn their own income, or enact contracts. They were legally under the complete dominion of their husbands.

Most families during this period did bear children who survived until adulthood and bore their own children. Life expectancies, particularly in the South, increased during this period as did the population in the colonies. Women, however, did NOT set the moral standards for their children, nor did they decide how the children were to be educated or trained. Those duties were considered the husband's responsibilities, although it was the wife's duty to enforce her husband's decisions where children were concerned.

Finally, the vast majority of families did live in rural areas. Most colonial cities were in reality small towns. Even the largest, such as Boston, New York, and Philadelphia, had fewer than 20,000 inhabitants. While the cities expanded greatly during this period, over 90 percent of the colonies' inhabitants lived in small, rural villages and towns.

19. **(E)** The French and Indian War was an overwhelming victory for the English and the American colonies. It resulted in the French being totally driven from the North American continent. It ended the American Indian tactic of playing one European power against another. It also led to Spain, a French ally, ceding Florida to England. The net result was that the American colonists no longer had to fear direct threats by a major foreign power. Colonists fighting side by side with the English had learned much about America, the English, and themselves. They learned that the British were not invincible. They learned to resent the arrogant attitudes of the British toward the colonists. They also gained confidence in themselves and gained a corps of well-trained officers who honed their skills fighting for the British. This led to a more independent, knowledgeable, and assertive attitude by Americans who now felt more free in their ability to challenge the British and resist British efforts to restrict their activities.

20. **(C)** All of the other choices were true. Most New England immigrants arrived as family units. This provided the New England colonies with a relatively stable social structure from their inception. In Chesapeake Bay, most colonists were single young males, many of whom were indentured servants. The ratio of men to women was 6 to 1 before 1640. This made it exceedingly difficult to find eligible mates and start families. In addition, the climate in the Chesapeake Bay region was an unhealthy climate. Men and women died between 10 to 20 years earlier on average than they did in New England, leaving them little time to start families when they did find mates. This severely limited population growth in Chesapeake Bay, where the population increases were entirely due to continued immigration rather than indigenous colonists. A population whose growth depends on a continuous flood of newcomers is not nearly as stable as a population whose growth is based on established couples having children and raising them in stable family environments as occurred in New England.

The only choice that was untrue was choice (C). There were basically no differences in the way women were viewed (in terms of their social role or their rights) in New England or Chesapeake Bay. In fact, some historians argue that because women were so rare and in such demand in the Chesapeake region, they were more likely to be treated more as equals than women in New England, who were plentiful and more likely to be locked into the traditional wifely role. A woman in Chesapeake Bay might succeed in rebelling against social norms simply because she was so badly needed; males couldn't afford to reject her. A woman in New England who rebelled against social expectations had no chance of being accepted by males who could find plenty of other women who were willing to "accept their place" in society.

21.　**(D)**　The original settlers of the Plymouth Colony actually had purchased a tract of land in northern Virginia from the Virginia Company. They lost their course in crossing the Atlantic and upon arriving at Cape Cod decided to stay. The settlers feared that because they were occupying land not legally granted to them they would be forced to return to England. As a result, they drew up a contract among all the settlers called the Mayflower Compact to legally establish their existence. The Pilgrim settlers in Plymouth did not establish religious freedom as they only desired freedom for their religion and came to America to erect a religious utopia. In addition, Plymouth did not become part of Massachusetts until 1692, and indeed Puritans and Pilgrims had much dislike for each other and lived as separate, often hostile, colonies until 1692. Rhode Island was founded in 1644 by Roger Williams.

22.　**(E)**　In recent years, students of population analysis, demographers, have greatly revised the long accepted population estimates of James Mooney in 1925 for the Amerindian in pre-Columbian times. Mooney has estimated that less than 25 million Indians resided in the Americas around the year 1500. The main problem with Mooney's figures is that they were based primarily upon white European eyewitness accounts of the sixteenth and seventeenth centuries. Today archaeological findings and sophisticated demographic analysis using the computer have established the Indian population of the Western Hemisphere at nearly 100 million prior to Columbus' arrival. It should be noted that the Indian population stood at its lowest ebb in America in 1886 when there were less than 250,000 Amerindians. In the 1980 census, the Amerindian population had grown to 1.2 million.

23.　**(E)**　In his contract with the Spanish monarchy, Columbus established that he and his heirs would receive 40 percent of all wealth taken from the lands he was about to sail to; he would receive the title, Admiral of the Ocean Seas; and he would be named governor of any uncharted areas he came into contact with. Columbus' motives are clear from this contract as power, glory, and wealth. Few educated people in Europe believed that the Earth was flat and Columbus had no desire to serve as a missionary for Christianity. Columbus did not come to America as an explorer; he came as a colonizer, seeking wealth and power. Once he landed in the Americas in 1492, he had proven Ptolemy wrong; a fact little mentioned by Columbus during the remainder of his lifetime.

24. **(B)** The establishment of Jamestown in 1607 as the first permanent English settlement in North America came dangerously close to failure. England had already failed in its initial venture in the 1580s at Roanoke in Virginia. Upon the first arrival of Jamestown settlers, they indicated they had learned little from Roanoke and repeated the myopic quest for gold and silver rather than plant and secure a food supply. As with Roanoke, during the first harsh winter more than half the settlers perished. Hostile Indians did not bode well for the colony either. It was the combination of the efforts of John Smith and the discovery of tobacco as a cash crop for export to Europe that made the colony able to be economically profitable. According to most historians, the Anglican faith played a minimal role in Virginia throughout the seventeenth century.

25. **(B)** Roger Williams was forced to flee Massachusetts because of his unorthodox religious beliefs. Although a Puritan minister, Williams warned the ministry in Massachusetts that they exerted too much political power and were being corrupted by their theocracy. He was to be put on trial for heresy when he fled to Rhode Island, not New Hampshire. Williams allowed complete religious toleration to all settlers. He died well before the Salem witch trials of 1692–1694. He never served as governor of Massachusetts.

26. **(E)** Recent historical research has indicated that indentured servants, popular myths to the contrary, remained for the most part in the lower sections of colonial society throughout their lives. The low social status was especially true in the Southern colonies throughout the colonial period. Indentured servants generally signed a contract with their masters, trading their labor for room and board, and the learning of a skilled craft for a set number of years (usually seven years). The servants were in many cases treated harshly by their masters and emerged from their servitude impoverished with few skills mastered. Although servants supported Bacon in his rebellion in Virginia, they never gained political power throughout the colonial period. Most servants were very hostile toward black slaves in the South and showed little sympathy for the slaves' loss of legal status as a human, a condition never applied to the indentured servant. In sum, the indentured generally arrived in America on the edge of poverty and remained there for the bulk of their lives.

27. **(B)** Slavery as an institution grew very slowly in America, unlike in the British West Indies. Although the first American slaves arrived in 1619 in Jamestown, it was not until the 1690s that slavery as an institution grew substantially. Throughout the 1600s, most Southerners had yet to determine if they would seek their labor pool through white servants or black slaves. The incident of Bacon's Rebellion convinced many Southern planters that slaves ultimately were easier to control. Few Americans imported their slaves directly from West Africa, preferring their slaves from this region to have been seasoned a few years in the British West Indies. Unlike North American slavery, the slave system in the West Indies was exceptionally brutal, often working slaves to death within

seven years of purchase. The children of slaves were always born slaves in the American slave system.

28.   **(A)**   Pennsylvania offered religious liberty and did not restrict land ownership. In fact, Pennsylvania served as a refuge for members of persecuted religions throughout Europe. Delaware was at first a part of the colony of Pennsylvania, and while it was granted a separate legislature by William Penn, the governor of Pennsylvania also remained governor of Delaware. German immigrants settled in what is now central Pennsylvania, where land was readily available. Penn was notable among colonial leaders for dealing peacefully with the Indians. Pennsylvania exported grain to Europe and the West Indies.

29.   **(C)**   William Penn established a frame of government that granted the bulk of power to the Penn family and their advisors. Only reluctantly, and after much difficulty with the settlers, did Penn allow them a small voice in government in the colony. Indeed, the term "democracy" was used as a pejorative term throughout the colonial and Revolutionary periods. For the most part, democracy was a nineteenth and twentieth century political development in America. Few colonials believed the people capable of self-rule without some elite guidance and most used the term synonymously with "mobocracy." Penn did establish religious toleration under Quaker control in Pennsylvania and during his lifetime the colony enjoyed peaceful relations with the Indians. Penn always envisioned the colony as part of the British Empire and was adamant about making the colony a financial success, which was achieved.

30.   **(C)**   In 1763, William Pitt had led England to a great victory over France. As he entered the peace talks, Pitt was debating the French offer of all of Canada and the West Indies sugar islands with the exception of Martinique and Guadeloupe as his fruits of victory. Although Pitt knew England was on the verge of bankruptcy and needed the revenue of the islands, he opted for Canada. This combination of a removed French menace from the North and a growing concern over the British national debt would ultimately prove two long-term causes of the American Revolution. France controlled neither Florida, Louisiana, nor the slave trade at the time of the peace.

31.   **(A)**   The health of the American colonies in the eighteenth century was proven to most Americans by the evidence of their explosive population growth that doubled every generation. In the eighteenth century, a rapidly growing population was considered the ultimate sign of a healthy nation. Along with their rapid growth, the colonies were growing more diverse as a people. New arrivals to America from areas other than England (Germans, Scotch-Irish, and Africans) made the middle and southern colonies more pluralistic. The African-American population now comprised about 20 percent of the total population, indicating the South's increased reliance upon slaves as a labor source. The five largest Ameri-

can cities in the eighteenth century held less than 10 percent of the total population but enjoyed a major role in colonial affairs. Life expectancies for men still remained at or about 70 years of age throughout the colonies.

32. **(A)** Seventeenth century married and single women were denied the right to vote in colonial elections. According to 17th century law, married women (*feme coverts*) did retain the authority to divorce their husbands by proving just cause (i.e., extreme physical cruelty, abandonment, impious behavior). Also, mothers were considered equal partners with fathers in following the New England practice of parental arrangements of marriage for their children as a means of socio-economic mobility. Finally, women were allowed to own personal property while married, and in many cases land and businesses as well. The denial of political rights to women in colonial America was based on the belief that women were unable to know public affairs as they were restricted in their affairs to the private domain of the household.

33. **(A)** The Carolinas were granted to supporters of the Stuarts as a reward for their loyalty during the Stuarts' exile during the English civil war. With the Stuarts' restoration to the throne, eight courtiers loyal to the Stuarts were granted proprietorship of the land extending from Virginia to Florida.

34. **(D)** While smuggling (A) was a problem, most smuggling was designed to obtain goods without paying stiff English tariffs. As such, smuggling was a problem for the English, but in many ways helped the colonial economy in America.

The colonies had no trade surplus (B) at this time. In fact, the situation was just the opposite. By 1760, the English colonies had amassed a trade deficit of over 2 million British pounds (sterling), a huge debt for that time. Although the colonial economy was exporting nearly all the excess agricultural goods it could produce, the colonies had developed a huge appetite for fine quality British manufactured goods. This appetite was leading to such massive imports of English goods to the colonies that the fledgling, mostly agricultural, colonial economy could not keep pace. This imbalance led to a shortage of "hard" cash to pay for the imported goods, creating severe problems keeping the economy solvent. Thus, choice (D) describes the biggest problem with the colonial economy.

35. **(E)** James II detested legislative bodies, and the English government felt that the New England legislatures were already too powerful and too independent. Perhaps the major reason for the restructuring of the New England colonial governments into a single autocratically controlled Dominion was to limit the power of the colonial legislatures and increase their subservence to Parliament and the throne.

1500–1763
REVIEW

1. THE AGE OF EXPLORATION

The Treaty of Tordesillas

Excited by the gold Columbus had brought back from America (after Amerigo Vespucci, an Italian member of a Portuguese expedition to South America whose widely reprinted report suggested a new world had been found), Ferdinand and Isabella, joint monarchs of Spain, sought formal confirmation of their ownership of these new lands. They feared the interference of Portugal, which was at that time a powerful seafaring nation and had been active in overseas exploration. At Spain's urging, the pope drew a "Line of Demarcation" 100 leagues west of the Cape Verde Islands, dividing the heathen world into two equal parts—that east of the line for Portugal and that west of it for Spain.

Because this line tended to be unduly favorable to Spain, and because Portugal had the stronger navy, the two countries worked out the Treaty of Tordesillas (1494), by which the line was moved farther west. As a result, Brazil eventually became a Portuguese colony, while Spain maintained claims to the rest of the Americas. As other European nations joined the hunt for colonies, they tended to ignore the Treaty of Tordesillas.

The Spanish Conquistadores

To conquer the Americas the Spanish monarchs used their powerful army, led by independent Spanish adventurers known as *conquistadores*. At first the *conquistadores* confined their attentions to the Caribbean islands, where the European diseases they unwittingly carried with them devastated the local Indian populations, who had no immunities against such diseases.

After about 1510 the *conquistadores* turned their attention to the American mainland. In 1513 Vasco Nuñez de Balboa crossed the isthmus of Panama and became the first European to see the Pacific Ocean. The same year Juan Ponce de Leon explored Florida in search of gold and a fabled fountain of youth. He found neither but claimed Florida for Spain. In 1519 Hernando (Hernan) Cortes led his dramatic expedition against the Aztecs of Mexico. Aided by the fact that the Indians at first mistook him for a god, as well as by firearms, armor, horses, and (unbeknownst to him) smallpox germs, all previously unknown in America, Cortes destroyed the Aztec empire and won enormous riches. By the 1550s other such fortune seekers had conquered much of South America.

In North America the Spaniards sought in vain for riches. In 1528 Panfilio de Narvaez led a disastrous expedition through the Gulf Coast region from which only four of the original 400 men returned. One of them, Cabeza de Vaca, brought with him a story of seven great cities full of gold (the "Seven Cities of

Cibola") somewhere to the north. In response to this, two Spanish expeditions explored the interior of North America. Hernando de Soto led a 600-man expedition (1539–1541) through what is now the southeastern United States, penetrating as far west as Oklahoma and discovering the Mississippi River, on whose banks de Soto was buried. Francisco Vasquez de Coronado led an expedition (1540–1542) from Mexico, north across the Rio Grande and through New Mexico, Arizona, Texas, Oklahoma, and Kansas. Some of Coronado's men were the first Europeans to see the Grand Canyon. While neither expedition discovered rich Indian civilizations to plunder, both increased Europe's knowledge of the interior of North America and asserted Spain's territorial claims to the continent.

New Spain

Spain administered its new holdings as an autocratic, rigidly controlled empire in which everything was to benefit the parent country. Tight control of even mundane matters was carried out by a suffocating bureaucracy run directly from Madrid. Annual treasure fleets carried the riches of the New World to Spain for the furtherance of its military-political goals in Europe.

As population pressures were low in sixteenth-century Spain, only about 200,000 Spaniards came to America during that time. To deal with the consequent labor shortages and as a reward to successful *conquistadores,* the Spaniards developed a system of large manors or estates (*encomiendas*) with Indian slaves ruthlessly managed for the benefit of the *conquistadores*. The *encomienda* system was later replaced by the similar, but somewhat milder, *hacienda* system. As the Indian population died from overwork and European diseases, Spaniards began importing African slaves to supply their labor needs. Society in New Spain was rigidly stratified, with the highest level reserved for natives of Spain (*peninsulares*) and the next for those of Spanish parentage born in the New World (*creoles*). Those of mixed (*mestizo*) or Indian blood occupied lower levels.

English and French Beginnings

In 1497, the Italian, John Cabot (Giovanni Caboto), sailing under the sponsorship of the king of England in search of a Northwest Passage (a water route to the Orient through or around the North American continent), became the first European, since the Viking voyages over four centuries earlier, to reach the mainland of North America, which he claimed for England.

In 1524, the king of France authorized another Italian, Giovannia da Verrazano, to undertake a mission similar to Cabot's. Endeavoring to duplicate the achievement of Spaniard Ferdinand Magellan, who had five years earlier found a way around the southern tip of South America, Verrazano followed the American coast from present-day North Carolina to Maine.

Beginning in 1534, Jacques Cartier, also authorized by the king of France, mounted three expeditions to the area of the St. Lawrence River, which he believed might be the hoped-for Northwest Passage. He explored up the river as far as the site of Montreal, where rapids prevented him, as he thought, from continuing to China. He claimed the area for France before abandoning his last expedition and returning to France in 1542. France made no further attempts to explore or colonize in America for 65 years.

England showed little interest in America as well during most of the sixteenth century. But when the English finally did begin colonization, commercial capitalism in England had advanced to the point that the English efforts were supported by private rather than government funds, allowing the English colonists to enjoy a greater degree of freedom from government interference.

Partially as a result of the New World rivalries and partially through differences between Protestant and Catholic countries, the sixteenth century was a violent time both in Europe and in America. French Protestants, called Huguenots, who attempted to escape persecution in Catholic France by settling in the New World, were massacred by the Spaniards. One such incident led the Spaniards, nervous about any possible encroachment on what they considered to be their exclusive holdings in America, to build a fort that became the beginning of a settlement at St. Augustine, Florida, the oldest city in North America. Spanish priests ventured north from St. Augustine, but no permanent settlements were built in the interior.

French and especially English sea captains made great sport of and considerable profit from plundering the Spaniards of the wealth they had first plundered from the Indians. One of the most successful English captains, Francis Drake, sailed around South America and raided the Spanish settlements on the Pacific coast of Central America before continuing on to California, which he claimed for England and named Nova Albion. Drake then returned to England by sailing around the world. England's Queen Elizabeth, sister and Protestant successor to Mary, had been quietly investing in Drake's highly profitable voyages. On Drake's return from his round-the-world voyage, Elizabeth openly showed her approval.

Angered by this as well as by Elizabeth's support of the Protestant cause in Europe, Spain's King Philip II in 1588 dispatched a mighty fleet, the Spanish Armada, to conquer England. Instead, the Armada was defeated by the English navy and largely destroyed by storms in the North Sea. This victory established England as a great power and moved it a step closer to overseas colonization, although the war with Spain continued until 1604.

Gilbert, Raleigh, and the First English Attempts

English nobleman Sir Humphrey Gilbert believed England should found colonies and find a Northwest Passage. In 1576 he sent English sea captain Martin Frobisher to look for such a passage. Frobisher scouted along the inhospitable northeastern coast of Canada and brought back large amounts of a yellow metal that turned out to be fool's gold. In 1578, Gilbert obtained a charter allowing him to found a colony with his own funds and guaranteeing the prospective colonists all the rights of those born and residing in England, thus setting an important precedent for future colonial charters. His attempts to found a colony in Newfoundland failed, and while pursuing these endeavors he was lost at sea.

With the queen's permission, Gilbert's work was taken up by his half-brother, Sir Walter Raleigh. Raleigh turned his attention to a more southerly portion of the North American coastline, which he named Virginia, in honor of England's unmarried queen. He selected as a site for the first settlement Roanoke Island just off the coast of present-day North Carolina.

After one abortive attempt, a group of 114 settlers—men, women, and children—were landed in July 1587. Shortly thereafter, Virginia Dare became the first English child born in America. Later that year the expedition's leader, John White, returned to England to secure additional supplies. Delayed by the war with Spain, he did not return until 1590, when he found the colony deserted. It is not known what became of the Roanoke settlers. After this failure, Raleigh was forced by financial constraints to abandon his attempts to colonize Virginia. Hampered by unrealistic expectations, inadequate financial resources, and the ongoing war with Spain, English interest in American colonization was submerged for 15 years.

QUESTION

What was the Northwest Passage?

EXPLANATION

The Northwest Passage was a water route through North America that would allow ships to reach Asia. Such a route was never found, but the search for it led to exploration of much of the east coast of America, discovery of the Great Lakes, and exploration of much of the interior of North America.

Drill 1: The Age of Exploration

1. The purpose of the Treaty of Tordesillas was

    (A) to divide the non-European world between Spain and Portugal.

    (B) to specify which parts of North America should be French and which parts should be Spanish.

    (C) to create an alliance of France, Holland, and England against Spanish designs in the New World.

    (D) to divide the New World between France and Spain.

    (E) to exclude any Portuguese colonization from the Western Hemisphere.

2. The chief significance of French explorer Samuel de Champlain's alienation of the Iroquois Indians was

    (A) to prevent the French from establishing a profitable fur trade in Canada.

(B)   to prevent Champlain from founding any permanent settlement along the St. Lawrence River.

(C)   to prevent Champlain from making it back to France alive.

(D)   to prevent New France from expanding southward into what is now the United States.

(E)   the creation of an alliance of British and French colonists against the Iroquois.

3.   Explorers who established French claims to the eastern United States included

I.   Giovanni da Verrazano.

II.   Martin Frobisher.

III.   Jacques Cartier.

IV.   John Cabot.

V.   Henry Hudson.

(A)   I only.   (B)   I and III.

(C)   I, II, and V.   (D)   I, III, IV, and V.

(E)   II only.

4.   The primary motive for European exploration in the fifteenth and sixteenth centuries was

(A)   to gain access to the wealth of the Far East.

(B)   to relieve population overcrowding.

(C)   to find a place outside of Europe for religious dissidents to be relocated.

(D)   to establish bases for defense against other European powers.

(E)   scientific curiosity.

5.   In the sixteenth and seventeenth centuries, the Europeans' greatest impact on the Americas was the

(A)   introduction of Christianity to American Indian tribes.

(B)   destruction of the massive American forests to make room for farms.

(C)   introduction of modern technology to American Indian tribes, allowing them to compete effectively with Europe.

(D)   introduction of European diseases to America, devastating many American Indian tribes.

(E)   introduction of slavery to the Americas.

2. THE BEGINNINGS OF COLONIZATION

Virginia

In the first decade of the 1600s, Englishmen, exhilarated by the recent victory over Spain and influenced by the writings of Richard Hakluyt (who urged American colonization as the way to national greatness and the spread of the gospel), once again undertook to plant colonies.

Two groups of merchants gained charters from James I, Queen Elizabeth's successor. One group of merchants was based in London and received a charter to North America between what are now the Hudson and the Cape Fear Rivers. The other was based in Plymouth and was granted the right to colonize in North America from the Potomac to the northern border of present-day Maine. They were called the Virginia Company of London and the Virginia Company of Plymouth, respectively. These were joint-stock companies, which raised their capital by the sale of shares of stock. Companies of this sort had already been used to finance and carry on English trade with Russia, Africa, and the Middle East.

The Plymouth Company, in 1607, attempted to plant a colony in Maine, but after one winter the colonists became discouraged and returned to Britain. Thereafter, the Plymouth Company folded.

The Virginia Company of London, in 1607, sent out an expedition of three ships with 104 men to plant a colony some 40 miles up the James River from Chesapeake Bay. Like the river on which it was located, the new settlement was named Jamestown in honor of England's king. It became the first permanent English settlement in North America, but for a time it appeared to be going the way of the earlier attempts. During the early years of Jamestown, the majority of the settlers died of starvation, various diseases, or hostile action by Indians. Though the losses were continuously replaced by new settlers, the colony's survival remained in doubt for a number of years.

There were several reasons for these difficulties. The entire colony was owned by the company, and all members shared the profits regardless of how much or how little they worked; thus, there was a lack of incentive. Many of the settlers were gentlemen, who considered themselves too good to work at growing the food the colony needed to survive. Others were simply unambitious and little inclined to work in any case. Furthermore, the settlers had come with the expectation of finding gold or other quick and easy riches and wasted much time looking for these while they should have been providing for their survival.

For purposes of defense, the settlement had been sited on a peninsula formed by a bend in the river; but this low and swampy location proved to be a breeding ground for all sorts of diseases and, at high tide, even contaminated the settlers' drinking supply with sea water. To make matters worse, relations with Powhatan, the powerful local Indian chief, were at best uncertain and often openly hostile, with disastrous results for the colonists.

In 1608 and 1609, the dynamic and ruthless leadership of John Smith kept the colony from collapsing. Smith's rule was, "He who works not, eats not." After Smith returned to England in late 1609, the condition of the colony again became critical.

In 1612, a Virginia resident named John Rolfe discovered that a superior strain of tobacco, native to the West Indies, could be grown in Virginia. There was a large market for this tobacco in Europe, and Rolfe's discovery gave Virginia a major cash crop.

To secure more settlers and boost Virginia's shrinking labor force, the company moved to make immigration possible for Britain's poor who were without economic opportunity at home or financial means to procure transportation to America. This was achieved by means of the indenture system, by which a poor worker's passage to America was paid by an American planter (or the company itself), who in exchange, was indentured to work for the planter (or the company) for a specified number of years. The system was open to abuse and often resulted in the mistreatment of the indentured servants.

To control the workers thus shipped to Virginia, as well as the often lazy and unruly colonists already present, the company gave its governors in America dictatorial powers. Governors such as Lord De La Warr, Sir Thomas Gates, and Sir Thomas Dale made use of such powers, imposing a harsh rule.

For such reasons, and its well-known reputation as a death trap, Virginia continued to attract inadequate numbers of immigrants. To solve this, a reform-minded faction within the company proposed a new approach, and under its leader Edwin Sandys made changes designed to attract more settlers. Colonists were promised the same rights they had in England. A representative assembly, the House of Burgesses, was founded in 1619—the first in America. Additionally, private ownership of land was instituted.

Despite these reforms, Virginia's unhealthy reputation kept many Englishmen away. Large numbers of indentured servants were brought in, especially young, single men. The first Africans were brought to Virginia in 1619 but were treated as indentured servants rather than slaves.

Virginia's Indian relations remained difficult. In 1622, an Indian massacre took the lives of 347 settlers. In 1644, the Indians struck again, massacring some 300 more. Shortly thereafter, the coastal Indians were subdued and no longer presented a serious threat.

Impressed by the potential profits from tobacco growing, King James I determined to have Virginia for himself. Using the high mortality and the 1622 massacre as a pretext, in 1624 he revoked the London Company's charter and made Virginia a royal colony. This pattern was followed throughout colonial history; both company colonies and proprietary colonies tended eventually to become royal colonies. Upon taking over Virginia, James revoked all political rights and the representative assembly—he did not believe in such things—but 15 years later his son, Charles I, was forced, by constant pressure from the Virginians and the continuing need to attract more settlers, to restore these rights.

New France

Shortly after England returned to the business of colonization, France renewed its interest in the areas previously visited by such French explorers as Jacques Cartier. The French opened with the Indians a lucrative trade in furs, plentiful in America and much sought after in Europe.

The St. Lawrence River was the French gateway to the interior of North America. In 1608, Samuel de Champlain established a trading post in Quebec, from which the rest of what became New France eventually spread.

Relatively small numbers of Frenchmen came to America, and partially because of this they were generally able to maintain good relations with the Indians. French Canadians were energetic in exploring and claiming new lands for France.

French exploration and settlement spread through the Great Lakes region and the valleys of the Mississippi and Ohio Rivers. In 1673, Jacques Marquette explored the Mississippi Valley, and, in 1682, Sieur de la Salle followed the river to its mouth. French settlements in the Midwest were not generally real towns, but rather forts and trading posts serving the fur trade.

Throughout its history, New France was handicapped by an inadequate population and a lack of support by the parent country.

New Netherlands

Other countries also took an interest in North America. In 1609, Holland sent an Englishman named Henry Hudson to explore for them in search of a Northwest Passage. In this endeavor Hudson discovered the river that bears his name.

Arrangements were made to trade with the Iroquois Indians for furs, especially beaver pelts for the hats then popular in Europe. In 1624, Dutch trading outposts were established on Manhattan Island (New Amsterdam) and at the site of present-day Albany (Fort Orange). A profitable fur trade was carried on and became the main source of revenue for the Dutch West India Company, the joint-stock company that ran the colony.

To encourage enough farming to keep the colony supplied with food, the Dutch instituted the patroon system, by which large landed estates would be given to wealthy men who transported at least 50 families to New Netherlands. These families would then become tenant farmers on the estate of the patroon who had transported them. As Holland's home economy was healthy, few Dutch felt desperate enough to take up such unattractive terms.

New Netherlands was, in any case, internally weak and unstable. It was poorly governed by inept and lazy governors; and its population was a mixture of people from all over Europe as well as many African slaves, forming what historians have called an "unstable pluralism."

The Pilgrims at Plymouth

Many Englishmen came from England for religious reasons. For the most part, these fell into two groups, Puritans and Separatists. Though similar in many respects to the Puritans, the Separatists believed the Church of England was beyond saving and so felt they must separate from it.

One group of Separatists, suffering government harassment, fled to Holland. Dissatisfied there, they decided to go to America and thus became the famous Pilgrims.

Led by William Bradford, they departed in 1620, having obtained from the London Company a charter to settle just south of the Hudson River. Driven by storms, their ship, the *Mayflower*, made landfall at Cape Cod in Massachusetts; and they decided it was God's will for them to settle in that area. This, however, put them outside the jurisdiction of any established government; and so before going ashore they drew up and signed the Mayflower Compact, establishing a foundation for orderly government based on the consent of the governed. After a difficult first winter that saw many die, the Pilgrims went on to establish a quiet and modestly prosperous colony. After a number of years of hard work they were able to buy out the investors who had originally financed their voyage and thus gain greater autonomy.

The Massachusetts Bay Colony

The Puritans were far more numerous than the Separatists. Contrary to stereotype, they did not dress in drab clothes and were not ignorant or bigoted. They did, however, take the Bible and their religion seriously and felt the Anglican Church still retained too many unscriptural practices left over from Roman Catholicism.

King James I had no use for the Puritans but refrained from bringing on a confrontation with their growing political power. His son, Charles I, determined in 1629 to persecute the Puritans aggressively and to rule without the Puritan-dominated Parliament. This course would lead eventually (ten years later) to civil war, but in the meantime some of the Puritans decided to set up a community in America.

To accomplish their purpose, they sought in 1629 to charter a joint-stock company to be called the Massachusetts Bay Company. Whether because Charles was glad to be rid of the Puritans or because he did not realize the special nature of this joint-stock company, the charter was granted. Further, the charter neglected to specify where the company's headquarters should be located. Taking advantage of this unusual omission, the Puritans determined to make their headquarters in the colony itself, 3,000 miles from meddlesome royal officials.

Under the leadership of John Winthrop, who taught that a new colony should provide the whole world with a model of what a Christian society ought to be, the Puritans carefully organized their venture and, upon arriving in Massachusetts in 1630, did not undergo the "starving time" that had often plagued other first-year colonies.

The government of Massachusetts developed to include a governor and a representative assembly (called the General Court) selected by the "freemen"— adult male church members. As Massachusetts' population increased (20,000 Puritans had come by 1642 in what came to be called the Great Migration), new towns were chartered, each town being granted a large tract of land by the Massachusetts government. As in European villages, these towns consisted of a number of houses clustered around the church house and the village green. Farmland was located around the outside of the town. In each new town the elect— those who testified of having experienced saving grace—covenanted together as a church.

Rhode Island, Connecticut, and New Hampshire

Puritans saw their colony not as a place to do whatever might strike one's fancy, but as a place to serve God and build His kingdom. Dissidents would only be tolerated insofar as they did not interfere with the colony's mission.

One such dissident was Roger Williams. A Puritan preacher, Williams was received warmly in Massachusetts in 1631; but he had a talent for carrying things to their logical (or sometimes not so logical) extreme. When his activities became disruptive, he was asked to leave the colony. To avoid having to return to England—where he would have been even less welcome—he fled to the wilderness around Narragansett Bay, bought land from the Indians, and founded the settlement of Providence (1636), soon populated by his many followers.

Another dissident was Anne Hutchinson, who openly taught things contrary to Puritan doctrine. Called before the General Court to answer for her teachings, she claimed to have had special revelations from God superseding the Bible. This was unthinkable in Puritan theology and led to Hutchinson's banishment from the colony. She also migrated to the area around Narragansett Bay and with her followers founded Portsmouth (1638). She later migrated still farther west and was killed by Indians.

In 1644 Roger Williams secured from Parliament a charter combining Providence, Portsmouth, and other settlements that had sprung up in the area into the colony of Rhode Island. Through Williams' influence the colony granted complete religious toleration. Rhode Island tended to be populated by such exiles and troublemakers as could not find welcome in the other colonies or in Europe. It suffered constant political turmoil.

Connecticut was founded by Puritans who had slight religious disagreements with the leadership of Massachusetts. In 1636 Thomas Hooker led a group of settlers westward to found Hartford. Hooker, though a good friend of Massachusetts Governor John Winthrop, felt he was exercising somewhat more authority than was good. Others also moved into Connecticut from Massachusetts. In 1639 the Fundamental Orders of Connecticut, the first written constitution in America, were drawn up, providing for representative government.

In 1637 a group of Puritans led by John Davenport founded the neighboring colony of New Haven. Davenport and his followers felt that Winthrop, far from being too strict, was not being strict enough. In 1662 a new charter combined both New Haven and Connecticut into an officially recognized colony of Connecticut.

New Hampshire's settlement did not involve any disagreement at all among the Puritans. It was simply settled as an overflow from Massachusetts. In 1677 King Charles II chartered the separate royal colony of New Hampshire. It remained economically dependent on Massachusetts.

QUESTION

> What was unique about Roger Williams' colony of Rhode Island?

EXPLANATION

Rhode Island was the first colony to establish religious toleration. At the time (1644) colonial governments did not tolerate dissent. Many dissenters from New England were forced to leave the colony, among them Roger Williams. He secured a charter from Parliament in New England for a new colony in what would be called Rhode Island. Other dissenters came to Rhode Island in order to enjoy religious toleration. As a result, it became the first colony with significant religious diversity.

Maryland

By the 1630s, the English crown was taking a more direct interest in exercising control over the colonies, and therefore turned away from the practice of granting charters to joint-stock companies, and towards granting such charters to single individuals or groups of individuals known as proprietors. The proprietors would actually own the colony, and would be directly responsible for it to the king, in an arrangement similar to the feudalism of medieval Europe. Though this was seen as providing more opportunity for royal control and less for autonomy on the part of the colonists, in practice proprietary colonies turned out much like the company colonies because settlers insisted on self-government.

The first proprietary colony was Maryland, granted in 1632 to George Calvert, Lord Baltimore. It was to be located just north of the Potomac River and to be at the same time a reward for Calvert's loyal service to the king as well as a refuge for English Catholics, of which Calvert was one. George Calvert died before the colony could be planted, but the venture was carried forward by his son Cecilius.

From the start more Protestants than Catholics came. To protect the Catholic minority, Calvert approved an Act of Religious Toleration (1649) guaranteeing political rights to Christians of all persuasions. Calvert also allowed a representative assembly. Economically and socially Maryland developed as a virtual carbon copy of neighboring Virginia.

QUESTION

What was the difference between a joint-stock colony and a proprietary colony?

EXPLANATION

Both were ways of financing a colonial settlement in the New World. A joint-stock company raised funds by selling shares of stock to investors, who expected to profit from the trade of the region. The stockholders held the charter to the colony. A proprietary colony was when a charter was granted by the crown to an individual or a group of individuals. A proprietary colony allowed the king more control of the colony, because the individuals were directly responsible to the crown.

The Carolinas

In 1663, Charles II, having recently been restored to the throne after a 20-year Puritan revolution that had seen his father beheaded, moved to reward eight of the noblemen who had helped him regain the crown by granting them a charter for all the lands lying south of Virginia and north of Spanish Florida.

The new colony was called Carolina, after the king. In hopes of attracting settlers, the proprietors came up with an elaborate plan for a hierarchical, almost feudal, society. Not surprisingly this proved unworkable, and despite offers of generous land grants to settlers, the Carolinas grew slowly.

The area of North Carolina developed as an overflow from Virginia with similar economic and cultural features. South Carolina was settled by English planters from the island of Barbados, who founded Charles Town (Charleston) in 1670. These planters brought with them their black slaves; thus, unlike the Chesapeake colonies of Virginia and Maryland, South Carolina had slavery as a fully developed institution from the outset. South Carolina eventually found rice to be a staple crop.

New York and New Jersey

Charles II, though immoral and dissolute, was cunning and had an eye for increasing Britain's power. The Dutch colony of New Netherlands lying between the Chesapeake and the New England colonies, caught his eye as a likely target for British expansion. In 1664 Charles gave his brother, James, Duke of York, title to all the Dutch lands in America, provided James conquered them first. To do this James sent an invasion fleet under the command of Colonel Richard Nicols. New Amsterdam fell almost without a shot and became New York.

James was adamantly opposed to representative assemblies and ordered that there should be none in New York. To avoid unrest Nicols shrewdly granted as many other civil and political rights as possible; but residents, particularly Puritans who had settled on Long Island, continued to agitate for self-government. Finally, in the 1680s, James relented, only to break his promise when he became king in 1685.

To add to the confusion in the newly renamed colony, James granted a part of his newly acquired domain to John Lord Berkeley and Sir George Carteret (two of the Carolina proprietors) who named their new proprietorship New Jersey. James neglected to tell Colonel Nicols of this, with the result that both Nicols, on the one hand, and Carteret and Berkeley, on the other, were granting title to the same land—to different settlers. Conflicting claims of land ownership plagued New Jersey for decades, being used by the crown in 1702 as a pretext to take over New Jersey as a royal colony.

Drill 2: The Beginnings of Colonization

1. The primary motive of those who founded the British colony in Virginia during the seventeenth century was

    (A) desire for economic gain.

    (B) desire for religious freedom.

    (C) desire to create a perfect religious commonwealth as an example to the rest of the world.

    (D) desire to recreate in the New World the story of feudalistic society that was fading in the Old World.

    (E) desire to increase the power and glory of Great Britain.

2. The patroon system was characteristic of which colony?

    (A) New France   (B) Virginia

    (C) Rhode Island   (D) New Netherlands

    (E) Massachusetts Bay

3. The Mayflower Compact could best be described as

    (A) a detailed frame of government.

    (B) a complete constitution.

    (C) a business contract.

    (D) a foundation for self-government.

    (E) an enumeration of the causes for leaving England and coming to the New World.

4. The most unusual feature of the charter of the Massachusetts Bay Colony was that it

    (A) provided that the colony should be run as a religious commonwealth.

    (B) made the colony completely independent of all English authority.

    (C) assured the colonists all the rights they would have had if they had been born and living in England.

    (D) did not specify where the company's headquarters should be.

    (E) specified that only Parliament, not the king, was to have authority over the colony.

5. During the first two decades of the seventeenth century all of the following aided in the establishment and growth of the colony at Jamestown, Virginia, EXCEPT

    (A) establishment of the Virginia House of Burgesses.

    (B) establishment of the ownership of private property.

    (C) the beginning of tobacco cultivation.

    (D) good relations with the local Indians.

    (E) large influxes of supplies and colonists from England.

3. THE COLONIAL WORLD

Life in the Colonies

New England grew not only from immigration but also from natural increase during the seventeenth century. The typical New England family had more children than the typical English or Chesapeake family, and more of those children survived to have families of their own. A New Englander could expect to live 15 to 20 years longer than his counterpart in the parent country and 25 to 30 years longer than his fellow colonist in the Chesapeake. Because of the continuity provided by these longer life spans, because the Puritans had migrated as intact family units, and because of the homogeneous nature of the Puritan New England colonies, New England enjoyed a much more stable and well-ordered society than did the Chesapeake colonies.

Puritans placed great importance on the family, which in their society was highly patriarchal. Young people were generally subject to their parents' direction in the matter of when and whom they would marry. Few defied this system, and illegitimate births were rare. Puritans also placed great importance on the ability to read, since they believed everyone should be able to read the Bible, God's word, himself. As a result, New England was ahead of the other colonies educationally and enjoyed extremely widespread literacy.

Since New England's climate and soil were unsuited to large-scale farming, the region developed a prosperous economy based on small farming, home industry, fishing, and especially trade and a large shipbuilding industry. Boston became a major international port.

Life in the Chesapeake colonies was drastically different. The typical Chesapeake colonist lived a shorter, less healthy life than his New England counterpart and was survived by fewer children. As a result the Chesapeake's population steadily declined despite a constant influx of settlers. Nor was Chesapeake society as stable as that of New England. Most Chesapeake settlers came as indentured servants; and since planters desired primarily male servants for work in the tobacco fields, men largely outnumbered women in Virginia and Maryland. This hindered the development of family life. The short life spans also contributed to the region's unstable family life as few children reached adulthood without experiencing the death of one or both parents. Remarriage resulted in households that contained children from several different marriages.

The system of indentured servitude was open to serious abuse, with masters sometimes treating their servants brutally or contriving through some technicality to lengthen their terms of indenture. In any case, 40 percent of the Chesapeake region's indentured servants failed to survive long enough to gain their freedom.

By the late seventeenth century life in the Chesapeake was beginning to stabilize, with death rates declining and life expectancies rising. As society stabilized, an elite group of wealthy families, such as the Byrds, Carters, Fitzhughs, Lees, and Randolphs, among others, began to dominate the social and political life of the region. Aping the life-style of the English country gentry, they built lavish manor houses from which to rule their vast plantations. For every one of these, however, there were many small farmers who worked hard for a living, showed deference to the great planters, and hoped someday they, or their children, might reach that level.

On the bottom rung of Southern society were the black slaves. During the first half of the seventeenth century blacks in the Chesapeake made up only a small percentage of the population and were treated more or less as indentured servants. In the decades between 1640 and 1670 this gradually changed, and blacks came to be seen and treated as life-long chattel slaves whose status would be inherited by their children. Larger numbers of them began to be imported and with this and rapid natural population growth they came by 1750 to compose 30 to 40 percent of the Chesapeake population.

While North Carolina tended to follow Virginia in its economic and social development (although with fewer great planters and more small farmers), South Carolina developed a society even more dominated by large plantations and chattel slavery. By the early decades of the eighteenth century, blacks had come to outnumber whites in that colony. South Carolina's economy remained dependent on the cultivation of its two staple crops, rice and, to a lesser extent, indigo.

How did the social structure in New England differ from that in Virginia in the seventeenth century?

EXPLANATION

New England had much less social stratification than Virginia. Most New England settlers were small farmers or manufactured products at home. Literacy and education was widespread. Virginia, on the other hand, had large plantations, where many indentured servants, and later slaves, worked. As a result, Virginia had more economic inequality than New England.

Mercantilism and the Navigation Acts

Beginning around 1650, British authorities began to take more interest in regulating American trade for the benefit of the mother country. A key idea that underlay this policy was the concept of mercantilism. Mercantilists believed the world's wealth was sharply limited, and therefore one nation's gain was automatically another nation's loss. Each nation's goal was to export more than it imported (i.e., to have a "favorable balance of trade"). The difference would be made up in gold and silver, which, so the theory ran, would make the nation strong both economically and militarily. To achieve their goals, mercantilists believed economic activity should be regulated by the government. Colonies could fit into England's mercantilist scheme by providing staple crops, such as rice, tobacco, sugar, and indigo, and raw materials, such as timber, that England would otherwise have been forced to import from other countries.

To make the colonies serve this purpose, Parliament passed a series of Navigation Acts (1651, 1660, 1663, and 1673). These were the foundation of England's worldwide commercial system and some of the most important pieces of imperial legislation during the colonial period. They were also intended as weapons in England's on-going struggle against its chief seventeenth century maritime rival, Holland. The system created by the Navigation Acts stipulated that trade with the colonies was to be carried on only in ships made in Britain or America and with at least 75 percent British or American crews. Additionally, when certain "enumerated" goods were shipped from an American port, they were to go only to Britain or to another American port. Finally, almost nothing could be imported to the colonies without going through Britain first.

Mercantilism's results were mixed. Though ostensibly for the benefit of all subjects of the British Empire, its provisions benefited some at the expense of others. It boosted the prosperity of New Englanders, who engaged in large-scale shipbuilding (something Britain's mercantilist policymakers chose to encourage), while it hurt the residents of the Chesapeake by driving down the price of tobacco (an enumerated item). On the whole, the Navigation Acts, as intended, transferred wealth from America to Britain by increasing the prices Americans had to pay for British goods and lowering the prices Americans received for the goods they produced. Mercantilism also helped bring on a series of three wars between England and Holland in the late 1600s.

Charles II and his advisors worked to tighten up the administration of colonies, particularly the enforcement of the Navigation Acts. In Virginia tempers grew short as tobacco prices plunged as a result. Virginians were also angry at Royal Governor Sir William Berkeley, whose high-handed, high-taxing ways they despised and who they believed was running the colony for the benefit of himself and his circle of cronies.

When in 1674, an impoverished nobleman of shady past by the name of Nathaniel Bacon came to Virginia and failed to gain admittance to Berkeley's inner circle with its financial advantages, he began to oppose Berkeley at every turn and came to head a faction of like-minded persons. In 1676 disagreement over Indian policy brought the matter to the point of armed conflict. Bacon and his men burned Jamestown, but then the whole matter came to an anticlimactic ending when Bacon died of dysentery.

The British authorities, hearing of the matter, sent ships, troops, and an investigating commission. Berkeley, who had 23 of the rebels hanged in reprisal, was removed; and thenceforth Virginia's royal governors had strict instructions to run the colony for the benefit of the mother country. In response, Virginia's gentry, who had been divided over Bacon's Rebellion, united to face this new threat to their local autonomy. By political means they consistently obstructed the governors' efforts to increase royal control.

The Half-Way Covenant

By the latter half of the seventeenth century many Puritans were coming to fear that New England was drifting away from its religious purpose. The children and grandchildren of the first generation were displaying more concern for making money than creating a godly society.

To deal with this, some clergymen in 1662 proposed the "Half-Way Covenant," providing a sort of half-way church membership for the children of members, even though those children, having reached adulthood, did not profess saving grace as was normally required for Puritan church membership. Those who embraced the Half-Way Covenant felt that in an increasingly materialistic society it would at least keep church membership rolls full and might preserve some of the church's influence in society.

Some communities rejected the Half-Way Covenant as an improper compromise, but in general the shift toward secular values continued, though slowly. Many Puritan ministers strongly denounced this trend in sermons that have come to be referred to as "jeremiads."

King Philip's War

As New England's population grew, local Indian tribes felt threatened, and conflict sometimes resulted. Puritans endeavored to convert Indians to Christianity. The Bible was translated into Algonquian; four villages were set up for converted Indians, who by 1650 numbered over a thousand. Still, most Indians remained unconverted.

In 1675, a Wampanoag chief named King Philip (Metacomet) led a war to exterminate the whites. Some 2,000 settlers lost their lives before King Philip was killed and his tribe subdued. New England continued to experience Indian troubles from time to time, though not as severe as those suffered by Virginia.

The Dominion of New England

The trend toward increasing imperial control of the colonies continued. In 1684 the Massachusetts charter was revoked in retaliation for that colony's large-scale evasion of the restrictions of the Navigation Acts.

The following year Charles II died and was succeeded by his brother, James II. James was prepared to go even farther in controlling the colonies, favoring the establishment of a unified government for all of New England, New York, and New Jersey. This was to be called the Dominion of New England, and the fact that it would abolish representative assemblies and facilitate the imposition of the Church of England on Congregationalist (Puritan) New England made it still more appealing to James.

To head the Dominion, James sent the obnoxious and dictatorial Sir Edmond Andros. Arriving in Boston in 1686, Andros quickly alienated the New Englanders. When news reached America of England's 1688 Glorious Revolution, replacing the Catholic James with his Protestant daughter Mary and her husband William of Orange, New Englanders cheerfully shipped Andros back to England.

Similar uprisings occurred in New York and Maryland. William and Mary's new government generally accepted these actions, though Jacob Leisler, leader of Leisler's Rebellion in New York, was executed for hesitating to turn over power to the new royal governor. This unfortunate incident poisoned the political climate of New York for many years.

The charter of Massachusetts, now including Plymouth, was restored in 1691, this time as a royal colony, though not as tightly controlled as others of that type.

The Salem Witch Trials

In 1692 Massachusetts was shaken by an unusual incident in which several young girls in Salem Village (now Danvers) claimed to be tormented by the occult activities of certain of their neighbors. Before the resulting Salem witch trials could be stopped by the intervention of Puritan ministers such as Cotton Mather, some 20 persons had been executed (19 by hanging and one crushed under a pile of rocks).

Pennsylvania and Delaware

Pennsylvania was founded as a refuge for Quakers. One of a number of radical religious sects that had sprung up about the time of the English Civil War, the Quakers held many controversial beliefs. They believed all persons had an "inner light" which allowed them to commune directly with God. They believed human institutions were, for the most part, unnecessary and, since they believed they could receive revelation directly from God, placed little importance on the Bible. They were also pacifists and declined to show customary deference to those who were considered to be their social superiors. This and their aggressiveness in denouncing established institutions brought them trouble in both Britain and America.

William Penn, a member of a prominent British family, converted to Quakerism as a young man. Desiring to found a colony as a refuge for Quakers, in 1681 he sought and received from Charles II a grant of land in America as payment of a large debt the king had owed Penn's late father.

Penn advertised his colony widely in Europe, offered generous terms on land, and guaranteed a representative assembly and full religious freedom. He personally went to America to set up his colony, laying out the city of Philadelphia. He succeeded in maintaining peaceful relations with the Indians.

In the years that followed, settlers flocked to Pennsylvania from all over Europe. The colony grew and prospered and its fertile soil made it not only attractive to settlers, but also a large exporter of grain to Europe and the West Indies.

Delaware, though at first part of Pennsylvania, was granted by Penn a separate legislature, but until the American Revolution, Pennsylvania's proprietary governors also functioned as governors of Delaware.

QUESTION

> What two conditions led to the success of the colony of Pennsylvania?

EXPLANATION

Pennsylvania offered settlers a fair amount of political and religious liberty, as well as fertile and productive soil. Thus, the colony attracted a large number of settlers from all over Europe and provided these settlers with an economic climate where they could become prosperous.

Drill 3: The Colonial World

1. "There is a twofold liberty, natural (I mean as our nature is now corrupt) and civil or federal. The first is common to man with beasts and other creatures. By this, man, as he stands in relation to man simply, hath liberty to do what he lists; it is a liberty to evil as well as to good.... The other kind of liberty I call civil or federal, it may also be termed moral, in reference to the covenant between God and man, in the moral law, and the politic

covenants and constitutions, amongst men themselves. This liberty is the proper end and object of authority, and cannot subsist without it; and it is a liberty to that only which is good, just, and honest."—John Winthrop, 1630.

In this passage, liberty is understood

(A) primarily in communal terms.

(B) as the most important value.

(C) as something incompatible with Puritan society.

(D) primarily in individual terms.

(E) as something to be achieved only in the future, not in the present.

2. Which of the following books was likely to be found in the home of a colonial New Englander?

(A) *The Scarlet Letter*   (B) *Walden*

(C) *Pilgrim's Progress*   (D) *The Holy Bible*, Douay version

(E) *Nature*

3. An indentured servant differed from a slave in that he or she

(A) received wages for their work.

(B) worked for a limited period of time, usually seven years, to repay their passage to America.

(C) was used only for agricultural work.

(D) was held in servitude for life.

(E) was ineligible for the 50 acres of land given under Virginia's head-right system.

4. Great Britain sought to control colonial trade because

(A) it did not want competition with its own manufacturers.

(B) colonial products were inferior to British products.

(C) colonial products were too expensive.

(D) the colonies were seeking political independence.

(E) the colonies were unable to establish trade with Spain and France.

5. The colonial South was divided into all of the following EXCEPT

(A) the Piedmont.   (B) the Great Plains.

(C) the Backcountry.   (D) the Tidewater.

(E) the Fall Line.

6. The term "Middle Colonies" refers to which of the following groupings?

   (A) New York, Pennsylvania, New Jersey, Delaware

   (B) Georgia, South Carolina, Virginia, Maryland

   (C) New Hampshire, New York, Virginia

   (D) Massachusetts, New Hampshire, Connecticut, Rhode Island

   (E) North Carolina, Virginia, Maryland, Delaware

7. Which of the following does NOT describe colonial government in America?

   (A) During the 1700s the assemblies became more powerful.

   (B) In royal colonies the governor could summon or dismiss the assembly.

   (C) Compared with England, the right to vote was limited to a few individuals.

   (D) The assemblies controlled the raising and spending of tax money.

   (E) In proprietary colonies the proprietor appointed the governor.

8. In founding the colony of Pennsylvania, William Penn's primary purpose was to

   (A) provide a refuge for persecuted English Quakers.

   (B) provide a refuge for persecuted Christians of all sects from all parts of Europe.

   (C) demonstrate the possibility and practicality of establishing truly friendly relations with the Indians.

   (D) make a financial profit.

   (E) provide a refuge for English debtors.

9. All of the following were main principles of the Navigation Acts EXCEPT

   (A) trade in the colonies was limited to only British or colonial merchants.

   (B) it prohibited the colonies from issuing their own paper currencies, greatly limiting their trading capabilities.

   (C) all foreign goods bound for the colonies had to be shipped through England where they were taxed with British import duties.

   (D) the colonists could not build or export products that directly competed with British export products.

   (E) colonial enumerated goods could only be sold in England.

10. The reason slavery flourished in the Southern English colonies and not in New England is

(A) most New England farms were too small for slaves to be economically necessary or viable whereas in the South the cultivation of staple crops, such as rice and tobacco, on large plantations necessitated the use of large numbers of indentured servants or slaves.

(B) blacks from the tropical climate of Africa could not adapt to the harsh New England winters. Their high death rates made their use as slave laborers unprofitable.

(C) a shortage of females in the Southern English colonies led to many female black Africans being imported as slaves and as potential wives for white planters in the region.

(D) whereas New England religious groups such as the Puritans forbade slavery on moral grounds, the Anglican church which dominated the Southern English colonies encouraged the belief that blacks were inferior, thus, not deserving of equal status.

(E) the Stono uprising in 1739 convinced New Englanders that the cost of controlling slaves was not worth their marginal economic benefits.

4. THE EIGHTEENTH CENTURY

Economy and Population

British authorities continued to regulate the colonial economy, though usually without going so far as to provoke unrest. An exception was the Molasses Act of 1733, which would have been disastrous for New England merchants. In this case, trouble was averted by the customs agents wisely declining to enforce the act stringently.

The constant drain of wealth from America to Britain, created by the mother country's mercantilistic policies, led to a corresponding drain in hard currency (gold and silver). The artificially low prices that this shortage of money created for American goods was even more advantageous to British buyers. When colonial legislatures responded by endeavoring to create paper money, British authorities blocked such moves. Despite these hindrances, the colonial American economy remained for the most part extremely prosperous.

America's population continued to grow rapidly, both from natural increases due to prosperity and a healthy environment, and from large-scale immigration, not only of English but also of such other groups as Scots-Irish and Germans.

The Germans were prompted to migrate by wars, poverty, and religious persecution in their homeland. They found Pennsylvania especially attractive and there settled fairly close to the frontier, where land was more readily available. They eventually came to be called the "Pennsylvania Dutch."

The Scots-Irish, Scottish Presbyterians who had been living in northern

Ireland for several generations, left their homes because of high rent and economic depression. In America they settled even farther west than the Germans, on or beyond the frontier in the Appalachians. They spread southward into the mountain valleys of Virginia and North Carolina.

QUESTION

> What effect did British economic policy have on the economy of the Amerian colonies in the eigtheenth century?

EXPLANATION

British policy was mercantilistic, where American colonies could trade, with few exceptions, only with Britain. This policy was of course advantageous to Britain and led to a drain of hard currency from the colonies. This led to a shortage of money in the colonies. Throughout the eighteenth century, Britain viewed the colonies as a source of revenue, and regulated the economy in order to maximize Britain's profit. This caused tension that ultimately led to the American Revolution.

The Early Wars of the Empire

Between 1689 and 1763 Britain and its American colonies fought a series of four wars with Spain, France, and France's Indian allies, in part to determine who would dominate North America.

Though the first war, known in America as King William's War (1689–1697) but in Europe as the War of the League of Augsburg, was a limited conflict involving no major battles in America, it did bring a number of bloody and terrifying border raids by Indians. It was ended by the Treaty of Ryswick, which made no major territorial changes.

The second war was known in America as Queen Anne's War (1702–1713), but in Europe as the War of the Spanish Succession, and brought America 12 years of sporadic fighting against France and Spain. It was ended by the Treaty of Utrecht, the terms of which gave Britain major territorial gains and trade advantages.

In 1739 war once again broke out with France and Spain. Known in America as King George's War, it was called the War of Jenkins' Ear in Europe and later the War of the Austrian Succession. American troops played an active role, accompanying the British on several important expeditions and suffering thousands of casualties. In 1745 an all New England army, led by William Pepperrell, captured the powerful French fortress of Louisbourg at the mouth of the St. Lawrence River. To the Americans' disgust, the British in the 1748 Treaty of Aix-la-Chapelle gave Louisbourg back to France in exchange for lands in India.

Georgia

With this almost constant imperial warfare in mind, it was decided to found a colony as a buffer between South Carolina and Spanish-held Florida. A group of British philanthropists, led by General James Oglethorpe, in 1732 obtained a charter for such a colony, to be located between the Savannah and Altamaha Rivers and to be populated by such poor as could not manage to make a living in Great Britain.

The philanthropist trustees, who were to control the colony for 21 years before it reverted to royal authority, made elaborate and detailed rules to mold the new colony's society as they felt best. As a result, relatively few settlers came, and those who did complained endlessly. By 1752 Oglethorpe and his colleagues were ready to acknowledge their efforts a failure. Thereafter, Georgia came to resemble South Carolina, though with more small farmers.

The Enlightenment

As the eighteenth century progressed, Americans came to be more or less influenced by European ways of thought, culture, and society. Some Americans embraced the European intellectual movement known as the "Enlightenment."

The key concept of the Enlightenment was rationalism—the belief that human reason was adequate to solve all of mankind's problems and, correspondingly, much less faith was needed in the central role of God as an active force in the universe.

A major English political philosopher of the Enlightenment was John Locke. Writing partially to justify England's 1688 Glorious Revolution, he strove to find in the social and political world the sort of natural laws Isaac Newton had recently discovered in the physical realm. He held that such natural laws included the rights of life, liberty, and property; that to secure these rights people submit to governments; and that governments which abuse these rights may justly be overthrown. His writings were enormously influential in America though usually indirectly, by way of early eighteenth-century English political philosophers. Americans tended to equate Locke's law of nature with the universal law of God.

The most notable Enlightenment man in America was Benjamin Franklin. While Franklin never denied the existence of God, he focused his attention on human reason and what it could accomplish. His renown spread to Europe both for the wit and wisdom of his *Poor Richard's Almanac* and for his scientific experiments.

The Great Awakening

Of much greater impact on the lives of the common people in America was the movement known as the Great Awakening. It consisted of a series of religious revivals occurring throughout the colonies from the 1720s to the 1740s. Preachers such as the Dutch Reformed Theodore Frelinghuysen, the Presbyterians William and Gilbert Tennent, and the Congregationalist Jonathan Edwards—best known for his sermon "Sinners in the Hands of an Angry God"—proclaimed a message of personal repentance and faith in Jesus Christ for salvation from an otherwise certain eternity in hell. The most dynamic preacher of the Great Awakening was the Englishman George Whitefield, who traveled through the colonies several times, speaking to crowds of up to 30,000.

The Great Awakening had several important results. America's religious community came to be divided between the "Old Lights," who rejected the Great Awakening, and the "New Lights," who accepted it—and sometimes suffered persecution because of their fervor. A number of colleges were founded (many of them today's "Ivy League" schools), primarily for the purpose of training New-Light ministers. The Great Awakening also fostered a greater readiness to lay the claims of established authority—in this case religious—alongside a fixed standard—in this case the Bible—and to reject such claims it found wanting.

The French and Indian War

The Treaty of Aix-la-Chapelle (1748), ending King George's War, provided little more than a breathing space before the next European and imperial war. England and France continued on a collision course as France determined to take complete control of the Ohio Valley and western Pennsylvania.

British authorities ordered colonial governors to resist this; and Virginia's Robert Dinwiddie, already involved in speculation on the Ohio Valley lands, was eager to comply. George Washington, a young major of the Virginia militia, was sent to western Pennsylvania to request the French to leave. When the French declined, Washington was sent in 1754 with 200 Virginia militiamen to expel them. After success in a small skirmish, Washington was forced by superior numbers to fall back on his hastily built Fort Necessity and then to surrender.

The war these operations initiated spread to Europe two years later, where it was known as the Seven Years' War. In America it later came to be known as the French and Indian War.

While Washington skirmished with the French in western Pennsylvania, delegates of seven colonies met in Albany, New York, to discuss common plans for defense. Delegate Benjamin Franklin proposed a plan for an intercolonial government. While the other colonies showed no support for the idea, it was an important precedent for the concept of uniting in the face of a common enemy.

To deal with the French threat, the British dispatched Major General Edward Braddock with several regiments of British regular troops. Braddock marched overland toward the French outpost of Fort Duquesne, at the place where the Monongahela and Allegheny Rivers join to form the Ohio. About eight miles short of his goal he was ambushed by a small force of French and Indians. Two-thirds of the British regulars, including Braddock himself, were killed. However, Britain bounced back from this humiliating defeat and several others that followed, and under the leadership of its capable and energetic prime minister, William Pitt, had by 1760 taken Quebec and Montreal and virtually liquidated the French empire in North America.

By the Treaty of Paris of 1763, which officially ended hostilities, Britain gained all of Canada and all of what is now the United States east of the Mississippi River. France lost all of its North American holdings.

Americans at the end of the French and Indian War were proud to be part of the victorious British Empire and proud of the important role they had played in making it so. They felt affection for Great Britain, and thoughts of independence had not yet crossed their minds.

Drill 4: The Eighteenth Century

1. The economic theory of mercantilism would be consistent with which of the following statements?

    (A) Economies will prosper most when trade is restricted as little as possible.

    (B) A government should seek to direct the economy so as to maximize exports.

    (C) Colonies are of little economic importance to the mother country.

    (D) It is vital that a country import more than it exports.

    (E) Tariff barriers should be avoided as much as possible.

2. Prior to 1763 the British policy of "salutary neglect"

    (A) did not enforce the Navigation Acts.

    (B) allowed royal colonies to elect their own governors.

    (C) took the Royal Navy off the high seas.

    (D) encouraged colonists to establish their own parliament.

    (E) withdrew British soldiers from North America.

3. The Proclamation of 1763

    (A) ordered that settlement be stopped west of the peaks of the Appalachians.

    (B) stated that those who broke the trade laws were to be tried in the admiralty courts.

    (C) ended the French and Indian War.

    (D) forbade trade with the French, Dutch, and Spanish West Indies.

    (E) established new taxes on trade.

4. The Great Awakening of the 1740s resulted in

    (A) the establishment of the Church of England.

    (B) a split between religious traditionalists and religious radicals.

(C) an outbreak of witch hunting, resulting in the Salem witchcraft trials.

(D) the hanging of Quakers in Boston.

(E) an increase in the number of Catholic immigrants to the colonies.

5. Jonathan Edwards was

(A) a preacher of the Great Awakening in New England.

(B) a mid-eighteenth century Pennsylvania Enlightenment philosopher.

(C) an early opponent of Parliamentary taxation of the American colonies.

(D) a transcendentalist thinker and writer.

(E) the founder of the communitarian experiment at New Harmony.

1500–1763
DRILLS

ANSWER KEY

Drill 1—The Age of Exploration

1. (A)   2. (D)   3. (A)   4. (A)   5. (D)

Drill 2—The Beginnings of Colonization

1. (A)   2. (D)   3. (D)   4. (D)   5. (D)

Drill 3—The Colonial World

1. (A)   2. (C)   3. (B)   4. (A)   5. (B)
6. (A)   7. (C)   8. (A)   9. (B)   10. (A)

Drill 4—The Eighteenth Century

1. (B)   2. (A)   3. (A)   4. (B)   5. (A)

GLOSSARY: 1500–1763

Chattel Slaves
Slaves whose status was life-long and would be passed on to their children.

Conquistadores
Independent Spanish adventurers, instrumental in the exploration of the New World.

Creoles
Those of Spanish parentage born in the New World.

Encomiendas
Large manors or estates given as rewards to Spanish *conquistadores*, with Indian slaves ruthlessly managed for their benefit.

Hacienda
An estate similar to the *encomiendas,* but somewhat milder.

Huguenots
French Protestants.

Indentured Servant
A person whose passage to the New World was paid for by an American planter or company in exchange for several years of labor.

Isthmus
A narrow strip of land connecting two larger land masses, with water on two sides.

Joint-Stock Company
A company which raises capital by the sale of shares of stock.

Mayflower Compact
A contract drawn up on board the *Mayflower* to lay the basis for governing Plymouth Colony.

Mercantilism
An economic system based on the belief that the world wealth was finite, and therefore where each nation strove to export more than it imported in order to receive gold and silver which would make the nation strong both militarily and economically.

Monarch
> A ruler, such as a king or a queen, who serves as head of state, and whose term of office is for life.

Northwest Passage
> A water route to the Orient through or around the North American continent.

Old Lights/New Lights
> Old Lights rejected the religious enthusiasm of the Great Awakening; New Lights accepted it.

Patroon
> A large landholder in New Netherlands (present-day New York) who had at least 50 tenant farmers working on his land.

Peninsulares
> Natives of Spain in the New World.

Pennsylvania Dutch
> Germans who settled in Pennsylvania.

Proprietary Colony
> A colony which was owned by an individual, rather than a company.

Puritans
> Calvinists who hoped to reform the Church of England.

Separatists
> English Protestants who did not believe the Church of England could be saved.

CHAPTER 3

1763–1787
THE AMERICAN REVOLUTION

➤ Diagnostic Test
➤ 1763–1787 Review & Drills
➤ Glossary

1763-1787
DIAGNOSTIC TEST

1. Ⓐ Ⓑ Ⓒ Ⓓ Ⓔ
2. Ⓐ Ⓑ Ⓒ Ⓓ Ⓔ
3. Ⓐ Ⓑ Ⓒ Ⓓ Ⓔ
4. Ⓐ Ⓑ Ⓒ Ⓓ Ⓔ
5. Ⓐ Ⓑ Ⓒ Ⓓ Ⓔ
6. Ⓐ Ⓑ Ⓒ Ⓓ Ⓔ
7. Ⓐ Ⓑ Ⓒ Ⓓ Ⓔ
8. Ⓐ Ⓑ Ⓒ Ⓓ Ⓔ
9. Ⓐ Ⓑ Ⓒ Ⓓ Ⓔ
10. Ⓐ Ⓑ Ⓒ Ⓓ Ⓔ
11. Ⓐ Ⓑ Ⓒ Ⓓ Ⓔ
12. Ⓐ Ⓑ Ⓒ Ⓓ Ⓔ
13. Ⓐ Ⓑ Ⓒ Ⓓ Ⓔ
14. Ⓐ Ⓑ Ⓒ Ⓓ Ⓔ
15. Ⓐ Ⓑ Ⓒ Ⓓ Ⓔ
16. Ⓐ Ⓑ Ⓒ Ⓓ Ⓔ
17. Ⓐ Ⓑ Ⓒ Ⓓ Ⓔ
18. Ⓐ Ⓑ Ⓒ Ⓓ Ⓔ
19. Ⓐ Ⓑ Ⓒ Ⓓ Ⓔ
20. Ⓐ Ⓑ Ⓒ Ⓓ Ⓔ
21. Ⓐ Ⓑ Ⓒ Ⓓ Ⓔ
22. Ⓐ Ⓑ Ⓒ Ⓓ Ⓔ
23. Ⓐ Ⓑ Ⓒ Ⓓ Ⓔ
24. Ⓐ Ⓑ Ⓒ Ⓓ Ⓔ
25. Ⓐ Ⓑ Ⓒ Ⓓ Ⓔ

1763–1787
DIAGNOSTIC TEST

This diagnostic test is designed to help you determine your strengths and weaknesses in your knowledge of the American Revolution (1763–1787). Follow the directions and check your answers.

> **Study this chapter for the following tests:**
> **AP U.S. History, CLEP General, CLEP United States History I,**
> **GED, Praxis Specialty Area, SAT: United States History**

25 Questions

DIRECTIONS: Choose the correct answer for each of the following questions. Fill in each answer on the answer sheet.

1. The Declaration of Independence stated that

   (A) men are created unequal.

   (B) governments derive their power from God.

   (C) it was not right that a small island should rule a large continent.

   (D) people have the right to abolish governments destructive of their rights.

   (E) there shall be no taxation without representation.

2. According to the Treaty of Paris of 1783, the boundaries of the United States were

   (A) Canada, the Gulf of Mexico, and the Mississippi River.

   (B) Canada, Florida, and the Mississippi River.

   (C) Canada, Florida, and the Missouri River.

   (D) Canada, Florida, and the Appalachian Mountains.

   (E) Canada, the Gulf of Mexico, and the Missouri River.

3. Which of the following is true of the Stamp Act Congress?

   (A) It was the first unified government for all the American colonies.

   (B) It provided an important opportunity for colonial stamp agents to discuss methods of enforcing the act.

    (C) It was attended only by Georgia, Virginia, and the Carolinas.

  • (D) It provided an important opportunity for colonial leaders to meet and establish ties with one another.

    (E) It rejected the assertion that the colonies ought to protest acts of Parliament deemed to be unconstitutional.

4.   The ordinances of 1785 and 1787 established all of the following EXCEPT

    (A) division of the Northwestern lands into townships.

    (B) reservation of one section in each township for support of public schools.

    (C) establishment of territorial government.

  • (D) protection of slavery.

    (E) a procedure for achieving statehood.

5.   The Newburgh Conspiracy was concerned with

    (A) betrayal of the plans for the vital fort at West Point, New York.

  • (B) the use of the Continental Army to create a more centralized Union of the states.

    (C) resistance to the collection of federal excise taxes in western Pennsylvania.

    (D) New England's threat to secede should the War of 1812 continue.

    (E) Aaron Burr's plot to detach the western United States as an empire for himself.

6.   The Molasses Act was intended to enforce England's mercantilist policies by

    (A) forcing the colonists to export solely to Great Britain.

  • (B) forcing the colonists to buy sugar from other British colonies rather than from foreign producers.

    (C) forbidding the colonists to engage in manufacturing activity in competition with British industries.

    (D) providing a favorable market for the products of the British East India Company.

    (E) creating an economic situation in which gold tended to flow from the colonies to the mother country.

7.   The British government imposed the Townshend Acts on the American colonies in the belief that

(A)   the American position regarding British taxation had changed.

(B)   it was necessary to provoke a military confrontation in order to teach the colonists a lesson.

(C)   its provisions were designed solely to enforce mercantilism.

(D)   it had been approved by the colonial legislatures.

(E)   the Americans would accept it as external rather than internal taxation.

8.   One of the purposes for writing the Declaration of Independence was to

(A)   persuade the still undecided American populace to accept a permanent break with Great Britain.

(B)   convince potential foreign allies of American determination to gain independence.

(C)   convince the British government to accept American independence.

(D)   protect captured American soldiers from possible treatment as traitors.

(E)   rally all the states behind a common cause.

Questions 9 and 10 refer to the following passage.

'Tis repugnant to reason, to the universal order of things, to all examples from former ages, to suppose that this Continent can long remain subject to any external power. The most sanguine in Britain doth not think so. The utmost stretch of human wisdom cannot, at this time, compass a plan, short of separation, which can promise the Continent even a year's security. Reconciliation is *now* a fallacious dream. Nature hath deserted the connection, and art cannot supply her place.

9.   This passage can be found in which of the following?

(A)   Thomas Jefferson's Declaration of Independence

(B)   George Washington's farewell address

(C)   Thomas Paine's *Crisis Papers*

(D)   Thomas Paine's *Common Sense*

(E)   John Dickinson's *Letters from a Farmer in Pennsylvania*

10.   The author wants primarily to convince readers that

(A)   it is a necessity of nature that America should be independent of Great Britain.

(B)   America should keep itself free from entangling alliances with European powers.

(C) Great Britain will soon give up the struggle to retain her North American colonies.

(D) parliamentary attempts to tax Americans without the consent of colonial legislatures are violations of the English constitution.

(E) Britain has given ample provocation for the colonies to declare their independence.

11. "For abolishing the free System of English Laws in a neighbouring Province, establishing therein an Arbitrary government, and enlarging its Boundaries so as to render it at once an example and fit instrument for introducing the same absolute rule into these Colonies."

In the above passage, Thomas Jefferson indicts King George III and Parliament for the

(A) Quartering Act.   (B) Prohibitory Act.

(C) Quebec Act.   (D) Stamp Act.

(E) Townshend Acts.

12. In writing "He has abdicated Government here, by declaring us out of his Protection and waging War against us," about which act or acts by King George III and Parliament is Thomas Jefferson complaining?

(A) The Declaratory Act   (B) The Coercive Acts

(C) The Intolerable Acts   (D) The Townshend Acts

(E) The Prohibitory Act

13. The fundamental goal of mercantilism in the 17th and 18th centuries was

(A) to eliminate the obstacles to free trade among the countries of Europe.

(B) to have "mother" countries serve as a source of raw materials and the colonies as a source of manufactured goods.

(C) to limit foreign imports and to encourage a favorable balance of trade.

(D) to encourage wealthy nations to provide economic assistance to the developing areas of the world.

(E) to discourage the growth of economic nationalism.

14. Parliament claimed the right to tax and legislate for England's American colonies whenever it desired, without direct American representation in Parliament, through passage of

(A) the Declaratory Act.   (B) the Proclamation of 1763.

(C)   the Townshend Acts.   (D)   the Intolerable Acts.

(E)   the Currency Act.

15.   England passed the Stamp Act in 1765 to

(A)   punish Americans for protests to the Sugar Act.

(B)   control the American press.

(C)   raise money to reduce England's national debt.

(D)   allow for illegal search-and-seizure of smugglers.

(E)   allow Americans to settle the Ohio River Valley.

16.   After the American Revolution, the Loyalists did NOT

(A)   return to Great Britain.

(B)   emigrate to Canada.

(C)   sue America for property loss.

(D)   settle in the West Indies.

• (E)   create their own American colony in Ohio.

17.   The Articles of Confederation created for the 13 states

(A)   a strong national government.

(B)   a sound national economy.

- (C)   a league of friendship among 13 independent countries.

(D)   the Bill of Rights.

(E)   interstate trade agreements.

18.   During the winter of 1786, Shays's Rebellion indicated to most Americans

(A)   the political dangers of the postwar recession.

(B)   the weaknesses of state government.

(C)   the need to reform the Articles of Confederation.

(D)   the desperation of the yeoman farmer in America.

(E)   all of the above.

19.   The passage of the Declaratory Act in 1766 by Parliament was greeted in America by

1774

(A)   the creation of the Continental Congress.

(B)   mob violence against British merchants.

(C) refusal to pay these new taxes.

‧ (D) little attention to its statement of parliamentary sovereignty.

(E) Tories fleeing to Canada.

20. At the close of the American Revolution, a group of American writers and artists sought to establish a distinctly American national culture. Which of the following do not belong to this movement?

(A) Noah Webster   (B) Philip Freneau

(C) Hector St. Jean Crèvecoeur   (D) Cotton Mather

(E) Joel Barlow

21. The key issue that prevented the American colonists from resolving their problems with England without open rebellion was

(A) the sovereignty of King George III over the colonies.

(B) the sovereignty of Parliament's edicts over the colonies.

(C) the stationing of British soldiers on American soil.

(D) American desire for total independence from Britain.

(E) the use of boycotts by American colonists to resist taxes passed by Parliament.

22. The battles of Lexington and Concord were significant because

(A) they convinced the British that the colonists could not be defeated militarily and led to the British abandonment of the port of Boston.

(B) they proved the superiority of European military tactics as well as the superiority of British regulars to the ragtag American militias.

(C) they marked the first organized battles between British regulars and colonial militiamen and ended any hopes for a peaceful resolution to the disagreement between England and its colonies.

(D) they marked the turning point of the American Revolution. After Concord, the British were never again able to regain the offensive against the Americans.

(E) they led to Benedict Arnold's betrayal of the American cause when he felt he wasn't given enough recognition for his role in leading the Americans to victory.

23. The Sugar Act and the Townshend Acts differed from the previously passed Navigation Acts in that

(A) the Navigation Acts taxed goods imported to the colonies directly from Britain, whereas the Sugar Act and the Townshend Acts taxed only goods imported to the colonies from outside of Britain.

(B) the Navigation Acts taxed only the ships on which goods were transported to the colonies, not the merchandise carried by those ships. The Sugar Act and the Townshend Acts taxed specific merchandise carried by ships to the colonies.

(C) the Navigation Acts taxed goods based on the distance the goods traveled to reach America, whereas the Sugar Act and the Townshend Acts taxed the goods themselves, regardless of how far they traveled to reach America.

(D) the Navigation Acts taxed only goods imported to the colonies from outside of Britain, whereas the Sugar Act and the Townshend Acts taxed goods imported to the colonies directly from Britain.

(E) the Sugar Act and the Townshend Acts put specific limits on which goods imported to the colonies could be taxed, whereas the Navigation Acts had taxed virtually everything transported by ship from Britain to the colonies.

24. The Coercive Acts were passed in reaction to

(A) the Seven Years' War.

(B) the Boston Massacre.

(C) the Declaration of Independence.

(D) the formation of the Sons of Liberty.

(E) the Boston Tea Party.

25. The primary reason for French aid to the American colonists was

(A) French belief in the ideals for which the American revolution stood.

(B) English attacks against French naval vessels along the French coast.

(C) American promises to restore Louisiana and Quebec to French control in return for French aid.

(D) French desires for revenge against England and hopes to regain much of the territory lost to the British in the Seven Years' War.

(E) French belief that aid to the Americans would force Britain to consider forming a confederation with France, allowing them to jointly dominate European affairs.

1763–1787
DIAGNOSTIC TEST

ANSWER KEY

1. (D)	6. (B)	11. (C)	16. (E)	21. (B)
2. (B)	7. (E)	12. (E)	17. (C)	22. (C)
3. (D)	8. (B)	13. (C)	18. (E)	23. (D)
4. (D)	9. (D)	14. (A)	19. (D)	24. (E)
5. (B)	10. (A)	15. (C)	20. (D)	25. (D)

DETAILED EXPLANATIONS OF ANSWERS

1.   **(D)**   The Declaration argued that all men are created equal and are endowed with rights, that government is instituted for the purpose of preserving these rights and gains its powers from the governed, and that people have the right of revolution when government becomes despotism. It was Thomas Paine's *Common Sense* that argued that a small island should not rule a large continent. No taxation without representation was a popular phrase of Americans after the Stamp Act of 1765.

2.   **(B)**   The Treaty recognized Canada, Florida, and the Mississippi River as the boundaries of the United States. Florida went to Spain. The Missouri River lies west of the Mississippi, while the Appalachians lay within the United States of 1783.

3.   **(D)**   One of the most important aspects of the Stamp Act Congress was the opportunity it provided for colonial leaders to meet and establish acquaintances with one another. Nine colonies—not merely Georgia, Virginia, and the Carolinas (C)—were represented at it, but far from being a unified government for all the American colonies (A); it simply passed mild resolutions protesting the Stamp Act. It was not therefore either a vehicle for enforcing the act (B) or opposed to American protests against the act (E).

4.   **(D)**   The Northwest Ordinance of 1787 barred slavery from the territories.

5.   **(B)**   The Newburgh Conspiracy was composed of army officers disgusted with a central government too weak to collect taxes to pay them and their troops. Betrayal of the plans for the fort at West Point (A) was Benedict Arnold's treason; resistance to the collection of federal excise taxes in western Pennsylvania (C); took the form of the Whiskey Rebellion of 1791. New England's threat to secede should the War of 1812 continue (D) was made at the 1814 Hartford Convention. Burr's strange plot (E) came to nothing.

6.   **(B)**   The Molasses Act was intended to force the colonists to buy sugar from more expensive British colonial sources rather than from foreign producers. Forcing the colonists to export solely to Great Britain (A), forbidding them to engage in manufacturing activity in competition with British industries (C), and creating an economic situation in which gold tended to flow from the colonies to the mother country (E) were also goals of mercantilism. Providing a favorable market for the products of the British East India Company (D) was the purpose of the Tea Act.

7.   **(E)**   The British government mistakenly thought the colonists would accept the Townshend Acts as an external tax after having rejected the previous Stamp Act, an internal tax. They were under no illusions about the American position on taxation having changed (A), and they had not yet decided to provoke a military confrontation to teach the colonists a lesson (B). The act was designed to collect revenue, not merely enforce mercantilism (C), and it had not been approved by the colonial legislatures (D), though in either case the Americans would probably have accepted it.

8.   **(B)**   One of the purposes for writing the Declaration of Independence was to convince potential foreign allies of American determination to gain independence. Such a declaration was not likely, after all that had been said already, to persuade many undecided Americans (A) nor to obtain greater unity among the states than was already the case (E). It also could not be expected to persuade the British to accept American independence (C) or to treat American prisoners of war decently (D).

9.   **(D)**   Thomas Paine argued that it was only common sense (the title of his 1776 pamphlet) for the American colonies to become independent from Great Britain. His argument is much more radical than that of John Dickinson in his *Letters from a Farmer in Pennsylvania* (E), written a decade earlier as a protest against the unconstitutional practices of the British government. Paine's *Crisis Papers* (C) were written about a year after *Common Sense* and were aimed not at convincing people to declare independence, which had already been done, but rather at persuading them to make sacrifices in order to win that independence.

10.   **(A)**   Paine's argument in this passage is that it is a necessity of nature that "this Continent"—America—should be independent of Great Britain. See also the explanation for number 9 above.

11.   **(C)**   The act Jefferson was attacking in this passage of the Declaration of Independence was the 1774 Quebec Act, establishing Roman Catholicism and authoritarian government in that province and extending it to embrace all of what is now the United States west of the Appalachians, north of the Ohio River, and east of the Mississippi. The Quartering Act (A), also of 1774, provided for the quartering of British troops in America at the expense of the colonists. The Prohibitory Act (B), issued late in 1775, declared the Americans to be no longer under the protection of King George III and amounted to a virtual declaration of war. The Stamp Act (D) of 1765, and the Townshend Acts (E) issued three years later, were attempts by Parliament to tax the American colonies.

12.   **(E)**   In this passage of the Declaration of Independence, Jefferson was complaining of the Prohibitory Act, by which King George III declared the Americans to be no longer under his protection and virtually declared war on them. Many Americans felt the withdrawal of the king's protection relieved them

of their debt of allegiance to the king and saw the act as his abdication of the government of the colonies.

13.   **(C)**   Mercantilism, the pursuit of economic power through national self-sufficiency, was the dominant economic doctrine in Western Europe by 1660. This doctrine encouraged the state to encourage manufacturers, to develop and protect its own shipping, and to make use of colonies as sources of raw materials and markets for its manufactured goods.

14.   **(A)**   The Declaratory Act, whose passage was coupled with the defeat of the detested Stamp Act, stated that Parliament had the right to tax any English colony when it chose and as it chose. The fact that the colonists had no representatives to Parliament was denied by Parliament's belief that IT represented all English citizens whether they lived in England itself or in England's overseas colonies. Therefore, Parliament believed that it alone had the right to tax England's colonies and could do so at will. Coupling the passage of this act with the repeal of the Stamp Act blunted the American reaction because Americans were so busy celebrating the repeal of the Stamp Act, most ignored the implications of the Declaratory Act.

15.   **(C)**   The primary purpose behind all of England's measures to raise a tax in America after 1763 was to reduce England's national debt. During the Seven Years' War with France, England was put on the verge of bankruptcy and could not tax its own subjects any higher. As a result, England turned to its colonies to raise the sorely needed revenue. The colonies had enjoyed the fruits of the empire and a policy of salutary neglect where they evaded taxes openly. The Stamp Act required all legal and published documents to bear a stamp issued from England with a small fee attached. Unlike the mild and sporadic protests against the Sugar Act earlier, Americans responded to the new tax with determined and forceful protests, led by merchants, lawyers, and printers. England had already angered the colonists by refusing their settlement west of Pennsylvania in the Ohio Territory by the Proclamation Line Act of 1763 and allowed illegal searches through the Writs of Assistance in 1760. The Stamp Act was not designed to control the American press.

16.   **(E)**   The Loyalists for the most part emigrated out of America. Many returned to England during the war rather than suffer political and economic persecution by the colonials. Some Loyalists founded new settlements during the Revolution and its aftermath in Canada and the West Indies. It is estimated that Loyalists comprised about 20 percent of the American population during the Revolution. For those who fled the country, England offered modest pensions. These pensions could not replace the loss of their confiscated property by the patriots, and issue of long-standing difference between England and America after the Revolutionary War. There was no Loyalist settlement in the Ohio Territory.

17.   **(C)**   The Articles of Confederation existed as the government of the United States from 1781 through 1788 when it was replaced by the United States Constitution. The Articles existed as a unicameral legislature in which each state had one vote. It was granted no coercive powers over the states and cannot be considered a national government, as it could not act directly on citizens. Because it could not raise taxes directly, but could only request moneys from the states, the Articles had little control over the states' finances. It paid for the war through an inflationary currency that at times was nearly worthless. After the war, the Articles proved unable to control interstate trade conflicts that led indirectly to the writing of the Constitution. The Bill of Rights was not ratified until 1791, two years after the Articles had expired. At best, it kept the 13 states from dividing through the use of a common enemy, England, during the war.

18.   **(E)**   In the immediate aftermath of the Revolutionary War in 1783, the British sought to do economically what they had been unsuccessful at militarily. British merchants indebted Americans heavily by extending credit and then in 1785 demanding full payment in gold. American merchants demanded full payment from yeoman farmers and would not accept barter payment as tender. The result was that by 1786, 35 percent of American farmers were in danger of losing their farms through mortgages. The farmers of western Massachusetts requested aid from the state government and when none came took matters into their own hands. The angry farmers closed down the courts to stop foreclosure proceedings against farmers. Massachusetts requested aid from the Articles, but the central government was unable to assist Massachusetts. Massachusetts eventually put down the rebellion with a show of force and the rebels scattered. Shays's Rebellion shocked most conservatives in America into recognizing that the Articles were sorely in need of reform. A convention was called for the summer of 1787 to meet in Philadelphia. The 55 delegates to that convention produced the Constitution of the United States.

19.   **(D)**   The Declaratory Act was largely ignored by Americans because of their rejoicing over the repeal of the hated Stamp Act of 1765. As its title indicates, the Declaratory Act simply stated that although the notorious Stamp Act had been repealed, Parliament still retained its sovereignty over the American colonies. As a result, the Declaratory Act did not add new taxes, resulted in the temporary "end" of American protests, and actually strengthened the position of the Tories who were loyal to British authority in America. The creation of America's first Continental Congress, as the creation of an extralegal form of government, was an extremely radical act and did not occur until 1774.

20.   **(D)**   Cotton Mather was a leading Puritan minister and intellectual who died a half-century prior to the American Revolution. Mather was a leading figure in the Salem witch trials of 1692–1694 and earned great fame for the publication of his book *Magnalia Christi Americana*, which was a homage to great Puritan Americans, in 1704. Noah Webster was one of the greatest champions of an American culture in late eighteenth-century America and designed his

dictionary to create a national language. Freneau, Crèvecoeur, and Barlow all sought to exalt a new American culture at the close of the Revolution. Through their essays, poems, and plays, each supported the view of a special historical mission for America and its people for the cause of freedom and liberty in world history.

21.   **(B)**   The whole "taxation without representation" issue revolved around Parliament's belief that its laws were sovereign (unchallengeable) in all parts of the empire, including the colonies. This sovereignty of parliamentary rule meant that Parliament could pass any taxes or laws in regard to the colonies and the colonies could not legally resist the enactment of these taxes or laws. The colonists, however, believed that without direct representation in Parliament, their rights as English citizens were being violated. In their view the Parliament had no right to tax them or regulate them unless they were given direct parliamentary representation. Neither side was willing to compromise on the issue and without compromise, no solution to the problems related to this conflict could be developed.

22.   **(C)**   The shots fired at Lexington have been labeled "the shots heard round the world." Up until this time, many colonists and English rulers still believed some type of compromise short of violence could be worked out. Many Englishmen believed just a strong "show of force" by the British military would send rebellious colonists scurrying back to their farms. The British rout at Concord proved that however ragtag the colonial forces looked, they were willing to fight and die for their cause and could even beat the British in the right circumstances. While the British at this point considered the debacle at Concord to be a fluke, the violence marked the end of any hope of a nonviolent settlement to the British-American conflict. Britain would now have to attempt to militarily crush the colonies, and the colonists were committed to open rebellion from the motherland.

23.   **(D)**   The Navigation Acts were passed in the mid-seventeenth century to coerce the colonies into trading directly with their mother country, England. These acts were not designed to raise money for England. However, the Sugar Act and the Townshend Acts represented a shifting of English policy toward the colonies. These acts were designed to raise money from the colonies by taxing goods imported directly from England. The purpose of taxing the colonies this way was to raise money to cover the costs to Britain for defending and administering the American colonies.

24.   **(E)**   The Coercive Acts, or Intolerable Acts, were punitive measures aimed at Massachusetts in particular, and the colonies in general, for resistance to the Tea Act of 1773. This resistance had culminated in the Boston Tea Party. The Coercive Acts closed the port of Boston until the tea dumped into Boston Harbor by Bostonians was paid for. The acts also reorganized the Massachusetts government, allowed officials accused of crimes while enforcing the law to be tried in

Canada or England, and required colonists to let their houses be used for troops' quarters when local military commanders requested it.

The incorrect choices all list events that were related to the growing split between Britain and America, but did not directly lead to the passage of the Coercive Acts. The Seven Years' War (A) (called the French and Indian War in America) had ended in 1763, ten years before the Coercive Acts, and had no connection with their passage. The Boston Massacre (B) occurred in 1770, and while it signaled the depth of antagonism between Britain and Bostonians, it was followed by three years of calm. As such, it was not a direct cause of the passage of the Coercive Acts, although it was certainly indirectly related. The Declaration of Independence (C) would not be written for another three years. Finally, the formation of the Sons of Liberty (D) took place in 1765. While they were involved in the Tea Party, their formation was not related to the passage of the Coercive Acts.

25.   **(D)**   The French saw the American Revolution as a chance to get even with England for past losses. Once the Americans had shown that they could withstand English assaults and that England would be overextended and tied down in a protracted struggle with its colonies, the French saw intervention as the best opportunity they would ever have to restore the balance of power in Europe between Britain and France. The French also hoped that an American victory would drive Britain from North America, leaving a weak and unstable American nation in its place. The inherent weakness and potential collapse of any American government surviving the revolution could open the door to renewed French domination of North America.

1763–1787
REVIEW

1. THE COMING OF THE AMERICAN REVOLUTION

Writs of Assistance

While Americans' feelings toward Great Britain were pride and affection, British officials felt contemptuous of Americans and anxious to increase imperial control over them beyond anything that had previously been attempted. This drive to gain new authority over the colonies, beginning in 1763, led directly to American independence.

Even before that time the Writs of Assistance cases had demonstrated that Americans would not accept a reduction of their freedom.

In 1761 a young Boston lawyer named James Otis argued before a Massachusetts court that Writs of Assistance (general search warrants issued to help royal officials stop evasion of Britain's mercantilist trade restrictions) were contrary to natural law. He made his point though he lost his case, and others in the colonies joined in protesting against the Writs.

Grenville and the Stamp Act

In 1763 the strongly anti-American George Grenville became prime minister and set out to solve some of the empire's more pressing problems. Chief of these was the large national debt incurred in the recent war.

Of related concern was the cost of defending the American frontier, recently the scene of a bloody Indian uprising led by an Ottowa chief named Pontiac. Goaded by French traders, Pontiac had aimed to drive the entire white population into the sea. While failing in that endeavor, he had succeeded in killing a large number of settlers along the frontier.

Grenville created a comprehensive program to deal with these problems and moved energetically to put it into effect. He sent the Royal Navy to suppress American smuggling and enforce vigorously the Navigation Acts. He also issued the Proclamation of 1763, forbidding white settlement west of the crest of the Appalachians, in hopes of keeping the Indians happy and the settlers close to the coast and thus easier to control.

In 1764, Grenville pushed through Parliament the Sugar Act (also known as the Revenue Act) aimed at raising revenue by taxes on goods imported by the Americans. It lowered by one-half the duties imposed by the Molasses Act but was intended to raise revenue rather than control trade. Unlike the Molasses Act, it was stringently enforced, with accused violators facing trial in admiralty courts without benefit of jury or the normal protections of due process.

Grenville determined to maintain up to 10,000 British regulars in America to control both colonists and Indians and secured passage of the Quartering Act, requiring the colonies in which British troops were stationed to pay for their maintenance. Americans had never before been required to support a standing army in their midst.

Grenville also saw through the passage of his Currency Act of 1764, which forbade once and for all any colonial attempts to issue currency not redeemable in gold or silver, making it more difficult for Americans to avoid the constant drain of money that Britain's mercantilist policies were designed to create in the colonies.

Most important, however, Grenville got Parliament to pass the Stamp Act (1765), imposing a direct tax on Americans for the first time. The Stamp Act required Americans to purchase revenue stamps on everything from newspapers to legal documents and would have created an impossible drain on hard currency in the colonies. Because it overlooked the advantage already provided by Britain's mercantilist exploitation of the colonies, Grenville's policy was shortsighted and foolish; but few in Parliament were inclined to see this.

Americans reacted first with restrained and respectful petitions and pamphlets, in which they pointed out that "taxation without representation is tyranny." From there resistance progressed to stronger and stronger protests that eventually became violent and involved intimidation of those Americans who had contracted to be the agents for distributing the stamps.

Resistance was particularly intense in Massachusetts, where it was led first by James Otis and then by Samuel Adams who formed the organization known as the Sons of Liberty.

Other colonies copied Massachusetts' successful tactics while adding some of their own. In Virginia, a young Burgess named Patrick Henry introduced seven resolutions denouncing the Stamp Act. Though only the four most moderate of them were passed by the House of Burgesses, newspapers picked up all seven and circulated them widely through the colonies, giving the impression all seven had been adopted. By their denial of Parliament's authority to tax the colonies, they encouraged other colonial legislatures to issue strongly worded statements.

In October 1765, delegates from nine colonies met as the Stamp Act Congress. Called by the Massachusetts legislature at the instigation of James Otis, the Stamp Act Congress passed moderate resolutions against the act, asserting that Americans could not be taxed without their consent, given by their representatives. They pointed out that Americans were not, and because of their location could not practically be, represented in Parliament and concluded by calling for the repeal of both the Stamp and Sugar Acts. Most important, however, the Stamp Act Congress showed that representatives of the colonies could work together and gave political leaders in the various colonies a chance to become acquainted with each other.

Most effective in achieving repeal of the Stamp Act was colonial merchants' nonimportation (boycott) of British goods. Begun as an agreement among New York merchants, the boycott spread throughout the colonies and had a powerful effect on British merchants and manufacturers, who began clamoring for the act's repeal.

Meanwhile, the fickle King George III had dismissed Grenville over an unrelated disagreement and replaced him with a cabinet headed by Charles Lord Rockingham. In March 1766, under the leadership of the new ministry, Parliament repealed the Stamp Act. At the same time, however, it passed the Declaratory Act, claiming power to tax or make laws for the Americans "in all cases whatsoever."

Though the Declaratory Act denied exactly the principle Americans had just been at such pains to assert—that of no taxation without representation—the Americans generally ignored it in their exuberant celebration of the repeal of the Stamp Act. Americans eagerly proclaimed their loyalty to Great Britain.

QUESTION

> Why did American colonists resist the Stamp Act?

EXPLANATION

A familiar way to summarize the reason behind opposition to the Stamp Act is "no taxation without representation." The Stamp Act was the first direct tax on American colonists, and many felt that this burden was unjust given the already considerable cost of mercantile policies to the colonists. Americans felt that the imposition of a tax by Parliament, where there was no colonial representation, was unfair and unjust.

The Townshend Acts

The Rockingham ministry proved to be even shorter lived than that of Grenville. It was replaced with a cabinet dominated by Chancellor of the Exchequer Charles Townshend. Townshend had boasted that he could successfully tax the colonies, and in 1766 Parliament gave him his chance by passing his program of taxes on items imported into the colonies. These taxes came to be known as the Townshend Duties. Townshend mistakenly believed the Americans would accept this method while rejecting the use of direct internal taxes.

The Townshend Acts also included the use of admiralty courts to try those accused of violations, the use of writs of assistance, and the paying of customs officials out of the fines they levied. Townshend also had the New York legislature suspended for noncompliance with the Quartering Act.

American reaction was at first slow. Philadelphia lawyer John Dickinson wrote an anonymous pamphlet entitled *Letters from a Farmer in Pennsylvania*, in which he pointed out in moderate terms that the Townshend Acts violated the principle of no taxation without representation and that if Parliament could suspend the New York legislature it could do the same to others. At the same time he urged a restrained response on the part of his fellow Americans.

In February 1768, the Massachusetts legislature, at the urging of Samuel Adams, passed the Massachusetts Circular Letter, reiterating Dickinson's mild arguments and urging other colonial legislatures to pass petitions calling on Parliament to repeal the acts. Had the British government done nothing, the matter might have passed quietly.

Instead, British authorities acted. They ordered that if the letter was not withdrawn, the Massachusetts legislature should be dissolved and new elections held. They forbade the other colonial legislatures to take up the matter, and they also sent four regiments of troops to Boston to prevent intimidation of royal officials and to intimidate the populace instead.

The last of these actions was in response to the repeated pleas of the Boston customs agents. Corrupt agents had used technicalities of the confusing and poorly written Sugar and Townshend Acts to entrap innocent merchants and line their own pockets. Mob violence had threatened when agents had seized the ship *Liberty*, belonging to Boston merchant John Hancock. Such incidents prompted the call for troops.

The sending of troops, along with the British authorities' repressive response to the Massachusetts Circular Letter aroused the Americans to resistance. Non-importation was again instituted, and soon British merchants were calling on Parliament to repeal the acts. In March 1770, Parliament, under the new prime minister, Frederick Lord North, repealed all of the taxes except that on tea, which was retained to prove Parliament had the right to tax the colonies if it so desired.

By the time of the repeal, however, friction between British soldiers and Boston citizens had led to an incident in which five Bostonians were killed. Although the British soldiers had acted more or less in self-defense, Samuel Adams labeled the incident the "Boston Massacre" and publicized it widely. At their trial the British soldiers were defended by prominent Massachusetts lawyer John Adams and were acquitted on the charge of murder.

In the years that followed, American orators desiring to stir up anti-British feeling often alluded to the Boston Massacre.

The Return of Relative Peace

Following the repeal of the Townshend duties, a period of relative peace set in. The tax on tea remained as a reminder of Parliament's claims, but it could be easily avoided by smuggling.

Much goodwill had been lost, and colonists remained suspicious of the British government. Many Americans believed the events of the past decade to have been the work of a deliberate conspiracy to take their liberty.

Occasional incidents marred the relative peace. One such was the burning, by a seagoing mob of Rhode Islanders disguised as Indians, of the *Gaspee,* a British customs schooner that had run aground off shore. The *Gaspee's* captain and crew had alienated Rhode Islanders by their extreme zeal for catching smugglers as well as by their theft and vandalism when ashore.

In response to this incident British authorities appointed a commission to find the guilty parties and bring them to England for trial. Though those responsible for the burning of the *Gaspee* were never found, this action on the part of the British prompted the colonial legislatures to form committees of correspondence to communicate with each other regarding possible threats from the British government.

The Tea Act

The relative peace was brought to an end by the Tea Act of 1773.

In desperate financial condition—partially because the Americans were buying smuggled Dutch tea rather than the taxed British product—the British East India Company sought and obtained from Parliament concessions allowing it to ship tea directly to the colonies rather than only by way of Britain. The result would be that East India Company tea, even with the tax, would be cheaper than smuggled Dutch tea. The colonists would thus, it was hoped, buy the tea, tax and all. The East India Company would be saved and the Americans would be tacitly accepting Parliament's right to tax them.

The Americans, however, proved resistant to this approach; and rather than see to admit Parliament's right to tax, they vigorously resisted the cheaper tea. Various methods, including tar and feathers, were used to prevent the collection of the tax on tea. In most ports Americans did not allow the tea to be landed.

In Boston, however, pro-British Governor Thomas Hutchinson forced a confrontation by ordering Royal Navy vessels to prevent the tea ships from leaving the harbor. After 20 days this would, by law, result in the cargoes being sold at auction and the tax paid. The night before the time was to expire, December 16, 1773, Bostonians thinly disguised as Indians boarded the ships and threw the tea into the harbor.

Many Americans felt this—the destruction of private property—was going too far, but the reaction of Lord North and Parliament quickly united Americans in support of Boston and opposition to Britain.

QUESTION

Why did Americans refuse to buy tea from the British East India Company?

EXPLANATION

The tea from the British East India Company would have been less expensive than smuggled Dutch tea. However, the British tea was taxed, and purchasing the tea would have meant that the Americans were conceding that the British had the right to directly tax the colonists. In order to avoid the tax and deny the right of the British government to tax the American colonists, the colonists often refused ships carrying the tea to land in port.

The Intolerable Acts

The British responded with four acts collectively referred to as the Coercive Acts. First, the Boston Port Act closed the port of Boston to all trade until local citizens would agree to pay for the lost tea (they would not). Secondly, the Massachusetts Government Act greatly increased the power of Massachusetts' royal governor at the expense of the legislature. Thirdly, the Administration of Justice Act provided that royal officials accused of crimes in Massachusetts could be tried elsewhere, where chances of acquittal might be greater. Finally, a strengthened Quartering Act allowed the new governor, General Thomas Gage, to quarter his troops anywhere, including unoccupied private homes.

A further act of Parliament also angered and alarmed Americans. This was the Quebec Act, which extended the province of Quebec to the Ohio River, established Roman Catholicism as Quebec's official religion, and set up for Quebec a government without a representative assembly.

For Americans this was a denial of the hopes and expectations of westward expansion for which they had fought the French and Indian War. Also, New Englanders especially saw it as a threat that in their colonies too, Parliament could establish autocratic government and the hated Church of England.

Americans lumped the Quebec Act together with the Coercive Acts and referred to them all as the Intolerable Acts.

In response to the Coercive Acts, the First Continental Congress was called and met in Philadelphia in September, 1774. It once again petitioned Parliament for relief but also passed the Suffolk Resolves (so called because they were first passed in Suffolk County, Massachusetts), denouncing the Intolerable Acts and calling for strict nonimportation and rigorous preparation of local militia companies in case the British should resort to military force.

The congress then narrowly rejected a plan, submitted by Joseph Galloway of Pennsylvania, calling for a union of the colonies within the empire and a rearrangement of relations with Parliament. Most of the delegates felt matters had already gone too far for such a mild measure. Finally, before adjournment, it was agreed that there should be a Second Continental Congress to meet in May of the following year if the colonies' grievances had not been righted by then.

Drill 1: The Coming of the American Revolution

1. The first armed conflict in 1775 between the Americans and British soldiers took place at

   (A) Fort Ticonderoga.

   (B) Bunker Hill.

   (C) Lexington-Concord.

   (D) Boston.

   (E) Yorktown.

2. Which of the following was a response to the Stamp Act?

   (A) The Boston Tea Party

   (B) The Battle of Lexington

   (C) The Paxton Boys' march on Philadelphia

   (D) Nonimportation of British goods

   (E) The Boston Massacre

3. During the 1760s and 1770s the most effective American tactic in gaining the repeal of the Stamp and Townshend Acts was

   (A) tarring and feathering British tax agents.

   (B) sending petitions to the king and Parliament.

   (C) boycotting British goods.

   (D) destroying private property, such as tea, on which a tax was to be levied.

   (E) using death threats to intimidate British tax agents.

4. One of the purposes of the 1773 Tea Act was to

   (A) prevent overconsumption of tea in America.

   (B) lower the price of tea in Great Britain by decreasing the demand for it in America.

   (C) save the British East India Company from financial ruin.

   (D) create a long-term shift in wealth from Britain's North American colonies to its colony in India.

   (E) calm labor unrest in India.

5. *Common Sense* was written by

   (A) Thomas Paine.   (B) Patrick Henry.

   (C) John Locke.   (D) Thomas Jefferson.

   (E) John Adams.

6. The Intolerable Acts of 1774 included all of the following EXCEPT

   (A) the closing of Boston harbor.

   (B) new taxes on glass, tea, lead, and paper.

   (C) making the Massachusetts council and judiciary appointive.

   (D) allowing trials of accused colonial officials to be moved to England.

   (E) authorizing the governor to limit town meetings to as few as one a year.

7. The major result of England's attempts to tighten the enforcement of its mercantilist policies in America after the French and Indian War was to

    (A) increase England's prosperity.

    (B) increase the amount of revenue collected in the colonies.

    (C) increase England's control of the colonial governments.

    (D) encourage French colonization in North America.

    (E) push the colonists toward open resistance to English rule.

8. When colonial Massachusetts' governor Thomas Hutchinson attempted to force the sale of taxed tea in Boston in 1773, Bostonians reacted with the

    (A) Boston Massacre.

    (B) Boston Tea Party.

    (C) Declaration of Independence.

    (D) Articles of Confederation.

    (E) Massachusetts Circular Letter.

9. American resistance to Parliament's Townshend Acts led directly to the

    (A) Boston Massacre.   (B) Boston Tea Party.

    (C) First Continental Congress.   (D) Declaratory Act.

    (E) battles of Lexington and Concord.

10. "The rule that a British subject shall not be bound by laws, or liable to taxes, but what he has consented to by his representatives, must be confined to the inhabitants of Great Britain only; and is not strictly true even there."

    The above statement is most likely to have been made by

    (A) Samuel Adams in denouncing the Stamp Act.

    (B) Francis Bernard as royal governor of Massachusetts.

    (C) John Adams in defending British soldiers accused of murder in the Boston Massacre.

    (D) John Dickinson in counseling against haste in declaring independence.

    (E) John Hancock in reference to the seizure of his ship by customs agents.

2. THE WAR FOR INDEPENDENCE

Lexington and Concord

The British government paid little attention to the First Continental Congress, having decided to teach the Americans a military lesson. More troops were sent to Massachusetts, which was officially declared to be in a state of rebellion. Orders were sent to General Gage to arrest the leaders of the resistance or, failing that, to provoke any sort of confrontation that would allow him to turn British military might loose on the Americans.

Gage decided on a reconnaissance-in-force to find and destroy a reported stockpile of colonial arms and ammunition at Concord. Seven hundred British troops set out on this mission on the night of April 18, 1775. Their movement was detected by American surveillance, and news was spread throughout the countryside by dispatch riders Paul Revere and William Dawes.

At the little village of Lexington, Captain John Parker and some 70 Minutemen (militiamen trained to respond at a moment's notice) awaited the British on the village green. As the British approached, a British officer shouted at the Minutemen to lay down their arms and disperse. The Minutemen did not lay down their arms but did turn to file off the green. A shot was fired, and then the British opened fire and charged. Eight Americans were killed and several others wounded, most shot in the back.

The British continued to Concord only to find that nearly all of the military supplies they had expected to find had already been moved. Attacked by growing numbers of Minutemen, they began to retreat toward Boston. As the British retreated, Minutemen, swarming from every village for miles around, fired on the column from behind rocks, trees, and stone fences. Only a relief force of additional British troops saved the first column from destruction.

Open warfare had begun, and the myth of British invincibility was destroyed. Militia came in large numbers from all the New England colonies to join the force besieging Gage and his army in Boston.

Bunker Hill

In May 1775, three more British generals, William Howe, Henry Clinton, and John Burgoyne, arrived in Boston urging Gage to further aggressive action. The following month the Americans tightened the noose around Boston by fortifying Breed's Hill (a spur of Bunker Hill), from which they could, if necessary, bombard Boston.

The British determined to remove them by a frontal attack that would demonstrate the awesome power of British arms. Twice the British were thrown back and finally succeeded as the Americans ran out of ammunition. Over a thousand British soldiers were killed or wounded in what turned out to be the bloodiest battle of the war (June 17, 1775). Yet the British had gained very little and remained bottled up in Boston.

Meanwhile in May 1775, American forces under Ethan Allen and Benedict Arnold took Fort Ticonderoga on Lake Champlain.

Congress, hoping Canada would join in the resistance against Britain, authorized two expeditions into Quebec. One, under General Richard Montgomery took Montreal and then turned toward the city of Quebec. It was met there by the second expedition under Benedict Arnold. The attack on Quebec (December 31, 1775) failed, Montgomery was killed, Arnold wounded, and American hopes for Canada ended.

The Second Continental Congress

While these events were taking place in New England and Canada, the Second Continental Congress met in Philadelphia in May 1775. Congress was divided into two main factions. One was composed mostly of New Englanders and leaned toward declaring independence from Britain. The other drew its strength primarily from the middle colonies and was not yet ready to go that far. It was led by John Dickinson of Pennsylvania.

Congress took action to deal with the difficult situation facing the colonies. It adopted the New England army around Boston, calling on the other colonies to send troops and sending George Washington to command it, adopted a "Declaration of the Causes and Necessity for Taking up Arms" and adopted the "Olive Branch Petition" pleading with King George III to intercede with Parliament to restore peace.

This last overture was ignored in Britain, where the king gave his approval to the Prohibitory Act, declaring the colonies in rebellion and no longer under his protection. Preparations were made for full-scale war against America.

Throughout 1775, Americans remained deeply loyal to Britain and King George III despite the king's proclamations declaring them to be in revolt. In Congress, moderates still resisted independence.

In January 1776, Thomas Paine published a pamphlet entitled *Common Sense,* calling for immediate independence. Its arguments were extreme and sometimes illogical and its language intemperate, but it sold widely and may have had much influence in favor of independence. Continued evidence of Britain's intention to carry on the war throughout the colonies also weakened the moderates' resistance to independence. The Prohibitory Act, with its virtual declaration of war against America, convinced many that no further moral scruples need stand in the way of such a step.

On June 7, 1776, Richard Henry Lee of Virginia introduced a series of formal resolutions in Congress calling for independence and a national government. Accepting these ideas, Congress named two committees. One, headed by John Dickinson, was to work out a framework for a national government. The other was to draft a statement of the reasons for declaring independence. This statement, the Declaration of Independence, was primarily the work of Thomas Jefferson of Virginia. It was a restatement of political ideas, by then commonplace in America, showing why the former colonists felt justified in separating from Great Britain. It was formally adopted by Congress on July 4, 1776.

QUESTION

What did the pamphlet *Common Sense,* by Thomas Paine, advocate?

EXPLANATION

Common Sense was written in order to gain support for American independence by the colonists. It was a piece of propaganda that argued for complete and immediate independence. At the time it was written, most Americans were more moderate in their aims, wishing only for the British government to redress specific grievances.

Washington Takes Command

Britain meanwhile was preparing a massive effort to conquer the United States. Gage was removed as being too timid, and top command went to Howe. To supplement the British army, large numbers of troops were hired from various German principalities. Since many of these Germans came from the state of Hesse-Kassel, Americans referred to all such troops as Hessians.

Although the London authorities desired a quick and smashing campaign, General Howe and his brother, British naval commander Richard, Admiral Lord Howe, intended to move slowly, using their powerful force to cow the Americans into signing loyalty oaths.

In March 1776, Washington placed on Dorchester Heights, overlooking Boston, some of the large cannons that had been captured at Ticonderoga, forcing the British to evacuate the city.

The British shipped their troops to Nova Scotia and then, together with large reinforcements from Britain, landed that summer at New York City. They hoped to find many loyalists there and make that city the key to their campaign to subdue America.

Washington anticipated the move and was waiting at New York, which Congress had ordered should be defended. However, the under-trained, under-equipped, and badly outnumbered American army was no match for the powerful forces under the Howes. Defeated at the Battle of Long Island (August 27, 1776), Washington narrowly avoided being trapped there (his escape partially due to the Howes' slowness). Defeated again at the Battle of Washington Heights (August 29–30, 1776) on Manhattan, Washington was forced to retreat across New Jersey with the aggressive British General Lord Cornwallis, a subordinate of Howe, in pursuit. By December what was left of Washington's army had made it into Pennsylvania.

With his victory almost complete, Howe decided to wait till spring to finish annihilating Washington's army. Scattering his troops in small detachments so as to hold all of New Jersey, he went into winter quarters.

Washington, with his small army melting away as demoralized soldiers deserted, decided on a bold stroke. On Christmas night 1776, his army crossed the Delaware River and struck the Hessians at Trenton. The Hessians, still groggy from their hard-drinking Christmas party, were easily defeated. A few days later Washington defeated a British force at Princeton (January 3, 1777).

Howe was so shocked by these two unexpected defeats that he pulled his outposts back close to New York. Much of New Jersey was regained. Those who had signed British loyalty oaths in the presence of Howe's army were now at the mercy of their patriot neighbors. And Washington's army was saved from disintegration.

Early in the war France began making covert shipments of arms to the Americans. This it did, not because the French government loved freedom (it did not), but because it hated Britain and saw the war as a way to weaken Britain by depriving it of its colonies. Arms shipments from France were vital for the Americans.

Saratoga and Valley Forge

For the summer of 1777 the British home authorities adopted an elaborate plan of campaign urged on them by General Burgoyne. According to the plan, Burgoyne himself would lead an army southward from Canada along the Lake Champlain corridor while another army under Howe moved up the Hudson River to join hands with Burgoyne at Albany. This, it was hoped, would cut off New England and allow the British to subdue that region, which they considered the hotbed of the "rebellion."

Howe had other ideas and shipped his army by sea to Chesapeake Bay, hoping to capture the American capital, Philadelphia, and destroy Washington's army at the same time. At Brandywine Creek (September 1, 1777) Washington tried but failed to stop Howe's advance. Yet the American army, though badly beaten, remained intact. Howe occupied Philadelphia as the Congress fled westward to York, Pennsylvania.

In early October, Washington attempted to drive Howe out of Philadelphia; but his attack at Germantown, though at first successful, failed at least partially due to thick fog and the still imperfect level of training in the American army, both of which contributed to confusion among the troops. Thereafter Howe settled down to comfortable winter quarters in Philadelphia, and Washington and his army to very uncomfortable ones at nearby Valley Forge, while far to the north, the British strategy that Howe had ignored was going badly awry.

Burgoyne's advance began well but slowed as the Americans placed obstructions on the rough wilderness trails by which his army, including numerous cannons and much bulky baggage, had to advance. A diversionary force of British troops and Iroquois Indians under the command of Colonel Barry St. Leger swung east of Burgoyne's column, but although it defeated and killed American General Nicholas Herkimer at the Battle of Oriskany (August 6, 1777), it was finally forced to withdraw to Canada.

In mid-August, a detachment of Burgoyne's force was defeated by New England militia under General John Stark near Bennington in what is now Vermont. By autumn Burgoyne found his way blocked by an American army: continentals (American regular troops such as those that made up most of Washington's army, paid, in theory at least, by Congress); and New England militia, under General Horatio Gates, at Saratoga, about 30 miles north of Albany. Burgoyne's two attempts to break through (September 19 and October 7, 1777) were turned back by the Americans under the brilliant battlefield leadership of Benedict Arnold. On October 17, 1777, Burgoyne surrendered to Gates.

The American victory at Saratoga convinced the French to join openly in the war against England. Eventually, the Spanish (1779) and the Dutch (1780) joined as well, and England was faced with a world war.

QUESTION

What took place in Valley Forge during the winter of 1777–78?

EXPLANATION

George Washington's army spent that winter there. Conditions were brutal, as there was little food or shelter for most of the troops. Morale suffered throughout the winter, but Washington was able to keep the army together while training the inexperienced troops. The training led to an improvement in the military capabilities of the troops.

The British Move South

The new circumstances brought a change in British strategy. With fewer troops available for service in America, the British would have to depend more on loyalists, and since they imagined that larger numbers of these existed in the South than elsewhere, it was there they turned their attention.

Howe was relieved and replaced by General Henry Clinton, who was ordered to abandon Philadelphia and march to New York. In doing so, he narrowly avoided defeat at the hands of Washington's army—much improved after a winter's drilling at Valley Forge under the direction of Baron von Steuben—at the Battle of Monmouth, New Jersey (June 28, 1778).

Clinton was thenceforth to maintain New York as Britain's main base in America while detaching troops to carry out the new Southern strategy. In November, 1778, the British easily conquered Georgia. Later the following year Clinton moved on South Carolina with a land and naval force, and in May 1780, U.S. General Benjamin Lincoln surrendered Charleston. Clinton then returned to New York, leaving Cornwallis to continue the Southern campaign.

Congress, alarmed at the British successes, sent General Horatio Gates to lead the forces opposing Cornwallis. Gates blundered to a resounding defeat at the Battle of Camden, in South Carolina (August 16, 1780).

The general outlook seemed bad for America at that point in the war. Washington's officers grumbled about their pay in arrears. The army was under-strength and then suffered successive mutinies among the Pennsylvania and New Jersey troops. Benedict Arnold went over to the British. In short, the British seemed to be winning the contest of endurance. This outlook was soon to change.

In the West, George Rogers Clark, acting under the auspices of the state of Virginia, led an expedition down the Ohio River and into the area of present-day Illinois and Indiana, defeating a British force at Vincennes, Indiana, and securing the area north of the Ohio River for the United States.

In the South, Cornwallis began to move northward toward North Carolina, but on October 7, 1780 a detachment of his force under Major Patrick Ferguson was defeated by American frontiersmen at the Battle of Kings Mountain in northern South Carolina. To further increase the problems facing the British, Cornwallis had unwisely moved north without bothering to secure South Carolina first. The result was that the British would no sooner leave an area than American militia or guerrilla bands, such as that under Francis Marion (the "Swamp Fox"), were once again in control and able to deal with those who had expressed loyalty to Britain in the presence of Cornwallis's army.

To command the continental forces in the South, Washington sent his most able subordinate, military genius Nathaniel Greene. Greene's brilliant strategy led to a crushing victory at Cowpens, South Carolina (January 17, 1781) by troops under Greene's subordinate, General Daniel Morgan of Virginia. It also led to a near victory by Greene's own force at Guilford Court House, North Carolina (March 15, 1781).

Yorktown

The frustrated and impetuous Cornwallis now abandoned the Southern strategy and moved north into Virginia. Clinton, disgusted at this departure from the plan, sent instructions for Cornwallis to take up a defensive position and await further orders. Against his better judgment Cornwallis did so, selecting Yorktown, Virginia, on a peninsula that reaches into Chesapeake Bay between the York and James Rivers.

Washington now saw and seized the opportunity this presented. With the aid of a French fleet which took control of Chesapeake Bay and a French army that joined him in sealing off the land approaches to Yorktown, Washington succeeded in trapping Cornwallis. After three weeks of siege, Cornwallis surrendered on October 17, 1781.

The War at Sea

Britain had other problems as well. Ships of the small but daring U.S. Navy as well as privateers (privately owned vessels outfitted with guns and authorized by a warring government to capture enemy merchant ships for profit) preyed on the British merchant marine. John Paul Jones, the most famous of the American naval leaders, captured ships and carried out audacious raids along the coast of Britain itself. French and Spanish naval forces also struck against various outposts of the British Empire.

The Treaty of Paris of 1783

News of the debacle at Yorktown brought the collapse of Lord North's ministry, and the new cabinet opened peace negotiations. The extremely able American negotiating team was composed of Benjamin Franklin, John Adams, and John Jay. The negotiations continued for some time, delayed by French and Spanish maneuvering. When it became apparent that France and Spain were planning to achieve an agreement unfavorable to the United States, the American envoys negotiated a separate treaty with Britain.

The final agreement became known as the Treaty of Paris of 1783. Its terms stipulated the following: 1) The United States was recognized as an independent nation by the major European powers, including Britain; 2) Its western boundary was set at the Mississippi River; 3) Its southern boundary was set at 31° north latitude (the northern boundary of Florida); 4) Britain retained Canada but had to surrender Florida to Spain; 5) Private British creditors would be free to collect any debts owed by citizens; and 6) Congress was to recommend that the states restore confiscated loyalist property.

Drill 2: The War for Independence

1. The American Revolutionaries gained help from which of the following?

    (A) France

    (B) Mexico

    (C) Canada

    (D) Italy

    (E) Germany

2. In seeking diplomatic recognition from foreign powers during the War for Independence, the American government found it necessary to

    (A) make large financial payments to the governments of France, Spain, and Holland.

    (B) promise to cede large tracts of American territory to France upon a victorious conclusion of the war.

    (C) demonstrate its financial stability and self-sufficiency.

    (D) demonstrate a determination and potential to win independence.

    (E) agree to grant France a specially favored trading status.

3. During the American War of Independence, the battle of Saratoga was most significant because it

    (A) left the British with inadequate resources to carry on the war.

    (B) prevented the British from ever mounting another successful invasion of American territory.

(C) allowed American forces to seize large portions of Canada.

(D) persuaded France to begin supporting the Americans openly.

(E) caused Holland to delay its decision to enter the war on the side of the British.

4. George Washington's army faced which of the following problems during the American Revolution?

(A) The British public unanimously supported the policy of its government.

(B) Two-thirds of the colonists opposed the war.

(C) The army was dependent on poorly trained militia.

(D) The army used conventional military tactics.

(E) The British government was able to give its full attention to the war.

5. Which of the following battles effectively ended the American Revolution?

(A) Yorktown   (B) Brandywine Creek

(C) Saratoga   (D) Princeton

(E) King's Mountain

6. Congress's most successful and effective method of financing the War of Independence was

(A) printing large amounts of paper money.

(B) obtaining grants and loans from France and the Netherlands.

(C) levying heavy direct taxes.

(D) issuing paper securities backed by the promise of western land grants.

(E) appealing to the states for voluntary contributions.

7. Thomas Jefferson's philosophy of government, as expressed in the Declaration of Independence, most closely reflects the views of

(A) Thomas Hobbes.   (B) Jean Jacques Rousseau.

(C) John Locke.   (D) Jean Paul Marat.

(E) Karl Marx.

8. Which of the following was NOT a provision of the Paris Peace Treaty ending the American Revolution?

(A) Louisiana was returned to French control.

(B) Florida was returned to Spanish control.

(C) The United States was recognized as an independent nation.

(D) The lands between the Mississippi and the Appalachians were given to the U.S. in disregard for the rights of Indian tribes living in those regions.

(E) The British granted the Americans fishing rights off the coast of Newfoundland.

9. Which Revolutionary War battle is considered the "turning point" in the war because it led to direct French assistance for the Americans?

(A) Trenton   (B) Bunker Hill

(C) Princeton   (D) Yorktown

(E) Saratoga

10. The American commitment to the "unalienable rights" of "life, liberty, and the pursuit of happiness" is most clearly expressed in

(A) the U.S. Constitution.

(B) the Declaration of Independence.

(C) the Bill of Rights

(D) the Twenty-fifth Amendment.

(E) *Plessy v. Ferguson.*

3. THE CREATION OF NEW GOVERNMENTS

The State Constitutions

After the collapse of British authority in 1775, it became necessary to form new state governments. By the end of 1777, ten new state constitutions had been formed.

Connecticut and Rhode Island kept their colonial charters, which were republican in nature, simply deleting references to British sovereignty. Massachusetts waited until 1780 to complete the adoption of its new constitution. The constitutions ranged from such extremely democratic models as the virtually unworkable Pennsylvania constitution (soon abandoned), in which a unicameral legislature ruled with little check or balance, to more reasonable frameworks such as those of Maryland and Virginia, which included more safeguards against popular excesses.

Massachusetts voters set an important example by insisting that a constitution should be made by a special convention rather than the legislature. This would make the constitution superior to the legislature and, hopefully, assure that the legislature would be subject to the constitution.

Most state constitutions included bills of rights—lists of things the government was not supposed to do to the people.

The Articles of Confederation

In the summer of 1776, Congress appointed a committee to begin devising a framework for national government. When completed, this document was known as the Articles of Confederation. John Dickinson, who had played a leading role in writing the Articles, felt a strong national government was needed; but by the time Congress finished revising them, the Articles went to the opposite extreme of preserving the sovereignty of the states and creating a very weak national government.

The Articles of Confederation provided for a unicameral Congress in which each state would have one vote, as had been the case in the Continental Congress. Executive authority under the Articles would be vested in a committee of 13, one member from each state. In order to amend the Articles, the unanimous consent of all the states was required.

The Articles of Confederation government was empowered to make war, make treaties, determine the amount of troops and money each state should contribute to the war effort, settle disputes between states, admit new states to the Union, and borrow money. More importantly, however, was that it was not empowered to levy taxes, raise troops, or regulate commerce.

Ratification of the Articles of Confederation was delayed by a disagreement over the future status of the lands that lay to the west of the original 13 states. Some states, notably Virginia, held extensive claims to these lands based on their original colonial charters. Maryland, which had no such claim, withheld ratification until in 1781 Virginia agreed to surrender its western claims to the new national government.

Meanwhile, the country was on its way to deep financial trouble. Unable to tax, Congress resorted to printing large amounts of paper money to finance the war; but these inflated "Continentals" were soon worthless. Other financial schemes fell through, and only grants and loans from France and the Netherlands staved off complete financial collapse. A plan to amend the Articles to give Congress power to tax was stopped by the lone opposition of Rhode Island. The army, whose pay was far in arrears, threatened mutiny. Some of those who favored a stronger national government welcomed this development and, in what became known as the Newburgh Conspiracy (1783), consulted with army second-in-command Horatio Gates as to the possibility of using the army to force the states to surrender more power to the national government. This movement was stopped by a moving appeal to the officers by Washington himself.

QUESTION

What was the most important feature of the Articles of Confederation?

EXPLANATION

The Articles of Confederation profited by a weak federal, or national government, and strong state governments. The federal government was empowered to control foreign policy, settle disputes between states, borrow money, and admit new states to the Union. However, it could not raise troops of its own or levy taxes. In addition, each state had considerable power to keep the national government from even doing what it was authorized to do. After several years of financial difficulty and instability, many people decided a stronger national government was needed.

The Trans-Appalachian West and the Northwest Ordinance

For many Americans the enormous trans-Appalachian frontier represented an opportunity to escape the economic hard times that followed the end of the war.

In 1775, Daniel Boone opened the "Wilderness Road" through the Cumberland Gap and on to the "Bluegrass" region of Kentucky. Others scouted down the Ohio River from Pittsburgh. By 1790, over 100,000 had settled in Kentucky and Tennessee, despite the risk of violent death at the hands of Indians. This risk was made worse by the presence of the British in northwestern military posts that should have been evacuated at the end of the war. From these posts they supplied the Indians with guns and encouraged them to use them on Americans. The Spaniards on the Florida frontier behaved in much the same way.

The settlement of Kentucky and Tennessee increased the pressure for the opening of the lands north of the Ohio River. To facilitate this Congress passed three land ordinances in the years from 1784 to 1787.

The Land Ordinance of 1784 provided for territorial government and an orderly system by which each territory could progress to full statehood (this ordinance is sometimes considered part of the Land Ordinance of 1785).

The Land Ordinance of 1785 provided for the orderly surveying and distribution of land in townships six miles square, each composed of 36 one-square-mile (640 acre) sections, of which one should be set aside for the support of education. (This ordinance is sometimes referred to as the "Northwest Ordinance of 1785.")

The Northwest Ordinance of 1787 provided a bill of rights for settlers and forbade slavery north of the Ohio River.

These ordinances were probably the most important legislation of the Articles of Confederation government.

The Jay-Gardoqui Negotiations

Economic depression followed the end of the war as the United States remained locked into the disadvantageous commercial system of the British Empire but without the trade advantages that system had provided.

One man who thought he saw a way out of the economic quagmire was Congress's secretary of foreign affairs, John Jay. In 1784, Jay began negotiating with Spanish minister Gardoqui a treaty that would have granted lucrative commercial privileges—benefiting large East Coast merchants such as Jay—in exchange for U.S. acceptance of Spain's closure of the Mississippi River as an outlet for the agricultural goods of the rapidly growing settlements in Kentucky and Tennessee. This the Spanish desired because they feared that extensive settlement in what was then the western part of the United States might lead to American hunger for Spanish-held lands.

When Jay reported this to Congress in the summer of 1786, the West and South were outraged. Negotiations were broken off. Some, angered that Jay could show so little concern for the other sections of the country, talked of dissolving the Union; and this helped spur to action those who desired not the dissolution but the strengthening of the Union.

Shays's Rebellion

Nationalists were further stimulated to action by Shays's Rebellion (1786). Economic hard times coupled with high taxes intended to pay off the state's war debt drove western Massachusetts farmers to desperation. Led by war veteran Daniel Shays, they shut down courts to prevent judges from seizing property or condemning people to debtors' prison for failing to pay their taxes.

The unrest created a disproportionate amount of panic in the rest of the state and the nation. The citizens of Boston subscribed money to raise an army to suppress the rebels. The success of this army together with timely tax relief caused the "rebellion" to fizzle out fairly quickly.

Amid the panic caused by the news of the uprising, many came to feel that a stronger government was needed to control such violent public outbursts as those of the western Massachusetts farmers.

QUESTION

Why did Shays's Rebellion (1786) contribute to support for a stronger national government?

EXPLANATION

Shays's Rebellion shut down courthouses in western Massachusetts and prevented the seizure of property and the condemning of people to debtor's prison during the economic hardships of the 1780s. While the rebellion itself did not threaten the rest of the state, it did lead to panic, and many people felt that the existing governments could not adequately ensure the safety and property of American citizens. This concern spread to other parts of the country as well, as many came to fear violent public outbursts. Many Americans desired a strong government to maintain order as the British did before war for independence.

Drill 3: The Creation of New Governments

1. The main dispute that delayed ratification of the Articles of Confederation by the newly independent states of the United States was

   (A) disagreement about the nature and composition of the national legislature.

   (B) disagreement about the powers and method of selecting a national president.

   (C) the refusal of some states to give up separate treaties made independently between themselves and foreign countries.

   (D) the refusal of some states to give up extensive claims to the lands west of the Appalachians.

   (E) the reluctance of slaveholding states to join in a union with states that considered slavery to be evil.

2. Under the Articles of Confederation, the Congress lacked the power to

   (A) control foreign affairs.   (B) coin money.

   (C) settle disputes among states. (D) tax.

   (E) borrow money.

3. The following table represents the amount of continental currency required to buy $1.00 in specie. In what year did the currency's value decline by the largest percentage?

1777	January	1.25	October	3.00
1778	January	4.00	October	5.00
1779	January	8.00	October	30.00
1780	January	42.50	October	77.50
1781	January	100.00	April	167.50

   (A) 1777   (B) 1778

   (C) 1779   (D) 1780

   (E) 1781

4. The group most likely to approve of the Articles of Confederation would be

   (A) former officers in the Continental army.

   (B) those who feared strong central government.

   (C) those who held U.S. government securities.

   (D) bankers, merchants, and financiers.

   (E) those who feared the dangers of unrestrained democracy.

5. The primary issue in dispute in Shays's Rebellion was

   (A) the jailing of individuals or seizure of their property for failure to pay taxes during a time of economic hardship.

   (B) the underrepresentation of western Massachusetts in the state legislature leading to accusations of "taxation without representation."

   (C) the failure of Massachusetts to pay a promised postwar bonus to soldiers who had served in its forces during the Revolution.

   (D) the failure of Massachusetts authorities to take adequate steps to protect the western part of the state from the depredations of raiding Indians.

   (E) economic oppression practiced by the banking interests of eastern Massachusetts.

6. All of the following were weaknesses of the Articles of Confederation government EXCEPT

   (A) it lacked the power to levy taxes.

   (B) it lacked the power to regulate commerce.

   (C) it lacked the power to borrow money.

   (D) it could not compel the states to abide by the terms of international treaties it had made.

   (E) it lacked a strong executive.

7. The Newburgh Conspiracy resulted from

   (A) attempts to bring Kansas into the Union as a slave state.

   (B) a plot by the Nationalist faction to overthrow the Articles of Confederation and replace the Continental Congress with a strong central government headed by a European-style monarch.

   (C) fears, at the conclusion of the Revolutionary War, that the Continental Congress would disband the army without funding the soldiers' pensions.

(D) plans by Aaron Burr to create a separate republic, with himself as the leader, in the American lands west of the Appalachians.

(E) schemes by France to regain dominance in the Mississippi Valley by enlisting the aid of several prominent Americans, promising them large tracts of land in the region in return for their assistance in the scheme.

8. Shays's Rebellion served to

(A) convince people of the need for slavery to be prohibited within the United States.

(B) point out the need to reform corrupt territorial governments in the American West.

(C) point out the need for reform in the way peaceful American Indians were treated on Indian reservations by corrupt government agents and greedy, dishonest businessmen.

(D) highlight the inadequacies of the United States government under the Articles of Confederation and point out the need for drastic reform.

(E) convince Americans still loyal to Britain during the Revolutionary War that they would not be accepted here once the war was over.

9. Women emerged from the American Revolution with the prescribed new responsibility of

(A) enjoying the vote.

(B) serving in local political office.

(C) becoming public school teachers.

(D) raising sons and daughters as good republican citizens.

(E) All of the above.

10. The 1784 negotiations between Secretary of Foreign Affairs Jay and Spanish Minister Gardoqui resulted in a treaty that would have

(A) provided for the purchase of territory west of the Mississippi River.

(B) received Spanish cooperation for defense of the newly independent nation.

(C) closed the Mississippi River as an outlet for agricultural goods of Kentucky and Tennessee.

(D) granted the U.S. the territory of Florida in exchange for claims of territory west of the Appalachians.

(E) granted loans from Spain to the U.S. for building roads and canals.

1763–1787
DRILLS

ANSWER KEY

Drill 1—The Coming of the American Revolution

1. (C)	2. (D)	3. (C)	4. (C)	5. (A)
6. (B)	7. (E)	8. (B)	9. (A)	10. (B)

Drill 2—The War for Independence

1. (A)	2. (D)	3. (D)	4. (C)	5. (A)
6. (B)	7. (C)	8. (A)	9. (E)	10. (B)

Drill 3—The Creation of New Governments

1. (D)	2. (D)	3. (C)	4. (B)	5. (A)
6. (C)	7. (C)	8. (D)	9. (D)	10. (D)

GLOSSARY: 1763–1787

Boycott
Merchant's refusal to important British goods.

Continentals
Regular soldiers paid by the Continental Congress.

Declaratory Act
An act that, while following the repeal of the Stamp Act, proclaimed the right of Parliament to tax or make laws for the American colonies.

The Enlightenment
An eighteenth-century intellectual movement that emphasized rationalism and human reason as adequate to solve humankind's problems.

Hessians
German mercenaries hired by the British to fight in the American Revolution.

Intolerable Acts
The Coercive Acts were laws passed by Britain to respond to the Boston Tea Party and other acts of American rebellion. The Quebec Act declared Roman Catholicism the official religion of Quebec. These two sets of acts together were called the Intolerable Acts by the American colonists.

Loyalists
American colonists who sided with the British in the American Revolution.

Militia
Citizen-soldiers.

Privateers
Privately owned vessels outfitted with guns and authorized by a warring government to capture enemy merchant ships for profit.

Quartering Act
A law requiring American colonists to provide housing for British troops.

Stamp Act
A direct tax on the American colonies that required stamps to be purchased on everything from newspapers to legal documents.

Sugar Act

A tax on goods imported into the Americas. (Also known as the Revenue Act.)

Tea Act

An act providing for the direct importation of taxed tea from India to America.

Townshend Acts

A program of taxes on the American colonies on imported goods.

Unicameral Legislature

A legislature with one body.

Writs of Assistance

General search warrants issued to help officers stop evasion of Britain's mercantilist trade restrictions.

CHAPTER 4

1787–1789
THE UNITED STATES CONSTITUTION

➤ Diagnostic Test
➤ 1787–1789 Review & Drills
➤ Glossary

1787-1789
DIAGNOSTIC TEST

1. Ⓐ Ⓑ Ⓒ Ⓓ Ⓔ
2. Ⓐ Ⓑ Ⓒ Ⓓ Ⓔ
3. Ⓐ Ⓑ Ⓒ Ⓓ Ⓔ
4. Ⓐ Ⓑ Ⓒ Ⓓ Ⓔ
5. Ⓐ Ⓑ Ⓒ Ⓓ Ⓔ
6. Ⓐ Ⓑ Ⓒ Ⓓ Ⓔ
7. Ⓐ Ⓑ Ⓒ Ⓓ Ⓔ
8. Ⓐ Ⓑ Ⓒ Ⓓ Ⓔ
9. Ⓐ Ⓑ Ⓒ Ⓓ Ⓔ
10. Ⓐ Ⓑ Ⓒ Ⓓ Ⓔ
11. Ⓐ Ⓑ Ⓒ Ⓓ Ⓔ
12. Ⓐ Ⓑ Ⓒ Ⓓ Ⓔ
13. Ⓐ Ⓑ Ⓒ Ⓓ Ⓔ
14. Ⓐ Ⓑ Ⓒ Ⓓ Ⓔ
15. Ⓐ Ⓑ Ⓒ Ⓓ Ⓔ
16. Ⓐ Ⓑ Ⓒ Ⓓ Ⓔ
17. Ⓐ Ⓑ Ⓒ Ⓓ Ⓔ
18. Ⓐ Ⓑ Ⓒ Ⓓ Ⓔ
19. Ⓐ Ⓑ Ⓒ Ⓓ Ⓔ
20. Ⓐ Ⓑ Ⓒ Ⓓ Ⓔ
21. Ⓐ Ⓑ Ⓒ Ⓓ Ⓔ
22. Ⓐ Ⓑ Ⓒ Ⓓ Ⓔ
23. Ⓐ Ⓑ Ⓒ Ⓓ Ⓔ
24. Ⓐ Ⓑ Ⓒ Ⓓ Ⓔ
25. Ⓐ Ⓑ Ⓒ Ⓓ Ⓔ

1787–1789
DIAGNOSTIC TEST

This diagnostic test is designed to help you determine your strengths and weaknesses in your knowledge of the United States Constitution (1787–1789). Follow the directions and check your answers.

Study this chapter for the following tests:
AP U.S. History, CLEP General, CLEP United States History I,
GED, Praxis Specialty Area, SAT: United States History

---

25 Questions

DIRECTIONS: Choose the correct answer for each of the following questions. Fill in each answer on the answer sheet.

1. Alexander Hamilton's legislative program for the new republic included all of the following EXCEPT

   UNIT 3

   (A) the Bank of the United States.

   (B) organization of the federal judiciary.

   (C) assumption of Confederation and state debts.

   (D) promotion of domestic manufacturing.

   (E) a system of excise taxes.

2. The Federal Constitution

   (A) abolished slavery.

   (B) did not count slaves for purposes of representation.

   (C) counted 3/5 of each slave for purposes of representation.

   (D) explicitly legalized slavery.

   (E) counted all slaves for purposes of representation.

3. The Northwest Ordinance of 1787 established what precedent for new territories?

   (A) Support for public education

(B) Equality of new states with old

(C) Fair treatment of Indians

(D) Prohibition of slavery

(E) Popular sovereignty

4. The central compromise of the Constitutional Convention involved the issue of

(A) balance of powers within the federal government.

(B) relationship of state and federal powers.

(C) abandonment of the Articles of Confederation.

(D) representation of large and small states.

(E) powers of the presidency.

5. Debate over ratification of the Constitution in New York resulted in the publication of

(A) *The American Commonwealth.*

(B) *The Federalist Papers.*

(C) *Common Sense.*

(D) *The Age of Reason.*

(E) *Defense of the Constitutions of Government of the United States of America.*

6. Regarding interpretation of the Constitution, Alexander Hamilton wrote: "It leaves, therefore, a criterion of what is constitutional, and of what is not so. This criterion is the *end*, to which the measure relates as a *means*. If the *end* be clearly comprehended within any of the specified powers, and if the measure have an obvious relation to that *end*, and is not forbidden by any particular provision of the Constitution, it may safely be deemed to come within the compass of the national authority."

In this passage Hamilton is arguing that

(A) the Constitution delegates implied powers to the federal government.

(B) the Constitution must specifically state that the federal government has the power to take a particular action.

(C) constitutional questions are to be settled by the Supreme Court.

(D) all implied powers are reserved to the states.

(E) the Constitution states both the ends and means of government action.

Questions 7 and 8 refer to the following passage.

The proposed Constitution, so far from implying an abolition of the State governments, makes them constituent parts of the national sovereignty, by allowing them a direct representation in the Senate, and leaves in their possession certain exclusive and very important portions of sovereign power.

7. The above passage is most likely to be found in which of the following?

    (A) Washington's farewell address

    (B) Jefferson's *Kentucky Resolutions*

    (C) Montesquieu's *Spirit of the Laws*

    (D) Tocqueville's *Democracy in America*

    (E) Hamilton, Madison, and Jay's *The Federalist Papers*

8. The author wants primarily to convince readers that

    (A) a balanced government is the best form of government.

    (B) the U.S. Constitution would preserve the rights and powers of the states.

    (C) the U.S. Constitution is a form of government uniquely suited to the American character.

    (D) the U.S. Constitution would effectively eliminate state governments.

    (E) the United States should keep itself free from entangling alliances with European countries.

9. One of the chief reasons for the failure of the Articles of Confederation was

    (A) their focus on the separation of powers within the federal branch of government.

    (B) their failure to adequately curb the powers of the executive branch of government.

    (C) their failure to provide women and free blacks with the right to vote.

    (D) their lack of an adequate mechanism for Congress to force states to comply with its decisions.

    (E) their strict tax collections provisions. These raised resentments among the people in the smaller states who believed that they were being overtaxed while residents of the larger states were being undertaxed.

10. During the campaign to ratify the Constitution, the Federalists argued

    (A) for a return to the Articles of Confederation as the framework of federal government.

(B) that a bill of rights, to correct flaws in the Constitution, must be in place before the Constitution could be ratified.

(C) for rejection of the Constitution and the convening of a new Constitutional Convention to come up with a better framework for government.

◦ (D) for ratification of the Constitution, with a possible bill of rights to be discussed after ratification.

(E) against a strong national government of any kind and an increase in the powers of states to govern themselves.

11. In order for a treaty to become law, the _____ must ratify the treaty after it has been negotiated by the_____.

(A) House of Representatives...Senate

(B) Congress...president

(C) Supreme Court...Senate

◦(D) Senate...president

(E) president...Senate

12. The Fourteenth Amendment to the Constitution was important because it

(A) prohibited slavery within the United States.

(B) guaranteed equal protection under the law for every American citizen.

(C) prohibited any state from denying an American citizen the right to vote based on race/ethnic background, color, or having previously been a slave.

(D) prohibited any state from denying women the right to vote.

(E) provided Congress with the power to establish and collect income taxes.

13. What is the minimum number of years of citizenship required to serve as a justice on the U.S. Supreme Court?

(A) 5   (B) 7

(C) 14   (D) 20

(E) None of the above.

14. In the impeachment process against the president, the ____ determine(s) the guilt or innocence of the president.

(A) House of Representatives   • (B) Senate

(C) Supreme Court   (D) Cabinet

(E) American people

15. The right to a speedy trial is guaranteed Americans by

(A) the Declaration of Independence.

(B) the First Amendment.

(C) the Third Amendment.

(D) the Sixth Amendment.

(E) Article II of the Constitution.

16. The U.S. House of Representatives contains _____ members.

(A) 100   . (B) 435

(C) 535   (D) 120

(E) 648

17. According to Article II of the U.S. Constitution, the sole authority to suspend the writ of *habeas corpus* resides in

(A) the Supreme Court.   (B) the president.

(C) the attorney general.   (D) the Congress.

(E) the state governors.   *Federalist #10*

18. In James Madison's tenth *Federalist*, the most dangerous threat to the U.S. Constitution was presented by

(A) the president's war powers.   (B) factions.

(C) the Supreme Court.   (D) a standing army.

(E) freedom of speech.

19. At the Philadelphia Convention of 1787, the author of the Great Compromise to the U.S. Constitution was

(A) Patrick Henry.   (B) John Adams.

(C) Thomas Jefferson.   . (D) Roger Sherman.

(E) James Madison.

20. During the ratification contest, the Antifederalist critique of the proposed U.S. Constitution contained all of the following arguments EXCEPT

(A) a lack of a written Bill of Rights.

(B) the lack of a popular vote for the presidency.

- (C) the location of the new government in Washington, D.C.

(D) the powers of the Supreme Court.

(E) the large territory of the United States.

21. The Constitutional Convention took place in 1787 in what city?

(A) New York   · (B) Philadelphia

(C) Washington, D.C.   (D) Baltimore

(E) Boston

22. According to the Constitution as passed in 1787 and ratified in 1789, a slave was equal to what fraction of a citizen for purposes of representation?

· (A) 3/5   (B) 1/4

(C) 2/5   (D) 1/2

(E) 3/4

23. The Constitutional Convention of 1787

I.   was dominated by Thomas Jefferson, Patrick Henry, John Adams, and George Washington.

II.   published daily summaries of its debates in the Philadelphia newspapers.

III. was called by the Confederation Congress for the sole purpose of revising/amending the Articles of Confederation.

IV.   outlawed the foreign slave trade.

(A) I only   (B) II only

· (C) III only   (D) I, II, and IV only

(E) I, II, III, and IV

24. The Bill of Rights

(A) is the first ten amendments to the Constitution.

(B) limited the powers of the federal government to those specifically named in the Constitution.

(C) gave citizens freedom of religion, assembly, speech and press, and the right of petition.

(D) guaranteed the rights of persons accused of crime.

· (E) All of the above.

25. *The Federalist Papers*

   (A) were written anonymously by Alexander Hamilton, John Jay, and James Madison.

   (B) argued that under the Constitution the states would relinquish too much sovereignty.

   (C) opposed ratification of the Constitution without the addition of a bill of rights.

   (D) convinced Patrick Henry to support the Constitution.

   (E) stressed that the Constitutional Convention was instructed to revise the Articles of Confederation, not to write a new constitution.

1787–1789
DIAGNOSTIC TEST

ANSWER KEY

1. (B)	6. (A)	11. (D)	16. (B)	21. (B)
2. (C)	7. (E)	12. (B)	17. (D)	22. (A)
3. (B)	8. (B)	13. (E)	18. (B)	23. (C)
4. (D)	9. (D)	14. (B)	19. (D)	24. (E)
5. (B)	10. (D)	15. (D)	20. (C)	25. (A)

DETAILED EXPLANATIONS
OF ANSWERS

1.   **(B)**   As secretary of the treasury, Hamilton was concerned with economic issues, thus he promoted the Bank of the United States, assumption of confederation and state debts, excise taxes, and manufacturing, though the latter was unsuccessful in Congress. Congress passed the Judiciary Act in 1789, but it was not Hamilton's proposal.

2.   **(C)**   The Constitution in Article 1, Section 2 counted 3/5 of "other persons" than free persons for the purposes of representation. It otherwise ignored the issue of slavery, except for providing for the return of runaway slaves in Article 1, Section 9.

3.   **(B)**   While the Northwest Ordinance provided support for public education, prohibited slavery, and sought fair treatment of Indians, the only precedent it established was a procedure for a territory to become a state equal with all existing states. Popular sovereignty emerged later as a policy to allow states to decide for themselves whether to be slave or free.

4.   **(D)**   The central compromise was the agreement that all states would be represented equally in the Senate and by population in the House. There was general agreement that the Articles must be abandoned, that the federal government must be more powerful than the states, and that the legislative and executive powers must be balanced.

5.   **(B)**   *The Federalist Papers* were written by John Jay, Alexander Hamilton, and James Madison to support ratification of the Constitution in New York state. Thomas Paine wrote *Common Sense* during the conflict with Great Britain and *The Age of Reason* to support rational religion. James Bryce, an Englishman, wrote *The American Commonwealth* in the late nineteenth century. John Adams's *Defense of the Constitutions of Government of the United States of America* was a history of republican government.

6.   **(A)**   Alexander Hamilton was arguing for "broad construction" of the Constitution, asserting that as long as the Constitution did not prohibit an action it was allowable when it carried out an end or goal of the Constitution. Thomas Jefferson argued for "strict construction," saying that the Constitution must specifically give the federal government a power in order for that power to be constitutional. Hamilton was saying nothing about the Supreme Court and rejected the idea that implied powers were reserved to the states.

7.   **(E)**   *The Federalist Papers* were a series of 85 letters written to newspapers by Hamilton, Madison, and Jay. The passage comes from the tenth *Federal-*

ist, written by James Madison. Its purpose was to explain, and ease people's minds about, the proposed U.S. Constitution.

8.   **(B)**   In order to set people's minds at ease about the proposed U.S. Constitution and thus secure its ratification, Hamilton sought to demonstrate that the Constitution would preserve the rights and powers of the states (the opposite of (D)). Hamilton, along with the other Federalists, did believe that a balanced government was the best form of government (A) and that the U.S. Constitution offered a form of government especially suited to the American character (C), but these facts are not the point of the argument presented here. That the United States should keep itself free from entangling alliances with European countries (E) was the advice of George Washington in his farewell address.

9.   **(D)**   The greatest obstacle faced by the United States Congress operating under the Articles of Confederation was that for any law to be enacted, all of the states had to agree to its enactment. Unanimous consent was difficult to obtain. When American representatives signed treaties, etc., individual states would refuse to obey treaty provisions if they disagreed with them. The Articles gave Congress no enforcement powers to force compliance. This limitation affected taxation, defense, commerce, and foreign relations. Without increased power to the national government, the country could not grow and prosper as a single unified entity. Concerns about the sovereignty of individual states had led to the Articles being imbalanced toward states' power, crippling the national government.

10.   **(D)**   The Federalists' name implied that they did not support a strong national government. However, the leaders of the Federalist movement believed strongly in the necessity of a relatively strong central government. They strongly supported ratification of the Constitution and believed that discussion of a bill of rights should be delayed until after the Constitution was ratified. Alexander Hamilton, James Madison, and John Jay wrote a series of essays contained within *The Federalist Papers* which brilliantly argued the Federalist position and captured support of all the nation's major newspapers. This campaign made the difference in the battles for ratification in several key states.

The chief opponents of ratification, the Antifederalists, argued against ratification primarily on the basis of choice (B), that a bill of rights needed to be in place before ratification of the Constitution. Many Antifederalists opposed the Constitution entirely based on the belief in choice (E), that no strong national government could or should ever exist. They believed that a strong national government would become corrupt and lose touch with the needs of the local people. They believed that the best path was for the states to govern themselves within the framework of an extremely limited national government. Few people wanted either choice (A), a return to Articles of Confederation which had clearly not worked, or (C), a new constitutional convention.

11.   **(D)**   According to Article II, Section 2 (II,2) of the United States Constitution, the Senate is granted the sole authority to ratify a treaty while the presi-

dent, or any delegated representative he appoints, alone can negotiate treaties with a foreign nation. This division of power is part of the elaborate checks and balances established in our Constitution by the founding fathers in 1787. This principle is one of the key characteristics of a republican form of government. The system was utilized to prevent one branch of government from becoming too powerful and dictatorial. Neither the Supreme Court nor the House of Representatives was included in this process. In recent years, American presidents have utilized increasingly the device of "executive agreements" with foreign nations to bypass the requirement of Senate approval of treaties. In 1937, the Supreme Court ruled in *United States v. Belmont* that although executive agreements are approved only by the president, they enjoy the same legal status as treaties.

12.   **(B)**   Many legal scholars consider the Fourteenth Amendment to the Constitution the most important amendment. It mandates that the federal government must provide equal protection under the law for every American citizen. This amendment was drawn up by Congress during Andrew Johnson's administration in an attempt to guarantee that civil rights legislation would be enforced. At the time, Johnson was accused, accurately, of not enforcing laws designed to protect the rights of freed blacks and former slaves. By passing this amendment, Congress hoped to guarantee enforcement of these laws. To ensure that the returning Southern states would not block overall ratification of the amendment, Congress mandated that states seeking readmission must ratify the amendment as a precondition for readmission.

13.   **(E)**   There are no qualifications to hold office as a justice of the Supreme Court specified in Article III of the Constitution beyond the "good behavior" clause. Thus, justices do not have to hold a law degree (40 percent of the justices have had no law degree) or serve as a judge on the lower courts. There presently is a bill before the House of Representatives to specify office qualifications for the Court, as is done in the Constitution for presidents and members of Congress. As many historians have pointed out, the founding fathers were extremely vague in drawing up the Supreme Court in the United States Constitution in 1787.

14.   **(B)**   The impeachment process in American government is actually a two-part process. In Article I, Section 2 (I,2), the House of Representatives holds the sole right to initiate impeachment against a president. The House acts as a grand jury in this phase and its impeachment of a president only amounts to an announcement to the Senate that the second phase of the process must begin. According to I,3, the Senate, with the Chief Justice of the Supreme Court presiding, begins a trial on the guilt or innocence of a president regarding the bill of impeachment. If found guilty, the president is removed from office. Thus, the Senate acts as a petit jury and determines innocence and guilt. Andrew Johnson, the seventeenth president, has been the only president impeached by the House of Representatives in 1867. He escaped removal from office by the Senate by a

single vote. President Richard Nixon was neither impeached nor removed from office by this process.

15.   **(D)**   It is in the Sixth Amendement that Americans are guaranteed the right to a "speedy trial." The entire amendment deals specifically with the rights of the accused in a criminal procedure. The amendment reflects the fears of the Antifederalists that "justice delayed was justice denied" and that the key to the survival of the Constitution, as with all republics, lay foremost in its capacity to administer justice to its citizens. Although the Declaration of Independence advances principles on the fundamental rights of all people, these rights are stated generally and lack the specific language of the Sixth Amendment. The First Amendment focuses on free speech, assembly, religion, and the right to petition, while the Third Amendment deals with the illegal quartering of soldiers in private homes. Article II focuses on the president of the United States and not individual rights.

16.   **(B)**   The House of Representatives is permanently frozen at 435 members. Originally, the number of members of the House was to be set at one representative per every 25,000 inhabitants. But as the American population grew, so did the House. Out of fear that the House would grow too unwieldy because of too many representatives, the House established a practice of one representative for every 500,000 inhabitants as a minimum guideline with membership not to exceed 435 members. It is the House's policy to adjust representative districts and members every ten years upon the completion of the federal census. It is important to recall that the House's formula for membership was part of the Great Compromise authored by Roger Sherman of Connecticut at the Philadelphia Convention in 1787. There Sherman settled the differences between large and small states by making the legislative branch bicameral: the Senate would be based on equal representation regardless of a state's population, while the House would base its membership on a state's population and thus favor the large states. Today, there are 100 members of the U.S. Senate (two per state) and 435 members of the House of Representatives, whose delegations vary by the size of their state's population.

17.   **(D)**   Only Congress has the authorization to suspend the writ of *habeas corpus*. The writ is one of our judicial system's basic protections for citizens from arbitrary arrest. The writ demands that arresting officers must present their evidence before a court official within 48 hours after the arrest of a suspect. Thus, the accused is presented with charges and evidence quickly to preserve the principle of innocent until proven guilty. The only American president to suspend the writ without Congressional authorization was Abraham Lincoln, who during the Civil War suspended it in Maryland and Tennessee. This action was later approved by Congress as an emergency wartime action. The attorney general was granted similar emergency powers regarding the writ by Congress in the McCarran Internal Security Act of 1950. This power ceased to function in 1970. Neither the

Supreme Court nor the state governors have ever been granted this power temporarily by Congress.

18. **(B)** According to most political scientists, James Madison's tenth *Federalist* ranks behind only the Declaration of Independence and the U.S. Constitution as a document fundamental to American government. During the ratification contest over the Constitution in New York, Madison, along with Alexander Hamilton and John Jay, authored a series of letters in defense of the Constitution that were signed under the pseudonym "Publius." It was Madison's tenth letter that showed how the Constitution differed from all previous political systems in that it allowed for expansive freedom for its citizens, yet still provided an energetic government. According to Madison, however, the only serious threat to the Constitution would arise from a single interest group, or faction, becoming dominant in our government. Madison believed a large territory and diverse population would prevent that from ever occurring. Madison supported a strong president and Supreme Court, and authored the Bill of Rights in 1790–1791.

19. **(D)** Roger Sherman was the author of the Great Compromise at the Philadelphia Convention. The issue at hand was the proposed Virginia Plan versus the New Jersey Plan at the convention. The delegates were equally divided between support of the Virginia Plan (a legislature based on population and favoring the large/populous states) and the New Jersey Plan (a legislature granting each state an equal vote and favoring the small states). This division resulted in a deadlock and threatened the ability to produce a new government for the nation. The deadlock was broken when Sherman proposed the creation of a two house (bicameral) legislature/congress, with the Senate based on the New Jersey Plan (two senators per state) and the House of Representatives based on the Virginia Plan (one representative per 25,000 inhabitants). With the approval of the compromise, the 55 delegates were able to produce the U.S. Constitution. Patrick Henry, as an Antifederalist, never attended the convention. Adams and Jefferson also were not in attendance as they were serving overseas as America's ambassadors to England and France, respectively. James Madison, as one of the authors of the Virginia Plan, did not author the compromise.

20. **(C)** The Antifederalists never voiced concern in 1788–1789 over the location of the government in Washington, D.C. because Washington, D.C. was not proposed as the new seat of government until 1790 with the accepted Constitution already in operation. During the newspaper debates over the Constitution, the Antifederalists expressly and vehemently denounced the powers of the Supreme Court as too broad and that the national court would overshadow the state courts under the Constitution. These opponents of the Constitution also feared the indirect election of the president through the electoral college system as one that would encourage plots and conspiracies. Finally, the two gravest defects of the Constitution in the eyes of the Antifederalists were that it did not guarantee the rights of its citizens in writing (ultimately, this complaint would lead to the Bill

of Rights as the first 10 amendments to the Constitution) and that no single republican form of government could effectively rule over such a large territory as the original American states.

21.   **(B)**   The Constitutional Convention met in Philadelphia from May 14 to September 17, 1787. Washington, D.C. did not yet exist.

22.   **(A)**   Three-fifths of the slaves were to be counted for purposes of both representation and taxation. This was a compromise between Southerners who wanted to count the slave for representation but not taxation and Northerners who took the opposite position.

23.   **(C)**   The Confederation Congress endorsed the calling of a convention as "expedient" but stipulated that the convention should be called "for the sole and express purpose of revising the Articles of Confederation." Conspicuous by their absence from the convention were Thomas Jefferson, John Adams, Patrick Henry, and John Hancock. The delegates to the convention voted to hold their deliberations in secret. During their deliberations, the delegates failed to deal with the emancipation of slaves.

24.   **(E)**   The Bill of Rights, the first ten amendments to the Constitution, was proposed by Congress (1789) and ratified by the states (1791). The first nine limited Congress by forbidding it to encroach upon certain basic rights—freedom of religion, speech, and press; immunity from arbitrary arrest; and trial by jury. The Tenth Amendment reserved to the states all powers except those specifically withheld from them or delegated to the federal government.

25.   **(A)**   *The Federalist Papers,* a collection of 85 essays, were written anonymously by Alexander Hamilton, John Jay, and James Madison. Seventy-seven of the essays originally appeared in New York newspapers under the pseudonym "Publius." These essays argued for the ratification of the Constitution by stressing the inadequacies of the Articles of Confederation.

1787–1789
REVIEW

1. DEVELOPMENT AND RATIFICATION OF THE CONSTITUTION

Toward a New Constitution

As time went on, the inadequacy of the Articles of Confederation became increasingly apparent. Congress could not compel the states to comply with the terms of the Treaty of Paris of 1783 regarding debts and loyalists' property. The British used this as an excuse for not evacuating their Northwestern posts, hoping to be on hand to make the most of the situation when, as they not unreasonably expected, the new government fell to pieces. In any case, Congress could do nothing to force them out of the posts, nor to solve any of the nation's other increasingly pressing problems.

In these dismal straits, some called for disunion, others for monarchy. Still others felt that republican government could still work if given a better constitution, and they made it their goal to achieve this.

In 1785 a meeting of representatives of Virginia, Maryland, Pennsylvania, and Delaware was held at George Washington's residence, Mt. Vernon, for the purpose of discussing current problems of interstate commerce. At their suggestion the Virginia legislature issued a call for a convention of all the states on the same subject, to meet the following summer in Annapolis, Maryland.

The Annapolis Convention met in September of 1786, but only five states were represented. Among those present, however, were such nationalists as Alexander Hamilton, John Dickinson, and James Madison. With so few states represented it was decided instead to call for a convention of all the states to meet the following summer in Philadelphia for the purpose of revising the Articles of Confederation.

The Constitutional Convention

The men who met in Philadelphia in 1787 were remarkably able, highly educated, and exceptionally accomplished. For the most part they were lawyers, merchants, and planters. Though representing individual states, most thought in national terms. Prominent among them were James Madison, Alexander Hamilton, Governor Morris, Robert Morris, John Dickinson, and Benjamin Franklin.

George Washington was unanimously elected to preside, and the enormous respect that he commanded helped hold the convention together through difficult times and make the product of the convention's work more attractive to the rest of the nation. The delegates then voted that the convention's discussions should be secret, to avoid the distorting and confusing influence of the press and publicity.

The delegates shared a basic belief in the innate selfishness of man, which must somehow be kept from abusing the power of government. For this purpose the document that they finally produced contained many checks and balances, designed to prevent the government, or any one branch of the government, from gaining too much power.

Madison, who has been called the "father of the Constitution," devised a plan of national government and persuaded fellow Virginian Edmund Randolph, who was more skilled at public speaking, to introduce it. Known as the "Virginia Plan," it called for an executive branch and two houses of Congress, each based on population.

Smaller states, who would thus have seen their influence decreased, objected and countered with William Paterson's "New Jersey Plan," calling for the continuation of a unicameral legislature with equal representation for the states as well as sharply increased powers for the national government.

A temporary impasse developed that threatened to break up the convention. At this point Benjamin Franklin played an important role in reconciling the often heated delegates, suggesting that the sessions of the convention henceforth begin with prayer (they did) and making various other suggestions that eventually helped the convention arrive at the "Great Compromise." The Great Compromise provided for a presidency, a Senate with all states represented equally (by two senators each), and a House of Representatives with representation according to population.

Another crisis involved North-South disagreement over the issue of slavery. Here also a compromise was reached. Slavery was neither endorsed nor condemned by the Constitution. Each slave was to count as three-fifths of a person for purposes of apportioning representation and direct taxation on the states (the Three-Fifths Compromise). The federal government was prohibited from stopping the importation of slaves prior to 1808.

The third major area of compromise was the nature of the presidency. This was made easier by the virtual certainty that George Washington would be the first president and the universal trust that he would not abuse the powers of the office or set a bad example for his successors. The result was a strong presidency with control of foreign policy and the power to veto Congress's legislation. Should the president commit an actual crime, Congress would have the power to impeach him. Otherwise the president would serve for a term of four years and be re-electable without limit. As a check to the possible excesses of democracy, the president was to be elected by an electoral college, in which each state would have the same number of electors as it did senators and representatives combined. The person with the second highest total in the electoral college would be vice president. If no one gained a majority in the electoral college, the president would be chosen by the House of Representatives.

The new Constitution was to take effect when nine states, through special state conventions, had ratified it.

QUESTION

> Describe how the principle of "checks and balances" prevents the abuse of government's power.

EXPLANATION

"Checks and balances" divides the government into three branches: legislative, judicial, and executive. For each power a particular branch has, another branch has the power to "check" it. In addition, all the branches theoretically have "balanced" power, that is, no one branch can dominate the others. In this way, the government has the authority to do what it must to effectively govern the nation, but the people are protected from the abuse of power.

The Struggle for Ratification

As the struggle over ratification got under way, those favoring the Constitution astutely took for themselves the name Federalists (i.e., advocates of centralized power) and labeled their opponents Antifederalists. The Federalists were effective in explaining the convention and the document it had produced. *The Federalist Papers,* written as a series of 85 newspaper articles by Alexander Hamilton, James Madison, and John Jay, brilliantly expounded the Constitution and demonstrated how it was designed to prevent the abuse of power from any direction. These essays are considered to be the best commentary on the Constitution by those who helped write it.

At first, ratification progressed smoothly, with five states approving in quick succession. In Massachusetts, however, a tough fight developed. By skillful maneuvering, Federalists were able to win over to their side such popular opponents of the Constitution as Samuel Adams and John Hancock. Others were won over by the promise that a bill of rights would be added to the Constitution, limiting the federal government just as the state governments were limited by their bills of rights. With such promises, Massachusetts ratified by a narrow margin.

By June 21, 1788, the required nine states had ratified, but the crucial states of New York and Virginia still held out. In Virginia, where George Mason and Patrick Henry opposed the Constitution, the influence of George Washington and the promise of a bill of rights finally prevailed and ratification was achieved there as well. In New York, where Alexander Hamilton led the fight for ratification, *The Federalist Papers*, the promise of a bill of rights, and the news of Virginia's ratification were enough to carry the day.

Only North Carolina and Rhode Island still held out, but they both ratified within the next 15 months.

In March 1789, George Washington was inaugurated as the nation's first president.

Drill 1: Development and Ratification of the Constitution

1. Those who supported ratification of the Constitution were called

    (A) Federalists.   (B) Democrates.

    (C) Whigs.   (D) Antifederalists.

    (E) Republicans.

2. Which of the following groups tended to support the Federalists?

    (A) Small farmers

    (B) Small businessmen

    (C) Wealthy merchants

    (D) Baptist and Methodist ministers

    (E) Skilled craftsmen

3. Alexander Hamilton believed that the United States should

    (A) repudiate the debts of the Confederation but assume those of the states.

    (B) assume the debts of the Confederation but not those of the states.

    (C) assume the debts of both the Confederation and the states.

    (D) repudiate the debts of both the Confederation and the states.

    (E) assume the debts of the Confederation, the states, and local governments.

4. The Constitutional Convention took place in

    (A) 1776.   (B) 1789.

    (C) 1787.   (D) 1781.

    (E) 1800.

5. The man responsible for laying out the groundwork of the Constitution and author of the principle of "checks and balances" included in what became known as the "Virginia Plan" was

    (A) Thomas Jefferson.   (B) James Monroe.

    (C) Alexander Hamilton.   (D) James Madison.

    (E) John Jay.

2. OUTLINE OF THE UNITED STATES CONSTITUTION

Articles of the Constitution

Preamble

"We the People of the United States, in order to form a more perfect Union, establish justice, insure domestic tranquility, provide for the common defense, promote the general welfare, and secure the blessings of liberty to ourselves and our posterity, do ordain and establish this Constitution for the United States of America."

Article I - Legislature

The legislature is divided into two parts—the House of Representatives (435 members currently; determined by proportional representation of the population) and the Senate (100 members currently; two from each state).

The House of Representatives may bring impeachment charges. All bills which concern money must originate in the House. Because of the size of the body, debate is limited except in special cases, where all representatives may meet as the Committee of the Whole. The Speaker of the House presides over the proceedings. Elected terms of representatives are two years, re-electable without limit, to persons who are at least 25 years of age.

The Senate, originally elected by state legislatures but now by direct election (Seventeenth Amendment), approves or rejects presidential nominations and treaties, and serves as the court and jury in impeachment proceedings. Debate within the Senate is unlimited. The president pro tempore usually presides, but the vice president of the United States is the presiding officer, and may vote to break a tie. Senate elected terms are for six years, re-electable without limit, to persons who are at least 30 years of age.

Article II - Executive

The president of the United States is elected for a four-year term, originally electable without limit (the Twenty-second Amendment limits election to two terms), and must be at least 35 years old.

Responsibilities for the president as outlined in the Constitution include acting as the chief of state, the chief executive, commander in chief of the Armed Forces, and the chief diplomat.

Article III - Judiciary

While the Constitution describes the Supreme Court in Article III, the actual construction of the court system was accomplished by the Judiciary Act of 1789.

The Supreme Court has jurisdiction for federal courts and appellate cases on appeal from lower courts.

Article IV - Interstate Relations

This article guarantees that court decisions and other legal actions (marriage, incorporation, etc.) valid in one state are valid in another. Extradition of criminals (and, originally, runaway slaves) and the exchange of citizenship benefits are likewise guaranteed. Article IV also provides for the admission of new states and guarantees federal protection against invasion and violence for each state. States admitted maintain the same status as the original states. All states are guaranteed a republican form of government.

Article V - Amendment Process

Amendments are proposed by a two-thirds vote of each house of Congress or by a special convention called by Congress upon the request of two-thirds of the state legislatures. Amendments are ratified by three-fourths of the state legislatures or state conventions.

Article VI - Supremacy Clause

Article VI sets up the hierarchy of laws in the United States. The Constitution is the "supreme law of the land" and supercedes treaties. Treaties supercede federal laws, federal laws (later to include federal regulatory agency directives) supercede state constitutions, state laws and local laws respectively. All federal and state officials, including judges, must take an oath to support and defend the Constitution.

Article VII - Ratification

This article specifies the ratification process necessary for the Constitution to take effect. Nine of the original 13 states had to ratify the Constitution before it became operative.

Amendments to the Constitution

The Amendments to the Constitution guarantee certain individual rights and amend original dictates of the Constitution. The first ten amendments are known as the Bill of Rights.

1. Freedom of religion, speech, press, assembly, and government petition (1791)
2. Right to bear arms in a regulated militia (on a state basis; it was not intended to guarantee an individual's rights) (1791)
3. Troops will not be quartered (housed) in private citizens' homes (1791)
4. Protects against unreasonable search and seizure (need for search warrant) (1791)

5. Protects the rights for the accused, including required indictments, double jeopardy, self-incrimination, due process, and just compensation (1791)
6. Guarantees a speedy and public trial, the confrontation by witnesses, and the right to call one's own witnesses on behalf (1791)
7. Guarantees a jury trial (1791)
8. Protects against excessive bail and cruel and unusual punishment (1791)
9. States that all rights not enumerated are nonetheless retained by the people (1791)
10. States that all powers not specifically delegated to the federal government are retained by the states (1791)
11. States may not be sued by individuals (1798)
12. Dictates that electors will cast separate ballots for president and vice president; in the event of no clear winner, the House will select the president and the Senate the vice president (1804)
13. Abolishes slavery (1865)
14. Extends citizenship to all persons; makes Confederate debt void and Confederate leaders ineligible for public office; states which denied voting rights to qualified citizens (blacks) would have their representation in Congress reduced; confers "dual" citizenship (both of the United States and of a specific state) on all citizens (1868)
15. Extends voting rights to blacks (1870)
16. Legalizes the income tax (1913)
17. Provides for the direct election of senators (1913)
18. Prohibits the general manufacture, sale, and use of alcoholic beverages (1919)
19. Extends voting rights to women (1920)
20. Changes inauguration date from March 4 to January 20; eliminated the "lame duck" session of Congress (after the November elections) (1933)
21. Repeals the Eighteenth Amendment (1933)
22. Limits presidents to two terms (1951)
23. Gives presidential electoral votes to the District of Columbia (1961)
24. Prohibits poll taxes (1964)
25. Changes the order of the presidential line of succession and provided guidelines for presidential disability (1967)
26. Extends voting rights to eighteen-year-olds (1971)
27. Ensures that congressional salary adjustments do not take effect until after the following election (1992)

Separation and Limitation of Powers

Powers Reserved for the Federal Government Only

- Foreign commerce regulation
- Interstate commerce regulation
- Mint money
- Create and establish post offices
- Regulate naturalization and immigration

- Grant copyrights and patents
- Declare and wage war, declare peace
- Admit new states
- Fix standards for weights and measures
- Raise and maintain an army and navy
- Govern the federal city (Washington, D.C.)
- Conduct relations with foreign powers
- Universalize bankruptcy laws

Powers Reserved for the State Governments Only

- Conduct and monitor elections
- Establish voter qualifications
- Provide for local governments
- Ratify proposed amendments to the Constitution
- Regulate contracts and wills
- Regulate intrastate commerce
- Provide education for its citizens
- Levy direct taxes (the Sixteenth Amendment permits the federal government to levy direct taxes)
- Maintain police power over public health, safety, and morals
- Maintain integrity of state borders

Powers Shared by Federal and State Governments

- Taxing, borrowing, and spending money
- Controlling the militia
- Acting directly on individuals

Restrictions on the Federal Government

- No *ex post facto* laws
- No bills of attainder
- Two-year limit on appropriation for the military
- No suspension of *habeas corpus* (except in a crisis)
- One port may not be favored over another
- All guarantees as stated in the Bill of Rights

Restrictions on State Governments

- Treaties, alliances, or confederations may not be entered into
- Letters of marque and reprisal may not be granted
- Contracts may not be impaired
- Money may not be printed or bills of credit emitted
- No import or export taxes
- May not wage war (unless invaded)

Required Percentages of Voting

Actions which require a simple majority include raising taxes, requesting appropriations, declaring war, increasing the national debt, instituting a draft, and introducing impeachment charge (House).

Actions which require a two-thirds majority include overriding a presidential veto, proposing amendments to the Constitution, expelling a member of Congress (in the individual house only), ratifying treaties (Senate), acting as a jury for impeachment (Senate), and ratifying presidential appointments (Senate).

The action which requires a three-fourths majority is approving a proposed constitutional amendment (states).

QUESTION

Why is the First Amendment considered so important in the United States?

EXPLANATION

The First Amendment guarantees some of the most important basic political liberties in the United States. By ensuring the basic freedoms of speech, press, assembly, religion, and the right to petition government, the amendment allows the people to freely criticize the government, and thus provides a way for citizens to keep those in government responsive to their needs. It also assures that citizens can have a broad range of opinions when called upon to make choices in a democracy.

Drill 2: Outline of the United States Constitution

1. When no presidential candidate obtains a majority of the electoral vote, who chooses the president?

    (A) The Senate

    (B) The House of Representatives

    (C) The Supreme Court

    (D) The Senate and the House of Representatives combined

    (E) The electoral college

2. The Bill of Rights guarantees all of the following EXCEPT

    (A) the freedom of religion.

    (B) the right to a fair trial.

    (C) powers not delegated to the federal government by the Constitution are reserved to the states.

    (D) the right to bear arms.

    (E) the right of women to vote.

3.   According to the Constitution, the president is chosen by

    (A) the House of Representatives.

    (B) popular vote of the people.

    (C) the electoral college.

    (D) the Senate.

    (E) both houses of Congress.

4.   The Fourteenth Amendment to the Constitution provided for which of the following?

    (A) Gave blacks federal and state citizenship

    (B) Disallowed any former Confederate officeholder from becoming a U.S. senator under any circumstances

    (C) Repudiated federal war debts

    (D) Allowed a state to limit the voting of blacks

    (E) Required the former Confederate states to pay off their debts incurred during the Civil War

5.   Article I of the U.S. Constitution establishes

    (A) freedom of speech.

    (B) the powers of the presidency.

    (C) freedom of assembly.

    (D) the powers of Congress.

    (E) the powers of the Supreme Court.

1787–1789
DRILLS

Drill 1—Development and Ratification of the Constitution

1. (A) 2. (C) 3. (C) 4. (C) 5. (D)

Drill 2—Outline of the United States Constitution

1. (B) 2. (E) 3. (C) 4. (A) 5. (D)

GLOSSARY: 1787–1789

Bill of Rights

The first ten amendments to the Constitution, limiting the power of the federal government.

Federalists

Those favoring ratification of the Constitution.

Great Compromise

A plan for the U.S. Constitution that called for a presidency, a Senate with all states represented equally, and a House of Representatives with representation according to population.

New Jersey Plan

A plan for the U.S. Constitution that called for a unicameral legislature with equal representation of the states and sharply increased powers for the national government.

Virginia Plan

A plan for the U.S. Constitution that called for an executive branch and two houses of Congress, each based on population.

CHAPTER 5

1789–1824
THE NEW NATION

➤ Diagnostic Test
➤ 1789–1824 Review & Drills
➤ Glossary

1789-1824
DIAGNOSTIC TEST

1. Ⓐ Ⓑ Ⓒ Ⓓ Ⓔ		21. Ⓐ Ⓑ Ⓒ Ⓓ Ⓔ
2. Ⓐ Ⓑ Ⓒ Ⓓ Ⓔ		22. Ⓐ Ⓑ Ⓒ Ⓓ Ⓔ
3. Ⓐ Ⓑ Ⓒ Ⓓ Ⓔ		23. Ⓐ Ⓑ Ⓒ Ⓓ Ⓔ
4. Ⓐ Ⓑ Ⓒ Ⓓ Ⓔ		24. Ⓐ Ⓑ Ⓒ Ⓓ Ⓔ
5. Ⓐ Ⓑ Ⓒ Ⓓ Ⓔ		25. Ⓐ Ⓑ Ⓒ Ⓓ Ⓔ
6. Ⓐ Ⓑ Ⓒ Ⓓ Ⓔ		26. Ⓐ Ⓑ Ⓒ Ⓓ Ⓔ
7. Ⓐ Ⓑ Ⓒ Ⓓ Ⓔ		27. Ⓐ Ⓑ Ⓒ Ⓓ Ⓔ
8. Ⓐ Ⓑ Ⓒ Ⓓ Ⓔ		28. Ⓐ Ⓑ Ⓒ Ⓓ Ⓔ
9. Ⓐ Ⓑ Ⓒ Ⓓ Ⓔ		29. Ⓐ Ⓑ Ⓒ Ⓓ Ⓔ
10. Ⓐ Ⓑ Ⓒ Ⓓ Ⓔ		30. Ⓐ Ⓑ Ⓒ Ⓓ Ⓔ
11. Ⓐ Ⓑ Ⓒ Ⓓ Ⓔ		31. Ⓐ Ⓑ Ⓒ Ⓓ Ⓔ
12. Ⓐ Ⓑ Ⓒ Ⓓ Ⓔ		32. Ⓐ Ⓑ Ⓒ Ⓓ Ⓔ
13. Ⓐ Ⓑ Ⓒ Ⓓ Ⓔ		33. Ⓐ Ⓑ Ⓒ Ⓓ Ⓔ
14. Ⓐ Ⓑ Ⓒ Ⓓ Ⓔ		34. Ⓐ Ⓑ Ⓒ Ⓓ Ⓔ
15. Ⓐ Ⓑ Ⓒ Ⓓ Ⓔ		35. Ⓐ Ⓑ Ⓒ Ⓓ Ⓔ
16. Ⓐ Ⓑ Ⓒ Ⓓ Ⓔ		36. Ⓐ Ⓑ Ⓒ Ⓓ Ⓔ
17. Ⓐ Ⓑ Ⓒ Ⓓ Ⓔ		37. Ⓐ Ⓑ Ⓒ Ⓓ Ⓔ
18. Ⓐ Ⓑ Ⓒ Ⓓ Ⓔ		38. Ⓐ Ⓑ Ⓒ Ⓓ Ⓔ
19. Ⓐ Ⓑ Ⓒ Ⓓ Ⓔ		39. Ⓐ Ⓑ Ⓒ Ⓓ Ⓔ
20. Ⓐ Ⓑ Ⓒ Ⓓ Ⓔ		40. Ⓐ Ⓑ Ⓒ Ⓓ Ⓔ

1789–1824
DIAGNOSTIC TEST

This diagnostic test is designed to help you determine your strengths and weaknesses in your knowledge of the new nation (1789–1824). Follow the directions and check your answers.

Study this chapter for the following tests:
AP U.S. History, CLEP General, CLEP United States History I,
GED, Praxis Specialty Area, SAT: United States History

---

40 Questions

DIRECTIONS: Choose the correct answer for each of the following questions. Fill in each answer on the answer sheet.

1. Which of the following was the first important means of transportation in the United States after independence?

    (A) Canals   (B) Turnpikes

    (C) Steamboats   (D) Railroads

    (E) Clipper ships

2. The Second Bank of the United States performed all of the following functions EXCEPT

    (A) receiving and paying out federal funds.

    (B) stabilizing the money supply.

    (C) shifting funds from the West and South to the Northeast.

    (D) keeping a check on the loans of other banks.

    (E) making loans to the federal government.

3. The Waltham system

    (A) purified melted iron with oxygen.

    (B) combined spinning and weaving in a single factory.

    (C) introduced the idea of interchangeable parts.

(D) combined public and private capital in business enterprise.

(E) established government bounties for the creation of new business.

4. The Judiciary Act of 1789 established

(A) a nine-judge Supreme Court.

(B) thirteen circuit courts.

(C) three district courts.

(D) the office of attorney general.

(E) the power of the Supreme Court to review the constitutionality of federal laws.

5. Which Supreme Court chief justice oversaw the development of the Court's power to judge the constitutionality of acts of Congress?

(A) John Marshall   (B) John Jay

(C) Roger Taney   (D) Alexander Hamilton

(E) Oliver Wendell Holmes, Jr.

6. Which of the following best describes the First Bank of the United States?

(A) It was solely a private business enterprise.

(B) It was solely a federal government enterprise.

(C) It was a joint private-public enterprise.

(D) It was a joint state-federal government enterprise.

(E) It was a joint state-private enterprise.

7. The Kentucky and Virginia Resolutions of 1798 introduced which of the following ideas?

(A) That Federal laws take precedence over state wishes

(B) That the years of residence required for naturalization be increased from five to fourteen

(C) That it is illegal to make "false, scandalous, malicious" statements against the federal government

(D) That individual states could nullify or set aside federal laws with which they disagreed

(E) That a protective tariff was harmful to the economic interests of the South

8. The Whiskey Rebellion of 1794 protested

    (A) prohibition.

    (B) a 25 percent tax on whiskey.

    (C) government regulation of whiskey production.

    (D) the lifting of import duties on whiskey.

    (E) a 30 percent drop in whiskey prices.

9. Besides mass production through the use of interchangeable parts, Eli Whitney also influenced American history by his invention of the

    (A) practical river steamboat. *1807 Fulton*

    (B) cotton gin.

    (C) incandescent light bulb. *Edison*

    (D) telegraph. *Morse*

    (E) steam locomotive.

10. The Republican response to the 1798 Alien and Sedition Acts included

    (A) South Carolina's nullification of the acts.

    (B) the Virginia and Kentucky Resolutions.

    (C) the Hartford Convention.

    (D) the Ostend Manifesto.

    (E) the Mulligan Letters.

11. The greatest significance of the Supreme Court's decision in *Marbury v. Madison* was that it

    (A) claimed for the first time that the Supreme Court could issue directives to the president.

    (B) claimed that the Supreme Court alone was empowered to say what the Constitution meant.

    (C) claimed for the first time that the Supreme Court could declare an act of Congress to be unconstitutional.

    (D) was openly defied by President Thomas Jefferson.

    (E) resulted in a major realignment of the first American party system.

12. All of the following reflect the views of Americans expressed by Alexis de Tocqueville and other early nineteenth century European visitors EXCEPT

    (A) daily life in America was highly politicized.

4

(B) Americans exhibited a strong sense of national pride.

(C) Americans were highly individualistic.

(D) Americans exhibited a strong sense of social deference.

(E) Americans valued personal freedom.

13. Art of the Hudson River School may be described as

(A) classically romantic, expressing an air of wonder at the mystery of nature.

(B) brutally realistic in its depiction of often unpleasant subjects.

(C) concentrating on grimy scenes of everyday life in crowded New York City tenements.

(D) almost completely abstract.

(E) concerned with portraiture to the exclusion of significant landscape painting.

14. The following map depicts the United States as it was immediately after the

(A) passage of the Compromise of 1850.

(B) passage of the Missouri Compromise.

(C) passage of the Northwest Ordinance.

(D) settlement of the Mexican War.

(E) negotiation of the Webster-Ashburton Treaty.

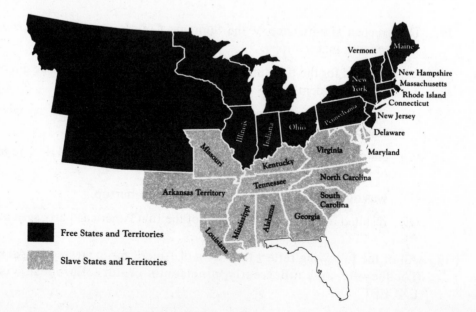

UNIT 4

15. Which of the following best describes the attitudes of Southern whites toward slavery during the eigtheenth and the beginning of the nineteenth century?

    (A) Slavery was a national sin.

    (B) Slavery was acceptable only if the slaves voluntarily chose to remain with their masters.

    (C) Slavery was a benefit to both whites and blacks. *SHIFT in 1830s after Turners Rebellon*

    (D) Slavery should be immediately abolished.

    (E) Slavery was a necessary evil.

1789–1809

16. During the first two decades under the United States Constitution, the main factor that separated Federalists from Republicans was

    (A) whether they accepted the Constitution or opposed it.

    (B) whether they favored the French Revolution or opposed it. *? LATER*

    (C) whether they leaned more toward states' rights or national sovereignty.

    (D) their personal like or dislike for the personalities of Thomas Jefferson and Alexander Hamilton.

    (E) whether they had been Patriots or Loyalists during the American War of Independence.

17. The international incident known as the XYZ Affair involved

    (A) a French foreign minister's demand for a bribe before he would meet with American envoys.

    (B) the British refusal to evacuate their forts on American territory.

    (C) General Andrew Jackson's incursion into Spanish-held Florida.

    (D) the British seizure of American crewmen from a U.S. Navy warship in Chesapeake Bay.

    (E) Aaron Burr's secret plot to detach the western United States in order to create a new nation of which he would be ruler.

Questions 18 and 19 refer to the following passage.

All combinations and associations, under whatever plausible character, with the real design to direct...the constituted authorities, are destructive of this fundamental principle and of fatal tendency. They serve to organize faction; to give it an artificial and extraordinary force; to put in the place of the delegated will of the nation the will of a party, often a small but artful and enterprising minority of the community, and, according to the alternate triumphs of different parties, to make the public administration the mirror of the ill-considered and incongruous projects of faction rather than the organ of consistent and wholesome plans, digested by common counsels and modified by mutual interests.

18. The passage on the previous page is most likely to be found in which of the following?

    (A) Hamilton, Madison, and Jay's *Federalist Papers*

    (B) Washington's farewell address

    (C) Jefferson's first inaugural address

    (D) Lincoln's first inaugural address

    (E) Jefferson's Declaration of Independence

19. The author wants primarily to convince his audience that

    (A) political parties are harmful.

    (B) the British have undermined free government in America.

    (C) party strife need not lead to civil conflict.

    (D) party strife should be forgotten once the will of the people has been expressed in an election.

    (E) the Constitution contains adequate safeguards against the dangers of faction.

20. Historians generally consider which of the following to have been an advocate of a strong national government?

    (A) Thomas Jefferson   (B) John C. Calhoun

    (C) Jefferson Davis   (D) Roger B. Taney

    (E) John Marshall

21. Which of the following did NOT characterize the early nineteenth century religious movement known as the Second Great Awakening?

    (A) Extreme displays of emotion

    (B) An emphasis on individual conversion

    (C) Increased interest in social reforms such as the temperance movement

    (D) Acceptance of slavery as ordained by God

    (E) Extensive involvement by women and African-Americans

22. President Tyler broke with the Whig party on all of the following issues EXCEPT

    (A) the creation of the Second Bank of the United States.

    (B) the ending of the Independent Treasury system.

    (C) the sale of public lands in the West.

    (D) a high protective tariff.

    (E) federal financing of internal improvements.

23. Which of the following was NOT one of the purposes of the Lewis and Clark expedition?

    (A) Establishing friendly relations with the western Indians

    (B) Gaining geographic knowledge about the western part of North America

  •(C) Discovering sources of gold   *1848*

    (D) Gaining scientific knowledge about the flora and fauna of western North America

    (E) Finding a water route to the Pacific Ocean across North America

24. Purposes of Alexander Hamilton's tax, tariff, and debt manipulation schemes during the presidency of George Washington included   *cf #6*

    (A) ridding the federal government of debt as soon as possible.

    (B) ending undue government interference in the economy.

  •(C) binding the interests of the moneyed class to the new federal government.

    (D) maintaining the United States as an agrarian society.

    (E) promoting the importation of British manufactured goods.

Questions 25 and 26 refer to the following passage.

During the contest of opinion through which we have passed the animation of discussions and of exertions has sometimes worn an aspect which might impose on strangers unused to think freely and to speak and to write what they think; but this being now decided by the voice of the nation, announced according to the rules of the Constitution, all will, of course, arrange themselves under the will of the law, and unite in common efforts for the common good.... Let us, then, fellow-citizens, unite with one heart and one mind.... We have called by different names brethren of the same principle.

25. The above passage is most likely to be found in which of the following?

    (A) Washington's farewell address

    (B) Lincoln's first inaugural address

we are Au;
Fs/R's

(C)   Jackson's first inaugural address

(D)   Jefferson's first inaugural address

(E)   The Declaration of Independence

26.   The author wants primarily to convince his audience that

(A)   political parties are harmful.

(B)   political strife is foreign to the American character.

(C)   party strife is indicative of fundamental philosophical differences.

(D)   party strife should be forgotten once the will of the people has been expressed in an election.

(E)   only the members of his party are acting in accordance with the rules of the Constitution.

27.   The Louisiana Purchase resulted primarily from

(A)   efforts to prevent Spain from closing off westward expansion by the United States.

LATER

(B)   glowing reports of the vast beauty and potential of the region as reported by Lewis and Clark on their return from their famous exploration of the region.

(C)   American efforts to prevent war with France over control of the Louisiana Territory and secure American commerce rights in New Orleans and along the Mississippi River. *Spain had ceded to Napolen, in 1801*

(D)   Federalist desires to establish a strong confederation of antislavery states west of the Mississippi River and further limit the power of the southern Republicans. *Pinckney Treaty "Ignorance" in 1802*

(E)   Republican desires to further dilute the Federalist power base in New England by expanding the country and reducing Federalist influence.

28.   The War of 1812 had all of the following effects EXCEPT

(A)   it strengthened American industrial and manufacturing production.

(B)   it virtually destroyed the Federalist party as a credible opposition to the Republican party.

(C)   it restored a sense of pride in most Americans and led to a wave of nationalism throughout the country after the conclusion of the war.

(D)   it destroyed the power of the Indian tribes in the Northwest Territory.

(E)   it led to an increased and more active American role in world politics.

29. The Treaty of Ghent signaled the end of the

   (A) Revolutionary War.   (B) Spanish-American War.

   ˒(C) War of 1812.   (D) Mexican-American War.

   (E) quasi-war with France.

30. The American system of manufacturing, which emerged in the early 1800s, was successful because of its use of

   (A) slave labor.

   (B) handmade, individually crafted, high-quality items.

   (C) the "putting out" system—distributing raw materials and collecting finished products for distribution.

   (D) early electric power to provide cheap energy for new factories.

   ˒(E) interchangeable parts to allow for mass production of high-quality items.

31. The "Era of Good Feeling" referred to _____ presidency.

   ˒(A) James Monroe's   (B) James Madison's

   (C) John Quincy Adams'   (D) William Henry Harrison's

   (E) Andrew Jackson's

32. During the Washington administration, Secretary of the Treasury, Alexander Hamilton, proposed an economic program which included all of the following EXCEPT

   (A) the establishment of close ties between the national government and American business.

   (B) the establishment of a national bank.

   ˄(C) having the states pay off the total war debt. *national gvt. assumed*

   (D) the imposition of new taxes through customs duties and excise taxes.

   (E) retirement of the full national debt and deficit government spending.

33. During the 1790s, Federalists and Republicans openly disagreed over

   (A) the extent of popular control of government.

   (B) foreign policy toward England and France.

   (C) the activities of Citizen Genet.

   (D) the fiscal policies of the national government.

   (E) All of the above.

34. The Alien and Sedition Acts included all of the following EXCEPT

    (A) increasing the residency requirements for U.S. citizenship.

    (B) extended presidential powers to remove foreign residents of the United States.

    (C) a threat to the jury system.

    (D) restriction of an opposition press.

    (E) the curtailment of free speech in America.

35. President John Adams' "Midnight Appointments" was the primary issue in the Supreme Court's ruling in

    (A) *Marbury v. Madison.*   (B) *Gibbons v. Ogden.*

    (C) *Martin v. Hunter's Lessee.*   (D) *Dartmouth v. Woodward.*

    (E) *Fletcher v. Peck.*

36. Chief Justice John Marshall established the power of judicial review for the Supreme Court in 1803. This doctrine grants

    (A) the Court the power of original jurisdiction.

    (B) the power of strict constructionalism.

    (C) the power of the government to regulate big business.

    (D) the power of the Court to determine what the laws of America are.

    (E) the power of the Court to select its own members.

37. "We prefer war to the putrescent pool of ignominious peace" best represents the attitudes of which group during the War of 1812?

    (A) Oliver Ellsworth and New England merchants

    (B) Henry Clay and westerners

    (C) The British nobility

    (D) James Madison and the Republicans

    (E) Harrison Gray Otis and the Federalists

38. The primary goal of the Hartford Convention was

    (A) to have New England secede from the United States.

    (B) to assert a doctrine of states' rights.

    (C) to establish a public school system in the nation.

    (D) to establish direct trade with Japan.

    (E) to plan the invasion of Cuba.

UNIT 4

39. The American Colonization Society was an antislavery organization that

(A) advocated racial equality.

(B) sought full political rights for blacks.

(C) favored immediate emancipation.

(D) advocated the forced shipment of freed slaves to Africa.

(E) relied upon governmental action to end slavery.

40. The doctrine of Manifest Destiny argued that   UNIT 4

(A) it was America's natural right to occupy all lands to the Pacific coast.

(B) the American economy needed new lands for new markets.

(C) America should remain first and foremost a nation of farmers.

(D) the nation needed new lands to safeguard democracy.

(E) All of the above.

1789–1824
DIAGNOSTIC TEST

ANSWER KEY

1.	(B)	9.	(B)	17.	(A)	25.	(D)	33. (E)
2.	(C)	10.	(B)	18.	(B)	26.	(D)	34. (C)
3.	(B)	11.	(C)	19.	(A)	27.	(C)	35. (A)
4.	(D)	12.	(D)	20.	(E)	28.	(E)	36. (D)
5.	(A)	13.	(A)	21.	(D)	29.	(C)	37. (B)
6.	(C)	14.	(B)	22.	(B)	30.	(E)	38. (B)
7.	(D)	15.	(E)	23.	(C)	31.	(A)	39. (D)
8.	(B)	16.	(B)	24.	(C)	32.	(E)	40. (E)

DETAILED EXPLANATIONS
OF ANSWERS

1. **(B)** Turnpikes became popular in the 1790s, and canals after completion of the Erie Canal in 1825. The steamboat was introduced in 1807 and became particularly popular in the 1830s.

2. **(C)** The Second Bank of the United States shifted funds from the wealthy East for investment in the underdeveloped West and South.

3. **(B)** In 1814, Francis Cabot Lowell built the first integrated textile factory at Waltham, Massachusetts. In 1851 William Kelly developed a method for purifying iron with oxygen. Eli Whitney and Simeon North were associated with interchangeable parts in the early nineteenth century. Many nineteenth century businesses used both private and public capital. Alexander Hamilton had proposed government bounties for the establishment of new manufacturing businesses.

4. **(D)** The Judiciary Act of 1789 provided for a six-judge Supreme Court, thirteen district courts, three circuit courts, and the office of attorney general. It gave the Supreme Court the power to review state laws that conflicted with federal statutes.

5. **(A)** John Marshall served as chief justice from 1801 to 1835, during which time the Court successfully claimed the power to determine the constitutionality of acts of Congress. John Jay served as chief justice from 1789 to 1794 and Roger B. Taney served from 1836 to 1864. Alexander Hamilton never served on the Supreme Court.

6. **(C)** The First Bank of the United States was a joint private-public enterprise, with stock owned by both the federal government and private individuals and with representatives of the government and private sector serving as directors.

7. **(D)** The Kentucky and Virginia Resolutions (1798) introduced the idea of nullification in response to the Alien and Sedition Acts (1798), which changed the years of residence necessary for naturalization and placed sharp limits on freedom of speech.

8. **(B)** The 1794 Whiskey Rebellion opposed a 25 percent tax on whiskey proposed by Hamilton and passed by Congress; government regulation of whiskey production, import duties, and prohibition did not emerge as issues until much later.

9. **(B)** Eli Whitney had an enormous influence on American history through his invention of the cotton gin. The steamboat (A) was invented by Whitney's

contemporary Robert Fulton, the steam locomotive (E) and the telegraph (D) somewhat later in the nineteenth century, and the incandescent light bulb (C), by Thomas Edison, near the end of the century.

10. **(B)** The Virginia and Kentucky Resolutions were the centerpiece of the Republican response to the Alien and Sedition Acts. The 1814 Hartford Convention (C), on the other hand, was a Federalist response to Republican policies. South Carolina's nullification (A) was aimed at the highly protective Tariff of 1828. The 1854 Ostend Manifesto (D) dealt with U.S. desires to acquire Cuba from Spain; and the Mulligan Letters (E) incriminated 1884 Republican presidential candidate James G. Blaine in an unsavory stock scheme.

11. **(C)** *Marbury v. Madison* asserted for the first time the Supreme Court's right to declare an act of Congress unconstitutional. It did not, however, go so far as to claim that the Supreme Court alone was empowered to say what the Constitution meant (B). In the decision of this case, Chief Justice John Marshall wisely avoided issuing a directive (A) that President Thomas Jefferson would have defied (D) had it been issued. The case did not bring any major political realignment.

12. **(D)** Tocqueville found the Americans had little or no sense of social deference. They were politicized (A) and individualistic (C), proud of their country (B), and placed a high value on personal freedom (E).

13. **(A)** The art of the Hudson River School was romantic in the early nineteenth century sense, expressing an air of wonder at the mystery of nature. Brutally realistic art (B) dealing with squalid scenes (C) was more characteristic of late nineteenth century American painting. Emphasis on portraiture (E) to one degree or another was prevalent in the eighteenth century, while most of the abstract art (D) has been produced in the twentieth century.

14. **(B)** This map depicts the United States as it was after the Missouri Compromise in 1820. Maine and Missouri have become states, and the territory remaining from the Louisiana Purchase has been divided between slave and free areas along the line of 36°30'. Arkansas and Michigan have not yet become states as would have been the case before the Webster-Ashburton Treaty (E). The Mexican Cession has not yet been added as would have been the case after the settlement of the Mexican War (D) or the Compromise of 1850 (A). However, at the time of the Northwest Ordinance (C), the Louisiana Purchase area would not yet have been added.

15. **(E)** During this period most Southerners tended to see slavery as a necessary evil. It was only later that a large number came to see it as a positive good (C). Northern abolitionists believed that slavery was a national sin (A) and should immediately be abolished (D).

16. **(B)** Though many factors might contribute to an individual's choice of party—including, perhaps, the character of the party's leader (D) and the party's stand on such issues as states' rights (C)—the chief factor during this period was acceptance or rejection of the French Revolution. Jefferson and his supporters saw it as good, while Hamilton and the Federalists did not. By this time, the Constitution had virtually universal acceptance in the U.S. (A). Though during the days of the fight over ratification, those favoring the Constitution were known as Federalists, they are not to be confused with the political party bearing the same name that gradually took form AFTER the Constitution was in effect. Patriot and Loyalist divisions came to mean increasingly less (E).

17. **(A)** The XYZ Affair involved the demand of French foreign minister Talleyrand that he receive a bribe before meeting with American envoys. Immediately following the War of Independence, the British did refuse to evacuate their forts on American territory, particularly on the northwestern frontier (B). In 1818, Andrew Jackson did lead an incursion into Spanish-held Florida (C) in pursuit of raiding Indians. The 1807 British seizure of American crewmen from a U.S. Navy warship in Chesapeake Bay (D) was the *Chesapeake-Leopard* Incident. Finally, Aaron Burr did indeed seem to have some sort of bizarre plot in mind during the first decade of the 1800s though nothing came of it (E).

18. **(B)** The passage is from Washington's 1796 farewell address, in which he announced his decision not to accept a third term as president and offered advice for the future shaping of national policy.

19. **(A)** In this passage, Washington wanted to convey that political parties—or "factions" as he called them—were harmful. Along with the rest of the Founding Fathers, Washington did not envision the present system of political parties; so he could not have been discussing party strife (C), (D); by the same token, the Constitution does not address the dangers of faction (E). Washington might have felt that Britain wanted to undermine the American system of government (B), but this passage does not discuss that topic.

20. **(E)** John Marshall, who served as chief justice of the United States for a third of a century, was a steadfast champion of the cause of national sovereignty and an enemy of the doctrine of states' rights. His successor, the almost equally long-tenured Roger B. Taney (D), held the opposite viewpoint; so did Thomas Jefferson (A) and Confederate president Jefferson Davis (C). However, the most renowned advocate of states' rights in nineteenth-century America by far was South Carolina politician John C. Calhoun (B).

21. **(D)** One of the most significant social impacts of the Second Great Awakening was the impetus it gave to the antislavery movement in the North. While the South as a region came to assert that slavery was ordained by God, this view collided with the trend of religious feeling at the time. The Second Great Awakening did include extreme displays of emotion (A), an emphasis on indi-

vidual conversion (B), an increased interest in social reforms such as the temperance and abolition movements (C), and the involvement of women and African-Americans (E).

22. **(B)** Although he stood at odds with his fellow Whigs on the bank issue (A); the Whigs' complicated tariff scheme which combined, among other things, the sale of public land (C) and a high tariff rate (D); and federal expenditure on internal improvements (E), President Tyler, realizing the need for financial reform, signed into law the destruction of the Independent Treasury system in early 1841. This measure, however, was only the calm before the storm for Tyler and the Whigs; before the middle of his term not only had his entire cabinet resigned (except Secretary of State Webster), but Tyler had been disowned by his party.

23. **(C)** In sending out the Lewis and Clark expedition, President Thomas Jefferson was not concerned with the possibility that they might discover gold (they did not). He did desire that they establish friendly relations with the western Indians (A), gain both geographic (B) and scientific (D) knowledge about western North America, and find a water route to the Pacific Ocean across the continent (E).

24. **(C)** Perhaps the most important purpose of Hamilton's economic program was binding the interests of the moneyed class to the new federal government. By making the government a banker and, more important, a debtor, the opposite of (A), he would ensure that the federal government's survival would be a condition of the repayment of the deposits of wealthy and powerful men. He also desired to promote manufacturing in America, the opposite of (D), by protecting it from the competition of imports, the opposite of (E). Hamilton did not believe that the government should refrain from "interfering" in the economy (B).

25. **(D)** The passage is from Jefferson's first inaugural address, March 1801. Coming after the extremely heated electoral campaign of 1800, it was followed immediately by Jefferson's famous statement, "We are all Republicans, we are all Federalists."

26. **(D)** Jefferson was trying to convince his audience that party strife should be forgotten once the will of the people has been expressed in an election (D). Jefferson recognized the inevitability of party politics in a democratic system, so he would not have argued against them (A), or that the strife caused by parties is foreign to the American character (B). Fundamental philosophical differences (C) are what give rise to different parties and are not the topic of this passage; nor is Jefferson arguing that only his party acts in accordance with the Constitution (E).

27. **(C)** Up until 1801, Spain had controlled the Louisiana Territory. While Spanish control theoretically threatened U.S. Mississippi River commerce and blocked westward U.S. expansion, in reality the Spanish kept the Mississippi

open to American commerce. Also, Spain was a weak power whose future looked bleak. It was commonly believed that Louisiana could be "obtained" from Spain one way or another whenever it suited American purposes. However, in 1801 Spain secretly turned over control of Louisiana to Napoleon and the French. Napoleon had openly discussed a French empire in North America and in 1802 the Port of New Orleans was closed to American shipping. This precipitated a crisis for Jefferson. A French empire blocking U.S. westward expansion was unacceptable as was French blocking of U.S. trade along the Mississippi. Jefferson considered joining with England in an effort to drive out the French militarily, but decided to try negotiations first. Due to a variety of factors, Napoleon decided the vast Louisiana Territory was not worth the cost of possession and maintenance. He thereby stunned American negotiators by offering the entire Louisiana Territory to the U.S. for approximately four cents an acre ($15 million). The purchase secured U.S. trading rights along the Mississippi and opened up the trans-Mississippi West to American exploration and expansion.

28.   **(E)**   The psychological reaction of most Americans to the Napoleonic Wars that drew America into the War of 1812 was one of withdrawal. Most people remembered Washington's words of being wary of European entanglements, and the war confirmed in their minds that Washington had been correct. Rather than seeking a more active and dominant role in European "intrigues," most Americans sought isolationism and avoidance of European commitments. Others wished to further reduce U.S. involvement with Europe by keeping Europe out of the Americas. This wish was expressed nine years after the conclusion of the 1812 war in the Monroe Doctrine.

29.   **(C)**   The War of 1812 officially ended with the Treaty of Ghent, signed in the Belgian city of Ghent on December 24, 1814. The treaty gave neither side what it initially demanded and effectively returned matters to their prewar standing.

30.   **(E)**   Innovations by Eli Whitney and Simeon North in the use of interchangeable parts to produce small arms for the military pioneered the beginnings of the machine tool industry. The use of precision-engineered, high-quality interchangeable parts led to the mass production of a wide variety of high-quality products not previously available to consumers. This brought the United States slowly but steadily into the Industrial Revolution and laid the groundwork for the American manufacturing colossus which emerged by the end of the nineteenth century.

31.   **(A)**   With the collapse of the Federalist party as a national political force following the War of 1812, President James Monroe (1816–1824) took over a country with essentially a one-party political system. The term "Era of Good Feeling" reflects Monroe's call for unity through his "American Plan" to promote national growth both economically and politically. It also reflects the existence of a powerful sense of nationalism that united the country at this time. There were

clear gains in foreign policy with the acquisition of Florida from Spain and the settling of disputes with Britain regarding territorial disputes along the Canadian border. While there were still political conflicts aplenty, the clearly drawn battle lines, which had existed before the Federalist collapse, were lacking. This period came to an abrupt end with the economic collapse of 1819 and the issue of slavery clouding Missouri's application for statehood. By this point, the Republican party had degenerated into a series of rebellious factions, making it difficult for Monroe to accomplish anything. The rise of sectionalism and partisanship, which accompanied the Missouri Compromise, would lay the foundation for the strong national parties that emerged in the 1820s and 1830s.

32.   **(E)**   Although Hamilton publicly advocated retirement of the bulk of America's wartime debt to restore faith, he desired to retain a portion of the debt to cement creditors closer to the national government out of their self-interest. As a result, Hamilton supported the notion of deficit spending as a means of attracting creditors to the national government. It was imperative to Hamilton that business interests be attracted to the national and not state governments. As a result, Hamilton demanded that the new national government assume the war debt of each individual state. In order to pay this sum, he proposed the raising of a revenue through customs duties and excise taxes. To conclude his plan, Hamilton sought to create a national bank with business leaders and government officials in the controlling interest. By these means, Hamilton sought to achieve his goal of uniting business leaders to the new national government during the 1790s. His program was directly opposed by Jefferson and Madison.

33.   **(E)**   Political parties burst across the nation's political horizon in the 1790s. The existence of political parties had been denounced by the Revolutionary War generation as evil and opposed to the common good of the republic. As a result, political parties virtually were non-existent prior to 1790. However, with the emergence of the Hamiltonian economic program and the start of war between England and France, two viewpoints of the "common good" of America emerged: the Federalists who supported Hamilton, favored England over France, and desired a government dominated by an elite group of politicians; the Democratic-Republicans who supported a nation of small farmers rather than business class, supported Revolutionary France over England, and expressed deep faith in democracy. The two parties openly split over the arrival of the new French minister to the United States in 1793, Edmund "Citizen" Genet. Genet sought to use American public opinion to swing support to France rather than maintain the course of neutrality under Washington.

34.   **(C)**   The Alien and Sedition Acts of 1797-1798 were a direct and bold attempt by President Adams to crush the opposition party of Madison-Jefferson, the Democratic-Republicans. Adams feared that Jefferson's party was bent on establishing a French-styled class revolution in America. To ensure that his party, the Federalists, remained in power, Adams pushed a series of laws known as the

Alien and Sedition Acts through the Federalist Congress. These Acts increased the residency requirement for citizenship from five to fourteen years. (Thus, new immigrants to America who tended to support Jefferson would be disenfranchised for fourteen years.) In addition, the president was granted broad powers to remove "undesirable" aliens, thus putting a political muzzle on aliens. In addition, the laws established large monetary fines and prison sentences to prison for anyone who attacked the American government (the Adams administration) in print or speech. The laws never included an attack on the jury system and indeed relied upon juries to determine guilt or innocence in all seditious libel cases.

35. **(A)**   After losing the election of 1800 to Thomas Jefferson and the Democratic-Republicans, President John Adams sought to use the national courts to block Jefferson from radical programs over the next four years. On the night before Jefferson's inaugural, Adams appointed several new federal judges from the Federalist party. Upon learning of this later, Jefferson sought to remove the midnight appointments through a test case of one appointment, William Marbury. In 1803, Marbury sued Secretary of State James Madison for his judgeship and petitioned the Supreme Court. In *Marbury v. Madison*, Chief Justice John Marshall correctly ruled that the issue was a matter not for the Supreme Court but for Congress. In so doing, however, Marshall declared the Judiciary Act of 1789 unconstitutional and granted the Supreme Court the power of judicial review. (This power allows the Court to be the final arbiter on the constitutionality of all laws enacted by Congress.) In *Fletcher* (1810), Marshall extended the Court's power of judicial review over state governments; in *Gibbons* (1824), Marshall extended governmental power over commerce; in *Martin* (1816), Marshall extended judicial review to the state courts; in *Dartmouth* (1819), Marshall offered views of contracts and corporations that would greatly influence the economy throughout the nineteenth century.

36. **(D)**   The power of judicial review allows the Supreme Court as the last voice on the constitutionality of law in America. Only the U.S. Constitution grants the Court the power of original jurisdiction in Article III. "Strict constructionalism" is a judicial viewpoint of recent years that argues one cannot liberally interpret pre-existing laws to decide a case. As a result, it is a theory and not a power. The Court does not select its own members; Article II provides that presidents nominate justices upon the advice and consent of the U.S. Senate's approval of a nominee. Finally, the Court's ability to regulate big business was never granted; the regulation of big business comes under the domain of congressional and Executive Department regulatory agencies (Federal Trade Commission, Environmental Protection Agency, Federal Communications Commission, etc.).

37. **(B)**   The speech cited was delivered by Henry Clay to his western supporters in Congress in 1811. Clay and his group, nicknamed the "War Hawks," supported American war with Great Britain to advance the westward push of the

country and thereby enhance their land speculations in this region and also end the "Indian menace." The Federalists and New England merchants were both vehemently opposed to the War of 1812. President Madison sought to negotiate a peaceful settlement with England; he reluctantly went to war in 1812. The British nobility generally were opposed to the war as well.

38.   **(B)**   New England dissatisfaction with the War of 1812 was evident from the start. Because of the trade embargoes of Jefferson and Madison, the New England merchant community was suffering from a depression that affected the entire region economically. New Englanders called for a meeting in Hartford, Connecticut in 1814 to discuss the region's options. Few delegates supported a movement to secede from the nation. Instead, the delegates, under the leadership of the Federalist party, advanced a view of states' rights identical to the position of the South during the Civil War. Tired of being treated as a neglected minority in the nation under Republican presidents, the New England delegates accomplished little at the convention. The news of the Treaty and the Battle of New Orleans doomed the convention and the Federalists as unpatriotic in the eyes of most Americans. Neither Japanese trade nor a Cuban invasion were ever discussed at the Convention.

39.   **(D)**   In 1817, Benjamin Lundy formed the American Colonization Society as the first antislavery organization in America. The group advocated gradual emancipation of slaves on an individual basis and refused to see abolition of slavery as a political affair. Comprised mostly of ministers, the Society sought to appeal to the Christian consciences of slave owners to emancipate their slaves. Once freed, the ex-slaves would then be shipped back immediately to Africa as the Society was extremely racist in its views of the inherent inferiority of blacks to whites. The Society believed there was no place for African-Americans in the nation and sought to remove all blacks from American soil rather than promote racial equality and full political rights for blacks.

40.   **(E)**   The rise of the doctrine of Manifest Destiny in the 1820s and 1830s championed the viewpoint that it was America's natural, God-given destiny to create a mighty nation stretching from the Atlantic to the Pacific shores. The advocates of this view contended that the health of the American economy demanded new markets from this push westward and that an expanding frontier guaranteed that the nation would remain a democracy of small, independent yeoman farmers. This belief remained powerful in the country throughout the nineteenth century.

1789–1824
REVIEW

1. THE FEDERALIST ERA

The results of the first elections held under the new Constitution made it clear that the fledgling government was going to be managed by those who had drawn up the document and by their supporters. Few Antifederalists were elected to Congress, and many of the new legislators had served as delegates to the Philadelphia Convention two years before. This Federalist majority immediately set about to draft legislation, which would fill in the gaps left by the convention, and to erect the structure of a strong central government.

The New Executive

There had never been any doubt as to who would be the first president. George Washington received virtually all the votes of the presidential electors, and John Adams received the next highest number, thus becoming the vice president. After a triumphal journey from Mount Vernon, Washington was inaugurated in New York City, the temporary seat of government, on April 30, 1789.

Congress Erects the Structure of Government

The new national legislature immediately acted to honor the Federalist pledge of a bill of rights made to those voters who had hesitated to ratify the new Constitution. Twelve amendments were drafted; these embodied the guarantees of personal liberties, most of which had been traditionally enjoyed by English citizens. Ten of these were ratified by the states by the end of 1791, and they became the Bill of Rights. The first nine spelled out specific guarantees of personal freedoms, such as religion, speech, press, assembly, petition, and a speedy trial by one's peers; and the Tenth Amendment reserved to the states all those powers not specifically withheld, or granted to the federal government. This last was a concession to those who feared the potential of the central government to usurp the sovereignty of the individual states.

The Establishment of the Federal Court System

The Judiciary Act of 1789 provided for a Supreme Court, with six justices, and invested it with the power to rule on the constitutional validity of state laws. It was to be the interpreter of the "supreme law of the land." The act established a system of district courts to serve as courts of original jurisdiction, and also provided for three courts of appeal.

The Establishment of Executive Departments

The Constitution had not specified the names or number of the departments of the executive branch. Congress established three—state, treasury, and war—and also the offices of attorney general and postmaster general. President Washington immediately appointed Thomas Jefferson, Alexander Hamilton, and Henry Knox, respectively, to fill the executive posts, and Edmund Randolph became attorney general. These four men were called upon regularly by the president for advice, and they later formed the nucleus of what became known as the Cabinet, although no provision for such was made in the Constitution.

Washington's Administration, 1789–1797

Hamilton's Financial Program

Treasury Secretary Alexander Hamilton, in his "Report on the Public Credit," proposed the funding of the national debt at face value, federal assumption of state debts, and the establishment of a national bank. In his "Report on Manufactures," Hamilton proposed an extensive program for federal stimulation of industrial development through subsidies and tax incentives. The money needed to fund these programs, proposed Hamilton, would come from an excise tax on distillers and from tariffs on imports.

Opposition to Hamilton's Program

Jefferson and others objected to the funding proposal because it obviously would benefit speculators who had bought up state and confederation obligations at depressed prices and who now would profit handsomely by their redemption at face value. The original purchasers, they claimed, should at least share in the windfall. They opposed the tax program because it would fall primarily on the small farmers. They saw Hamilton's entire program as enriching a small elite group at the expense of the more worthy common citizen.

The Appearance of Political Parties

Political parties had been considered a detrimental force by the founding fathers, since they were seen to contribute to the rise of "factions;" thus, no mention of such was made in the Constitution. But differences in philosophy very quickly began to drive the leaders of government into opposing camps—the Federalists and the Republicans.

Alexander Hamilton and the Federalists

Hamilton, as the theorist of the group who favored a strong central government, interpreted the Constitution as having vested extensive powers in the federal government. This "implied powers" stance claimed that the government was given all powers that were not expressly denied to it. This is the "broad" interpretation.

Thomas Jefferson and the Republicans

Jefferson and Madison held the view that any action not specifically permitted in the Constitution was thereby prohibited. This is the "strict" interpretation, and the Republicans opposed the establishment of Hamilton's national bank on this view of government. The Jeffersonian supporters, primarily under the guidance of James Madison, began to organize political groups in opposition to the Federalist program, and called themselves Republicans.

Sources of Partisan Support

The Federalists received their strongest support from the business and financial groups in the commercial centers of the Northeast and in the port cities of the South. The strength of the Republicans lay primarily in the rural and frontier areas of the South and West.

QUESTION

> What forces led to the development of political parties in the United States?

EXPLANATION

The U.S. Constitution did not provide for political parties and, to this day, the Constitution does not mention them. In some sense, political parties may be seen as a carry-over from the debates concerning ratification of the Constitution. As at least two distinct philosophies of government emerged even more strongly during Washington's administration, those who shared similar philosophies saw an advantage in allying with one another. The source of the first distinction was between a strict interpretation of the Constitution, which held that anything not specifically permitted to the federal government by the Constitution was therefore prohibited, and the "implied powers" position, which held that only powers specifically denied to the federal government by the Constitution were not given to it.

Foreign and Frontier Affairs

The French Revolution

When revolutionary France went to war with the European powers in 1792, Washington's response was a Proclamation of Neutrality. Citizen Genet violated that policy by trying to encourage popular support in this country for the French government and embarrassed the president. American merchants traded with both sides, though the most lucrative business was carried on with the French West Indies. This brought retaliation by the British, who began to seize American merchant ships and force their crews into service with the British navy.

Jay's Treaty with Britain (1794)

John Jay negotiated a treaty with the British which attempted to settle the conflict at sea, as well as to curtail English agitation of their Indian allies on the western borders. The agreement actually settled few of the issues and merely bought time for the new nation in the worsening international conflict. Jay was severely criticized for his efforts and was even hanged in effigy, but the Senate accepted the treaty as the best possible under the circumstances.

The Treaty with Spain (1795)

Thomas Pinckney was invited to the Spanish court to strengthen what Madrid perceived to be her deteriorating position on the American frontier. The result was the Pinckney Treaty, ratified by the Senate in 1796, in which the Spanish opened the Mississippi River to American traffic, including the right of deposit in the port city of New Orleans, and recognized the 31st parallel as the northern boundary of Florida.

Frontier Problems

Indian tribes on the Northwest and Southwest borders were increasingly resisting the encroachments on their lands by the American settlers. British authorities in Canada were encouraging the Indians in their depredations against frontier settlements. In 1794, General Anthony Wayne decisively defeated the Indians at the Battle of Fallen Timbers, and the resulting Treaty of Greenville cleared the Ohio territory of Indian tribes.

Internal Problems

The Whiskey Rebellion (1794)

Western farmers refused to pay the excise tax on whiskey, which formed the backbone of Hamilton's revenue program. When a group of Pennsylvania farmers terrorized the tax collectors, President Washington sent out a federalized militia force of some 15,000 men, and the rebellion evaporated, thus strengthening the credibility of the young government.

Land Policy

As the original 13 states ceded their western land claims to the new federal government, new states were organized and admitted to the Union, thus strengthening the ties of the western farmers to the central government (Vermont, 1791; Kentucky, 1792; and Tennessee, 1796).

Drill 1: The Federalist Era

1. The American public protested the Jay Treaty of 1794 because

    (A) it failed to get British soldiers out of the northwest posts.

    (B) it arranged compensation for slaves freed by the British during the Revolution.

    (C) it allowed extensive trade with the West Indies.

    (D) it did nothing about British seizure of American vessels in the French West Indies.

    (E) it settled Canadian boundary questions.

2. The Pinckney Treaty with Spain in 1795 gave Americans the "right of deposit" at New Orleans. This meant that

    (A) Americans could land goods at New Orleans and ship them out again without paying taxes.

    (B) America had full trading rights with the Spanish.

    (C) Americans could ship their goods in Spanish vessels.

    (D) New Orleans became an American possession.

    (E) American banks could be established in New Orleans.

3. A revolution in what country made American neutrality an issue in the 1790s?

    (A) Great Britain   (B) Spain

    (C) Netherlands   (D) France

    (E) Germany

4. The most controversial portion of Alexander Hamilton's economic program was

    (A) federal assumption of state debts.

    (B) assessment of direct taxes on the states.

    (C) creation of the Bank of the United States.

    (D) imposition of high protective tariffs.

    (E) establishment of a bimetallic system.

5. All of the following were part of Alexander Hamilton's economic program EXCEPT

   (A) excise taxes.

   (B) subsidies to farmers.

   (C) federal assumption of state debts.

   (D) protective tariffs.

   (E) a national bank.

6. In the 1790s' political conflict between Thomas Jefferson and Alexander Hamilton, Jefferson would have been more likely to

   (A) take a narrow view of the Constitution.

   (B) favor Britain over France in the European wars.

   (C) favor the establishment of a national bank.

   (D) win the cooperation of presidents George Washington and John Adams.

   (E) oppose the efforts of Citizen Genet in America.

7. Which of the following was NOT true of the Northwest Ordinance of 1787?

   (A) It recognized the territorial claims of the various Indian tribes within the Northwest Territory.

   (B) It guaranteed freedom of religion to settlers in the Northwest Territory.

   (C) It guaranteed the right to a jury trial to settlers in the Northwest Territory.

   (D) It prohibited slavery within the Northwest Territory.

   (E) It specified procedures through which settlers could organize state governments and eventually apply for full statehood.

8. A leader of the Nationalist movement in the United States in the 1780s was

   (A) Alexander Hamilton. (B) Thomas Jefferson.

   (C) Samuel Adams. (D) Richard Henry Lee.

   (E) Thomas Payne.

9. Opposition to the Jay Treaty in the U.S. Senate centered around

   (A) the opening of American trade with the West Indies.

   (B) the British refusal to withdraw troops from American soil.

(C)   the settlement of American debts to British merchants.

(D)   its inability to stop the practice of British impressment.

(E)   none of the above.

10.   The Whiskey Rebellion of 1794 protested

(A)   Prohibition.

(B)   a 25% tax on whiskey.

(C)   government regualtion of whiskey production.

(D)   the lifting of import duties on whiskey.

(E)   a 30% drop in whiskey prices.

2. JOHN ADAMS' ADMINISTRATION AND THE JEFFERSONIAN ERA

The Election of 1796

John Adams was the Federalist candidate, and Thomas Jefferson ran under the opposition banner of the Republicans. Since Jefferson received the second highest number of electoral votes, he became vice president. Thus, a Federalist president and a Republican vice president served together, an obviously awkward arrangement. Adams was a brilliant lawyer and statesman, but too dogmatic and uncompromising to be an effective politician, and he endured a very frustrating and unproductive term in office.

The XYZ Affair

A three-man delegation was sent to France in 1798 to persuade the French to stop harassing American shipping. When they were solicited for a bribe by three subordinates of the French Minister Talleyrand, they indignantly refused, and their report of this insult produced outrage at home. The cry "millions for defense, but not one cent for tribute" was raised, and public feelings against the French ran high. Since Talleyrand's officials were unnamed in the dispatches, the incident became known as the "XYZ affair."

Quasi-War (1798–1799)

This uproar moved Adams to suspend all trade with the French, and American ship captains were authorized to attack and capture armed French vessels. Congress created a Department of the Navy, and war seemed imminent. In 1800, the new French government, now under Napoleon, signed a new treaty, and the peace was restored.

Repression and Protest

The Alien and Sedition Acts

The elections in 1798 had increased the Federalist majorities in both houses of Congress, and they used their "mandate" to enact legislation to stifle foreign influences. The Alien Act raised new hurdles in the path of immigrants trying to obtain citizenship, and the Sedition Act widened the powers of the Adams administration to muzzle its newspaper critics. Both bills were aimed at actual or potential Republican opposition, and a number of editors were actually jailed for printing critical editorials.

The Kentucky and Virginia Resolves

Republican leaders were convinced that the Alien and Sedition Acts were unconstitutional, but the process of deciding on the constitutionality of federal laws was as yet undefined. Jefferson and Madison decided that the state legislatures should have that power, and they drew up a series of resolutions which were presented to the Kentucky and Virginia legislatures, respectively. They proposed that John Locke's "compact theory" be applied, which would empower the state bodies to "nullify" federal laws within those states. These resolutions were adopted, but only in those two states; and so the issue died, but a principle was put forward which was later to bear fruit in the nullification controversy of the 1830s and finally in the secession crisis of 1860–61.

The Revolution of 1800

The Election

Thomas Jefferson and Aaron Burr ran on the Republican ticket, against John Adams and Charles Pinckney, who ran for the Federalists. The Republican candidates won handily, but both received the same number of electoral votes, thus throwing the selection of the president into the House of Representatives. After a lengthy deadlock, Alexander Hamilton threw his support to Jefferson, and Burr had to accept the vice presidency, the result obviously intended by the electorate. This increased the ill-will between Hamilton and Burr and contributed to their famous duel in 1804.

Packing the Judiciary

The Federalist Congress passed a new Judiciary Act early in 1801 and President Adams filled the newly created vacancies with party supporters, many of them with last-minute commissions. John Marshall was then appointed chief justice of the U.S. Supreme Court, thus guaranteeing continuation of Federalist policies from the bench of the high court.

The Jeffersonian Era

Thomas Jefferson and his Republican followers envisioned a society in vivid contrast to that of Hamilton and the Federalists. They dreamed of a nation of independent farmers, living under a central government that exercised a minimum of control over their lives and served merely to protect the individual liberties guaranteed by the Constitution. This agrarian paradise would be free from the industrial smoke and urban blight of Europe and would serve as a beacon light of Enlightenment rationalism to a world searching for direction. That vision was to prove a mirage, and Jefferson was to preside over a nation that was growing more industrialized and urban and which seemed to need an ever stronger hand at the presidential tiller.

The New Federal City

The city of Washington had been designed by Pierre L'Enfant and was briefly occupied by the Adams administration. When Jefferson moved in, it was still a straggling provincial town with muddy streets and muggy summers. Most of its inhabitants moved out when Congress was not in session.

Jefferson the President

The new president tried to project an image of democratic simplicity, sometimes appearing so casually dressed as to appear slovenly. But he was a brilliant thinker and a shrewd politician. He appointed men to his cabinet who agreed with his political philosophy: James Madison as secretary of state and Albert Gallatin as secretary of the treasury.

Conflict with the Judges

Marbury vs. Madison

William Marbury, one of Adams' "midnight appointments," sued Secretary of State Madison to force delivery of his commission as a justice of the peace in the federal district. John Marshall, as Supreme Court justice, refused to rule on the request, claiming that the law which gave the Supreme Court jurisdiction over such matters had exceeded the Constitutional grant of powers and thus was unconstitutional. Marshall thus asserted the power of judicial review over federal legislation, a power which has become the foundation of the Supreme Court's check on the other two branches of government.

The Impeachment Episodes

Jefferson began a campaign to remove Federalist judges by impeachment. One district judge was removed, and proceedings were begun to impeach Supreme Court Justice Samuel Chase. That effort failed, but the threat had encouraged the judiciary to be less blatantly political.

QUESTION

Why is the Supreme Court decision *Marbury v. Madison* important?

EXPLANATION

Marbury v. Madison established the precedent of judicial review, which gave the Supreme Court the power to interpret the Constitution, declaring acts of Congress unconstitutional and therefore illegal. This has enhanced the power of the Supreme Court, providing it with an important check on the power of Congress.

Domestic Affairs

Enforcement of the Alien and Sedition Acts was immediately suspended, and the men convicted under those laws were released.

The federal bureaucracy was reduced and expenses were drastically cut. The size of the army was reduced and the expansion program of the Navy was canceled.

The excise taxes were repealed and federal income was limited to land sale proceeds and customs duties. Federal land sale policy was liberalized, smaller parcels were authorized, and less cash was required—policies which benefited small farmers.

The Twelfth Amendment was adopted and ratified in 1804, ensuring that a tie vote between candidates of the same party could not again cause the confusion of the Jefferson-Burr affair.

Following the Constitutional mandate, the importation of slaves was stopped by law in 1808.

The Louisiana Purchase

Napoleon, in an effort to regain some of France's New World empire, had obtained the old French trans-Mississippi territory from Spain by political pressure. Jefferson sent a delegation to Paris to try to buy New Orleans, lest the new French officials close it to American traffic. Napoleon's defeat in Santo Domingo persuaded him that Louisiana could not be exploited, and indeed was now subject to potential American incursions. So he offered to sell the entire territory to the United States for $15 million. The American delegation accepted the offer in April 1803, even though they had no authority to buy more than the city of New Orleans.

The Constitutional Dilemma

Jefferson's stand on the strict interpretation of the Constitution would not permit him to purchase land without Congressional approval. But he accepted his advisors' counsel that his treaty-making powers included the authority to buy the land. Congress concurred, after the fact, and the purchase price was appropriated, thus doubling the territory of the nation overnight.

Exploring the West

Even before Napoleon's offer, Jefferson had authorized an expedition to explore the Western territory to the Pacific. The Lewis and Clark group, with 48 men, left St. Louis in 1804, and returned two years later with a wealth of scientific and anthropological information, and having strengthened the United States' claim to the Oregon territory. At the same time, Zebulon Pike and others had been traversing the middle parts of Louisiana and mapping the land.

The Essex Junto (1804)

Some New England Federalists saw the western expansion as a threat to their position in the Union, and they tried to organize a secessionist movement. They courted Aaron Burr's support by offering to back him in a bid for the governorship of New York. Hamilton led the opposition to that campaign and when Burr lost the election, he challenged Hamilton to a duel, which resulted in Hamilton's death.

The Burr Conspiracy

Aaron Burr was now a fugitive, without a political future. He became involved in a scheme to take Mexico from Spain and establish a new nation in the West.

In the fall of 1806, he led a group of armed men down the Mississippi River system toward New Orleans. He was arrested in Natchez and tried for treason in Richmond, Virginia. Judge John Marshall's decision for acquittal helped to narrow the legal definition of treason. Jefferson's attempts to influence and prejudice the trial were justified by his claims of "executive privilege," but they were fruitless.

John Randolph and the Yazoo Claims

Jefferson's Republican opponents, under the leadership of his cousin John Randolph of Roanoke, called themselves the "Quids." They accused the president of complicity in the Yazoo Land controversy which had followed Georgia's cession of her western lands to the federal government. This created serious strife within the Republican party and weakened Jefferson's effectiveness in his second term.

International Involvement

The Barbary War

In 1801, Jefferson sent a naval force to the Mediterranean to break the North African Muslim rulers' practice of exacting tribute from Western merchant ships. Intermittent undeclared war dragged on until 1805, with no decisive settlement.

The Napoleonic Wars

War continued in Europe between France, under Napoleon, and the European powers, led by Britain. Both sides tried to prevent their enemies from trading with neutral powers, especially the United States. Napoleon's "Continental System" was answered by Britain's "Orders in Council." American ships were seized by both sides; and American sailors were even "impressed" into the British navy.

The Chesapeake-Leopard Affair (1807)

The British ship H.M.S. *Leopard* stopped the U.S.S. *Chesapeake* off the Chesapeake Bay, and four alleged British deserters were taken off the ship. Public outcry for war followed, and Jefferson was hard pressed to remain neutral.

The Embargo of 1807

Jefferson's response to the cry for war was to draft a law prohibiting American ships from leaving port for any foreign destination, thus avoiding contact with vessels of either belligerent. The result was economic depression, particularly in the heavily commercial Northeast. This proved to be his most unpopular policy of both terms in office.

Madison's Administration, 1809–1817

The Election of 1808

Republican James Madison won the election over Federalist Charles Pinckney, but the Federalists gained seats in both houses of the Congress. The embargo-induced depression was obviously a heavy political liability, and Madison was to face growing pressures to deal with the international crisis. He was a brilliant man but with few social or political skills. His greatest asset was probably his wife, the vivacious and energetic Dolly.

The War of 1812

Just before Madison's inauguration, Congress had passed a modified embargo known as the Non-Intercourse Act, which opened trade to all nations except France and Britain. When it expired in 1810, it was replaced by Macon's Bill No. 2, which gave the president power to prohibit trade with any nation when they violated U.S. neutrality.

The Indian tribes of the Northwest and the Mississippi Valley were resentful of the government's policy of pressured removal to the West, and the British authorities in Canada were exploiting their discontent by encouraging border raids against the American settlements.

The Shawnee chief Tecumseh set out to unite the Mississippi Valley tribes and reestablish Indian dominance in the Old Northwest. With the help of his brother, the Prophet, and the timely New Madrid earthquake, he persuaded a sizable force of warriors to join him. On November 11, 1811, however, General William Henry Harrison destroyed Tecumseh's village on Tippecanoe Creek and dashed his hopes for an Indian confederacy.

Southern frontiersmen coveted Spanish Florida, which included the southern ranges of Alabama, Mississippi, and Louisiana. They resented Spanish support of Indian depredations against the borderlands, and since Spain was Britain's ally, they saw Britain as the background cause of their problems.

The Congress in 1811 contained a strong pro-war group called the War Hawks, led by Henry Clay and John C. Calhoun. They gained control of both houses and began agitating for war with the British. On June 1, 1812, President Madison asked for a declaration of war and Congress complied.

A three-pronged invasion of Canada met with disaster on all three fronts, and the Americans fell back to their own borders. At sea, American privateers and frigates, including "Old Ironsides," scored early victories over British warships, but were soon driven back into their home ports and blockaded by the powerful British ships-of-the-line.

Admiral Oliver Hazard Perry constructed a fleet of ships on Lake Erie; and on September 10, 1813, he defeated a British force at Put-In Bay and established control of the lake. His flagship flew the banner, "Don't Give Up the Ship." This victory opened the way for William Henry Harrison to invade Canada in October and defeat a combination British and Indian force at the Battle of the Thames.

The War in the Southwest

Andrew Jackson led a force of frontier militia into Alabama in pursuit of Creek Indians who had massacred the white inhabitants of Fort Mims. On March 27, 1814, he crushed the Indians at Horseshoe Bend and then seized the Spanish garrison at Pensacola.

British Strategy Changes (1814)

A British force came down Lake Champlain and met defeat at Plattsburgh, New York in September. A British armada sailed up the Cheasapeake Bay and sacked and burned Washington, D.C. They then proceeded up the bay toward Baltimore, which was guarded by Fort McHenry. That fort held firm through the British bombardment, inspiring Key's "Star Spangled Banner."

The Battle of New Orleans

The most serious British threat came at the port of New Orleans. A powerful invasion force was sent there to close the mouth of the Mississippi River, but Andrew Jackson decisively defeated it with a polyglot army of frontiersmen, Blacks, Creoles, and pirates. The battle was fought on January 8, 1815, two weeks after a peace treaty had been signed at the city of Ghent, in Belgium.

The Treaty of Ghent, Christmas Eve 1814

With the European wars ended, the major causes for the dispute with Britain had ceased to be important; so both sides were eager for peace. The treaty provided for the acceptance of the status quo at the beginning of hostilities; and so both sides restored their wartime conquests to the other.

The Hartford Convention, December 1814

The Federalists had become increasingly a minority party. They vehemently opposed the war and Daniel Webster and other New England congressmen consistently blocked the administration's efforts to prosecute the war effort. On December 15, 1814, delegates from the New England states met in Hartford, Connecticut, and drafted a set of resolutions suggesting nullification—and even secession—if their interests were not protected against the growing influence of the South and the West.

Soon after the convention adjourned, the news of the victory at New Orleans was announced and their actions were discredited. The Federalist party ceased to be a political force from this point.

QUESTION

> What impact did the War of 1812 have on the Federalist party?

EXPLANATION

The war weakened the Federalist party. The Federalists had increasingly become a regional party, representing the Northeast. The Federalists had opposed the war, since the economic interests of the Northeast were to maintain relations with Great Britain, and worked to block the Republican government's war efforts. While the outcome of the war was to preserve the status quo, news of Andrew Jackson's victory in New Orleans discredited those who had opposed the war.

Post-War Developments

Protective Tariff (1816)

In 1816, the first protective tariff in the nation's history was passed to slow the flood of cheap British manufactures into the country.

Rush-Bagot Treaty (1817)

In 1817, an agreement was reached between Britain and the United States to stop maintaining armed fleets on the Great Lakes. This first "disarmament" agreement is still in effect.

Jackson's Florida Invasion (1817)

Indian troubles in the newly acquired areas of western Florida prompted General Andrew Jackson, acting under dubious authority, to invade Spanish East Florida and to hang two British subjects whom he suspected of selling guns and supplies to the Indians. Then he re-occupied Pensacola and raised the American flag, a clear violation of international law. Only wide public support prevented his arrest and prosecution by the government.

Indian Policy

The government began to systematically pressure all the Indian tribes remaining in the East to cede their lands and accept new homes west of the Mississippi, a policy which met with disappointing results. Most declined the offer.

The Barbary Wars (1815)

In response to continued piracy and extortion in the Mediterranean, Congress declared war on the Muslim state of Algiers in 1815 and dispatched a naval force to the area under Stephen Decatur. He quickly defeated the North African pirates and forced them to pay indemnities for past tribute they had exacted from American ship captains. This action finally gained the United States free access to the Mediterranean basin.

The Adams-Onis Treaty (1819)

Spain had decided to sell the remainder of the Florida territory to the Americans before they took it anyway. Under this agreement, the Spanish surrendered all their claims to the territory and drew the boundary of Mexico all the way to the Pacific. In exchange, the United States agreed to assume $5 million in debts owed to American merchants.

The Monroe Doctrine

Around 1810, national revolutions had begun in Latin America: so the colonial populations refused to accept the rule of the new Napoleonic governments in Europe. Leaders like San Martin and Bolivar had declared independence for their countries and, after Napoleon's fall in 1814, were defying the restored Hapsburg and Bourbon rulers of Europe.

British and American leaders feared that the new European governments would try to restore the former New World colonies to their erstwhile royal owners.

In his annual message to Congress in December 1823, President Monroe included a statement that the American hemisphere was "henceforth not to be considered as subjects for future colonization by any European powers." Thus began a 30-year period of freedom from serious foreign involvement for the United States.

Drill 2: John Adams' Administration and the Jeffersonian Era

1. Which of the following does NOT describe the Louisiana Purchase of 1803?

    (A) The United States purchased Louisiana from France for $15 million.

    (B) Jefferson expanded the powers of the presidency.

    (C) French power expanded in the Western Hemisphere.

    (D) The United States doubled in size.

    (E) The treaty of cession left some of the boundaries vague.

2. Between 1806 and 1809, non-importation, non-intercourse, and embargo acts sought to

    (A) bring peace between France and Great Britain.

    (B) encourage domestic American manufacturing.

    (C) force Great Britain to recognize American rights.

    (D) balance Southern and Northern economic power.

    (E) help Britain in the Napoleonic wars.

3. In 1819 the United States obtained Florida from

    (A) Great Britain.　　　　　(B) Spain.

    (C) France.　　　　　(D) Mexico.

    (E) Portugal.

4. The *Marbury v. Madison* decision of 1803 established the principle that

    (A) the federal government had the power to regulate commerce.

(B) the Supreme Court had the power to declare acts of Congress unconstitutional.

(C) the federal government had the power to protect property rights under the contract clause.

(D) a state lacked the power to block the operation of a federal agency.

(E) states had the power to determine whether acts of Congress applied within their borders.

5. Who helped guide the Lewis and Clark expedition and aided in dealing with Indians?

(A) Sacajawea

(B) Zebulon Pike

(C) Sitting Bull

(D) James Wilkinson

(E) Tecumseh

6. The "Revolution of 1800" resulted in the election of

(A) John Adams.

(B) Thomas Jefferson.

(C) James Monroe.

(D) James Madison.

(E) John Quincy Adams.

7. The War of 1812 resulted in which of the following?

(A) New territory for the United States

(B) Resumption of the status quo prior to the war

(C) Defeat of the United States

(D) The strengthening of the Federalist party

(E) Loss of United States territory

8. All of the following contributed to the coming of the War of 1812 EXCEPT

(A) the *Chesapeake-Leopard* incident.

(B) British impressment of American seamen from American ships on the high seas.

(C) the concerns of western Americans that the Indian raids they suffered were being carried out with British encouragement.

(D) the Congressional "War Hawks'" desire to annex Canada.

(E) the armed confrontation between U.S. and British forces along the Maine-Canada border.

9. The Monroe Doctrine stated that the United States

   (A) was not concerned with the type of government other countries might have.

   (B) was concerned only with the type of government that the countries of the Western Hemisphere might have.

   (C) would not tolerate any new European colonization in the New World.

   (D) claimed the Western Hemisphere as its exclusive zone of influence.

   (E) was prepared to drive out by force any European power that did not give up its colonies in the Western Hemisphere.

10. The XYZ Affair was important in that it

   (A) underlined the importance of a strong, impartial federal judiciary in resolving Constitutional disputes between the state and federal governments.

   (B) led to U.S. abrogation of the 1778 peace treaty and brought the U.S. into a quasi-war with France.

   (C) nearly brought Britain into the Civil War on the side of the Confederacy.

   (D) discredited Aaron Burr and forced his removal from the 1800 presidential election ticket as Thomas Jefferson's running mate.

   (E) led the U.S. to seek a declaration of war against Britain in 1812 for impressing American seamen onto British ships.

3. INTERNAL DEVELOPMENT

The years following the War of 1812 were years of rapid economic and social development. Too rapid, in fact, and they were followed by a severe depression in 1819. But this slump was temporary, and it became obvious that the country was moving rapidly from its agrarian origins toward an industrial, urban future. Westward expansion accelerated, and the mood of the people became very positive. In fact, these years were referred to as the "Era of Good Feelings."

The Monroe Presidency (1817-1823)

James Monroe, the last of the "Virginia Dynasty," had been hand-picked by the retiring Madison and he was elected with only one opposed electoral vote: a symbol of national unity.

Postwar Boom

The years following the war were characterized by a high foreign demand for American cotton, grain, and tobacco; commerce flourished. The Second National Bank, through its overly liberal credit policies, proved to be an inflationary influence and the price level rose rapidly.

The Depression of 1819

Inventories of British manufactured goods had built up during the war, and English merchants began to dump their products on the American market at cut-rate prices. American manufacturers suffered from this influx of imports. The U.S. Bank tried to slow the inflationary spiral by tightening credit, and a sharp business slump resulted. This depression was most severe in the newly expanding West, partly because of its economic dependency, partly because of heavy speculation in Western lands.

The Marshall Court

John Marshall delivered the majority opinions in a number of critical decisions in these formative years, all of which served to strengthen the power of the federal government and restrict the powers of state governments.

Marbury v. Madison (1803)

This case established the precedent of the Supreme Court's power to rule on the constitutionality of federal laws.

Fletcher v. Peck (1810)

The Georgia legislature had issued extensive land grants in a shady deal with the Yazoo Land Company. A subsequent legislative session repealed that action because of the corruption that had attended the original grant. The Court decided that the original action by the Georgia Assembly had constituted a valid contract which could not be broken regardless of the corruption which had followed. This was the first time a state law was voided on the grounds that it violated a principle of the U.S. Constitution.

Dartmouth College v. Woodward (1819)

The quarrel between the president and the trustees of the New Hampshire college became a political issue when the Republicans backed the president and the Federalists supported the trustees. The president tried to change Dartmouth from a private to a public institution by having its charter revoked. The Court ruled that the charter, though issued by the king during colonial days, still constituted a contract, and thus could not be arbitrarily changed or revoked without the consent of both parties. The result of this decision was to limit severely the power of state governments to control the corporation, which was the emerging form of business organization.

McCulloch v. Maryland (1819)

The state of Maryland had tried to levy a tax on the Baltimore branch of the Bank of the United States and thereby protect the competitive position of its own state banks. Marshall's ruling declared that no state has the right to control an agency of the federal government. Since "the power to tax is the power to destroy," such state action violated Congress' "implied powers" to establish and operate a national bank.

Gibbons v. Ogden (1824)

The State of New York had granted a monopoly to Ogden to operate a steamboat between New York and New Jersey. Gibbons obtained a Congressional permit to operate a steamboat line in the same waters. When Ogden sued to maintain his monopoly, the New York courts ruled in his favor. Gibbons' appeal went to the Supreme Court. John Marshall ruled that commerce included navigation and that only Congress has the right to regulate commerce among states. Thus, the state-granted monopoly was void.

The Missouri Compromise (1820)

The Missouri Territory, the first to be organized from the Louisiana Purchase, applied for statehood in 1819. Since the Senate membership was evenly divided between slave holding and free states at that time, the admission of a new state was obviously going to give the voting advantage either to the North or to the South. Slavery was already well-established in the new territory; so the Southern states were confident in their advantage, until Representative Tallmadge of New York proposed an amendment to the bill which would prohibit slavery in Missouri. The Southern outcry was immediate, and the ensuing debate grew hot. The Senate was dead-locked.

Henry Clay's Compromise Solution

As the debate dragged on, the northern territory of Massachusetts applied for admission as the state of Maine. This offered a way out of the dilemma, and House Speaker Clay formulated a package that both sides could accept. The two admission bills were combined, with Maine coming in free and Missouri as a slave state. To make the package palatable for the House, a provision was added to prohibit slavery in the remainder of the Louisiana Territory, north of the southern boundary of Missouri (latitude 36° 30'). Clay guided this bill through the House and it became law, thus maintaining the balance of power.

The debates in Congress had reminded everyone of the deep division between the sections, and some saw it as evidence of trouble to come. Thomas Jefferson, in retirement at Monticello, remarked that the news from Washington was like a "fire-bell in the night."

The Expanding Economy

The Growing Population

Population continued to double every 25 years. The migration of people to the West increased in volume; and by 1840, over one-third of all Americans lived west of the Alleghenies. Immigration from abroad was not significant until 1820; then it began to increase rapidly, mostly from the British Isles.

The Farming Sector

As markets for farm products grew in the expanding cities, coupled with liberal land sale policies by the federal government, the growing of staple agricultural crops became more profitable. More and more land was put into cultivation, and the prevailing system of clearing and planting became more wasteful of timber as well as of the fertility of the land.

The Cotton Kingdom

The new lands in the Southwest, then made up by Alabama, Mississippi, Louisiana, and Texas, proved ideal for the production of short-staple cotton. Eli Whitney's invention of the cotton "gin" solved the problem of separating the seeds from the fibers, and the cotton boom was under way.

The growing market for food and work animals in the cotton South provided the opportunity for the new eastern farmers to specialize in those items and further stimulated the westward movement.

Fishing

New England and Chesapeake fishing proved very profitable. Deep-sea whaling became a significant enterprise, particularly from the Massachusetts/Rhode Island ports.

Lumbering

The expanding population created a need for building materials, and timber remained a profitable export item. Shipbuilding thrived in a number of Eastern Seaboard and Gulf Coast ports.

Fur Trade

John Jacob Astor and others opened up business all the way to the Northwest Coast. "Mountain men" probed deeper and deeper into the Rocky Mountain ranges in search of the beaver.

Trade with the Spanish

The Santa Fe Trail, which ran from New Mexico northeast to Independence, Missouri, became an active trading corridor, opening up the Spanish territories to American migration and influence and also providing the basis for future territorial claims.

QUESTION

> How did the cotton boom lead to growth in the non-cotton growing states of the American West?

EXPLANATION

Profits from cotton were high, in part because the invention of the cotton gin made separation of the seeds from the fibers inexpensive. Therefore, most of the arable land was devoted to cotton growing. The cotton boom also led to an increase in the population of the South; the South depended on western farmers for food and other agricultural products of the West.

The Transportation Revolution

The first half of the nineteenth century witnessed an extraordinary sequence of inventions and innovations which produced a true revolution in transport and communications.

River Traffic

The steamboats built by Robert Fulton, the *Clermont* in 1807 and the *New Orleans* in 1811, transformed river transport. As shipment times and freight rates both plummeted, regular steam service was established on all the major river systems.

Road building

By 1818, the National Road, which was built with federal funds, had been completed from Cumberland, Maryland to Wheeling, Virginia, linking the Potomac with the Ohio River. A network of privately owned toll roads (turnpikes) began to reach out from every sizable city. They were usually built for only a few miles out; and while they never accounted for a significant share of the total freight tonnage moved, they formed the nucleus for a growing road system in the new nation.

The Canal Era

The Erie Canal, linking the Hudson River at Albany, New York, with Lake Erie, was completed in 1825 and became the first and most successful example of a canal. It was followed by a rash of construction until canals linked every major waterway system east of the Mississippi River.

Canals were the first development projects to receive large amounts of public funding. They ran east-west and so tied the new West to the old East, with later implications for sectional divisions.

The Rise of New York City

Its location as a transport hub, coupled with innovations in business practices, boosted New York City into becoming a primary trade center, and America's largest city, by 1830. One such innovation was the packet boat, which operated on a guaranteed schedule and helped to rationalize commerce, both internal and international.

New York soon dominated the domestic market for cotton, a situation which progressively reduced the South to the status of an economic colony.

QUESTION

> In what important way did the federal government get involved in the economy in the 1820s and 1830s?

EXPLANATION

The government contributed large amounts of public money to the building of canals. An extensive network of canals was constructed, linking every major waterway east of the Mississippi. This increased the speed of transportation of goods between the Northeast and the West, connecting the economy of these two regions more closely than either region would be connected to the South.

Industrialization

The Rise of the Factory System

Samuel Slater migrated from Britain in 1789, after having served as an apprentice under inventor Richard Arkwright and then as a mill manager. He used his knowledge to build the first successful cotton-spinning mill in this country. The first cotton manufacturing plant in the world to include all the elements of manufacturing under one roof was built in Boston in 1813.

Eli Whitney's development and application of the principle of interchangeable parts, first used in his firearms factories, helped to speed the growth of mass-production operations.

The expansion of markets in Latin America and the Far East, as well as domestic markets, both resulted from and helped to develop the factory system.

Manufacturers and industrialists found it necessary to organize banks, insurance companies, and real estate firms to meet the needs of their growing business organizations.

The Corporation

The corporate form, with its limited liability and its potential for raising and utilizing large amounts of capital, became the typical type of business organization. By the 1830s, most states had enacted general laws for incorporating.

The Labor Supply

In the early days, the "Lowell System" became a popular way to staff the New England factories. Young women were hired from the surrounding countryside, brought to town, and housed in dormitories in the mill towns. They were paid low wages for hard work under poor conditions, but they were only working for a short time to earn a dowry or help out with the family income; so they soon went back home. This "rotating labor supply" was ideal for the owners, since the girls were not motivated to agitate for better wages and conditions.

Labor was always in short supply in this country; so the system depended on technology to increase production. This situation always placed a premium on innovation in machinery and technique.

The Growth of Unions

The factory system separated the owners from the workers and thus depersonalized the workplace. It also made the skilled artisan less important, since the repetitive processes of the mill could be performed by relatively unskilled laborers.

Although the first organized strike took place in 1828 in Paterson, New Jersey, by child workers, periodic economic downturns helped keep workers relatively dependent and passive until the 1850s.

A major goal of early unions was the 10-hour day, and this effort sparked a period of growth in organized labor which was later effectively quenched by the depression of 1837.

Educational Development

The Growth of Public Schools

Before 1815, there were no public schools to speak of in this country. Some states had endorsed the idea of free schools for the people, but they shrank from the task of financing such a system. Jefferson had outlined such a plan for Virginia, but it came to nothing.

Schools were primarily sponsored by private institutions—corporate academies in the Northeast and religious institutions in the South and mid-Atlantic states. Most were aristocratic in orientation—training the nation's leaders—and few had any interest in schooling the children of the poor.

Women were likewise considered unfit for academic training, and those female schools which existed concentrated on homemaking skills and the fine arts, which would make "ornaments" of the young ladies enrolled.

The New York Free School, one of those rare examples of a school for the poor, experimented for a time with the Lancastrian system, in which older students tutored the younger ones, thus stretching the scarce budget dollars.

Higher Education

Although the numbers of institutions of higher learning increased sharply in the early years of the nineteenth century, none was truly public. All relied upon high tuition rates for survival; so less than one in ten young men, and no women, ever attended a college or university.

The training these schools provided was very limited as well. The only professional training was in theology, and only a smattering of colleges offered brief courses of study in law or medicine. The University of Pennsylvania, for example, offered one year of medical schooling, after which a person could obtain a license to practice the healing arts. Needless to say, medical practice was quite primitive.

The Growth of Cultural Nationalism

Jeffersonian Americans tried to demonstrate their newly won independence by championing a strong sense of cultural nationalism, a feeling that their young republic represented the "final stage" of civilization, the "last great hope of mankind."

Literary Nationalism

Although most Americans had access to one or more newspapers, the market for native authors was quite limited. Publishers preferred to print works from British authors or to import books from Europe. A few Americans, who were willing to pay the costs of publishing their own works, found a growing number of readers.

Significant American Authors

Washington Irving was by far the best-known native writer in America. He excelled in the telling of folktales and local color stories and is best remembered for his portraits of Hudson River characters.

Mercy Otis Warren, the revolutionary pamphleteer, published a multi-volume *History of the Revolution* in 1805.

"Parson" Mason Weems wrote the best-seller *Life of Washington* in 1806, which was short on historical accuracy but long on nationalistic hero-worship.

Educational Literature

Early schoolbooks, like Noah Webster's "Blue Backed Speller," as well as his dictionary of the "American" language, reflected the intense desire to promote patriotism and a feeling of national identity.

Developments in Religious Life

The Post-Revolution Years

The Revolutionary War weakened the position of the traditional, established churches. The doctrines of the Enlightenment became very popular, and its religious expression, deism, gained a considerable following among the educated classes. Rationalism, Unitarianism, and Universalism all saw a period of popularity. Thomas Paine's exposition of the rationalist posture, *The Age of Reason*, attacked the traditional Christian values and was read widely.

The Second Great Awakening

The reaction to the trend toward rationalism, the decline in church membership, and the lack of piety was a renewal of personal, heart-felt evangelicalism. It began in 1801 at Cane Ridge, Kentucky, in the first "camp meeting."

As the revival spread, its characteristics became more uniform—an emphasis on personal salvation, an emotional response to God's grace, an individualistic faith. Women took a major part in the movement. Blacks were also heavily involved, and the individualistic emphasis created unrest among their ranks, particularly in the slaveholding South.

The revival produced strong nationalistic overtones, and the Protestant ideas of a "called nation" were to flourish later in some of the Manifest Destiny doctrines of expansionism. The social overtones of this religious renewal were to spark the great reform movements of the 1830s and 1840s.

Drill 3: Internal Development

1. The Missouri Compromise of 1820 did all of the following EXCEPT

    (A) bring in Maine as a free state.

    (B) bring in Missouri as a slave state.

    (C) prohibit slavery north of latitude 36° 30'.

    (D) maintain the balance of slave and free states.

    (E) establish the principle of popular sovereignty south of 36° 30'.

2. Factors promoting the beginnings of American industrialization during the early nineteenth century included all of the following EXCEPT

   (A) high protective tariffs.

   (B) improvements in transportation.

   (C) large-scale immigration.

   (D) the absence of craft organizations that tied artisans to a single trade.

   (E) close and friendly relations with already industrialized Great Britain.

3. In what decision did Chief Justice John Marshall rule that only Congress has the right to regualte commerce among the states?

   (A) *Dartmouth College v. Woodward*

   (B) *Marbury v. Madison*

   (C) *McCulloch v. Maryland*

   (D) *Gibbons v. Ogden*

   (E) *Fletcher v. Peck*

Average Inland Freight Rates in the U.S., 1800-1830

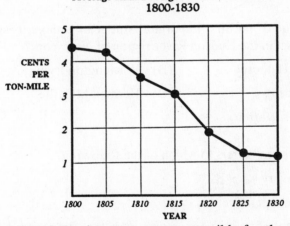

4. Which of the following was most responsible for the change shown on the graph between 1815 and 1830?

   (A) The development of practical steam-powered railroad trains

   (B) The development of a network of canals linking important cities and waterways

   (C) The growth in the nation's mileage of improved roads and turnpikes

   (D) Improvements in the design of keelboats and flatboats

   (E) The development of steamboats

5. Which of the following does NOT describe American education prior to 1815?

    (A) Fewer than 1/10 of American young men attended at college or university.

    (B) There were virtually no free public schools in the nation.

    (C) Female schools concentrated on non-academic subjects such as home-making and the fine arts.

    (D) Private elementary and secondary schools concentrated on educating the poor.

    (E) Theology was the only complete professional training available in higher education.

6. The most active people in the religious revivals of the mid-nineteenthth century were

    (A) Roman Catholics.   (B) Jews.

    (C) mainstream Protestants.   (D) Quakers.

    (E) evangelical Christians.

7. Who became one of the first important American authors, best known for writing stories set in the Hudson River region of New York?

    (A) Nathaniel Hathorne   (B) Washington Irving

    (C) Parson Weems   (D) Herman Melville

    (E) Mercy Otis Warren

8. The "Lowell System" refers to which of the following?

    (A) Chattel slavery

    (B) Worker's cooperative

    (C) Employment of young women who were then housed in dormitories

    (D) An early American labor union

    (E) A business organization with limited liability for its owners

9. All of the following describe the American economy between 1815 and 1819 EXCEPT

    (A) liberal credit policies led to inflation.

    (B) English merchants dumped their products at low prices on the American market.

    (C) tightened credit led to a depression in 1819.

(D) there was high demand for American cotton, grain, and tobacco.

(E) factory production became more important than agriculture.

10. Rationalism, Deism, and Unitarianism were characteristic of

(A) the Enlightenment.

(B) Cultural Nationalism.

(C) evangelicalism.

(D) the romantic movement.

(E) Republicanism.

1789–1824

DRILLS

ANSWER KEY

Drill 1—The Federalist Era

1. (D)	2. (A)	3. (D)	4. (C)	5. (B)
6. (A)	7 (A)	8. (A)	9. (D)	10. (B)

Drill 2—John Adams' Administration and the Jeffersonian Era

1. (C)	2. (C)	3. (B)	4. (B)	5. (A)
6. (B)	7 (B)	8. (E)	9. (C)	10. (B)

Drill 3—Internal Development

1. (E)	2. (E)	3. (D)	4. (E)	5. (D)
6. (E)	7 (B)	8. (C)	9. (E)	10. (A)

GLOSSARY: 1789–1824

Broad Interpretation
> An interpretation of the Constitution as having vested extensive powers in the federal government.

Cabinet
> Officials who serve as advisors to the President as well as run the executive department.

Corporation
> A business organization used to raise capital and ensure limited liability for its participants.

Cotton Gin
> A device used to separate the seeds from the fibers of the cotton plant quickly.

Faction
> A group of individuals with shared interests, not taking into account the interests of the society at large.

Mandate
> An overwhelming election victory that gives the winner political credit.

Monroe Doctrine
> Monroe's statement that European powers could not interfere in the affairs of the American hemisphere.

Nullify
> To declare federal law void within a state.

Quids
> Republican opponents of Jefferson who accused him of complicity in the Yazoo controversy.

Strict Interpretationn
> An interpretation of the Constitution holding that any action not specifically permitted was thereby prohibited.

Turnpike
> A privately owned toll road.

CHAPTER 6

1824–1850
JACKSONIAN DEMOCRACY AND WESTWARD EXPANSION

➤ Diagnostic Test
➤ 1824–1850 Review & Drills
➤ Glossary

1824-1850
DIAGNOSTIC TEST

1. (A) (B) (C) (D) (E)
2. (A) (B) (C) (D) (E)
3. (A) (B) (C) (D) (E)
4. (A) (B) (C) (D) (E)
5. (A) (B) (C) (D) (E)
6. (A) (B) (C) (D) (E)
7. (A) (B) (C) (D) (E)
8. (A) (B) (C) (D) (E)
9. (A) (B) (C) (D) (E)
10. (A) (B) (C) (D) (E)
11. (A) (B) (C) (D) (E)
12. (A) (B) (C) (D) (E)
13. (A) (B) (C) (D) (E)
14. (A) (B) (C) (D) (E)
15. (A) (B) (C) (D) (E)
16. (A) (B) (C) (D) (E)
17. (A) (B) (C) (D) (E)
18. (A) (B) (C) (D) (E)
19. (A) (B) (C) (D) (E)
20. (A) (B) (C) (D) (E)

21. (A) (B) (C) (D) (E)
22. (A) (B) (C) (D) (E)
23. (A) (B) (C) (D) (E)
24. (A) (B) (C) (D) (E)
25. (A) (B) (C) (D) (E)
26. (A) (B) (C) (D) (E)
27. (A) (B) (C) (D) (E)
28. (A) (B) (C) (D) (E)
29. (A) (B) (C) (D) (E)
30. (A) (B) (C) (D) (E)
31. (A) (B) (C) (D) (E)
32. (A) (B) (C) (D) (E)
33. (A) (B) (C) (D) (E)
34. (A) (B) (C) (D) (E)
35. (A) (B) (C) (D) (E)
36. (A) (B) (C) (D) (E)
37. (A) (B) (C) (D) (E)
38. (A) (B) (C) (D) (E)
39. (A) (B) (C) (D) (E)
40. (A) (B) (C) (D) (E)

1824–1850
DIAGNOSTIC TEST

This diagnostic test is designed to help you determine your strengths and weaknesses in your knowledge of the Jacksonian democracy and westward expansion (1824–1850). Follow the directions and check your answers.

Study this chapter for the following tests:
AP U.S. History, CLEP General, CLEP United States History I,
GED, Praxis Specialty Area, SAT: United States History

---

40 Questions

DIRECTIONS: Choose the correct answer for each of the following questions. Fill in each answer on the answer sheet.

1. Which of the following correctly describes women's rights in mid-nineteenth-century America?

   (A) A married woman controlled her own property.

   (B) Husbands were forbidden to beat their wives.

   (C) Women could freely enter professions such as medicine.

   (D) Women could not claim money they had earned.

   (E) Women had the right to vote in federal elections.

2. Which of the following territories was won from Mexico in 1848?

   (A) Oregon *Spain*   (B) California

   (C) Texas *plains*   (D) Florida *Spain*

   (E) Louisiana *1803*

   Transcontinental Treaty – 1819

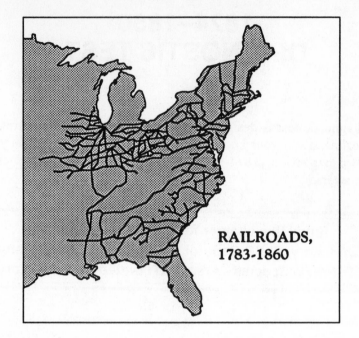

**RAILROADS,
1783-1860**

3. According to the above map, which of the following statements is most correct?

    (A) The South had the most extensively developed railroad system.

    (B) The transportation system ran primarily east-west.

    (C) The West had a poorly developed transportation system.

    (D) The South depended upon canals for transportation.

    (E) The United States had developed few railroad lines prior to 1860.

4. What territory gained independence in 1836?

    (A) California *1844*   (B) Oregon

    (C) Texas   (D) Kansas-Nebraska

    (E) Missouri *1820*

5. After which of the following dates was there little criticism of slavery within the South?

    (A) 1776   (B) 1789

    (C) 1815   (D) 1832 *POSITIVE GOOD*
                                              After Nat Turner

    (E) 1850

6. Which of the following was NOT a cause of the Panic of 1837?

    (A) The building up of surpluses in the nation's factories

(B) The destruction of the second Bank of the United States

(C) Over extension of bank credit

(D) A poor wheat crop

(E) The Specie Circular of 1836

7. The principle of "popular sovereignty" was

   (A) first conceived by Senator Stephen A. Douglas.

   (B) applied as part of the Missouri Compromise.

   (C) a central feature of the Kansas-Nebraska Act.

   (D) a policy favored by the Whig party during the late 1840s and early 1850s.

   (E) successful in solving the impasse over the status of slavery in the territories.

8. Which of the following best describes the attitudes of Southern whites toward slavery during the mid-nineteenth century (ca. 1835–1865)?

   (A) Slavery was a necessary evil.

   (B) Slavery should be immediately abolished.

   (C) Slavery was a benefit to both whites and blacks.

   (D) Slavery should gradually be phased out and the freed slaves colonized to some place outside the United States.

   (E) Slavery was a national sin.

9. The Wilmot Proviso stipulated that

   (A) slavery should be prohibited in the lands acquired as a result of the Mexican War.

   (B) no lands should be annexed to the United States as a result of the Mexican War.

   (C) California should be a free state while the rest of the Mexican Cession should be reserved for the formation of slave states.

   (D) the status of slavery in the Mexican Cession should be decided on the basis of "popular sovereignty."

   (E) the Missouri Compromise line should be extended through the Mexican Cession to the Pacific, lands north of it being closed to slavery.

10. The Whig party turned against President John Tyler because

   (A) he was felt to be ineffective in pushing the Whig agenda through Congress.

(B)   he spoke out in favor of the annexation of Texas.

(C)   he opposed the entire Whig legislative program.

(D)   he criticized Henry Clay's handling of the Nullification Crisis.

(E)   he aggressively favored the expansion of slavery.

11.   All of the following were causes of the Mexican War EXCEPT

(A)   American desire for California.

(B)   Mexican failure to pay debts and damages owed to the U.S.

(C)   U.S. annexation of the formerly Mexican-held Republic of Texas.

(D)   Mexican desire to annex Louisiana.

(E)   the disputed southern boundary of Texas.

12.   The Missouri Compromise provided that Missouri be admitted as a slave state, Maine be admitted as a free state, and

(A)   all of the Louisiana Territory north of the northern boundary of Missouri be closed to slavery.

(B)   all of the Louisiana Territory north of 36°30' be closed to slavery.

(C)   the entire Louisiana Territory be opened to slavery.

(D)   the lands south of 36°30' be guaranteed to slavery and the lands north of it be negotiable.

(E)   all of the Louisiana Territory north of the southern boundary of Missouri be closed to slavery for 30 years.

13.   The term "Trail of Tears" refers to

(A)   the Mormon migration from Nauvoo, Illinois, to what is now Utah.

(B)   the forced migration of the Cherokee tribe from the southern Appalachians to what is now Oklahoma.

(C)   the westward migration along the Oregon Trail.

(D)   the migration into Kentucky along the Wilderness Road.

(E)   the migration of German settlers southward from Pennsylvania into the Shenandoah Valley of Virginia.

14.   The most forceful Southern protest against high protective tariffs during the first half of the nineteenth century was the

(A)   Hayne-Webster Debate.

(B)   Virginia and Kentucky Resolutions.

(C)   Nullification Controversy.

(D) resignation of Vice President John C. Calhoun.

(E) imposition of the congressional "gag rule."

15. Which of the following was NOT a new religious group that emerged in America during the nineteenth century?

(A) Latter-day Saints   (B) Adventists

(C) Methodists   (D) Spiritualists

(E) Christian Scientists

"NO HIGHER LAW."

16. The point of view expressed in the above cartoon would have pleased

(A) Daniel Webster.   (B) Henry Clay.

(C) William Lloyd Garrison.   (D) John C. Calhoun.

(E) George Fitzhugh.

17. All of the following were among President Andrew Jackson's objections to the First Bank of the United States EXCEPT

(A) it allowed the economic power of the government to be controlled by private individuals.

(B) it threatened the integrity of the democratic system.

(C) it was preventing the government from achieving its policy of creating inflation.

(D) it could be used irresponsibly to create financial hardship for the nation.

(E) it benefited a small group of wealthy and privileged persons at the expense of the rest of the country.

18. The Nullification Controversy directly involved South Carolina's opposition to which of the following federal policies?

   (A) The Alien and Sedition Acts (B) The protective tariff

   (C) The Missouri Compromise   (D) The Civil Rights Act of 1866

   (E) The Compromise of 1850

19. The most divisive and controversial aspect of the slavery issue during the first half of the nineteenth century was

   (A) the status of slavery in the District of Columbia.

   (B) the right of abolitionists to send their literature through the U.S. mail.

   (C) the enforcement of the draconian Fugitive Slave Law.

   (D) the status of slavery in the territories.

   (E) the prohibition of international slave trade.

20. Which of the following would an 1850s Southern plantation owner have been most likely to approve of?

   (A) George Fitzhugh's *Cannibals All!*

   (B) Hinton Rowan Helper's *The Impending Crisis of the South*

   (C) Frederick Law Olmstead's *The Cotton Kingdom*

   (D) William Lloyd Garrison's *The Liberator*

   (E) Harriet Beecher Stowe's *Uncle Tom's Cabin*

Questions 21–23 refer to the map below.

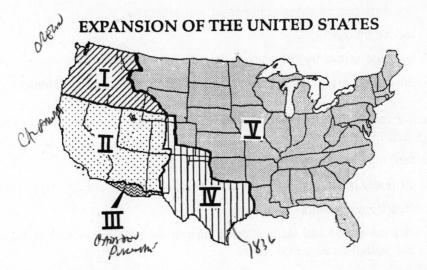

EXPANSION OF THE UNITED STATES

21. In which area(s) of the map was slavery in existence prior to its annexation by the United States?

    (A) II, III, and IV   (B) II and III

    (C) IV only   (D) II only

    (E) III only

22. Which area(s) of the map became part of the United States as a direct result of the Mexican War?

    (A) IV only   (B) III and IV

    (C) III only   (D) II, III, and IV

    (E) II only

23. Which of the following is true of Area III?

    (A) Its acquisition was a direct result of the Mexican-American War.

    (B) It contained a possible route for a southern transatlantic railroad.

    (C) Its purchase was authorized by President Polk.

    (D) It automatically entered the Union as slave territory.

    (E) The area gained statehood during the Cleveland and Harrison administrations.

24. The 1832–1833 Nullification Crisis involved all of the following EXCEPT

    (A) federal tariff policy.

    (B) Southern fear of federal tampering with slavery.

    (C) federal land policy.

    (D) personal animosity between Andrew Jackson and John C. Calhoun.

    (E) the rights of individual states versus those of the federal government.

25. A major reason for prejudice against Irish immigrants to America in the 1840s and 1850s was

    (A) their high rates of alcoholism.

    (B) difficulty in understanding them because of their accent.

    (C) their Roman Catholicism.

    (D) their education and skills allowed them to take skilled jobs away from less skilled American workers.

    (E) their tendency to gravitate toward rural farming communities and take over the most desired farmland, often dominating the communities in which they settled.

26. The paternalistic view of slavery held that

    (A) slavery was a necessary evil that should be phased out as soon as was economically possible.

    (B) slavery was a totally unjustifiable abuse of humanity demanding immediate abolition.

    (C) slavery was an artifact of a more primitive past that would eventually fade out on its own.

    (D) slavery was necessary to protect blacks from the mistreatment and abuse they would receive if they were freed.

    (E) slavery was necessary to keep blacks from developing their superior potential and eventually dominating the white race.

27. The slogan "Fifty-four forty or fight," which helped get James K. Polk elected president, referred to

    (A) the dispute over the northernmost boundary to which slavery would be allowed within the United States.

    (B) the border dispute between Mexico and the United States over the southwestern border of Texas.

    (C) the dispute between Britain and the United States over the border between American Oregon and British Canada.

(D) disputes with Russia over control of northern California, which the Russians claimed as their own territory.

(E) the dispute between the United States and Britain over the border between American Maine and British Canada. *E/137*

28. In the mid-eighteenth century, the first wave of non-English speaking immigrants (other than African slaves) arrived in the English colonies. They were ethnic

(A) Poles.

(B) Scandinavians.

•(C) Germans.

(D) Italians.

(E) Russians.

Common Man

29. Andrew Jackson's election in 1828 is seen by many historians to represent

(A) the end of the Federalist party in America.

-(B) the rise of individualism and popular democracy in America.

(C) the first true consolidation of federal power over the states since the drafting of the Constitution.

(D) the beginnings of a genuine American aristocracy in government.

(E) the low point of power for the executive branch of government in the 1800s.

30. Henry David Thoreau, Nathaniel Hawthorne, Ralph Waldo Emerson, James Fenimore Cooper, Herman Melville, Margaret Fuller, and Theodore Parker were all involved in developing the transcendentalist philosophy of the

(A) Shaker community in New Lebanon, New York. *celibacy*

(B) Mormon community in Palmyra, New York.

(C) New Harmony community in Indiana. *Utopian factory Robert Owen*

(D) Oneida community in upstate New York.

- (E) Brook Farm community in Roxbury, Massachusetts.

31. In the 1830s and 1840s, the primary difference between the Whigs and the Democrats was that

(A) the Whigs favored economic expansion while the Democrats favored a stable but retracted economy.

(B) the Democrats favored the abolition of slavery while the Whigs favored retaining the current system of slavery being allowed in the Southern states that desired it, but no further expansion of slavery north of the Mason-Dixon line.

(C)   the Whigs favored an expanded, activist federal government while the Democrats favored a limited non interventionist federal government.

(D)   the Democrats were strongly supported by evangelical Christians and supported a wide range of moral reforms while the Whigs were supported by westerners who favored individual choice over morally based restrictions on behavior.

(E)   the Whigs favored limitations on westward expansion while the Democrats favored the concept of "manifest destiny" and expansion to the Pacific Ocean.

32.   The Nullification Crisis of 1832 revolved around

   (A)   states' rights to overrule or disallow any federal legislation they found unacceptable.

   (B)   the federal government's right to nullify any antislavery legislation passed by the territories west of the Mississippi.

   (C)   the Supreme Court's right to nullify Congressional legislation deemed unconstitutional.

   (D)   the refusal of state militias to submit themselves to federal control in time of war.

   (E)   the right of Congress to override a presidential veto on matters of foreign policy.

33.   The first presidential election that relied upon the popular vote to select the electoral college was held in

   (A)   1789.   (B)   1800.

   (C)   1824.   (D)   1916.

   (E)   1928.

34.   The popular theology of Charles Finney during the Second Great Awakening stressed

   (A)   human perfectibility.   (B)   an Old Testament God.

   (C)   original sin.   (D)   rational Christianity.

   (E)   none of the above.

35.   Which of the following American authors sought to recreate the everyday experiences of ordinary Americans in his writings?

   (A)   Edgar Allan Poe   (B)   Nathaniel Hawthorne

   (C)   Herman Melville   (D)   Walt Whitman

   (E)   Frances Trollope

36. The Tariff Act of 1832 resulted in

    (A) near war between the United States and South Carolina.

    (B) a rift between President Jackson and Vice President Calhoun.

    (C) the revival of a states' rights doctrine.

    (D) a compromise solution proposed by Henry Clay.

    (E) all of the above.

37. Which of the following events occurred first?

    (A) The Kansas-Nebraska Act *1854*

    (B) The Nat Turner Rebellion *1831*

    (C) The Seneca Falls Convention *1848* *E Cady Stanton*

    (D) The Lincoln-Douglas debates *1858*

    (E) The Homestead Act *1862 settlement of the West*

38. "I wish to speak today, not as a Massachusetts man, nor as a Northern man, but as an American for the preservation of the Union." Daniel Webster delivered this speech in defense of

    (A) Dartmouth College.   (B) the Charles River Bridge.

    (C) Abraham Lincoln.   (D) the Compromise of 1850.

    (E) the Second Bank of the United States.

39. Stephen Douglas' advocacy of popular sovereignty in the Kansas-Nebraska Act ignited rather than dispelled the flames of sectionalism. Popular sovereignty sought to

    (A) allow blacks to vote in the Kansas-Nebraska territories.

    (B) let the residents of Kansas-Nebraska areas determine their own laws on slavery through elections.

    (C) force the Supreme Court to rule on slavery's constitutionality.

    (D) remove the slavery issue from politics.

    (E) None of the above.

40. The "Secret Six" were the financial supporters of

    (A) the attack on Fort Sumter.

    (B) John Brown's raid on Harper's Ferry. *1859*

    (C) Lincoln's presidential

    (D) Southern secession. candidacy.

    (E) King Cotton Diplomacy.

1824–1850
DIAGNOSTIC TEST

ANSWER KEY

1. (D)	9. (A)	17. (C)	25. (C)	33. (C)
2. (B)	10. (C)	18. (B)	26. (D)	34. (A)
3. (B)	11. (D)	19. (D)	27. (C)	35. (D)
4. (C)	12. (B)	20. (A)	28. (C)	36. (E)
5. (D)	13. (B)	21. (C)	29. (B)	37. (B)
6. (A)	14. (C)	22. (E)	30. (E)	38. (D)
7. (C)	15. (C)	23. (B)	31. (C)	39. (B)
8. (C)	16. (C)	24. (C)	32. (A)	40. (B)

DETAILED EXPLANATIONS OF ANSWERS

1. **(D)** In most states women had no claim to money they earned; it was controlled by their husbands, as was their own property. Husbands could legally beat their wives "with a reasonable instrument." And the professions were largely closed to women. Women did not have the right to vote in federal elections until the passage of the Nineteenth Amendment in 1920.

2. **(B)** The Oregon boundary was settled with Britain in 1846. Louisiana was purchased from France in 1803 and Florida from Spain in 1819. Texas had won its independence from Mexico in 1836 and was annexed by the United States in 1845.

3. **(B)** There were few roads or railroad lines connecting the North and South in 1860. Most transportation routes in both the North and South ran east-west.

4. **(C)** Texas won independence from Mexico in 1836 through rebellion. California briefly became independent in 1846. The other territories never became independent.

5. **(D)** After 1832 there was little Southern criticism of the institution of slavery. The Nat Turner Rebellion took place in 1831 and the Virginia legislature debated the abolition of slavery in 1832 but took no action.

6. **(A)** The United States still had a basically agricultural economy, hence factories had only a marginal effect on the total economy. The destruction of the Bank of the United States took away the major control over the state chartered banks, and many of them became over extended. Many banks failed after the 1836 Specie Circular. A poor wheat crop also forced the U.S. to use gold and silver to purchase grain from other countries.

7. **(C)** The principle of "popular sovereignty" was a central feature of the Kansas-Nebraska Act. Though championed by Senator Stephen A. Douglas (A), it had previously been put forward by 1848 Democratic presidential candidate Lewis Cass. A favorite policy of Democrats—not Whigs (D)—during the late 1840s and early 1850s, it proved a failure in solving the impasse over the status of slavery in the territories (E). It differed from the system of congressionally specified free and slave areas used in the Missouri Compromise (B).

8. **(C)** During the period from 1835–1865 Southerners generally defended slavery as a positive benefit to society and even to the slaves themselves. That slavery was a necessary evil (A) and should be gradually phased out as the slaves

were colonized outside the United States (D) was the attitude of an earlier generation of white Southerners, including Thomas Jefferson. That slavery was a national sin (E) and should be immediately abolished (B) was the view of the abolitionists, a minority even in the North during this period.

9. **(A)** The Wilmot Proviso was intended to prohibit slavery in the area acquired through the Mexican War. Congress generally agreed that the United States would acquire some territory from the war (B). That California should be a free state while the rest of the Mexican Cession was reserved for slavery (C), that the status of slavery in the Mexican Cession should be decided on the basis of "popular sovereignty" (D), and that the Missouri Compromise line should be extended to the Pacific (E) were all suggestions for a compromise that might calm the furor aroused by the Wilmot Proviso.

10. **(C)** The Whigs turned on Tyler because he opposed their entire legislative program. He did speak out in favor of Texas annexation (B) and he seemed to favor expansion of slavery (E), but these offenses would have been relatively minor in Whig eyes by comparison.

11. **(D)** Mexico did expect to win the war, invade the U.S., and dictate a peace in Washington, but whatever desire, if any, the Mexicans may have had for the state of Louisiana was not a factor in the coming of the war. The U.S. did, however, desire to annex California (A) and did annex Texas (C); Mexico did refuse to pay its debts (B) and did claim Texas (C); and the southern boundary of Texas was in dispute (E). All of these contributed to the coming of the war.

12. **(B)** As part of the 1820 Missouri Compromise, all of the Louisiana Territory north of 36°30'—that is, the southern (A) boundary of most of Missouri—was closed (C) to slavery. According to the compromise this was to be permanent, though subsequent behavior on the part of some politicians—the 1854 Kansas-Nebraska Act—might lead one to believe the free areas had been left negotiable (D) or closed to slavery only for 30 years (E)—but such was not the case.

13. **(B)** The term "Trail of Tears" is used to describe the relocation of the Cherokee tribe from the southern Appalachians to what is now Oklahoma. The migration of Mormons from Nauvoo, Illinois, to the Great Salt Lake in Utah (A), the westward movements along the Oregon Trail (C) and, much earlier, the Wilderness Road (D), and the migration of German settlers into the Shenandoah Valley (E)—earlier still—all took place and could at times be as unpleasant as the Cherokees' trek. They were, however, voluntary and therefore did not earn such sad titles as the "Trail of Tears."

14. **(C)** The most forceful Southern protest against the high protective tariffs of the first half of the nineteenth century came in 1832 when South Carolina claimed that it had nullified—suspended the operation of—the tariff laws within

its boundaries. The Hayne-Webster Debate (A) dealt with this and related issues, and the resignation of Vice President John C. Calhoun (D) may have been at least in part influenced by disagreements over tariffs. The Virginia and Kentucky Resolutions (B) were a protest against the Alien and Sedition Acts of the late 1790s, not the tariff, and the "gag rule" (E) dealt with slavery.

15. **(C)** The Methodists came to America during the late colonial period. Latter-day Saints or Mormons began about 1830 under the leadership of Joseph Smith. Adventists grouped around William Miller's prediction that Christ would return in 1844. Modern Spiritualism began with the "rappings" experienced by the Fox sisters in 1848. Christian Science was founded in 1866 by Mary Baker Eddy.

16. **(C)** William Lloyd Garrison was a leading abolitionist who would have approved of this cartoon condemning the Fugitive Slave Law of 1850. Daniel Webster (portrayed in the cartoon) and Henry Clay both played roles in bringing about the Compromise of 1850, of which the law was a part. John C. Calhoun and George Fitzhugh were staunch defenders of slavery.

17. **(C)** Jackson did NOT object to the bank's preventing inflation, though some of his followers may have. Jackson, on the other hand, desired a gold standard. He believed the bank allowed the economic power of the government to be wielded by private individuals (A), the bank's directors. He believed it benefited this small and wealthy group, and their friends, at the expense of the rest of the country (E). He believed it could create economic hardship for the nation (D) and had in 1819, and he believed it threatened the integrity of the democratic system by using its influence in elections (B).

18. **(B)** The Nullification Controversy directly involved South Carolina's opposition to the protective tariff. It may indirectly have involved South Carolina's opposition to the antislavery debate in Congress and therefore to the Missouri Compromise (C). The Civil Rights Act of 1866 (D) and the Compromise of 1850 had not occurred when the Nullification Crisis began in 1832. The South's—and the Republican party's—response to the 1798 Alien and Sedition Acts (A) was contained in the Virginia and Kentucky Resolutions.

19. **(D)** The status of slavery in the territories proved the most divisive aspect of the slavery issue. Relatively little controversy surrounded international slave trade (E), and Congress prohibited it in 1808, as soon as it was constitutionally empowered to do so. The status of slavery in the District of Columbia (A), the right to send antislavery literature through the mail (B), and the enforcement of the Fugitive Slave Law (C) were all highly controversial and divisive issues though ultimately not to the degree of the territorial issue that eventually led to civil war.

20. **(A)** George Fitzhugh's *Cannibals All!*, in which he argued that slavery

was more humane than wage-labor, would have been far more likely to be approved by an 1850s Southern planter than any of the other books listed. *Uncle Tom's Cabin* (E) and *The Impending Crisis of the South* (B) were both 1850s books attacking slavery. *The Cotton Kingdom* (C) was not flattering in its depiction of Southern culture, and *The Liberator* (D) was an abolitionist newspaper so hated in the South that a man found in the South with a copy in his possession risked being killed.

21.   **(C)**   Area IV of the map represents the Republic of Texas, which had legalized slavery during the nine years of its existence as an independent nation, prior to its 1845 annexation by the United States. Slavery never existed in the Oregon country (I), nor did it exist in the Mexican Cession (II) or the Gadsden Purchase (III) before U.S. annexation.

22.   **(E)**   The only area that became part of the United States as a direct result of the Mexican War was the Mexican Cession (II), purchased by the United States for the sum of $18,250,000 under the terms of the treaty that ended the war. Texas (IV) was annexed in 1845, shortly before the Mexican War. Oregon (I) was acquired in a deal with Great Britain in 1846, the same year that war broke out with Mexico. The Gadsden Purchase (III) was bought from Mexico several years after the end of the war.

23.   **(B)**   The United States bought Area III, the Gadsden Purchase, from Mexico in 1853, mainly to accomplish the goal of a southern transcontinental railroad to link the bulk of the United States with the newly acquired territories on the Pacific Coast. The Southern Pacific Railroad, which ran from Houston through El Paso and Tucson to Los Angeles, was completed in 1882. The government made the purchase five years after President Polk left office (C), and six years after the end of the Mexican-American War, through which Polk added much of northern Mexico to the United States (A). The region was not purchased as slave or free territory (D); according to the Compromise of 1850, the decision would be left to the territory. The region became part of the states of Arizona and New Mexico in 1912 (E), almost a quarter of a century after Cleveland and Harrison added seven states to the Union.

24.   **(C)**   The Nullification Crisis did not involve federal land policy. It was primarily a question of the constitutionality of tariffs (A) and the right of states to set aside federal laws (E), driven by Southern fear of possible future federal tampering with slavery (B). Animosity between South Carolina politician John C. Calhoun and President Andrew Jackson (D) also played a role in the crisis.

25.   **(C)**   Anti-Catholicism had been a factor of American life since the days of the Puritans. Catholicism was identified with religious tyranny and intolerance in the eyes of most Americans and there were real fears of the power of the pope and the Catholic Church. When Irish immigrants came to America in vast numbers in the 1840s, the overwhelming majority of them were Catholic. This raised

fears of their potential to launch some sort of Catholic insurrection in the cities where they settled in large numbers, simply because there seemed to be so many of them. Fears of Catholicism led people to blame the Irish for virtually every poverty-related problem that existed in the American coastal cities. Since the Irish were newcomers, and Catholic, they made easy scapegoats and suffered accordingly.

26. **(D)** The paternalistic view of slavery, held by most Southern plantation owners, held that blacks were inferior, mentally weak and ignorant, requiring "protection" from the evils that could befall them if they were left on their own. In this view, slaveowners were benevolent protectors who took care of their black slaves almost as parents take care of children. This was a comforting myth that most slaveholders really appear to have believed. It was comforting in that if they were really protectors of their poor black "children," then holding slaves wasn't sinful at all. It was, rather, a social service providing a good for everybody involved. Unfortunately, this twisted rationalization denied the fact that slaves were horribly mistreated and often abused or killed for little or no provocation. If they were ignorant or childlike, it is only because they were denied educational opportunities and many slaves learned that acting with childlike deference to their "master" often got them better treatment. In other words, their childishness was often an act based on a powerful instinct to survive rather than any limitations of mental capacity.

27. **(C)** The slogan "Fifty-four forty or fight" was used by James K. Polk's supporters in his election campaign of 1844. It referred to the simmering dispute between the United States and Britain over who should control Oregon, which until that point had been jointly controlled by Britain and the United States. Many Americans wanted control of the entire Oregon Territory, which had its northern border at 54°40'. Thus, the slogan "Fifty-four forty or fight" implied that Britain should give the United States all of Oregon or prepare to fight to keep it. Polk, who had bigger concerns with Mexico in regard to Texas and the American Southwest, did not look forward to fighting simultaneous wars with Britain and Mexico. He also wasn't in favor of adding another free state (as opposed to a slave state) to the Union. Finally, he didn't see northern Oregon as very suitable for American settlement. For these reasons he decided to negotiate with Britain rather than go to war. The final border was established at 49° latitude, continuing the northern border of the Wisconsin and Iowa Territories (now Minnesota, North Dakota, and Montana) to Puget Sound and the Pacific Ocean.

28. **(C)** The first wave of immigration to the English colonies by non-English speaking people was dominated by ethnic Germans fleeing from the Rhine region of what is now Germany. Most were farmers fleeing from war and starvation in their homeland. Some were seeking a respite from religious persecution. Many of them settled in western Pennsylvania and began successful farming communities where they were inaccurately labeled "the Pennsylvania Dutch."

While the ethnic groups listed in the remaining choices were all involved in waves of immigration to the New World, they all came at later dates, mostly after the mid-nineteenth century.

29.   **(B)**   Andrew Jackson's election marked the culmination of a movement whose roots lay in the philosophy of Thomas Jefferson that the country was best governed when people were allowed to govern themselves and the federal government interfered as little as possible. Following the activist presidency of John Quincy Adams in which he tried to expand federal power, Andrew Jackson swung the pendulum in the reverse direction. He was a frontiersman, the first truly common man elected to the presidency. He was a self-made man. He was a rugged individualist who was committed to reducing the concentration of political and economic power in Washington, D.C. and returning that power to the states and to the people where (in his opinion) it was less likely to be abused. His election was symbolic of the rise of the notion of "popular sovereignty" which asserted that the people could do no wrong and didn't need an elite aristocratic class to lead them.

30.   **(E)**   All of the choices are utopian communities which evolved as part of the religious revivals, or the Second Great Awakening, of the 1820s, 1830s, and 1840s. But only one of those communities, Brook Farm, was the source of the transcendentalist philosophy espoused by Thoreau, Melville, and others who lived and worked there. Brook Farm focused on the importance of spiritualism over materialism. Members of the community lived a communal life-style, and all shared in the upkeep of the community. The writers who lived there explored the workings of nature and the individual and became some of the most prominent American writers of the nineteenth century. During their prime they were a part of what is now called the American Renaissance.

31.   **(C)**   In the 1830s and 1840s, the Democrats supported the Jeffersonian principles of limited power to the federal government. They felt that what power the government wielded should be exercised at the state and local level. Democrats distrusted a strong, centralized government and opposed policies which would give the federal government support for private industry.

Their opponents, the Whigs, favored all of these policies. The Whigs believed in using the power of the federal government to help build the country and expand the nation's economy. The Whigs supported policies favored by business owners, the middle class, and the wealthy.

32.   **(A)**   The doctrine of nullification was developed in South Carolina as a means of protecting residents from what they saw as the "tyranny of the majority." This doctrine claimed that individual states could choose to ignore federal mandates or laws if they found those laws offensive or unfair to their interests. This issue became a crisis in 1832 when South Carolina invoked nullification in regard to an unpopular federal tariff. Andrew Jackson forced the tariff to be collected and some South Carolinians began discussing secession. The crisis was

resolved through the passage of a compromise tariff leading to the repeal of the nullification law by South Carolina. While a more serious crisis had been averted, this incident set the stage for further talk of secessionism as the slavery issue escalated tensions throughout the 1840s and 1850s.

33.   **(C)**   In the election of 1824, the members of the electoral college were selected by popular vote for the first time. Despite the public's misconceptions, the American president is selected by the electoral college and not the popular vote. Prior to 1824 members of the electoral college were selected by some agency of state government and as a result, the American electorate had little direct say in presidential elections. Today, a candidate requires 270 out of 535 electoral votes to become president. Members of the electoral college are chosen on a state-by-state basis according to party affiliation with the candidate. Each state is granted the same number of electors as its membership in Congress. In a winner-take-all format, a vote for a presidential candidate really is a vote for his party's state candidates to the electoral college and an indication to the electors from your state as to your candidate of choice. The November presidential election really is an election of the electoral college who meet in December to select the president.

34.   **(A)**   The tremendous religious revival that swept through America during the 1830s was largely the result of the new theology offered by Charles Finney. Finney touched off this Second Great Awakening in western New York state where he offered a view of human perfectibility that rejected the older Calvinistic theology. Finney exhorted his audiences to achieve perfection through God's love and to overcome original sin in their lives. Finney's God was a New Testament God of love, rather than the vengeful Old Testament God depicted in the First Great Awakening in the 1730s. Finney stressed each person's emotional bonds to God and downplayed approaching religion through dry abstract reasoning. As a result, many of his revivals became scenes of emotional outpourings. His appeal to a "self-made" Christian obviously struck a chord with a society advocating the self-made man.

35.   **(D)**   In his essay "The American Scholar," Ralph Waldo Emerson implored American writers to cast their works in the everyday lives of ordinary Americans. The only American writer of the group listed who followed that charge proved to be Walt Whitman whose poems were odes to the average American. Whitman depicted the typical American as a noble individual who lived a great morality play in his everyday workings. Hawthorne, Poe, and Melville all used either exotic settings (the distant past and ocean voyages) and focused on unusual characters (Captain Ahab and Hester Prynne) to focus on the human weaknesses of pride, guilt, and revenge. Poe especially focused on the theme of decline and regression rather than progress, i.e., *The Fall of the House of Usher*, 1839. Hawthorne's *House of the Seven Gables* (1850) and *The Scarlett Letter* (1851) both re-examined the Puritan past as one complete with misgivings and

doom. In Melville's *Moby Dick* (1851), pessimism about the human character prevails and results in tragedy.

36. **(E)** The Tariff Act of 1832 led directly to the Nullification Crisis between South Carolina and the United States. The Tariff Act established high import fees for all European manufactured goods in an effort to protect Northern industries. South Carolina balked at the policy which offered no protection for Southern farmers and forced them to pay higher prices as consumers. Under the leadership of Vice President John C. Calhoun, South Carolina re-established the states' rights view (the doctrine argues that the states and not the national government is sovereign and therefore each state can decide which national laws to obey) and refused to pay the tariff by nullifying it. President Jackson threatened to force South Carolina to obey by armed invasion, and South Carolina threatened to secede from the nation. Speaker of the House of Representatives Henry Clay intervened in the matter averting war with a compromise solution that effectively allowed South Carolina to avoid paying the tariff duties without advancing states' rights doctrines.

37. **(B)** The Nat Turner Rebellion occurred in 1831 as the bloodiest slave uprising in American history when 55 whites were killed by about 15 slaves in Virginia. The Kansas-Nebraska Act was passed in 1854 and sought to establish the principle of popular sovereignty in the two territories on the issue of slavery to promote the presidential ambitions of Senator Stephen Douglas of Illinois. The Seneca Falls Convention convened in 1848 as a militant expression of women's rights led by Lucretia Mott and Elizabeth Cady Stanton. The Lincoln-Douglas debates took place in 1858 as both candidates vied for the Senate seat in Illinois. The Homestead Act was passed by Congress in 1862 and granted a free 160-acre farm in the Far West (Great Plains region) to any American citizen 21 years of age or older who would work the land for five years.

38. **(D)** This speech by Daniel Webster delivered in defense of the Compromise of 1850 on the floor of the House of Representatives is considered one of the most famous speeches in American history. As Webster was closing out his illustrious political career, he ushered forth all his political and rhetorical skills to combat the growing spirit of sectionalism that was threatening his beloved America. Webster used all his power to gain passage of the act and completed his efforts with this brilliant appeal to patriotic nationalism. His defense of Dartmouth College before the Supreme Court gave rise to a rhetorical flourish of "only a small college, but there are, sirs, those who love it." Webster never delivered major addresses on Lincoln, the Bank, or the Bridge case.

39. **(B)** In 1854, Stephen Douglas harbored ambitions for the presidency in 1856. In order to attract the Southern votes required for his victory, Douglas proposed an act to amend the Missouri Compromise line of 36°30' in the case of the Kansas-Nebraska territories. Although both areas were north of the line, Douglas argued the settlers of the regions should decide for themselves on sla-

very. The result was civil war in the two regions as pro-Southern settlers openly battled with antislavery forces over the next two years. Douglas never was a champion of the black vote and believed Congress, not the Supreme Court, could solve the slave crisis.

40.   **(B)**   The Secret Six were a group of New York millionaires who provided the financial backing for John Brown's raid on Harper's Ferry, Virginia in 1859, Brown, a militant abolitionist, sought to seize a federal arsenal in the South and distribute weapons to slaves to lead a massive slave uprising. When information about Brown's ties to the Secret Six surfaced during his trial, the South began to seriously consider secession as its only course of action against the abolitionists. The Secret Six felt Lincoln was much too soft on slavery in 1860 to offer him support. In fact, their support of Brown's raid displays their view that violence and not politics would end slavery in America.

1824–1850
REVIEW

1. THE JACKSONIAN DEMOCRACY, 1829–1841

While the "Age of Jackson" did not bring perfect political, social, or economic equality to all Americans, it did mark a transformation in the political life of the nation that attracted the notice of European travelers and observers. Alexis de Tocqueville observed an "equality of condition" here that existed nowhere else in the world, and an egalitarian spirit among the people that was unique. Certainly the electorate had become broadened so that all white males had access to the polls, even if blacks and women were still outside the system. It was, in that sense, the "age of the common man." As to whether Andrew Jackson and his party were actually working for the good of those common men is another matter.

The Election of 1824

The Expansion of the Electorate

Most states had already eliminated the property qualifications for voting before the campaigns for this election began. The new Massachusetts state constitution of 1820 had led the way in this liberalization of the franchise, and most Northern states followed soon after, usually with some conservative opposition, but not violent reactions. In Rhode Island, Thomas Dorr led a bloodless "rebellion" in an effort to expand the franchise in that state, and though he was briefly imprisoned for his efforts, the incident led the conservative legislature to relent and grant the vote to non-property owners. The movement for reform was much slower in the Southern states.

Free blacks were excluded from the polls across the South and in most of the Northern states. In those areas where they had held the franchise, they were gradually excluded from the social and economic mainstream as well as from the political arena in the early years of this period.

National elections had never attracted much enthusiasm until 1824. Legislative caucuses had made the presidential nominations and kept the ruling cliques in power by excluding the voters from the process. But this year the system failed, and the caucuses were bypassed.

The members of the electoral college were now being almost universally elected by the people, rather than by the state legislatures, as in the early days.

The Candidates

Secretary of the Treasury William H. Crawford of Georgia was the pick of the Congressional caucus. Secretary of State John Quincy Adams held the job which traditionally had been the stepping-stone to the executive office. Speaker of the House Henry Clay presented the only coherent program to the voters, the "American System," which provided a high tariff on imports to finance an extensive internal improvement package. Andrew Jackson of Tennessee presented himself as a war hero from the 1812 conflict. All four candidates claimed to be Republicans.

The Election

Jackson won 43 percent of the popular vote, but the four-way split meant that he only received 38 percent of the electoral votes. Under the provisions of the Twelfth Amendment, the top three candidates were voted on by the House of Representatives. This left Henry Clay out of the running, and he threw his support to Adams. The votes had no sooner been counted, when the new president, Adams, appointed Henry Clay his secretary of state.

Andrew Jackson and his supporters immediately cried "foul!" and accused Clay of making a deal for his vote. The rallying cry of "corrupt bargain" became the impetus for their immediate initiation of the campaign for the 1828 election.

The Adams Administration

The new president pushed for an active federal government in areas like internal improvements and Indian affairs. These policies proved unpopular in an age of increasing sectional jealousies and conflicts over states' rights.

Adams was frustrated at every turn by his Jacksonian opposition, and his unwillingness, or inability, to compromise further antagonized his political enemies. For example, his refusal to endorse and enforce the Creek Indians' land cession to the state of Georgia was negated by their re-cession of their lands under pressure from Georgia's Jacksonian government.

John C. Calhoun and Nullification

In 1828, Congress passed a new tariff bill which was originally supported by Southern congressmen in order to embarrass the administration. The finished bill, however, included higher import duties for many goods which were bought by Southern planters, so they bitterly denounced the law as the "Tariff of Abominations."

John C. Calhoun was serving as Adams' vice president, so to protest the tariff and still protect his position, he anonymously published the "South Carolina Exposition and Protest," which outlined his theory of the "concurrent majority": a federal law which was deemed harmful to the interests of an individual state could be declared null and void within that state by a convention of the people. Thus, a state holding a minority position could ignore a law enacted by the majority which they considered unconstitutional (shades of Thomas Jefferson).

The Election of 1828

Adams' supporters now called themselves the National Republicans, and Jackson's party ran as the Democratic Republicans. Andrew Jackson had aggressively campaigned since his defeat in the House in 1825.

It was a dirty campaign. Adams' people accused Jackson of adultery and of the murder of several militiamen who had been executed for desertion during the War of 1812. Jackson's followers in turn defamed Adams and his programs and accused him of extravagance with public funds.

When the votes were counted, Jackson had won 56 percent of the popular vote and swept 178 of the 261 electoral votes. John Calhoun was elected vice president.

Andrew Jackson as President

Jackson was popular with the common man. He seemed to be the prototype of the self-made Westerner: rough-hewn, violent, vindictive, with few ideas but strong convictions. He ignored his appointed cabinet officers and relied instead on the counsel of his "Kitchen Cabinet," a group of partisan supporters who had the ear and the confidence of the president.

Jackson expressed the conviction that government operations could be performed by untrained, common folk, and he threatened the dismissal of large numbers of government employees, to replace them with his supporters. Actually, he talked more about this "spoils system" than he acted on it.

He exercised his veto power more than any other president before him. A famous example was the Maysville Road, a project in Kentucky which would require a federal subsidy. Jackson opposed it because it would exist only within the boundaries of a single state.

Jacksonian Indian Policy

Jackson supported the removal of all Indian tribes to west of the Mississippi River. The Indian Removal Act in 1830 provided for federal enforcement of that process.

The portion of the Cherokee Nation which occupied northern Georgia claimed to be a sovereign political entity within the boundaries of that state. The Supreme Court supported that claim in its decision in *Worcester v. Georgia* (1832), but President Jackson refused to enforce the court's decision.

The result of this policy was the Trail of Tears, the forced march, under U.S. Army escort, of thousands of Cherokees to the West. A quarter or more of the Indians, mostly women and children, perished on the journey.

QUESTION

What is "Jacksonian democracy"?

EXPLANATION

"Jacksonian democracy" is a term used to describe the impact of the expansion of the franchise during the 1820s and 1830s. Not only were more people able to vote with the elimination of many property qualifications, democratic elections were becoming more important. For instance, electors to the electoral college were chosen by popular vote, instead of by state legislators. Because of this, the status of the "common man" was on the rise, as was Americans' attachment to the idea of equality.

The Webster-Hayne Debate (1830)

Federal Land Policy

The method of disposing of government land raised sectional differences. Westerners wanted cheap lands available to the masses. Northeasterners opposed this policy because it would lure away their labor supply and drive up wages. Southerners supported the West, hoping to weaken the ties between East and West.

The Senate Confrontation

Senator Robert Hayne of South Carolina made a speech in support of cheap land, and he used Calhoun's anti-tariff arguments to support his position. In his remarks, he referred to the possibility of nullification.

Daniel Webster's famous replies to this argument moved the debate from the issue of land policy to the nature of the Union and states' rights within it. Webster argued for the Union as indissoluble and sovereign over the individual states. His concluding statements have become a part of our rhetorical heritage: "It is, Sir, the people's Constitution, the people's government, made for the people, made by the people, and answerable to the people…. Liberty and Union, now and forever, one and inseparable!"

The Second Nullification Crisis

The final split between Andrew Jackson and his vice president, John C. Calhoun, came over the new Tariff of 1832, and over Mrs. Calhoun's snub of Peggy Eaton, the wife of Secretary of War John Eaton.

Mrs. Eaton was a commoner, and the aristocratic Mrs. Calhoun refused to include her on the guest lists for the Washington parties. Jackson, no doubt remembering the slights to his own dear Rachel, defended his friends Peggy and John and demanded that they be included in the social life of the capitol.

Jackson was a defender of states' rights, but within the context of a dominant Union. When he supported the higher rates of the new tariff, Calhoun resigned his office in a huff and went home to South Carolina. There he composed an Ordinance of Nullification, which was duly approved by a special convention, and the customs officials were ordered to stop collecting the duties at the port of Charleston.

Jackson's response was immediate and decisive. He obtained a Force Bill from Congress (1833), which empowered him to use federal troops to enforce the collection of the taxes. And he suggested the possibility of hanging Calhoun. At the same time, he offered a gradual reduction in the levels of the duties. Calhoun backed down, both sides claimed victory, and the crisis was averted.

The War on the Bank

The Controversy

The Bank of the United States had operated under the direction of Nicholas Biddle since 1823. He was a cautious man, and his conservative economic policy enforced conservatism among the state and private banks—which many bankers resented. Many of the Bank's enemies opposed it simply because it was big and powerful. Many still disputed its constitutionality.

The Election of 1832

Andrew Jackson freely voiced his antagonism toward the Bank, and his intention to destroy it. During the campaign for the presidency in 1832, Henry Clay and Daniel Webster promoted a bill to recharter the Bank, even though its charter did not expire until 1836. They feared that Jackson would gain support over time and could kill the Bank as a parting shot as he retired. The Congress passed the recharter bill, but Jackson vetoed it. This left that institution a lame duck agency.

Jackson soundly defeated Henry Clay in the presidential race, and he considered his victory a mandate from the people to destroy the Bank. His first move was to remove the federal government's deposits from Biddle's vaults and distribute the funds to various state and local banks, called by his critics the "pet banks." Biddle responded by tightening up on credit and calling in loans, hoping to embarrass the government and force a withdrawal by Jackson. Jackson stood firm and the result was a financial recession.

The Panic of 1837

When Biddle was forced to relent through pressure from business interests, the economy immediately rebounded. With credit policies relaxed, inflation began to pick up. The government contributed to this expansion by offering millions of acres of Western land for sale to settlers at low prices.

In 1836, Jackson ordered a distribution of surplus funds and thus helped to further fuel the inflationary rise in prices. Finally, even Jackson recognized the danger and tried to slow the spiral by issuing the Specie Circular, which required payment for public land in hard money; no more paper or credit. Depression quickly followed this move.

The business recession lasted well into the 1840s. Our national economy was by this time so tied in with international business and finance that the downturn affected the entire Atlantic community, and was in turn worsened by the global impact. But most Americans blamed everyone in power, including Jackson, institutions, and business practices. This disillusionment helped to initiate and intensify the reform movement which so occupied this nation in the nineteenth century's second quarter.

The Election of 1836

Jackson had hand-picked his Democratic successor, Martin Van Buren of New York. The Whigs ran three regional candidates in hopes of upsetting the Jacksonians. The Whig party had emerged from the ruins of the National Republicans and other groups who opposed Jackson's policies. The name was taken from the British Whig tradition, which simply refers to the "opposition."

Van Buren's Presidency

Van Buren, known as Old Kinderhook (O.K.), inherited all the problems and resentments generated by his mentor. He spent most of his term in office dealing with the financial chaos left by the death of the second bank. The best he could do was to eventually persuade Congress to establish an independent treasury to handle government funds. It began functioning in 1840.

The Election of 1840

The Candidates

The Whigs nominated William Henry Harrison, "Old Tippecanoe," a western Indian fighter. Their choice for vice president was John Tyler, a former Democrat from Virginia. The Democrats put up Van Buren again, but they could not agree on a vice presidential candidate, so they ran no one.

The Campaign

This election saw the largest voter turnout to date. The campaign was a dramatic one. The Whigs stressed the depression and the opulent life-style of the incumbent in contrast to the simple "log cabin" origins of their candidate.

Harrison won a narrow popular victory, but swept 80 percent of the electoral vote. Unfortunately for the Whigs, President Harrison died only a month after the inauguration, having served the shortest term in presidential history.

The Meaning of Jacksonian Politics

The Party System

The Age of Jackson was the beginning of the modern two-party system. Popular politics, based on emotional appeal, became the accepted style. The practice of meeting in mass conventions to nominate national candidates for office was established during these Jackson years.

The Strong Executive

Jackson, more than any president before him, used his office to dominate his party and the government to such an extent that he was called "King Andrew" by his critics.

The Changing Emphasis Towards States' Rights

Andrew Jackson supported the authority of the states against the national government, but he drew the line at the concept of nullification. He advocated a strong union made up of sovereign states, and that created some dissonance in his political thinking.

The Supreme Court reflected this shift in thinking in its decision on the Charles River Bridge case in 1837, delivered by Jackson's new chief justice, Roger Taney. He ruled that a state could abrogate a grant of monopoly if that original grant had ceased to be in the best interests of the community. This was clearly a reversal of the Dartmouth College principal of the sanctity of contracts, if the general welfare was involved.

Party Philosophies

The Democrats opposed big government and the requirements of modernization: urbanization and industrialization. Their support came from the working classes, small merchants, and small farmers.

The Whigs promoted government participation in commercial and industrial development, the encouragement of banking and corporations, and a cautious approach to westward expansion. Their support came largely from Northern business and manufacturing interests, and from large Southern planters. Calhoun, Clay, and Webster dominated the Whig party during these early decades of the nineteenth century.

Tocqueville's *Democracy in America*

Alexis de Tocqueville, a French civil servant, traveled to this country in the early 1830s to study the American prison system, which was one of the more innovative systems in the world. His book, *Democracy in America*, published in 1835, was the result of his observations, and it reflected a broad interest in the entire spectrum of the American democratic process and the society in which it had developed. His insightful commentary on the American way of life has proven to be almost prophetic in many respects, and provides the modern reader with an outsider's objective view of what this country was like in the Age of Jackson.

QUESTION

> Why did political parties develop at the same time as the growth of democracy?

EXPLANATION

While political parties developed in the United States almost from the election of George Washington to the presidencies, they became much like their modern equivalents during the Age of Jacksonian Democracy. Parties were able to make appeals to a broad base of people, using emotional appeals and simple, easy to understand messages. The party convention served the important function of communicating these messages to the American people.

Drill 1: The Jacksonian Democracy, 1829–1841

1. In the controversy over the lands belonging by treaty to the "Five Civilized Tribes," the Jackson administration

   (A) destroyed the tribes militarily.

   (B) forced Georgia to restore the lands to the Indians.

   (C) forced the Indians to be removed to the West.

   (D) called upon the Supreme Court to decide the issue.

   (E) divided the lands between Georgia and the Indians.

2. President Andrew Jackson's Specie Circular stipulated that

   (A) inefficient employees of the federal government should be immediately dismissed regardless of their political affiliation.

   (B) federal government deposits should be withdrawn from the second Bank of the United States.

   (C) no federal funds should be spent on internal improvements.

   (D) paper money should not be accepted in payment for federal government lands sold.

   (E) the government would use force if necessary to collect the tariff in South Carolina.

3.   Which of the following opposed rechartering the Second Bank of the United States?

(A)   Nicholas Biddle   (B)   Henry Clay

(C)   Daniel Webster   (D)   Andrew Jackson

(E)   John Marshall

4.   The Nullification Controversy of 1828 to 1833 arose in response to congressional support for

(A)   restrictions on slavery.

(B)   protective tariffs.

(C)   internal improvements.

(D)   the second Bank of the United States.

(E)   popular sovereignty.

5.   The followers of Andrew Jackson established what political party?

(A)   Whig   (B)   Republican

(C)   Democratic   (D)   Federalist

(E)   Populist

6.   Andrew Jackson's Specie Circular sought to

(A)   pay off the government debts.

(B)   slow down speculation in public land.

(C)   replace the Bank of the United States with an independent treasury.

(D)   end the financial panic of 1837.

(E)   establish the free coinage of silver.

7.   Henry Clay's "American System" advocated all of the following EXCEPT

(A)   federal funding for the building of roads.

(B)   a national bank.

(C)   high protective tariffs.

(D)   an independent treasury.

(E)   federal funding for the building of canals.

8.   President Andrew Jackson's Maysville Road Veto dealt with

(A)   federally financed internal improvements.

(B)   foreign policy.

    (C)   the power of the Second Bank of the United States relative to that of other financial institutions.

    (D)   the efficiency and honesty of government employees.

    (E)   the purchase of government land with paper money.

9.   When President Andrew Jackson's enemies spoke of the "Kitchen Cabinet," they were referring to

    (A)   a group of old friends and unofficial advisors of the president.

    (B)   a number of persons of low social standing, including a former cook, who were appointed by Jackson to high cabinet positions.

    (C)   a suggestion as to where Jackson might keep the federal government's money if he removed it from the Bank of the United States.

    (D)   a coterie of Jackson supporters in the U.S. Senate.

    (E)   several state governors who supported Jackson.

10.   The LEAST important issue during the era of "Jacksonian Democracy" was

    (A)   the removal of Indians from southeastern states.

    (B)   federal financing of internal improvements.

    (C)   the right of states to nullify federal laws.

    (D)   the growing trend toward industrialization.

    (E)   the reopening of trade with the British West Indies.

2. ANTEBELLUM CULTURE

The American people in 1840 found themselves living in an era of transition and instability. The society was changing and traditional values were being challenged. The responses to this uncertainty were twofold: a movement toward reform and a rising desire for order and control.

We have a fairly vivid picture of what Americans were like in this period of time, from accounts by hundreds of foreign visitors who came to this country to observe our society-in-the-making. These observers noted a restless population, always on the move, compulsive joiners of associations, committed to progress, hard-working and hard-playing, driven relentlessly by a desire for wealth. They believed in and talked about equality, but the reality was that the system was increasingly creating a class society. Americans seemed to lean toward violence, and mob incidents were common.

The Reform Impulse: Major Sources of Reform

Romanticism held a belief in the innate goodness of man, thus in his improvability. This movement had its roots in turn-of-the-century Europe, and it emphasized the emotions and feelings over rationality. It appeared as a reaction against the excesses of the Enlightenment which had put strong emphasis on reason, to the exclusion of feelings.

There was also a growing need perceived for stability and control over the social order and the forces which were threatening the traditional values.

Both of these major streams of reform activity were centered in the Northeast, especially in New England.

The Flowering of Literature

Northern Writers and Themes

James Fenimore Cooper's *Leatherstocking Tales* emphasized the independence of the individual, and also the importance of a stable social order.

Walt Whitman's *Leaves of Grass* likewise celebrated the importance of individualism.

Henry Wadsworth Longfellow's epic poems *Evangeline* and *Hiawatha* spoke of the value of tradition and the impact of the past on the present.

Herman Melville's classic stories—*Typee, Billy Budd, Moby Dick*—all lashed out at the popular optimism of his day. He believed in the Puritan doctrine of original sin and his characters spoke of the mystery of life.

Historian and nationalist Francis Parkman vividly portrayed the struggle for empire between France and Britain in his *Montcalm and Wolfe*. *The Oregon Trail* described the opening frontier of the Rocky Mountains and beyond.

James Russell Lowell, poet and editor, wrote the *Bigelow Papers* and the *Commemoration Ode*, honoring Civil War casualties of Harvard.

A writer of romances and tales, Nathaniel Hawthorne is best remembered for his criticism of Puritan bigotry in *The Scarlet Letter*.

Southern Writers and Themes

Author of *The Raven, Tamerlane*, and many tales of terror and darkness, Edgar Allen Poe explored the world of the spirit and the emotions.

South Carolina poet William Gilmore Simms changed from a staunch nationalist to a defender of the slave system and the uniqueness of the Southern way of life.

A Georgia storyteller, Augustus Longstreet used vulgar, earthy language and themes to paint the common folk of the South.

The Fine Arts

Artists and Themes

The Hudson River School was a group of landscape painters who portrayed the awesomeness of nature in America, the New World. George Catlin painted the American Indian, whom he saw as a vanishing race. John James Audubon painted the wide array of American birds and animals.

Music and the Theater

The theater was popular, but generally condemned by the church and conservatives as a "vagabond profession." The only original American contribution was the blackface minstrel show.

The Transcendentalists

Major Themes

This movement had its origins in Concord, Massachusetts. The basic objective of these thinkers was to transcend the bounds of the intellect and to strive for emotional understanding, to attain unity with God, without the help of the institutional church, which they saw as reactionary and stifling to self-expression.

Major Writers

Ralph Waldo Emerson, essayist and lecturer, authored "Nature" and "Self-Reliance." Henry David Thoreau, best known for his *Walden*, repudiated the repression of society and preached civil disobedience to protest unjust laws.

QUESTION

How is transcendentalism related to romanticism?

EXPLANATION

Transcendentalism was a specific kind of romanticism. It stressed individualism, self-reliance, and freedom from social and institutional constraints. Like romanticism, transcendentalists believed that human beings were best fulfilled by transcending the intellect and emphasizing one's emotions.

The Utopians

Their Purpose

The cooperative community was their attempt to improve the life of the common man in the face of increasing impersonal industrialism.

The Utopian Communities

Brook Farm, in Massachusetts, was the earliest commune in America, and it was short-lived. Nathaniel Hawthorne was a short-term resident, and his *Blithedale*

Romance was drawn from that experience. This work and *The Scarlet Letter* were both condemnations of the life of social isolation.

New Harmony, Indiana, was founded by Robert Owen, of the New Lanark experiment in Wales, but it failed after two years. He attacked religion, marriage, and the institution of private property, so he encountered resistance from neighboring communities.

Nashola was in the environs of Memphis, Tennessee, established by the free-thinking Englishwoman Frances Wright as a communal haven for freed slaves. Needless to say, her community experiment encountered fierce opposition from her slave-holding neighbors, and it survived only briefly.

Oneida Community in New York was based on free love and open marriages.

The Shakers were directed by Mother Ann Lee. The communities were socialistic experiments which practiced celibacy, sexual equality, and social discipline. The name was given them by onlookers at their community dancing sessions.

Amana Community, in Iowa, was another socialist experiment, with a rigidly ordered society.

The Mormons

The Origins of the Movement

Joseph Smith received the "sacred" writings in New York state in 1830 and organized the Church of Jesus Christ of Latter-day Saints. They were not popular with their neighbors, primarily because of their practice of polygamy, and so were forced to move about, first to Missouri, then to Nauvoo, Illinois. There Smith was killed by a mob, and the community was led to the Great Salt Lake by their new leader, Brigham Young, in one of the great epic migrations to the West.

The Church

The Mormons were the most successful of the communal experiments. They established a highly organized, centrally controlled system, which provided security and order for the faithful. They held a strong belief in human perfectibility, and so were in the mainstream of romantic utopians.

Remaking Society: Organized Reform

Sources of Inspiration

Transcendentalism, as a branch of European romanticism, spawned a great deal of interest in remaking society into more humane forms.

Protestant Revivalism was a powerful force for the improvement of society. Evangelist Charles G. Finney, through his "social gospel," offered salvation to all. A strong sectarian spirit split the Protestant movement into many groups; e.g., the Cumberland Presbyterians. Also evident was a strong anti-Catholic element, which was strengthened by the new waves of immigration from Catholic Ireland and southern Germany after 1830.

Temperance

The American Society for Promotion of Temperance was organized in 1826. It was strongly supported by Protestants, but just as strongly opposed by the new Catholic immigrants.

Public Schools

The motivations for the free school crusade were mixed. Some wanted to provide opportunity for all children to learn the skills for self-fulfillment and success in a republic. Others wanted to use schools as agencies for social control—to Americanize the new immigrant children as well as to Protestantize the Catholics, and to defuse the growing problems of urbanization. The stated purpose of the public schools was to instill social values: thrift, order, discipline, and democracy.

Public apathy and even opposition met the early reformers: Horace Mann, the first secretary of the Massachusetts Board of Education, and Henry Barnard, his counterpart in Connecticut and Rhode Island.

The movement picked up momentum in the 1830s, but was very spotty. Few public schools were available in the West, fewer still for Southern whites, and none at all for Southern blacks.

Higher Education

In 1839, the first state-supported school for women, Troy Female Seminary, was founded in Troy, New York. Oberlin College in Ohio was the nation's first co-educational college. The Perkins School for the Blind in Boston was the first of its kind in the United States.

Asylums for the Mentally Ill

Dorothea Dix led the fight for these institutions, advocating more humane treatment for the mentally incompetent.

Prison Reform

The purpose of the new penitentiaries was not to just punish, but to rehabilitate. The first was built in Auburn, New York, in 1821.

Feminism

The Seneca Falls, New York, meeting in 1848, and its "Declaration of Sentiments and Resolutions," were the beginning of the modern feminist movement. The Grimke sisters, Elizabeth Cady Stanton, and Harriet Beecher Stowe were active in these early days. The movement was linked with that of the abolitionists, but suffered because it was considered to be of secondary importance.

The Abolitionist Movement

The early antislavery movement was benign, advocating only the purchase and colonization of slaves. The American Colonization Society was organized in 1817 and established the colony of Liberia in 1830, but by that time the movement had reached a dead end.

In 1831, William Lloyd Garrison started his paper, *The Liberator*, and began to advocate total and immediate emancipation, thus giving new life to the movement. He founded the New England Anti-slavery Society in 1832 and the American Anti-slavery Society in 1833. Theodore Weld pursued the same goals, but advocated more gradual means.

Frederick Douglass, having escaped from his Maryland owner, became a fiery orator for the movement and published his own newspaper, the *North Star*.

There were frequent outbursts of anti-abolition violence in the 1830s, against the fanaticism of the radicals. Abolitionist editor Elijah Lovejoy was killed by a mob in Illinois.

The movement split into two wings: Garrison's radical followers, and the moderates who favored "moral suasion" and petitions to Congress. In 1840, the Liberty party, the first national antislavery party, fielded a presidential candidate on the platform of "free soil," non-expansion of slavery into the new western territories.

The literary crusade continued with Harriet Beecher Stowe's *Uncle Tom's Cabin* being the most influential among the many books which presented the abolitionist message.

Educating the Public

This was the golden age of oratory. Speechmaking drew huge and patient crowds, and four-hour-long orations were not uncommon, especially at public events like the 4th of July celebrations.

Newspapers and magazines multiplied and were available to everyone.

Women more and more became the market for magazines oriented to their interests. Periodicals like *Godey's Ladies Book* reached mass circulation figures.

Colleges sprang up everywhere, the products of religious sectarianism as well as local pride, which produced "booster colleges" in every new community as population moved west. Many of these were poorly funded and managed; many did not survive longer than a few years.

Informal educational "lyceums" became popular, where the public could gather for cultural enrichment.

Diverging Societies—Life in the North

Although the United States was a political entity, with all of the institutions of government and society shared among the peoples of the various states, there had always been a wide diversity of cultural and economic goals among the various states of the union. As the nineteenth century progressed, that diversity seemed to grow more pronounced, and the collection of states seemed to polarize more into the two sections we call the North and the South, with the expanding West becoming ever more identified with the North.

Population Growth (1790–1860)

The new West was the fastest growing area of the country, with population tending to move along parallels westward. From four million in 1790, population had reached 32 million in 1860 with one-half living in states and territories which did not even exist in Washington's administration.

Natural Increase

Birth rates began to drop after 1800, more rapidly in the cities than in the rural areas. Families who had averaged six children in 1800 only had five in 1860. Some of the reasons were economic: children were becoming liabilities rather than assets. The new "cult of domesticity" reflected a shift in family responsibilities. Father was out of the home working, and the burden of child-rearing fell more heavily on mother. Primitive birth control methods were used, and abortion was becoming common enough that several states passed laws restricting it. One result of all this was an aging population with the median age rising from 16 to 20 years.

Immigration

The influx of immigrants had slowed during the conflicts with France and England, but the flow increased between 1815 and 1837, when the economic downturn again sharply reduced their numbers. Thus, the overall rise in population during these years was due more to incoming foreigners than to natural increase. Most of the newcomers were from Britain, Germany, and southern Ireland. The Germans usually fared best, since they brought more money and more skills. Discrimination was common in the job market, primarily directed against the Catholics. "Irish Need Not Apply" signs were common. However, the persistent labor shortage prevented the natives from totally excluding the foreign elements. These newcomers huddled in ethnic neighborhoods in the cities, or those who could moved west to try their hand at farming.

Growth of the Cities

In 1790 five percent of the U.S. population lived in cities of 2,500 or more. By 1860, that figure had risen to 25 percent. This rapid urbanization created an array of problems.

Problems of Urbanization

The rapid growth in urban areas was not matched by the growth of services. Clean water, trash removal, housing, and public transportation all lagged behind, and the wealthy got them first. Bad water and poor sanitation produced poor health, and epidemics of typhoid fever, typhus, and cholera were common. Police and fire protection were usually inadequate, and the development of professional forces was resisted because of the cost and the potential for political patronage and corruption.

Social Unrest

Rapid growth helped to produce a wave of violence in the cities. In New York City in 1834, the Democrats fought the Whigs with such vigor that the state militia had to be called in. New York and Philadelphia witnessed race riots in the mid-1830s, and a New York mob attacked a Catholic convent in 1834. In the 1830s, 115 major incidents of mob violence were recorded. Street crime was common in all the major cities.

The Role of Minorities

Women

Women were treated as minors before the law. In most states the woman's property became her husband's with marriage. Political activity was limited to the formation of associations in support of various pious causes, such as abolition, and religious and benevolent activity. Professional employment was largely limited to school teaching; that occupation became dominated by women. The women's rights movement focused on social and legal discrimination, and women like Lucretia Mott and Sojourner Truth became well-known figures on the speakers' circuit.

Blacks

By 1850, 200,000 free blacks lived in the North and West. Their lives were restricted everywhere by prejudice, and "Jim Crow" laws separated the races. Black citizens organized separate churches and fraternal orders. The African Methodist Episcopal Church, for example, had been organized in 1794 in Philadelphia and flourished in the major Northern cities. Black Masonic and Odd Fellows lodges were likewise established. The economic security of the free blacks was constantly threatened by the newly-arrived immigrants, who were willing to work at the least desirable jobs for less wages. Racial violence was a daily threat.

The Growth of Industry

By 1850, the value of industrial output had surpassed that of agricultural production. The Northeastern states led the way in this movement. Over one-half of the manufacturing establishments were located there, and most of the larger enterprises. Seventy percent of the workers who were employed in manufacturing lived in New England and the middle states, and the Northeast produced more than two-thirds of the manufactured goods.

Inventions and Technology

The level of technology used in American manufacturing already exceeded that of European industry. Eli Whitney's applications of interchangeable parts were being introduced into a wide variety of manufacturing processes. Coal was replacing water as the major source of industrial power. Machine tools were reaching a high level of sophistication. Much of this progress was due to the contributions of America's inventors. Between 1830 and 1850 the number of patents issued for industrial inventions almost doubled. Charles Goodyear's process of vulcanizing rubber was put to 500 different uses and formed the basis for an entire new industry. Elias Howe's sewing machine was to revolutionize the clothing industry. The mass production of iron, with its new techniques and uses, created a new array of businesses, of which the new railroad industry was the largest consumer. Samuel F.B. Morse's new electric telegraph was first used in 1840 to transmit business news and information.

The Rise of Unions

The growth of the factory system was accompanied by the growth of the corporate form of business ownership, which in turn further separated the owners from the workers. One result was the organization of worker groups to fight for benefits, an early example of which was the 10-hour day. In 1835, Boston construction craftsmen struck for seven months to win a 10-hour work day, and in Paterson, New Jersey, textile workers became the first factory workers to strike for shorter hours. The federal government's introduction of the 10-hour day for federal projects, in 1840, helped to speed the acceptance of this goal. The influx of immigrants who were willing to work for low wages helped to spur the drive for unions, and in turn their numbers helped to weaken the bargaining position of union members.

The Revolution in Agriculture

Farm and industry reinforced each other and developed simultaneously. As more urban workers became dependent on food grown by others, the potential profits of farming increased. Many of the technological developments and inventions were applied to farm machinery, which in turn enabled farmers to produce more food more cheaply for the urban workers. As in industry, specialization and mechanization became the rule in agriculture, particularly on the newly opening western prairies of Illinois, Iowa, and Kansas.

Inventions and Technology

Large-scale farming on the prairies spurred critical inventions. McCormick's mechanical reaper, patented in 1834, enabled a crew of six men to harvest in one day as much wheat as 15 men could using older methods. John Deere's steel plow, patented in 1837, provided a more durable tool to break the heavy prairie sod. Jerome Case's threshing machine multiplied the bushels of grain that could be separated from the stalk in a day's time.

The New Market Economy

These developments not only made large-scale production possible, they also shifted the major emphasis from corn to small grain production, and made farming for the international market feasible, which in turn made the Western farmer dependent on economic forces over which he had no control. This dependence produced the rising demand for government provision of free land and the agricultural colleges which later were provided by the Homestead and Morrill bills during the Civil War.

In the East, the trend was toward truck farming for the nearby burgeoning urban areas, and the production of milk, fruits, and berries. Here, as in the West, there was much interest in innovative practices which could increase production efficiency and profits.

The Revolution in Commerce

Before the coming of the railroad, coastal sailing ships practically monopolized domestic trade. The canal construction boom of the 1830s had taken commercial traffic from the river systems, but by 1840 the railroad had begun to emerge as the carrier of the future. Pennsylvania and New York State contained most of the 3,328 miles of track, but the rail system was rapidly expanding across the northern tier of states, tying the industrializing East to the expanding, agricultural West.

Everyday Life in the North

Between 1800 and 1860 output of goods and services increased twelve-fold and the purchasing power of the average worker doubled. The household labor system was breaking down, and the number of wage-earners exceeded for the first time the number of independent, self-employed Americans. Even so, everyday living was still quite primitive. Most people bathed only infrequently, washed clothes and dishes even less. Housing was primitive for most, consisting of one- or two-room cabins, heated by open fireplaces, with water carried in from springs or public faucets. For the working man, rural or urban, life was hard.

Diverging Societies—Life in the South

The Southern states experienced dramatic growth in the second quarter of the nineteenth century. The economy grew more productive and more prosperous, but still the section called the South was basically agrarian, with few important cities and scattered industry. The plantation system, with its cash crop production driven by the use of slave labor, remained the dominant institution. In the words of one historian, "The South grew, but it did not develop." And so the South grew more unlike the North, and it became more defensive of its distinctive way of life.

The Cotton Kingdom

The most important economic phenomenon of the early decades of the nineteenth century was the shift in population and production from the old "upper South" of Virginia and the Carolinas to the "lower South" of the newly opened Gulf states of Alabama, Mississippi, and Louisiana. This shift was the direct result of the increasing importance of cotton. In the older Atlantic states, tobacco retained its importance, but had shifted westward to the Piedmont, and was replaced in the east by food grains. The southern Atlantic coast continued to produce rice, and southern Louisiana and east Texas retained their emphasis on sugar cane. But the rich black soil of the new Gulf states proved ideal for the production of short-staple cotton, especially after the invention of the "gin," and cotton became the center of the Southern economy. Nearly three million bales were being produced annually by 1850.

By 1860, cotton was to account for two-thirds of the value of U.S. exports. In the words of a Southern legislator of that era, "Cotton is King!"

Classes in the South

Although the large plantation with its white-columned mansion and its aristocratic owners is frequently seen as typical of Southern life, the truth is quite different.

The Planter Class

Owners of large farms who also owned 50 or more slaves actually formed a small minority of the Southern population. Three-fourths of Southern whites owned no slaves at all, almost half of slave-owning families owned fewer than six, and 12 percent owned 20 or more. But this minority of large slaveowners exercised political and economic power far beyond what their numbers would indicate. They became a class to which all others paid deference, and they dominated the political and social life of their region.

The Yeoman Farmers

The largest group of Southern whites were the independent small farmers who worked their land with their family, sometimes side by side with one or two slaves, to produce their own food, with sometimes enough surplus to sell for a little extra cash. These simple folk predominated in the upland South and constituted a sizable element even in the lower cotton-producing states. Their major crop was corn, and indeed the South's corn crop was more valuable than its cotton, but the corn was used at home for dinner tables and for animal feed, and so ranked behind cotton as an item of export. These people were generally poorer than their Northern counterparts.

The Poor Whites

Perhaps a half-million white Southerners lived on the edge of the agrarian economy, in varying degrees of poverty. These "crackers," or "sandhillers," occupied the barren soils of the red hills or sandy bottoms, and they lived in squalor worse than the slaves. They formed a true underclass.

The Institution of Slavery

As the necessary concomitant of this expanding plantation system, the "Peculiar Institution" of black slavery fastened itself upon the Southern people, even as it isolated them from the rest of the world.

Slavery as a Labor System

The utilization of slave labor varied according to the region and the size of the growing unit. The large plantations growing cotton, sugar, or tobacco used the gang system, in which white overseers directed black drivers, who supervised large groups of workers in the fields, all performing the same operation. In the culture of rice, and on the smaller farms, slaves·were assigned specific tasks, and when those tasks were finished, the worker had the remainder of the day to himself.

House servants usually were considered the most favored, since they were spared the hardest physical labor and enjoyed the most intimate relationship with the owner's family. This could be considered a drawback, since they were frequently deprived of the social communion of the other slaves, enjoyed less privacy, and were more likely to suffer the direct wrath of a dissatisfied mistress.

Urban Slavery

A sizable number of slaves worked in the towns, serving as factory hands, domestics, artisans, and construction workers. They lived fairly independent lives and indeed a good number purchased their freedom with their savings, or quietly crossed the color line and disappeared into the general population. As the nineteenth century progressed, these people were increasingly seen as a bad model and a threat to the institution, and so urban slavery practically disappeared.

The Slave Trade

The most significant demographic shift in these decades was the movement of blacks from the Old South to the new Southwest. Traders shipped servants by the thousands to the newly opened cotton lands of the Gulf states. A prime field hand fetched an average price of $800, as high as $1,500 in peak years. Families were frequently split apart by this miserable traffic. Planters freely engaged in this trade, but assigned very low status to the traders who carried it out.

Although the importation of slaves from abroad had been outlawed by Congress since 1808, they continued to be smuggled in until the 1850s. The import ban kept the price up and encouraged the continuation of the internal trade.

Slaves' Reaction to Slavery

Blacks in bondage suffered varying degrees of repression and deprivation. The harsh slave codes were comprehensive in their restrictions on individual freedom, but they were unevenly applied, and so there was considerable variety in the severity of life. The typical slave probably received a rough but adequate diet and enjoyed crude but sufficient housing and clothing.

But the loss of freedom and the injustice of the system produced a variety of responses. Many "soldiered" on the job and refused to work hard, or they found ways to sabotage the machinery or the crops. There was an underground system of ridicule toward the masters which was nurtured, as reflected in such oral literature as the "Brer Rabbit" tales.

Violent reaction to repression was not uncommon. Gabriel Prosser in Richmond (1800), Denmark Vesey in Charleston (1822), and Nat Turner in coastal Virginia (1831) all plotted or led uprisings of blacks against their white masters. Rumors of such uprisings kept whites in a state of constant apprehension.

The ultimate rebellion was to simply leave, and many tried to run away, some successfully. Especially from the states bordering the North, an ever increasing number of slaves fled to freedom, many with the aid of the "underground railroad" and smugglers such as Harriet Tubman, who led over 300 of her family and friends to freedom after she herself had escaped.

Most of those in bondage, however, were forced to simply adapt, and they did. A rich culture was developed within the confines of the system, and included distinctive patterns of language, music, and religion. Kinship ties were probably strengthened in the face of the onslaughts of sale and separation of family members. In the face of incredible odds, the slaves developed a distinctive network of tradition and interdependence, and they survived.

Commerce and Industry

The lack of manufacturing and business development has frequently been blamed for the South's losing its bid for independence in 1861–1865. Actually, the South was highly industrialized for its day, and compared favorably with most European nations in the development of manufacturing capacity. Obviously, it trailed far behind the North, so much so that when war erupted in 1861, the Northern states owned 81 percent of the factory capacity in the United States.

Manufacturing

The Southern states saw considerable development in the 1820s and 1830s in textiles and iron production and in flour milling. Richmond's Tredegar Iron Works compared favorably with the best in the North. Montgomery Bell's forges in Tennessee produced a good proportion of the ironware used in the upper South. Even so, most of the goods manufactured in these plants were for plantation consumption rather than for export, and they never exceeded two percent of the value of the cotton crop.

Commercial Activity

The businessmen of the South worked primarily with the needs and products of the plantation, and the factors of New Orleans and Charleston had to serve as bankers and insurance brokers as well as the agents for the planters. An organized network of commerce never developed in the South, even though the planters themselves must be recognized as businessmen, since they operated large, complex staple-producing units.

Voices for Change

There were those who saw their native South sinking ever more into the position of dependency upon Northern bankers and businessmen, and they cried out for reform. James B. D. DeBow's *Review* advocated commercial development and agricultural diversification, but his cries largely fell on deaf ears.

Why were Southerners so wedded to the plantation system, in the face of much evidence that it was retarding development? Certainly one reason is that cotton was profitable. Over the long run, capital return on plantation agriculture was at least as good as on Northern industrial capital. Even though skilled slaves abounded and could have manned factories, they were more profitable in the field.

Since most of the planter's capital was tied up in land and slaves, there was little left to invest in commerce or manufacturing. Most important, perhaps, was the value system of the Southern people, who put great store in traditional rural ideals: chivalry, leisure, genteel elegance. Even the yeoman farmer held these values, and hoped some day to attain to the position the planters held.

QUESTION

How did the antebellum North and South differ in terms of industrial development?

EXPLANATION

Both regions had developed industry in the first half of the nineteenth century. However, the South only produced manufactured goods for consumption, not export. The economy as a whole was still dominated by agriculture. In the North, industry was coming to dominate the economy. Most technological innovations in manufacturing were being developed in the North. The North was also able to export manufactured goods.

Life in the Southern States

The Role of Women

The position of the Southern woman was similar in many ways to her Northern counterpart, but also very different. They had fewer opportunities for anything but home life. The middle-class wife was heavily involved in the operation of the farm, and served as supervisor and nurse for the servants as well as manager of the household, while the upper-class women served merely as ornaments. Education was rare and centered on the "domestic arts." High birth and death rates took their toll on childbearing women, and many men outlived several wives. The half-breed slave children were constant reminders of the planters' dalliances and produced constant tension and frustration among plantation wives.

Education

Schooling beyond literacy training was available only to the sons of the well-to-do. Academies and colleges abounded, but not for the working classes. And what public schools there were, were usually inferior and ill-supported. By 1860, one-half of all the illiterates in the United States lived in the South.

Daily Life in the South

The accounts of travelers in the Southern states provide us with vivid pictures of living conditions on the average homestead. Housing was primitive, one- or two-room cabins being the rule. Corn, sweet potatoes, and pork formed the staples of the Southern diet, and health problems reflected the resulting vitamin deficiencies. Rickets and pellagra were common ailments.

Although the prevalence of violence has probably been overstated, it certainly existed, and the duel remained an accepted avenue for settling differences well into the nineteenth century.

Southern Response to the Antislavery Movement

As the crusade for abolition intensified in the North, the South assumed an ever more defensive position. Biblical texts were used to justify the enslavement of an "inferior race." Scientific arguments were advanced to prove the inherent inferiority of the black African. Southern postal authorities refused to deliver any mail that contained information antagonistic to the slave system. Any kind of dissent was brutally suppressed, and the South became more and more a closed society. Literature and scholarship shriveled, and creative writers like Edgar Allen

Poe and William Gilmore Simms became the rare exception.

The last serious Southern debate over the institution of slavery took place in the Virginia legislature in 1832, in the aftermath of Nat Turner's revolt. That discussion squelched any move toward emancipation. In 1836, Southern members of the U.S. House of Representatives pushed through the infamous "gag rule," which forbade any discussion on the question of slavery on the floor of the House. That rule remained in effect until 1844.

The most elaborate product of this ferment was John C. Calhoun's theory of the "concurrent majority," in which states in the minority would form an alliance to nullify laws passed by the majority, thereby placing limits on majority rule. This was intended to curb the power of the growing North.

Beginning in 1837, regular conventions were held across the South to discuss ways to escape Northern economic and political hegemony. As the decade of the 1840s opened, the two sections were becoming more and more estranged, and the channels of compromise were becoming more and more poisoned by the emotional responses to black slavery. The development which contributed most to keeping the sore festering was westward expansion.

Drill 2: Antebellum Culture

1. Which of the following best characterizes Southern society before the Civil War?

    (A) Half of the slave owners owned five or fewer slaves.

    (B) Most white families owned slaves.

    (C) Most slave owners owned several hundred slaves.

    (D) The percentage of slave owners was consistent throughout the South.

    (E) Most slave owners lived in urban areas.

2. The "minstrel shows" of the early and mid-nineteenth century featured

    (A) readings of serious poetry of a distinctly American nature.

    (B) operatic performances in the English language and focusing on American themes.

    (C) the exhibition of collections of rare and curious objects from exotic parts of the world.

    (D) melodramas with plots resembling those of the sentimental novels then popular.

    (E) white men, with makeup-blackened faces, singing, dancing, and performing humorous skits.

3. What do Gabriel Prosser, Denmark Vesey, and Nat Tumer have in common?

   (A) They were active in the Second Great Awakening.

   (B) They were early railroad tycoons.

   (C) They organized slave rebellions.

   (D) They helped form the Whig party.

   (E) They were leading New England abolitionists.

4. American factory workers of the pre-Civil War period

   (A) formed powerful unions.

   (B) worked long hours.

   (C) had excellent working conditions.

   (D) included few children.

   (E) were attracted to socialism.

5. Beginning in the 1830s, William Lloyd Garrison called for

   (A) colonization of slaves.

   (B) immediate emancipation of slaves.

   (C) free soil.

   (D) step-by-step emancipation of slaves.

   (E) popular sovereignty.

6. Which of the following was NOT a major writer of the pre-Civil War period?

   (A) Ralph Waldo Emerson   (B) William Dean Howells

   (C) Nathaniel Hawthorne   (D) Herman Melville

   (E) Washington Irving

7. Which of the following was NOT a women's rights reformer?

   (A) Mother Ann Lee   (B) Lucretia Mott

   (C) Elizabeth Cady Stanton   (D) Susan B. Anthony

   (E) Margaret Fuller

8. What became the South's major cash crop for sale in the international market in the 19th century?

   (A) Tobacco   (B) Cotton

(C) Corn   (D) Rice

(E) Indigo

9. The "spoils system" refers to

(A) the practice of supporting government projects for one's own congressional district.

(B) the practice of appointing relatives to political office.

(C) the practice of giving government jobs to one's political supporters.

(D) the practice of turning to unofficial advisors for council regarding official actions.

(E) the practice of turning to political action committees for campaign funds.

10. Dorothea Dix was associated with which of the following reforms?

(A) Education   (B) Temperance

(C) Care of the mentally ill   (D) Health

(E) Anti-slavery

3. WESTWARD EXPANSION

Although the term "Manifest Destiny" was not actually coined until 1844, the belief that the American nation was destined to eventually expand all the way to the Pacific Ocean, and to possibly embrace Canada to the north, and Mexico to the south, had been voiced for years by many who believed that American liberty and ideals should be shared with everyone possible, by force if necessary. The rising sense of nationalism which followed the War of 1812 was fed by the rapidly expanding population, the reform impulse of the 1830s, and the desire to acquire new markets and resources for the burgeoning economy of "Young America."

Louisiana and the Far West Fur Trade

The Lewis and Clark expedition had scarcely filed its reports before a variety of adventurous entrepreneurs began to penetrate the newly acquired territory and the lands beyond. "Mountain men" like Jim Bridges trapped the Rocky Mountain streams and the headwaters of the Missouri River system for the greatly prized beaver pelts, while explorers like Jedediah Smith mapped the vast territory which stretched from the Rockies to the Sierra Nevada range and on into California. John Jacob Astor established a fur post at the mouth of the Columbia River which he named Astoria and challenged the British claim to the northwest. Though he was forced to sell out his establishment to the British, he lobbied Congress to pass trade restrictions against British furs, and eventually became the first American millionaire from the profits of the American Fur Company. The growing trade with the Orient in furs and other specialty goods was sharpening the desire of many businessmen for American ports on the Pacific coast.

The Oregon Country

The Adams-Onis Treaty of 1819 had set the northern boundary of Spanish possessions near the present northern border of California. The territory north of that line and west of the vague boundaries of the Louisiana Territory had been claimed over the years by Spain, England, Russia, France, and the United States. By the 1820s, all these claims had been yielded to Britain and the United States. The Hudson's Bay Company had established a fur trading station at Fort Vancouver and claimed control south to the Columbia River. The United States claimed all the way north to the 54°40' parallel. Unable to settle the dispute, they had agreed on a joint occupation of the disputed land.

In the 1830s American missionaries followed the traders and trappers to the Oregon country, and began to publicize the richness and beauty of the land, sending back official reports on their work, which were published in the new inexpensive "penny press" papers. Everyone read these reports, and the result was the "Oregon Fever" of the 1840s, as thousands of settlers trekked across the Great Plains and the Rocky Mountains to settle the new Shangri-La.

The Texas Question (1836–1845)

Texas had been a state in the Republic of Mexico since 1822, following the Mexican revolution against Spanish control. The United States had offered to buy the territory at the time, since it had renounced its claim to the area in the Adams-Onis Treaty of 1819. The new Mexican government indignantly refused to sell, but immediately began to invite immigration from the north by offering land grants to Stephen Austin and other Americans. They needed to increase the population of the area and to produce revenue for the infant government. The Americans responded in great numbers, and by 1835 approximately 35,000 "gringos" were homesteading on Texas land.

The Mexican officials saw their power base eroding as the foreigners flooded in, and so they moved to tighten control, through restrictions on new immigration and through tax increases. The Texans responded in 1836 by proclaiming independence and establishing a new republic. The ensuing war was short-lived. The Mexican dictator, Santa Anna, advanced north and annihilated the Texan garrisons at the Alamo and at Goliad. On April 23, 1836, Sam Houston defeated him at San Jacinto, and the Mexicans were forced to let Texas go its way.

Houston immediately asked the American government for recognition and annexation, but President Andrew Jackson feared the revival of the slavery issue since the new state would come in on the slave-holding side of the political balance, and he also feared war with Mexico, so he did nothing. When Van Buren followed suit, the new republic sought foreign recognition and support, which the European nations eagerly provided, hoping thereby to create a counterbalance to rising American power and influence in the Southwest. France and England both quickly concluded trade agreements with the Texans.

QUESTION

Why did the U.S. wait ten years before annexing Texas?

EXPLANATION

There were two reasons why the United States was reluctant to annex the newly independent Republic of Texas. The first had to do with slavery. Texas would be admitted as a slave state, and thus upset the balance of the Senate. The second was that Mexico threatened to go to war with the U.S. if it annexed Texas.

New Mexico and California

The district of New Mexico had, like Texas, encouraged American immigration, and for the same reasons. Soon that state was more American than Mexican. The Santa Fe Trail—from Independence, Missouri, to the town of Santa Fe—created a prosperous trade in mules, gold and silver, and furs which moved north in exchange for manufactured goods which went south. American settlements sprang up all along the route.

Though the Mexican officials in California had not encouraged it, American immigration nevertheless had been substantial. First traders and whaling crews, then merchants, arrived to set up stores and developed a brisk trade. As the decade of the 1830s passed, the number of newcomers increased. Since the Missouri Compromise had established the northern limits for slavery at the 36°30' parallel, most of this Mexican territory lay in the potential slave-holding domain, and many of the settlers had carried their bondsmen with them.

Manifest Destiny and Sectional Stress

The question of expansion was universally discussed. Although the strongest sentiment was found in the North and West, the South had its own ambitions, and they usually involved the extension of their "peculiar institution."

The Democrats generally favored the use of force, if necessary, to extend American borders. The Whigs favored more peaceful means, through diplomacy. Some Whigs, like Henry Clay, feared expansion under any circumstances, because of its potential for aggravating the slavery issue.

Clay was closest to the truth. As the decade of the 1840s opened, the questions of Texas, California, and the New Mexican territory were increasingly prominent, and the sectional tension which they produced was destined to light the fires of civil war.

Tyler, Polk, and Continued Westward Expansion

Tyler and the Whigs

When William Henry Harrison became president, he immediately began to rely on Whig leader Henry Clay for advice and direction, just as Clay had planned and expected he would. He appointed to his cabinet those whom Clay suggested, and at Clay's behest he called a special session of Congress to vote the Whig legislative program into action. To the Whigs' dismay, Harrison died of pneumonia just one month into his term, to be replaced by Vice President John Tyler.

A states' rights Southerner and a strict constitutionalist who had been placed on the Whig ticket to draw Southern votes, Tyler rejected the entire Whig program of a national bank, high protective tariffs, and federally funded internal improvements (roads, canals, etc.). Clay stubbornly determined to push the program through anyway. In the resulting legislative confrontations, Tyler vetoed a number of Whig-sponsored bills.

The Whigs were furious. Every cabinet member but one resigned in protest. Tyler was officially expelled from the party and made the target of the first serious impeachment attempt. (It failed.) In opposition to Tyler, over the next few years, the Whigs, under the leadership of Clay, transformed themselves from a loose grouping of diverse factions to a coherent political party with an elaborate organization.

One piece of important legislation that did get passed during Tyler's administration was the Preemption Act (1841), allowing settlers who had squatted on unsurveyed federal lands first chance to buy the land (up to 160 acres at low prices) once it was put on the market.

The Webster-Ashburton Treaty

The member of Tyler's cabinet who did not immediately resign in protest was Secretary of State Daniel Webster. He stayed on to negotiate the Webster-Ashburton Treaty with Great Britain.

There were at this time several causes of tension between the U.S. and Great Britain:

1) The Canada-Maine boundary in the area of the Aroostook Valley was disputed. British efforts to build a military road through the disputed area led to reaction by Maine militia in a bloodless confrontation known as the "Aroostook War" (1838).
2) The Caroline Affair (1837) involved an American ship, the *Caroline*, that had been carrying supplies to Canadian rebels. It was burned by Canadian loyalists who crossed the U.S. border in order to do so.
3) In the Creole Incident, Britain declined to return escaped slaves who had taken over a U.S. merchant ship, the *Creole*, and sailed to the British-owned Bahamas.

4) British naval vessels, patrolling the African coast to suppress slave-smuggling, sometimes stopped and searched American ships.

The Webster-Ashburton Treaty (1842) dealt with these problems in a spirit of mutual concession and forbearance:

1) Conflicting claims along the Canada-Maine boundary were compromised.
2) The British expressed regret for the destruction of the *Caroline*.
3) The British promised to avoid "officious interference" in freeing slaves in cases such as that of the *Creole*.
4) Both countries agreed to cooperate in patrolling the African coast to prevent slave-smuggling.

The Webster-Ashburton Treaty was also important in that it helped create an atmosphere of compromise and forbearance in U.S.-British relations.

After negotiating the treaty, Webster too resigned from Tyler's cabinet.

The Texas Issue

Rejected by the Whigs and without ties to the Democrats, Tyler was a politician without a party but not without ambitions. Hoping to gather a political following of his own, he sought an issue with powerful appeal and believed he had found it in the question of Texas annexation.

The Republic of Texas had gained its independence from Mexico in 1836 and, since most of its settlers had come from the U.S., immediately sought admission as a state. It was rejected because antislavery forces in Congress resented the presence of slavery in Texas and because Mexico threatened war should the U.S. annex Texas.

To excite American jealousy and thus hasten annexation, Texas President Sam Houston made much show of negotiating for closer relations with Great Britain. Southerners feared that Britain, which opposed slavery, might bring about its abolition in Texas and then use Texas as a base from which to undermine slavery in the American South. Other Americans were disturbed at the possibility of a British presence in Texas because of the obstacle it would present to what many Americans were coming to believe—and what New York journalist John L. O'Sullivan would soon express—as America's "manifest destiny to overspread the continent."

Tyler's new secretary of state, John C. Calhoun, negotiated an annexation treaty with Texas. Calhoun's identification with extreme pro-slavery forces and his insertion in the treaty of pro-slavery statements brought the treaty's rejection by the Senate (1844). Nevertheless, the Texas issue had been injected into national politics and could not be made to go away.

The Election of 1844

Democratic front-runner Martin Van Buren and Whig front-runner Henry Clay agreed privately that neither would endorse Texas annexation and that it would not become a campaign issue, but expansionists at the Democratic convention succeeded in dumping Van Buren in favor of James K. Polk. Polk, called "Young Hickory" by his supporters, was a staunch Jacksonian who opposed protective tariffs and a national bank but, most important, favored territorial expansion, including not only annexation of Texas but also occupation of all the Oregon country (up to latitude 54°40') hitherto jointly occupied by the U.S. and Britain. The latter claim was expressed in his campaign slogan, "Fifty-four forty or fight."

Tyler, despite his introduction of the issue that was to decide that year's presidential campaign, was unable to build a party of his own and withdrew from the race.

The Whigs nominated Clay, who continued to oppose Texas annexation but, sensing the mood of the country was against him, began to equivocate. His wavering cost him votes among those Northerners who were extremely sensitive to the issue of slavery and believed that the settlement, independence, and proposed annexation of Texas was a gigantic plot to add slave states to the Union. Some of these voters shifted to the Liberty party.

The antislavery Liberty party nominated James G. Birney. Apparently, because of Clay's wavering on the Texas issue, Birney was able to take enough votes away from Clay in New York to give that state, and thus the election, to Polk.

Tyler, as a lame-duck president, made one more attempt to achieve Texas annexation before leaving office. By means of a joint resolution, which unlike a treaty required only a simple majority rather than a two-thirds vote, he was successful in getting the measure through Congress. Texas was finally admitted to the Union (1845).

Polk as President

Though a relatively unknown "dark horse" at the time of his nomination for the presidency, Polk had considerable political experience within his home state of Tennessee and was an adept politician. He turned out to be a skillful and effective president.

As a good Jacksonian, Polk favored a low, revenue-only tariff rather than a high, protective tariff. This he obtained in the Walker Tariff (1846). He also opposed a national debt and a national bank and re-established Van Buren's Independent Sub-Treasury system, which then remained in effect until 1920.

The Settlement of Oregon

A major issue in the election campaign of 1844, Oregon at this time comprised all the land bounded on the east by the Rockies, the west by the Pacific, the south by latitude 42°, and the north by the boundary of Russian-held Alaska at 54°40'. Oregon had been visited by Lewis and Clark and in later years by American fur traders and especially missionaries such as Jason Lee and Marcus Whitman. Their reports sparked interest in Oregon's favorable soil and climate.

During the first half of the 1840s, some 6,000 Americans had taken the 2,000-mile, six-month journey on the Oregon Trail, from Independence, Missouri, across the plains along the Platte River, through the Rockies at South Pass, and down the Snake River to their new homesteads. Most of them settled in the Willamette Valley, south of the Columbia River.

The area had been under the joint occupation of the U.S. and Great Britain since 1818, but Democrats in the election of 1844 had called for U.S. ownership of all of Oregon. Though this stand had helped him win the election, Polk had little desire to fight the British for land he considered unsuitable for agriculture and unavailable for slavery, which he favored. This was all the more so since trouble seemed to be brewing with Mexico over territory Polk considered far more desirable.

The British, for their part, hoped to obtain the area north of the Columbia River, including the natural harbor of Puget Sound (one of only three on the Pacific coast), with its adjoining Strait of Juan de Fuca.

By the terms of the Oregon Treaty (1846), a compromise solution was reached. The current U.S.-Canada boundary east of the Rockies (49°) was extended westward to the Pacific, thus securing Puget Sound and shared use of the Strait of Juan de Fuca for the U.S. Some northern Democrats were angered and felt betrayed by Polk's failure to insist on all of Oregon, but the Senate readily accepted the treaty.

The Mormon Migration

Aside from the thousands of Americans who streamed west on the Oregon Trail during the early 1840s and the smaller number who migrated to what was then Mexican-held California, another large group of Americans moved west but to a different destination and for different reasons. These were the Mormons.

Members of a unique religion founded by Joseph Smith at Palmyra, New York, in the 1820s, Mormons, often in trouble with their neighbors, had been forced to migrate to Kirtland, Ohio; Clay County, Missouri; and finally, Nauvoo, Illinois. There, on the banks of the Mississippi River, they built the largest city in the state, had their own militia, and were a political force to be reckoned with.

In 1844 Mormon dissidents published a newspaper critical of church leader Smith and his newly announced doctrine of polygamy. Smith had their printing press destroyed. Arrested by Illinois authorities, Smith and his brother were confined to a jail in Carthage, Illinois, but later killed by a crowd of hostile non-Mormons who forced their way into the jail.

The Mormons then decided to migrate to the Far West, preferably someplace outside U.S. jurisdiction. Their decision to leave was hastened by pressure from their non-Mormon neighbors, among whom anti-Mormon feeling ran high as a response to polygamy and the Mormons' monolithic social and political structure.

Under the leadership of new church leader Brigham Young some 85,000 Mormons trekked overland in 1846 to settle near the Great Salt Lake in what is now Utah (but was then owned by Mexico). Young founded the Mormon republic of Deseret and openly preached (and practiced) polygamy.

After Deseret's annexation by the U.S. as part of the Mexican Cession, Young was made territorial governor of Utah. Nevertheless, friction developed with the federal government. By 1857 public outrage over polygamy prompted then President James Buchanan to replace Young with a non-Mormon governor. Threats of Mormon defiance led Buchanan to send 2,500 army troops to compel Mormon obedience to federal law. Young responded by calling out the Mormon militia and blocking the passes through which the army would have to advance. This standoff, known as the "Mormon War," was resolved in 1858, with the Mormons accepting the new governor and Buchanan issuing a general pardon.

The Coming of War with Mexico

For some time American interest had been growing in the far western lands then held by Mexico:

1) Since the 1820s Americans had been trading with Santa Fe and other Mexican settlements along the Rio Grande by means of the Santa Fe Trail. Though not extensive enough to be of economic importance, the trade aroused further American interest in the area.
2) Also, since the 1820s, American "mountain men," trappers who sought beaver pelts in the streams of the Rockies, had explored the mountains of the Far West, opening new trails and discovering fertile lands. They later served as guides for settlers moving west.
3) At the same time, whaling ships and other American vessels had carried on a thriving trade with the Mexican settlements on the coast of California.
4) Beginning in 1841, American settlers came overland to California by means of the California Trail, a branch from the Oregon Trail that turned southwest in the Rockies and crossed Nevada along the Humbolt River. By 1846 several hundred Americans lived in California.

The steady flow of American pioneers into Mexican-held areas of the Far West led to conflicting territorial desires and was thus an underlying cause of the Mexican War. Several more immediate causes existed:

1) Mexico's ineffective government was unable to protect the lives and property of American citizens in Mexico during the country's frequent and recurring revolutions and repeatedly declined to pay American claims for damages even when such claims were supported by the findings of mutually agreed upon arbitration.
2) Mexico had not reconciled itself to the loss of Texas and considered its annexation by the U.S. a hostile act.
3) The southern boundary of Texas was disputed. Whereas first the independent Republic of Texas and now the U.S. claimed the Rio Grande as

the boundary, Mexico claimed the Nueces River, 130 miles farther north, which had been the boundary of the province of Texas when it had been part of Mexico.

4) Mexican suspicions had been aroused regarding U.S. designs on California when, in 1842, a U.S. naval force under Commodore Thomas Catsby Jones had seized the province in the mistaken belief that war had broken out between the U.S. and Mexico. When the mistake was discovered, the province was returned and apologies made.

5) Mexican politicians had so inflamed the Mexican people against the U.S. that no Mexican leader could afford to take the risk of appearing to make concessions to the U.S. for fear of being overthrown.

Though Mexico broke diplomatic relations with the U.S. immediately upon Texas' admission to the Union, there still seemed to be some hope of a peaceful settlement. In the fall of 1845 Polk sent John Slidell to Mexico City with a proposal for a peaceful settlement of the differences between the two countries. Slidell was empowered to cancel the damage claims and pay $5,000,000 for the disputed land in southern Texas. He was also authorized to offer $25,000,000 for California and $5,000,000 for other Mexican territory in the Far West. Polk was especially anxious to obtain California because he feared the British would snatch it from Mexico's extremely weak grasp.

Nothing came of these attempts at negotiation. Racked by coup and countercoup, the Mexican government refused even to receive Slidell.

Polk thereupon sent U.S. troops into the disputed territory in southern Texas. A force under General Zachary Taylor (who was nicknamed "Old Rough and Ready") took up a position just north of the Rio Grande. Eight days later, April 5, 1846, Mexican troops attacked an American patrol. When news of the clash reached Washington, Polk sought and received from Congress a declaration of war against Mexico, May 13, 1846.

The Mexican War

Americans were sharply divided about the war. Some favored it because they felt Mexico had provoked the war or because they felt it was the destiny of America to spread the blessings of freedom to oppressed peoples. Others opposed the war. Some, primarily Polk's political enemies the Whigs, accused the president of having provoked it. Others, generally Northern abolitionists, saw in the war the work of a vast conspiracy of Southern slaveholders greedy for more slave territory.

In planning military strategy, Polk showed genuine skill. American strategy consisted originally of a three-pronged attack, consisting of a land movement westward through New Mexico into California, a sea movement against California, and a land movement southward into Mexico.

The first prong of this three-pronged strategy, the advance through New Mexico and into California, was led by Colonel Stephen W. Kearny. Kearny's force easily secured New Mexico, entering Santa Fe August 16, 1846, before continuing west to California. There American settlers, aided by an army exploring party under John C. Frémont, had already revolted against Mexico's weak rule in what was called the Bear Flag Revolt.

As part of the second prong of U.S. strategy, naval forces under Commodore John D. Sloat had seized Monterey and declared California to be part of the United States. Forces put ashore by Commodore Robert Stockton joined with Kearny's troops to defeat the Mexicans at the Battle of San Gabriel, January 1847, and complete the conquest of California.

The third prong of the American strategy, an advance southward into Mexico, was itself divided into two parts:

1) Troops under Colonel Alexander W. Doniphan defeated Mexicans at El Brazito (December 25–28, 1846) to take El Paso, and then proceeded southward, winning the Battle of Sacramento (February 28, 1847) to take the city of Chihuahua, the capital of the Mexican province of that name.

2) The main southward thrust, however, was made by a much larger American army under General Zachary Taylor. After badly defeating larger Mexican forces at the battles of Palo Alto (May 7, 1846) and Resaca de la Palma (May 8, 1846), Taylor advanced into Mexico and defeated an even larger Mexican force at the Battle of Monterey (September 20–24, 1846). Then, after substantial numbers of his troops had been transferred to other sectors of the war, he successfully withstood, though badly outnumbered, an attack by a Mexican force under Antonia Lopez de Santa Anna at the Battle of Buena Vista, February 22–23, 1847.

Despite the success of all three parts of the American strategy, the Mexicans refused to negotiate. Polk therefore ordered U.S. forces under General Winfield Scott to land on the east coast of Mexico, march inland, and take Mexico City.

Scott landed at Veracruz on March 9, 1847, and by March 27 had captured the city with the loss of only 20 American lives. He advanced from there, being careful to maintain good discipline and avoid atrocities in the countryside. At Cerro Gordo (April 18, 1847), in what has been called "the most important single battle of the war," Scott outflanked and soundly defeated a superior enemy force in a seemingly impregnable position. After beating another Mexican army at Churubusco (August 19–20, 1847), Scott paused outside Mexico City to offer the Mexicans another chance to negotiate. When they declined, U.S. forces stormed the fortress of Chapultepec (September 13, 1847) and the next day entered Mexico City. Still Mexico refused to negotiate a peace and instead carried on guerrilla warfare.

Negotiated peace finally came about when the State Department clerk Nicholas Trist, though his authority had been revoked and he had been ordered back to Washington two months earlier, negotiated and signed the Treaty of Guadalupe-Hidalgo (February 2, 1848), ending the Mexican War. Under the terms of the treaty, Mexico ceded to the U.S. the territory Polk had originally sought to buy, this time in exchange for a payment of $15,000,000 and the assumption of $3,250,000 in American citizens' claims against the Mexican government. This territory, the Mexican Cession, included the natural harbors at San Francisco and San Diego, thus giving the U.S. all three of the major West-Coast natural harbors.

Many, including Polk, felt the treaty was far too generous. There had been talk of annexing all of Mexico or of forcing Mexico to pay an indemnity for the cost of the war. Still, Polk felt compelled to accept the treaty as it was, and the Senate subsequently ratified it.

On the home front many Americans supported the war enthusiastically and flocked to volunteer. Some criticized the war, among them Henry David Thoreau, who, to display his protest, went to live at Walden Pond and refused to pay his taxes. Jailed for this, he wrote "Civil Disobedience."

Although the Mexican War increased the nation's territory by one-third, it also brought to the surface serious political issues that threatened to divide the country, particularly the question of slavery in the new territories.

Drill 3: Westward Expansion

1. In coining the phrase "Manifest Destiny," journalist John L. O'Sullivan meant that

    (A) the struggle for racial equality was the ultimate goal of America's existence.

    (B) America was certain to become an independent country sooner or later.

    (C) it was the destiny of America to overspread the continent.

    (D) America must eventually become either all slave or all free.

    (E) America should seek to acquire an overseas empire.

2. Northerners were interested in the Oregon Territory for all of the following reasons EXCEPT

    (A) it would maintain the balance of slave and free territory.

    (B) it had a large amount of rich farmland.

    (C) it offered excellent harbors.

    (D) the Russians were expressing interest in the area.

    (E) missionary reports described the territory in glowing terms.

3. The slogan "Fifty-four forty or fight" had to do with

   (A) the so called "Aroostook War," involving a boundary dispute between Maine and New Brunswick, Canada.

   (B) the demand for the annexation of all of the Oregon country.

   (C) the demand for the readjustment of the boundary with Mexico.

   (D) the demand of free-soil Northerners that some limit be placed on the spread of slavery in the territories.

   (E) the demand of Southerners that the Missouri Compromise line be extended through the Mexican Cession.

4. The 1840s Preemption Act, signed by President John Tyler, provided that

   (A) the status of slavery in a territory was to be decided by the settlers there.

   (B) slave law preempted free law in disputes involving escaped slaves.

   (C) settlers who had squatted on government land would have first chance to buy it.

   (D) the vice president automatically became president upon the death of the president.

   (E) federal law preempted state law in matters pertaining to slavery.

5. The most significant aspect of the Mexican-American War on the United States during the 20 years following the war was that it

   (A) led to the development of the idea of "passive resistance" among those who opposed the war.

   (B) ended years of hostility between the United States and Mexico.

   (C) reignited the slavery conflict in regards to all the territories newly acquired from Mexico.

   (D) gave America undisputed control over Mexican foreign policy for the next 20 years.

   (E) revealed the shocking ineptitude of American military forces, leading to massive reforms in military training and procedures throughout the 1850s.

1824–1850
DRILLS

ANSWER KEY

Drill 1—The Jacksonian Democracy 1829-1841

1.	(C)	2.	(D)	3.	(D)	4.	(B)	5.	(C)
6.	(B)	7.	(D)	8.	(A)	9.	(A)	10.	(D)

Drill 2—Antebellum Culture

1.	(A)	2.	(E)	3.	(C)	4.	(B)	5.	(B)
6.	(B)	7.	(A)	8.	(B)	9.	(C)	10.	(C)

Drill 3—Westward Expansion

1.	(C)	2.	(D)	3.	(B)	4.	(C)	5.	(C)

GLOSSARY: 1824 –1850

Abolitionism
A movement opposed to slavery.

American System
The platform of Henry Clay, providing a high tariff on imports to finance internal improvements.

Kitchen Cabinet
Andrew Jackson's unofficial advisors.

Labor Union
A worker group that fights for better wages and working conditions.

Manifest Destiny
The belief that the American nation was destined to expand all the way to the Pacific Ocean, and possibly embrace Canada to the north and Mexico to the south.

Mountain Men
Men who trapped beavers in the Rocky Mountains for beaver pelts.

Peculiar Institution
The Southern term for slavery.

Romanticism
An intellectual movement that held a belief in the innate goodness of man, thus in his improvability. It emphasizes emotions and feelings over rationality.

Social Gospel
A religious movement that offered universal salvation.

Spoils System
Giving jobs and other benefits to one's partisan supporters.

Temperance
Opposition to consumption of alcoholic beverages.

Transcendentalism
An intellectual movement that sought to transcend the bounds of the intellect, to strive for emotional understanding, and to attain unity with God, without the help of the organized religion.

Underground Railroad

A way that slaves, with the assistance of sympathizers, could escape plantations in the South for the North.

Utopia

A small, cooperative community designed to improve life by rejecting impersonal industrialism.

Yeoman Farmer

A small, independent farmer in the antebellum South.

CHAPTER 7

1850–1861
SECTIONAL CONFLICT

➤ Diagnostic Test
➤ 1850–1861 Review & Drills
➤ Glossary

1850-1861
DIAGNOSTIC TEST

1. Ⓐ Ⓑ Ⓒ Ⓓ Ⓔ
2. Ⓐ Ⓑ Ⓒ Ⓓ Ⓔ
3. Ⓐ Ⓑ Ⓒ Ⓓ Ⓔ
4. Ⓐ Ⓑ Ⓒ Ⓓ Ⓔ
5. Ⓐ Ⓑ Ⓒ Ⓓ Ⓔ
6. Ⓐ Ⓑ Ⓒ Ⓓ Ⓔ
7. Ⓐ Ⓑ Ⓒ Ⓓ Ⓔ
8. Ⓐ Ⓑ Ⓒ Ⓓ Ⓔ
9. Ⓐ Ⓑ Ⓒ Ⓓ Ⓔ
10. Ⓐ Ⓑ Ⓒ Ⓓ Ⓔ
11. Ⓐ Ⓑ Ⓒ Ⓓ Ⓔ
12. Ⓐ Ⓑ Ⓒ Ⓓ Ⓔ
13. Ⓐ Ⓑ Ⓒ Ⓓ Ⓔ
14. Ⓐ Ⓑ Ⓒ Ⓓ Ⓔ
15. Ⓐ Ⓑ Ⓒ Ⓓ Ⓔ
16. Ⓐ Ⓑ Ⓒ Ⓓ Ⓔ
17. Ⓐ Ⓑ Ⓒ Ⓓ Ⓔ
18. Ⓐ Ⓑ Ⓒ Ⓓ Ⓔ
19. Ⓐ Ⓑ Ⓒ Ⓓ Ⓔ
20. Ⓐ Ⓑ Ⓒ Ⓓ Ⓔ
21. Ⓐ Ⓑ Ⓒ Ⓓ Ⓔ
22. Ⓐ Ⓑ Ⓒ Ⓓ Ⓔ
23. Ⓐ Ⓑ Ⓒ Ⓓ Ⓔ
24. Ⓐ Ⓑ Ⓒ Ⓓ Ⓔ
25. Ⓐ Ⓑ Ⓒ Ⓓ Ⓔ

1850–1861
DIAGNOSTIC TEST

This diagnostic test is designed to help you determine your strengths and weaknesses in your knowledge of Sectional Conflict (1850–1861). Follow the directions and check your answers.

Study this chapter for the following tests:
AP U.S. History, CLEP General, CLEP United States History I,
GED, Praxis Specialty Area, SAT: United States History

---

25 Questions

DIRECTIONS: Choose the correct answer for each of the following questions. Fill in each answer on the answer sheet.

1. Which of the following was NOT characteristic of pre-Civil War American cities?

    (A) Rapidly rising death rates   (B) Increase of crime

    (C) Extensive sewer systems   (D) Growth of slums

    (E) Increase of population

2. By opening the territory north of 36°30' to slavery, the Kansas-Nebraska Act repealed the

    (A) Dred Scott decision.   (B) Compromise of 1850.

    (C) Wilmot Proviso.   (D) Missouri Compromise.

    (E) Northwest Ordinance.

3. In 1858 at Freeport, Illinois, Stephen Douglas argued that

    (A) Congress should bar slavery from the territories.

    (B) slavery should be abolished in Washington, D.C.

    (C) slavery could not be kept out of the territories if people in the territories failed to pass laws to protect it.

    (D) the slave trade should be declared illegal.

(E)   slavery should be allowed in all the territories.

4.   Which of the following statements is true of the Kansas-Nebraska Act?

(A)   It led to the disintegration of the Democratic party.

(B)   It was a measure that the South had been demanding for decades.

(C)   It led directly to the formation of the Republican party.

(D)   By applying "popular sovereignty" to territories formerly closed to slavery by the Missouri Compromise, it succeeded in maintaining the tenuous sectional peace that had been created by the Compromise of 1850.

(E)   It assured that its sponsor, Senator Stephen A. Douglas, would receive the 1856 Democratic presidential nomination.

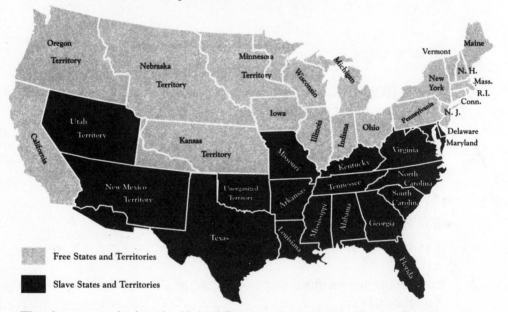

Free States and Territories

Slave States and Territories

5.   The above map depicts the United States as it was immediately after the

(A)   passage of the Compromise of 1850.

(B)   negotiation of the Webster-Ashburton Treaty.

(C)   passage of the Northwest Ordinance.

(D)   settlement of the Mexican War.

(E)   passage of the Missouri Compromise.

6.   The most common form of resistance on the part of black American slaves prior to the Civil War was

(A)   violent uprisings in which many persons were killed.

(B) attempts to escape and reach Canada by means of the "Underground Railroad."

, (C) passive resistance, including breaking tools and slightly slowing the pace of work.

(D) arson of plantation buildings and cotton gins.

(E) poisoning of the food consumed by their white masters.

7. For farmers and planters in the South, the 1850s was a period of *Econome "Climate"*

   (A) low prices for agricultural products.

   ✓(B) rapid and violent fluctuations in crop prices.

   (C) high crop prices due to repeated crop failures.

   , (D) high crop prices and sustained prosperity.

   (E) desperate poverty culminating in the Panic of 1857.

8. William Lloyd Garrison in his publication *The Liberator* was outspoken in calling for

   (A) the gradual and compensated emancipation of slaves.

   (B) colonization of slaves to some place outside the boundaries of the United States. *Moms Ormy, Lincoln, others*

   (C) repeal of the congressional "gag rule." *John Q. Adams*

   ⌐(D) immediate and uncompensated emancipation of slaves.

   (E) the strict maintenance of the constitutional doctrine of states' rights.

9. The Congressional "gag rule" stipulated that

   (A) no law could be passed prohibiting slavery in the territories.

   (B) no member of Congress could make statements or speeches outside of Congress pertaining to slavery.

   (C) no antislavery materials could be sent through the mail to addresses in Southern states.

   ⌐(D) no antislavery petitions would be formally received by Congress.

   (E) no bills pertaining to slavery would be considered.

10. In its decision in the case of *Dred Scott v. Sanford* the Supreme Court held that *opinion of Taney*

    (A) separate facilities for different races were inherently unequal and therefore unconstitutional.

    • (B) no black slave could be a citizen of the United States.

(C) separate but equal facilities for different races were constitutional.

(D) Affirmative Action programs were acceptable only when it could be proven that specific previous cases of discrimination had occurred within the institution or business in question.

(E) imposition of a literacy test imposed an unconstitutional barrier to the right to vote.

11. The most significant improvement to America's system of transportation during the 1850s was

   (A) the completion of the Erie Canal.

   (B) a surge in turnpike building.

   (C) the completion of the transcontinental railroad.

   (D) the invention of the steamboat.

   (E) a surge in railroad building.

12. During the 1850s tobacco was grown primarily in the

   (A) Deep South states such as Alabama and Mississippi.

   (B) Upper South states such as Virginia and Kentucky.

   (C) Midwestern states such as Illinois and Indiana.

   (D) Northeastern states such as New Jersey and New York.

   (E) Far Western states such as California and Oregon.

13. The most valuable export from the United States in 1860 was

   (A) wheat.   (B) corn.

   (C) hemp.   (D) iron ore.

   (E) cotton.

Questions 14 and 15 refer to the following passage.

An Act of Congress which deprives a person of the United States of his liberty or property merely because he came himself or brought his property into a particular Territory of the United States, and who had committed no offense against the laws, could hardly be dignified with the name of due process of law....

14. The preceding passage is most likely to have been written by

   (A) Roger B. Taney.   (B) Abraham Lincoln.

   (C) Stephen A. Douglas.   (D) Zachary Taylor.

   (E) Thomas Jefferson.

15. The author wants primarily to convince readers that

    (A) each territory has the right to allow or prohibit slavery within its boundaries.

    • (B) the Constitution protects slavery in all U.S. territories.

    (C) slavery is a moral evil that should not be allowed to spread into any new territories.

    (D) slavery is a necessary evil, the spread of which should be limited as much as possible.

    (E) the constutional requirements of due process of law mandates that slaves brought into free territories be immediately liberated.

16. The demise of the Whig party and the rise of the Republican party resulted primarily from

    (A) John Brown's raid.   (B) the Missouri Compromise.

    (C) the Compromise of 1850.   • (D) the Kansas-Nebraska Act.

    (E) the Lincoln-Douglas debates.

17. The Kansas-Nebraska Act of 1854 created a firestorm of opposition because it

    (A) prohibited slavery in Kansas and Nebraska as well as confirming the rights of New Mexico and Arizona settlers to prohibit slavery.

    (B) extending the northernmost boundary for slavery, as defined in the Missouri Compromise, from the southern border of Missouri and the western border of the Louisiana Territory to the Pacific Ocean.

    • (C) allowed slavery north of the line agreed upon in the Missouri Compromise, effectively repealing it.

    (D) mandated the extension of slavery in all Western territories except California in return for the creation of the Nebraska and Kansas territories.

    (E) legally repealed the doctrine of popular sovereignty in the Western territories.

18. The slavery as a "positive good" argument was presented by

    (A) Benjamin Lundy.   (B) Henry Clay.

    • (C) George Fitzhugh.   (D) Stephen Douglas.

    (E) William Lloyd Garrison.

19. Which of the following events occurred last?

    (A) The Kansas-Nebraska Act   (B) The Nat Turner Rebellion

    (C) The Seneca Falls Convention (D) The Lincoln-Douglas debates

    (E) The Homestead Act

20. The Dred Scott decision in 1857 by Chief Justice Roger Taney declared

    (A) African-Americans were citizens.

    (B) slaves legally could sue in federal courts.

    (C) slaves were not property.

    (D) the Missouri Compromise was unconstitutional.

    (E) all of the above.

21. In the election of 1860, Abraham Lincoln's total of the popular vote was

    (A) 80 percent.   (B) 70 percent.

    (C) 60 percent.   (D) 50 percent.

    (E) 40 percent.

22. The most important difference between the South and other sections of the United States prior to 1860 was which of the following?

    (A) Slavery

    (B) Economic diversification

    (C) Rural patterns of living

    (D) Development of transportation systems

    (E) Population growth

23. By 1860 approximately how many slaves lived in the South?

    (A) 2 million   (B) 3 million

    (C) 4 million   (D) 5 million

    (E) 6 million

24. The Ostend Manifesto of 1854 concerned which of the following?

    (A) Hawaii   (B) Alaska

    (C) Puerto Rico   (D) Cuba

    (E) Guam

25. The Panic of 1857 fundamentally resulted from

   (A) the violence in Kansas.

   (B) the economic impact of gold from California.

   (C) the Dred Scott decision.

   • (D) excessive investments in railroads.

   (E) the secessionist movement in the South.

1850–1861
DIAGNOSTIC TEST

ANSWER KEY

1. (C)	6. (C)	11. (E)	16. (D)	21. (E)
2. (D)	7. (D)	12. (B)	17. (C)	22. (A)
3. (C)	8. (D)	13. (E)	18. (C)	23. (C)
4. (C)	9. (D)	14. (A)	19. (E)	24. (D)
5. (A)	10. (B)	15. (B)	20. (D)	25. (D)

DETAILED EXPLANATIONS
OF ANSWERS

1. **(C)** The population growth of pre-Civil War cities generally outdistanced the sewer systems. This contributed to the increasing death rate, especially in the growing slums. With the growth of slums came an increase in crime.

2. **(D)** By organizing Kansas-Nebraska on the basis of popular sovereignty, the Kansas-Nebraska Act repealed the Missouri Compromise of 1820 which had barred slavery north of 36°30'. The Wilmot Proviso was not passed by Congress. The Compromise of 1850 had nothing directly to do with slavery north of 36°30'. The Dred Scott case would not be decided until 1857. The Northwest Ordinance of 1787 had outlawed slavery in the western lands given up by the original 13 states.

3. **(C)** In response to Lincoln's question of how he could support both popular sovereignty and the Dred Scott decision, Stephen Douglas said that slavery could not be kept out of the territories if people there failed to pass laws to protect it. This became known as the Freeport Doctrine and lost Douglas support in the South.

4. **(C)** The Republican party came into being primarily out of the controversy stirred up by the Kansas-Nebraska Act. While this same controversy did cause a sizable splinter faction to leave the Democratic party and join the newly formed Republican party, it did not cause the disintegration of the Democratic party (A), which continued as a political force up to and beyond the Civil War. It is also true that the Kansas-Nebraska Act applied popular sovereignty to territory north of the Missouri Compromise line for the first time, but far from preserving the nation's fragile sectional harmony (D), it had quite the opposite effect. Although the South generally supported the act, most Southerners had given the area little thought before Douglas introduced the issue (B). Douglas did obtain the Democratic presidential nomination in 1860—rather than 1856 (E)—but the Kansas-Nebraska Act probably did more to hurt his political career than otherwise.

5. **(A)** The map depicts the United States after the Compromise of 1850. The states of Texas and California as well as the Utah and New Mexico Territories were not part of the United States at the time of the 1842 Webster-Ashburton Treaty (B), dealing with the Maine-New Brunswick boundary; the 1787 Northwest Ordinance (C), organizing what was to become the states of Ohio, Indiana, Illinois, Michigan, and Wisconsin; and the 1820 Missouri Compromise (E), regulating the status of slavery in the territory gained by the Louisiana Purchase. California and the two territories were gained as a result of the Mexican War (D), but California statehood, as well as territorial status for Utah and New Mexico,

had to await the Compromise of 1850.

6.   **(C)**   Blacks most commonly resisted slavery passively, if at all. The Underground Railroad (B), though celebrated in popular history, involved a relatively minute number of slaves. Arson (D), poisoning (E), and violent uprising (A), though they did sometimes occur and were the subject of much fear on the part of white Southerners, were also relatively rare.

7.   **(D)**   Farmers and planters in the South enjoyed high crop prices and sustained prosperity during the 1850s. Crops were large (C) and prices were high and steady (A) and (B). Southerners saw this as a sign of the superiority of their slave economy over that of the North, hard hit as it was by the Panic of 1857 (E).

8.   **(D)**   Garrison called for the immediate and uncompensated emancipation of all slaves. He was not particularly in favor of states' rights (E), and he definitely opposed either gradualism or compensation (A). He also opposed colonization (B). Though he opposed the congressional "gag rule" (C), its repeal was not his main issue of concern.

9.   **(D)**   The congressional "gag rule" held that no antislavery petitions would be formally received by Congress. It did not directly govern the laws that could be considered (A) and (E) nor did it limit what a member could say outside of Congress (B). Antislavery materials sent through the mail would not be delivered to Southern addresses (C), but this was a separate matter.

10.   **(B)**   In the 1857 case *Dred Scott v. Sanford,* the Supreme Court held that no black slave could be a citizen of the United States. It was in the 1954 case *Brown v. Topeka Board of Education* that the court held separate facilities for the races to be unconstitutional (A). The reverse (C) was the court's holding in the 1896 case *Plessy v. Ferguson.* Literacy tests were overturned (E) in the 1960s, and Affirmative Action was limited (D) in the 1970s and '80s.

11.   **(E)**   The most significant transportation improvement in 1850s America was a surge in railroad building. The days of canal (A) and turnpike (B) building, as well as the invention of the steamboat (D), were past by that time, and the transcontinental railroad (C) was still a decade in the future.

12.   **(B)**   Tobacco was a crop of the Upper South. The Deep South grew primarily cotton. The Midwest (C) produced grain and livestock, and the Far West (E) produced various crops.

13.   **(E)**   From 1856 to 1860, cotton accounted for over fifty percent of the total exports of the United States. In contrast, domestic manufacturers during this period accounted for only 12 percent of the total exports. In 1860, the total value of goods exported from the United States was $333,576,000 and the value of the cotton exported was $191,806,555.

14. **(A)** The passage was written by U.S. Chief Justice Roger B. Taney as part of the Supreme Court's majority opinion in the 1857 case of *Dred Scott v. Sanford*. Taney held 1) that slaveholders could take up residence with their slaves in free states without thereby losing title to their human chattels; and 2) that neither Congress nor any territorial legislature could prohibit slavery in any territory of the United States. He justified this opinion on the basis that 1) the U.S. Constitution recognized slaves as property; and 2) forbidding the ownership of slaves in territories amounted to depriving the slaveholders of their property without due process of law.

15. **(B)** As in number 14 above, Taney's argument was that slavery, as a form of property recognized by the Constitution, could not be prohibited by Congress or any other authority, in any of the territories of the United States.

16. **(D)** The Kansas-Nebraska Act, with its provisions nullifying the Missouri Compromise and allowing slavery in the northern half of the Louisiana Territory, was so divisive that it virtually destroyed the Whig party. Whigs who supported the Kansas-Nebraska Act joined the Democratic party. Those who opposed it left the Whig party in frustration and helped found a new party, the Republican party. The Republicans built their power base upon the issue of limiting the westward expansion of slavery, and they were extremely successful. By 1854 they had captured a majority of Northern seats in the House of Representatives. The Democratic party was also affected by the Kansas-Nebraska Act. Up until this time, both the Democratic and Whig parties had been parties with national bases of political support. With the dissension following the Kansas-Nebraska Act, the Democrats lost most of their Northern political support base while increasing their support base in the South. With the Whigs gone and the Republicans drawing almost all their support from antislavery and "free soil" forces, primarily in the North, the country now had two parties with sectional strength rather than national support. This development tended to increase the sectionalism already present, and the parties were no longer in a position to moderate sectional differences as they had done when they had constituents to satisfy in every section of the country.

17. **(C)** While the Kansas-Nebraska Act did not mandate slavery in the Western territories, nor did it prohibit slavery in those territories, it gave settlers the right to decide for themselves whether they wanted to prohibit slavery. This extended the notion of "popular sovereignty" into the Kansas and Nebraska territories. Unfortunately, this left open the possibility of both territories allowing slavery. Since both territories were north of Missouri's southern border, and both were comprised of land from the original Louisiana Purchase, this arrangement violated the Missouri Compromise which forbade slavery in this part of the Louisiana Territory. Abolitionist forces were enraged and saw the new policy as a "sellout" to the "slave power" and a betrayal of principle. The outrage led to increased debate between North and South and left many Northerners convinced

that no compromise on slavery could now be trusted. Extremists argued that the Kansas-Nebraska Act was part of a larger plot to spread slavery across the entire West, and eventually the entire country. This legislation politically split the country more than any other legal act in American history. From this point on there would be no further compromises between North and South regarding slavery.

18. **(C)** In the 1850s, the most ardent defender of Southern slavery was George Fitzhugh. In works such as *Cannibals All!*, Fitzhugh pointed out that all great empires and civilizations of the past had relied upon slavery and that slave owners actually were civilizing "savage" Africans as much as could be expected under slavery. Fitzhugh also pointed out that unlike the treatment of "wage slaves" up north (factory workers), slaves were cared for while aged and infirm by the slave owner. It was Fitzhugh's view that because of the community of interest under slavery, slavery actually proved more human toward its workers (slaves) than Northern capitalism did toward its workers. Benjamin Lundy sought to end slavery through the American Colonization Society, as did William Lloyd Garrison through the abolitionists or American Anti-slavery Society. Both Henry Clay and Stephen Douglas sought compromise solutions to the political crisis of slavery that adopted a strong stance on neither side of the slavery issue.

19. **(E)** The Nat Turner Rebellion occurred in 1831 as the bloodiest slave uprising in American history when 55 whites were killed by about 15 slaves in Virginia. The Kansas-Nebraska Act was passed in 1854 and sought to establish the principle of popular sovereignty in the two territories on the issue of slavery to promote the presidential ambition of Senator Stephen Douglas of Illinois. The Seneca Falls Convention convened in 1848 as a militant expression of women's rights led by Lucretia Mott and Elizabeth Cady Stanton. The Lincoln-Douglas debates took place in 1858 as both candidates vied for the Senate seat in Illinois. The Homestead Act was passed by Congress in 1862 and granted a free 160-acre farm in the Far West (Great Plains region) to any American citizen 21 years of age or older who would work the land for five years.

20. **(D)** In 1857, the Supreme Court under Roger Taney sought to offer a final solution to the crisis over slavery in the Dred Scott case. Here a black slave sued for his freedom on the grounds he was in Northern territory which had outlawed slavery. Taney ruled that Scott could not sue in the Court because blacks were not and could never become citizens of the United States. In addition, Taney ruled the Missouri Compromise of 1819 and all other laws prohibiting slavery unconstitutional as violations of the "due process clause" of the Fifth Amendment regarding property.

21. **(E)** In the election of 1860, the strength of sectionalism in the country was apparent with the nomination of four sectional candidates for president. As the Republican party's candidate, Lincoln mustered only 40 percent of the popular vote but carried a majority of electoral college votes to win the election. John Breckinridge for the Southern Democrats earned 18 percent of the popular vote,

while Stephen Douglas and the Northern Democrats earned 30 percent of the vote. John Bell of the Constutional Union party was able to gather only 13 percent of the vote. Thus, Lincoln was seen as a minority president lacking a national mandate and representing only the interests of the North.

22.   **(A)**   Although there may be some disagreement among historians, most see slavery as the key element underlying other differences such as the lack of industrialization, rural patterns of living, and slow development of a transportation system, particularly railroads. The existence of slavery also made the South less attractive to immigrants.

23.   **(C)**   By 1860 the South had nearly 4 million slaves.

24.   **(D)**   In 1854 the American ministers to Great Britain, France, and Spain met in Ostend, Belgium and issued a statement that became known as the Ostend Manifesto. It said that if Spain would not sell Cuba to the United States, the U.S. had the right to seize the island by force.

25.   **(D)**   The Panic of 1857 resulted primarily from overspeculation in railroad stocks. Many banks failed across the nation, although the North suffered the most and the South the least. By 1858 the economy began picking up, bolstered by European demand for foodstuffs and cotton.

1850–1861
REVIEW

1. THE CRISIS OF 1850

The Wilmot Proviso

The Mexican War had no more than started when, on August 8, 1846, freshman Democratic Congressman David Wilmot of Pennsylvania introduced his Wilmot Proviso as a proposed amendment to a war appropriations bill. It stipulated that "neither slavery nor involuntary servitude shall ever exist" in any territory to be acquired from Mexico. It was passed by the House, and though rejected by the Senate, it was reintroduced again and again amid increasingly acrimonious debate.

The Wilmot Proviso aroused intense sectional feelings. Southerners, who had supported the war enthusiastically, felt they were being treated unfairly. Northerners, some of whom had been inclined to see the war as a slaveholders' plot to extend slavery, felt they saw their worst suspicions confirmed by the Southerners' furious opposition to the Wilmot Proviso. There came to be four views regarding the status of slavery in the newly acquired territories.

The Southern position was expressed by John C. Calhoun, now serving as senator from South Carolina. He argued that the territories were the property not of the U.S. federal government, but of all the states together, and therefore Congress had no right to prohibit in any territory any type of "property" (by which he meant slaves) that was legal in any of the states.

Antislavery Northerners, pointing to the Northwest Ordinance of 1787 and the Missouri Compromise of 1820 as precedents, argued that Congress had the right to make what laws it saw fit for the territories, including, if it so chose, laws prohibiting slavery.

A compromise proposal favored by President Polk and many moderate Southerners called for the extension of the 36°30' line of the Missouri Compromise westward through the Mexican Cession to the Pacific, with territory north of the line to be closed to slavery and territory south of it opened to slavery.

Another compromise solution, favored by Northern Democrats such as Lewis Cass of Michigan and Stephen A. Douglas of Illinois, was known as "squatter sovereignty" and later as "popular sovereignty." It held that the residents of each territory should be permitted to decide for themselves whether or not to allow slavery, but it was vague as to when they might exercise that right.

The Election of 1848

Both parties sought to avoid as much as possible the hot issue of slavery in the territories as they prepared for the 1848 election campaign.

The Democrats nominated Lewis Cass, and their platform endorsed his middle-of-the-road popular sovereignty position with regard to slavery in the territories.

The Whigs dodged the issue even more effectively by nominating General Zachary Taylor, whose fame in the Mexican War made him a strong candidate. Taylor knew nothing of politics, had never voted, and liked to think of himself as above politics. He took no position at all with respect to slavery in the territories.

Some antislavery Northern Whigs and Democrats, disgusted with their parties' failure to take a clear stand against the spread of slavery, deserted the party ranks to form another antislavery third party. They were known as "Conscience" Whigs (because they voted their conscience) and "Barnburner" Democrats (because they were willing to burn down the whole Democratic "barn" to get rid of the pro slavery "rats"). Their party was called the Free-Soil party, since it stood for keeping the soil of new western territories free of slavery. Its candidate was Martin Van Buren.

The election excited relatively little public interest. Taylor won a narrow victory, apparently because Van Buren took enough votes from Cass in New York and Pennsylvania to throw those states into Taylor's column.

Gold in California

The question of slavery's status in the Western territories was made more immediate when, on January 24, 1848, gold was discovered at Sutter's Mill, not far from Sacramento, California. The next year gold-seekers from the eastern U.S. and from many foreign countries swelled California's population from 14,000 to 100,000.

Once in the gold fields these "forty-niners" proved to contain some rough characters, and that fact, along with the presence, or at least the expectation, of quick and easy riches, made California a wild and lawless place. No territorial government had been organized since the U.S. had received the land as part of the Mexican Cession, and all that existed was an inadequate military government. In September 1849, having more than the requisite population and being much in need of better government, California petitioned for admission to the Union as a state.

Since few slaveholders had chosen to risk their valuable investments in human property in the turbulent atmosphere of California, the people of the area not surprisingly sought admission as a free state, touching off a serious sectional crisis back east.

The Compromise of 1850

President Zachary Taylor, though himself a Louisiana slaveholder, opposed the further spread of slavery. Hoping to sidestep the dangerously divisive issue of slavery in the territories, he encouraged California as well as the rest of the Mexican Cession to organize and seek admission directly as states, thus completely bypassing the territorial stage.

Southerners were furious. They saw admission of California as a free-state as a back-door implementation of the hated Wilmot Proviso they had fought so hard to turn back in Congress. They were also growing increasingly alarmed at what was becoming the minority status of their section within the country. Long outnumbered in the House of Representatives, the South would now find itself, should California be admitted as a free state, also outvoted in the Senate.

Other matters created friction between North and South. A large tract of land was disputed between Texas, a slave state, and the as yet unorganized New Mexico Territory, where slavery's future was at best uncertain. Southerners were angered by the small-scale but much talked about efforts of Northern abolitionists, "underground railroad" to aid escaped slaves in reaching permanent freedom in Canada. Northerners were disgusted by the presence of slave pens and slave markets in the nation's capital. Radical Southerners talked of secession and scheduled an all-Southern convention to meet in Nashville in June 1850 to propose ways of protecting Southern interests, inside or outside the Union. At this point the aged Henry Clay attempted to compromise the various matters of contention between North and South. He proposed an eight-part package deal that he hoped would appeal to both sides.

For the North, the package contained these aspects: California would be admitted as a free state; the land in dispute between Texas and New Mexico would go to New Mexico; New Mexico and Utah Territories (all of the Mexican Cession outside of California) would not be specifically reserved for slavery, but its status there would be decided by popular sovereignty and, the slave trade would be abolished in the District of Columbia.

For the South, the package offered the following: A tougher Fugitive Slave Law would be enacted; the federal government would pay Texas' $10,000,000 pre-annexation debt; Congress would declare that it did not have jurisdiction over the interstate slave trade; and Congress would promise not to abolish slavery itself in the District of Columbia.

What followed the introduction of Clay's compromise proposal was eight months of heated debate, during which Clay, Calhoun, and Daniel Webster, the three great figures of Congress during the first half of the nineteenth century—all three aged and none of them with more than two years to live—made some of their greatest speeches. Clay called for compromise and "mutual forbearance." Calhoun gravely warned that the only way to save the Union was for the North to grant all the South's demands and keep quiet on the issue of slavery. Webster abandoned his previous opposition to the spread of slavery (as well as most of his popularity back in his home state of Massachusetts) to support the compromise in an eloquent speech.

The opponents of the compromise were many and powerful and ranged from President Taylor, who demanded admission of California without reference to slavery, to Northern extremists such as Senator William Seward of New York, who spoke of a "higher law" than the Constitution, forbidding the spread of slavery, to Southern extremists such as Calhoun or Senator Jefferson Davis of Mississippi. By mid-summer all seemed lost for the compromise, and Clay left Washington exhausted and discouraged.

Then the situation changed dramatically. President Taylor died (apparently of gastroenteritis) on July 9, 1850, and was succeeded by Vice President Millard Fillmore, a quiet but efficient politician and a strong supporter of compromise. In Congress the fight for the compromise was taken up by Senator Stephen A. Douglas of Illinois. Called the "Little Giant" for his small stature but large political skills, Douglas broke Clay's proposal into its component parts so that he could use varying coalitions to push each part through Congress. This method proved successful, and the compromise was adopted.

The Compromise of 1850 was received with joy by most of the nation. Sectional harmony returned, for the most part, and the issue of slavery in the territories seemed to have been permanently settled. That this was an illusion became apparent within a few years.

The Election of 1852

The 1852 Democratic convention deadlocked between Cass and Douglas and so instead settled on dark horse Franklin Pierce of New Hampshire. The Whigs, true to form, chose General Winfield Scott, a war hero with no political background.

The result was an easy victory for Pierce, largely because the Whig party, badly divided along North-South lines as a result of the battle over the Compromise of 1850, was beginning to come apart. The Free-Soil party's candidate, John P. Hale of New Hampshire, fared poorly, demonstrating the electorate's weariness with the slavery issue.

Pierce and "Young America"

Americans eagerly turned their attention to railroads, cotton, clipper ships, and commerce. The world seemed to be opening up to American trade and influence.

President Pierce expressed the nation's hope that a new era of sectional peace was beginning. To assure this he sought to distract the nation's attention from the slavery issue to an aggressive program of foreign economic and territorial expansion known as "Young America."

In 1853 Commodore Matthew Perry led a U.S. naval force into Tokyo Bay on a peaceful mission to open Japan—previously closed to the outside world—to American diplomacy and commerce.

By means of the Reciprocity Treaty (1854), Pierce succeeded in opening Canada to greater U.S. trade. He also sought to annex Hawaii, increase U.S. interest in Central America, and acquire territories from Mexico and Spain.

From Mexico he acquired in 1853 the Gadsden Purchase, a strip of land in what is now southern New Mexico and Arizona along the Gila River. The purpose of this purchase was to provide a good route for a transcontinental railroad across the southern part of the country.

Pierce sought to buy Cuba from Spain. When Spain declined, three of Pierce's diplomats, meeting in Ostend, Belgium, sent him the Ostend Manifesto urging military seizure of Cuba should Spain remain intransigent.

Pierce was the first "doughface" president—"a northern man with southern principles"—and his expansionist goals, situated as they were in the South, aroused suspicion and hostility in antislavery Northerners. Pierce's administration appeared to be dominated by Southerners, such as Secretary of War Jefferson Davis, and whether in seeking a southern route for a transcontinental railroad or seeking to annex potential slave territory such as Cuba, it seemed to be working for the good of the South.

Economic Growth

The chief factor in the economic transformation of America during the 1840s and 1850s was the dynamic rise of the railroads. In 1840 America had less than 3,000 miles of railroad track. By 1860 that number had risen to over 30,000 miles. Railroads pioneered big-business techniques, and by improving transportation, helped create a nationwide market. They also helped link the Midwest to the Northeast rather than the South, as would have been the case had only water transportation been available.

Water transportation during the 1850s saw the heyday of the steamboat on inland rivers and the clipper ship on the high seas. The period also saw rapid and sustained industrial growth. The factory system began in the textile industry, where Elias Howe's invention of the sewing machine (1846) and Isaac Singer's improved model (1851) aided the process of mechanization, and spread to other industries.

Agriculture varied according to region. In the South, large plantations and small farms existed side by side for the most part, and both prospered enormously during the 1850s from the production of cotton. Southern leaders referred to the fiber as "King Cotton," an economic power that no one would dare fight against.

In the North the main centers of agricultural production shifted from the Middle Atlantic states to the more fertile lands of the Midwest. The main unit of agriculture was the family farm, and the main products were grain and livestock. Unlike the South where 3,500,000 slaves provided abundant labor, the North faced incentives to introduce labor-saving machines. Cyrus McCormick's mechanical reaper came into wide use, and by 1860 over 100,000 were in operation on Midwestern farms. Mechanical threshers also came into increasing use.

QUESTION

Why did Western farmers have closer ties with the Northeast by the 1850s?

EXPLANATION

The most important tie between the West and the Northeast was economic. The economic tie developed because canals and railroads, the most important ways to move freight, generally ran along east west routes. The West grew food for the Northeast, and the Northeast sold manufactured goods to the West.

Decline of the Two-Party System

Meanwhile, ominous developments were taking place in politics. America's second two-party system, which had developed during the 1830s, was in the process of breaking down. The Whig party, whose dismal performance in the election of 1852 had signaled its weakness, was now in the process of complete disintegration. Partially this was the result of the issue of slavery, which tended to divide the party along North-South lines. Partially, though, it may have been the result of the nativist movement.

The nativist movement and its political party, the American, or, as it was called, the Know-Nothing party, grew out of alarm on the part of native-born Americans at the rising tide of German and Irish immigration during the late 1840s and early 1850s. The Know-Nothing party, so called because its members were told to answer "I know nothing" when asked about its secret proceedings, was anti-foreign and, since many of the foreigners were Catholic, also anti-Catholic. It surged briefly to become the country's second largest party by 1855 but faded even more quickly due to the ineptness of its leaders and the growing urgency of the slavery question, which, though ignored by the Know-Nothing party, was rapidly coming to overshadow all other issues. To some extent the Know-Nothing movement may simply have benefited from the already progressing disintegration of the Whig party, but it may also have helped to complete that disintegration.

All of this was ominous because the collapse of a viable nationwide two-party system made it much more difficult for the nation's political process to contain the explosive issue of slavery.

QUESTION

> What impact did the successive compromises regarding slavery ultimately have on the United States?

EXPLANATION

Compromises only served to delay the secession of the South from the Union. The problem was that each compromise sought to avoid facing a permanent solution to the slavery issue; no such compromise would ever satisfy everyone. Instead, they only dealt with the specific crisis that the United States was facing. The various compromises were only short term, temporary solutions.

Drill 1: The Crisis of 1850

1. According to this map and table, which state had the greatest degree of urbanization in 1860?

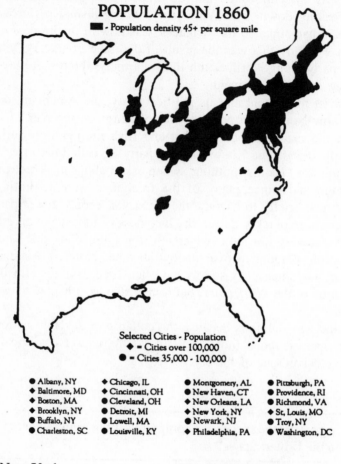

POPULATION 1860

■ - Population density 45+ per square mile

Selected Cities - Population
◆ = Cities over 100,000
● = Cities 35,000 - 100,000

● Albany, NY	◆ Chicago, IL	● Montgomery, AL	● Pittsburgh, PA
◆ Baltimore, MD	◆ Cincinnati, OH	● New Haven, CT	● Providence, RI
◆ Boston, MA	● Cleveland, OH	◆ New Orleans, LA	● Richmond, VA
◆ Brooklyn, NY	● Detroit, MI	◆ New York, NY	◆ St. Louis, MO
● Buffalo, NY	● Lowell, MA	● Newark, NJ	● Troy, NY
● Charleston, SC	● Louisville, KY	◆ Philadelphia, PA	● Washington, DC

(A) New York

(B) Pennsylvania

(C) Illinois

(D) Massachusetts

(E) Virginia

2. Which of the following was part of the Compromise of 1850?

    (A) Abolition of the slave trade

    (B) A new fugitive slave law

    (C) California's entry into the Union on the basis of popular sovereignty

    (D) Utah and New Mexico territories to be free

    (E) A new eastern border for Texas

3. Improvements in America's transportation system during the 1850s were primarily the result of

   (A) the expansion of the canal network.

   (B) the expansion of the railroad network.

   (C) improvement in the design of steamboats.

   (D) construction of improved paved roads.

   (E) invention of the automobile.

4. Government subsidies for the building of transcontinental railroads during the nineteenth century mainly took the form of

   (A) large cash payments based on the mileage of track built.

   (B) a one-time blanket appropriation for the building of each separate transcontinental line.

   (C) generous land grants along the railroad's right-of-way.

   (D) the option of drawing supplies and materials from government depots.

   (E) the provision of large amounts of convict labor at no charge to the railroad company.

5. All of the following are true of the Compromise of 1850 EXCEPT

   (A) it provided for the admission of California to the Union as a free state.

   (B) it included a tougher fugitive slave law.

   (C) it prohibited slavery in the lands acquired as a result of the Mexican War.

   (D) it stipulated that land in dispute between the state of Texas and the territory of New Mexico should be ceded to New Mexico.

   (E) it ended the slave trade in the District of Columbia.

6. The main issue of the 1850s Free-Soil party was that

   (A) the federal government should permit no further spread of slavery in the territories.

   (B) a homestead act should be passed, granting 160 acres of government land in the West free to anyone who would settle on it and improve it for five years.

   (C) the federal government should oversee immediate and uncompensated abolition of slavery.

   (D) freed slaves should be provided with 40 acres and two mules to provide them the economic means of independent self-support.

(E)   the United States should annex Cuba.

7.   The Wilmot Proviso was most likely to be supported by

(A)   Jacksonian Democrats.

(B)   advocates of nullification.

(C)   secessionists.

(D)   Free-Soilers.

(E)   advocates of popular sovereignty.

8.   The Wilmot Proviso stipulated that

(A)   slavery should be prohibited in the lands acquired as a result of the Mexican War.

(B)   no lands should be annexed to the United States as a result of the Mexican War.

(C)   California should be a free state while the rest of the Mexican Cession should be reserved for the formation of slave states.

(D)   the status of slavery in the Mexican Cession should be decided on the basis of "popular sovereignty."

(E)   the Missouri Compromise line should be extended through the Mexican Cession to the Pacific, lands north of it being closed to slavery.

9.   The Compromise of 1850 had the effect of

(A)   providing a compromise that offered only limited expansion of slavery into territories west of the Mississippi, satisfying both pro-slavery Southerners and abolitionist Northerners, and resolving the issue of slavery west of the Mississippi.

(B)   postponing and evading, rather than resolving, the problems related to slavery in American territories west of the Mississippi.

(C)   ending Southern demands for the expansion of slavery into American territories west of the Mississippi.

(D)   ending Northern demands for the prohibition of slavery in American territories west of the Mississippi.

(E)   providing a compromise that allowed all American territories west of the Mississippi to decide the slavery issue for themselves.

10.   Northern denunciation of the Compromise of 1850 was directed primarily toward

(A)   the Fugitive Slave Law.

(B)   statehood for California.

(C)   the acquisition of New Mexico and Utah as slave territories.

(D)   the "gag rule" in the House of Representatives.

(E)   continuation of the African slave trade.

2. THE RETURN OF SECTIONAL CONFLICT

Continuing Sources of Tension

While Americans hailed the apparent sectional harmony created by the Compromise of 1850 and enjoyed the rapid economic growth of the decade that followed, two items which continued to create tension centered on the issue of slavery.

The Strengthened Fugitive Slave Law

The more important of these was a part of the compromise itself, the strengthened federal Fugitive Slave Law. The law enraged Northerners, many of whom believed it little better than a legalization of kidnapping. Under its provisions blacks living in the North and claimed by slave catchers were denied trial by jury and many of the other protections of due process. Even more distasteful to antislavery Northerners was the provision that required all U.S. citizens to aid, when called upon, in the capture and return of alleged fugitives. So violent was Northern feeling against the law that several riots erupted as a result of attempts to enforce it. Some Northern states passed personal liberty laws in an attempt to prevent the working of the Fugitive Slave Law.

The effect of all this was to polarize the country even further. Many Northerners who had not previously taken an interest in the slavery issue now became opponents of slavery as a result of having its injustices forcibly brought home to them by the Fugitive Slave Law. Southerners saw in Northern resistance to the law further proof that the North was determined to tamper with the institution of slavery.

Publishing of Uncle Tom's Cabin

One Northerner who was outraged by the Fugitive Slave Act was Harriet Beecher Stowe. In response, she wrote *Uncle Tom's Cabin*, a fictional book depicting what she perceived as the evils of slavery. Furiously denounced in the South, the book became an overnight bestseller in the North, where it turned many toward active opposition to slavery. This, too, was a note of harsh discord among the seemingly harmonious sectional relations of the early 1850s.

The Kansas-Nebraska Act

All illusion of sectional peace ended abruptly when in 1854 Senator Stephen A. Douglas of Illinois introduced a bill in Congress to organize the area west of Missouri and Iowa as the territories of Kansas and Nebraska. Douglas, who apparently had no moral convictions on slavery one way or the other, hoped organizing the territories would facilitate the building of a transcontinental railroad on a central route, something that would benefit him and his Illinois constituents.

Though he sought to avoid directly addressing the touchy issue of slavery, Douglas was compelled by pressure from Southern senators such as David Atchison of Missouri to include in the bill an explicit repeal of the Missouri Compromise (which banned slavery in the areas in question) and a provision that the status of slavery in the newly organized territories be decided by popular sovereignty.

The bill was opposed by most Northern Democrats and a majority of the remaining Whigs, but with the support of the Southern-dominated Pierce administration it was passed and signed into law.

The Republican Party

The Kansas-Nebraska Act aroused a storm of outrage in the North, where the repeal of the Missouri Compromise was seen as the breaking of a solemn agreement. It hastened the disintegration of the Whig party and divided the Democratic party along North-South lines.

In the North, many Democrats left the party and were joined by former Whigs and Know-Nothings in the newly created Republican party. Springing to life almost overnight as a result of Northern fury at the Kansas-Nebraska Act, the Republican party included diverse elements whose sole unifying principle was the firm belief that slavery should be banned from all the nation's territories, confined to the states where it already existed, and allowed to spread no further.

Though its popularity was confined almost entirely to the North, the Republican party quickly became a major power in national politics.

QUESTION

In what way did the Kansas-Nebraska Act repeal the Missouri Compromise?

EXPLANATION

The Missouri Compromise stated that all territories organized west of the Mississippi River and north of 36°30' except the state of Missouri would prohibit slavery. The Kansas-Nebraska Act said that the status of slavery in these territories would be decided by popular sovereignty, thus allowing for the possibility of slavery there.

"Bleeding Kansas"

With the status of Kansas (Nebraska was never in much doubt) to be decided by the voters there, North and South began competing to see which could send the greatest number. Northerners formed the New England Emigrant Aid Company to promote the settling of antislavery men in Kansas, and Southerners responded in kind. Despite these efforts the majority of Kansas settlers were Midwesterners who were generally opposed to the spread of slavery but were more concerned with finding good farmland than deciding the national debate over slavery in the territories.

Despite this large antislavery majority, large-scale election fraud, especially on the part of heavily armed Missouri "border ruffians" who crossed into Kansas on election day to vote their pro-slavery principles early and often, led to the creation of a virulently pro-slavery territorial government. When the presidentially appointed territorial governor protested this gross fraud, Pierce removed him from office.

Free-Soil Kansans responded by denouncing the pro-slavery government as illegitimate and forming their own free-soil government in an election which the pro-slavery faction boycotted. Kansas now had two rival governments, each claiming to be the only lawful one.

Both sides began arming themselves and soon the territory was being referred to in the Northern press as "Bleeding Kansas" as full-scale guerrilla war erupted. In May 1856, Missouri border ruffians sacked the free-soil town of Lawrence, killing two and destroying homes, businesses, and printing presses. Two days later a small band of antislavery zealots under the leadership of fanatical abolitionist John Brown retaliated by killing and mutilating five unarmed men and boys at a pro-slavery settlement on Pottawatomie Creek. In all, some 200 died in the months of guerrilla fighting that followed.

Meanwhile, violence had spread even to Congress itself. In the same month as the Sack of Lawrence and the Pottawatomie Massacre, Senator Charles Sumner of Massachusetts made a two-day speech entitled "The Crime Against Kansas," in which he not only denounced slavery but also made degrading personal references to aged South Carolina Senator Andrew Butler. Two days later Butler's nephew, Congressman Preston Brooks, also of South Carolina, entered the Senate chamber and, coming on Sumner from behind, beat him about the head and shoulders with a cane, leaving him bloody and unconscious.

Once again the North was outraged, while in the South, Brooks was hailed as a hero. New canes were sent to him to replace the one he had broken over Sumner's head. Denounced by Northerners, he resigned his seat and was overwhelmingly re-elected. Northerners were further incensed and bought thousands of copies of Sumner's inflammatory speech.

The Election of 1856

The election of 1856 was a three-way contest that pitted Democrats, Know-Nothings, and Republicans against each other.

The Democrats dropped Pierce and passed over Douglas to nominate James Buchanan of Pennsylvania. Though a veteran of 40 years of politics, Buchanan was a weak and vacillating man whose chief qualification for the nomination was that during the slavery squabbles of the past few years he had been out of the country as American minister to Great Britain and therefore had not been forced to take public positions on the controversial issues.

The Know-Nothings, including the remnant of the Whigs, nominated Millard Fillmore. However, choice of a Southerner for the nomination of vice president so alienated Northern Know-Nothings that many shifted their support to the Republican candidate.

The Republicans nominated John C. Frémont of California. A former officer in the army's Corps of Topographical Engineers, Frémont was known as "the Pathfinder" for his explorations in the Rockies and the Far West. The Republican platform called for high tariffs, free Western homesteads (160 acres) for settlers, and, most important, no further spread of slavery. Their slogan was "Free Soil, Free Men, and Frémont." Southerners denounced the Republican party as an abolitionist organization and threatened secession should it win the election.

Against divided opposition Buchanan won with apparent ease. However, his victory was largely based on the support of the South, since Frémont carried most of the Northern states. Had the Republicans won Pennsylvania and either Illinois or Indiana, Frémont would have been elected. In the election the Republicans demonstrated surprising strength for a political party only two years old and made clear that they, and not the Know-Nothings, would replace the moribund Whigs as the other major party along with the Democrats.

The Dred Scott Case

Meanwhile, there had been rising through the court system a case that would give the Supreme Court a chance to state its opinion on the question of slavery in the territories. The case was *Dred Scott v. Sanford* and involved a Missouri slave, Dred Scott, who had been encouraged by abolitionists to sue for his freedom on the basis that his owner, an army doctor, had taken him for a stay of several years in a free state, Illinois, and then in a free territory, Wisconsin. By 1856 the case had made its way to the Supreme Court, and by March of the following year the Court was ready to render its decision.

The justices were at first inclined to rule simply that Scott, as a slave, was not a citizen and could not sue in court. Buchanan, however, shortly before his inauguration urged the justices to go farther and attempt to settle the whole slavery issue once and for all, thus removing it from the realm of politics where it might prove embarrassing to the president.

The Court obliged. Under the domination of aging pro-Southern Chief Justice Roger B. Taney of Maryland, it attempted to read the extreme Southern position on slavery into the Constitution, ruling not only that Scott had no standing to sue in federal court, but also that temporary residence in a free state, even for several years, did not make a slave free, and that the Missouri Compromise (already a dead letter by that time) had been unconstitutional all along because

Congress did not have the authority to exclude slavery from any territory whatsoever. Nor did territorial governments, which were considered to receive their power from Congress, have the right to prohibit slavery.

Far from settling the sectional controversy, the Dred Scott case only made it worse. Southerners were encouraged to take an extreme position and refuse compromise, while antislavery Northerners became more convinced than ever that there was a pro-slavery conspiracy controlling all branches of government, and expressed an unwillingness to accept the Court's dictate as final.

Buchanan and Kansas

Later in 1857 the pro-slavery government in Kansas, through largely fraudulent means, arranged for a heavily pro-slavery constitutional convention to meet at the town of Lecompton. The result was a state constitution that allowed slavery. To obtain a pretense of popular approval for this constitution, the convention provided for a referendum in which the voters were to be given a choice only to prohibit the entry of additional slaves into the state.

Disgusted Free-Soilers boycotted the referendum, and the result was a constitution that put no restrictions at all on slavery. Touting this Lecompton constitution, the pro-slavery territorial government petitioned Congress for admission to the Union as a slave state. Meanwhile the free-soilers drafted a constitution of their own and submitted it to Congress as the legitimate one for the prospective state of Kansas.

Eager to appease the South, which had started talking of secession again, and equally eager to suppress antislavery agitation in the North, Buchanan vigorously backed the Lecompton constitution. Douglas, appalled at this travesty of popular sovereignty, broke with the administration to oppose it. He and Buchanan became bitter political enemies, with the president determined to use all the power of the Democratic organization to crush Douglas politically.

After extremely bitter and acrimonious debate, the Senate approved the Lecompton constitution, but the House insisted that Kansans be given a chance to vote on the entire document. Southern congressmen did succeed in managing to apply pressure to the Kansas voters by adding the stipulation that should the Lecompton constitution be approved, Kansas would receive a generous grant of federal land, but should it be voted down, Kansas would remain a territory.

Nevertheless, Kansas voters, when given a chance to express themselves in a fair election, turned down the Lecompton constitution by an overwhelming margin, choosing to remain a territory rather than become a slave state. Kansas was finally admitted as a free state in 1861.

The Panic of 1857

In 1857 the country was struck by a short but severe depression. There were three basic causes for this "Panic of 1857": several years of overspeculation in railroads and lands, faulty banking practices, and an interruption in the flow of European capital into American investments as a result of the Crimean War. The

North blamed the Panic on low tariffs, while the South, which had suffered much less than the industrial North, saw the Panic as proof of the superiority of the Southern economy in general and slavery in particular.

The Lincoln-Douglas Debates

The 1858 Illinois senatorial campaign produced a series of debates that got to the heart of the issues that were threatening to divide the nation. In that race incumbent Democratic Senator and front-runner for the 1860 presidential nomination Stephen A. Douglas was opposed by a Springfield lawyer, little known outside the state, by the name of Abraham Lincoln.

Though Douglas had been hailed in some free-soil circles for his opposition to the Lecompton constitution, Lincoln, in a series of seven debates that the candidates agreed to hold during the course of the campaign, stressed that Douglas's doctrine of popular sovereignty failed to recognize slavery for the moral wrong it was. Again and again Lincoln hammered home the theme that Douglas was a secret defender of slavery because he did not take a moral stand against it.

Douglas, for his part, maintained that his guiding principle was democracy, not any moral standard of right or wrong with respect to slavery. The people could, as far as he was concerned, "vote it up or vote it down." At the same time he strove to depict Lincoln as a radical and an abolitionist who believed in racial equality and race mixing.

At the debate held in Freeport, Illinois, Lincoln pressed Douglas to reconcile the principle of popular sovereignty to the Supreme Court's decision in the Dred Scott case. How could the people "vote it up or vote it down" if, as the Supreme Court alleged, no territorial government could prohibit slavery? Douglas, in what came to be called his "Freeport Doctrine," replied that the people of any territory could exclude slavery simply by declining to pass any of the special laws that slave jurisdictions usually passed for their protection.

Douglas's answer was good enough to win him re-election to the Senate, although by the narrowest of margins, but hurt him in the coming presidential campaign. The Lecompton fight had already destroyed Douglas's hopes of uniting the Democratic party and defusing the slave issue. It had also damaged his 1860 presidential hopes by alienating the South. Now his Freeport Doctrine hardened the opposition of Southerners already angered by his anti-Lecompton stand.

For Lincoln, despite the failure to win the Senate seat, the debates were a major success, propelling him into the national spotlight and strengthening the backbone of the Republican party to resist compromise on the free-soil issue.

Drill 2: The Return of Sectional Conflict

1. According to the Dred Scott decision,

    (A) only people living within a territory could forbid slavery there.

    (B) slaves were citizens of the United States.

    (C) Congress had no power over slavery in the territories.

    (D) the Missouri Compromise was constitutional.

    (E) slaves taken temporarily into a free state were free.

2. In his famous "Freeport Doctrine" set forth in his debate with Abraham Lincoln at Freeport, Illinois, Stephen A. Douglas stated that

    (A) any territory desiring to exclude slavery could do so simply by declining to pass laws protecting it.

    (B) any state wishing to secede from the Union could do so simply by the vote of a special state constitutional convention.

    (C) no state had the right to obstruct the operation of the Fugitive Slave Act by the passage of "personal liberty laws."

    (D) the Dred Scott decision prohibited any territorial legislature from excluding slavery until a state constitution was drawn up for approval by Congress.

    (E) any slaveholder was free to take his slaves anywhere within the United States without hindrance by state, federal, or territorial governments.

Question 3 refers to the following map.

277

3. The map on the previous page depicts the status of slavery in America after the

(A) Dred Scott decision.   (B) Missouri Compromise.

(C) Compromise of 1850.   (D) Kansas-Nebraska Act.

(E) Civil War.

4. The political party that ran on a strong antiforeign platform was

(A) the American party of 1856.

(B) the Liberty party of 1844.

(C) the Free-Soil party of 1848 and 1852.

(D) the States' Rights Democratic party of 1948.

(E) the People's party of 1892.

5. The Dred Scott case was notable because

(A) it guaranteed the rights of U.S. citizenship to freed blacks and former slaves who succeeded in fleeing to "free states" where slavery was prohibited.

(B) imposed a "gag rule" on Congressional legislation regarding slavery, making it virtually impossible to introduce antislavery legislation.

(C) nullified the Fugitive Slave Act, making it impossible to apprehend runaway slaves who succeeded in fleeing to "free states" where slavery was prohibited.

(D) it ruled that states did not have the Constitutional right to secede from the Union and upheld Congress' right to prohibit slavery in the Western territories.

(E) denied the rights of citizenship to former slaves and prohibited Congress from enacting restrictions against slavery in the Western territories.

3. THE COMING OF THE CIVIL WAR

John Brown's Raid

On the night of October 16, 1859, John Brown, the Pottawatomie Creek murderer, led 18 followers in seizing the federal arsenal at Harpers Ferry, Virginia (now West Virginia), taking hostages, and endeavoring to incite a slave uprising. Brown, supported and bankrolled by several prominent Northern abolitionists (later referred to as "the Secret Six"), planned to arm local slaves and then spread his uprising across the South. His scheme was ill-conceived and had little chance of success. Quickly cornered by Virginia militia, he was eventually captured by a force of U.S. Marines under the command of Army Colonel Robert

E. Lee. Ten of Brown's 18 men were killed in the fight, and Brown himself was wounded.

Charged under Virginia law with treason and various other crimes, Brown was quickly tried, convicted, sentenced, and, on December 2, 1859, hanged. Throughout his trial and at his execution, he conducted himself with fanatical resolution, making eloquent and grandiose statements that convinced many Northerners that he was a martyr rather than a criminal. His death was marked in the North by signs of public mourning.

Though responsible Northerners such as Lincoln denounced Brown's raid as a criminal act that deserved to be punished by death, many Southerners became convinced that the entire Northern public approved of Brown's action and that the only safety for the South lay in a separate Southern confederacy. This was all the more so because Brown, in threatening to create a slave revolt, had touched on the foremost fear of white Southerners.

Hinton Rowan Helper's Book

The second greatest fear of Southern slaveholders was that Southern whites who did not own slaves, by far the majority of the Southern population, would come to see the continuation of slavery as not being in their best interest. This fear was touched on by a book, *The Impending Crisis in the South*, by a North Carolinian named Hinton Rowan Helper. In it Helper argued that slavery was economically harmful to the South and that it enriched the large planter at the expense of the yeoman farmer.

Southerners were enraged, and more so when the Republicans reissued a condensed version of the book as campaign literature. When the new House of Representatives met in December 1859 for the first time since the 1858 elections, angry Southerners determined that no Republican who had endorsed the book should be elected speaker.

The Republicans were the most numerous party in the House although they did not hold a majority. Their candidate for speaker, John Sherman of Ohio, had endorsed Helper's book. A rancorous two-month battle ensued in which the House was unable even to organize itself, let alone transact any business. Secession was talked of openly by Southerners, and as tensions rose congressmen came to the sessions carrying revolvers and Bowie knives. The matter was finally resolved by the withdrawal of Sherman and the election of a moderate Republican as speaker. Tensions remained fairly high.

The Election of 1860

In this mood the country approached the election of 1860, a campaign that eventually became a four-man contest.

The Democrats met in Charleston, South Carolina. Douglas had a majority of the delegates, but at that time a party rule required a two-thirds vote for the nomination. Douglas, faced with the bitter opposition of the Southerners and the Buchanan faction, could not gain this majority. Finally, the convention split up when Southern "fire-eaters" led by William L. Yancey walked out in protest of the convention's refusal to include in the platform a plank demanding federal protection of slavery in all the territories.

A second Democratic convention several weeks later in Baltimore also failed to reach a consensus, and the sundered halves of the party nominated separate candidates. The Southern wing of the party nominated Buchanan's vice president, John C. Breckinridge of Kentucky, on a platform calling for a federal slave code in all the territories. What was left of the national Democratic party nominated Douglas on a platform of popular sovereignty.

The Republicans met in Chicago, confident of victory and determined to do nothing to jeopardize their favorable position. Accordingly, they rejected as too radical front-running New York Senator William H. Seward in favor of Illinois favorite son Abraham Lincoln. The platform was designed to have something for all Northerners, including the provisions of the 1856 Republican platform as well as a call for federal support of a transcontinental railroad. Once again, its center-piece was a call for the containment of slavery.

A third presidential candidate was added by the Constitutional Union party, a collection of aging former Whigs and Know-Nothings from the southern and border states as well as a handful of moderate Southern Democrats. It nominated John Bell of Tennessee on a platform that sidestepped the issues and called simply for the Constitution, the Union, and the enforcement of the laws.

Douglas, believing only his victory could reconcile North and South, became the first U.S. presidential candidate to make a vigorous nationwide speaking tour. In his speeches he urged support for the Union and opposition to any extremist candidates that might endanger its survival, by which he meant Lincoln and Breckinridge.

On election day the voting went along strictly sectional lines. Breckinridge carried the Deep South; Bell, the border states; and Lincoln, the North. Douglas, although second in popular votes, carried only a single state and part of another. Lincoln led in popular votes, and though he was short of a majority in that category, he did have the needed majority in electoral votes and was elected.

The Secession Crisis

Lincoln had declared he had no intention of disturbing slavery where it already existed, but many Southerners thought otherwise. They also feared further raids of the sort John Brown had attempted and felt their pride injured by the election of a president for whom no Southerner had voted.

On December 20, 1860, South Carolina, by vote of a special convention made up of delegates elected by the people of the state, declared itself out of the Union. By February 1, 1861, six more states (Alabama, Georgia, Florida, Mississippi, Louisiana, and Texas) had followed suit.

Representatives of the seven seceded states met in Montgomery, Alabama, in February 1861 and declared themselves to be the Confederate States of America. They elected former Secretary of War and U.S. Senator Jefferson Davis of Mississippi as president and Alexander Stephens of Georgia as vice president. They also adopted a constitution for the Confederate States which, while similar to the U.S. Constitution in many ways, contained several important differences:

1) Slavery was specifically recognized, and the right to move slaves from one state to another was guaranteed.
2) Protective tariffs were prohibited.
3) The president was to serve for a single non-renewable six-year term.
4) The president was given the right to veto individual items within an appropriations bill.
5) State sovereignty was specifically recognized.

In the North reaction was mixed. Some, such as prominent Republican Horace Greeley of the *New York Tribune,* counseled, "Let erring sisters go in peace." President Buchanan, now a lame duck, seemed to be of this mind, since he declared secession to be unconstitutional but at the same time stated his belief that it was unconstitutional for the federal government to do anything to stop states from seceding. Taking his own advice, he did nothing.

Others, led by Senator John J. Crittenden of Kentucky, strove for a compromise that would preserve the Union. Throughout the period of several weeks as the Southern states one by one declared their secession, Crittenden worked desperately with a congressional compromise committee in hopes of working out some form of agreement.

The compromise proposals centered on the passage of a constitutional amendment forever prohibiting federal meddling with slavery in the states where it existed as well as the extension of the Missouri Compromise line (36°30') to the Pacific, with slavery specifically protected in all the territories south of it.

Some Congressional Republicans were inclined to accept this compromise, but president-elect Lincoln urged them to stand firm for no further spread of slavery. Southerners would consider no compromise that did not provide for the spread of slavery, and talks broke down.

QUESTION

> What was Lincoln's position regarding slavery when he was elected to the presidency?

EXPLANATION

Lincoln opposed slavery, but the official position of the Republican party and Lincoln was that slavery would continue where it was already in place, but should not be allowed to expand into the territories. Southerners did not trust Lincoln or the Republicans, believing that their actual intention was to eliminate slavery.

Drill 3: The Coming of the Civil War

1. In the election of 1860, Abraham Lincoln won

    (A) a majority of the popular vote.

    (B) the electoral votes of Kentucky and Maryland.

    (C) less than half of the electoral vote

    (D) the Northern and Midwestern states.

    (E) the electoral votes of Virginia and Tennessee.

2. Which of he following BEST describes the election of 1860?

    (A) Democrat Douglas ran far behind Republican Lincoln in the popular vote, but much closer in the electoral vote.

    (B) Lincoln polled a clear majority of all votes cast.

    (C) Southern Democrat Breckenridge was a secessionist who carried most of the slave states.

    (D) The Southern states were prepared to secede if Lincoln won.

    (E) Union candidate Bell received no support in the South.

3. Lincoln won the 1860 presidential election primarily because

    (A) there was overwhelming support throughout the country for the Republicans' antislavery platform.

    (B) he was seen as a moderate, by both Northerners and Southerners, who could possibly negotiate a compromise between abolitionists and slaveholders.

    (C) he gathered overwhelming support in the highly populated Northern states while his three opponents divided the anti-Lincoln vote in the North, West, and South.

    (D) the Know-Nothing party gave Lincoln its endorsement, and combined with Republican support, the two parties were able to outpoll the politically isolated Democrats.

    (E) he was able to discredit his chief opponent, Stephen Douglas, as a "closet abolitionist."

4. John Brown's raid on the federal arsenal at Harper's Ferry and his subsequent trial and execution had the effect of

    (A) making a martyr of John Brown and convincing many Southerners that secession from the Union was the only way they could prevent the increasingly abolitionist North from interfering with slavery in the South.

   (B) discrediting the abolitionist movement in the eyes of most people and convincing most Southerners that the North would not support forceful efforts to end slavery, despite verbal attacks on slavery by Northern abolitionists.

   (C) inciting a series of slave revolts that resulted in the deaths of thousands of Southern slaves, further enraging both Northern abolitionists and Southern slaveholders.

   (D) sparking a virtual civil war in the state of Nebraska over the issue of slavery.

   (E) exposing a pro-slavery plot to assassinate the leaders of several abolitionist groups and discrediting the prosecution despite Brown being found guilty.

5.   Select the statement which BEST represents Abraham Lincoln's public position on slavery in the election of 1860.

   (A) "We must purge this land by blood."

   (B) "We consider the slaveholder a relentless tyrant."

   (C) "On the issue of slavery I will not retreat a single inch."

   (D) "If I can maintain the Union with slavery I shall; if I can maintain the Union without slavery I shall."

   (E) "Slavery is the most dreaded disease known to civilized mankind."

1850–1861
DRILLS

ANSWER KEY

Drill 1—The Crisis of 1850

1.	(A)	2.	(B)	3.	(B)	4.	(C)	5.	(C)
6.	(A)	7.	(D)	8.	(A)	9.	(B)	10.	(A)

Drill 2—The Return of Sectional Conflict

1.	(C)	2.	(A)	3.	(D)	4.	(A)	5.	(E)

Drill 3—The Coming of the Civil War

1.	(D)	2.	(D)	3.	(C)	4.	(A)	5.	(D)

GLOSSARY: 1850–1861

Fireeaters

Southern delegates to the Democratic party convention who walked out in protest of the convention's refusal to include a platform plan demanding federal protection of slavery in all the territories.

Forty-Niners

Gold seekers from the eastern U.S. who went to California.

Free-Soil Party

A political party that stood for prohibiting slavery from newly acquired territories.

Nativists

Americans who were alarmed about increasing immigration from Germany and Ireland.

Popular Sovereignty

A process where the residents of a territory would decide whether slavery was to be permitted when the territory became a state.

Young America

An aggressive program of economic and territorial expansion.

1861–1877

DIAGNOSTIC TEST

CHAPTER 8

1861–1877

THE CIVIL WAR AND RECONSTRUCTION

➤ Diagnostic Test
➤ 1861–1877 Review & Drills
➤ Glossary

1861-1877
DIAGNOSTIC TEST

1. Ⓐ Ⓑ Ⓒ Ⓓ Ⓔ		19. Ⓐ Ⓑ Ⓒ Ⓓ Ⓔ
2. Ⓐ Ⓑ Ⓒ Ⓓ Ⓔ		20. Ⓐ Ⓑ Ⓒ Ⓓ Ⓔ
3. Ⓐ Ⓑ Ⓒ Ⓓ Ⓔ		21. Ⓐ Ⓑ Ⓒ Ⓓ Ⓔ
4. Ⓐ Ⓑ Ⓒ Ⓓ Ⓔ		22. Ⓐ Ⓑ Ⓒ Ⓓ Ⓔ
5. Ⓐ Ⓑ Ⓒ Ⓓ Ⓔ		23. Ⓐ Ⓑ Ⓒ Ⓓ Ⓔ
6. Ⓐ Ⓑ Ⓒ Ⓓ Ⓔ		24. Ⓐ Ⓑ Ⓒ Ⓓ Ⓔ
7. Ⓐ Ⓑ Ⓒ Ⓓ Ⓔ		25. Ⓐ Ⓑ Ⓒ Ⓓ Ⓔ
8. Ⓐ Ⓑ Ⓒ Ⓓ Ⓔ		26. Ⓐ Ⓑ Ⓒ Ⓓ Ⓔ
9. Ⓐ Ⓑ Ⓒ Ⓓ Ⓔ		27. Ⓐ Ⓑ Ⓒ Ⓓ Ⓔ
10. Ⓐ Ⓑ Ⓒ Ⓓ Ⓔ		28. Ⓐ Ⓑ Ⓒ Ⓓ Ⓔ
11. Ⓐ Ⓑ Ⓒ Ⓓ Ⓔ		29. Ⓐ Ⓑ Ⓒ Ⓓ Ⓔ
12. Ⓐ Ⓑ Ⓒ Ⓓ Ⓔ		30. Ⓐ Ⓑ Ⓒ Ⓓ Ⓔ
13. Ⓐ Ⓑ Ⓒ Ⓓ Ⓔ		31. Ⓐ Ⓑ Ⓒ Ⓓ Ⓔ
14. Ⓐ Ⓑ Ⓒ Ⓓ Ⓔ		32. Ⓐ Ⓑ Ⓒ Ⓓ Ⓔ
15. Ⓐ Ⓑ Ⓒ Ⓓ Ⓔ		33. Ⓐ Ⓑ Ⓒ Ⓓ Ⓔ
16. Ⓐ Ⓑ Ⓒ Ⓓ Ⓔ		34. Ⓐ Ⓑ Ⓒ Ⓓ Ⓔ
17. Ⓐ Ⓑ Ⓒ Ⓓ Ⓔ		35. Ⓐ Ⓑ Ⓒ Ⓓ Ⓔ
18. Ⓐ Ⓑ Ⓒ Ⓓ Ⓔ		

1861–1877
DIAGNOSTIC TEST

This diagnostic test is designed to help you determine your strengths and weaknesses in your knowledge of the Civil War and Reconstruction (1861–1877). Follow the directions and check your answers.

Study this chapter for the following tests:
AP U.S. History, CLEP General, CLEP United States History I,
CLEP United States History II, GED, Praxis Specialty Area,
SAT: United States History

---

35 Questions

DIRECTIONS: Choose the correct answer for each of the following questions. Fill in each answer on the answer sheet.

1. Most modern historians believe that Reconstruction was characterized by

   (A) extensive military occupation of the South.

   (B) black misrule of the South.

   (C) government corruption of the South.

   (D) limited military occupation of the South.

   (E) Northern takeover of the economy and government of the South.

2. The Confederacy raised money for its war effort by all of the following EXCEPT

   (A) borrowing money from abroad.

   (B) raising taxes.

   (C) printing money *greenbacks*

   (D) establishing an income tax.

   (E) borrowing money from its citizens.

3. In issuing the Emancipation Proclamation, one of Lincoln's goals was to

   (A) gain the active aid of Britain and France in restoring the Union.

(B) stir up enthusiasm for the war in such border states as Maryland and Kentucky.

(C) please the Radicals in the North by abolishing slavery in areas of the South already under the control of Union armies.

(D) please Russia, one of the Union's few overseas friends, where the serfs had been emancipated the previous year.

(E) keep Britain and France from intervening on the side of the Confederacy.

4. Organizations such as the Ku Klux Klan were organized in a number of Southern states after the Civil War for the purpose of

(A) extorting large amounts of money from former slaves.

(B) promoting the return of former slaves to Africa.

(C) preventing the former slaves from voting.

(D) commemorating those who had died in the war.

(E) preparing for another armed uprising against the federal government.

5. Which of the following statements is true of Lincoln's Ten Percent Plan?

(A) It stipulated that at least ten percent of former slaves must be accorded the right to vote within a given Southern state before that state could be readmitted to the Union.

(B) It allowed the rights of citizenship only to those Southerners who could take an oath that they had never been disloyal to the Union.

(C) It allowed high-ranking rebel officials to regain the right to vote and hold office by simply promising future good behavior.

(D) It was silent on the issue of slavery.

(E) It provided for the restoration of loyal governments for the erstwhile Confederate states now under Union control.

6. All of the following were parts of Andrew Johnson's plan for Reconstruction EXCEPT

(A) recommending to the Southern states that the vote be extended to the recently freed slaves.

(B) requiring ratification of the Thirteenth Amendment.

(C) requiring payment of monetary reparations for the damage caused by the war.

(D) requiring renunciation of secession.

(E) requiring repudiation of the Confederate debt.

PLANS for
Reconstruction
Lincoln, Johnson, Reps/Dems

7. The term "Seward's Folly" referred to Secretary of State William Seward's

   (A) advocacy of a lenient policy toward the defeated Southern states.

   (B) break with the majority Radical faction of the Republican party in order to back President Andrew Johnson.

   (C) belief that the Civil War could be avoided and the Union restored by provoking a war with Britain and France.

   (D) purchase of Alaska from Russia. *1867 – $7 million*

   (E) attempt to gain the presidency in 1860.

8. A major threat to the Monroe Doctrine during the 1860s was posed by

   (A) British sale of war materials to the Confederacy.

   (B) French loans to the Confederacy.

   (C) the presence of British troops in Central and South America.

   (D) Russian ownership of Alaska.

   (E) the presence of French troops and a puppet emperor in Mexico.

9. In response to President Andrew Johnson's relatively mild Reconstruction program, the Southern states did all of the following EXCEPT

   (A) refuse to repudiate the Confederate debt.

   (B) elect many former high-ranking Confederates to Congress and other top positions.

   (C) refuse to grant blacks the right to vote.

   (D) attempt to reinstitute slavery.

   (E) pass special "black codes" restricting the legal rights of blacks.

10. Andrew Johnson was impeached and nearly removed from office on the grounds of his

   (A) refusal to carry out the provisions of the Military Reconstruction Act.

   (B) alleged involvement in a corrupt stock-manipulating scheme carried out by one of his associates.

   (C) refusal to carry out the provisions of the Civil Rights Act of 1866.

   (D) violation of the Tenure of Office Act in removing Secretary of War Edwin M. Stanton.

   (E) general failure to cooperate with the Radical Republicans in their efforts to carry out Reconstruction.

11. In speaking of "redemption" in a political sense, white Southerners of the Reconstruction era made reference to

- (A) ridding the South of the Reconstruction governments.

- (B) atoning for their society's sin of slavery by granting full legal and social equality to blacks.

- (C) atoning for the Southern states' secession by displaying extreme patriotism to the restored United States.

- (D) regaining personal rights of citizenship by taking an oath of allegiance to the Union.

- (E) buying back from the federal government plantations confiscated during the war.

12. The primary underlying reason that Reconstruction ended in 1877 was that

- (A) Southerners had succeeded in electing anti-Reconstruction governments in all the former Confederate states.

- (B) all the goals set by the Radical Republicans at the end of the Civil War had been accomplished.

- (C) leading Radicals in the North had become convinced that Reconstruction had been unconstitutional.

- (D) Northern voters had grown weary of the effort to Reconstruct the South and generally lost interest.

- (E) Republican political managers had come to see further agitation of North-South differences arising from the Civil War as a political liability.

13. "Waving the bloody shirt" was the name given to the practice of

- (A) scaring black potential voters into staying away from the polls.

- (B) voting large appropriations of federal funds for unnecessary projects in a powerful congressman's district.

- (C) using animosities stirred up by the Civil War to gain election in the post-war North.

- (D) inciting the country to go to war with Spain.

- (E) machine politics as practiced in many major cities during the late nineteenth century.

14. All of the following are true of the Confederate war effort during the Civil War EXCEPT

- (A) Confederate industry was never able to adequately supply Confederate soldiers with the armaments they needed to successfully fight the war.

(B) Confederate agriculture was never able to adequately supply the people of the South with the food they needed.

(C) inflation became a major problem in the South as the Confederate government was forced to print more paper currency than it could support with gold or other tangible assets.

(D) the inadequate railroad system of the South hindered movement of soldiers, supplies, and food from the places they were stationed (or produced) to the places in which they were most needed.

(E) tremendous resentment at the military draft developed among poor and middle-class Southerners because wealthy Southern males could pay to have a substitute take their place in the army.

15. The main reason that President Grant's administration is considered a failure is

(A) he failed to retreat from the radical Reconstruction policies of his predecessors.

(B) he failed to effectively quell the Indian uprisings in the Western territories.

(C) his failure to control the corruption permeating his administration.

(D) he attempted to destroy the Democratic party and return the country to a one-party system.

(E) he failed to be reelected after serving his first term in office.

16. After the collapse of the Reconstruction governments, the men who came to power in the "New South" were called

(A) carpetbaggers   (B) scalawags.

(C) copperheads.   (D) freedmen.

(E) redeemers.

17. The biggest failure of Reconstruction governments was that they

(A) failed to reestablish an effective plantation system to rejuvenate the South's devastated economy.

(B) were dominated by blacks, which aroused such white hostility that, combined with the inexperience of black legislators, doomed Reconstruction governments to failure.

(C) failed to reestablish an effective public education system in the occupied South.

    (D) failed to effectively industrialize the South.

  *(E) failed to change basic white attitudes in the South and they were unable to effectively reorganize the South's social structure.

18. In announcing the Emancipation Proclamation, Lincoln's immediate purpose was to

    (A) free black slaves in all of the slave states. *not possible*

    (B) free black slaves in only the border slave states which had remained loyal to the Union.

    (C) let the Southern states know that whether or not they chose to secede from the Union, slavery would not be tolerated by his administration once he took office.

  ·(D) rally Northern morale by giving the war a higher moral purpose than just preserving the Union.

    (E) recruit freed blacks into the Union army and overcome the shortage of white soldiers in the army at that time.

19. The <u>final</u> four states to secede from the United States after the firing on Fort Sumter were *7| first*

  (A) Alabama, Georgia, South Carolina, and North Carolina.

  ·(B) Virginia, Arkansas, Tennessee, and North Carolina.

  (C) Georgia, Mississippi, South Carolina, and Texas.

  (D) South Carolina, Kentucky, Maryland, and Delaware.

  (E) Florida, Georgia, Maryland, and South Carolina.

20. During the Civil War, the "copperheads" were

    (A) anti-Lincoln Republicans.   (B) Northern pro-war Democrats.

    (C) pro-Union Southerners.   ·(D) Northern antiwar Democrats.

    (E) none of the above.

21. The Southern strategy of gaining a European ally against the North was attempted through a policy referred to as

    (A) the Stars and Bars.   (B) the war of attrition.

  ·(C) King Cotton Diplomacy.   (D) nullification.

    (E) mercantilism.

22. The Great Plains Indian culture can best be described in the 1840s as

    (A) nomadic.

    (B) centered around the buffalo.

    (C) at its zenith.

    (D) animistic in its reverence for the spiritual power of nature.

    · (E) all of the above.

23. Lincoln's Reconstruction plan for the defeated Southern states included all of the following EXCEPT

    10 %
    Governing

    (A) abolition of slavery.

    (B) free education for ex-slaves.

    (C) republican state governments.

    (D) a required 10 percent of all voters in a state to take a loyalty oath to the United States.

    (E) citizenship for ex-slaves. *Later – 14ᵗʰ Amendment*

24. The Wade-Davis Bill best represents the views of

    (A) President Andrew Johnson. · (B) the Radical Republicans.

    (C) the carpetbaggers.   (D) the scalawags.

    (E) the Democratic party.

25. The Fifteenth Amendment established

    13 – Ends Slavery
    14 – Citizenship
    15 – Voting

    (A) the legal end of slavery in America.

    (B) the two-term presidency.

    · (C) the right to vote for ex-slaves.

    (D) the income tax.

    (E) female suffrage.

26. In trying to impeach President Andrew Johnson, Congress used the

    (A) Morrill Act. *used against*   · (B) Tenure of Office Act.

    (C) Civil Rights Act.   (D) *Ex Parte Milligan.*

    (E) None of the above

27. The Trent Affair was important because

    (A) it discredited the revolutionary government in France in the eyes of most Americans.

(B) it prevented the Confederacy from being able to purchase several warships from Britain and France for use against Union shipping.

(C) it was the first clear case of treason by a United States official and it
badly embarrassed the administration of John Adams.

(D) it resulted in the sinking of the Confederate raider, the *Alabama.*

· (E) it nearly led to British recognition of the Confederacy and war between Britain and the Union.

28. Andrew Johnson was impeached primarily because

(A) he was an alcoholic and made several major speeches while totally
drunk.

(B) angry Northern congressmen resented the fact that Johnson, a Southerner (from Tennessee) had become president following Lincoln's death
and was administering Southern Reconstruction.

(C) members of Congress felt that Johnson's Reconstruction policies were
too harsh and unfairly penalized former Confederate leaders trying to
rebuild their homeland.

(D) he demanded suffrage for blacks in addition to the abolition of slavery.

. . (E) he obstructed the enforcement of congressional Reconstruction policies that he felt were too harsh.

29. Which of the following factors came closest to giving the Confederacy what
could have been a decisive foreign policy success during the Civil War?

(A) The U.S. Navy's seizure of Confederate emissaries James M. Mason
and John Slidell from the British Mail steamer *Trent.*

(B) French objections to the Union blockade.

(C) The acute economic dislocation in Britain and France caused by the
cut-off of cotton imports from the South.

(D) The concerns of French financial interests that had loaned large amounts
of money to the Confederacy.

(E) The skillful negotiating of Confederate diplomats in Europe.

30. Abraham Lincoln took the Union into war against the Confederate States of
America with the stated purpose of

(A) protecting federal installations in Confederate territories.

(B) freeing the slaves and abolishing slavery from American soil.

✓ (C) preserving the Union.

(D) punishing the South for its arrogance, rebelliousness, and enslavement of blacks by Southern slaveholders.

(E) protecting the Union from Southern attacks on Union territories in the border states remaining loyal to the Union.

31. Secretary of State William Seward's purchase of Alaska from the Russians in 1867 was based primarily on

(A) his realization that fishing rights in Alaskan waters would be a boon to American fishermen.

(B) his desire to secure the vast oil reserves rumored to be hidden deep within Alaska's forbidding interior. *nobody knew*

(C) fears of Russian attempts to expand their control into western Canada and possibly the northwestern United States.

(D) his desires to help the Russians, who desperately needed the money they would get for dumping this "wasteland" on the Americans.

(E) his dream of an American empire that would subsume all of North America, including Canada, Mexico, and Greenland. *MANIFEST DESTINY*

32. The battle between the *Monitor* and the *Merrimac* was important because

(A) it was the first successful effort by the Confederate navy to break the Union naval blockade.

(B) it signified the last major effort by the Confederate navy to break the Union naval blockade.

(C) it broke the Union stranglehold on Hampton Roads, Virginia, and opened the door for General Lee's offensive into Maryland.

(D) it signaled the end of the wooden warship as the ultimate naval vessel and marked the beginning of the age of iron/steel warships.

(E) the *Merrimac's* failure to break the Union naval blockade cost the Confederacy its last hope of achieving official recognition by France or Britain.

33. In general, state governments in the South during Reconstruction

(A) were ineffective because they were dominated by freed slaves and others who were incompetent to hold office.

(B) were totally ineffective because of the restrictive rule of the Union military bureaucracy, which kept a tight reign on state governments.

(C) accomplished some notable items, but basically squandered their opportunity to effectively rebuild the South because of the greed and corruption of "scalawags" and Yankee "carpetbaggers."

(D) were much more successful than the pre-Civil War governments that preceded them.

• (E) accomplished some notable achievements and were comparable in their effectiveness to the pre-Civil War governments that preceded them.

no more corrupt

34. The Emancipation Proclamation immediately freed the slaves

(A) throughout the United States. *No one*

(B) only in the border states.

(C) throughout the South only.

(D) in Maryland and Tennessee.

• (E) None of the above

35. Because of its acceptance of the States' Rights doctrine, the Confederacy most closely resembled

(A) the British Constitution.

• (B) the Articles of Confederation.

(C) Napoleonic France.

(D) the United States Constitution.

(E) None of the above.

1861–1877
DIAGNOSTIC TEST

ANSWER KEY

1. (D)	8. (E)	15. (C)	22. (E)	29. (A)
2. (D)	9. (D)	16. (E)	23. (E)	30. (C)
3. (E)	10. (D)	17. (E)	24. (B)	31. (E)
4. (C)	11. (A)	18. (D)	25. (C)	32. (D)
5. (E)	12. (D)	19. (B)	26. (B)	33. (E)
6. (C)	13. (C)	20. (D)	27. (E)	34. (E)
7. (D)	14. (A)	21. (C)	28. (E)	35. (B)

DETAILED EXPLANATIONS
OF ANSWERS

1.   **(D)**   Modern historians have generally rejected the traditional view that Reconstruction of the South was characterized by black misrule, government corruption, Northern takeover of the Southern government and economy, and extensive military occupation. Only about 20,000 troops were stationed in the South and that number was only for a short time.

2.   **(D)**   The Confederacy borrowed about $15 million from abroad and $100 million from its citizens, raised over $100 million through taxation, and printed over $1 billion in paper currency. No income tax was established.

3.   **(E)**   One of Lincoln's reasons for issuing the Emancipation Proclamation was keeping Britain and France from intervening on the side of the Confederacy. Lincoln neither needed, wanted, nor could have obtained the active aid of these countries in restoring the Union (A), and Russia, which had indeed freed its serfs the previous year, would have been a U.S. ally regardless (D). The Radicals in the North would indeed have been pleased had Lincoln freed the slaves in areas of the South already under the control of Union armies (C), but it was precisely that which the Emancipation Proclamation did not do, largely out of concern for the more-or-less loyal slaveholding border states such as Maryland and Kentucky, who were not at all enthused about Lincoln's action even as it was (B).

4.   **(C)**   The purpose of the Ku Klux Klan and similar organizations was intimidating blacks out of voting. While this represented defiance of the federal government, it was not preparation for another uprising (E), and while such groups may have commemorated dead Confederates (D) from time to time as struck their fancy, that was hardly their purpose. Nor was there much point in extorting money from the near-penniless former slaves (A), and by this time there was little talk of returning the former slaves to Africa (B).

5.   **(E)**   Lincoln's Ten Percent Plan provided for the restoration of loyal government in states formerly in rebellion. It did not require that any of the former slaves be given the right to vote (A). It allowed Southerners to participate in the political process provided they would take an oath of future, not past (B), loyalty to the Union and acceptance of the abolition of slavery (D). High ranking Confederates were excepted from this provision (C) and had to apply separately to the president for pardon.

6.   **(C)**   Johnson did not require former Confederate states to pay reparations, but he did recommend they extend the vote to blacks (A), and he did

require them to ratify the Thirteenth Amendment (B), renounce secession (D), and repudiate the Confederate debt (E).

7.   **(D)**   "Seward's Folly" was the name given to the purchase of Alaska. Seward had indeed believed that the Civil War could be avoided and the Union restored by provoking a war with Britain and France (C)—a foolish belief but not well known enough to gain a label. He had attempted to gain the presidency in 1860 and failed (E), though no one would have labeled his campaign folly. Seward also favored a lenient policy toward the defeated South (A) and broke with the majority wing of his party to support President Andrew Johnson (B), though whether that was folly or courage remains debatable.

8.   **(E)**   The greatest threat to the Monroe Doctrine during the 1860s was France's attempt to set up a puppet empire in Mexico. Britain did sell war supplies to the Confederacy (A) and France did loan it money (B) but these, while highly unfriendly acts toward the United States, were not violations of the Monroe Doctrine. Russia did own Alaska until 1867 (D) and British troops were present in the pre-existing British colonies in Central and South America (C), but these, too, were not violations of the Monroe Doctrine.

9.   **(D)**   The Southern states did not attempt to reinstitute slavery, but some or all of them did refuse to repudiate the Confederate debt (A), elect former Confederates to high position (B), refuse to grant blacks the right to vote (C), and pass special "black codes" restricting the legal rights of blacks (E), resulting in the imposition of harsh congressional Reconstruction despite Johnson's efforts to prevent it.

10.   **(D)**   It was for violation of the Tenure of Office Act in removing Secretary of War Stanton that Johnson was impeached and almost removed from office. His refusal to cooperate with the Radical Republicans (E) or to carry out the spirit, if not the letter, of the Military Reconstruction Act (A) and the Civil Rights Act (C) were the reasons the heavily radical Congress was anxious to be rid of him, but even they could not bring themselves to impeach him without some actual breach of a law—thus, the Tenure of Office Act. It was Grant, rather than Johnson, whose associates were involved in not one but a number of highly questionable schemes (B).

11.   **(A)**   When white Southerners during the era of Reconstruction spoke of "redemption" in political terms they meant ridding their states of the Reconstruction governments. They would hardly have thought it necessary to atone for slavery or secession (B) and (C), and regaining personal rights (D) was relatively easy for the great majority of Southerners who had not held high positions in the Confederacy or in the U.S. government before joining the Confederacy. Very few, if any, plantations were confiscated as a result of the war (E).

12.   **(D)**   Northern voters simply lost interest and grew tired of Reconstruc-

tion. Leading Radicals in the North had never cared much whether Reconstruction was constitutional or not (C) but many of them were dead by 1877. Agitating wartime animosities was still a useful electoral tactic (E), but it did not necessarily need to be linked to reconstructing the South. The goals of the Radical Republicans had not been accomplished (B), but neither had the Southerners regained all the state governments (A).

13. **(C)** "Waving the bloody shirt" was the practice of using wartime animosities to gain election in the North. Machine politics were practiced in many cities during the late nineteenth century (E), though there is no special name for this other than "corruption." The voting of large appropriations of federal funds for unnecessary projects in a powerful congressman's district (B) might also be called corruption but is more often referred to as a "pork barrel scheme," a general term for a politician's buying of votes with government appropriations. Inciting the country to go to war with Spain (D) was one of the things accomplished just before the turn of the century by "yellow journalism."

14. **(A)** Contrary to myth, Confederate industry did a masterful job in producing weapons and ammunition for the Confederate military during the war. While it is true that the Confederates never had the abundance of weapons possessed by Union forces, particularly in artillery, it was only near the end of the war, when Union forces had overrun many production centers and totally destroyed the South's transportation network, that severe shortages of ammunition and weapons developed. It is also true that in the beginning of the war Confederate industry could not arm everyone who volunteered for military service, the Union had that same problem. Most Southerners had their own weapons so that despite the lack of government-produced weapons, there was no shortage of available weapons for soldiers. The biggest problem faced by the Confederate armies in regard to weapons and ammunition was a lack of uniformity for the vast array of "home grown" weapons and ammunition used by their soldiers, not a shortage of weapons themselves.

15. **(C)** Grant was an intensely loyal man who was, sadly, not the best judge of character in choosing his administrative appointees. During his first term in office, his administration was beset with financial scandals involving the vice president, Grant's brother-in-law, and a well-known financial entrepreneur named Jay Gould. In his second term, the "whiskey ring" scandal implicated Grant's private secretary. His secretary of war was implicated in a bribery scandal. While few believed Grant to be corrupt, Grant's loyalty to his corrupt associates tarnished his image in virtually everyone's eyes. It also crippled the effectiveness of his administration.

16. **(E)** During the waning years of Reconstruction, when Southern voters voted Reconstructionist Republicans out of office and replaced them with Democrats, Southerners said that the state had been "redeemed." In other words, the state was said to have been saved from the "clutches" of Yankee Reconstruction-

ism. Thus, the leaders of this new post-Reconstruction, Democratic administrations were called "redeemers." Since many of these "redeemers" came from the former ruling elites, to others wishing to return the South to "the good old days," the presence of these "old school" leaders must have seemed like political redemption for the South.

17. **(E)** The biggest failure of Reconstruction in the South was its failure to effectively change Southern social structure and eliminate the racism inherent within. When Reconstruction ended, the Republican governments which had run the South during Reconstruction were universally voted out of office. When they were gone, the South was in many ways little different than it had been before the war. Most of the wealth was still concentrated in the hands of a few white landowners. While blacks were no longer technically slaves, they owned no land. Various restrictions and lack of capital effectively prevented them from acquiring land. Without land and money, blacks remained targets of white exploitation. New "black codes" limited their voting rights, education rights, property rights, and their rights to use public facilities. The passage of these new codes symbolized how little attitudes had changed. Blacks were still economic slaves, if not legal slaves, and lived in terror of white oppression. Whites still felt that blacks were inferior and, in many cases, blamed blacks (and Yankees) for the Civil War as well as every other problem experienced since the war. As a result, while the Civil War held the Union together and ended legalized slavery, it would be another 80 years after the end of Reconstruction before types of social changes hoped for at the start of Reconstruction could begin.

18. **(D)** Lincoln's immediate purpose in announcing the Emancipation Proclamation was to rally flagging Northern morale. Lincoln waited until after a major Union victory, at Antietam in 1862, so he couldn't be charged with making the announcement as an act of desperation. He recognized that the costs of the war had reached a point where preserving the Union would not be a powerful enough reason to motivate many Northerners to continue the war. Framing the war as a war against slavery would mobilize powerful abolitionist forces in the North and perhaps create an atmosphere of a "holy crusade" rather than one of using war to resolve a political conflict.

While the Emancipation Proclamation had the announced purpose of freeing the slaves, Lincoln himself indirectly stated that freeing the slaves was a means to a greater end, preserving the Union. In a statement released before the Emancipation Proclamation Lincoln asserted, "If I could save the Union without freeing any slave I would do it, and if I could save it by freeing all the slaves I would do it... What I do about slavery, and the colored race I do because I believe it helps to save the Union."

19. **(B)** On April 12, 1861, the Confederate forces began their bombardment on Fort Sumter. With the Fort's surrender and Lincoln's proclamation that an insurrection existed, the states of the Upper South (Virginia, Arkansas, Tennessee, and North Carolina) joined the Lower South (South Carolina, Alabama,

Mississippi, Florida, Georgia, Louisiana, and Texas) who had seceded in February 1861, to form the Confederate States of America.

20.   **(D)**   The American Civil War was an unpopular war in the North. Lincoln constantly was troubled by draft riots and the treats of Northern antiwar Democrats, called the copperheads. Anti-Lincoln Republicans adopted the name, Radical Republicans, and pro-Union Southerners were labeled scalawags after the war. Lincoln masterfully was able to maintain control over his party during the war and narrowly was re-elected in 1864, in large part owing to some eleventh-hour Northern military victories. At the close of the war, the copperheads were treated with severe hatred in the North, especially after Lincoln's assassination.

21.   **(C)**   King Cotton Diplomacy was the sole foreign policy strategy of the Confederacy. The South refused to export cotton to Europe in the hopes that this embargo would lead to a depression in the European textile industry and force western Europe to ally with the South because of their dependance upon cotton. This strategy failed because Europeans had been stockpiling American cotton since 1855 in anticipation of the Civil War and found a new source of cotton in Egypt. The Stars and Bars was the nickname for the Confederate flag, while a war of attrition was General Grant's military strategy for ending the Civil War. Mercantilism was Great Britain's economic policy toward its American colonies in the seventeenth and eighteenth centuries, while nullification was the attempt by South Carolina not to pay new tariff rates in 1831.

22.   **(E)**   In the 1840s, the Indians of the Great Plains were at their height as a civilization. Not yet in close contact with whites, the Plains Indians lived a nomadic existence hunting the plentiful buffalo who provided the Indians with food, clothing, and shelter. The Plains tribes were noted for their deep reverence of the forces of nature and believed all natural elements held a soul and were to be treated with respect.

23.   **(E)**   In 1864, Lincoln announced his plan to allow the South to re-enter the Union. The plan, known as his Reconstruction Plan, was extremely lenient to the defeated South. Lincoln proposed the South re-enter on a state-by-state basis after having agreed to abolish slavery, educate the ex-slaves, establish republican state government, and have 10 percent of Southern citizens take an oath of loyalty to the Union. The Radical Republicans in Congress opposed Lincoln's plan as too lenient and criticized the plan for not allowing for the citizenship of the ex-slaves which the Radicals established under the Fourteenth Amendment in 1867.

24.   **(B)**   In 1864, the Radical Republicans openly broke from President Lincoln's Reconstruction plans with the passage of the Wade-Davis Act. This act presented the Radicals' Reconstruction plans and sought to treat the South as a conquered territory under military rule. Rather than the quick readmission of

Southern states that Lincoln envisioned, the act demanded readmission only after 50 percent of the voters of each state could prove their loyalty to the Union during the Civil War. Lincoln vetoed the act. President Johnson did not support Wade-Davis, nor did the Democratic party. Both scalawags and carpetbaggers had little association with the measure as Southerners who cooperated during Reconstruction with the North and carpetbaggers who went down South to work on rebuilding the devastated South after the war.

25.　**(C)**　Slavery was ended by Congress' ratification of the Thirteenth Amendment to the U.S. Constitution in 1865. The Radical Republicans were in control of Congress and passed the amendment in the aftermath of Lincoln's assassination by John Wilkes Booth. The Fifteenth Amendment (1867) extends the vote to ex-slaves, who were granted citizenship under the Fourteenth amendment in 1867. The Nineteenth Amendment (1920) extends the vote to women, while the Sixteenth Amendment (1913) established the federal income tax. The Twenty-second Amendment in 1951 established the two-term limit on the presidency.

26.　**(B)**　In the impeachment proceedings against President Johnson, Congress cited his violation of the Tenure of Office Act in removing Secretary of War Stanton without Senate approval. Of the 11 charges of impeachment brought by the House against Johnson, nine were based on the Tenure of Office Act. The Morrill Act was passed in 1862 to establish publicly financed land grant colleges in the states. The Civil Rights Act was passed in 1866 and directed against the "black codes" in Southern governments, not Johnson. *Ex Parte Milligan* (1866) ruled that civilian courts should have been allowed to function during the Civil War rather than the military tribunals Lincoln established. The case was a decision by the Supreme Court of the United States.

27.　**(E)**　The Trent Affair resulted from the overaggressive pursuit of two Confederate ambassadors to England by an American naval officer. The two Confederates, John Mason and James Slidell, were on their way to Europe aboard a British packet ship to become permanent envoys to England and France. The captain of the Union vessel, the *San Jacinto*, found out that the Confederate envoys were on the British vessel. He intercepted the British ship in international waters, stopping and boarding the vessel and removing the two Confederate envoys, who were returned as prisoners to the United States. The British vehemently protested the seizure as a violation of their maritime rights. They threatened war with the United States, which would have included recognition of the Confederacy, if the two diplomats were not returned. Many in the North were determined to keep the diplomats whether it meant war with Britain or not. Fortunately, Lincoln had a more realistic assessment of the situation. He realized that the Union could not afford a war with England while simultaneously trying to subdue the Confederacy. He also realized that turning the diplomats over to England immediately would cause a firestorm of protest at home. So he stalled for time, posturing to the British to make it sound like the U.S. would never back down. After a few weeks, when tensions had subsided at home and people's attention had shifted to other matters, he quietly arranged the release of the two diplomats to the British. While the incident was a dangerous gaffe by the Union, and was a major short-term embarrassment, in the long-term, Lincoln's handling of the matter earned him much respect in Britain and laid the groundwork for better future relations between the two powers. It did not, however, prevent the Confederacy from purchasing several warships such as the *Alabama* from the British before the war was over.

28.   **(E)**   Under Johnson's Reconstruction policies, many Southern states attempted to reenter the Union led by former Confederates, pardoned by Johnson. Once in office, these ex-Confederates helped legislate a new wave of "black codes" that limited the rights of blacks. They also did little or nothing to ensure that the rights of freed slaves were protected. Johnson was willing to let the old Southern ruling elites take power again as long as they understood that they could not reinstitute slavery, nor could they secede. Since Johnson, himself, did not see blacks as equals, he was not willing to demand any further gurantees that black rights be protected. Northern congressmen saw the new "black codes" as a new type of economic and political slavery. They felt that the old ruling elites of the South should be punished for their actions and should be forbidden from holding public office.

Efforts by Southern leaders to restrict black rights convinced many congressional leaders that Southern leaders had failed to learn from their military defeat. When Congress implemented its own, tougher reconstruction policy, Johnson fought it by replacing appointed officials who attempted to enforce congressional Reconstruction policy. When Johnson attempted to replace a member of his cabinet, Edward Stanton, in disregard of congressional legislation requiring Senate approval of the removal of any cabinet member by the president, the House of Representatives voted for impeachment. The impeachment trial was close, but Johnson survived it by one vote. Despite his close victory in the trial, Johnson enforced congressional Reconstruction policies for the remainder of his term.

29.   **(A)**   The U.S. Navy's seizure of Confederate emissaries James M. Mason and John Slidell from the British mail Steamer *Trent* came closest to giving the Confederacy the foreign help it needed by nearly bringing on a war between Great Britain and the United States. Confederate diplomats were not, on the whole, very skillful negotiators (E). There was some objection in Europe to the Union blockade (B), but Britain, the only country that could have done anything about it, favored permissive rules for blockading. Large prewar stocks of cotton in Britain and France along with the discovery of alternate sources of cotton prevented the economic dislocation in those countries that Confederate leaders had hoped would bring their aid (C). Some French financiers did float a bond issue for the Confederacy (D), but they slyly made sure they got their money first, assuring that if anyong got bilked it would be the small, uninfluential investors.

30.　**(C)**　Lincoln firmly believed that the Southern states did not have the constitutional right to secede from the Union. He only went to war when Southerners attacked Fort Sumter, and then he mobilized Union forces to put down "a state of insurrection" in the Southern states. Throughout the war Lincoln repeatedly emphasized that his purpose in warring with the South was to preserve the Union of which he felt the Southern states were an integral part.

31.　**(E)**　William Seward was a fervent believer in the concept of Manifest Destiny. He was an extremist in this regard who firmly believed that one day the United States would govern all of North and Central America, including the Caribbean, Greenland, and even Iceland. Obtaining Alaska from the Russians not only removed one more European influence from American shores, but it brought the U.S. one step closer to Seward's expansionist dreams. While Seward's dream has not yet been realized, and will probably never be, it was the driving force behind his support of the Alaska purchase.

32.　**(D)**　The battle between the *Monitor* and *Merrimac* ushered in a whole new age of warship construction. The ease with which the *Merrimac* had destroyed the Union's wooden warships the day before it met the *Monitor*, proved that the old wooden ships were obsolete in comparison to this new iron monster. While wooden warships would still be a major part of the naval forces of both sides for the remainder of the war, increasingly the new warships were made with metal plating on their sides and many of the old ones were retrofitted with metal plating. The day of the wooden warship was clearly over.

33.　**(E)**　The state governments in the South during Reconstruction actually did a remarkable job, given the conditions under which they labored. The office holders were at least as qualified as those who preceded them. The legions of freed slaves were mostly illiterate, but no more so than the poor white rural farmers who had the right to vote before the Civil War. While greed and corruption certainly existed in Reconstruction governments, there is no evidence that it was much worse than the corruption that existed in Southern state governments before or during the Civil War. Reconstruction governments did a surprisingly effective job beginning the Herculean task of rebuilding the South's infrastructure. Housing, roads, railroads, and industry all needed to be rebuilt almost from scratch. The plantation system was in ruins, as was the entire Southern economy. Any government would have had difficulties operating in this environment. Despite this, Reconstruction governments founded the South's first adequate public education systems and helped establish a whole range of public services such as facilities to care for the poor or the mentally ill. Voting rights were expanded and for the first time, the poor and middle class could elect representatives from their own economic class. While these governments were not demonstrably superior to the governments which preceded them, they were certainly comparable. Many of the problems keeping Reconstruction governments from doing a better job were related to inexperience and, in many cases, corruption. However, more often than not, problems stemmed from active resistance to needed reforms by Southern whites who resented reforms and particularly resented being represented by "Yankees" or blacks. Unfortunately, many of the notable reforms enacted by these governments were wiped out by conservative white Democrats who regained power after Reconstruction ended.

34.   **(E)**   Lincoln's issuance of the Emancipation Proclamation in January 1863, was greeted with joyous celebration in the North. However, a strict legal reading of the document indicates that it effectively did not free a slave. Lincoln's proclamation freed only those slaves in territories in rebellion against the United States, an area which by definition Lincoln had no authority. The proclamation was silent on those slaves who were held in Maryland and Tennessee, two areas under Lincoln's control. Slavery finally was ended by an act of Congress in 1865 through the Thirteenth Amendment to the Constitution.

35.   **(B)**   The Confederate government's adoption of a states' rights system of government most closely represents the Articles of Confederation from 1784–1788. Both systems of government rely on the friendly cooperation of its member states, have no coercive power over the states, and cannot act directly on its citizens but must go through the states. The British Constitution, U.S. Constitution, and Napoleonic France all established strong central/national governments with local government units that are subordinate to the national government. Another term for the Confederacy and the Articles used by political scientists is state-centered federalism.

1861–1877
REVIEW

1. HOSTILITIES BEGIN

Fort Sumter

Lincoln did his best to avoid angering the slave states that had not yet seceded. In his inaugural address he urged Southerners to reconsider their actions but warned that the Union was perpetual, that states could not secede, and that he would therefore hold the federal forts and installations in the South.

Of these only two remained in federal hands: Fort Pickens, off Pensacola, Florida; and Fort Sumter, in the harbor of Charleston, South Carolina. Lincoln soon received word from Major Robert Anderson, commanding the small garrison at Sumter, that supplies were running low. Desiring to send in the needed supplies, Lincoln informed the governor of South Carolina of his intention but promised that no attempt would be made to send arms, ammunition, or reinforcements unless Southerners initiated hostilities.

Not satisfied, Southerners determined to take the fort. Confederate General P. G. T. Beauregard, acting on orders from President Davis, demanded Anderson's surrender. Anderson said he would if not resupplied. Knowing supplies were on the way, the Confederates opened fire at 4:30 a.m. on April 12, 1861. The next day the fort surrendered.

The day following Sumter's surrender Lincoln declared the existence of an insurrection and called for the states to provide 75,000 volunteers to put it down. In response to this, Virginia, Tennessee, North Carolina, and Arkansas declared their secession.

The remaining slave states, Delaware, Kentucky, Maryland, and Missouri, wavered to varying degrees but stayed with the Union. Delaware, which had few slaves, gave little serious consideration to the idea of secession. Kentucky declared itself neutral and then sided with the North when the South failed to respect this neutrality. Maryland's incipient secession movement was crushed by Lincoln's timely imposition of martial law. Missouri was saved for the Union by the quick and decisive use of federal troops as well as the sizable population of pro-Union, antislavery German immigrants living in St. Louis.

QUESTION

> What action by Lincoln led to the secession of Virginia, Tennessee, North Carolina, and Arkansas?

EXPLANATION

Lincoln declared that the South was in a state of insurrection and called for troops to put it down. In response, the four states seceded. The raising of troops was considered an act hostile to the South.

Relative Strengths at the Outset

An assessment of available assets at the beginning of the war would not have looked favorable for the South.

The North enjoyed at least five major advantages over the South. It had overwhelming preponderance in wealth and thus was better able to finance the enormous expense of the war. The North was also vastly superior in industry and thus capable of producing the needed war materials; while the South, as a primarily agricultural society, often had to improvise or do without.

The North furthermore had an advantage of almost three to one in manpower, and over one-third of the South's population was composed of slaves, whom Southerners would not use as soldiers. Unlike the South, the North received large numbers of immigrants during the war. The North retained control of the U.S. Navy, and thus would command the sea and be able, by blockading, to cut the South off from outside sources of supply.

Finally, the North enjoyed a much superior system of railroads, while the South's relatively sparse railroad network was composed of a number of smaller railroads, often not interconnected and with varying gauges of track, more useful for carrying cotton from the interior to port cities than for moving large amounts of war supplies or troops around the country.

The South did, however, have several advantages of its own. It was vast in size, and this would make it difficult to conquer; it did not need to conquer the North, but only resist being conquered itself. Its troops would also be fighting on their own ground, a fact that would give them the advantage of familiarity with the terrain as well as the added motivation of defending their homes and families. Its armies would often have the opportunity of fighting on the defensive, a major advantage in the warfare of that day.

At the outset of the war, the South drew a number of highly qualified senior officers, such as Robert E. Lee, Joseph E. Johnston, and Albert Sidney Johnston, from the U.S. Army. By contrast, the Union command structure was already set when the war began, with the aged Winfield Scott, of Mexican War fame, at the top. It took young and talented officers, such as Ulysses S. Grant and William T. Sherman, time to work up to high rank. Meanwhile Union armies were often led by inferior commanders as Lincoln experimented in search of good generals.

At first glance, the South might also have seemed to have an advantage in its president. Jefferson Davis had extensive military and political experience and was acquainted with the nation's top military men and, presumably, with their relative abilities. On the other hand, Lincoln had been, up until his election to the presidency, less successful politically and had virtually no military experience. In fact, Lincoln was much superior to Davis as a war leader, showing firmness, flexibility, mental toughness, great political skill, and, eventually, an excellent grasp of strategy.

Opposing Strategies

Both sides were full of enthusiasm for the war. In the North the battle cry was "On to Richmond," the new Confederate capital established after the secession of Virginia. In the South it was "On to Washington." Yielding to popular demand, Lincoln ordered General Irvin McDowell to advance on Richmond with his army. At a creek called Bull Run near the town of Manassas Junction, Virginia, just southwest of Washington, D.C., they met a Confederate force under generals P.G.T. Beauregard and Joseph E. Johnston on July 21, 1861. In the First Battle of Bull Run (called First Manassas in the South), the Union army was forced to retreat in confusion back to Washington.

Bull Run demonstrated the unpreparedness and inexperience of both sides. It also demonstrated that the war would be long and hard, and, particularly in the North, that greater efforts would be required. Lincoln would need an overall strategy. To supply this, Winfield Scott suggested his Anaconda Plan to squeeze the life out of the Confederacy which included a naval blockade to shut out supplies from Europe, a campaign to take the Mississippi River, splitting the South in two, and the taking a few strategic points and waiting for pro-Union sentiment in the South to overthrow the secessionists. Lincoln liked the first two points of Scott's strategy but considered the third point unrealistic.

He ordered a naval blockade, an overwhelming task considering the South's long coastline. Yet under Secretary of the Navy Gideon Welles the navy was expanded enormously and the blockade, derided in the early days as a "paper blockade," became increasingly effective.

Lincoln also ordered a campaign to take the Mississippi River. A major step in this direction was taken when naval forces under Captain David G. Farragut took New Orleans in April 1862.

Rather than waiting for pro-Unionists in the South to gain control, Lincoln hoped to raise huge armies and apply overwhelming pressure from all sides at once until the Confederacy collapsed. The strategy was good; the problem was finding good generals to carry it out.

Drill 1: Hostilities Begin

1. By February 1, 1861 what group of states had seceded from the Union?

    (A) Mississippi, Florida, Alabama, Georgia, Louisiana, Texas, and South Carolina

    (B) Mississippi, Arkansas, Missouri, Alabama, Georgia, and Florida

    (C) Arkansas, Tennessee, North Carolina, and Virginia

    (D) Texas, Louisiana, Arkansas, Mississippi, and Alabama

    (E) Kentucky, Mississippi, Arkansas, Missouri, Alabama, and Georgia

2.   Which of the following served as president of the Confederate States of America?

    (A) Robert E. Lee   (B) Robert E. Lee

    (C) Robert Y. Hayne   (D) Jefferson Davis

    (E) Alexander H. Stephens

3.   Which of the following was NOT a Northern advantage in the Civil War?

    (A) It was fighting a defensive war.

    (B) It had greater manufacturing capacity.

    (C) It owned greater railroad trackage.

    (D) It had a larger population.

    (E) The mountain chains ran north and south.

4.   Who served as a Union General?

    (A) Joseph Johnston   (B) Thomas Jackson

    (C) William T. Sherman   (E) Robert E. Lee

    (E) J.E.B. Stuart

5.   The overall strategic policy of the Union to destroy the Confederacy through a combination of constant pressure and slowly wearing down the South's ability to wage war was called

    (A) the Nutcracker Plan.   (B) the Anaconda Plan.

    (C) the Squeeze Plan.   (D) the Attrition Plan.

    (E) the Sausolito Plan.

2. THE UNION PRESERVED

Union Defeats McClellan

To replace the discredited McDowell, Lincoln chose General George B. McClellan. McClellan was a good trainer and organizer and was loved by the troops, but was unable to use effectively the powerful army (now called the Army of the Potomac) he had built up. Despite much prodding from Lincoln, McClellan hesitated to advance, badly overestimating his enemy's numbers.

Finally, in the spring of 1862, he took the Army of the Potomac by water down Chesapeake Bay to land between the York and James Rivers in Virginia.

His plan was to advance up the peninsula formed by these rivers directly to Richmond.

The operations that followed were known as the Peninsula Campaign. McClellan advanced slowly and cautiously toward Richmond, while his equally cautious Confederate opponent, General Joseph E. Johnston, drew back to the outskirts of the city before turning to fight at the Battle of Seven Pines. In this inconclusive battle, Johnston was wounded. To replace him Jefferson Davis appointed his military advisor, General Robert E. Lee.

Lee summoned General Thomas J. "Stonewall" Jackson and his army from the Shenandoah Valley (where Jackson had just finished defeating several superior federal forces, causing consternation in Washington) and with the combined forces attacked McClellan.

After two days of bloody but inconclusive fighting, McClellan lost his nerve and began to retreat. In the remainder of what came to be called the Battle of the Seven Days, Lee continued to attack McClellan, forcing him back to his base, though at great cost in lives. McClellan's army was loaded back onto its ships and taken back to Washington.

Before McClellan's army could reach Washington and be completely deployed in northern Virginia, Lee saw and took an opportunity to thrash Union General John Pope, who was operating in northern Virginia with another Northern army, at the Second Battle of Bull Run.

Union Victories in the West

In the western area of the war's operations, essentially everything west of the Appalachian Mountains, matters were proceeding in a much different fashion. The Northern commanders there, Henry W. Halleck and Don Carlos Buell, were no more enterprising than McClellan, but Halleck's subordinate, Ulysses S. Grant, definitely was.

Seeking and obtaining permission from Halleck, Grant mounted a combined operation—army troops and navy gunboats—against two vital Confederate strongholds, Forts Henry and Donelson, which guarded the Tennessee and Cumberland Rivers in northern Tennessee, and which were the weak point of the thin-stretched Confederate line under General Albert Sidney Johnson. When Grant captured the forts in February 1862, Johnston was forced to retreat to Corinth in northern Mississippi.

Grant pursued but, ordered by Halleck to wait until all was in readiness before proceeding, Grant halted his troops at Pittsburgh Landing on the Tennessee River, 25 miles north of Corinth. On April 6, 1862, Johnston, who had received reinforcements and been joined by General P. G. T. Beauregard, surprised Grant there, but in the two-day battle that followed (Shiloh) failed to defeat him. Johnston himself was among the many killed in what was, up to this point, the bloodiest battle in American history.

Grant was severely criticized in the North for having been taken by surprise. Yet with other Union victories and Farragut's capture of New Orleans, the North had taken all of the Mississippi River except for a 110-mile stretch between the Confederate fortresses of Vicksburg, Mississippi, and Port Hudson, Louisiana.

The Success of Northern Diplomacy

Many Southerners believed Britain and France would rejoice in seeing a divided and weakened America. The two countries would likewise be driven by the need of their factories for cotton and thus intervene on the Confederacy's behalf. So strongly was this view held that during the early days of the war, when the Union blockade was still too weak to be very effective, the Confederate government itself prohibited the export of cotton in order to hasten British and French intervention.

This view proved mistaken for several reasons. Britain already had on hand large stocks of cotton from the bumper crops of the years immediately prior to the war. During the war the British were successful in finding alternative sources of cotton, importing the fiber from India and Egypt. British leaders may also have weighed their country's need to import wheat from the northern United States against its desire for cotton from the Southern states. Finally, British public opinion opposed slavery.

Skillful Northern diplomacy had a great impact. In this, Lincoln had the extremely able assistance of Secretary of State William Seward, who took a hard line in warning Europeans not to interfere, and of Ambassador to Great Britain Charles Francis Adams. Britain therefore remained neutral and other European countries, France in particular, followed its lead.

One incident nevertheless came close to fulfilling Southern hopes for British intervention. In November 1861 Captain Charles Wilkes of the U.S.S *San Jacinto* stopped the British mail and passenger ship *Trent* and forcibly removed Confederate emissaries James M. Mason and John Slidell. News of Wilkes' action brought great rejoicing in the North but outrage in Great Britain, where it was viewed as a violation of Britain's rights on the high seas. Lincoln and Seward, faced with British threats of war at a time the North could ill afford it, wisely chose to release the envoys and smooth things over with Britain.

The Confederacy was able to obtain some loans and to purchase small amounts of arms, ammunition, and even commerce-raiding ships such as the highly successful C.S.S. *Alabama*. However, Union naval superiority kept such supplies to a minimum.

The War at Sea

The Confederacy's major bid to challenge the Union's naval superiority was based on the employment of a technological innovation, the ironclad ship. The first and most successful of the Confederate ironclads was the C.S.S. *Virginia*. Built on the hull of the abandoned Union frigate *Merrimac*, the *Virginia* was protected from cannon fire by iron plates bolted over her sloping wooden sides. In May 1862 she destroyed two wooden warships of the Union naval force at Hampton Roads, Virginia, and was seriously threatening to destroy the rest of the squadron before being met and fought to a standstill by the Union ironclad U.S.S. *Monitor*.

The Home Front

The war on the home front dealt with the problems of maintaining public morale, supplying the armies of the field, and resolving constitutional questions regarding authority and the ability of the respective governments to deal with crises.

For the general purpose of maintaining public morale but also as items many Republicans had advocated even before the war, Congress in 1862 passed two highly important acts dealing with domestic affairs in the North.

The Homestead Act granted 160 acres of government land free of charge to any person who would farm it for at least five years. Much of the West was eventually settled under the provisions of this act. The Morrill Land Grant Act offered large amounts of the federal government's land to states that would establish "agricultural and mechanical" colleges. Many of the nation's large state universities were founded in later years under the provisions of this act.

Keeping the people relatively satisfied was made more difficult by the necessity, apparent by 1863, of imposing conscription in order to obtain adequate manpower for the huge armies that would be needed to crush the South. Especially hated by many working class Northerners was the provision of the conscription act that allowed a drafted individual to avoid service by hiring a substitute or paying $300. Resistance to the draft led to riots in New York City in which hundreds were killed.

The Confederacy, with its much smaller manpower pool on which to draw, had instituted conscription in 1862. Here, too, it did not always meet with cooperation. Some Southern governors objected to it on doctrinaire states' rights grounds, doing all they could to obstruct its operation. A provision of the Southern conscription act allowing one man to stay home as overseer for every 20 slaves led the non-slaveholding whites who made up most of the Southern population to grumble that it was a "rich man's war and a poor man's fight." Draft-dodging and desertion became epidemic in the South by the latter part of the war.

Scarcity of food and other consumer goods in the South as well as high prices led to further desertion as soldiers left the ranks to care for their starving families. Discontent also manifested itself in the form of a "bread riot" in Richmond.

Supplying the war placed an enormous strain on both societies, but one the North was better able to bear.

To finance the Northern side of the war, high tariffs and an income tax (the nation's first) were resorted to, yet even more money was needed. The Treasury Department, under Secretary of the Treasury Salmon P. Chase, issued "greenbacks," an unbacked fiat currency that nevertheless fared better than the Southern paper money because of greater confidence in Northern victory. To facilitate the financing of the war through credit expansion, the National Banking Act was passed in 1863.

The South, with its scant financial resources, found it all but impossible to cope with the expense of war. Excise and income taxes were levied and some small loans were obtained in Europe, yet the Southern Congress still felt compelled to issue paper money in such quantities that it became virtually worthless. That, and the scarcity of almost everything created by the war and its disruption of the economy, led to skyrocketing prices.

The Confederate government responded to the inflation it created by imposing taxes-in-kind and impressment, the seizing of produce, livestock, etc., by Confederate agents in return for payment according to an artificially set schedule of prices. Since payment was in worthless inflated currency, this amounted to confiscation and soon resulted in goods of all sorts becoming even scarcer than otherwise when a Confederate impressment agent was known to be in the neighborhood.

Questions of constitutional authority to deal with crises plagued both presidents.

To deal with the emergency of secession, Lincoln stretched the presidential powers to the limit, or perhaps beyond the limit, of the Constitution. To quell the threat of secession in Maryland, Lincoln suspended the writ of *habeas corpus* and imprisoned numerous suspected secessionists without charges or trial, ignoring the insistence of pro-Southern Chief Justice Roger B. Taney in *Ex Parte Merryman* (1861) that such action was unconstitutional.

"Copperheads," Northerners such as Clement L. Vallandigham of Ohio who opposed the war, denounced Lincoln as a tyrant and would-be dictator but remained a minority. Though occasionally subject to arrest and/or deportation for their activities, they were generally allowed a considerable degree of latitude.

Davis encountered obstructionism from various state governors, the Confederate Congress, and even his own vice president, who denounced him as a tyrant for assuming too much power and failing to respect states' rights. Hampered by such attitudes, the Confederate government proved less effective than it might have been.

The Emancipation Proclamation

By mid-1862, Lincoln, under pressure from radical elements of his own party and hoping to create a favorable impression on foreign public opinion, determined to issue the Emancipation Proclamation, declaring free all slaves in areas still in rebellion as of January 1, 1863. In order that this not appear an act of panic and desperation in view of the string of defeats the North had recently suffered on the battlefields of Virginia, Lincoln, at Seward's recommendation, waited to announce the proclamation until the North should win some sort of victory. This was provided by the Battle of Antietam on September 17, 1863.

Though the Radical Republicans, prewar abolitionists for the most part, had for some time been urging Lincoln to take such a step, Northern public opinion as a whole was less enthusiastic, as the Republicans suffered major losses in the November 1862 congressional elections.

The Turning Point in the East

After his victory of the Second Battle of Bull Run, Lee moved north and crossed into Maryland, where he hoped to win a decisive victory that would force the North to recognize Southern independence.

He was confronted by the Army of the Potomac, once again under the command of General George B. McClellan. Through a stroke of good fortune early in the campaign, detailed plans for Lee's entire audacious operation fell into McClellan's hands, but the Northern general, by extreme caution and slowness, threw away this incomparable chance to annihilate Lee and win—or at least shorten—the war.

The armies finally met along Antietam Creek, just east of the town of Sharpsburg in western Maryland. In a bloody but inconclusive day-long battle, known as Antietam in the North but as Sharpsburg in the South, McClellan's timidity led him to miss another excellent chance to destroy Lee's cornered and badly outnumbered army. After the battle Lee retreated to Virginia, and Lincoln, besides issuing the Emancipation Proclamation, removed McClellan from command.

To replace him, Lincoln chose General Ambrose E. Burnside, who promptly demonstrated his unfitness for command by blundering into a lopsided defeat at Fredericksburg, Virginia, on December 13, 1862.

Lincoln then replaced Burnside with General Joseph "Fighting Joe" Hooker. Handsome and hard-drinking, Hooker had bragged of what he would do to "Bobby Lee" when he got at him; but when he took his army south, "Fighting Joe" quickly lost his nerve. He was out-generaled and soundly beaten at the Battle of Chancellorsville, May 5–6, 1863. At this battle the brilliant Southern general "Stonewall" Jackson was accidentally shot by his own men and died several days later.

Lee, anxious to shift the scene of the fighting out of his beloved Virginia, sought and received permission from President Davis to invade Pennsylvania. He was pursued by the Army of the Potomac, now under the command of General George G. Meade, whom Lincoln had selected to replace the discredited Hooker. They met at Gettysburg; and in a three-day battle (July 1–3, 1863) that was the bloodiest of the entire war, Lee, who sorely missed the services of Jackson and whose cavalry leader, the normally reliable J. E. B. Stuart, failed to provide him with timely reconnaissance, was defeated. However, he was allowed by the victorious Meade to retreat to Virginia with his army intact if battered, much to Lincoln's disgust. Still, Lee would never again have the strength to mount such an invasion.

Lincoln Finds Grant

Meanwhile Grant undertook to take Vicksburg, one of the two last Confederate bastions on the Mississippi River. In a brilliant campaign he bottled up the Confederate forces of General John C. Pemberton inside the city and placed them under siege. After six weeks of siege, the defenders surrendered on July 4, 1863.

Five days later Port Hudson surrendered as well, giving the Union complete control of the Mississippi.

After Union forces under General William Rosecrans suffered an embarrassing defeat at the Battle of Chickamauga in northwestern Georgia, September 19–20, 1863, Lincoln named Grant overall commander of Union forces in the West.

Grant went to Chattanooga, Tennessee, where Confederate forces under General Braxton Bragg were virtually besieging Rosecrans, and immediately took control of the situation. Gathering Union forces from other portions of the western theater and combining them with reinforcements from the East, Grant won a resounding victory at the Battle of Chattanooga (November 23–25, 1863), in which federal forces stormed seemingly impregnable Confederate positions on Lookout Mountain and Missionary Ridge. This victory put Union forces in position for a drive into Georgia, which began the following spring.

Early in 1864 Lincoln made Grant commander of all Union armies. Grant devised a coordinated plan for constant pressure on the Confederacy. General William T. Sherman would lead a drive toward Atlanta, Georgia, with the goal of destroying the Confederate army under General Joseph E. Johnston (who had replaced Bragg). Grant himself would accompany Meade and the Army of the Potomac in advancing toward Richmond with the goal of destroying Lee's Confederate army.

In a series of bloody battles (the Wilderness, Spotsylvania, Cold Harbor) in May and June of 1864, Grant drove Lee to the outskirts of Richmond. Still unable to take the city or get Lee at a disadvantage, Grant circled around to try to take both by way of the back door, attacking Petersburg, Virginia, an important railroad junction just south of Richmond and the key to that city's—and Lee's—supply lines. Once again turned back by entrenched Confederate troops, Grant settled down to besiege Petersburg and Richmond in a stalemate that lasted some nine months.

Sherman had been advancing simultaneously in Georgia. He maneuvered Johnston back to the outskirts of Atlanta with relatively little fighting. At that point Confederate President Davis lost patience with Johnston and replaced him with the aggressive General John B. Hood. Hood and Sherman fought three fierce but inconclusive battles around Atlanta in late July, then settled down to a siege of their own during the month of August.

The Election of 1864 and Northern Victory

In the North discontentment grew with the long casualty lists and seeming lack of results. Yet the South could stand the grinding war even less. By late 1864 Jefferson Davis had reached the point of calling for the use of blacks in the Confederate armies, though the war ended before black troops could see action for the Confederacy. The South's best hope was that Northern war-weariness would bring the defeat of Lincoln and the victory of a peace candidate in the election of 1864.

Lincoln ran on the ticket of the National Union party, essentially the Republican party with loyal or "War" Democrats. His vice-presidential candidate was Andrew Johnson, a loyal Democrat from Tennessee.

The Democratic party's presidential candidate was General George B. McClellan, who, with some misgivings, ran on a platform labeling the war a failure and calling for a negotiated peace settlement even it that meant Southern independence.

The outlook was bleak for a time, and even Lincoln himself believed that he would be defeated. Then in September 1864 word came that Sherman had taken Atlanta. The capture of this vital Southern rail and manufacturing center brought an enormous boost to Northern morale. Along with other Northern victories that summer and fall, it insured a resounding election victory for Lincoln and the continuation of the war to complete victory for the North.

To speed that victory, Sherman marched through Georgia from Atlanta to the sea, arriving at Savannah in December 1864 and turning north into the Carolinas, leaving behind a 60-mile-wide swath of destruction. His goal was to impress on Southerners that continuation of the war could only mean ruin for all of them. He and Grant planned that his army should press on through the Carolinas and into Virginia to join Grant in finishing off Lee.

Before Sherman's troops could arrive, Lee abandoned Richmond (April 3, 1865) and attempted to escape with what was left of his army. Pursued by Grant, he was cornered and forced to surrender at Appomattox, Virginia, April 9, 1865. Other Confederate armies still holding out in various parts of the South surrendered over the next few weeks.

Lincoln did not live to receive news of the final surrenders. On April 14, 1865, he was shot in the back of the head while watching a play in Ford's Theater in Washington. His assassin, pro-Southern actor John Wilkes Booth, injured his ankle in making his escape. Hunted down by Union cavalry several days later, he died of a gunshot wound, apparently self-inflicted. Several other individuals were tried, convicted, and hanged by a military tribunal for participating with Booth in a conspiracy to assassinate not only Lincoln, but also Vice President Johnson and Secretary of State Seward.

QUESTION

Why did Lincoln win reelection in 1864?

EXPLANATION

Lincoln did not expect to win the election in 1864, as many in the North were tired of the war and did not see the possibility of it ending. However, William T. Sherman won a decisive battle that took the city of Atlanta, and combined with other victories, it appeared that the North could win the war sooner than many had thought at first. This shifted public opinion behind Lincoln, and he won the election fairly easily.

Drill 2: The Union Preserved

1. Robert E. Lee surrendered to Ulysses Grant at

    (A) Spotsylvania.
    (B) Appomattox.
    (C) Cold Harbor.
    (D) Raleigh.
    (E) Richmond.

2. The Homestead Act provided

    (A) that Indians should henceforth own their lands as individuals rather than collectively as tribes.

    (B) 160 acres of free land within the public domain to any head of household who would settle on it and improve it over a period of five years.

    (C) large amounts of federal government land to Great Plains cattle ranchers who would contract to provide beef for the Union army.

    (D) 40 acres of land to each former slave above the age of 21.

    (E) that the land of former Confederates should not be confiscated.

3. Which of the following battles of the American Civil War was NOT a Confederate victory?

    (A) Antietam
    (B) Chickamaugua
    (C) Chancellorsville
    (D) Fredericksburg
    (E) First Bull Run

4. The key event that guaranteed Lincoln's reelection in 1864 was

    (A) the fall of Vicksburg to General Grant.

    (B) the capture of New Orleans by Admiral Farragut.

    (C) the defeat of Lee's army by General Meade at Gettysburg.

    (D) the fall of Atlanta to General Sherman.

    (E) the successful defense of Nashville by General Thomas against repeated Confederate counterattacks.

5. The battle that is considered to be the "turning point" of the Civil War and the last chance at a military victory by the Confederacy is

    (A) Antietam.
    (B) Shiloh.
    (C) Gettysburg.
    (D) Chattanooga.
    (E) Chickamaugua.

3. THE ORDEAL OF RECONSTRUCTION

Lincoln's Plan of Reconstruction

Reconstruction began well before fighting of the Civil War came to an end. It brought a time of difficult adjustments in the South.

Among those who faced such adjustments were the recently freed slaves, who flocked into Union lines or followed advancing Union armies or whose plantations were part of the growing area of the South that came under Union military control. Some slaves had left their plantations, and thus their only means of livelihood, in order to obtain freedom within Union lines. Many felt they had to leave their plantations in order to be truly free, and some sought to find relatives separated during the days of slavery. Some former slaves also seemed to misunderstand the meaning of freedom, thinking they need never work again.

To ease the adjustment for these recently freed slaves, Congress in 1865 created the Freedman's Bureau, to provide food, clothing, and education, and generally look after the interests of former slaves.

Even before the need to deal with this problem had forced itself on the Northern government's awareness, steps had been taken to deal with another major adjustment of Reconstruction, the restoration of loyal governments to the seceded states. By 1863 substantial portions of several Southern states had come under Northern military control, and Lincoln had set forth a policy for re-establishing governments in those states.

Lincoln's policy, known as the Ten Percent Plan, stipulated that Southerners, except for high-ranking rebel officials, could take an oath promising future loyalty to the Union and acceptance of the end of slavery. When the number of those who had taken this oath within any one state reached ten percent of the number who had been registered to vote in that state in 1860, a loyal state government could be formed. Only those who had taken the oath could vote or participate in the new government.

Tennessee, Arkansas, and Louisiana met the requirements and formed loyal governments but were refused recognition by Congress, which was dominated by Radical Republicans.

The Radical Republicans, such as Thaddeus Stevens of Pennsylvania, believed Lincoln's plan did not adequately punish the South, restructure Southern society, and boost the political prospects of the Republican party. The loyal Southern states were denied representation in Congress and electoral votes in the election of 1864.

Instead, the Radicals in Congress drew up the Wade-Davis Bill. Under its stringent terms a majority of the number who had been alive and registered to vote in 1860 would have to swear an "ironclad" oath stating that they were now loyal and had never been disloyal. This was obviously impossible in any former Confederate state unless blacks were given the right to vote, something Radical Republicans desired but Southerners definitely did not. Unless the requisite number swore the "ironclad" oath, Congress would not allow the state to have a government.

Lincoln killed the Wade-Davis Bill with a "pocket veto," and the Radicals were furious. When Lincoln was assassinated the Radicals rejoiced, believing Vice President Andrew Johnson would be less generous to the South or at least easier to control.

Johnson's Attempt at Reconstruction

To the dismay of the Radicals, Johnson followed Lincoln's policies very closely, making them only slightly more stringent by requiring ratification of the Thirteenth Amendment (officially abolishing slavery), repudiation of Confederate debts, and renunciation of secession. He also recommended the right to vote be given to blacks.

Southern states proved reluctant to accept these conditions, some declining to repudiate Confederate debts or ratify the Thirteenth Amendment (it nevertheless received the ratification of the necessary number of states and was declared part of the Constitution in December 1865). No Southern state extended the right to vote to blacks (at this time no Northern state did, either). Instead, the Southern states promulgated "black codes," imposing various restrictions on the freedom of the former slaves.

Foreign Policy Under Johnson

On coming into office Johnson had inherited a foreign policy problem involving Mexico and France. The French Emperor, Napoleon III, had made Mexico the target of one of his many grandiose foreign adventures. In 1862, while the U.S. was occupied with the Civil War and therefore unable to prevent this violation of the Monroe Doctrine, Napoleon III had Archduke Maximilian of Austria installed as a puppet emperor of Mexico, supported by French troops. The U.S. had protested but for the time could do nothing.

With the war over, Johnson and Secretary of State Seward were able to take more vigorous steps. General Philip Sheridan was sent to the Rio Grande with a military force. At the same time Mexican revolutionary leader Benito Juarez was given the tacit recognition of the U.S. government. Johnson and Seward continued to invoke the Monroe Doctrine and to place quiet pressure on Napoleon III to withdraw his troops. In May 1866, facing difficulties of his own in Europe, the French emperor did so, leaving the unfortunate Maximilian to face a Mexican firing squad.

Johnson's and Seward's course of action in preventing the extension of the French Empire into the Western Hemisphere strengthened America's commitment to and the rest of the world's respect for the Monroe Doctrine.

In 1866 the Russian minister approached Seward with an offer to sell Alaska to the U.S. The Russians desired to sell Alaska because its fur resources had been largely exhausted and because they feared that in a possible war with Great Britain (something that seemed likely at the time) they would lose Alaska anyway.

Seward, who was an ardent expansionist, pushed hard for the purchase of

Alaska, known as "Seward's Folly" by its critics, and it was largely through his efforts that it was pushed through Congress. It was urged that purchasing Alaska would reward the Russians for their friendly stance toward the U.S. government during the Civil War at a time when Britain and France had seemed to favor the Confederacy.

In 1867 the sale went through and Alaska was purchased for $7,200,000.

Congressional Reconstruction

Southern intransigence in the face of Johnson's relatively mild plan of Reconstruction manifested in the refusal of some states to repudiate the Confederate debt and ratify the Thirteenth Amendment. The refusal to give the vote to blacks, the passage of black codes, and the election of many former high-ranking Confederates to Congress and other top positions in the Southern states, played into the hands of the Radicals, who were anxious to impose harsh rule on the South. They could now assert that the South was refusing to accept the verdict of the war.

Once again Congress excluded the representatives of the Southern states. Determined to reconstruct the South as it saw fit, Congress passed a Civil Rights Act and extended the authority of the Freedman's Bureau, giving it both quasi-judicial and quasi-executive powers.

Johnson vetoed both bills, claiming they were unconstitutional; but Congress overrode the vetoes. Fearing that the Supreme Court would agree with Johnson and overturn the laws, Congress approved and sent on to the states for ratification (June 1866) the Fourteenth Amendment, making constitutional the laws Congress had just passed. The Fourteenth Amendment defined citizenship and forbade states to deny various rights to citizens, reduced the representation in Congress of states that did not allow blacks to vote, forbade the paying of the Confederate debt, and made former Confederates ineligible to hold public office.

With only one Southern state, Tennessee, ratifying, the amendment failed to receive the necessary approval of three-fourths of the states. But the Radicals in Congress were not finished. Strengthened by victory in the 1866 elections, they passed, over Johnson's veto, the Military Reconstruction Act, dividing the South into five military districts to be ruled by military governors with almost dictatorial powers. Tennessee, having ratified the Fourteenth Amendment, was spared the wrath of the Radicals. The rest of the Southern states were ordered to produce constitutions giving the vote to blacks and to ratify the Fourteenth Amendment before they could be "readmitted." In this manner the Fourteenth Amendment was ratified.

Realizing the unprecedented nature of these actions, Congress moved to prevent any check or balance from the other two branches of government. Steps were taken toward limiting the jurisdiction of the Supreme Court so that it could not review cases pertaining to congressional Reconstruction policies. This proved unnecessary as the Court, now headed by Chief Justice Salmon P. Chase in place of the deceased Taney, readily acquiesced and declined to overturn the Reconstruction acts.

To control the president, Congress passed the Army Act, reducing the president's control over the army. In obtaining the cooperation of the army the Radicals had the aid of General Grant, who already had his eye on the 1868 Republican presidential nomination. Congress also passed the Tenure of Office Act, forbidding Johnson to dismiss cabinet members without the Senate's permission. In passing the latter act, Congress was especially thinking of Radical Secretary of War Edwin M. Stanton, a Lincoln holdover whom Johnson desired to dismiss.

Johnson obeyed the letter but not the spirit of the Reconstruction acts, and Congress, angry at his refusal to cooperate, sought in vain for grounds to impeach him until in August 1867, Johnson violated the Tenure of Office Act (by dismissing Stanton) in order to test its constitutionality. The matter was not tested in the courts, however, but in Congress, where Johnson was impeached by the House of Representatives and came within one vote of being removed by the Senate. For the remaining months of his term, he offered little further resistance to the Radicals.

QUESTION

How did Congress force the South to ratify the Fourteenth Amendment?

EXPLANATION

When first submitted to the states, all the Southern states except for Tennessee refused to ratify it, and therefore it did not pass. In response, Congress divided the South into five military districts, governed by military governors who had considerable power. In addition, the military governments denied Southerners basic Constitutional rights. Only by passing the Fourteenth Amendment could the states be readmitted to the Union. In this way, Congress forced passage of the Fourteenth Amendment.

The Election of 1868 and the Fifteenth Amendment

In 1868 the Republican convention, dominated by the Radicals, drew up a platform endorsing Radical Reconstruction. For president, the Republicans nominated Ulysses S. Grant, who had no political record and whose views—if any—on national issues were unknown. The vice-presidential nominee was Schuyler Colfax.

Though the Democratic nomination was sought by Andrew Johnson, the party knew he could not win and instead nominated former Governor Horatio Seymour of New York for president and Francis P. Blair, Jr. of Missouri for vice president. Both had been Union generals during the war. The Democratic platform mildly criticized the excesses of Radical Reconstruction and called for continued payment of the war debt in greenbacks, although Seymour himself was a hard-money man.

Grant, despite his enormous popularity as a war hero, won by only a narrow margin, drawing only 300,000 more popular votes than Seymour. Some 700,000 blacks had voted in the Southern states under the auspices of army occupation, and since all of these had almost certainly voted for Grant, it was clear that he had not received a majority of the white vote.

The narrow victory of even such a strong candidate as Grant prompted Republican leaders to decide that it would be politically expedient to give the vote to all blacks, North as well as South. For this purpose the Fifteenth Amendment was drawn up and submitted to the states. Ironically, the idea was so unpopular in the North that it won the necessary three-fourths approval only with its ratification by Southern states required to do so by Congress.

Post-War Life in the South

Reconstruction was a difficult time in the South. During the war approximately one in ten Southern men had been killed. Many more were maimed for life. Those who returned from the war found destruction and poverty. Property of the Confederate government was confiscated by the federal government, and dishonest Treasury agents confiscated private property as well. Capital invested in slaves or in Confederate war bonds was lost. Property values fell to one-tenth of their prewar level. The economic results of the war stayed with the South for decades.

The political results were less long-lived but more immediately disturbing to Southerners. Southerners complained of widespread corruption in governments sustained by federal troops and composed of "carpetbaggers," "scalawags" (respectively the Southern names for Northerners who came to the South to participate in Reconstruction governments and Southerners who supported the Reconstruction regimes), and recently freed blacks.

Under the Reconstruction governments, social programs were greatly expanded, leading to higher taxes and growing state debts. Some of the financial problems were due to corruption, a problem in both North and South in this era when political machines, such as William Marcy "Boss" Tweed's Tammany Hall machine in New York, dominated many Northern city governments and grew rich.

Southern whites sometimes responded to Reconstruction governments with violence, carried out by groups such as the Ku Klux Klan, aimed at intimidating blacks and white Republicans out of voting. The activities of these organizations were sometimes a response to those of the Union League, an organization used by Southern Republicans to control the black vote. The goal of Southerners not allied with the Reconstruction governments, whether members of the Klan or not, was "redemption" (i.e., the end of the Reconstruction governments).

By 1876 Southern whites had been successful, by legal means or otherwise, in "redeeming" all but three Southern states. The following year the federal government ended its policy of Reconstruction and the troops were withdrawn, leading to a return to power of white Southerners in the remaining states.

Reconstruction ended primarily because the North lost interest. Corruption in government, economic hard times brought on by the Panic of 1873, and general weariness on the part of Northern voters with the effort to remake Southern society all sapped the will to continue. Diehard Radicals such as Thaddeus Stevens and Charles Sumner were dead.

Corruption Under Grant

Having arrived in the presidency with no firm political positions, Grant found that the only principle he had to guide his actions was his instinctive loyalty to his old friends and the politicians who had propelled him into office. This principle did not serve him well as president. Though personally of unquestioned integrity, he naively placed his faith in a number of thoroughly dishonest men. His administration was rocked by one scandalous revelation of government corruption after another. Not every scandal involved members of the executive branch, but together they tended to taint the entire period of Grant's administration as one of unparalleled corruption.

The "Black Friday" Scandal

In the "Black Friday" scandal, two unscrupulous businessmen, Jim Fiske and Jay Gould, schemed to corner the gold market. To further their designs, they got Grant's brother-in-law to convince the president that stopping government gold sales would be good for farmers. Grant naively complied, and many businessmen were ruined as the price of gold was bid up furiously on "Black Friday." By the time Grant realized what was happening, much damage had already been done.

The Credit Mobilier Scandal

In the Credit Mobilier scandal, officials of the Union Pacific Railroad used a dummy construction company called Credit Mobilier to skim off millions of dollars of the subsidies the government was paying the Union Pacific for building a transcontinental railroad. To ensure that Congress would take a benevolent attitude toward all this, the officials bribed many of its members lavishly. Though much of this took place before Grant came into office, its revelation in an 1872 congressional investigation created a general scandal.

The "Salary Grab Act"

In the "Salary Grab Act" of 1873, Congress voted a 100 percent pay raise for the president and a 50 percent increase for itself and made both retroactive two years back. Public outrage led to a Democratic victory in the next congressional election and the law was repealed.

The Sanborn Contract Fraud

In the Sanborn Contract fraud, a politician named Sanborn was given a contract to collect $427,000 in unpaid taxes for a 50 percent commission. The commission found its way into Republican campaign funds.

The Whiskey Ring Fraud

In the Whiskey Ring fraud, distillers and treasury officials conspired to defraud the government of large amounts of money from the excise tax on whiskey. Grant's personal secretary was in on the plot, and Grant himself naively accepted gifts of a questionable nature. When the matter came under investigation, Grant endeavored to shield his secretary.

The Bribing of Belknap

Grant's secretary of war, W.W. Belknap, accepted bribes from corrupt agents involved in his department's administration of Indian affairs. When the matter came out, he resigned to escape impeachment.

The Liberal Republicans

Discontentment within Republican ranks with regard to some of the earlier scandals as well as with the Radicals' vindictive Reconstruction policies led a faction of the party to separate and constitute itself as the Liberal Republicans. Besides opposing corruption and favoring sectional harmony, the Liberal Republicans favored hard money and a laissez-faire approach to economic issues. For the election of 1872, they nominated *New York Tribune* editor Horace Greeley for president. Eccentric, controversial, and ineffective as a campaigner, Greeley proved a poor choice. Though nominated by the Democrats as well as the Liberal Republicans, he was easily defeated by Grant, who was again the nominee of the Radicals.

Economic Issues Under Grant

Many of the economic difficulties the country faced during Grant's administration were caused by the necessary readjustments from a wartime back to a peacetime economy.

The central economic question was deflation versus inflation or, more specifically, whether to retire the unbacked paper money, greenbacks, printed to meet the wartime emergency, or to print more.

Economic conservatives, creditors, and business interests usually favored retirement of the greenbacks and an early return to the gold standard.

Debtors, who had looked forward to paying off their obligations in depreciated paper money worth less than the gold-backed money they had borrowed, favored a continuation of currency inflation through the use of more greenbacks. The deflation that would come through the retirement of existing greenbacks would make debts contracted during or immediately after the war much harder to pay.

Generally, Grant's policy was to let the greenbacks float until they were on par with gold and could then be retired without economic dislocation.

Early in Grant's second term the country was hit by an economic depression known as the Panic of 1873. Brought on by the overexpansive tendencies of railroad builders and businessmen during the immediate postwar boom, the panic was triggered by economic downturns in Europe and, more immediately, by the failure of Jay Cooke and Company, a major American financial firm.

The financial hardship brought on by the panic led to renewed clamor for the printing of more greenbacks. In 1874 Congress authorized a small new issue of greenbacks, but it was vetoed by Grant. Pro-inflation forces were further enraged when Congress in 1873 demonetized silver, going to a straight gold standard. Silver was becoming more plentiful due to western mining and was seen by some as a potential source of inflation. Pro-inflation forces referred to the demonetization of silver as the "Crime of '73."

In 1875 Congress took a further step toward retirement of the greenbacks and return to a working gold standard when, under the leadership of John Sherman, it passed the Specie Resumption Act, calling for the resumption of specie payments (i.e., the redeemability of the nation's paper money in gold) by January 1, 1879.

Disgruntled proponents of inflation formed the Greenback party and nominated Peter Cooper for president in 1876. However, they gained only an insignificant number of votes.

QUESTION

> Why would farmers favor the monetarization of silver?

EXPLANATION

Farmers favored the monetarization of silver because it was an inflationary fiscal policy. Inflation would increase farm prices, as well as make it more expensive for farmers to pay off debt that they had often acquired to buy their land.

The Disputed Election of 1876

In the election of 1876, the Democrats campaigned against corruption and nominated New York Governor Samuel J. Tilden, who had broken the Tweed political machine of New York City.

The Republicans passed over Grant, who was interested in another term and had the backing of the remaining hard-core Radicals, and turned instead to Governor Rutherford B. Hayes of Ohio. Like Tilden, Hayes was decent, honest, in favor of hard money and civil service reform, and opposed to government regulation of the economy. In their campaigning, the Republicans resorted to a tactic known as "waving the bloody shirt." Successfully used in the last two presidential elections, this meant basically playing on wartime animosities, urging Northerners to vote the way they had shot, and suggested that a Democratic victory and a Confederate victory would be about the same thing.

This time the tactic was less successful. Tilden won the popular vote and led in the electoral vote 184 to 165. However, 185 electoral votes were needed for election, and 20 votes, from the three Southern states still occupied by federal troops and run by Republican governments, were disputed.

Though there had been extensive fraud on both sides, Tilden undoubtedly deserved at least the one vote he needed to win. Congress created a special commission to decide the matter. It was to be composed of five members each from the Senate, the House, and the Supreme Court. Of these, seven were to be Republicans, seven Democrats, and one an independent. The Republicans arranged, however, for the independent justice's state legislature to elect him to the Senate. When the justice resigned to take his Senate seat, it left all the remaining Supreme Court justices Republican. One of them was chosen, and in a series of eight-to-seven votes along straight party lines, the commission voted to give all 20 disputed votes—and the election—to Hayes.

When outraged congressional Democrats threatened to reject these obviously fraudulent results, a compromise was worked out. In the Compromise of 1877, Hayes promised to show consideration for Southern interests, end Reconstruction, and withdraw the remaining federal troops from the South in exchange for Democratic acquiescence in his election. Reconstruction would probably have ended anyway, since the North had already lost interest in it.

Drill 3: The Ordeal of Reconstruction

1. Under Lincoln's plan of Reconstruction, Southern states could resume their part in the Union after

    (A) 50 percent of the voters as of 1860 took an oath of allegiance.

    (B) 10 percent of the voters as of 1860 took an oath of allegiance.

    (C) allowing blacks to vote.

    (D) adopting the Thirteenth Amendment which abolished slavery.

    (E) repudiating debts accumulated under the Confederacy.

RE-CONSTRUCTION,
OR "A WHITE MAN'S GOVERNMENT".

2. Which of the following best expresses the point of view of the above cartoon?

    (A) Southern whites and blacks can never be reconciled.

    (B) Southern whites would willingly be reconciled with blacks.

    (C) Blacks have no interest in reconciliation with Southern whites.

    (D) The president must take a forceful role in reconciling Southern whites and blacks.

    (E) Reconciliation of Southern whites and blacks is simply a matter of recognizing the new realities.

3. The Compromise of 1877

    (A) provided guarantees for the maintenance of full civil rights for Southern blacks.

    (B) dealt with the issue of slavery in the territories.

    (C) brought an end to Congressional Reconstruction.

    (D) worked out the differences between the free-silver and the gold standard wings of the Republican party.

    (E) stipulated all federal troops stationed in the South should be withdrawn by 1890.

4. In response to Southern intransigence in the face of President Andrew Johnson's mild Reconstruction plan, Congress did all of the following EXCEPT

    (A) exclude Southern representatives and senators from participating in Congress.

    (B) pass the Civil Rights Act of 1866.

    (C) order the arrest and imprisonment of former Confederate leaders.

    (D) approve and send on to the states the Fourteenth Amendment.

    (E) divide the South into five districts to be ruled by military governors with almost dictatorial powers.

5. When President Andrew Johnson removed Secretary of War Edwin M. Stanton without the approval of the Senate, contrary to the terms of the recently passed Tenure of Office Act, he

    (A) was impeached and removed from office.

    (B) came within one vote of being impeached.

    (C) was impeached and came within one vote of being removed from office.

    (D) resigned to avoid impeachment and was subsequently pardoned by his successor.

    (E) was impeached, refused to resign, and his term ended before a vote could be taken on his removal from office.

6. In speaking of "scalawags," white Southerners of the Reconstruction era make reference to

    (A) former slaves who had risen to high positions within the Reconstruction governments of the Southern states.

    (B) Northerners who had come south to take up high positions within the Reconstruction governments of the Southern states.

    (C) the U.S. Army generals who served as military governors in the South.

    (D) the Radical Republicans in Congress who imposed the Reconstruction regimes on the South.

    (E) Southerners who supported or participated in the Reconstruction regimes.

7. By the Compromise of 1877 the Democrats agreed to allow the Republican candidate to become president in exchange for

    (A) a promise that they would be allowed to win the next two presidential elections.

(B)   an end to Reconstruction.

(C)   large personal bribes to leading Democrats.

(D)   a substantial lowering of protective tariffs.

(E)   retroactive compensation for freed slaves.

8.   This 1871 cartoon by Thomas Nast suggests that

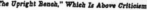

"The Upright Bench," Which Is Above Criticism.

(A)   justice prevails in New York.

(B)   political influence is sold for cash.

(C)   the wealthy control New York politics.

(D)   New York government is inefficient.

(E)   the people are being well-served by New York government.

9.   Which of the following did NOT take place during the Grant presidency?

(A)   John Wesley Powell's exploration of the Grand Canyon

(B)   Last federal troops removed from the South

    (C) Settlement of the Alabama claims

    (D) Completion of the first transcontinental railroad

    (E) Credit Mobilier

10. During the period of Reconstruction, most of the states of the former Confederacy, in order to regain admission to the Union, were required to

    (A) grant blacks all the civil rights that Northern states had granted them.

    (B) ratify the Fourteenth Amendment.

    (C) provide integrated public schools.

    (D) ratify the Sixteenth Amendment.

    (E) provide free land and farming utensils for the recently freed slaves.

1861–1877
DRILLS

ANSWER KEY

Drill 1—Hostilities Begin

1. (A)   2. (D)   3. (A)   4. (C)   5. (B)

Drill 2—The Union Preserved

1. (B)   2. (B)   3. (A)   4. (D)   5. (C)

Drill 3—The Ordeal of Reconstruction

1. (B)   2. (E)   3. (C)   4. (C)   5. (C)
6. (E)   7. (B)   8. (B)   9. (B)   10. (B)

GLOSSARY: 1861–1877

Anaconda Plan
  The Northern strategy for the Civil War. It included a naval blockade to shut out supplies from Europe, a campaign to take the Mississippi River, and the taking of a few strategic points and waiting for pro-Union sentiment in the South to overthrow the secessionists.

Carpetbaggers
  Northerners who came to the South to participate in Reconstruction governments.

Copperheads
  Northerners who opposed the war.

Crime of '73
  What pro-inflation forces called the demonetization of silver.

Greenbacks
  An unbacked fiat currency issued by the Union to help fund the Civil War.

Ironclad Oath
  An oath required by Radical Republicans, that a requisite number of Southerners would have to take before the state could be readmitted to the Union. It states that the Southerner was now loyal and had never been disloyal to the Union.

Ironclad Ship
  A technological innovation, during the Civil War where a ship was protected from cannon fire by iron plates bolted on the wooden sides.

Laissez-faire
  The belief that government should not interfere in the economy.

Pocket Veto
  Preventing a bill from becoming law by letting the bill expire without signing it.

Reconstruction
  The process by which the defeated Southern states would be admitted back into the Union.

Redemption
  The end of Reconstruction governments.

Scalawags
  Southerners who supported Reconstruction programs.

CHAPTER 9

1877–1912

INDUSTRIALISM AND THE PROGRESSIVE ERA

➤ Diagnostic Test
➤ 1877–1912 Review & Drills
➤ Glossary

1877-1912
DIAGNOSTIC TEST

1. Ⓐ Ⓑ Ⓒ Ⓓ Ⓔ
2. Ⓐ Ⓑ Ⓒ Ⓓ Ⓔ
3. Ⓐ Ⓑ Ⓒ Ⓓ Ⓔ
4. Ⓐ Ⓑ Ⓒ Ⓓ Ⓔ
5. Ⓐ Ⓑ Ⓒ Ⓓ Ⓔ
6. Ⓐ Ⓑ Ⓒ Ⓓ Ⓔ
7. Ⓐ Ⓑ Ⓒ Ⓓ Ⓔ
8. Ⓐ Ⓑ Ⓒ Ⓓ Ⓔ
9. Ⓐ Ⓑ Ⓒ Ⓓ Ⓔ
10. Ⓐ Ⓑ Ⓒ Ⓓ Ⓔ
11. Ⓐ Ⓑ Ⓒ Ⓓ Ⓔ
12. Ⓐ Ⓑ Ⓒ Ⓓ Ⓔ
13. Ⓐ Ⓑ Ⓒ Ⓓ Ⓔ
14. Ⓐ Ⓑ Ⓒ Ⓓ Ⓔ
15. Ⓐ Ⓑ Ⓒ Ⓓ Ⓔ
16. Ⓐ Ⓑ Ⓒ Ⓓ Ⓔ
17. Ⓐ Ⓑ Ⓒ Ⓓ Ⓔ
18. Ⓐ Ⓑ Ⓒ Ⓓ Ⓔ
19. Ⓐ Ⓑ Ⓒ Ⓓ Ⓔ
20. Ⓐ Ⓑ Ⓒ Ⓓ Ⓔ
21. Ⓐ Ⓑ Ⓒ Ⓓ Ⓔ
22. Ⓐ Ⓑ Ⓒ Ⓓ Ⓔ
23. Ⓐ Ⓑ Ⓒ Ⓓ Ⓔ
24. Ⓐ Ⓑ Ⓒ Ⓓ Ⓔ
25. Ⓐ Ⓑ Ⓒ Ⓓ Ⓔ

26. Ⓐ Ⓑ Ⓒ Ⓓ Ⓔ
27. Ⓐ Ⓑ Ⓒ Ⓓ Ⓔ
28. Ⓐ Ⓑ Ⓒ Ⓓ Ⓔ
29. Ⓐ Ⓑ Ⓒ Ⓓ Ⓔ
30. Ⓐ Ⓑ Ⓒ Ⓓ Ⓔ
31. Ⓐ Ⓑ Ⓒ Ⓓ Ⓔ
32. Ⓐ Ⓑ Ⓒ Ⓓ Ⓔ
33. Ⓐ Ⓑ Ⓒ Ⓓ Ⓔ
34. Ⓐ Ⓑ Ⓒ Ⓓ Ⓔ
35. Ⓐ Ⓑ Ⓒ Ⓓ Ⓔ
36. Ⓐ Ⓑ Ⓒ Ⓓ Ⓔ
37. Ⓐ Ⓑ Ⓒ Ⓓ Ⓔ
38. Ⓐ Ⓑ Ⓒ Ⓓ Ⓔ
39. Ⓐ Ⓑ Ⓒ Ⓓ Ⓔ
40. Ⓐ Ⓑ Ⓒ Ⓓ Ⓔ
41. Ⓐ Ⓑ Ⓒ Ⓓ Ⓔ
42. Ⓐ Ⓑ Ⓒ Ⓓ Ⓔ
43. Ⓐ Ⓑ Ⓒ Ⓓ Ⓔ
44. Ⓐ Ⓑ Ⓒ Ⓓ Ⓔ
45. Ⓐ Ⓑ Ⓒ Ⓓ Ⓔ
46. Ⓐ Ⓑ Ⓒ Ⓓ Ⓔ
47. Ⓐ Ⓑ Ⓒ Ⓓ Ⓔ
48. Ⓐ Ⓑ Ⓒ Ⓓ Ⓔ
49. Ⓐ Ⓑ Ⓒ Ⓓ Ⓔ
50. Ⓐ Ⓑ Ⓒ Ⓓ Ⓔ

1877–1912
DIAGNOSTIC TEST

This diagnostic test is designed to help you determine your strengths and weaknesses in your knowledge of Industrialism and the Progressive Era (1877–1912). Follow the directions and check your answers.

Study this chapter for the following tests:
AP U.S. History, CLEP General, CLEP United States History I,
GED, Praxis Specialty Area, SAT: United States History

50 Questions

DIRECTIONS: Choose the correct answer for each of the following questions. Fill in each answer on the answer sheet.

1. Which of the following was NOT characteristic of American industry in the post-Civil War period?

   (A) Government successfully broke up large business concentrations.

   (B) The corporation became an increasingly popular form of organization.

   (C) Trusts and holding companies emerged.

   (D) Trade names began appearing for the first time.

   (E) Monopolies were formed both horizontally and vertically.

2. Adoption of the "direct primary" by every state changed which of the following?

   (A) The procedure for choosing a presidential candidate

   (B) The procedure for recalling an elected official

   (C) The procedure for making new laws

   (D) The procedure for selecting candidates for governor and other high state offices

   (E) The procedure for forcing the state legislature to hear a particular bill

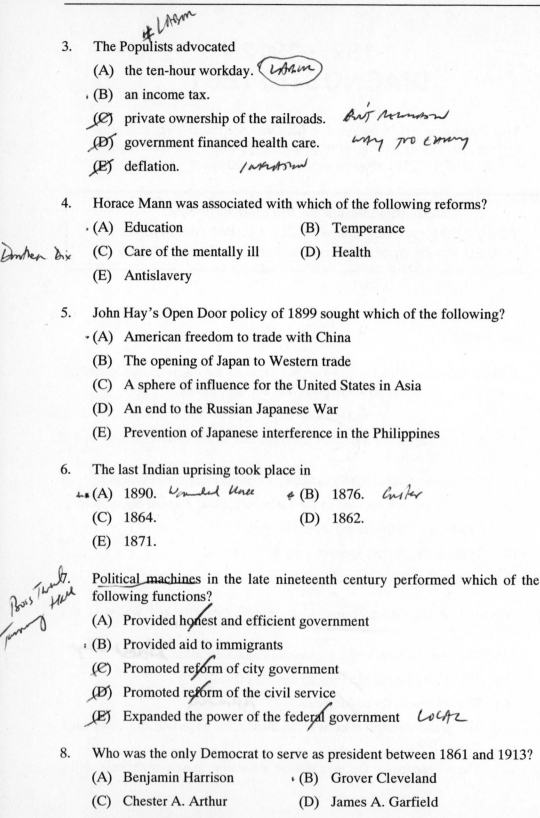

3. The Populists advocated

    (A) the ten-hour workday.

    (B) an income tax.

    (C) private ownership of the railroads.

    (D) government financed health care.

    (E) deflation.

4. Horace Mann was associated with which of the following reforms?

    (A) Education   (B) Temperance

    (C) Care of the mentally ill   (D) Health

    (E) Antislavery

5. John Hay's Open Door policy of 1899 sought which of the following?

    (A) American freedom to trade with China

    (B) The opening of Japan to Western trade

    (C) A sphere of influence for the United States in Asia

    (D) An end to the Russian Japanese War

    (E) Prevention of Japanese interference in the Philippines

6. The last Indian uprising took place in

    (A) 1890.   (B) 1876.

    (C) 1864.   (D) 1862.

    (E) 1871.

7. Political machines in the late nineteenth century performed which of the following functions?

    (A) Provided honest and efficient government

    (B) Provided aid to immigrants

    (C) Promoted reform of city government

    (D) Promoted reform of the civil service

    (E) Expanded the power of the federal government

8. Who was the only Democrat to serve as president between 1861 and 1913?

    (A) Benjamin Harrison   (B) Grover Cleveland

    (C) Chester A. Arthur   (D) James A. Garfield

    (E) Rutherford B. Hayes

9. "In all things that are purely social we can be separate as the fingers, yet one as the hand in all things essential to human progress." This statement reflects the philosophy of which of the following?

   (A) A. Philip Randolph   (B) W.E.B. DuBois

   (C) Booker T. Washington   (D) Martin Luther King

   (E) Frederick Douglass

10. The Spanish-American War resulted in which of the following?

    (A) A guerrilla war between Americans and Filipinos

    (B) American colonization of Cuba

    (C) Theodore Roosevelt's election as president in 1900

    (D) The decline of the anti-imperialist movement

    (E) Independence of Puerto Rico

11. The Ballenger-Pinchot affair involved which of the following issues?

    (A) Reduction of tariff rates

    (B) The Insurgents' move against Speaker of the House Joseph Cannon

    (C) Conservation of public lands

    (D) Regulation of the railroads

    (E) Importation of farm products from Canada without tariff duties

12. "Underneath the surface...the activity of privilege appears, the privileges of the street railways, the gas, the water, the telephone, and the electric-lighting companies. The connection of these industries with politics explains the power of the boss and the machine." Who would most likely have made this statement?

    (A) A Puritan   (B) A muckraker

    (C) A Populist   (D) A transcendentalist

    (E) An isolationist

13. Which of the following correctly describes American railroads in the late nineteenth century?

    (A) All shippers received rebates on their freight charges.

    (B) Railroads had little influence in Congress.

    (C) Railroads received public land.

    (D) After 1886 the states had the power to regulate railroads.

    (E) Railroads were built only to serve population centers.

14. Immigrants coming to America from Eastern and Southern Europe during the late nineteenth century were most likely to

    (A) settle in large cities in the Northeast or Midwest.

    (B) settle on farms in the upper Midwest.

    (C) seek to file on homesteads on the Great Plains.

    (D) migrate to the South and Southwest.

    (E) return to their homelands after only a brief stay in the U.S.

15. The main idea of Theodore Roosevelt's proposed "New Nationalism" was to

    (A) make the federal government an instrument of domestic reform.

    (B) undertake an aggressive new foreign policy.

    (C) increase economic competition by breaking up all trusts and large business combinations.

    (D) seek to establish a large overseas empire.

    (E) take an isolationist position in foreign policy while maintaining the status quo domestically.

16. The Haymarket Incident involved

    (A) a riot between striking workers and police.

    (B) a scandal involving corruption within the Grant administration.

    (C) allegations of corruption on the part of Republican presidential candidate James G. Blaine.

    (D) a disastrous fire that pointed out the hazardous working conditions in some factories.

    (E) an early challenge to the authority of states to regulate the railroad industry.

17. The "New Immigration" was made up primarily of

    (A) Europeans who came for economic rather than religious reasons.

    (B) Europeans who were better off financially than those of the "Old Immigration."

    (C) persons from Northern and Western Europe.

    (D) persons from Southern and Eastern Europe.

    (E) persons from Asia, Africa, and the Americas.

18. As a result of the Spanish-American War, the United States gained possession of Puerto Rico, Guam, and

    (A) the Philippines.

    (B) Cuba.

    (C) Bermuda.

    (D) the Panama Canal Zone.

    (E) Hawaii.

19. Which of the following was a goal of the Populist movement?

    (A) Free coinage of silver

    (B) Reform of child labor laws *later*

    (C) Using modern science to solve social problems

    (D) Eliminating the electoral college as a method of choosing the nation's president

    (E) National legislation outlawing racial discrimination

20. The settlement-house movement drew its workers primarily from which of the following groups? *Social work / Jane Addams*

    (A) Young, affluent, college-educated women

    (B) Poor Eastern European immigrants

    (C) Disabled veterans of the Spanish-American War

    (D) Idealistic young men who came to the city largely from rural areas

    (E) Often illiterate members of the urban working class

21. The "yellow journalism" of the late nineteenth century might best be described as

    (A) focusing on the influx of Chinese immigrants to the West Coast and calling for restrictions on such immigration.

    (B) attempting to alarm the public about the supposed "Yellow Peril" of Japan's growing naval and industrial might.

    (C) focusing exclusively on corruptions and abuses in government and big business.

    (D) reporting the news in an exaggerated, distorted, and sensationalized manner. *jingoism led to Spanish-American War   Hearst*

    (E) dominated by the funding of large corporations so as to take a stance consistently favorable to big business.

22. Which of the following was among the objectives of Booker T. Washington?

    (A) To keep up a constant agitation of questions of racial equality

    (B)   To encourage blacks to be more militant in demanding their rights

    (C)   To encourage blacks to work hard, acquire property, and prove they were worthy of their rights

    (D)   To urge blacks not to accept separate but equal facilities

    (E)   To form an organization to advance the rights of blacks

23.   The Morrill Land Grant Act provided

    (A)   160 acres of free land within the public domain to any head of household who would settle on it and improve it over a period of five years.

    (B)   large amounts of federal government land to states that would establish agricultural and mechanical colleges.

    (C)   40 acres of land to former slaves.

    (D)   that the land of former Confederates should not be confiscated.

    (E)   large reservations for the Indians of the Great Plains.

24.   The Sherman Silver Purchase Act of 1890

    (A)   required the federal government to purchase silver.

    (B)   forbade the federal government to purchase silver.

    (C)   made it illegal for private citizens to purchase silver.

    (D)   made it illegal for private citizens to purchase federal lands with anything but silver.

    (E)   allowed the federal government to buy silver at the discretion of the president.

25.   All of the following were characteristic of life on a pioneer farm on the Great Plains during the late nineteenth century EXCEPT

    (A)   living in a sod house.

    (B)   burning buffalo chips for heating and cooking.

    (C)   splitting rails to make fences.

    (D)   practicing new dry-lands farming techniques.

    (E)   growing large crops of wheat or corn.

26.   According to the following table, by what year did the major source of immigration to the United States shift from Northern and Western Europe to Southern and Eastern Europe?

Year	North & West Eur.	South & East Eur.
1870	318,792	5,409
1880	658,904	21,211
1890	459,246	103,357
1900	103,719	206,134
1910	202,198	465,366

(A) 1870   (B) 1880

(C) 1890   - (D) 1900

(E) 1910

27. Which of the following worked for women's suffrage in the latter part of the nineteenth century?

(A) Abigail Adams *18th century*   (B) Margaret Fuller *transcendentalist 1840s*

(C) Dorothea Dix *asylum reform* . (D) Lucy Stone

(E) Germaine Greer *1960s*   *+ Elizabeth Cady Stanton*

28. The Farmers' Alliances of the 1880s appealed primarily to

(A) small farmers in the Northeast who found themselves unable to compete with large Western farms.

. (B) Southern and Great Plains farmers frustrated with low crop prices and mired in the sharecrop and crop-lien systems.

(C) established and well-to-do farmers who desired to limit production in order to sustain high prices.

(D) owners of the giant "bonanza" farms of the Northern Plains states who sought special advantages from the government.

(E) Chinese immigrants serving as agricultural workers with low pay and poor working conditions, primarily in the Eastern states.

29. Which of the following regions was most heavily represented among immigrants to the United States during the years from 1865 to 1890?

- (A) Northern and Western Europe

(B) Southern and Eastern Europe

(C) Asia

(D) Africa

(E) Central and South America

30. All of the following are true of William H. Taft EXCEPT

    (A) he was an able and efficient administrator.

    (B) he was little inclined to making rousing speeches or engage in political conflict.

    ·(C) he reversed Theodore Roosevelt's conservationist policies.

    (D) he disliked publicity.

    (E) his administration was more active in prosecuting trusts than Roosevelt's had been.

31. Which of the following groups was the first target of congressional legislation restricting immigration?

    (A) Northern and Western Europeans

    (B) Southern and Eastern Europeans *1920's*

    ·(C) Asians *Chinese Exclusion Act, 1882*

    (D) Africans

    (E) Central and South Americans

32. During the late nineteenth and early twentieth centuries, Republicans generally favored

    ·(A) high protective tariffs.

    (B) low, revenue-only tariffs.

    (C) completely free trade.

    (D) high tariffs on farm produce but none on manufactured goods.

    (E) only such tariffs as would be beneficial to agriculture.

33. Which of the following statements is LEAST true about immigration to the U.S. between 1880 and 1900?

    (A) Most immigrants were unskilled day laborers.

    (B) Immigration increased steadily during these years.

    (C) Immigrants tended to be Catholic, Eastern Orthodox, or Jewish.

    (D) Most immigrants came from Northern and Western Europe.

    (E) Chinese immigrants were excluded by law during most of these years.

34. Which of the following gave the greatest impetus to national civil service reform?

    (A) President Hayes's halt to Southern Reconstruction

(B)   The renomination of President Arthur in 1884

(C)   The continued Stalwart-Half Breed battles of the Republican party

(D)   The assassination of President Garfield

(E)   The prosecution and eventual conviction of Boss Tweed

35.   Which of the following circumstances was most significant in bringing an end to Reconstruction in 1877?

(A)   The installation of a Republican administration

(B)   The deaths of many leading Radical politicians in the North

(C)   The increasing interest in economic issues rather than racial or sectional ones

(D)   The violent resistance of Southerners in such organizations as the Ku Klux Klan

(E)   The Northern electorate's fatigue with the effort to remake Southern society

36.   All of the following improved the situation of the American farmer during the late nineteenth century EXCEPT

(A)   an expanding money supply based on the gold standard.

(B)   the escalating food demands of a growing urban population.

(C)   the declining rate at which new acreage became available for cultivation.

(D)   early government programs subsidizing farmers and stabilizing commodities markets.

(E)   a constant supply of farm laborers.

37.   Late nineteenth century works by American naturalists included

I.   Henry James's *The Portrait of a Lady.*

II.   Frank Norris's *The Octopus.*

III.   Herman Melville's *Billy Budd.*

IV.   Theodore Dreiser's *Sister Carrie.*

V.   Thomas Nelson Page's "Marse Chan."

(A)   I, II, and IV   (B)   I, II, and III

(C)   II, III, and IV   (D)   II and IV

(E)   II and V

38. "He sulkily admitted now that there was no more escape, but he lay and detested the grind of the real-estate business, and disliked his family, and disliked himself for disliking them. The evening before, he had played poker at Vergil Gunch's till midnight, and after such holidays he was irritable before breakfast. It may have been the tremendous home-brewed beer of the prohibition era and the cigars to which that beer enticed him; it may have been resentment of return from this fine, bold man-world to a restricted region of wives and stenographers, and of suggestions not to smoke so much."

This passage was most likely written by

(A) William Dean Howells.   (B) David Phillips.

(C) Sinclair Lewis.   (D) F. Scott Fitzgerald.

(E) Washington Irving.

39. One of the major effects of the Industrial Revolution of the late nineteenth century in the United States was

(A) an increased emphasis on worker health and safety issues.

(B) an increased emphasis on speed rather than quality of work.

(C) an increased emphasis on high-quality, error free work.

(D) an increase in the number of small industrial facilities, which could operate more efficiently than larger, more costly industrial plants.

(E) a decrease in worker productivity as a result of continuous clashes between unions and management.

40. The policy promoted by Theodore Roosevelt, most blatantly pursued in Central America, was the

(A) New Deal policy.   (B) Big Stick policy.

(C) Good Neighbor policy.   (D) Fair Deal policy.

(E) Square Deal policy.

41. All of the following were major problems with turn-of-the-century American cities EXCEPT

(A) poverty.   (B) pollution.

(C) lack of adequate housing.   (D) crime.

(E) unemployment.

42. U.S. presidents between 1876 and 1900 were considered among the weakest in American history. A major reason for this was that

    (A) none of them served more than one term in office.

    (B) they considered themselves caretakers, not dynamic initiators of new legislation.

    (C) Congress enacted several new laws restricting presidential power during this period.

    (D) they were the products of machine politics, political followers who were typically incompetent leaders.

    (E) they were limited in their actions by the overwhelming Populist sentiment of their time.

43. Which of the following best describes the Industrial Workers of the World?

    (A) They were a third party that ran candidates for political office.

    ·(B) They were among the most radical labor unions in the early twentieth century.

    (C) They appealed to most American workers.

    (D) They agitated for U.S. involvement in World War I.

    (E) They supported William Taft in the election of 1908.

44. The sharecropping system in the South following Reconstruction had the effect of

    (A) allowing many former slaves and poor white tenant farmers, who could have never otherwise owned land, to buy their own farms.

    (B) moving many former slaves and poor white tenant farmers into the middle class.

    ·(C) pushing tenant farmers and poor independent farmers into deep levels of debt to large landowners and merchants.

    (D) helping to limit the power of former plantation owners and Northern business interests.

    (E) changing the basic attitudes of whites and blacks who were now forced to work side-by-side farming the same land.

45. The political machines such as Tammany Hall which ran American cities at the turn of the century derived their strongest support from

    (A) industrial leaders and business elites.

    (B) organized religion.

    (C) wealthy landowners living in rural areas outside the cities.

(D) the middle class.

(E) poor immigrants and ethnic communities in the inner city.

46. What was the reaction of most Filipinos when they were liberated from Spanish control and occupied by American forces following the Spanish-American War?

(A) They applied for statehood, but their application was rejected by Congress which feared that the Philippines were too far away to effectively govern.

(B) They welcomed the Americans as heroes and were thrilled when the United States government announced that the Philippines would eventually be granted its independence when the people had been educated and trained in running their own government.

(C) Their reaction was relatively neutral. They had known nothing but colonial status for hundreds of years and had become resigned to their fate.

(D) While there was some resentment at the American refusal to grant them immediate independence, there was little violence. Most Philippine hostility was expressed in a few scattered peaceful protests.

• (E) Filipinos, angered at American actions, declared themselves independent and launched a violent rebellion that killed thousands and took two years to quell.

47. Education in turn-of-the-century schools was primarily aimed at

(A) giving students an opportunity for personal growth and development.

(B) teaching children basic religious values.

(C) developing individualism so that each student would have the personal character necessary to survive in a capitalistic society.

(D) teaching children management skills necessary to run their own business.

• (E) teaching children punctuality and discipline necessary for factory work.

48. The black leader at the turn of the century who refused to accept second-class citizenship for blacks and founded the National Association for the Advancement of Colored People (NAACP) for the purpose of fighting racial discrimination through the courts was

(A) Marcus Garvey. (B) Booker T. Washington.

(C) George Washington Carver. • (D) W.E.B. DuBois.

(E) Hiram Revels.

49. In the nineteenth century, American farmers supported an economic policy of inflation because inflation generally favors

- (A) debtor groups.
(B) creditor groups.
(C) high food costs.
(D) a dynamic monetary system.
(E) a barter system.

50. The late-nineteenth-century labor union most identified with the motto "pure and simple unionism" was

(A) the Knights of Labor.
(B) the American Federation of Labor.
(C) the National Labor Union.
(D) the IWW.
(E) the Molly Maguires.

1877–1912
DIAGNOSTIC TEST

ANSWER KEY

1. (A)	11. (C)	21. (D)	31. (B)	41. (E)
2. (D)	12. (B)	22. (C)	32. (A)	42. (B)
3. (B)	13. (C)	23. (B)	33. (D)	43. (B)
4. (A)	14. (A)	24. (A)	34. (D)	44. (C)
5. (A)	15. (A)	25. (C)	35. (E)	45. (E)
6. (A)	16. (A)	26. (D)	36. (D)	46. (E)
7. (B)	17. (D)	27. (D)	37. (D)	47. (E)
8. (B)	18. (A)	28. (B)	38. (C)	48. (D)
9. (C)	19. (A)	29. (A)	39. (B)	49. (A)
10. (A)	20. (A)	30. (C)	40. (B)	50. (B)

DETAILED EXPLANATIONS
OF ANSWERS

1. **(A)** Although the Sherman Antitrust Act of 1890 gave the government power to break up large business combinations, the Supreme Court in *United States v. E.C. Knight Co.* (1895) took away that power.

2. **(D)** The direct primary replaced the party caucus as the procedure for choosing candidates for governor and other high state offices. Adopted by most states during the Progressive period, it was more popular than the initiative (E), referendum (C), and recall (B). Not all states use the primary in choosing presidential candidates.

3. **(B)** The Populist party, which emerged in the late 1880s and early 1890s, called for the eight-hour day, an income tax, and government ownership of the railroads, as well as restrictions on immigration, the secret ballot, popular election of senators, and freeing the money supply from the price of gold.

4. **(A)** Horace Mann served as secretary of the Massachusetts State Board of Education; Lyman Beecher advocated temperance reforms; Dorothea Dix promoted better care of the mentally ill; and Sylvester Graham pushed health reform.

5. **(A)** The Open Door policy sought to establish American freedom of trade with China, where European powers had established "spheres of influence." Japan had been "opened" in 1854. The Treaty of Portsmouth (1905) ended the Russo-Japanese War, while the Japanese in 1905 agreed not to interfere in the Philippines.

6. **(A)** The last Indian uprising took place in 1890, ending at Wounded Knee, South Dakota. In 1862 the Sioux went on the warpath in the northern Great Plains. In 1864 militia attacked Cheyenne and Arapaho at Sand Creek, Colorado. Custer's "Last Stand" occurred in 1876, and the Arapaho-Apache War took place in 1871.

7. **(B)** The political machines served as a crude welfare system for the immigrant population, although they were corrupt and expensive. Reformers sought to wrest control away from the machines.

8. **(B)** Grover Cleveland is also the only president to serve two split terms 1885–1889 and 1893–1897.

9. **(C)** Booker T. Washington made this statement in his "Atlanta Compromise" speech of 1895. His contemporary, W.E.B. DuBois, strongly opposed

Washington's compromise approach in favor of strong advocacy of civil rights. Frederick Douglass was active in the pre-Civil War antislavery movement, while Martin Luther King was a civil rights leader of the 1950s and 1960s.

10. **(A)** When the U.S. refused to grant independence to the Philippines, Filipino rebels mounted guerrilla warfare against the Americans until defeated in 1902. Cuba became an American protectorate rather than a colony, while Puerto Rico became an unincorporated U.S. territory. Anti-imperialism grew as a result of the war and its aftermath. Roosevelt was elected vice president in 1900.

11. **(C)** Of the various controversies that took place during the Taft presidency (1909–1913), the Ballenger-Pinchot affair dealt with conservation. Taft supported the regulation of railroads (Mann-Elkins Act, 1910) but compromised on the Payne-Aldrich Tariff. He sided with Cannon in a losing battle with the "insurgents" in Congress, and his proposal for tariff-free Canadian farm products stirred up even more controversy.

12. **(B)** In the 1890s and early twentieth century, muckraking journalists uncovered the corruption lying underneath the surface of American politics and business. The Populists had been primarily concerned with the problems of the farmers.

13. **(C)** The railroads received large land grants from the federal government. They paid rebates only to their large customers and had considerable influence in Congress. In 1886 the Supreme Court decided that only the federal government had the right to regulate the railroads. Railroads were often built to encourage growth of new cities rather than serve existing ones.

14. **(A)** For whatever reasons, immigrants of the "New Immigration" tended to settle in the large cities of the Northeast and Midwest. Very few of them settled on farms (B), filed on homesteads (C), or migrated to the South and Southwest (D). While some eventually returned to their countries of origin, the majority did not (E).

15. **(A)** Roosevelt's New Nationalism pertained to domestic reform. Unrelated was the fact that Roosevelt always favored an aggressive foreign policy (B), including the establishment of an overseas empire (D). He would, of course, have opposed either isolationism or the holding of the status quo (E). Though he gained a reputation as a trust-buster, Roosevelt was by no means in favor of breaking up all trusts and large business combinations (C).

16. **(A)** The Haymarket Incident involved the throwing of a bomb at Chicago police and a subsequent riot involving police and striking workers. There were plenty of scandals within the Grant administration (B), but this was not one of them. Allegations of corruption on the part of Republican presidential candidate James G. Blaine (C) were contained in the Mulligan Letters. The disastrous

fire that pointed out the hazardous working conditions in some factories (D) was New York's Triangle Factory fire. An early challenge to the authority of states to regulate the railroad industry (E) was contained in the Supreme Court case of *Munn v. Illinois.*

17. **(D)** The "New Immigration" was made up primarily of persons from Southern and Eastern Europe. Some, such as persecuted Russian Jews, came for religious reasons (A). The great majority were financially less well off (B) than those of the "Old Immigration," who came from Northern and Western Europe (C). Persons from Asia, Africa, and the Americas would not generally be considered part of the "New Immigration."

18. **(A)** The U.S. gained possession of the Philippines through the Spanish-American War. Cuba (B), though originally the primary issue of contention between Spain and the United States, was not annexed but rather granted its independence under the terms of the Platte Amendment. Hawaii (E) and the Panama Canal Zone (D) were acquired within a few years of the Spanish-American War but in unrelated incidents and not from Spain. Bermuda (C) has never been acquired by the United States.

19. **(A)** The Populists desired free coinage of silver. They also desired direct election of U.S. senators, not necessarily an end to the electoral college (D). The Progressive movement, which followed Populism, favored reform of child labor laws (B) and using modern science to solve social problems (C). In general, Populists were more likely to favor racial discrimination than to oppose it (E).

20. **(A)** The settlement-house workers were often young, affluent, college-educated women such as Jane Addams. Poor immigrants (B), disabled veterans (C), and illiterate workers (E) would have had less opportunity for such things. Idealistic young men (D) were apparently drawn to such enterprises in smaller numbers.

21. **(D)** "Yellow journalism" is the reporting of the news in an exaggerated, distorted, and sensationalized manner. The Muckrakers focused on corruptions and abuses in government and big business (C). While popular concern in one part of the country or another might from time to time focus on the supposed dangers of Chinese immigration (A) or Japanese power (B), and while a large corporation might occasionally have a paper as its mouthpiece (E), none of these characterized a school of journalism in itself.

22. **(C)** Booker T. Washington encouraged his fellow blacks to work hard, acquire property, and prove they were worthy of their rights. Washington's contemporary and critic W.E.B. DuBois urged his fellow blacks to agitate questions of racial equality (A), be more militant in demanding their rights (B), not to accept separate but equal facilities (D), and to form an organization to advance the rights of blacks (E).

23. **(B)** The Morrill Land Grant Act provided large amounts of federal government land to states that would establish agricultural and mechanical colleges. It was the Homestead Act that granted 160-acre farms free to those who would settle on them (A). After the Civil War there was some talk of providing former slaves with "40 acres and a mule," but nothing came of it (C). Even without a special act of Congress to prevent it, in fact very little land of former Confederates was confiscated (D). Various acts of Congress and decisions of presidents throughout the 1800s dealt with the disposition of the Great Plains Indians (E).

24. **(A)** The Sherman Silver Purchase Act required the federal government to purchase a certain specified amount of silver each month (B). The president had no discretion in the matter (E). Private citizens were not directly affected by the act (C) and (D).

25. **(C)** Splitting rails would not have been part of the life of a Great Plains pioneer, since one of the difficulties of such a life was the absence of trees. For this reason houses were made of sod (A) rather than wood, and heating and cooking were done over fires of buffalo chips (B). Using dry-land farming techniques (D) and growing wheat and corn (E) would also have characterized the life of a Great Plains farmer.

26. **(D)** In 1900 there were nearly twice as many immigrants from Southern and Eastern Europe as there were from Northern and Western Europe. This shift is called the "New Immigration."

27. **(D)** Lucy Stone was a leader in the women's suffrage movement from the 1840s until her death in 1893. Abigail Adams was the wife of John Adams and Margaret Fuller was active in the transcendentalist movement of the 1830s and 1840s, while Dorothea Dix campaigned about the same time for better treatment of the mentally ill. Germaine Greer was active in the women's movement of the 1960s and 1970s.

28. **(B)** Farmers of the Great Plains and the South often saw the Alliance movement as the only way to get out of the seemingly endless cycle of debt (crop liens), sharecropping, and/or low commodity prices. Small farmers in the Northeast could not, in fact, compete with Western farms, but they had no need to since they could concentrate on production of perishable items for nearby metropolitan areas (A). This was also the age of the giant "bonanza" farms of the Northern Plains, but neither the owners of such farms (D) nor established, well-to-do farmers (C) had any need for the kind of government help the Farmers' Alliances sought. There were also a number of Chinese immigrants in the Western states at this time, not, however, in the Farmers' Alliances (E).

29. **(A)** Surprisingly, the "Old Immigration," made up of those from Northern and Western Europe, still predominated after the Civil War until about 1890.

Thereafter, the "New Immigration," composed primarily of those from Southern and Eastern Europe (B), was most prevalent.

30. **(C)** Taft did not reverse Theodore Roosevelt's conservationist policies but, in fact, advanced them more than Roosevelt had. He did this, however, in a quiet way, since he disliked publicity (D) and was little inclined to make rousing speeches or engage in political conflict (B). In much the same way he went about prosecuting trusts to a greater degree than Roosevelt had done (E). He was also an able administrator (A).

31. **(B)** The first target of congressional legislation restricting immigration were those of the "New Immigration," primarily from Southern and Eastern Europe, whose influx had spurred Congress to impose the limits. Relatively few limits were placed on those from Northern and Western Europe (A), though eventually severe immigration restrictions were placed on those coming from most of the rest of the world (C), (D), and (E).

32. **(A)** Republicans of the late nineteenth and early twentieth centuries favored high protective tariffs in order to benefit American manufacturers at the expense of the rest of the U.S. economy. They opposed low tariffs (B) or free trade (C). Tariffs could not benefit farmers in the U.S. since the U.S. was an exporter, rather than even a potential importer, of farm produce (D) and (E).

33. **(D)** The "New Immigration" of 1880–1900 predominantly consisted of immigrants from Eastern and Southern Europe, rather than Northern and Western Europe. The "New Immigrants" were largely unskilled day laborers (A) and came from non-Protestant religions (C); as a result, quotas were established to keep these "inferior" immigrants out. Immigration did increase steadily over these years (B), although the Chinese remained excluded (E) from the immigration boom by the Chinese Exclusion Act of 1882, which was renewed upon its expiration in 1892 and remained in effect for the rest of the century.

34. **(D)** The assassination of Garfield by a disgruntled office seeker shocked the nation and provoked the Pendleton Act of 1883, which, among other reforms required a competitive test for entry into jobs "classified" by the president and prohibited financial assessments of jobholders. While the Stalwart-Half Breed battles in the Republican party exemplified the problems of the spoils system (C), they had been going on for years before Garfield was shot, without reforms. Tweed's conviction (E), while long in coming, spurred no national movement for reform; Hayes's ending of Reconstruction (A) was not a civil service issue. Chester Arthur did not win renomination in 1884 (B).

35. **(E)** Reconstruction came to an end in 1877, primarily because the Northern electorate had grown tired of the effort to remake Southern society. Many leading Radical politicians in the North had died (B), but it was the electorate's fatigue with Reconstruction (E) that prevented others from rising to take their

place. The violence of organizations such as the Ku Klux Klan (D) actually increased after the withdrawal of federal troops from the South, and it was the end of Reconstruction that allowed the nation to shift its interest from racial and sectional issues to economic ones (C).

36. **(D)** Despite the efforts of the Populists, government programs to aid farmers did not become reality during the late nineteenth century. However, the lot of the farmer was bettered by a combination of circumstances including an expanding money supply based on the gold standard (A), the escalating food demands of a growing urban population (B), a declining rate at which new acreage became available for cultivation (C), and a constant (rather than rapidly growing) supply of farm laborers (E).

37. **(D)** American naturalism in the late nineteenth and early twentieth centuries was an outgrowth of realism, which de-emphasized didactic and moral ends in favor of an "objective" depiction of life. To this end naturalists wrote meditations on evolution, historical determinism, and mechanistic philosophy, along with a concern for social justice. Frank Norris (II), author of *The Octopus* and *McTeague,* and Theodore Dreiser (IV), author of *Sister Carrie* and *An American Tragedy,* are perhaps the most famous American naturalists. Herman Melville (III) addressed metaphysical concerns and often had pessimistic leanings, but did not write in the naturalist tradition. Thomas Nelson Page (V) wrote mainly about the South; he belonged to the realist tradition although his stories and novels were heavily sentimental. Henry James (I) was perhaps the most famous American writer of the late nineteenth century, but, as opposed to realists and naturalists who focused strictly on the reproduction of reality in fiction, James was preoccupied with formal problems and aimed for psychological realism in his work.

38. **(C)** The passage, which refers to events of small-town Midwestern life in the 1920s, is from Sinclair Lewis's novel *Babbitt* (1922), which describes the life of George Babbitt, a businessman and in many ways the personification of the narrowness of small-town America. David Phillips (B) was a muckraking journalist and author of "The Treason of the Senate" (1906), which exposed special-interest-related corruption in that body. F. Scott Fitzgerald's (D) subjects belonged to the Jazz Age rather than to small-town America. The works of William Dean Howells (A) are concerned with the growth of industrialization that was an issue of Gilded Age politics. Washington Irving (E), author of *The Sketch Book,* wrote during the earliest part of the nineteenth century.

39. **(B)** There were many major changes resulting from the rapid industrial development in the United States from 1860 through 1900. First, there was a shift to building larger and larger industrial facilities to accommodate the new machine technologies coming into existence. Small factories could not absorb the cost of much of the machinery and did not produce enough to make the machin-

ery profitable. So contrary to choice (D), there was an increase in large industrial plants and a relative decline in small factories.

40. **(B)** Roosevelt's most memorable line was also the underpinning of his foreign policy strategy in Central America: "Speak softly but carry a big stick." The thrust of this policy was that the United States wouldn't waste a lot of energy on words in settling issues in Central America. Instead, there would be a focus on action. This served to warn Central American countries to watch their behavior or they would face U.S. political and military intervention to insure that things were returned to "proper order." Basically, Roosevelt's policy was an expansion of the Monroe Doctrine and served notice that the United States intended to be the policeman of the Caribbean. Roosevelt, true to form, backed up his words with action. The U.S. sent troops into six different Latin American nations between 1900 and 1930. U.S. economic intervention was even more prevalent. Regrettably, while this policy allowed America to flex its muscles and solved many short-term problems, it ignored the sensitivities of Latin Americans, building deep resentments that linger today.

41. **(E)** About the only thing that wasn't a major problem was unemployment. There were plenty of jobs available and almost anyone could find some type of work if he or she looked long enough. The biggest problem was that most of the available work paid very poor wages. So while unemployment wasn't an issue, poverty related to low-paying employment was a major problem. Even then, debates raged about how much assistance should be given to help the poor. While some assistance was made available, most people had to fend for themselves or rely on extended family to survive.

Housing construction was aimed primarily at the expanding middle class, and the poor were relegated to tenement housing. Crime was perhaps the biggest concern for city dwellers. Finally, pollution was a major problem. Plumbing and sewage facilities were inadequate. The quality of drinking water was often substandard. Garbage disposal was a major problem and often created disease problems for city residents. The air was often choked with fumes from the coal-fired boilers of local industry. Even horse droppings were a health menace until the advent of the automobile.

42. **(B)** The years between 1876–1900 were years of relative political equality between the Republicans and Democrats. It was also a time when most Americans were rejecting or resisting the cries for reform by political activists. Most people wanted the federal government to remain inactive and uninvolved as much as possible. The concept of laissez-faire leadership was flourishing. This resulted in little significant reform legislation from the Congress. It also led to the election of presidents who saw themselves as political caretakers of the office of the presidency, rather than advocates of social or political reform. The equality between the two parties at this time also made it difficult for any president to push for major changes, because the political base of support was too evenly

divided to provide the necessary votes in Congress for effective action. While none of these presidents were incompetent (as asserted by choice (D)), they just didn't see the presidency as an office appropriate for taking strong initiatives. They believed their major job was to insure Congressional legislation was effectively carried out and to veto any legislation in which they felt Congress had exceeded its powers. Such an attitude does not tend to lead to inspirational, dynamic leadership. Their style was such that they believed the LESS they were noticed the better they were doing their job. This has left the long-term impression of them being "weak" presidents.

43. **(B)** The Industrial Workers of the World, also known as the Wobblies, were a radical labor organization that supported revolution. They were also involved in strikes and other important labor activities. They did not run candidates for political offices, nor did they have much appeal to most American workers. They did not seek U.S. involvement in World War I, nor is it at all likely that they would have supported Taft for President.

44. **(C)** The sharecropping system allowed poor tenant farmers and poor independent farmers to borrow seed, equipment, and supplies for planting and harvesting a crop. In return, sharecroppers had to pledge their crop, or a portion of their crop, as collateral. While this arrangement allowed sharecroppers to continue to farm the land and squeeze out a minimal survival, the costs charged to farmers for supplies and equipment as well as the exorbitant interest rates charged for loaning those supplies effectively kept sharecroppers in permanent debt. Interest rates ranged as high as 200 percent. Most sharecroppers never accumulated enough cash to work their way out from under the tremendous debt load they incurred trying to work their small plots of lands. The only ones who got wealthy from this system were the landowners and the merchants who controlled the sharecroppers. This system did nothing to bring poor farmers into the middle class. Neither did it expand the number of independently owned farms in the South. It had no restrictive effect on the power of former plantation owners or Northern business interests. Finally, it did nothing to enhance the relationship between blacks and whites as it did not force them to work side by side. In fact, in many ways it was used by Southern ruling elites to maintain the old social and racial order.

45. **(E)** Political machines and the politics of political bosses dominated the workings of city governments at the turn of the century. Many of these organizations stayed in power through bribery, graft, and other corrupt practices. In return, however, the machines took care of the interests of many of their most influential constituents. They provided many services which helped the poor survive in return for support at the polls. Many reformers, mostly from the middle and upper classes, demanding changes to end the corruption, found themselves stymied at the polls by large blocks of poor and immigrant voters who supported the political machines. The machines were often successfully able to portray themselves as protectors of the poor who fought against upper-class

reformers interested only in themselves.

While the political machines were able to enlist the support of some industrial leaders, and sometimes got indirect support from organized religion, they got little support from the middle class and virtually no support from wealthy landowners living outside the city.

46. **(E)** Philippine nationalists believed that when the United States drove out the Spanish, the Philippines would be given independence. Comments by the commander of the U.S. naval forces in the region, Commodore Dewey, were interpreted as promises of independence. When the U.S. began formal occupation of the islands and it became clear that independence was not forthcoming, the nationalists began agitating against U.S. rule. In addition, Americans treated the Filipinos with contempt. Much of this was in large part due to latent racism against the nonwhite Filipinos. Racial slurs were commonly used, and they were treated in much the same manner as Southerners treated ex-slaves after the Civil War.

Frustration soon reached a boiling point and in 1899 the leader of the nationalists, Emilo Aguinaldo, declared Philippine independence and launched an insurrection against American control. The rebellion took over two years to control, and it resulted in countless atrocities by both Filipinos and Americans. The ensuing bloodbath cost over 500,000 Filipinos killed and approximately 5,000 Americans.

While the Filipinos lost the revolution, it did lead to reforms in U.S. policy. In 1916, the Filipinos were promised that they would be granted their independence (when the United States felt they were capable of successfully governing themselves).

47. **(E)** Turn-of-the-century educational reform was often prompted by industrialists seeking better quality workers to fill job openings in the factories. Thus, most educational reforms in this era were aimed at teaching students the disciplined, punctual, conformist skills and behaviors they would need to be good factory workers, which is what the future held for most urban schoolchildren. While individual initiative was rewarded through grades, those grades could only be obtained by channeling initiative within the strict limits of school objectives. So, while initiative was rewarded, it was a noncreative, conformist initiative that didn't allow for challenging basic rules or assumptions. This mirrored the situation in which most factory workers operated. Creativity wasn't necessary nor was it helpful on an assembly line. Individual growth was not a major issue for American schools until the late 1960s and early 1970s. The goal of the school in 1900 was to produce educated, trainable workers. Management techniques would be reserved for those males who went on to colleges or universities as part of their advanced education or were learned on the job. While individual initiative was rewarded, too much individualism was usually frowned upon. Schools rarely rewarded people who didn't follow the rules precisely, and individualists are not usually very good at following other people's rules. While individualism had been a hallmark of America's westward expansion, in public schools it was a

distant ideal to be discussed but certainly not practiced. After all, an individualist on the factory assembly line could turn into a real troublemaker and possibly sow discontent among other workers.

48.   **(D)**   W.E.B. DuBois was a leading black progressive leader. He was a well-educated (Ph.D. from Harvard), articulate spokesman for blacks who refused to accept continued subjugation by whites. He believed that for blacks to achieve equality, an elite group of talented, trained, and well-educated blacks would have to "lead the way," setting an example whites could not dismiss and blacks could proudly follow. His lofty goals led to his founding the NAACP as a vehicle to promote black rights through the courts and to focus concerns on black needs and black issues. An idealistic intellectual, his style and words often alienated him from the majority of impoverished, uneducated black Americans of his day. He found more support among progressive, liberal white intellectuals than among blacks. However, he did set the example talked about in his ideals, a strong black American leader whom whites could not easily dismiss and who blacks could follow proudly.

49.   **(A)**   In the American economic system, a person who holds a fixed rate loan is aided by inflation. Inflation, as a condition where too many dollars are chasing too few goods, actually reduces the real purchasing power of the dollar over time. Therefore, a person who is indebted over 20 years would be paying the same dollar amount per year from year one to year 20. Yet, the value of year 20 dollars would be worth much less than year one dollars because of inflation. Because nineteenth century American farmers always borrowed money on the promise of a future harvest, they were traditionally a debtor group. Because all loans of the nineteenth century were at fixed interest rates, farmers supported inflationary policies to better their financial condition. Although food costs do rise under inflation, there is no guarantee that the producer of the food (the farmer) would receive more profit in a commercial agricultural system. Also, the farmer would suffer higher costs under inflation as do all consumers. A dynamic monetary system and a barter system by themselves do nothing to better the farmer economically. In short, inflation assisted the debtor and not the creditor in the nineteenth century.

50.   **(B)**   Of all labor unions in the late nineteenth century, only Samuel Gompers' skilled craftsman union, the American Federation of Labor, claimed a partnership in capitalism with management and saw itself as "pure and simple unionism" in its quest for higher wages and other bread and butter issues. The Industrial Workers of the World preached one great union for all workers and worker ownership of the means of production as did the Knights of Labor. The National Labor Union held onto an idealistic vision of the American craftsman as the rugged individual entrepreneur that was an anachronism in the late nineteenth century. The Molly Maguires were a group of unionists active in the coal industry who preached the violent overthrow of the managerial class to gain worker benefits.

1877–1912
REVIEW

1. THE NEW INDUSTRIAL ERA, 1877-1882

The structure of modern American society was erected by democratic, capitalistic, and technological forces in the post-Civil War era. Between the 1870s and 1890s, "Gilded Age" America emerged as the world's leading industrial and agricultural producer.

Politics of the Period, 1877–1882

The presidencies of Abraham Lincoln and Theodore Roosevelt mark the boundaries of a half century of relatively weak executive leadership, and legislative domination by Congress and the Republican party.

The Compromise of 1877

With Southern Democratic acceptance of Rutherford B. Hayes' Republican presidency, the last remaining Union troops were withdrawn from the Old Confederacy (South Carolina, Florida, Louisiana), and the country was at last reunified as a modern nation-state led by corporate and industrial interests. The Hayes election arrangement also marked the government's abandonment of its earlier vague commitment to African-American equality.

Republican Factions

"Stalwarts" led by New York Senator Roscoe Conkling favored the old spoils system of political patronage. "Half-Breeds" headed by Maine Senator James G. Blaine pushed for civil service reform and merit appointments to government posts.

Election of 1880

James A. Garfield of Ohio, a Half-Breed, and his vice presidential running mate Chester A. Arthur of New York, a Stalwart, defeated the Democratic candidates, General Winfield S. Hancock of Pennsylvania and former Indiana congressman William English. Tragically, the Garfield administration was but an interlude, for the president was assassinated in 1881 by a mentally disturbed patronage seeker, Charles Guiteau. Although without much executive experience, the Stalwart Arthur had the courage to endorse reform of the political spoils system by supporting passage of the Pendleton Act (1883) which established open competitive examinations for civil service positions.

The Greenback-Labor Party

This third-party movement polled over one million votes in 1878, and elected 14 members to Congress in an effort to promote the inflation of farm prices, and the cooperative marketing of agricultural produce. In 1880, the party's presidential candidate, James Weaver of Iowa, advocated public control and regulation of private enterprises such as railroads in the common interest of more equitable competition. Weaver theorized that because railroads were so essential, they should be treated as a public utility. He polled only three percent of the vote.

The Economy, 1877–1882

Industrial expansion and technology assumed major proportions in this period. Between 1860 and 1894 the United States moved from the fourth largest manufacturing nation to the world's leader through capital accumulation, natural resources, especially in iron, oil and coal. Also, an abundance of labor was helped by massive immigration, railway transportation and communications (the telephone was introduced by Alexander Graham Bell in 1876), and major technical innovations such as the development of the modern steel industry by Andrew Carnegie, and electrical energy by Thomas Edison. In the petroleum industry, John D. Rockefeller controlled 95 percent of the U.S. oil refineries by 1877.

The New South

By 1880, Northern capital erected the modern textile industry in the New South by bringing factories to the cotton fields. Birmingham, Alabama, emerged as the South's leading steel producer, and the introduction of machine-made cigarettes propelled the Duke family to prominence as tobacco producers.

Standard of Living

Throughout the U.S. the standard of living rose sharply, but the distribution of wealth was very uneven. Increasingly, an elite of about 10 percent of the population controlled 90 percent of the nation's wealth.

Social Darwinism

Many industrial leaders used the doctrines associated with the "Gospel of Wealth" to justify the unequal distribution of national wealth. Self-justification by the wealthy was based on the notion that God had granted wealth as He had given grace for material and spiritual salvation of the select few. These few, according to William Graham Sumner, relied heavily on the survival-of-the-fittest philosophy associated with Charles Darwin.

Labor Unrest

When capital overexpansion and overspeculation led to the economic panic of 1873, massive labor disorders spread through the country leading to the paralyzing railroad strike of 1877. Unemployment and salary reductions caused major class conflict. President Hayes used federal troops to restore order after dozens of workers were killed. Immigrant workers began fighting among themselves in California where Irish and Chinese laborers fought for economic survival.

Labor Unions

The depression of the 1870s undermined national labor organizations. The National Labor Union (1866) had a membership of 600,000 but failed to withstand the impact of economic adversity. The Knights of Labor (1869) managed to open its membership to not only white native American workers, but immigrants, women, and African-Americans as well. Although they claimed one million members, they too could not weather the hard times of the 1870s, and eventually went under in 1886 in the wake of the bloody Haymarket Riot in Chicago.

Agricultural Militancy

Agrarian discontent expressed through the activities of the National Grange and the Farmers' Alliances in the West and South showed greater lasting power. During the Civil War, many farmers had overexpanded their operations, purchased more land and machinery, and gone heavily into debt. When the relatively high wartime agricultural prices collapsed in the decades after the war, farmers worked collectively to promote currency inflation, higher farm prices, silver and gold bimetalism, debt relief, cooperative farm marketing ventures, and regulation of monopolies and railroads by the federal and state governments. Although not very successful in the 1870s, farmer militancy continued to be a powerful political and economic force in the decades of the 1880s and 1890s.

Social and Cultural Developments, 1877–1882

Urbanization was the primary social and cultural phenomenon of the period. Both internal and external migrations contributed to an industrial urban state that grew from 40 million people in 1870 to almost 80 million in 1900. New York, Chicago, and Philadelphia emerged as cities of over one million people.

Skyscrapers and Immigrants

Cities grew both up and out as the skyscraper made its appearance after the introduction of the mechanical elevator by Elisha Otis. The city also grew outward into a large, impersonal metropolis divided into various business, industrial and residential sectors, usually segregated by ethnic group, social class, and race. Slums and tenements sprang up within walking distance of department stores and townhouses. Two million immigrants from Northern Europe poured into the U.S. during the 1870s. In the 1880s another five million entered the country, but by this time they were coming from Southern and Eastern Europe. Many people faced the dual difficulty of migration from one culture to another, and also migration from a predominantly rural life-style to an urban one in the United States.

Lack of Government Policy

There were few programs to deal with the vast influx of humanity other than the prohibition of the criminal and the insane. City governments soon developed the primary responsibility for immigrants —often trading employment, housing, and social services for political support.

Social Gospel

In time, advocates of the "social gospel" such as Jane Addams and Washington Gladden urged the creation of settlement houses and better health and education services to accommodate the new immigrants. New religious groups also appeared including the Salvation Army and Mary Baker Eddy's Church of Christian Science in 1879.

Education

Public education continued to expand, especially on the secondary level. Private Catholic parochial schools and teaching colleges grew in number as well. Adult education and English instruction became important functions of both public and private schooling.

African-American Leaders

Booker T. Washington emerged in 1881 as the president of Tuskegee Institute in Alabama, a school devoted to teaching and vocational education for African-Americans with a mission to encourage self-respect and economic equality of the races. It was at Tuskegee that George Washington Carver emerged in subsequent years as an agricultural chemist who did much to find industrial applications for agricultural products.

Feminism

The new urban environment encouraged feminist activism. Millions of women worked outside the home and continued to demand voting rights. Many women became active in social reform movements such as the prohibitionist Women's Christian Temperance Movement, planned parenthood, humane societies, antiprostitution crusades, and equal rights for all regardless of gender, race, and class.

Literature

Important books appeared such as Henry George's *Progress and Poverty* (1879), a three-million copy seller that advocated one single tax on land as the means to redistribute wealth for greater social and economic justice. In fiction

Lew Wallace's *Ben Hur* (1880), and the many Horatio Alger stories promoting values such as hard work, honesty, and a touch of good fortune sold many millions of copies. Other famous works of the era included Mark Twain's *The Gilded Age* (1873) and *The Adventures of Tom Sawyer* (1876), Bret Harte's stories of the old West, William Dean Howell's social commentaries, and Henry James' *Daisy Miller* (1879) and *The Portrait of the Lady* (1881).

Foreign Relations, 1877–1882

The United States gradually became involved in the "new imperialism" of the 1870s geared to finding markets for surplus industrial production, access to needed raw materials, and opportunities for overseas investment during a time of domestic economic depression. Unlike European territorial colonialism, however, the United States preferred market expansion without the political liability of military occupation.

Latin America

President Hayes recognized the government of dictator Porfirio Diaz in Mexico thus encouraging not only trade expansion, but U.S. investment in railroads, mines, agriculture, and oil.

Pan Americanism

In 1881 Secretary of State James G. Blaine advocated the creation of an International Bureau of American Republics to promote a customs union of trade and political stability for the Western Hemisphere. The assassination of President Garfield temporarily kept Blaine from forming this organization until 1889. The Bureau subsequently evolved into the Pan American Union in 1910 and the Organization of American States in 1948.

Mediation of Border Disputes

The United States offered its good offices to promote the peaceful resolution of border conflicts between a number of states: in 1876 between Argentina and Paraguay; in 1880 between Colombia and Chile; in 1881 between Mexico and Guatemala, Argentina and Chile, and Peru and Chile. The United States also worked to bring an end to the War of the Pacific (1879–1884) fought between Chile and the alliance of Peru and Bolivia.

Canal Project

In 1876 the Interoceanic Canal Commission recommended a Nicaraguan route for a canal to link the Atlantic and Pacific Oceans. In the 1880s, the U.S. officially took a hostile position against the French Panama Canal project.

The Pacific

In 1878, the United States ratified a treaty with Samoa giving the U.S. trading rights and a naval base at Pago Pago.

Japan

In 1878, the United States was the first country to negotiate a treaty granting tariff autonomy to Japan, and set a precedent for ending the practice by Western nations of controlling customs house collections in Asian states.

Korea

Commodore Shufeldt opened trade and diplomatic relations with the Hermit Kingdom in 1882. The United States promoted the principles of equal opportunity of trade and the sovereignty of Korea (later known as open door policies) which had earlier been advocated as desirable in China.

Native Americans

Westward expansion and the discovery of gold in South Dakota in the early 1870s led to the Sioux War, 1876–1877, and George A. Custer's "last stand." In 1877 the Nez Perce War in Idaho resulted from similar causes. The Apache in Arizona and New Mexico fought as well.

Reservations

The Indian tribes were eventually vanquished and compelled to live on isolated reservations. In addition to superior U.S. military force, disease, railway construction, alcoholism, and the virtual extermination of the bison contributed to their defeat. In 1881 Helen Hunt Jackson's *A Century of Dishonor* chronicled the tragic policy pursued against the Native Americans.

The Reaction to Corporate Industrialism, 1882–1887

The rise of big business and monopoly capitalism—especially in banking, railroads, mining, and the oil and steel industries—generated a reaction on the part of working class Americans in the form of new labor organizations and collective political action. Most Americans, however, were not opposed to free enterprise economics, but simply wanted an opportunity to share in the profits.

Politics of the Period, 1882–1887

The only Democrat elected president in the half century after the Civil War was Grover Cleveland.

Election of 1884

The Republicans nominated James G. Blaine (Maine) for president and

John Logan (Illinois) for vice president. The Democrats chose New York governor Grover Cleveland and Thomas A. Hendricks (Indiana). The defection of Independent Republicans supporting civil service reforms, known as "Mugwumps" (such as E.L. Godkin and Carl Schurz), to the Cleveland camp cost Blaine, the former Speaker of the House, the election. The Democrats held control of the House, and the Republicans controlled the Senate.

Presidential Succession Act of 1886

The death of Vice President Hendricks in 1885 led to a decision to change the line of succession (established in 1792) from the president *pro tempore* of the Senate to the Cabinet officers in order of creation of their departments to maintain party leadership. This system lasted until 1947 when the Speaker of the House was declared third in line.

Executive Appointments

President Cleveland insisted that executive appointments and removals were the prerogative of the executive and not the Senate. This was the first time since Andrew Johnson that a president had strengthened the independence of his office.

The Economy, 1882–1887

Large, efficient corporations prospered. Captains of industry, or robber barons, such as John D. Rockefeller in oil, J. P. Morgan in banking, Gustavus Swift in meat processing, Andrew Carnegie in steel, and E. H. Harriman in railroads, put together major industrial empires.

Big Business

The concentration of wealth and power in the hands of a relatively small number of giant firms in many industries led to monopoly capitalism that minimized competition. This process, in turn, led to a demand by smaller businessmen, farmers, and laborers for government regulation of the economy in order to promote capital competition for the salvation of free enterprise economics.

The Interstate Commerce Act (1887)

Popular resentment of railroad abuses such as price fixing, kickbacks, and discriminatory freight rates created demands for state regulation of the railway industry. When the Supreme Court ruled individual state laws unconstitutional (Wabash Case, 1886) because only Congress had the right to control interstate commerce, the Interstate Commerce Act was passed providing that a commission be established to oversee fair and just railway rates, prohibit rebates, end discriminatory practices, and require annual reports and financial statements. The Supreme Court, however, remained a friend of special interests, and often undermined the work of the I.C.C.

Expanding Cultivation

Agrarians and ranchers continued their westward expansion. The amount of land under cultivation between 1870 and 1890 more than doubled from 408 to 840 million acres. Transcontinental railroads, modern farm machinery, and soil conservation practices contributed to national prosperity.

Low Farm Prices

Despite success many farmers were concerned about capital indebtedness, low farm prices resulting from surplus production, railroad rate discrimination, and the lack of sufficient silver currency to promote price inflation. Agrarian groups such as the National Grange and the Farmers' Alliances called for government regulation of the economy to redress their grievances. To a certain extent, however, many of these problems were determined by participation of American agriculture in global markets. Farmers did not completely understand all the risks in an international free market economy.

American Federation of Labor (1886)

Confronted by big business, Samuel Gompers and Adolph Strasser put together a combination of national craft unions to represent the material interests of labor in the matter of wages, hours, and safety conditions. The A.F. of L. philosophy was pragmatic and not directly influenced by the dogmatic Marxism of some European labor movements. Although militant in its use of the strike, and its demand for collective bargaining in labor contracts with large corporations such as those in railroads, mining, and manufacturing, the A.F. of L. did not intend violent revolution nor political radicalism.

Scientific Management

After graduating from Stevens Institute of Technology in 1883, Frederick W. Taylor, the father of scientific management, introduced modern concepts of industrial engineering, plant management, time and motion studies, efficiency experts, and a separate class of managers in industrial manufacturing.

Tariff Policy

Although still protecting many American industries, the tariff of 1883 lowered duty schedules by an average five percent.

QUESTION

How did large corporations undermine economic competition in the nineteenth century?

EXPLANATION

During this period, large corporations strove to dominate their market, driving out competition. By establishing a monopoly, companies could raise prices and increase profits. Companies worked to eliminate competition, and ironically, government intervention through measures such as the Sherman Anti-Trust Act was used to restore free markets.

Social and Cultural Developments, 1882–1887

The continued growth of urban America contributed to the dissemination of knowledge and information in many fields.

Newspapers and Magazines

The linotype machine (1886) invented by Otto Mergenthaler cut printing costs dramatically. Press associations flourished and publishing became big business. In 1884, Joseph Pulitzer, an Hungarian-born immigrant, was the first publisher to reach a mass audience selling 100,000 copies of the *New York World*. New magazines such as *Forum* appeared in 1886 with a hard-hitting editorial style that emphasized investigatory journalism and controversial subjects.

Higher Education

Colleges and universities expanded and introduced a more modern curriculum. Graduate study emphasized meticulous research and the seminar method as pioneered in the United States at Johns Hopkins University. A complex society required a more professional and specialized education.

Women's Colleges

Bryn Mawr (1885) was established and soon found a place among such schools as Vassar, Wellesley, and Mount Holyoke in advancing education for women.

Natural Science

Albert Michelson at the University of Chicago, working on the speed of light, contributed in the 1880s to theories which helped prepare the way for Einstein's Theory of Relativity. In 1907, Michelson was the first American to win a Nobel Prize.

The New Social Science

Richard T. Ely studied the ethical implications of economic problems. Henry C. Adams and Simon Patten put forth theories to justify government regulation and planning in the economy. In sociology, Lester Frank Ward's *Dynamic Sociology* (1883) stressed intelligent planning and decision making over genetic determinism as promoted by Social Darwinists such as William Graham Sumner. Woodrow Wilson's *Congressional Government* was a critique of the committee system in Congress and called for a better working relationship between the executive and legislative branches of government. After winning the presidency in 1912, Wilson would be in a position to put his ideas into practice.

Literary Realism

Romanticism declined in favor of a more realistic approach to literature. Novelists explored social problems such as crime and political corruption, urban ghetto life, class conflict, evolution, and the environment. Mark Twain's master-piece *Huckleberry Finn* appeared in 1884. In 1885, William Dean Howell's *The Rise of Silas Lapham* presented the theme of business ethics in a competitive society. *The Bostonians* (1886) by Henry James attempted a complex psychologi-cal study of female behavior.

Art

Realism could also be seen in the artistic works of Thomas Eakins, Mary Cassatt, Winslow Homer, and James Whistler. Museums and art schools ex-panded. Wealthy patrons spent fortunes on personal art collections. Immigrant artists attracted enthusiastic crowds to settlement house exhibits.

Foreign Relations, 1882–1887

Contrary to popular belief, the United States was not an isolationist nation in the 1880s. Trade expansion and the protection of markets were primary con-cerns.

Modern Navy

In 1883 Congress authorized the construction of new steel ships that would take the U.S. Navy in a 20-year period from twelfth to third in world naval ranking. In 1884, the U.S. Naval War College was established in Newport, Rhode Island—the first of its kind.

Europe

Problems existed with Britain over violence in Ireland and England. In 1886, the U.S. refused to extradite an Irish national accused of terrorist activity in London.

Diseased meat products in the European market led to British and German bans against uninspected American meat exports. Congress soon provided for government regulation and inspection of meat for export. This action would set a precedent for systematic food and drug inspection in later years.

Africa

The United States participated in the Berlin Conference (1884) concerning trade in the Congo. The U.S. also took part in the Third International Red Cross Conference.

Asia and the Pacific

In 1882, Congress passed a law suspending Chinese immigration to the U.S. for ten years. The act reflected racist attitudes and created friction with China.

In 1886, the U.S. obtained by treaty with Hawaii the Pearl Harbor Naval Base.

Missionaries

American Christian missionaries were active in the Pacific, Asia, Africa, Latin America, and the Middle East. Missionaries not only brought religion to many third world regions, but also Western education, exposure to science and technology, and commercial ventures. Some missionaries also took with them racist concepts of white supremacy.

Latin America

In 1884, the U.S. signed a short-lived pact with Nicaragua for joint ownership of an isthmian canal in Central America.

QUESTION

> What motivated American foreign policy during the 1880s and 1890s?

EXPLANATION

American foreign policy was primarily motivated by economics. As U.S. manufacturing output increased, there was a need for markets and raw materials. Americans were also looking for investment opportunities overseas. American foreign policy sought to protect those interests, not by annexing overseas territory, but rather through diplomacy and expansion of markets.

Drill 1: The New Industrial Era, 1877–1882

1. The Knights of Labor

   (A) excluded women and blacks.

   (B) organized workers by craft.

    (C)   were concerned only with wages, hours, and working conditions.

    (D)   admitted both skilled and unskilled workers into membership.

    (E)   advocated destruction of the federal government.

2.   After 1890 most immigrants to America came from

    (A)   Northern and Western Europe.

    (B)   Southern and Eastern Europe.

    (C)   Great Britain and Ireland.

    (D)   Asia.

    (E)   Mexico.

3.   Under the crop-lien system, a farmer

    (A)   borrowed money against his next harvest in order to buy more land.

    (B)   borrowed money against the previous year's harvest, which was stored in warehouses until the market was favorable for selling.

    (C)   was likely to diversify the crops he planted.

    (D)   mortgaged his next harvest to a merchant in order to buy seed and supplies and support his family.

    (E)   could usually become completely debt-free within seven to ten years.

4.   A member of the Social Gospel movement would probably

    (A)   consider such social sins as alcohol abuse and sexual permissiveness as society's most serious problems.

    (B)   assert that the poor were themselves at fault for their circumstances.

    (C)   maintain that abuses and social degradation resulted solely from a lack of willpower on the part of those who committed them.

    (D)   hold that religion is an entirely individualistic matter.

    (E)   argue that Christians should work to reorganize the industrial system and bring about international peace.

5.   Henry George's most famous book was

    (A)   *Looking Backward.*   (B)   *Progress and Poverty.*

    (C)   *The Jungle.*   (D)   *The Shame of the Cities.*

    (E)   *Sister Carrie.*

6. Which of the following statements is true of the Bland-Allison Act?

   (A) It gave the president discretion to purchase up to one million ounces of silver per year.

   (B) It required the government to purchase from two to four million dollars' worth of gold per month.

   (C) It was intended to raise the market price of gold and thus create a slight inflationary effect.

   (D) It provided for a floating rate of exchange between silver and gold.

   (E) It was vetoed by President Rutherford B. Hayes.

7. The Compromise of 1877 resulted in

   (A) the ascension of Republican Rutherford B. Hayes to the presidency in return for assurances that what was left of Reconstruction in the South would be ended.

   (B) the division of Dakota Territory into North Dakota and South Dakota.

   (C) government financing for a Southern transcontinental railroad route in return for financial grants allowing for the completion of the Great Northern Railroad from Minnesota to the Pacific Northwest.

   (D) the ascension of Republican Rutherford B. Hayes to the presidency in return for the passage of an Amnesty Act which would pardon former Confederate soldiers allowing them to regain their voting rights.

   (E) the formal separation of Virginia and West Virginia and the official acceptance of statehood for West Virginia.

8. The most important factor in the destruction of the Plains Indians' societies by whites in the late nineteenth century was

   (A) the use of modern weapons by white soldiers and cavalrymen.

   (B) the destruction of the buffalo herds by whites.

   (C) the introduction of alcohol by whites to Indian society.

   (D) the encroachment of railroads onto Indian lands.

   (E) the use of reservations by whites to limit the movements of Indians.

9. The only dominant, broad-based labor union in the United States from 1870–1890 was the

   (A) National Labor Union.

   (B) Industrial Workers of the World (IWW).

   (C) American Federation of Labor (AFL).

(D) Congress of Industrial Organization (CIO).

(E) Knights of Labor.

10. How did the U.S. government initially react toward movements to establish trade unions in businesses and factories in the latter half of the nineteenth century?

(A) It strongly supported the trade union movement and forced businesses to allow the development of unions.

(B) It mildly supported the development of trade unions but took no active measures to help establish unions until business abuses of workers became undeniable.

(C) It stayed out of business affairs, supporting neither businesses nor unions, unless one side or the other broke the law.

(D) It supported the establishment of unions in all businesses except defense industries and jobs which had civil service organizations.

(E) It actively supported business efforts to destroy unions before they could effectively establish themselves.

2. THE EMERGENCE OF THE REGIONAL EMPIRE, 1887–1892

Despite a protective tariff policy, the United States became increasingly international as it sought to export surplus manufactured and agricultural goods. Foreign markets were viewed as a safety valve for labor employment problems and agrarian unrest. The return of Secretary of State James G. Blaine in 1889 marked a major attempt by the United States to promote a regional empire in the Western Hemisphere and reciprocal trade programs.

Politics of the Period, 1887–1892

National politics became more controversial and turbulent in this era.

Election of 1888

Although the Democrat Grover Cleveland won the popular vote by about 100,000 over the Republican Benjamin Harrison, Harrison carried the electoral college 233–168, and was declared president after waging a vigorous campaign to protect American industrial interests with a high protective tariff. In Congress, Republicans won control of both the House and Senate.

Department of Agriculture

The Department of Agriculture (1889) was raised to Cabinet status with Norman Coleman as the first secretary.

House Rules of Operation

Republican Thomas B. Reed became Speaker of the House in 1890 and changed the rules of operation to make himself a veritable tsar with absolute control in running the House.

Force Bill (1890)

Senate objections kept Congress from protecting African-American voters in the South through federal supervision of state elections.

Dependent Pensions Act (1890)

Congress granted service pensions to Union veterans and their dependents for the first time.

The Economy, 1887–1892

Antimonopoly measures, protective tariffs and reciprocal trade, and a billion dollar budget became the order of the day.

Sherman Anti-Trust Act (1890)

Corporate monopolies (trusts) which controlled whole industries were subject to federal prosecution if they were found to be combinations or conspiracies in restraint of trade. Although supported by smaller businesses, labor unions, and farm associations, the Sherman Anti-Trust Act was in time interpreted by the Supreme Court to apply to labor unions and farmers' cooperatives as much as to large corporate combinations. Monopoly was still dominant over laissez-faire, free enterprise economics during the decade of the 1890s.

Sherman Silver Purchase Act (1890)

Pro-silver interests passed legislation authorizing Congress to buy 4.5 million ounces of silver each month at market prices and issue Treasury notes redeemable in gold and silver. The act created inflation and lowered gold reserves.

McKinley Tariff (1890)

This compromise protective tariff promised by the Republicans in 1888, and introduced by William McKinley of Ohio, was passed and extended to industrial and agricultural goods. The act also included reciprocal trade provisions that allowed the president to retaliate against nations that discriminated against U.S. products, and reward nations that opened their markets to American goods. Subsequent price increases led to a popular backlash and a Democratic House victory in the 1890 congressional elections.

Billion Dollar Budget

Congress depleted the Treasury surplus with the first peacetime billion dollar appropriation of funds for state tax refunds, infrastructure improvements, navy modernization, and pension payments. The loss of Treasury reserves put the economy in a precarious position when an economic panic occurred in 1893.

Social and Cultural Developments, 1887–1892

Amusing the millions became a popular pastime.

Popular Amusements

In addition to the legitimate stage, vaudeville shows presenting variety acts became immensely popular. The circus expanded when Barnum and Bailey formed a partnership to present "the greatest show on earth." Distinctively American Wild West shows toured North America and Europe. To record these activities, George Eastman's newly invented roll-film camera became popular with spectators.

Sports

In 1888, professional baseball sent an all-star team to tour the world. Boxing adopted leather gloves in 1892. Croquet and bicycle racing were new crazes. Basketball was invented in 1891 by James Naismith, a Massachusetts Y.M.C.A. instructor. Organized intercollegiate sports such as football, basketball, and baseball created intense rivalries between colleges that attracted mass spectator interest.

Childrearing Practices

Parents became more supportive and sympathetic to their children and less authoritarian and restrictive. The 1880s were something of a golden age in children's literature. Mary Wells Smith depicted an agrarian ideal; Sidney Lanier wrote tales of heroic boys and girls; Howard Pyle's *Robin Hood* gained wide readership and Joel Chandler Harris' characters Brer Rabbit, Brer Fox, and Uncle Remus became very popular.

Religion

Many churches took issue with the growing emphasis on materialism in American society. Dwight Lyman Moody introduced urban revivalism comparable to earlier rural movements among Protestant denominations. In addition, the new immigrants generated significant growth for Roman Catholicism and Judaism. By 1890, there were about 150 religious denominations in the United States.

QUESTION

What kind of cultural developments were most important during the period 1887–1892?

EXPLANATION

Due to an increase in leisure time, popular culture dominated American cultural developments. Spectator sports, collegiate and professional, first became popular during this period. Traditional cultural institutions such as opera and theater were eclipsed by vaudeville shows and circuses.

Foreign Relations, 1887–1892

Following in the footsteps of William Seward as a major architect of American foreign policy, James G. Blaine promoted hemispheric solidarity with Latin America and economic expansionism.

Pan Americanism

As Secretary of State, Blaine was concerned with international trade, political stability, and excessive militarism in Latin America. His international Bureau of American Republics was designed to promote a Pan American customs union and peaceful conflict resolution. To achieve his aims, Blaine opposed U.S. military intervention in the hemisphere. To a certain extent, his policies were in the tradition of President James Monroe and his Secretary of State, John Quincy Adams.

Haiti

After the Haitian revolution of 1888–1889, Blaine resisted pressure for U.S. intervention to establish a naval base near Port-au-Prince. The noted African-American Frederick Douglass played a key role in advising Blaine as U.S. minister to Haiti.

Chilean Revolution

When American sailors from the U.S.S. *Baltimore* were killed in Valparaiso (1891), President Harrison threatened war with the anti-American revolutionary government of President Balmaceda. Secretary Blaine helped to bring about a Chilean apology and preserve his Pan American policy.

Asia and the Pacific

The medical missionary/diplomat Horace Allen promoted peaceful American investment and trade with Korea.

In 1889, the United States upheld its interests against German expansion in the Samoan Islands by establishing a three-party protectorate over Samoa with Britain and Germany. The United States retained the port of Pago Pago.

In 1891, Queen Liliuokalani resisted American attempts to promote a protectorate over Hawaii. By 1893, pro-American sugar planters overthrew the native Hawaiian government and established a new government friendly to the United States.

Africa

In 1890, the United States refused to establish naval bases in the Portuguese colonies of Angola and Mozambique when Portugal was looking for allies against British expansion in Africa. Blaine opposed territorial expansion for the U.S. in Africa, but favored the development of commercial markets.

Theoretical Works

In 1890, Naval Captain Alfred Thayer Mahan published *The Influence of Sea Power on History* which argued that control of the seas was the means to world power. Josiah Strong's *Our Country* presented the thesis that Americans had a mission to fulfill by exporting the word of God around the world, especially to non-white populations. Frederick Jackson Turner's "Frontier Thesis" (1893) justified overseas economic expansion as a way to secure political power and prosperity. In *The Law of Civilization and Decay* (1895), Brooks Adams postulated that a nation must expand or face inevitable decline.

Europe

The murders of 11 Italian citizens in New Orleans (1891) brought the United States and Italy into confrontation. The United States defused the situation by compensating the families of the victims.

Drill 2: The Emergence of the Regional Empire, 1887–1892

1. In his book *The Influence of Sea Power Upon History* (1890), Alfred T. Mahan argued which of the following?

    (A) Colonial possessions are a drain on the nation's resources.

    (B) A strong merchant marine is less important than a navy.

    (C) Naval bases are unnecessary for the protection of colonial possessions.

    (D) Great empires are based on naval supremacy.

    (E) Land forces are more important than naval forces.

2. The Sherman Anti-Trust Act prohibited

   (A) verbal contracts.

   (B) monopolies found to be restraining trade.

   (C) strikes by labor unions.

   (D) immigrants from becoming citizens.

   (E) the circulation of paper money.

3. The Interstate Commerce Act of 1887 was aimed primarily at

   (A) increasing interstate trade by forbidding states from levying tariffs on goods transported from other states.

   (B) curbing abusive pricing and hauling policies by the nation's railroads.

   (C) increasing interstate trade through government assistance in efforts to build new canals, roads, and railroads.

   (D) curbing abusive pricing and hauling policies by the nation's ocean-going, river-going, and canal-going shipping companies.

   (E) increasing interstate commerce by offering financial incentives to companies that operated offices or manufacturing plants in more than one state.

4. Which of the following was used as "scientific evidence" by wealthy American industrialists in the latter half of the nineteenth century to prove that they deserved the wealth they had accumulated?

   (A) Broca's research into the functioning of various centers of the human brain

   (B) Darwin's theory of natural selection

   (C) Freud's theories of human psychology

   (D) The research of Louis Pasteur on biological processes

   (E) Karl Marx's research on the economic development of societies

5. In the 1880s the issue of tariffs on imported goods became a major controversy because

   (A) the free trade policies in effect at that time were allowing underpriced foreign goods to destroy fledgling American industries and virtually eliminate American crop exports to Europe.

   (B) individual states refused to give up their right to enact tariffs on goods brought across state lines from neighboring states.

   (C) high tariffs were resulting in unnecessarily high prices on manufactured goods, hurting both farmers and consumers while protecting several wealthy manufacturers.

(D) Democrats forced the enactment of free trade legislation in the U.S. but European countries responded by raising their tariffs on U.S. manufactured goods throwing the U.S. economy into a depression.

(E) Democrats allowed tariffs to be enacted only on imported farm goods, which protected American farmers but left U.S. manufacturers vulnerable to European tariffs.

3. ECONOMIC DEPRESSION AND SOCIAL CRISIS, 1892–1897

The economic depression that began in 1893 brought about a collective response from organized labor, militant agriculture, and the business community. Each group called for economic safeguards and a more humane free enterprise system that would expand economic opportunities in an equitable manner.

Politics of the Period, 1892–1897

The most marked development in American politics was the emergence of a viable third-party movement in the form of the essentially agrarian Populist party.

Election of 1892

Democrat Grover Cleveland (New York) and his vice presidential running mate Adlai E. Stevenson (Illinois) regained the White House by defeating the Republican President Benjamin Harrison (Indiana) and Vice President Whitelaw Reid (New York). Voters generally reacted against the inflationary McKinley Tariff. Cleveland's conservative economic stand in favor of the gold standard brought him the support of various business interests. The Democrats won control of both houses of Congress.

Populist Party

The People's party (Populist) nominated James Weaver (Iowa) for president and James Field (Virginia) for vice president in 1892. The party platform put together by such Populist leaders as Ignatius Donnally (Minnesota), Thomas Watson (Georgia), Mary Lease (Kansas), and "Sockless" Jerry Simpson (Kansas) called for the enactment of a program espoused by agrarians, but also for a coalition with urban workers and the middle class. Specific goals were the coinage of silver to gold at a ratio of 16 to 1; federal loans to farmers; a graduated income tax; postal savings banks; public ownership of railroads, telephone, and telegraph systems; prohibition of alien land ownership; immigration restriction; a ban on private armies used by corporations to break up strikes; an eight-hour working day; a single six-year term for president, and direct election of senators; the right of initiative and referendum; and the use of the secret ballot.

Although the Populists were considered radical by some, they actually wanted to reform the system from within and allow for a fairer distribution of wealth. In a society in which 10 percent of the population controlled 90 percent of the nation's wealth, the Populists were able to garner about one million votes (out of 11 million votes cast), and 22 electoral votes. By 1894, Populists had elected 4 senators, 4 congressmen, 21 state executive officials, 150 state senators, and 315 state representatives, primarily in the West and South. After the 1893 depression, the Populists planned a serious bid for national power in the 1896 election.

Repeal of Sherman Silver Purchase Act (1893)

After the economic panic of 1893, Cleveland tried to limit the outflow of gold reserves by asking Congress to repeal the Sherman Silver Act which had provided for notes redemptive in either gold or silver. Congress did repeal the act, but the Democratic party split over the issue.

Election of 1896

The Republicans nominated William McKinley (Ohio) for president and Garrett Hobart (New Jersey) for vice president on a platform calling for maintaining the gold standard and protective tariffs. The Democratic party repudiated Cleveland's conservative economics and nominated William Jennings Bryan (Nebraska) and Arthur Sewell (Maine) for president and vice president on a platform similar to the Populists: 1) coinage of silver at a ratio of 16 to 1; 2) condemnation of monopolies, protective tariffs, and anti-union court injunctions; 3) criticism of the Supreme Court's removal of a graduated income tax from the Wilson-Gorman tariff bill (1894). Bryan delivered one of the most famous speeches in American history when he declared that the people must not be "crucified upon a cross of gold."

The Populist party also nominated Bryan, but chose Thomas Watson (Georgia) for vice president. Having been out-maneuvered by the Silver Democrats, the Populists lost the opportunity to become a permanent political force.

McKinley won a hard fought election by only about one-half million votes as Republicans succeeded in creating fear among business groups and middle-class voters that Bryan represented a revolutionary challenge to the American system. The manipulation of higher farm prices, and the warning to labor unions that they would face unemployment if Bryan won the election helped to tilt the vote in favor of McKinley. An often forgotten issue in 1896 was the Republican promise to stabilize the ongoing Cuban revolution. This pledge would eventually lead the U.S. into war with Spain (1898) for Cuban independence. The Republicans retained control over Congress which they had gained in 1894.

QUESTION

> What prevented the Populist party from becoming a permanent political force during the election of 1896?

EXPLANATION

The Democrats adopted much of the Populist party platform themselves, and both parties nominated the same presidential candidate, William Jennings Bryan. Bryan lost to the Republican candidate, William McKinley, in part because the Republicans exploited the fears of many middle-class Americans that the Populist program represented a radical challenge to the American way of life. Both factors contributed to the marginalization of the Populist party.

The Economy, 1892–1897

The 1890s was a period of economic depression and labor agitation.

Homestead Strike (1892)

Iron- and steelworkers went on strike in Pennsylvania against the Carnegie Steel Company to protest salary reductions. Carnegie employed strike-breaking Pinkerton security guards. Management-labor warfare led to a number of deaths on both sides.

Depression of 1893

The primary causes for the Depression of 1893 were the dramatic growth of the federal deficit; withdrawal of British investments from the American market and the outward transfer of gold; loss of business confidence; and the bankruptcy of the National Cordage Company was the first among thousands of U.S. corporations that closed banks and businesses. As a consequence, 20 percent of the work force was eventually unemployed. The depression would last four years. Recovery would be helped by war preparation.

March of Unemployed (1894)

The Populist businessman Jacob Coxey led a march of hundreds of unemployed workers on Washington asking for a government work relief program. The government met the marchers with force and arrested their leaders.

Pullman Strike (1894)

Eugene Debs' American Railway Union struck the Pullman Palace Car Co. in Chicago over wage cuts and job losses. President Cleveland broke the violent strike with federal troops. Popular opinion deplored violence and militant labor tactics.

Wilson-Gorman Tariff (1894)

This protective tariff did little to promote overseas trade as a way to ease the depression. A provision amended to create a graduated income tax was stricken by the Supreme Court as unconstitutional (*Pollack v. Farmers' Loan and Trust Co.*, 1895).

Dingley Tariff (1897)

The Dingley Tariff raised protection to new highs for certain commodities.

Surplus Production and Foreign Trade

Anxiety over domestic class warfare, and the desire to sell surplus manufactured goods overseas led many business interests to encourage the U.S. government to find new international markets. Carnegie Steel and Standard Oil lobbied the State Department for better trade promotion policies as a way to recover from the depression and provide jobs for American workers. Ironically, special business interests often undercut efforts to establish reciprocal trade agreements and free trade in favor of politically motivated tariff protection.

Social and Cultural Developments, 1892–1897

Economic depression and war dominated thought and literature in the decade of the 1890s.

Literature

Lester Frank Ward of Brown University presented a critique of excessive competition in favor of social planning in *The Psychic Factors of Civilization*, 1893. William Dean Howells' *A Hazard of New Fortunes*, 1890, was a broad attack on urban living conditions in industrial America, and the callous treatment of workers by wealthy tycoons. Stephen Crane wrote about the abuse of control of women in *Maggie, A Girl of the Streets*, 1892, and the pain of war in *The Red Badge of Courage*, 1895. Edward Bellamy's *Looking Backward* presented a science fiction look into a prosperous, but regimented future.

Americans also began to read such European realists as Dostoevsky, Ibsen, Tolstoy, and Zola.

William James' *Principles of Psychology* introduced the discipline to American readers as a modern science of the human mind.

Prohibition of Alcohol

The Anti-Saloon League was formed in 1893. Women were especially concerned about the increase of drunkenness during the depression.

Immigration

Immigration declined by almost 400,000 during the depression. Jane Addams' Hull House in Chicago continued to function as a means of settling poor immigrants from Greece, Germany, Italy, Poland, Russia, and elsewhere into American society. Lillian Wald's Henry Street Settlement in New York, and Robert Wood's South End House in Boston performed similar functions. Such institutions also lobbied against sweatshop labor conditions and for bans on child labor.

Chautauqua Movement

Home study courses growing out of the Chautauqua Movement in New York State became popular.

Chicago World's Fair (1893)

Beautifying the cities was the fair's main theme. One lasting development was the expansion of urban public parks.

Radio and Film

Nathan Stubblefield transmitted voice over the air without wires in 1892. Thomas Edison's kinetoscope permitted the viewing of motion pictures in 1893.

Foreign Relations, 1892–1897

In addition to the economic depression, three international events in 1895 that propelled the United States foreign policy were the Cuban war for independence against Spain, Britain's boundary dispute with Venezuela, and the settlement of the Sino-Japanese War.

Cuba and Spain

The Cuban revolt against Spain in 1895 impacted the U.S. in that Americans had about $50 million invested in the Cuban economy and did an annual business of over $100 million in Cuba. During the election of 1896, McKinley promised to stabilize the situation and work for an end to hostilities. Sensational "yellow journalism" and nationalistic statements from officials such as Assistant Secretary of the Navy, Theodore Roosevelt, encouraged popular support for direct American military intervention on behalf of Cuban independence. President McKinley, however, proceeded cautiously through 1897.

Britain and Venezuela (1895)

The dispute over the border of Britain's colony of Guiana threatened war with Venezuela, especially after gold was discovered in the area. Although initially at odds with Britain, the United States eventually came to support British claims against Venezuela when Britain agreed to recognize the Monroe Doctrine in Latin America. Britain also sought U.S. cooperation in its dispute with Germany in South Africa. This rivalry would in time lead to the Boer War. The realignment of the United States and Britain would play a significant role during World War I.

The Sino-Japanese War (1894–1895)

Japan's easy victory over China signaled to the United States and other nations trading in Asia that China's weakness might result in its colonization by industrial powers and the closing of the China market. The U.S. resolved to seek a naval base in the Pacific to protect its interests. The opportunity to annex the Philippines after the war with Spain was in part motivated by the desire to protect America's trade and future potential in Asia. This concern would also lead the U.S. to announce the "Open Door" policy with China in 1899 and 1900 designed to protect equal opportunity of trade and China's political independence.

Latin America

When revolutions broke out in 1894 in both Brazil and Nicaragua, the United States supported the existing governments in power to maintain political stability and favorable trade treaties. Secretaries of State Walter Q. Gresham, Richard Olney, and John Sherman continued to support James G. Blaine's Pan American policy.

The Pacific

The United States intervened in the Hawaiian revolution (1893) to overthrow the anti-American government of Queen Liliuokalani. President Cleveland rejected American annexation of Hawaii in 1894, but President McKinley agreed to annex it in 1898.

QUESTION

What role did the Monroe Doctrine play in American foreign policy between 1882–1897?

EXPLANATION

The Monroe Doctrine provided justification for U.S. involvement in the affair of other nations of the Western Hemisphere. The Pan-American alliance emerged from these hemispheric concerns. However, the U.S. could support European powers. For example, during a border dispute between the British colony of Guiana and Venezuela, the U.S. supported the British in exchange for British recognition of the Monroe Doctrine.

Drill 3: Economic Depression and Social Crisis, 1892–1897

1. This cartoon blames the depression of 1893–1896 on which of the following?

    (A) Foreign competition with American products

    (B) The power of the trusts

    (C) The failure to coin silver after 1873

    (D) The lack of labor unions

    (E) The indebtedness of farmers

2. Edward Bellamy's book *Looking Backward* was

    (A) a fictional exposé of the meatpacking industry.

    (B) a detailed program for social reform.

    (C) the catalyst of the Social Gospel movement.

    (D) a denunciation of machine politics in big city government.

    (E) a futuristic utopian fantasy.

3. The Sino-Japanese War affected the United States in which of the following ways?

    (A) It led to U.S. aid for Russia.

    (B) It increased the need for rapid naval transportation between the Atlantic and Pacific Oceans.

    (C) It convinced the U.S. that it needed to increase its presence in the Pacific to protect its interests.

    (D) It increased isolationism in the United States.

    (E) It led the U.S. to re-emphasize the Monroe Doctrine.

4. Who supported the free coinage of silver in the 1890s?

    (A) Large corporations   (B) Bankers

    (C) Populists   (D) Republicans

    (E) International traders

5. Frederick Jackson Turner's "Frontier Thesis" included all of the following EXCEPT

    (A) American democracy developed out of the frontier experience.

    (B) the frontier acted as a safety-valve for social ferment.

    (C) the frontier moved throughout American history.

    (D) the frontier had disappeared by 1890.

    (E) the frontier contributed to higher levels of civilization.

6. "You shall not crucify mankind on a cross of gold" was what candidate's rallying cry in the election of 1896?

    (A) William McKinley   (B) Eugene Debs

    (C) William Jennings Bryan (D) William Howard Taft

    (E) Theodore Roosevelt

7. One of the goals of the Populist movement was to induce the government to introduce

    (A) free coinage of silver.

    (B) prohibition of all immigration from China and Japan.

    (C) the building of a transcontinental railroad at government expense.

    (D) a "single tax" on land.

    (E) more stringent regulations for the health and safety of factory workers.

8. The Populist party was an outgrowth of

    (A) resentment over government farm policies.

    (B) the end of Reconstruction in the South.

    (C) the union movement in Eastern industrial centers.

    (D) efforts to obtain equal rights for women and minorities.

    (E) the second Great Awakening.

9. Which of the following was NOT a cause of the Depression of 1893?

    (A) The growth of the federal deficit

(B) Labor union activity

(C) Withdrawal of British investments from American markets

(D) Loss of business confidence

(E) The bankruptcy of the National Cordage Company

10. All the following Populist platform issues were later accepted by Americans EXCEPT

(A) the graduated income tax.

(B) direct election of United States senators.

(C) the use of the Australian ballot.

(D) the eight-hour day for labor.

(E) government ownership of the telegraph and telephone industries.

4. WAR AND THE AMERICANIZATION OF THE WORLD, 1897–1902

In 1900 an Englishman named William T. Stead authored a book entitled *The Americanization of the World* in which he predicted that American productivity and economic strength would propel the United States to the forefront of world leadership in the twentieth century. The Spanish-American War and the events following it indicated that the U.S. would be a force in the global balance of power for years to come. Few, however, would have predicted that as early as 1920 the U.S. would achieve the pinnacle of world power as a result of the debilitating policies pursued by European political leaders during World War I (1914–1919). One question remained: Would the American people be prepared to accept the responsibility of world leadership?

Politics of the Period, 1897–1902

President McKinley's wartime leadership and tragic assassination closed one door in American history, but opened another door to the leadership of Theodore Roosevelt, the first "progressive" president.

Election of 1900

The unexpected death of Vice President Garrett Hobart led the Republican party to choose the war hero and reform governor of New York, Theodore Roosevelt, as President William McKinley's vice presidential running mate. Riding the crest of victory against Spain, the G.O.P. platform called for upholding the gold standard for full economic recovery, promoting economic expansion and power in the Caribbean and the Pacific, and building a canal in Central America. The Democrats nominated once again William Jennings Bryan and Adlai Stevenson on a platform condemning imperialism and the gold standard. McKinley easily won reelection by about 1 million votes (7.2 million to 6.3 million), and the Republicans retained control of both houses of Congress.

Other Parties

The fading Populists nominated Wharton Barker (Pennsylvania) and Ignatius Donnelly (Minnesota) on a pro-inflation platform but only received 50,000 votes. The Socialist Democratic party nominated Eugene V. Debs (Indiana) and Job Harriman (California) on a platform urging the nationalization of major industries. Debs received 94,000 votes. The surprising Prohibition party nominated John Woolley (Illinois) and Henry Metcalf (Rhode Island) and called for a ban on alcohol production and consumption. They received 209,000 votes.

McKinley Assassination (1901)

While attending the Pan American Exposition in Buffalo, New York, the president was shot on September 6 by Leon Czolgosz, an anarchist sworn to destroy all governments. The president died on September 14 after many officials thought he would recover. Theodore Roosevelt became the nation's twenty-fifth president and its youngest to that time at age 42.

The Economy, 1897–1902

The war with Spain provided the impetus for economic recovery. President Roosevelt promised a "square deal" for all Americans, farmers, workers, consumers, and businessmen. Progressive economic reform was geared to the rejuvenation of free enterprise capitalism following the 1893 depression and the destruction of illegal monopolies. In this way, radicals would be denied an audience for more revolutionary and violent change.

War With Spain (1898)

The financial cost of the war was $250,000,000. Eastern and Midwestern industrial cities tended to favor war and benefit from it. Northeastern financial centers were more cautious about war until March 1898, and questioned the financial gains of wartime production at the expense of peacetime expansion and product/market development.

Federal Bankruptcy Act (1898)

This act reformed and standardized procedures for bankruptcy and the responsibilities of creditors and debtors.

Erdman Act (1898)

This act provided for mediation by the chair of the Interstate Commerce Commission and the commissioner of the Bureau of Labor in unresolved railroad labor controversies.

Currency Act (1900)

The United States standardized the amount of gold in the dollar at 25.8 grains, 9/10s fine. A separate gold reserve was set apart from other general funds, and government bonds were sold to maintain the reserve.

Technology

Between 1860 and 1900 railroad trackage grew from 36,800 miles to 193,350 miles. U.S. Steel Corp. was formed in 1901, Standard Oil Company of New Jersey in 1899.

Social and Cultural Developments, 1897–1902

Debates about the war and territorial acquisitions, and the state of the economy, tended to dominate thought and literature.

Yellow Journalism

Joseph Pulitzer's *New York World* and William Randolph Hearst's *New York Journal* competed fiercely to increase circulation through exaggeration of Spanish atrocities in Cuba. Such stories whipped up popular resentment of Spain and helped to create a climate of opinion receptive to war.

DeLôme Letter and Sinking of the Maine

On February 9, 1898, the newspapers published a letter written by the Spanish minister in Washington, Depuy de Lôme, personally criticizing President McKinley in insulting terms. On February 15, the battleship U.S.S. *Maine* was blown up in Havana harbor with a loss of 250 Americans. The popular demand for war with Spain grew significantly even though it was likely that the *Maine* was blown up by accident when spontaneous combustion in a coal bunker caused a powder magazine to explode.

U.S. Military

Facing its first war since the Civil War, the U.S. Army was not prepared for a full scale effort in 1898. Although 245,000 men served in the war (with over 5,000 deaths), the army at the outset consisted of only 28,000 troops. The volunteers who shaped up in the early stages were surprised to be issued winter uniforms to train in the tropics for war in Cuba. Cans of food stockpiled since the Civil War were reissued. After getting past these early problems, the War Department settled down to a more effective organizational procedure. Sadly, more deaths resulted from disease and food poisoning than from battlefield casualties. The U.S. Navy (26,000 men) was far better prepared for war as a result of past years of modernization.

Territories

After the United States had defeated Spain, it was faced with the issue of what to do with such captured territories as the Philippines, Puerto Rico, the Isle of Pines, and Guam. A major public debate ensued with critics of land acquisition forming the Anti-Imperialist League with the support of Mark Twain, William James, William Jennings Bryan, Grover Cleveland, Charles Francis Adams, Carl Schurz, Charles W. Eliot, David Starr Jordan, Andrew Carnegie, and Samuel Gompers among others. Supporters of colonialism included Theodore Roosevelt, Mark Hanna, Alfred Thayer Mahan, Henry Cabot Lodge, Albert Beveridge, President McKinley, and many others. Ironically, many individuals in both camps favored U.S. economic expansion, but had difficulty with the idea that a democracy would actually accept colonies and overseas armies of occupations.

Literature

Thorsten Veblen's *Theory of the Leisure Class* (1899) attacked the "predatory wealth" and "conspicuous consumption" of the new rich in the gilded age. Veblen added evidence and argument to a critique begun by Jacob Riis in *How the Other Half Lives* (1890) documenting the gnawing poverty, illness, crime, and despair of New York's slums. Frank Norris's *McTeague* (1899) chronicled a man's regression to brutish animal behavior in the dog-eat-dog world of unbridled and unregulated capitalist competition. His novel *The Octopus* (1901) condemned monopoly.

QUESTION

> Why would democracy be incompatible with colonial territories?

EXPLANATION

Democracy requires that the people themselves govern, but in a colony, a foreign government has ultimate sovereignty. The incompatibility was especially apparent to some Americans, who had fought their own revolution in order to overthrow a foreign government and establish democracy.

Foreign Policy, 1897–1902

The summer war with Spain and the expansion of American interests in Asia and the Caribbean were dominant factors.

Decision for War (1898)

Loss of markets, threats to Americans in Cuba, and the inability of both Spain and Cuba to resolve the Cuban revolution either by force or diplomacy led to McKinley's request of Congress for a declaration of war. The sinking of the *Maine* in February 1898, and the return of Vermont Senator Redfield Proctor from a fact-finding mission on March 17, 1898 revealed how poor the situation was in Cuba.

McKinley's Ultimatum

On March 27, President McKinley asked Spain to call an armistice, accept American mediation to end the war, and end the use of concentration camps in Cuba. When Spain refused to comply, McKinley requested Congress declare war. On April 21, Congress declared war on Spain with the objective of establishing Cuban independence (Teller Amendment).

Cuba

After the first U.S. forces landed in Cuba on June 22, 1898, the United States proceeded to victories at El Caney and San Juan Hill. By July 17, Admiral Sampson's North Atlantic Squadron destroyed the Spanish fleet, Santiago surrendered, and American troops quickly went on to capture Puerto Rico.

The Philippines

As early as December 1897, Commodore Perry's Asiatic Squadron was alerted to possible war with Spain. On May 1, 1898, the Spanish fleet in the Philippines was destroyed and Manila surrendered on August 13. Spain agreed to a peace conference to be held in Paris in October 1898.

Treaty of Paris

Secretary of State William Day led the American negotiating team, which secured Cuban independence, the ceding of the Philippines, Puerto Rico, and Guam to the U.S., and the payment of $20 million to Spain for the Philippines. The treaty was ratified by the Senate on February 6, 1900.

Philippines Insurrection

Filipino nationalists under Emilio Aguinaldo rebelled against the United States (February 1899) when they learned the Philippines would not be given independence. The United States used 70,000 men to suppress the revolutionaries by June 1902. A special U.S. commission recommended eventual self-government for the Philippines.

Hawaii and Wake Island

During the war with Spain, the U.S. annexed Hawaii on July 7, 1898. In 1900 the U.S. claimed Wake Island, 2,000 miles west of Hawaii.

China

Fearing the break-up of China into separate spheres of influence, Secretary of State John Hay called for acceptance of the Open Door notes by all nations trading in the China market to guarantee equal opportunity of trade (1899) and the sovereignty of the Manchu government of China (1900). With Manila as a base of operations, the United States was better able to protect its economic and political concerns in Asia. Such interests included the American China Development Co. (1898), a railway and mining concession in south China, and various oil, timber, and industrial investments in Manchuria.

Boxer Rebellion (1900)

Chinese nationalists ("Boxers") struck at foreign settlements in China and at the Ch'ing dynasty Manchu government in Beijing for allowing foreign industrial nations, such as Britain, Japan, Russia, France, Germany, Italy, Portugal, Belgium, The Netherlands, and the United States, large concessions within Chinese borders. An international army helped to put down the rebellion and enabled the Chinese government to remain in power.

Platt Amendment (1901)

Although Cuba was granted its independence, the Platt Amendment provided that Cuba become a virtual protectorate of the United States. Cuba could not 1) make a treaty with a foreign state impairing its independence, or 2) contract an excessive public debt. Cuba was required to 1) allow the U.S. to preserve order on the island, and 2) lease a naval base for 99 years to the U.S. at Guantanamo Bay.

Hay-Pauncefote Treaty (1901)

This treaty between the U.S. and Britain abrogated an earlier agreement (1850, Clayton-Bulwer Treaty) to build jointly an isthmian canal. The United States was free to unilaterally construct, fortify, and maintain a canal that would be open to all ships.

Insular Cases (1901–1903)

The Supreme Court decided that constitutional rights did not extend to territorial possessions, thus the Constitution did not follow the flag. Congress had the right to administer each island possession without constitutional restraint. Inhabitants of those possessions did not have the same rights as American citizens.

The New Diplomacy

As the beginning of the twentieth century foreshadowed the "Americanization of the world," a modern professional foreign service was being put into place to promote the political and economic policies of a technologically and democratically advanced society about to bid for world power.

Drill 4: War and the Americanization of the World, 1897–1902

1. Speaking of the need to expand American power into Central and South America, one nineteenth century American said, "...can anyone doubt that the result of this competition will be 'survival of the fittest'?" This statement reflects what philosophy?

    (A) Social Darwinism

    (B) Realism

    (C) Idealism

    (D) Communism

    (E) Anarchism

2. All of the following led to the Spanish-American War of 1898 EXCEPT

    (A) the de Lôme letter.

    (B) yellow journalism.

    (C) explosion of the *Maine.*

    (D) the push to annex Hawaii.

    (E) influence of Cuban exiles.

3. William Randolph Hearst achieved fame and wealth as a

    (A) radio commentator.

    (B) newspaper publisher.

    (C) photographer.

    (D) film producer.

    (E) political cartoonist.

4. Emilio Aguinaldo was

    (A) the commander of the Spanish fleet defeated at Manila Bay.

    (B) the Spanish general whose harsh tactics against Cuban rebels helped bring on the Spanish-American War.

    (C) the leader of the Philippine insurrection against first Spanish and then U.S. occupation.

    (D) the commander of the Spanish fleet destroyed at Santiago.

    (E) the Spanish foreign minister who negotiated the treaty ending the Spanish-American War.

5. The primary cause of the Spanish-American War was

    (A) Spanish occupation of the Panama Canal.

    (B) American expansionism and support for Cuban nationalism.

    (C) the murder of two U.S. diplomats in Spain on a peaceful diplomatic mission.

(D)   Spanish attacks on U.S. commercial ships off the coast of Cuba.

(E)   the sinking of the battleship *Maine* in Havana harbor supposedly by Spanish military agents.

5.   PROGRESSIVE REFORMS AND THE REGULATORY STATE, 1902–1912

As a Republican progressive reformer committed to honest and efficient government designed to serve all social classes in America, Theodore Roosevelt restored the presidency to the high eminence it had held through the Civil War era, and redressed the balance of power with old guard leaders in Congress.

Politics of the Period, 1902–1907

President Roosevelt did much to create a bipartisan coalition of liberal reformers whose objective was to restrain corporate monopoly and promote economic competition at home and abroad. Roosevelt won the support of enlightened business leaders, the middle class, consumers, and urban and rural workers with his promise of a "square deal" for all.

Roosevelt's Anti-Trust Policy (1902)

The president pledged strict enforcement of the Sherman Anti-Trust Act (1890) to break up illegal monopolies and regulate large corporations for the public good through honest federal government administration.

Progressive Reform in the States

Taking their cue from Washington, many states enacted laws creating honest and efficient political and economic regulatory standards. Political reforms included enacting laws establishing primary elections (Mississippi, Wisconsin), initiative and referendum (South Dakota, Oregon), and the rooting out of political bosses on the state and municipal levels (especially in New York, Ohio, Michigan, and California).

Commission Form of Government (1903)

After a hurricane and tidal wave destroyed much of Galveston, Texas, progressive businessmen and Texas state legislators removed the ineffective and corrupt mayor and city council and established a city government of five elected commissioners who were experts in their fields to rebuild Galveston. Numerous other cities adopted the commission form of government to replace the mayor/council format.

State Leaders

Significant state reformers in the period were Robert LaFollette of Wisconsin, Albert Cummins of Iowa, Charles Evans Hughes of New York, James M. Cox of Ohio, Hiram Johnson of California, William S. U'ren of Oregon, Albert Beveridge of Indiana, and Woodrow Wilson of New Jersey.

City Reformers

Urban leaders included John Purroy Mitchell of New York City, Tom L. Johnson and Newton Baker of Cleveland, Hazen Pingree of Detroit, Sam Jones of Toledo, and Joseph Folk of St. Louis.

Election of 1904

Having assured Republican party leaders that he wished to reform corporate monopolies and railroads, but not interfere with monetary policy or tariffs, Roosevelt was nominated for president along with Charles Fairbanks (Indiana) for vice president. The Democratic party nominated New York judge Alton B. Parker for president and Henry G. Davis (West Virginia) for vice president on a platform that endorsed Roosevelt's "trust-busting," which called for even greater power for such regulatory agencies as the Interstate Commerce Commission, and accepted the conservative gold standard as the basis for monetary policy. Roosevelt easily defeated Parker by about two million votes, and the Republicans retained control of both houses of Congress.

Hepburn Act (1906)

Membership of the Interstate Commerce Commission was increased from five to seven. The I.C.C. could set its own fair freight rates, had its regulatory power extended over pipelines, bridges, and express companies, and was empowered to require a uniform system of accounting by regulated transportation companies. This act and the Elkins Act (1903—reiterated illegality of railroad rebates) gave teeth to the original Interstate Commerce Act of 1887.

Pure Food and Drug Act (1906)

This act prohibited the manufacture, sale, and transportation of adulterated or fraudulently labeled foods and drugs in accordance with consumer demands to which Theodore Roosevelt was especially sensitive.

Meat Inspection Act (1906)

The Meat Inspection Act provided for federal and sanitary regulations and inspections in meatpacking facilities. Wartime scandals in 1898 relating to spoiled canned meats were a powerful force for reform.

Immunity of Witness Act (1906)

Corporate officials could no longer make a plea of immunity to avoid testifying in cases dealing with their corporation's illegal activities.

Conservation Laws

From 1902 to 1908 a series of laws and executive actions were enacted to create federal irrigation projects, national parks and forests, develop water power (Internal Waterways Commission), and establish the National Conservation Commission to oversee the nation's resources.

The Economy, 1902–1907

Anti-trust policy and government regulation of the economy gave way to a more lenient enforcement of federal laws after the panic of 1907. Recognition of the rights of labor unions was enhanced.

Anti-Trust Policy (1902)

In order to restore free competition, President Roosevelt ordered the Justice Department to prosecute corporations pursuing monopolistic practices. Attorney General P.C. Knox first brought suit against the Northern Securities Company, a railroad holding corporation put together by J.P. Morgan; then he moved against Rockefeller's Standard Oil Company. By the time he left office in 1909, Roosevelt brought indictments against 25 monopolies.

Department of Commerce and Labor (1903)

A new cabinet position was created to address the concerns of business and labor. Within the department, the Bureau of Corporations was empowered to investigate and report on the illegal activities of corporations.

Coal Strike (1902)

Roosevelt interceded with government mediation to bring about negotiations between the United Mine Workers union and the anthracite mine owners after a bitter strike over wages, safety conditions, and union recognition. This was the first time that the government intervened in a labor dispute without automatically siding with management.

Panic of 1907

A brief economic recession and panic occurred in 1907 as a result, in part, of questionable bank speculations, a lack of flexible monetary and credit policies, and a conservative gold standard. This event called attention to the need for banking reform which would lead to the Federal Reserve System in 1913. Although Roosevelt temporarily eased the pressure on anti-trust activity, he made it clear that reform of the economic system to promote free-enterprise capitalism would continue.

St. Louis World's Fair (1904)

The World's Fair of 1904 celebrated the centennial of the Louisiana Purchase and brought the participation of Asian nations to promote foreign trade.

Social and Cultural Developments, 1902–1907

Debate and discussion over the expanding role of the federal government commanded the attention of the nation.

Progressive Reforms

There was not one unified progressive movement, but a series of reform causes designed to address specific social, economic, and political problems. Middle-class men and women were especially active in attempting to correct the excessive powers of giant corporations, and the radical extremes of Marxist revolutionaries and radicals among intellectuals and labor activists. However, the mainstreams of the business community and the labor unions were moderate in their desires to preserve economic opportunities and the free enterprise system. Progressive reforms might best be described as evolutionary change from above rather than revolutionary upheaval from below.

Varieties of Reform

Progressive reform goals included not only honest government, economic regulation, environmental conservation, labor recognition, and new political structures. Reformers also called for gender equality for men and women in the work force (Oregon Ten Hour Law), an end to racial segregation (National Association for the Advancement of Colored People), child labor laws, prison reform, regulation of the stock market, direct election of senators, and a more efficient foreign service among other reform activities.

Muckrakers

Muckrakers (a term coined by Roosevelt) were investigative journalists and authors who were often the publicity agents for reforms. Popular magazines included McClure's, *Collier's, Cosmopolitan*, and *Everybody's*. Famous articles that led to reforms included "The Shame of the Cities" by Lincoln Steffens, "History of Standard Oil Company" by Ida Tarbell, "The Treason of the Senate" by David Phillips, and "Frenzied Finance" by Thomas Lawson.

Literature

Works of literature with a social message included *Following the Color Line* by Ray Stannard Baker, *The Bitter Cry of the Children* by John Spargo, *Poverty* by Robert Hunter, *The Story of Life Insurance* by Burton Hendrick, *The Financier* by Theodore Dreiser, *The Jungle* by Upton Sinclair, *The Boss* by Henry Lewis, *Call of the Wild, The Iron Heel,* and *The War of the Classes* by

Jack London, *A Certain Rich Man* by William Allen White, and *The Promise of American Life* by Herbert Croly.

Inventions

The Wright brothers made their first air flight at Kitty Hawk, North Carolina in 1903.

QUESTION

What general values did the progressive reformers of the early twentieth century share?

EXPLANATION

In general, the progressive reformers believed that human life could be improved through the application of rational society policy. They supported the basic political system of liberal democracy, but thought that it could be reformed by the use of experts and professionals. The agenda was not shaped by ideology, but by a view that institutions such as government and the educational system could be used to improve society.

Foreign Relations, 1902–1907

Theodore Roosevelt's "Big Stick" diplomacy and economic foreign policy were characteristics of the administration.

Panama Canal

Roosevelt used executive power to engineer the separation of Panama from Colombia, and the recognition of Panama as an independent country. The Hay-Bunau-Varilla Treaty of 1903 granted the United States control of the canal zone in Panama for $10 million and an annual fee of $250,000 beginning nine years after ratification of the treaty by both parties. Construction of the canal began in 1904 and was completed in 1914.

Roosevelt Corollary to the Monroe Doctrine

The U.S. reserved the right to intervene in the internal affairs of Latin American nations to keep European powers from using military force to collect debts in the Western Hemisphere. The U.S. eventually intervened in the affairs of Venezuela, Haiti, the Dominican Republic, Nicaragua, and Cuba by 1905 as an international policeman brandishing the "big stick" against Europeans and Latin Americans. Luis Drago of Argentina urged the adoption of an international agreement prohibiting the use of military force for the collection of debts.

Rio de Janeiro Conference (1906)

Secretary of State Elihu Root attempted to de-emphasize U.S. military and political intervention in order to promote economic and political goodwill, economic development, trade, and finances in Latin America. President Roosevelt was actually moving away from "big stick" diplomacy and toward "dollar diplomacy" before he left office. The United States also promoted the Pan American Railway project at this meeting of the International Bureau of American Republics.

China

In pursuit of the Open Door policy of equal opportunity of trade and the guaranteed independence of China, the United States continued to promote its trade interests in Asia. Segregation and restrictions of Chinese immigrants in California and other states led Chinese national leaders to call for a boycott in 1905 of U.S. goods and services in both China and the United States. The boycott ended in 1906 without significant changes in state laws.

Russo-Japanese War (1904–1905)

With American encouragement and financial loans, Japan pursued and won a war against tsarist Russia. Roosevelt negotiated the Treaty of Portsmouth, New Hampshire, which ended the war, and for which the president ironically received the Nobel Peace Prize in 1906. Japan, however, was disappointed at not receiving more territory and financial compensation from Russia and blamed the United States.

Taft-Katsura Memo (1905)

The United States and Japan pledged to maintain the Open Door principles in China. Japan recognized American control over the Philippines, and the United States granted a Japanese protectorate over Korea.

Gentleman's Agreement with Japan (1907)

After numerous incidents of racial discrimination against Japanese in California, Japan agreed to restrict the emigration of unskilled Japanese workers to the U.S.

Great White Fleet (1907)

In order to show American strength to Japan and China, Roosevelt sent the great white naval fleet to Asian parts.

Algeciras Conference (1906)

The United States participated with eight European states to guarantee for Morocco's equal opportunity of trade, and the independence of the sultan of Morocco in a manner reminiscent of the Open Door notes in China. The Conference, however, created tension between Germany and France which would be at war in the next decade.

The Second Hague Conference (1907)

Forty-six nations including the United States met in the Netherlands to discuss disarmament and the creation of an international court of justice. Little was accomplished except for the adoption of a resolution banning the use of military force for the collection of foreign debts.

QUESTION

How could one summarize Theodore Roosevelt's "Big Stick" diplomacy?

EXPLANATION

"Big Stick" diplomacy meant using force, or threatening to use force, especially in the Western Hemisphere in order to carry out the United States' foreign policy agenda. It also included acting as an "international policeman" in situations where European powers attempted to use force to collect Latin American debts. In other parts of the world, the U.S. also used displays of its military power to convince foreign nations that they would be better off avoiding a confrontation with the U.S.

The Regulatory State and the Ordered Society, 1907–1912

The progressive presidencies of Roosevelt, Taft, and Wilson brought the concept of big government to fruition. A complex corporate society needed rules and regulations as well as powerful agencies to enforce those measures necessary to maintain and enhance democratic free enterprise competition. The search for political, social, and economic standards designed to preserve order in American society while still guaranteeing political, social, and economic freedom was a difficult, but primary task. The nation increasingly looked to Washington to protect the less powerful segments of the republic from the special interests that had grown up in the late nineteenth century. A persistent problem for the federal government was how best to preserve order and standards in a complex technological society while not interfering with the basic liberties Americans came to cherish in the Constitution and throughout their history. The strain of World War I after 1914 would further complicate the problem.

Politics of the Period, 1907–1912

The continuation of progressive reforms by both Republican and Democratic leaders helped to form a consensus for the establishment of regulatory standards.

Election of 1908

Deciding not to run for re-election, Theodore Roosevelt opened the way for William H. Taft (Ohio) and James S. Sherman (New York) to run on a Republican platform calling for a continuation of anti-trust enforcement, environmental conservation, and a lower tariff policy to promote international trade. The Democrats nominated William Jennings Bryan for a third time with John Kern (Indiana) for vice president on an anti-monopoly and low tariff platform. The Socialists once again nominated Eugene Debs. Taft easily won by over a million votes, and the Republicans retained control of both houses of Congress. For the first time, the American Federation of Labor entered national politics officially with an endorsement of Bryan. This decision began a long alliance between organized labor and the Democratic party in the twentieth century.

Taft's Objectives

The president had two primary political goals in 1909. One was the continuation of Roosevelt's trust-busting policies, and the other was the reconciliation of the old guard conservatives and young progressive reformers in the Republican party.

Anti-Trust Policy

In pursuing anti-monopoly law enforcement, Taft chose as his attorney general George Wickersham, who brought 44 indictments in anti-trust suits.

Political Rift

Taft was less successful in healing the Republican split between conservatives and progressives over such issues as tariff reform, conservation, and the almost dictatorial power held by the reactionary Republican Speaker of the House Joseph Cannon (Illinois). Taft's inability to bring both wings of the party together led to the hardened division which would bring about a complete Democratic victory in the 1912 elections.

The Anti-Cannon Crusade

In 1910, Republican progressives joined with Democrats to strip Speaker Cannon of his power to appoint the Committee on Rules and serve on it himself. Although critical of Cannon, Taft failed to align himself with the progressives. Democrats gained control of the House in the 1910 elections, and a Republican-Democratic coalition ran the Senate.

Ballinger-Pinchot Dispute (1909–1910)

Progressives backed Gifford Pinchot, chief of the U.S. Forest Service, in his charge that the conservative Secretary of the Interior, Richard Ballinger, was giving away the nation's natural resources to private corporate interests. A congressional investigatory committee found that Ballinger had done nothing illegal, but did act in a manner contrary to the government's environmental policies. Taft had supported Ballinger through the controversy, but negative public opinion forced Ballinger to resign in 1911. Taft's political standing with progressive Republicans was hurt going into the election of 1912.

Government Efficiency

Taft promoted the idea of a national budgetary system. Although Congress refused to cooperate, by executive action the president saved over $40 million for the government, and set an example for many state and local governments.

The Sixteenth Amendment

Congress passed in 1909 a graduated income tax amendment to the Constitution which was ratified in 1913.

Mann-Elins Act (1910)

This act extended the regulatory function of the Interstate Commerce Commission over cable and wireless companies, and telephone and telegraph lines; gave the I.C.C. power to begin its own court proceedings and suspend questionable rates; and set up a separate but temporary commerce court to handle rate dispute cases.

Election of 1912

This election was one of the most dramatic in American history. President Taft's inability to maintain party harmony led Theodore Roosevelt to return to national politics. When denied the Republican nomination, Roosevelt and his supporters formed the Progressive party (Bull Moose) and nominated Roosevelt for president and Hiram Johnson (California) for vice president on a political platform nicknamed "The New Nationalism." It called for stricter regulation of large corporations, creation of a tariff commission, women's suffrage, minimum wages and benefits, direct election of senators, initiative, referendum and recall, presidential primaries, and prohibition of child labor. Roosevelt also called for a Federal Trade Commission to regulate the broader economy, a stronger executive, and more government planning. Theodore Roosevelt did not see big business as evil, but a permanent development that was necessary in a modern economy.

The Republicans

President Taft and Vice President Sherman retained control of the Republican party after challenges by Roosevelt and Robert LaFollette, and were nominated on a platform of "Quiet Confidence" calling for a continuation of progressive programs pursued by Taft over the past four years.

The Democrats

After 45 ballots without a nomination, the Democratic convention finally worked out a compromise whereby William Jennings Bryan gave his support to New Jersey Governor Woodrow Wilson on the forty-sixth ballot. Thomas Marshall (Indiana) was chosen as the vice presidential candidate. Wilson called his campaign the "New Freedom" based on progressive programs similar to those in the Progressive and Republican parties. Wilson, however, did not agree with Roosevelt on the issue of big business, which Wilson saw as morally evil. Therefore, Wilson called for breaking up large corporations rather than just regulating them. He differed from the other two-party candidates by favoring independence for the Philippines, and the exemption from prosecution of labor unions under the Sherman Anti-Trust Act. Wilson also supported such measures as lower tariffs, a graduated income tax, banking reform, and direct election of senators. Philosophically, Wilson was skeptical of big business and big government. In some respects, he hoped to return to an earlier and simpler concept of a free enterprise republic. After his selection, however, he would modify his views to conform more with those of Theodore Roosevelt.

Election Results

The Republican split clearly paved the way for Wilson's victory. Wilson received 6.2 million votes, Roosevelt 4.1 million, Taft 3.5 million, and the Socialist Debs 900,000 votes. In the electoral college, Wilson received 435 votes, Roosevelt 88, Taft 8. Although a minority president, Wilson garnered the largest electoral majority in American history to that time. Democrats won control of both houses of Congress.

The Wilson Presidency

The Wilson administration brought together many of the policies and initiatives of the previous Republican administrations, and reform efforts in Congress by both parties. Before the outbreak of World War I in 1914, President Wilson, working with cooperative majorities in both houses of Congress, achieved much of the remaining progressive agenda. By the end of Wilson's presidency, the New Freedom and the New Nationalism would merge into one government philosophy of regulation, order, and standardization in the interest of an increasingly diverse and pluralistic American nation.

The Economy, 1907–1912

The short-lived panic of 1907 revealed economic weaknesses in banking and currency policy addressed by Presidents Roosevelt, Taft, and Wilson, and by Congress. Significantly, the American economy was strengthened just in time to meet the challenges of World War I.

National Monetary Commission (1908)

Chaired by Senator Nelson Aldrich (Rhode Island), the 18 member commission recommended what later became the basis for the Federal Reserve System in 1913 with a secure Treasury reserve and branch banks to add and subtract currency from the monetary supply depending on the needs of the economy.

Payne-Aldrich Tariff (1909)

Despite the intention of lowering the tariff, enough amendments were added in the Senate to turn the bill into a protective measure. Progressive reformers felt betrayed by special interests opposed to consumer price concerns. President Taft made the political mistake of endorsing the tariff.

Postal Savings Banks (1910)

Recommended by President Taft, and one of the original Populist party goals, certain U.S. post offices were authorized to receive deposits and pay interest.

New Battleship Contract (1910)

The State Department arranged for Bethlehem Steel Corporation to receive a large contract to build battleships for Argentina. This was an example of Taft's "dollar diplomacy" in action.

Anti-Trust Proceedings

Although a friend to the business community, President Taft ordered 90 legal proceedings against monopolies and 44 anti-trust suits, including the one which broke up the American Tobacco Trust (1911). It was also under Taft that the government succeeded with its earlier suit against Standard Oil.

Canadian Reciprocity (1911)

A reciprocal trade agreement between the United States and Canada was repudiated by the Canadian legislature which feared economic and political domination by the United States.

New Cabinet Posts (1913)

The Department of Commerce and Labor was divided into two separate autonomous cabinet level positions.

Automobiles

In 1913 Henry Ford introduced the continuous flow process on the automobile assembly line.

Social and Cultural Developments, 1907–1912

The rationales for progressive reform and government activism were important themes in American society.

Social Programs

States led the way with programs such as public aid to mothers of dependent children (Illinois, 1911) and the first minimum wage law (Massachusetts, 1912).

Race and Ethnic Attitudes

Despite the creation of the NAACP in 1909, many progressive reformers tended to be Anglo-Saxon elitists critical of the lack of accomplishments of Native American Indians, African-Americans, and Asian, Southern and Eastern European immigrants. In 1905, the African-American intellectual militant W.E. B. DuBois founded the Niagara Movement calling for federal legislation to protect racial equality and provide full rights of citizenship.

Radical Labor

Although moderate labor unions as represented by the A.F. of L. functioned within the American system, a radical labor organization called the Industrial Workers of the World (I.W.W. or Wobblies, 1905–1924) was active in promoting violence and revolution. Led by colorful figures such as Carlo Tresca, Elizabeth Gurley Flynn (the Red Flame), Daniel DeLeon, "Mother" Mary Harris Jones, the maverick priest Father Thomas Hagerty, and Big Bill Haywood, among others, the I.W.W. organized effective strikes in the textile industry in 1912, and among a few Western miners groups, but generally had little appeal to the average American worker. After the Red Scare of 1919, the government worked to smash the I.W.W. and deport many of its immigrant leaders and members.

White Slave Trade

In 1910, Congress made interstate prostitution a federal crime with passage of the Mann Act.

Literature

Enthused by the self-confidence exuded by political reformers, writers remained optimistic in their realism, and their faith in the American people to solve social and economic problems with honest and efficient programs.

Motion Pictures

By 1912 Hollywood had replaced New York and New Jersey as the center for silent film production. There were 13,000 movie houses in the United States and Paramount Pictures had just been formed as a large studio resembling other large corporations. Serials, epic features, and Mack Sennett comedies were in production. All of these developments contributed to the "star system" in American film entertainment.

Science

The X-ray tube was developed by William Coolidge in 1913. Robert Goddard patented liquid rocket fuel in 1914. Plastics and synthetic fibers such as rayon were developed in 1909 by Arthur Little and Leo Baekeland, respectively. Adolphus Busch applied the diesel engine to the submarine in 1912.

Foreign Relations, 1907–1912

The expansion of American international interests through Taft's "dollar diplomacy" and world tensions foreshadowing the First World War were dominant themes.

Dollar Diplomacy

President Taft sought to avoid military intervention, especially in Latin America, by replacing "big stick" policies with "dollar diplomacy" in the expectation that American financial investments would encourage economic, social, and political stability. This idea proved an illusion as investments never really filtered through all levels of Latin American societies, nor did such investments generate democratic reforms.

Mexican Revolution (1910)

Francisco I. Madero overthrew the dictator Porfirio Diaz (1911) declaring himself a progressive revolutionary akin to reformers in the United States. American and European corporate interests (especially oil and mining) feared national interference with their investments in Mexico. President Taft recognized Madero's government, but stationed 10,000 troops on the Texas border (1912) to protect Americans from the continuing fighting. In 1913 Madero was assassinated by General Victoriano Huerta. Wilson urged Huerta to hold democratic elections and adopt a constitutional government. When Huerta refused his advice, Wilson invaded Mexico with troops at Vera Cruz in 1914. A second U.S. invasion came in northern Mexico in 1916. War between the U.S. and Mexico might have occurred had not World War I intervened.

Latin American Interventions

Although Taft and Secretary of State P.C. Knox created the Latin American Division of the State Department in 1909 to promote better relations, the United States kept a military presence in the Dominican Republic and Haiti, and intervened militarily in Nicaragua (1911) to quiet fears of revolution and help manage foreign financial problems.

Arbitration Treaties

Taking a page from Roosevelt's book, Taft promoted arbitration agreements as an alternative to war in Latin America and in Asia.

Lodge Corollary to the Monroe Doctrine (1911)

When a Japanese syndicate moved to purchase a large tract of land in Mexico's Lower California, Senator Lodge introduced a resolution to block the Japanese investment. The Corollary went further to exclude non-European powers from the Western Hemisphere under the Monroe Doctrine.

Bryan's Arbitration Treaties (1913–1915)

Wilson's Secretary of State William Jennings Bryan continued the policies of Roosevelt and Taft to promote arbitration of disputes in Latin America and elsewhere. Bryan negotiated about 30 such treaties.

Root-Takahira Agreement (1908)

This agreement reiterated the status quo in Asia established by the United States and Japan by the Taft-Katsura Memo (1905).

China Consortium (1909)

American bankers and the State Department demanded entry into an international banking association with Britain, France, and Germany to build a railway network (Hukuang) in southern and central China. Wilson withdrew the U.S. from participation in 1913 as the Chinese revolution deteriorated into greater instability.

Manchuria

President Taft and Secretary Knox attempted to force the sale of Japanese and Russian railroad interests in Manchuria to American investment interests. When this diplomacy failed, Knox moved to construct a competing rail system.

The Chinese government, however, refused to approve the American plan. Both Japan and Russia grew more suspicious of United States interests in Asia.

Chinese Revolution (1911)

Chinese nationalists overthrew the Manchu Dynasty and the last emperor of China, Henry Pu Yi. Although the military war lord Yuan Shih-Kai seized control, decades of factionalism, revolution, and civil war destabilized China and lessen its market potential for American and other foreign investors.

Drill 5: Progressive Reforms and the Regulatory State, 1902-1912

1. Which of the following states first gave women the right to vote?

    (A) Colorado

    (B) Wyoming

    (C) New York

    (D) Utah

    (E) Idaho

2. Which of the following statements best summarizes Theodore Roosevelt's position on trusts?

    (A) Trusts are an economic evil and should be destroyed in every case. *Wilson*

    (B) Only trusts in the railroad and oil industries are acceptable.

    (C) Good trusts should be tolerated while bad trusts are prevented from manipulating markets.

    (D) Only trusts in the meatpacking industry should be broken up.

    (E) Anything that stands in the way of complete and unrestricted economic competition is evil and should be removed.

3. Theodore Roosevelt contributed to the Progressive movement in all of the following EXCEPT

    (A) he strengthened the presidency.

    (B) he opposed trusts and other big business combinations.

    (C) he advertised progressive ideas.

    (D) he promoted conservation.

    (E) he expanded the power of the ICC.

4. Which of the following does NOT correctly describe the Progressives?

   (A) They favored government regulation of business on behalf of the public interest.

   (B) They were concerned with the social and economic conditions of the city.

   • (C) They represented farmers and the working class.

   (D) They advocated a more orderly and efficient society.

   (E) They called for a stronger state and federal government.

5. The Roosevelt corollary to the Monroe Doctrine established which of the following?

   (A) The right of European nations to forcefully collect debts in the Western Hemisphere.

   (B) The right of the United States to build and fortify an Atlantic-Pacific canal.

   (C) The independence of Panama from Colombia.

   • (D) The right of the U.S. to act as a police power in the Western Hemisphere nations.

   (E) The right of the United States to act as an arbitrator in European conflicts with Western Hemisphere nations.

6. The "Wisconsin Idea" of Robert LaFollette included which of the following?

   (A) Close cooperation with the University of Wisconsin in the writing of legislation

   (B) Strong support of labor unions

   (C) Reduction of business and income taxes

   (D) Subsidies to agriculture

   (E) Establishment of Social Security

7. During William H. Taft's administration, the federal government moved to strengthen its regulatory control over the railroad industry by

   (A) passage of the Mann-Elkins Act.

   (B) creation of the Federal Trade Commission.

   (C) passage of the "Granger Laws."

   (D) taking over and operating the railroads.

   (E) removal of former legal obstacles to consolidation of the railroads into giant corporations.

8. The Spanish-American War spurred building of the Panama Canal by

   - (A) demonstrating the need to shift naval forces quickly from the Atlantic to the Pacific.

   (B) demonstrating the ease with which Latin American countries could be overcome by U.S. military force.

   (C) discrediting congressional opponents of the project.

   (D) removing the threat that any possible canal could be blockaded by Spanish forces based in Cuba and Puerto Rico.

   (E) demonstrating that such tropical diseases as malaria and yellow fever could be controlled.

9. Which of the following is true of W.E.B. DuBois?

   - (A) He founded the National Association for the Advancement of Colored People.

   (B) He was the chief author of the Atlanta Compromise. *8T*

   (C) He was an outspoken critic of the Niagara Movement.

   (D) He believed that blacks should temporarily accommodate themselves to the whites.

   (E) He worked closely with Booker T. Washington.

10. In what way did the muckrakers contribute to the rise of Progressivism in the early years of the twentieth century?

   (A) Their lurid stories of European abuses led directly to American isolationism until World War I.

   (B) Their stories glorifying the rich and famous led to the supremacy of laissez-faire economic theories during this period.

   (C) Their horror stories of Marxist infiltration into workers' unions led to public support for crackdowns against reform-minded unions and alliances.

   - (D) Their exposés of government and business corruption, abuse, and mismanagement led to widely supported public demands for effective reform.

   (E) They created a repugnance for the national press that generalized into a distrust for all government and business institutions.

1877–1912
DRILLS

ANSWER KEY

Drill 1—The New Industrial Era, 1877–1882

1. (D)   2. (B)   3. (D)   4. (E)   5. (B)
6. (E)   7. (A)   8. (B)   9. (E)   10. (E)

Drill 2—The Emergence of the Regional Empire, 1887–1892

1. (D)   2. (B)   3. (B)   4. (B)   5. (C)

Drill 3—Economic Depression and Social Crisis, 1892–1897

1. (C)   2. (E)   3. (C)   4. (C)   5. (E)
6. (C)   7. (A)   8. (A)   9. (B)   10. (E)

Drill 4—War and the Americanization of the World, 1897–1902

1. (A)   2. (D)   3. (B)   4. (C)   5. (B)

Drill 5—Progressive Reforms and the Regulatory State, 1902–1912

1. (B)   2. (C)   3. (B)   4. (C)   5. (D)
6. (A)   7. (A)   8. (A)   9. (A)   10. (D)

GLOSSARY: 1877–1912

Big Stick Diplomacy
Using American military power to fortify the diplomatic policies of the United States.

Boxers
Chinese nationalists who fought against foreign interests in China.

Bull Moose Party
Another name for the Progressive party.

Dollar Diplomacy
Using American economic power to fortify the diplomatic policies of the United States.

Gilded Age
The period between the 1870s and 1890s when the United States emerged as the world's leading industrial and agricultural producer.

Half-Breeds
The Republican faction that pushed for civil service reform and merit appointments to government posts.

Muckrakers
Investigative journalists and authors who exposed corruption in business and government.

Mugwumps
Independent Republicans who favored civil service reforms.

New Imperialism
Expansion that replaced territorial colonialism with finding markets for surplus industrial production, access to raw materials, and opportunities for overseas investment during domestic economic depression.

Open Door Policy
Declared that trade with China should be open to all nations.

Populist
A political coalition of agrarians with urban workers and the middle class. Its goals included monetization of silver, a graduated income tax, public ownership of railroads, telegraph, and telephone systems, an eight-hour day, and a ban on private armies used to break up strikes.

Progressivism

A political movement calling for rejuvenation of free enterprise capitalism and the destruction of illegal monopolies. It also called for civil service reform and honest and efficient government.

Reservation

Isolated lands where Native Americans were compelled to live.

Social Darwinism

An application of Darwin's theory of evolution, survival of the fittest, to justify unequal distribution of wealth by claiming that God granted wealth to the fittest.

Stalwarts

The Republican faction that favored the spoils system of political patronage.

Yellow Journalism

Sensationalist newspapers that encouraged direct military intervention on behalf of Cuban independence.

CHAPTER 10

1912–1920

WILSON AND WORLD WAR I

➤ Diagnostic Test
➤ 1912–1920 Review & Drills
➤ Glossary

1912-1920
DIAGNOSTIC TEST

1. Ⓐ Ⓑ Ⓒ Ⓓ Ⓔ
2. Ⓐ Ⓑ Ⓒ Ⓓ Ⓔ
3. Ⓐ Ⓑ Ⓒ Ⓓ Ⓔ
4. Ⓐ Ⓑ Ⓒ Ⓓ Ⓔ
5. Ⓐ Ⓑ Ⓒ Ⓓ Ⓔ
6. Ⓐ Ⓑ Ⓒ Ⓓ Ⓔ
7. Ⓐ Ⓑ Ⓒ Ⓓ Ⓔ
8. Ⓐ Ⓑ Ⓒ Ⓓ Ⓔ
9. Ⓐ Ⓑ Ⓒ Ⓓ Ⓔ
10. Ⓐ Ⓑ Ⓒ Ⓓ Ⓔ
11. Ⓐ Ⓑ Ⓒ Ⓓ Ⓔ
12. Ⓐ Ⓑ Ⓒ Ⓓ Ⓔ
13. Ⓐ Ⓑ Ⓒ Ⓓ Ⓔ
14. Ⓐ Ⓑ Ⓒ Ⓓ Ⓔ
15. Ⓐ Ⓑ Ⓒ Ⓓ Ⓔ
16. Ⓐ Ⓑ Ⓒ Ⓓ Ⓔ
17. Ⓐ Ⓑ Ⓒ Ⓓ Ⓔ
18. Ⓐ Ⓑ Ⓒ Ⓓ Ⓔ
19. Ⓐ Ⓑ Ⓒ Ⓓ Ⓔ
20. Ⓐ Ⓑ Ⓒ Ⓓ Ⓔ

1912–1920
DIAGNOSTIC TEST

This diagnostic test is designed to help you determine your strengths and weaknesses in your knowledge of Wilson and World War I (1912–1920). Follow the directions and check your answers.

Study this chapter for the following tests:
AP U.S. History, CLEP General, CLEP United States History I,
GED, Praxis Specialty Area, SAT: United States History

---

20 Questions

DIRECTIONS: Choose the correct answer for each of the following questions. Fill in each answer on the answer sheet.

1. Who led the American expeditionary forces in Europe during World War I?

   (A) Douglas MacArthur   (B) George Dewey

   (C) John J. Pershing   (D) Leonard Wood

   (E) Dwight D. Eisenhower

2. In reaction to a perceived insult to the U.S. flag, and in order to hasten the downfall of Mexican leader Victoriano Huerta, President Woodrow Wilson

   (A) ordered General John J. Pershing to take U.S. troops across the border into northern Mexico.

   (B) withdrew previously granted U.S. diplomatic recognition of Huerta's regime.

   (C) ordered the occupation of Mexico City by U.S. troops.

   (D) ordered U.S. forces to occupy the Mexican port city of Vera Cruz.

   (E) sent a strong diplomatic protest.

3. Which of the following was most crucial in bringing about U.S. participation in the First World War?

   (A) British propaganda

   (B) German violation of Belgian neutrality

[handwritten: Sussex pledge]

- (C) German use of submarines against merchant and passenger ships

- (D) German atrocities against French and Belgian civilians in the occupied areas of those countries

- (E) Revelation of a German proposal to Mexico for a joint war against the United States *[handwritten: Zimmermann Telegram]*

4. All of the following were fully or partially realized points of Woodrow Wilson's Allied peace plan EXCEPT

    (A) the creation of an independent Poland.

  - (B) the extensive readjustment of national boundaries in the Middle East to create independent nations.

    (C) the restoration of Alsace-Lorraine to France.

    [handwritten: was created but didn't join] (D) the creation of a League of Nations to settle international disputes.

    (E) the creation of nations in the Balkans according to the principle of self-determination of peoples.

5. The event that was most important in transforming the U.S. from international debtor status to international creditor status was

    (A) the Civil War.

    (B) the formation of J. P. Morgan and Company.

  - (C) the First World War.

    (D) the passage of the Fordney-McCumber Tariff.

    (E) the Depression of the 1930s.

6. What proposal did President Woodrow Wilson make in 1918 that convinced the Germans they would be treated fairly if they surrendered?

    (A) The Twenty-One Demands

  - (B) The Fourteen Points

    (C) The Versailles Proposals

    (D) The Balfour Declaration

    (E) The "New Freedom" Policy *[handwritten: never ratified]*

7. What was the reaction in the U.S. Senate to the terms of the 1918 Treaty of Versailles?

    (A) The Senate overwhelmingly supported the major provisions of the treaty and only demanded a few minor adjustments before ratifying it.

    (B) The Senate felt that in many ways the treaty was too harsh on Germany, but that overall it was a good plan for postwar peace.

(C)   The Senate was angry at Wilson for the way he handled the negotiations, but felt that the treaty was too important to be destroyed by
partisan politics. As a result, the Senate narrowly passed the ratification measure making the treaty official.

(D)   The Senate was angry at Wilson for the way he handled the negotiations and had problems with several treaty Articles. As a result, the
Senate didn't ratify the treaty until the second time Wilson sent it to
them. Even then, the Senate refused to ratify the provisions calling for
U.S. membership in a League of Nations.

• (E)   The Senate was angry at Wilson for the way he handled the negotiations and for the treaty that the peace conference produced. Wilson
refused to compromise on various treaty provisions, and the Senators
rejected the treaty both times it was sent to them.

8.   The Zimmerman Note was infamous because it

(A)   exposed German atrocities against Jews and other prisoners of war
and contributed directly to the U.S. entry into World War I.

• (B)   exposed a German plot to enlist Mexico into an alliance with Germany
in a war against the United States.

(C)   exposed corruption in the U.S. Justice Department leading to a total
reorganization of the department and the formation of the FBI.

(D)   exposed a British plot to disguise their warships as American merchant
ships, encouraging German submarines to attack any ship flying the American flag, hopefully luring the United States into World War I.

(E)   revealed the existence of Communist spies in the highest levels of
American government, following World War I, and led to the "Red
Scare" in which hundreds of innocent people were victimized in witch
hunts trying to weed out Communists.

9.   The rejection of the Versailles Treaty by the United States Senate signaled
what future for American foreign policy?

• (A)   The United States retreated into isolationism and backed away from a
world leadership role.

(B)   The United States rejected playing a secondary role to the European
powers and took a more aggressive role in dominating world politics.

(C)   The United States began taking an active part in promoting internationalism through its leadership in the League of Nations.

(D)   The United States formed a defensive alliance with Britain and France
to protect against any further abuses by the Germans.

(E) The United States launched an aggressive campaign to force all the European powers to relinquish their colonial holdings to American control and eventual independence.

10. The "Red Scare" of 1919 was caused primarily by

(A) the release of the Zimmerman Note.

(B) bombings of government facilities and industrial plants by agents from Comintern.

(C) Lenin's promise to bury capitalism, starting with the United States.

(D) a rash of massive labor strikes and disputes affecting millions of American workers.

(E) the invasion of Poland by Soviet military forces.

11. President Woodrow Wilson sent troops into Mexico because

(A) Mexico would not pay its debts to the United States.

(B) Mexico nationalized the oil industry.

(C) Victoriano Huerta assassinated President Francisco Madera and seized power.

(D) Pancho Villa raided Columbus, New Mexico, killing 17 Americans.

(E) a Mexican official arrested American sailors near Tampico, Mexico.

12. Which of the following statements best describes American attitudes toward World War I prior to 1917?

(A) American sympathies were divided, but they supported the president's policy of neutrality.

(B) Americans generally opposed neutrality and wanted to enter the war on the side of the English.

(C) Americans believed that the war had nothing to do with the United States.

(D) Americans generally opposed neutrality and wanted to enter the war on the side of the Germans.

(E) Americans believed that Congress should forbid Americans from travelling on British and French ships and from selling war materials to nations at war.

13. Which of the following did NOT contribute to the outbreak of World War I?

(A) Nationalism   (B) Imperialism

(C) International rivalries   (D) Alliance systems

(E) Communism

14. According to Woodrow Wilson, what was the key element of the Treaty of Versailles?

    (A) The mandate system for Germany's former colonies

    (B) German agreement to pay reparations

    (C) The creation of new independent states

    (D) The League of Nations

    (E) The return of Alsace-Lorraine to France

15. A major point of disagreement between Europe and the United States after World War I concerned

    (A) the nationalization of U.S. businesses in Europe.

    (B) claims of copyright violations.

    (C) payment of European debts to the United States.

    (D) the recognition of the new Communist government of Russia.

    (E) the rearmament of Germany.

16. In 1914, Germany took the offensive and moved against France while violating the neutrality of

    (A) Great Britain.   (B) Spain.

    (C) Belgium.   (D) Switzerland.

    (E) France.

17. Black Americans during World War I, for the most part,

    (A) were treated with dignity in Europe.

    (B) suffered little discrimination at home.

    (C) believed integration was becoming a reality in American society.

    (D) refused to participate in the war effort.

    (E) endorsed the policy of nonviolent resistance.

18. Following World War I, Senator Henry Cabot Lodge led the fight against the

    (A) establishment of the new nations of Europe.

    (B) harsh treatment of Germany.

    (C) United States occupation of Germany.

    (D) discrimination of blacks and women.

    (E) League of Nations.

19. Woodrow Wilson's career included all of the following EXCEPT

    (A) serving as governor of New Jersey.

    (B) teaching political science.

    (C) serving as governor of Virginia. *Came from VA originally*

    (D) serving as president of Princeton University.

    (E) writing the Fourteen Points.

20. The scandal in 1919 that affected the integrity of major league baseball was

    (A) "The Red Sox Scam."

    (B) "The Yankee Giveaway."

    (C) "The Philadelphia Folly."

    (D) "The Red Stockings Cash Deal."

    (E) "The Black Sox Scandal."

1912–1920
DIAGNOSTIC TEST

ANSWER KEY

1. (C)	5. (C)	9. (A)	13. (E)	17. (A)
2. (D)	6. (B)	10. (D)	14. (D)	18. (E)
3. (C)	7. (E)	11. (D)	15. (C)	19. (C)
4. (B)	8. (B)	12. (A)	16. (C)	20. (E)

DETAILED EXPLANATIONS
OF ANSWERS

1.   **(C)**   Although Leonard Wood was the highest ranking officer at the time the U.S. entered World War I, he was passed over in favor of John J. Pershing to command U.S. forces in Europe. George Dewey was the admiral who defeated the Spanish in the Philippines during the Spanish-American War. Eisenhower and MacArthur were commanders during World War II.

2.   **(D)**   In response to a perceived insult to the U.S. flag and in order to hasten the downfall of Mexican leader Victoriano Huerta, Wilson ordered U.S. forces to occupy the port of Vera Cruz where the original incident had occurred. Anxious to be rid of Huerta, Wilson would probably not have considered a diplomatic protest (E) strong enough, though he did respond with such protests to German U-boat activities in the First World War. Wilson ordered Pershing into Mexico (A) two years later after Mexican bandit Pancho Villa had raided across the border into the United States. Wilson had never granted diplomatic recognition to Huerta's regime (B), and U.S. troops have not occupied Mexico City (C) since the end of the Mexican War in 1848.

3.   **(C)**   The German use of submarines against merchant and passenger ships was the most crucial factor in bringing the United States into the First World War. German violation of Belgian neutrality (B) helped bring Britain into the war, and British propaganda (A), which did play a role in securing U.S. involvement, made much of German atrocities in Belgium (D). The Zimmerman note, in which Germany suggested to Mexico a joint war against the United States, with promises of generous annexations by Mexico (E), was also a factor. However, torpedoing underarmed ships without giving warning and making provision for the safety of passengers and crew—which a submarine was incapable of doing in 1917—was seen as akin to piracy.

4.   **(B)**   While the Treaty of Versailles did forge an independent though short-lived, Polish nation (A), restore Alsace-Lorraine to France (C), create many nations in the Balkans according to the principle of self-determination (E), and create the League of Nations (D) (albeit without the participation of the United States), Wilson's Fourteen Points did not achieve independence for any Middle Eastern nations, let alone adjust national boundaries. Borders were readjusted and territories changed hands, but future Middle Eastern nations would remain part of European colonial empires until after World War II.

5.   **(C)**   The First World War was the single most important event in bringing the transition of the United States from a net international debtor nation to an international creditor, as European nations involved in the war liquidated their investments in the U.S. and then borrowed large sums that they were subse-

quently unable and/or unwilling to repay.

6.   **(B)**   In January 1918, Woodrow Wilson proposed Fourteen Points which enunciated his goals for the peace that would follow World War I. These were idealistic goals based on notions of open diplomacy, the elimination of secret treaties, self-determination, arms reduction, open trade, and a League of Nations to serve as an international forum to prevent future wars. The thrust of the Fourteen Points emphasized fairness and openness in international relationships. By November 1918, the Germans faced military and political collapse, but they approached an armistice with the Allies convinced that the postwar treaty would be a fair one based upon Wilson's Fourteen Points. They reasoned that since the United States had turned the tide and saved France and Britain from almost certain defeat, the United States would dominate the peace negotiations. Unfortunately, they reasoned incorrectly and the Treaty of Versailles reflected British and French desires for vengeance more than it reflected the Wilsonian principles elucidated in his Fourteen Points.

7.   **(E)**   When Woodrow Wilson left Washington for the Paris Peace Conference, he had already taken steps to insure Senate opposition to whatever treaty emerged from the negotiations. The Senate was dominated by Republicans and Wilson, a Democrat, neglected to ask any senators to accompany him to the negotiations. He also neglected to ask any Republicans to accompany him. These errors of omission guaranteed anger and resentment among Republicans in general and senators in particular. When the Treaty of Versailles was presented to the Senate, senators found plenty of grist to grind in opposing the treaty. Contrary to Wilson's pre-negotiation pledges, the treaty was punitive and failed to come close to approaching the principles of humanitarianism and self-determination that Wilson had so nobly espoused before and during the Paris Peace Conference. One senator prophetically called the treaty a "blueprint for another war."

Wilson made matters worse by refusing to compromise with the Senate on provisions senators found objectionable. Instead, he lectured them like a teacher would lecture some errant schoolchildren. Then, he embarked on a cross-country speaking tour by train to try to go "over the heads" of the senators and sell the treaty directly to the American people. During this trip he engaged in name-calling and direct attacks on the intelligence of the Senate. To a body of people as proud as those in the Senate, this was both insulting and infuriating, and their reaction was predictable. In addition, on his return to Washington, Wilson suffered a stroke which incapacitated him, and he refused to negotiate further with treaty critics. Not surprisingly, when the treaty came up for ratification in November 1919, it was voted down. It came up for a vote again in March 1920, but Wilson still refused to compromise and the treaty was again voted down. The treaty was never ratified in its original form. The United States later signed a separate peace treaty with Germany.

8.   **(B)**   In 1917, with the war going badly, Germany resumed its campaign of unrestricted submarine warfare against all ships entering British coastal wa-

ters. Since many of these ships were American and the United States had previously denounced unrestricted submarine warfare, the Germans anticipated that the policy would bring the United States into the war. Their main hope of victory was in disrupting British shipping so badly that the British could be driven out of the war before the Americans could effectively mobilize.

The Germans were aware that relations between the United States and Mexico were very tense at this time. Someone in the German government decided to take advantage of this in a manner that would hopefully delay meaningful U.S. intervention in the war. German Foreign Secretary Arthur Zimmerman sent a note to the German ambassador to Mexico outlining a proposal. In return for a military alliance with Germany in which Mexico would attack the United States (if the U.S. entered World War I), the Mexicans would recover all the land they had previously lost to the Americans after the Mexican-American War once the U.S. was defeated.

The ploy backfired when the British intercepted the telegram in which the plan was outlined and released it to the United States. It was the combination of the release of this telegram with the resumption of unrestricted submarine warfare by the Germans that led to the U.S. entry into World War I.

9.   **(A)**   The rejection of the Versailles Treaty by the United States Senate signaled not only anger and frustration at Woodrow Wilson, but a generalized rejection of his whole effort to make America an international leader. Many Americans, examining the provisions of the Versailles Treaty, felt betrayed by the European "Allies" whom we had saved from German domination. Many accurately feared that the harsh, punitive provisions against Germany would inevitably lead to another European war and, we would again be called upon to save the Europeans from themselves. Many felt that Wilson had allowed the United States to be "used" by the Europeans for their own purposes, and these people were determined never to let it happen again.

The result was not only the rejection of the Versailles Treaty, but a rejection of internationalism and a determination to return America to George Washington's principles of "avoiding European entanglements." American leaders sought a return to isolationism in the belief that the Atlantic Ocean provided a big buffer between the United States and Europe and from now on it was better that the Europeans stay on their side of it and we would stay on ours. The refusal of the United States Senate to allow U.S. entry into the League of Nations, for fear that League membership would allow Europe to draw American forces into future wars, epitomized American feelings at this time.

The election of Warren G. Harding in 1920, with his emphasis on domestic politics and economic prosperity, reflected the desires of most Americans to take care of the "home front" and let Europe take care of itself. During the 1920s, when weak European leadership might have been positively swayed by active American involvement in world affairs, the United States withdrew, letting the Europeans flounder. This would pose tremendous difficulties for Franklin Roosevelt in the late 1930s when he realized that Hitler and Nazi expansionism would have to be dealt with by American military force. Yet he could not convince the powerful forces of isolationism that America needed to prepare for war until it was nearly too late.

10.   **(D)**   When Russia signed a separate peace with Germany in January 1918, removing Russia from the war and allowing the Germans to transfer all of their forces to the western front, the Allies felt betrayed and treated the Russians as if they were German allies. The Bolshevik government, responsible for the pullout, was ostracized by Western Europe and the United States. A blockade was imposed on Russian ports, and Allied troops (including Americans) were sent to Russia to aid efforts by conservative Russians to overthrow the Bolsheviks.

In 1919, the Bolsheviks announced the formation of the Communist International movement (Comintern) to spread the revolution worldwide. This spread fear throughout non-Communist industrial nations and led to suspicions of Communist subversion whenever domestic problems arose, especially when those problems involved workers, where Communist organizers were believed to be most active.

In the United States in 1919, many management-labor disputes held in check during the war now boiled to the surface. Workers who didn't feel free to challenge the government or industry while the nation was fighting a war, now felt justified in pushing to resolve their grievances. As a result, more than 4,000,000 workers walked off the job in a total of over 3,000 different strikes. Bombs were mailed to several business and political leaders.

While the vast majority of these walkouts were due to simple, but serious, labor complaints about wages and working conditions, there was just enough involvement by known leftists and Communists to confirm in the minds of many people that all the strikes were part of a massive plot by Communists and Anarchists to bring down the United States government and America's capitalist economic system. At the federal level, the Federal Bureau of Investigation, headed by J. Edgar Hoover, was created to crush the "insurrection." Together with state and local police agencies, thousands of suspected Communists were arrested and charged with sedition. Hundreds of foreign nationals living in the United States were deported, some on very flimsy evidence. So many innocent people were charged in alleged conspiracies, and so many alleged plots and predictions of terrorism proved unfounded, that eventually the leaders of the anti-Communist crackdowns lost their credibility. The crackdowns ceased but had a chilling effect on liberalism and leftist political thought in the United States for several years.

11.   **(D)**   In 1916 President Wilson sent American troops, under General John J. Pershing, into Mexico after Pancho Villa had raided New Mexico. This took place after several years of revolutionary turmoil in Mexico, including the assassination of Madera in 1913 and the arrest of the American sailors in 1914.

12.   **(A)**   Because of their ethnic loyalties, American sympathies were divided, but they generally supported the president's policy of neutrality. William Jennings Bryan resigned as secretary of state in 1915, because he believed that

the U.S. should forbid Americans from traveling on British and French ships. He also wanted Congress to forbid Americans from selling war materials to nations at war. After the sinking of the *Lusitania*, most Americans realized that the war affected American interests.

13. **(E)** Communism was not yet a major contributor to international tensions. Nationalism among minority groups created problems in almost every European nation. The struggle for colonies divided European nations into "haves" and "have nots." International rivalries pitted nations against one another as they sought additional territory, and the alliance systems resulted in a chain of military actions once the Archduke of Austria-Hungary was assassinated at Sarajevo, Serbia.

14. **(D)** Woodrow Wilson believed that the League of Nations was the key to maintaining peace. His unwillingness to compromise with Henry Cabot Lodge, however, led to the defeat of the treaty in the U.S. Senate and fatally weakened the League.

15. **(C)** When the United States withdrew diplomatically from Europe at the end of World War I, American demands that European nations repay money borrowed from American sources during the war was a major issue. European nations saw this demand as an example of "Uncle Scrooge," who collected from his allies for his own war contributions. There were no discussions of the nationalization of industries (A); copyright violations (B); or the rearmament of Germany (E). In general, most of America's allies in the war did not consider recognition of the Communist government of Russia (D) immediately, although recognition came from Britain and France in the 1920s and the United States in 1933. In fact, during his period from 1918 to 1922, when civil war broke out between monarchists and Bolsheviks, the United States, Britain, France, and Japan sent troops into Russia ostensibly to aid in restoring order but with the secondary goal of toppling the Bolshevik government.

16. **(C)** In response to Austria's ultimatum on Serbia, Russia mobilized. The existing systems of alliances made the Russian mobilization tantamount to a declaration of general war. Therefore, Germany responded by mobilizing and putting into motion the "Schlieffen Plan." This plan called for an immediate attack on France. The German General Staff believed it a vital necessity to get at France by the shortest possible route. This route lay through Belgium.

17. **(A)** Black Americans, both military and civilian, were better treated in Europe than in the United States. Generally, they were not subjected to the discrimination and segregation they experienced in the United States.

18. **(E)** Henry Cabot Lodge, United States Senator from Massachusetts from 1893 to 1924, was a conservative Republican. Lodge was a bitter foe of Woodrow Wilson's Fourteen Points; and as the chairman of the Senate Foreign Relations

Committee, he led the attack on the Treaty of Versailles and the League of Nations.

19. **(C)** [Thomas] Woodrow Wilson was born in Staunton, Virginia, the son of a Presbyterian minister. Upon graduation from Princeton, he studied law at the University of Virginia. Wilson opened a law office in Atlanta, but he soon abandoned the practice of law to study government and history at Johns Hopkins University where he earned his Ph.D. After receiving his degree, he taught jurisprudence and political economy. In 1902, he was elected president of Princeton University, the first nonclerical head of the institution. Wilson was elected governor of New Jersey in 1910. As governor, he established a record which brought him to the forefront of national politics. In 1912, he received the Democratic presidential nomination and won the election. Wilson was reelected in 1916. Upon the outbreak of World War I, he was determined to keep the United States neutral. After the United States entered the war, Wilson proposed his Fourteen Points as a basis for peace (January 1918).

20. **(E)** The Chicago White Sox team was accused of intentionally losing the 1919 World Series.

1912–1920
REVIEW

1. WOODROW WILSON AND THE NEW FREEDOM

The New President

Wilson was only the second Democrat (Cleveland was the first) elected president since the Civil War. He was born in Virginia in 1856, the son of a Presbyterian minister, and was reared and educated in the South. After earning a doctorate at Johns Hopkins University, he taught history and political science at Princeton, and in 1902 became president of that university. In 1910 he was elected governor of New Jersey as a reform or progressive Democrat.

The Cabinet

The key appointments were William Jennings Bryan as secretary of state and William Gibbs McAdoo as secretary of the treasury.

The Inaugural Address

Wilson called the Congress, now controlled by Democrats, into a special session beginning April 7, 1913 to consider three topics:

1) Reduction of the tariff
2) Reform of the national banking and currency laws
3) Improvements in the antitrust laws

On April 8 he appeared personally before Congress, the first president since John Adams to do so, to promote his program.

The Underwood-Simmons Tariff Act of 1913

Average rates were reduced to about 29 percent as compared with 37 to 40 percent under the previous Payne-Aldrich Tariff. A graduated income tax was included in the law to compensate for lost tariff revenue. It ranged from a tax of one percent on personal and corporate incomes over $4,000, a figure well above the annual income of the average worker, to seven percent on incomes over $500,000. The Sixteenth Amendment to the Constitution, ratified in February 1913, authorized the income tax.

The Federal Reserve Act of 1913

Following the Panic of 1907, it was generally agreed that there was a need for more stability in the banking industry and for a currency supply which would expand and contract to meet business needs. Three points of view on the subject developed:

1) Most Republicans backed the proposal of a commission headed by Senator Nelson W. Aldrich for a large central bank controlled by private banks.

2) Bryanite Democrats, pointing to the Wall Street influence exposed by the 1913 Pujo Committee investigation of the money trust, wanted a reserve system and currency owned and controlled by the government.

3) Conservative Democrats favored a decentralized system privately owned and controlled but free from Wall Street.

The bill which finally passed in December 1913 was a compromise measure. Provisions of the law were as follows:

1) The nation was divided into 12 regions with a Federal Reserve Bank in each region.

2) Commercial banks in the region owned the Federal Reserve Bank by purchasing stock equal to six percent of their capital and surplus, and elected the directors of the bank. National banks were required to join the system, and state banks were invited to join.

3) The Federal Reserve Banks held the gold reserves of their members.

4) Federal Reserve Banks loaned money to member banks by rediscounting their commercial and agricultural paper. That is, the money was loaned at interest less than the public paid to the member banks, and the notes of indebtedness of businesses and farmers to the member banks were held as collateral. This allowed the Federal Reserve to control interest rates by raising or lowering the discount rate.

5) The money loaned to the member banks was in the form of a new currency, Federal Reserve Notes, which was backed 60 percent by commercial paper and 40 percent by gold. This currency was designed to expand and contract with the volume of business activity and borrowing.

6) Checks on member banks were cleared through the Federal Reserve System.

7) The Federal Reserve System serviced the financial needs of the federal government.

8) The system was supervised and policy was set by a national Federal Reserve Board composed of the secretary of the Treasury, the comptroller of the currency, and five other members appointed by the president of the United States.

QUESTION

What was the purpose of the Federal Reserve Bank?

EXPLANATION

The Federal Reserve Bank was designed to promote economic stability by an independent organization that would regulate the money supply, expanding it or contracting it as needed. The Federal Reserve Bank was owned by commercial banks in the region and supervised by government officials. It controlled the money supply by lending money to member banks.

The Clayton Antitrust Act of 1914

This law supplemented and interpreted the Sherman Antitrust Act of 1890. The principal provisions were as follows:

1) Stock ownership by a corporation in a competing corporation was prohibited.

2) Interlocking directorates of competing corporations were prohibited. That is, the same persons could not manage competing corporations.

3) Price discrimination (charging less in some regions than in others to undercut the competition) and exclusive contracts which reduced competition were prohibited.

4) Officers of corporations could be held personally responsible for violations of antitrust laws.

5) Labor unions and agricultural organizations were not to be considered "combinations or conspiracies in restraint of trade" as defined by the Sherman Antitrust Act.

The Federal Trade Commission Act of 1914

The law prohibited all unfair trade practices without defining them and created a commission of five members appointed by the president. The commission was empowered to issue cease and desist orders to corporations to stop actions considered to be in restraint of trade, and to bring suit in the courts if the orders were not obeyed. Firms could also contest the orders in court. Under previous antitrust legislation, the government could act against corporations only by bringing suit.

Evaluation

The Underwood-Simmons Tariff, the Federal Reserve Act, and the Clayton Act were clearly in accord with the principles of the New Freedom, but the Federal Trade Commission reflected a move toward the kind of government regulation advocated by Roosevelt in his New Nationalism. Nonetheless, in 1914 and 1915 Wilson continued to oppose federal government action in such matters as loans to farmers, child labor regulation, and women's suffrage.

The Triumph of New Nationalism

Political Background

The Progressive party dissolved rapidly after the election of 1912. The Republicans made major gains in Congress and in the state governments in the 1914 elections, and their victory in 1916 seemed probable. Early in 1916 Wilson and the Democrats abandoned most of their limited government and states' rights positions in favor of a legislative program of broad economic and social reforms designed to win the support of the former Progressives for the Democratic party in the election of 1916. The urgency of their concern was increased by the fact that Theodore Roosevelt intended to seek the Republican nomination in 1916.

The Brandeis Appointment

Wilson's first action marking the adoption of the new program was the appointment on January 28, 1916 of Louis D. Brandeis, considered by many to be the principal advocate of social justice in the nation, as an associate justice of the Supreme Court.

The Federal Farm Loan Act of 1916

The law divided the country into 12 regions and established a Federal Land Bank in each region. Funded primarily with federal money, the banks made farm mortgage loans at reasonable interest rates. Wilson had threatened to veto similar legislation in 1914.

The Child Labor Act of 1916

This law, earlier opposed by Wilson, forbade shipment in interstate commerce of products whose production had involved the labor of children under 14 or 16, depending on the products. The legislation was especially significant because it was the first time that Congress regulated labor within a state using the interstate commerce power. The law was declared unconstitutional by the Supreme Court in 1918 on the grounds that it interfered with the powers of the states.

The Adamson Act of 1916

This law mandated an eight-hour day for workers on interstate railroads with time-and-a-half for overtime and a maximum of sixteen hours in a shift. Its passage was a major victory for railroad unions and averted a railroad strike in September 1916.

The Kerr-McGillicuddy Act of 1916

This law initiated a program of workmen's compensation for federal employees.

The Election of 1916

The Democrats

The minority party nationally in terms of voter registration, the Democrats nominated Wilson and adopted his platform calling for continued progressive reforms and neutrality in the European war. "He kept us out of war" became the principal campaign slogan of Democratic politicians.

The Republicans

The convention bypassed Theodore Roosevelt, who had decided not to run as a Progressive and had sought the Republican nomination. On the first ballot, the party chose Charles Evans Hughes, an associate justice of the Supreme Court and formerly a progressive Republican governor of New York. Hughes, an ineffective campaigner, avoided the neutrality issue because of divisions among the Republicans, and found it difficult to attack the progressive reforms of the Democrats. He emphasized what he considered the inefficiency of the Democrats and failed to find a popular issue.

The Election

Wilson won the election with 277 electoral votes and 9,129,000 popular votes, almost three million more than he received in 1912. Hughes received 254 electoral votes and 8,538,221 popular votes. The Democrats controlled Congress by a narrow margin. While Wilson's victory seemed close, the fact that he had increased his popular vote by almost 50 percent over the previous four years was remarkable. It appears that most of his additional votes came from people who had voted for the Progressive or Socialist tickets in 1912.

Social Issues in the First Wilson Administration

Blacks

In 1913 Treasury Secretary William G. McAdoo and Postmaster General Albert S. Burleson segregated workers in some parts of their departments with no objection from Wilson. Many Northern blacks and whites protested, especially black leader W. E. B. DuBois, who had supported Wilson in 1912. William Monroe Trotter, militant editor of the Boston *Guardian,* led a protest delegation to Washington and clashed verbally with the president. No further segregation in government agencies was initiated, but Wilson had gained a reputation for being inimical to civil rights.

Women

The movement for women's suffrage, led by the National American Woman Suffrage Association, was increasing in momentum at the time Wilson became president, and several states had granted the right to vote to women. Wilson opposed a federal woman suffrage amendment, maintaining that the franchise should be controlled by the states. Later he changed his view and supported the Nineteenth Amendment.

Immigration

Wilson opposed immigration restrictions which were proposed by labor unions and some reformers. He vetoed a literacy test for immigrants in 1915, but in 1917 Congress overrode a similar veto.

Drill 1: Woodrow Wilson and the New Freedom

1. Which of the following was passed into law during the presidency of Woodrow Wilson?

    (A) The Pure Food and Drug Act (B) A progressive income tax

    (C) A high protective tariff   (D) A national old-age pension

    (E) The Sherman Antitrust Act

2. The Owen-Glass Federal Reserve Act of 1913 provided which of the following?

    (A) A commission to oversee big business

    (B) An enlarged list of illegal business activities

    (C) A graduated tax on income

    (D) The popular election of U.S. senators

    (E) A central banking system for the United States

3. The achievements of Woodrow Wilson's "New Freedom" program included

    (A) creation of the Federal Reserve Board.

    (B) creation of the Federal Trade Commission.

    (C) the first federal income tax.

    (D) the Clayton Antitrust Act.

    (E) all of the above.

4. Woodrow Wilson's "New Freedom" and Theodore Roosevelt's "New Nationalism" were similar in that both

    (A) removed restrictions on the rights of women and minorities.

(B)   removed restrictions on the rights of unions to organize within the workplace.

(C)   expanded the rights of states to regulate business operations within state borders.

(D)   expanded the government's role in regulating businesses and business monopolies.

(E)   expanded the notion of individualism inherent in their laissez-faire economic policies.

5.   The income tax was successfully included as a part of what piece of Wilsonian legislation?

(A)   Underwood Tariff Act   (B)   Federal Reserve Act

(C)   Clayton Antitrust Act   (D)   Federal Trade Commission Act

(E)   Smith-Lever Act

2.   WILSON'S FOREIGN POLICY AND THE ROAD TO WAR

Wilson's Basic Premise: New Freedom Policy

Wilson promised a more moral foreign policy than that of his predecessors, denouncing imperialism and dollar diplomacy, and advocating the advancement of democratic capitalist governments throughout the world.

Conciliation Treaties

Secretary Bryan negotiated treaties with 29 nations under which they agreed to submit disputes to international commissions for conciliation, not arbitration. They also included provisions for a cooling-off period, usually one year, before the nations would resort to war. While the treaties probably had no practical effect, they illustrated the idealism of the administration.

Dollar Diplomacy

Wilson signaled his repudiation of Taft's dollar diplomacy by withdrawing American involvement from the six-power loan consortium of China.

Japan

In 1913 Wilson failed to prevent passage of a California law prohibiting land ownership by Japanese aliens. The Japanese government and people were furious, and war seemed possible. Relations were smoothed over, but the issue was unresolved. In 1915 American diplomatic pressure made Japan back off from its 21 demands on China, but in 1917 the Lansing-Ishii Agreement was signed wherein Japan recognized the Open Door in China but the United States recognized Japan's special interest in that nation.

The Caribbean

Like his predecessors, Wilson sought to protect the Panama Canal, which opened in 1914, by maintaining stability in the area. He also wanted to encourage diplomacy and economic growth in the underdeveloped nations of the region. In applying his policy, he became an interventionist as were Roosevelt and Taft.

In 1912 American marines had landed in Nicaragua to maintain order, and an American financial expert had taken control of the customs. The Wilson administration kept the marines in Nicaragua, and negotiated the Bryan-Chamorro Treaty of 1914 which gave the United States an option to build a canal through the country. In effect, Nicaragua became an American protectorate, although treaty provisions authorizing such action were not ratified by the Senate.

Claiming that political anarchy existed in Haiti, Wilson sent marines in 1915 and imposed a treaty making the country a protectorate, with American control of its finances and constabulary. The marines remained until 1934.

In 1916 Wilson sent marines to the Dominican Republic to stop a civil war and established a military government under an American naval commander.

Wilson feared in 1915 that Germany might annex Denmark and its Caribbean possession, the Danish West Indies or Virgin Islands. After extended negotiations, the United States purchased the islands from Denmark by treaty on August 4, 1916 for $25 million and took possession of them on March 31, 1917.

In 1913 Wilson refused to recognize the government of Mexican military dictator Victoriano Huerta, and offered unsuccessfully to mediate between Huerta and his Constitutionalist opponent, Venustiano Carranza. When the Huerta government arrested several American seamen in Tampico in April 1914, American forces occupied the port of Vera Cruz, an action condemned by both Mexican political factions. In July 1914 Huerta abdicated his power to Carranza, who was soon opposed by his former general Francisco "Pancho" Villa. Seeking American intervention as a means of undermining Carranza, Villa shot 16 Americans on a train in northern Mexico in January 1916 and burned the border town of Columbus, New Mexico, in March 1916, killing 17 people. Carranza reluctantly consented to Wilson's request that the United States be allowed to pursue and capture Villa in Mexico, but did not expect the force of about 6,000 army troops under the command of General John J. Pershing which crossed the Rio Grande on March 18. The force advanced over 300 miles into Mexico, failed to capture Villa, and became, in effect, an army of occupation. The Carranza government demanded an American withdrawal, and several clashes with Mexican troops occurred. War threatened, but in January 1917 Wilson removed the American forces.

Pan American Mediation (1914)

John Barrett, head of the Pan American Union (formerly Blaine's International Bureau of American Republics) called for multilateral mediation to bring about a solution to Mexico's internal problems and extract the United States from its military presence in Mexico. Although Wilson initially refused, Argentina, Brazil, and Chile did mediate among the Mexican factions and Wilson withdrew American troops. Barrett hoped to replace the unilateral Monroe Doctrine with a multilateral Pan American policy to promote collective responses and mediation to difficult hemispheric problems. Wilson, however, refused to share power with Latin America.

QUESTION

In what way did Wilson's New Freedom Policy differ from that of his predecessors?

EXPLANATION

Wilson believed that the U.S. should use its power not simply to promote its own interests, but to promote American democratic values. Foreign policy was tied to moral values. Wilson believed that through enacting such a policy, peace and justice could thrive throughout the world. This idealism is seen most clearly in Wilson's Fourteen Point Plan for Peace following World War I.

The Road to War in Europe

American Neutrality

When World War I broke out in Europe, Wilson issued a proclamation of American neutrality on August 4, 1914. Despite that action, the United States drifted toward closer ties with the Allies, especially Britain and France. While many Americans were sympathetic to the Central Powers, the majority, including Wilson, hoped for an Allied victory. Although British naval power effectively prevented American trade with the Central Powers and European neutrals, often in violation of international law, the United States limited itself to formal diplomatic protests. The value of American trade with the Central Powers fell from $169 million in 1914 to almost nothing in 1916, but trade with the Allies rose from $825 million to $3.2 billion during the same period. In addition, the British and French had borrowed about $3.25 billion from American sources by 1917. The United States had become a major supplier of Allied munitions, food, and raw materials.

The Submarine Crisis of 1915

The Germans began the use of submarines in 1915, announced a submarine blockade of the Allies on February 4, and began to attack unarmed British passenger ships in the Atlantic. Wilson insisted to the Germans that Americans had a right as neutrals to travel safely on such ships, and that international law required a warship to arrange for the safe removal of passengers before attacking such a ship. The sinking of the British liner *Lusitania* off the coast of Ireland on May 7, 1915 with the loss of 1,198 lives, including 128 Americans, brought strong protests from Wilson. Secretary of State Bryan, who believed Americans should stay off belligerent ships, resigned rather than insist on questionable neutral rights, and was replaced by Robert Lansing. Following the sinking of another liner, the *Arabic*, on August 19, the Germans gave the "*Arabic* pledge" to stop attacks on unarmed passenger vessels.

The Gore-McLemore Resolution

During the latter part of 1915 the British began to arm their merchant ships. Many Americans thought it in the interest of United States neutrality that Americans not travel on the vessels of belligerents. Early in 1916 the Gore-McLemore Resolution to prohibit American travel on armed ships or on ships carrying munitions was introduced in Congress, but it was defeated in both houses after intensive politicking by Wilson.

The Sussex Pledge

When the unarmed French channel steamer *Sussex* was torpedoed but not sunk on March 24, 1916 with seven Americans injured, Wilson threatened to sever relations unless Germany ceased all surprise submarine attacks on all shipping, whether belligerent or neutral, armed or unarmed. Germany acceded with the "*Sussex* pledge" at the beginning of May, but threatened to resume submarine warfare if the British did not stop their violations of international law.

The House-Grey Memorandum

Early in 1915 Wilson sent his friend and adviser, Colonel Edward M. House, on an unsuccessful visit to the capitals of the belligerent nations on both sides to offer American mediation in the war. Late in the year, House returned to London to propose that Wilson call a peace conference, and, if Germany refused to attend or was uncooperative at the conference, the United States would probably enter the war on the Allied side. An agreement to that effect, called the House-Grey Memorandum, was signed by the British foreign secretary, Sir Edward Gray, on February 22, 1916.

Preparedness

In November 1915 Wilson proposed a major increase in the army and the activation of the National Guard as a preparedness measure. Americans divided on the issue, with organizations like the National Security League proposing stronger military forces, and others, like the League to Enforce Peace, opposing. After opposition by Southern and Western anti-preparedness Democrats, Congress passed a modified National Defense Act in June 1916 which increased the army from about 90,000 to 220,000, and enlarged the National Guard under federal control. In August over $500 million were appropriated for naval construction. The additional costs were met by increased taxes on the wealthy.

The Election of 1916

Wilson took the leadership on the peace issue, charging that the Republicans were the war party and that the election of Charles Evans Hughes would probably result in war with Germany and Mexico. His position was popular with many Democrats and Progressives, and the slogan "He kept us out of war" became the principal theme of Democratic campaign materials, presumably contributing to his election victory.

Wilson's Final Peace Efforts (1916–1917)

On December 12, 1916 the Germans, confident of their strong position, proposed a peace conference, a step which Wilson previously had advocated. When Wilson asked both sides to state their expectations, the British seemed agreeable to reasonable negotiations, but the Germans were evasive and stated that they did not want Wilson at the conference. In an address to Congress on January 22, 1917, Wilson made his last offer to serve as a neutral mediator. He proposed a "peace without victory," based not on a "balance of power" but on a "community of power," alluding to his proposal of May 1916 for an "association of nations."

Unlimited Submarine Warfare

Germany announced on January 31, 1917 that it would sink all ships, belligerent or neutral, without warning in a large war zone off the coasts of the Allied nations in the eastern Atlantic and the Mediterranean. The Germans realized that the United States might declare war, but they believed that, after cutting the flow of supplies to the Allies, they could win the war before the Americans could send any sizable force to Europe. Wilson broke diplomatic relations with Germany on February 3. During February and March, several American merchant ships were sunk by submarines.

The Zimmerman Telegram

The British intercepted a secret message from the German foreign secretary, Arthur Zimmerman, to the German minister in Mexico, and turned it over to the United States on February 24, 1917. The Germans proposed that, in the event of a war between the United States and Germany, Mexico attack the United States. After the war, the "lost territories" of Texas, New Mexico, and Arizona would be returned to Mexico. In addition, Japan would be invited to join the alliance against the United States. When the telegram was released to the press on March 1, many Americans became convinced that war with Germany was necessary.

The Declaration of War

Wilson, on March 2, 1917, called Congress to a special session beginning April 2. When Congress convened, he requested a declaration of war against Germany. The declaration was passed by the Senate on April 4 by a vote of 82 to 6 and by the House on April 6 by a vote of 373 to 50, and signed by Wilson on April 6.

Wilson's Reasons

Wilson's decision to ask for a declaration of war seems to have been based primarily on four considerations. He believed that the Zimmerman telegram showed that the Germans were not trustworthy and would eventually go to war against the United States. He also felt that armed neutrality could not adequately protect American shipping. The democratic government established in Russia after the revolution in March 1917 also proved more acceptable as an ally than the Tsarist government. Finally, he was convinced that the United States could hasten the end of the war and insure for itself a major role in designing a lasting peace.

Drill 2: Wilson's Foreign Policy and the Road to War

1. All of the following contributed to American entrance into World War I EXCEPT

    (A) German submarine warfare.

    (B) cultural and economic ties with Great Britain.

    (C) the Zimmerman telegram.

    (D) the presidential election of 1916.

    (E) the February 1917 revolution in Russia.

2. Which of the following had the greatest effect in moving the United States toward participation in the First World War?

    (A) The German disregard of treaty obligations in violating Belgian neutrality

    (B) Germany's declaration of its intent to wage unrestricted submarine warfare

    (C) A German offer to reward Mexico with U.S. territory should it join Germany in a war against the United States

(D)   The beginning of the Russian Revolution

(E)   The rapidly deteriorating situation for the Allies

3.   In 1913 Woodrow Wilson withheld recognition of the Huerta government of Mexico for which of the following reasons?

(A)   Huerta did not really control the country.

(B)   Huerta was unwilling to carry out his country's obligations to other countries.

(C)   Wilson disapproved of Huerta's actions.

(D)   Pancho Villa had raided Columbus, New Mexico.

(E)   American sailors had been arrested at Tampico.

4.   In the "*Arabic* pledge" of 1916, Germany promised not to

(A)   aid Mexico in any war against the United States.

(B)   attempt to buy war materials in the United States.

(C)   use submarines for any purpose but reconnaissance.

(D)   attempt to break the British blockade.

(E)   sink passenger ships without warning.

5.   What was the major factor which brought the United States into WW I?

(A)   Unrestricted submarine warfare by the British against shipping in German waters

(B)   Terror bombing of British cities by German airplanes and zeppelins

(C)   Reports of war atrocities by the German army such as the mass murders of British and French prisoners of war and the executions of millions of German Jews by the Kaiser

(D)   The belief that the British and French would eventually lose a war of attrition against Germany and that the U.S. had a moral obligation to prevent that from happening

(E)   Unrestricted submarine warfare by the Germans against shipping in British waters

3. WORLD WAR I: THE MILITARY CAMPAIGN

Raising an Army

Despite the enlistment of many volunteers, it was apparent that a draft would be necessary. The Selective Service Act was passed on May 18, 1917 after bitter opposition in the House led by the speaker, "Champ" Clark. Only a compromise outlawing the sale of liquor in or near military camps secured passage. Originally including all males 21 to 30, the limits were later extended to 17 and 46. The first drawing of 500,000 names was made on July 20, 1917. By the end of the war, 24,231,021 men had been registered and 2,810,296 had been inducted. In addition, about two million men and women volunteered.

Women and Minorities in the Military

Some women served as clerks in the navy or in the Signal Corps of the army. Originally nurses were part of the Red Cross, but eventually some were taken into the army. About 400,000 black men were drafted or enlisted, despite the objections of Southern political leaders. They were kept in segregated units, usually with white officers, which were used as labor battalions or for other support activities. Some black units did see combat, and a few blacks became officers, but did not command white troops.

The War at Sea

In 1917 German submarines sank 6.5 million tons of Allied and American shipping, while only 2.7 million tons were built. German hopes for victory were based on the destruction of Allied supply lines. The American navy furnished destroyers to fight the submarines, and, after overcoming great resistance from the British navy, finally began the use of the convoy system in July 1917. Shipping losses fell from almost 900,000 tons in April 1917 to about 400,000 tons in December 1917, and remained below 200,000 tons per month after April 1918. The American navy transported over 900,000 American soldiers to France, while British transports carried over one million. Only two of the well-guarded troop transports were sunk. The navy had over 2,000 ships and over half a million men by the end of the war.

The American Expeditionary Force

The soldiers and marines sent to France under the command of Major General John J. Pershing were called the American Expeditionary Force, or the AEF. From a small initial force which arrived in France in June 1917, the AEF increased to over two million by November 1918. Pershing resisted efforts by European commanders to amalgamate the Americans with the French and British armies, insisting that he maintain a separate command. American casualties included 112,432 dead, about half of whom died of disease, and 230,024 wounded.

Major Military Engagements

The American force of about 14,500 which had arrived in France by September 1917 was assigned a quiet section of the line near Verdun. As numbers increased, the American role became more significant. When the Germans mounted a major drive toward Paris in the spring of 1918, the Americans experienced their first important engagements. In June they prevented the Germans from crossing the Marne at Chateau-Thierry and cleared the area of Belleau Wood. In July, eight American divisions aided French troops in attacking the German line between Rheims and Soissons. The American First Army, with over half a million men under Pershing's immediate command, was assembled in August 1918 and began a major offensive at St. Mihiel on the southern part of the front on September 12. Following the successful operation, Pershing began a drive against the German defenses between Verdun and Sedan, an action called the Meuse-Argonne offensive, and reached Sedan on November 7. During the same period, the English in the north and the French along the central front also broke through the German lines. The fighting ended with the armistice on November 11, 1918.

Mobilizing the Home Front

Industry

The Council of National Defense, comprised of six cabinet members and a seven-member advisory commission of business and labor leaders, was established in 1916 before American entry into the war to coordinate industrial mobilization, but it had little authority. In July 1917 the council created the War Industries Board to control raw materials, production, prices, and labor relations. The military forces refused to cooperate with the civilian agency in purchasing their supplies, and the domestic war effort seemed on the point of collapse in December 1917 when a Congressional investigation began. In 1918 Wilson took stronger action under his emergency war powers which were reinforced by the Overman Act of May 1918. In March 1918 Wilson appointed Wall Street broker Bernard M. Baruch to head the WIB, assisted by an advisory committee of 100 businessmen. The WIB allocated raw materials, standardized manufactured products, instituted strict production and purchasing controls, and paid high prices to businesses for their products. Even so, American industry was just beginning to produce heavy armaments when the war ended. Most heavy equipment and munitions used by the American troops in France were produced in Britain or France.

Food

The United States had to supply not only its own food needs but those of Britain, France, and some of the other Allies as well. The problem was compounded by bad weather in 1916 and 1917 which had an adverse effect on agriculture. The Lever Act of 1917 gave the president broad control over the production, price, and distribution of food and fuel. Herbert Hoover was appointed by Wilson to head a newly created Food Administration. Hoover fixed high prices to encourage the production of wheat, pork, and other products, and encouraged the conservation of food through such voluntary programs as "Wheatless Mondays" and "Meatless Tuesdays." Despite the bad harvests in 1916 and 1917, food exports by 1919 were almost triple those of the prewar years, and real farm income was up almost 30 percent.

Fuel

The Fuel Administration under Harry A. Garfield was established in August 1917. It was concerned primarily with coal production and conservation because coal was the predominant fuel of the time and was in short supply during the severe winter of 1917–1918. "Fuelless Mondays" in nonessential industries to conserve coal and "Gasless Sundays" for automobile owners to save gasoline were instituted. Coal production increased about 35 percent from 1914 to 1918.

Railroads

The American railroad system, which provided most of the inter-city transportation in the country, seemed near collapse in December 1917 because of the wartime demands and heavy snows which slowed service. Wilson created the United States Railroad Administration under William G. McAdoo, Secretary of the Treasury, to take over and operate all the railroads in the nation as one system. The government paid the owners rent for the use of their lines, spent over $500 million on improved tracks and equipment, and achieved its objective of an efficient railroad system.

Maritime Shipping

The United States Shipping Board was authorized by Congress in September 1916, and in April 1917 it created a subsidiary, the Emergency Fleet Corporation, to buy, build, lease, and operate merchant ships for the war effort. Edward N. Hurley became the director in July 1917, and the corporation constructed several large shipyards which were just beginning to produce vessels when the war ended. By seizing German and Dutch ships, and by the purchase and requisition of private vessels, the board had accumulated a large fleet by September 1918.

Labor

To prevent strikes and work stoppages in war industries, the War Labor Board was created in April 1918 under the joint chairmanship of former president William Howard Taft and attorney Frank P. Walsh with members from both industry and labor. In hearing labor disputes, the WLB in effect prohibited strikes, but it also encouraged higher wages, the eight-hour day, and unionization. Union membership doubled during the war from about 2.5 million to about 5 million.

War Finance and Taxation

The war is estimated to have cost about $33.5 billion by 1920, excluding such future costs as veterans' benefits and debt service. Of that amount at least $7 billion was loaned to the Allies, with most of the money actually spent in the United States for supplies. The government raised about $10.5 billion in taxes and borrowed the remaining $23 billion. Taxes were raised substantially in 1917, and again in 1918. The Revenue Act of 1918, which did not take effect until 1919, imposed a personal income tax of six percent on incomes to $4,000, and 12 percent on incomes above that amount. In addition, a graduated surtax went to a maximum of 65 percent on large incomes, for a total of 77 percent. Corporations paid an excess profits tax of 65 percent, and excise taxes were levied on luxury items. Much public, peer, and employer pressure was exerted on citizens to buy Liberty Bonds which covered a major part of the borrowing. An inflation of about 100 percent from 1915 to 1920 contributed substantially to the cost of the war.

The Committee on Public Information

The committee, headed by journalist George Creel, was formed by Wilson in April 1917. Creel established a successful system of voluntary censorship of the press, and organized about 150,000 paid and volunteer writers, lecturers, artists, and other professionals in a propaganda campaign to build support for the American cause as an idealistic crusade, and to portray the Germans as barbaric and bestial Huns. The CPI set up volunteer Liberty Leagues in every community, and urged their members and citizens at large to spy on their neighbors, especially those with foreign names, and to report any suspicious words or actions to the Justice Department.

War Hysteria

A number of volunteer organizations sprang up around the country to search for draft dodgers, enforce the sale of bonds, and report any opinion or conversation considered suspicious. Perhaps the largest such organization was the American Protective League with about 250,000 members, which claimed the approval of the Justice Department. Such groups publicly humiliated people accused of not buying war bonds and persecuted, beat, and sometimes killed people of German descent. As a result of the activities of the CPI and the vigilante groups, German language instruction and German music were banned in many areas, German measles became "liberty measles," pretzels were prohibited in some cities, and the like. The anti-German and anti-subversive war hysteria in the United States far exceeded similar public moods in Britain and France during the war.

The Espionage and Sedition Acts

The Espionage Act of 1917 provided for fines and imprisonment for persons who made false statements which aided the enemy, incited rebellion in the military, or obstructed recruitment or the draft. Printed matter advocating treason or insurrection could be excluded from the mails. The Sedition Act of May 1918 forbade any criticism of the government, flag, or uniform, even if there were no detrimental consequences, and expanded the mail exclusion. The laws sounded reasonable, but they were applied in ways which trampled on civil liberties. Eugene V. Debs, the perennial Socialist candidate for president, was given a ten-year prison sentence for a speech at his party's convention in which he was critical of American policy in entering the war and warned of the dangers of militarism. Movie producer Robert Goldstein released the movie *The Spirit of '76* about the Revolutionary War. It naturally showed the British fighting the Americans. Goldstein was fined $10,000 and sentenced to ten years in prison because the film depicted the British, who were now fighting on the same side as the United States, in an unfavorable light. The Espionage Act was upheld by the Supreme Court in the case of *Schenck v. United States* in 1919. The opinion, written by Justice Oliver Wendell Holmes, Jr., stated that Congress could limit free speech when the words represented a "clear and present danger," and that a person cannot cry "fire" in a crowded theater. The Sedition Act was similarly upheld in *Abrams v. United States* a few months later. Ultimately, 2,168 persons were prosecuted under the laws, and 1,055 were convicted, of whom only ten were charged with actual sabotage.

QUESTION

Why were the Espionage and Sedition Acts controversial?

EXPLANATION

These acts restricted speech that criticized the government or could potentially harm the war effort. The laws were applied in ways that many Americans felt violated the First Amendment, freedom of speech. When the laws were found constitutional by the U.S. Supreme Court, they argued that in wartime, critical speech represented "a clear and present danger" to the security of the U.S. In short, the conflict was one between First Amendment rights and national security, and at the time, national security was considered the more important of the two.

Wartime Social Trends

Women

With approximately 16 percent of the normal labor force in uniform and demand for goods at a peak, large numbers of women, mostly white, were hired by factories and other enterprises in jobs never before open to them. They were often resented and ridiculed by male workers. When the war ended, almost all returned to traditional "women's jobs" or to homemaking. Returning veterans replaced them in the labor market. Women continued to campaign for woman suffrage. In 1917 six states, including the large and influential states of New York, Ohio, Indiana, and Michigan, gave the right to vote to women. Wilson changed his position in 1918 to advocate woman suffrage as a war measure. In January 1918 the House of Representatives adopted a suffrage amendment to the constitution which was defeated later in the year by Southern forces in the Senate. The way was paved for the victory of the suffragists after the war.

Racial Minorities

The labor shortage opened industrial jobs to Mexican-Americans and to blacks. W. E. B. DuBois, the most prominent black leader of the time, supported the war effort in the hope that the war that would make the world safe for democracy would bring a better life for blacks in the United States. About half a million rural Southern blacks migrated to cities, mainly in the North and Midwest, to obtain employment in war and other industries, especially in steel and meatpacking. Some white Southerners, fearing the loss of labor when cotton prices were high, tried forcibly to prevent their departure. Some white Northerners, fearing job competition and encroachment on white neighborhoods, resented their arrival. In 1917 there were race riots in 26 cities in the North and South, with the worst in East St. Louis, Illinois. Despite the opposition and their concentration in entry-level positions, there is evidence that the blacks who migrated generally improved themselves economically.

Prohibition

Proponents of prohibition stressed the need for military personnel to be sober and the need to conserve grain for food, and depicted the hated Germans as disgusting beer drinkers. In December 1917 a constitutional amendment to prohibit the manufacture and sale of alcoholic beverages in the United States was passed by Congress and submitted to the states for ratification. While alcohol consumption was being attacked, cigarette consumption climbed from 26 billion in 1916 to 48 billion in 1918.

Drill 3: World War I: The Military Campaign

1. The primary function of the Food Administration during the First World War was to

    (A) keep farm prices high by limiting the amount of food produced on American farms.

    (B) insure an adequate supply of food for American needs by arranging for imports from America's British and French allies.

    (C) oversee the production and allocation of foodstuffs to assure adequate supplies for the army and the Allies.

    (D) monitor the purity and wholesomeness of all food items shipped to France to feed the American army there.

    (E) create and operate large-scale government-owned farms.

2.   The Eighteenth Amendment to the United States Constitution

    (A) prohibits the sale of alcoholic beverages.

    (B) recognizes women's right to vote.

    (C) limits the president to two terms.

    (D) establishes the direct election of United States senators.

    (E) establishes the federal income tax.

3.   "Industrial boards" which helped mobilize the country's war efforts during World War I were

    (A) instrumental in preventing corruption and labor dissension from crippling the mobilization campaign.

    (B) so dominated by greedy businessmen cashing in on the war that they were disbanded and replaced by the War Industries Board.

    (C) the key to an efficient war effort following the collapse of the War Industries Board.

    (D) ruled unconstitutional by the conservative Supreme Court and were forced to reorganize as unfunded private consulting groups.

    (E) not formed until so late in the war effort that they had little impact other than to streamline the process for the transfer of men and equipment from the United States to France.

4.   What World War I battle, in which the Americans were involved, turned the tide against Germany?

    (A) Belleau Wood   (B) Somme Offensive

    (C) Second Battle of the Marne   (D) Saint Mihiel Salient

    (E) Meuse-Argonne Offensive

5.   What new technological development used in World War I made the observance of traditional international law virtually impossible?

    (A) Airplane   (B) Machine gun

    (C) Submarine   (D) Steamship

    (E) Armored tank

4. PEACEMAKING, DOMESTIC PROBLEMS, AND THE ELECTION OF 1920

The Fourteen Points

From the time of the American entry into the war, Wilson had maintained that the war would make the world safe for democracy. He insisted that there should be peace without victory, meaning that the victors would not be vindictive toward the losers, so that a fair and stable international situation in the postwar world would insure lasting peace. In an address to Congress on January 8, 1918, he presented his specific peace plan in the form of the Fourteen Points. The first five points called for open rather than secret peace treaties, freedom of the seas, free trade, arms reduction, and a fair adjustment of colonial claims. The next eight points were concerned with the national aspirations of various European peoples and the adjustment of boundaries, as, for example, in the creation of an independent Poland. The fourteenth point, which he considered the most important and had espoused as early as 1916, called for a "general association of nations" to preserve the peace. The plan was disdained by the Allied leadership, but it had great appeal for many people on both sides of the conflict in Europe and America.

The Election of 1918

On October 25, 1918, a few days before the congressional elections, Wilson appealed to the voters to elect a Democratic Congress, saying that to do otherwise would be a repudiation of his leadership in European affairs. Republicans, who had loyally supported his war programs, were affronted. The voters, probably influenced more by domestic and local issues than by foreign policy, gave the Republicans a slim margin in both houses in the election. Wilson's statement had undermined his political support at home and his stature in the eyes of world leaders.

The Armistice

The German Chancellor, Prince Max of Baden, on October 3, 1918 asked Wilson to begin peace negotiations based on his concepts of a just peace and the Fourteen Points. Wilson insisted that the Germans must evacuate Belgium and France and form a civilian government. By early November, the Allied and American armies were advancing rapidly and Germany was on the verge of collapse. The German Emperor fled to the Netherlands and abdicated. Representatives of the new German republic signed the armistice on November 11, 1918 to be effective at 11:00 A.M. that day, and agreed to withdraw German forces to the Rhine and to surrender military equipment, including 150 submarines.

The Versailles or Paris Peace Conference

Wilson decided that he would lead the American delegation to the peace conference which opened in Paris on January 12, 1919. In doing so, he became the first president to leave the country during his term of office. The other members of the delegation were Secretary of State Robert Lansing, General Tasker Bliss, Colonel Edward M. House, and attorney Henry White. Wilson made a serious mistake in not appointing any leading Republicans to the commission and in not consulting the Republican leadership in the Senate about the negotiations. In Paris, Wilson joined Prime Minister David Lloyd George of Great Britain, Premier Georges Clemenceau of France, and Prime Minister Vittorio Orlando of Italy to form the "Big Four" which dominated the conference. In the negotiations, which continued until May 1919, Wilson found it necessary to make many compromises in forging the text of the treaty.

The Soviet Influence

Russia was the only major participant in the war which was not represented at the peace conference. Following the Communist Revolution of 1917, Russia had made a separate peace with Germany in March 1918. Wilson had resisted Allied plans to send major military forces to Russia to oust the Communists and bring Russia back into the war. An American force of about 5,000 was sent to Murmansk in the summer of 1918 in association with British and French troops to prevent the Germans from taking military supplies, and was soon active in assisting Russian anti-Bolsheviks. It remained in the area until June 1919. In July 1918 Wilson also sent about 10,000 soldiers to Siberia where they took over the operation of the railroads to assist a Czech army which was escaping from the Germans by crossing Russia. They were also to counterbalance a larger Japanese force in the area, and remained until April 1920. Wilson believed that the spread of communism was the greatest threat to peace and international order. His concern made him reluctant to dispute too much with the other leaders at the Versailles Conference, and more agreeable to compromise, because he believed it imperative that the democracies remain united in the face of the communist threat.

The Versailles Treaty

In the drafting of the treaty, Wilson achieved some of the goals in the Fourteen Points, compromised on others, and failed to secure freedom of the seas, free trade, reduction of armaments, or the return of Russia to the society of free nations. Some major decisions were as follows:

1) The League of Nations was formed, implementing the point which Wilson considered the most important. Article X of the Covenant, or charter, of the League called on all members to protect the "territorial integrity" and "political independence" of all other members.
2) Germany was held responsible for causing the war; required to agree to

pay the Allies for all civilian damage and veterans' costs, which eventually were calculated at $33 billion; the German army and navy were limited to tiny defensive forces; and the west bank of the Rhine was declared a military-free zone forever and occupied by the French for 15 years. These decisions were clearly contrary to the idea of peace without victory.

3) New nations of Yugoslavia, Austria, Hungary, Czechoslovakia, Poland, Lithuania, Latvia, Estonia, and Finland partially fulfilled the idea of self-determination for all nationalities, but the boundaries drawn at the conference left many people under the control of other nationalities.

4) German colonies were made mandates of the League of Nations and given in trusteeship to France, Japan, and Britain and its Dominions.

The German delegates were allowed to come to Versailles in May 1919 after the completion of the treaty document. They expected to negotiate on the basis of the draft, but were told to sign it "or else," probably meaning an economic boycott of Germany. They protested, but signed the Versailles Treaty on June 28, 1919.

The Senate and the Treaty

Following a protest by 39 senators in February 1919, Wilson obtained some changes in the League structure to exempt the Monroe Doctrine and domestic matters from League jurisdiction. Then, on July 26, 1919, he presented the treaty with the League within it to the Senate for ratification. Almost all of the 47 Democrats supported Wilson and the treaty, but the 49 Republicans were divided. About a dozen were "irreconcilables" who thought that the United States should not be a member of the League under any circumstances. The remainder included 25 "strong" and 12 "mild" reservationists who would accept the treaty with some changes. The main objection centered on Article X of the League Covenant, where the reservationists wanted it understood that the United States would not go to war to defend a League member without the approval of Congress. The leader of the reservationists was Henry Cabot Lodge of Massachusetts, the chairman of the Foreign Relations Committee. More senators than the two-thirds necessary for ratification favored the treaty either as written or with reservations.

Wilson and the Senate

On September 3, 1919 Wilson set out on a national speaking tour to appeal to the people to support the treaty and the League, and to influence their senators. He collapsed after a speech in Pueblo, Colorado, on September 25, and returned to Washington where he suffered a severe stroke on October 2 which paralyzed his left side. He was seriously ill for several months and never fully recovered. In a letter to the Senate Democrats on November 18, Wilson urged them to oppose the treaty with the Lodge reservations. In votes the next day, the treaty failed to get a two-thirds majority either with or without the reservations.

The Final Vote

Many people, including British and French leaders, urged Wilson to compromise with Lodge on reservations, including the issue of Article X. Wilson, instead, wrote an open letter to Democrats on January 8, 1920 urging them to make the election of a Democratic president in 1920 a "great and solemn referendum" on the treaty as written. Such partisanship only exacerbated the situation. Many historians think that Wilson's ill health impaired his judgment, and that he would have worked out a compromise had he not had the stroke. The Senate took up the treaty again in February 1920, and on March 19 it was again defeated both with and without the reservations. The United States officially ended the war with Germany by a resolution of Congress signed on July 2, 1921, and a separate peace treaty was ratified on July 25. The United States did not join the League.

Consequences of War

The impact of the war was far-reaching in the twentieth century. The United States emerged as the economic and political leader of the world—even if the American people were not prepared to accept the responsibility. The Russian revolution overthrew the tsar and inaugurated a Communist dictatorship. Britain, France, Austria, and Turkey went into various states of decline. Germany was devastated at the Versailles Peace Conference. Revenge and bitterness would contribute to the rise of Adolph Hitler and the Nazi movement. The European industrial nations would never recover from the cost of the war. Lingering economic problems would contribute to the Crash of 1929 and the Great Depression of the 1930s. The seeds of World War II had been planted.

QUESTION

How did the Fourteen Points for Peace reflect Wilson's "New Freedom" approach to foreign policy?

EXPLANATION

Wilson's stated goal upon entering the war was to "make the world safe for democracy." The war was not to conquer territory or gain power and influence in the world. Wilson believed that by imposing his peace treaty, he could create a political climate that would reduce the chances of future wars. The points included guaranteeing the peoples of Europe their own governments and territorial integrity. Also included was the creation of a "League of Nations" where nations could resolve disputes without going to war.

Domestic Issues at the End of the Wilson Administration

Demobilization

The AEF was brought home as quickly as possible in early 1919, and members of the armed forces were rapidly discharged. Congress provided for wounded veterans through a system of veteran's hospitals under the Veteran's Bureau, and funded relief, especially food supplies, for war-torn Europe. The wartime agencies for the control of the economy, such as the War Industries Board, were soon disbanded. During 1919 Congress considered various plans to nationalize the railroads or continue their public operation, but then passed the Esch-Cummings or Transportation Act of 1920 which returned them to private ownership and operation. It did extend Interstate Commerce Commission control over their rates and financial affairs, and allowed supervised pooling. The fleet of ships accumulated by the Shipping Board during the war was sold to private owners at attractive prices.

Final Reforms of the Progressive Era

In January 1919 the Eighteenth Amendment to the Constitution prohibiting the manufacture, sale, transportation, or importation of intoxicating liquors was ratified by the states, and it became effective in January 1920. The Nineteenth Amendment providing for women's suffrage, which had been defeated in the Senate in 1918, was approved by Congress in 1919. It was ratified by the states in time for the election of 1920.

The Postwar Economy

Despite fear of unemployment with the return of veterans to the labor force and the end of war purchases, the American economy boomed during 1919 and the first half of 1920. Consumers had money from high wages during the war, and the European demand for American food and manufactured products continued for some months after the war. The demand for goods resulted in a rapid inflation. Prices in 1919 were 77 percent above the prewar level, and in 1920 they were 105 percent above that level.

Strikes

The great increase in prices prompted 2,655 strikes in 1919 involving about four million workers or 20 percent of the labor force. Unions were encouraged by the gains they had made during the war and thought they had the support of public opinion. However, the Communist Revolution in Russia in 1917 soon inspired in many Americans, including government officials, a fear of violence and revolution by workers. While most of the strikes in early 1919 were successful, the tide of opinion gradually shifted against the workers.

Four major strikes received particular attention. In January 1919 all unions in Seattle declared a general strike in support of a strike for higher pay by shipyard workers. The action was widely condemned, the federal government sent marines, and the strike was soon abandoned.

In September 1919 Boston police struck for the right to unionize. Governor Calvin Coolidge called out the National Guard and stated that there was "no right to strike against the public safety by anybody, anywhere, anytime." The police were fired and a new force was recruited.

The American Federation of Labor attempted to organize the steel industry in 1919. When Judge Elbert H. Gary, the head of U.S. Steel, refused to negotiate, the workers struck in September. After much violence and the use of federal and state troops, the strike was broken by January 1920.

The United Mine Workers of America under John L. Lewis struck for shorter hours and higher wages on November 1, 1919. Attorney General A. Mitchell Palmer obtained injunctions and the union called off the strike. An arbitration board later awarded the miners a wage increase.

The Red Scare

Americans feared the spread of the Russian Communist Revolution to the United States, and many interpreted the widespread strikes of 1919 as Communist-inspired and the beginning of the revolution. Bombs sent through the mail to prominent government and business leaders in April 1919 seemed to confirm their fears, although the origin of the bombs has never been determined. The membership of the two Communist parties founded in the United States in 1919 was less than 100,000, but many Americans were sure that many workers, all foreign-born persons, radicals, and members of the International Workers of the World, a radical union in the western states, were Communists. The anti-German hysteria of the war years was transformed into the anti-Communist and anti-foreign hysteria of 1919 and 1920, and continued in various forms through the twenties.

The Palmer Raids

Attorney General A. Mitchell Palmer was one of the targets of the anonymous bombers in the spring of 1919. He was also an aspirant for the Democratic nomination for president in 1920, and he realized that many Americans saw the threat of a Communist revolution as a grave danger. In August 1919 he named J. Edgar Hoover to head a new Intelligence Division in the Justice Department to collect information about radicals. In November 1919 Palmer's agents arrested almost 700 persons, mostly anarchists, and deported 43 of them as undesirable aliens. On January 2, 1920 Justice Department agents, local police, and vigilantes in 33 cities arrested about 4,000 people accused of being Communists. It appears that many people caught in the sweep were neither Communists nor aliens. Eventually 556 were shown to be Communists and aliens, and were deported. Palmer then announced that huge Communist riots were planned for major cities on May Day, May 1, 1920. Police and troops were alerted, but the day passed with no radical activity. Palmer was discredited and the Red Scare subsided.

The Race Riots of 1919

During the war about half a million blacks had migrated from the South to industrial cities, mostly in the North and Midwest, to find employment. After the war white hostility, based on competition for lower-paid jobs and black encroachment into neighborhoods, led to race riots in 25 cities with hundreds killed or wounded and millions of dollars in property damage. Beginning in Longview, Texas, the riots spread, among other places, to Washington, D.C., and Chicago. The Chicago riot in July was the worst, lasting 13 days and leaving 38 dead, 520 wounded, and 1,000 families homeless. Fear of returning black veterans in the South lead to an increase of lynchings from 34 in 1917 to 60 in 1918 and 70 in 1919. Some of the victims were veterans still in uniform.

QUESTION

What impact did the Russian Revolution have on the American labor movement?

EXPLANATION

The Russian Communist Revolution raised fears of a similar uprising in America. This "Red Scare" led to the shift of public opinion against labor. Many believed that labor unions were working to start such a revolution in the United States. A series of strikes in 1919 exacerbated these fears, and the government intervened against the striking workers.

The Election of 1920

It seemed to many political observers in 1920 that the Republicans had an excellent chance of victory. The Wilson administration was blamed by many for the wartime civil liberties abuses, the League of Nations controversy, and the strikes and inflation of the postwar period.

The Republican Convention

The principal contenders for the nomination were General Leonard Wood, who had the support of the followers of the deceased Theodore Roosevelt, and Governor Frank O. Lowden of Illinois, the pick of many of the party bosses. When the convention seemed to deadlock, Henry Cabot Lodge, the convention chairman, and several other leaders arranged for the name of Senator Warren G. Harding of Ohio to be introduced as a dark-horse candidate. Harding was nominated on the tenth ballot, and Governor Calvin Coolidge of Massachusetts was chosen as the vice presidential nominee. The platform opposed the League, and promised low taxes, high tariffs, immigration restriction, and aid to farmers.

The Democratic Convention

The front-runners were William Gibbs McAdoo, the secretary of the Treasury and Wilson's son-in-law, and Attorney General A. Mitchell Palmer. Governor James Cox of Ohio was entered as a favorite son. Wilson expected the convention to deadlock, at which point his name would be introduced and he would be nominated for a third term by acclamation. His plan never materialized. McAdoo and Palmer contended for 37 ballots with neither receiving the two-thirds necessary for nomination. Palmer then released his delegates, most of whom turned to Cox. Cox was nominated on the forty-fourth ballot, and Franklin D. Roosevelt, an assistant secretary of the navy and distant cousin of Theodore, was selected as his running mate. The platform endorsed the League, but left the door open for reservations.

The Campaign

Harding's managers decided that he should speak as little as possible, but he did address visiting delegations from his front porch in Marion, Ohio. It was impossible to tell where he stood on the League issue, but he struck a responsive chord in many people when he urged that the nation should abandon heroics, nostrums, and experiment, and return to what he called normalcy. Cox and Roosevelt traveled extensively, speaking mostly in support of the League. Many found neither presidential candidate impressive.

The Election

Harding received 16,152,200 popular votes, 61 percent of the total, for 404 electoral votes. Cox received 9,147,353 popular votes for 127 electoral votes. Socialist candidate Eugene V. Debs, in federal prison in Atlanta for an Espionage Act conviction, received 919,799 votes. The Democrats carried only states in the solid South, and even there lost Tennessee. It appears that people voted Republican more as a repudiation of Wilson's domestic policies than as a referendum on the League. Wilson had alienated German-Americans, Irish-Americans, antiwar Progressives, civil libertarians, and Midwestern farmers, all groups which had given the Democrats considerable support in 1916.

Drill 4: Peacemaking, Domestic Problems, and the Election of 1920

1. All of the following were part of Woodrow Wilson's Fourteen Points EXCEPT

   (A) self-determination.

   (B) open diplomacy.

   (C) freedom of the seas.

   (D) a League of Nations.

   (E) a restoration of the balance of power.

2. Woodrow Wilson failed to obtain ratification of the Versailles Treaty because

   (A) a majority of the senators opposed the treaty and the League of Nations under any circumstances.

   (B) he was unwilling to publicly campaign for the treaty.

   (C) he was unwilling to make any compromises with Henry Cabot Lodge.

   (D) the Republican senators wanted a stronger League of Nations.

   (E) he made too many compromises with the Republican opposition.

3. The Red Scare of 1919 was influenced by all of the following EXCEPT

   (A) the October Russian Revolution.

   (B) labor strikes in several areas of the U.S.

   (C) terrorist bombings.

   (D) the continuation of World War I.

   (E) formation of the American Communist party.

4. American involvement in World War I brought about which of the following social and economic changes in the United States?

   (A) Extensive black migration to the North

   (B) Decline of trade unions

   (C) A loosening of controls on freedom of speech

   (D) Reduction of the number of women in the workplace

   (E) A strengthening of antitrust laws

5. In the negotiations leading to the Treaty of Versailles, Woodrow Wilson was willing to sacrifice other portions of his Fourteen Points in order to gain Allied approval of

(A) a ban on secret diplomacy.

(B) a strengthening of the Austrian Empire in order to restore the balance of power.

(C) a union of Germany and Austria in accordance with the right of self-determination of peoples.

(D) new rules of blockade that would provide more complete freedom of the seas.

(E) a League of Nations.

1912–1920
DRILLS

ANSWER KEY

Drill 1—Woodrow Wilson and the New Freedom

1. (B)   2. (E)   3. (E)   4. (D)   5. (A)

Drill 2—Wilson's Foreign Policy and the Road to War

1. (D)   2. (B)   3. (C)   4. (E)   5. (E)

Drill 3—World War I: The Military Campaign

1. (C)   2. (A)   3. (D)   4. (C)   5. (C)

Drill 4—Peacemaking, Domestic Problems, and the Election of 1920

1. (E)   2. (C)   3. (D)   4. (A)   5. (E)

GLOSSARY: 1912–1920

Arabic Pledge

The German pledge to stop submarine attacks on unarmed passenger vessels.

League of Nations

An international organization to promote peaceful resolution of international conflicts. It called on all members to protect the territorial integrity and the political independence of all other members.

Liberty Bonds

Bonds sold to the American public to fund the federal wartime debt.

Prohibition

A Constitutional amendment which prohibited the sale and manufacture of alcoholic beverages in the United States.

Sussex Pledge

The German pledge to cease submarine attacks on all shipping.

CHAPTER 11

1920–1929

THE ROARING TWENTIES AND ECONOMIC COLLAPSE

➤ Diagnostic Test

➤ 1920–1929 Review & Drills

➤ Glossary

1920-1929
DIAGNOSTIC TEST

1. (A) (B) (C) (D) (E)
2. (A) (B) (C) (D) (E)
3. (A) (B) (C) (D) (E)
4. (A) (B) (C) (D) (E)
5. (A) (B) (C) (D) (E)
6. (A) (B) (C) (D) (E)
7. (A) (B) (C) (D) (E)
8. (A) (B) (C) (D) (E)
9. (A) (B) (C) (D) (E)
10. (A) (B) (C) (D) (E)
11. (A) (B) (C) (D) (E)
12. (A) (B) (C) (D) (E)
13. (A) (B) (C) (D) (E)
14. (A) (B) (C) (D) (E)
15. (A) (B) (C) (D) (E)
16. (A) (B) (C) (D) (E)
17. (A) (B) (C) (D) (E)
18. (A) (B) (C) (D) (E)
19. (A) (B) (C) (D) (E)
20. (A) (B) (C) (D) (E)
21. (A) (B) (C) (D) (E)
22. (A) (B) (C) (D) (E)
23. (A) (B) (C) (D) (E)
24. (A) (B) (C) (D) (E)
25. (A) (B) (C) (D) (E)

1920–1929
DIAGNOSTIC TEST

This diagnostic test is designed to help you determine your strengths and weaknesses in your knowledge of the Roaring Twenties and economic collapse (1920–1929). Follow the directions and check your answers.

Study this chapter for the following tests:
AP U.S. History, CLEP General, CLEP United States History I,
GED, Praxis Specialty Area, SAT: United States History

---

25 Questions

DIRECTIONS: Choose the correct answer for each of the following questions. Fill in each answer on the answer sheet.

1. The National Origins Act of 1924

   (A) restricted immigrants from Northern and Western Europe.

   (B) removed all immigration restrictions.

   (C) discriminated against immigrants from Southern and Eastern Europe.

   (D) opened up immigration to Asians.

   (E) restricted disproportionately against immigrants from the Eastern Hemisphere.

2. Which of the following characterized the economy of the 1920s?

   (A) An emphasis on heavy industry, such as the production of locomotives

   (B) An emphasis on cash rather than credit purchases

   (C) A drop in the real wages of workers

   (D) A shift to the production of consumer goods

   (E) Increasing wealth for the agricultural sector

3. All of the following are true of Calvin Coolidge EXCEPT

   (A) he was quiet and usually said little.

   (B) he generally continued Harding's policies.

   (C) he favored balanced budgets and frugal government.

   • (D) he was heavily involved in the corruption of the Harding administration.

   (E) he opposed government intervention in the economy.

4. By "normalcy'' President Warren G. Harding meant not only peace after the recent war but also

   (A) a renewal of the Progressivist reform movement.

   (B) a return to an emphasis on domestic reform in place of Wilson's foreign adventures.

   • (C) an end to idealistic crusades and efforts at large-scale reform.

   (D) the establishment of new norms of international behavior.

   (E) U.S. membership in the newly formed League of Nations.

5. Warren G. Harding may best be characterized as

   (A) a personally corrupt and dishonest man.

   (B) unsuccessful in foreign policy but highly successful in domestic affairs.

   • (C) having made a number of misjudgments in the men he appointed and with whom he associated.

   (D) probably more dedicated to Progressive reform than either Wilson or Roosevelt had been.

   (E) quiet and taciturn.

6. Factors helping to promote mass production and marketing in the 1920s included all of the following EXCEPT

   • (A) the prevalence of large chains of retail stores.

   (B) more individualistic, less bureaucratic structures of management within large corporations.

   (C) the extension of consumer credit through installment buying.

   (D) the development of assembly-line techniques.

   (E) aggressive advertising in mass media.

7. Writers such as F. Scott Fitzgerald, Ernest Hemingway, and H.L. Mencken

   (A) viewed American entrance into World War I as a result of bankers' and munitions makers' desire for wartime profits.

   (B) argued for the continuing relevance of traditional values.

   (C) attempted to revive the Progressive movement in the 1920s.

   (D) warned that the prosperity of the 1920s would be undermined by overproduction.

   • (E) questioned the basic assumptions of middle-class society.

8. The "Lost Generation" refers to

   (A) those young adults whose lives and families were devastated by the Great Depression of the 1930s.

   (B) the millions of young men killed in the senseless trench warfare of World War I.

   • (C) young writers disillusioned by the materialism, decadence, and conformity dominating 1920s America.

   (D) the thousands of workers killed or injured in efforts to form and promote worker safety in turn-of-the-century America.

   (E) the generation of young Americans caught up in the turmoil of war protests and moral collapse during the 1960s.

9. In 1924, Congress wrote into law the National Origins Act which

   (A) established the federal census every ten years.

   • (B) established immigration quotas that restricted immigration from Southern and Eastern Europe.

   (C) required all public officeholders to be native-born citizens.

   (D) created an open border policy between Canada and the United States.

   (E) required all Americans traveling abroad to acquire a passport.

10. Place the following four events in the proper order in which they occurred.

    1. The rise of the flapper *1920s*

    2. The creation of the National Organization for Women *1960s*

    3. *Roe v. Wade* *1973*

    4. The creation of "Rosie the Riveter" *WWII*

    (A) 4-2-3-1   • (B) 1-4-2-3

    (C) 1-4-3-2   (D) 2-1-4-3

    (E) 1-2-3-4

11. Harding's administration, in particular, was known for its

    (A) conservationism.   •(B) corruption.

    (C) integrity.   (D) Progressivism.

    (E) internationalism.

12. The Scopes Trial had the effect of

    (A) eliminating state restrictions on the teaching of evolution in schools.

    •(B) highlighting the intolerance of religious fundamentalism and its conflict with contemporary science and secularism.

    (C) emphasizing the importance of the First Amendment when a person's ideas are not popular among the majority of Americans.

    (D) pointing out the necessity of preventing the state from interfering in religious matters.

    (E) reestablishing the predominance of fundamentalist religious ideas over secular scientific pronouncements which had dominated American thought throughout the early 1920s.

    Questions 13–17: Each of these questions requires you to identify the correct American author with his/her work.

    (A) Sinclair Lewis   (B) John Dos Passos

    (C) Charlotte Perkins Gilman   (D) F. Scott Fitzgerald

    (E) T.S. Eliot

13. "The Waste Land"   E

14. *Main Street*   A

15. *The Big Money*   B/C

16. "The Yellow Wallpaper"

17. *The Great Gatsby*   D

18. Teapot Dome refers to

    (A) the code name for the atomic bomb during World War II.

    (B) a school of artistic realism that flourished in the 1920s.

    •(C) a political scandal during the Harding administration.

    (D) the sale of stocks on margin in 1929.

(E)   the migrant farm community in John Steinbeck's *Grapes of Wrath.*

19.   In the 1920s women were affected by all of the following EXCEPT

   *(A)   the Equal Rights Amendment.   *1970s*

   (B)   the right to vote in national elections.

   (C)   increasing opportunities for employment.

   (D)   labor-saving devices for the home.

   (E)   a new freedom in social roles.

20.   The Johnson Act of 1924 favored immigrants from

   (A)   Asia.   (B)   Latin America.

   (C)   Eastern Europe.   (D)   Southern Europe.

   • (E)   Northern Europe.

21.   What was the significance of the Immigration Acts of 1921 and 1924?

   (A)   They limited immigration from Mexico for the first time.

   (B)   They created a category of "special immigrants," which included relatives of U.S. citizens living abroad.

   (C)   They made immigration requirements qualitative, rather than quantitative.

   • (D)   They set quotas on immigration from certain areas of Europe, Asia, and Africa.

   (E)   They based annual quotas on a flat one-sixth of one percent of the national population in 1920.

22.   Sinclair Lewis generally depicted small-town America as   *Something negative*

   (A)   an island of sincerity amid the cynicism of American life.

   (B)   the home of such traditional virtues as honesty, hard work, and wholesomeness.

   (C)   merely a smaller scale version of big-city life.

   • (D)   dreary, prejudiced, and vulgar.

   (E)   open and accepting but naive and easily taken in.

23.   All of the following were cardinal features of U.S. foreign policy during the Harding and Coolidge administrations EXCEPT

   (A)   a strong interventionist policy in Latin America.

   (B)   an aversion to involvement in European political conflicts.

(C) a concrete naval disarmament treaty.

(D) rigidity in demanding repayment of Allied war debts.

(E) the negotiation of independence for the oil-rich Middle Eastern nations.

24. Georgia O'Keeffe, Thomas Hart Benton, and Edward Hopper were all

• (A) American painters of the 1920s.

(B) pioneers in the field of a distinctly American music.

(C) known for their abstract paintings of flowers and other objects.

(D) pioneers in the building of skyscrapers.

(E) American literary figures of the first decade of the twentieth century.

25. When the United States Supreme Court failed to rule favorably on New Deal legislation, President Franklin Roosevelt

• (A) introduced a judiciary reorganization bill that would increase the number of Supreme Court justices.

(B) attempted to circumvent the Court by having cases involving New Deal legislation appealed to state supreme courts.

(C) called for the election of federal judges.

(D) used his emergency powers and appointed three new justices to the Supreme Court.

(E) threatened to have Congress reduce the justices' salaries.

1920–1929
DIAGNOSTIC TEST

ANSWER KEY

1.	(C)	6.	(B)	11.	(B)	16.	(C)	21.	(D)
2.	(D)	7.	(E)	12.	(B)	17.	(D)	22.	(D)
3.	(D)	8.	(C)	13.	(E)	18.	(C)	23.	(E)
4.	(C)	9.	(B)	14.	(A)	19.	(A)	24.	(A)
5.	(C)	10.	(B)	15.	(B)	20.	(E)	25.	(A)

DETAILED EXPLANATIONS
OF ANSWERS

1.　**(C)**　The National Origins Act limited immigration to two percent of the foreign-born residing in the United States in 1890. This effectively discriminated against Southern and Eastern Europeans and Asians.

2.　**(D)**　In the 1920s consumer goods such as cars and radios became the dominant elements in the economy. Installment purchasing became popular. Real wages increased, but farming did not participate in the prosperity.

3.　**(D)**　Coolidge had no involvement whatsoever with the corruption of the Harding administration, and in fact established a considerable reputation for honesty. He was quiet (A), and he did continue Harding's policies (B), balance the budget (C), and oppose government intervention in the economy (E).

4.　**(C)**　"Normalcy" meant an end to idealist crusades and reformist agitation, definitely not a renewal of the Progressivist reform movement (A), a return to domestic reform (B), the establishment of new norms of international behavior (D) as Woodrow Wilson had tried to do, or U.S. membership in the League of Nations (E).

5.　**(C)**　Harding made misjudgments about the men around him. He was definitely not a Progressive (D). His administration's greatest accomplishments were in the field of foreign policy (B). He was sociable and talkative (E), unlike his quiet and taciturn vice president Calvin Coolidge, and he was apparently a personally honest man (A).

6.　**(B)**　Actually structures of management by this time were becoming more, not less, bureaucratic, and *that* lent itself to mass methods of production and marketing. Other factors included the growth of chain retail stores (A), the extension of consumer credit (C), the development of assembly-line techniques (D), and aggressive advertising in the mass media (E).

7.　**(E)**　Fitzgerald, Hemingway, and Mencken in various ways reflected the disillusionment with traditional values that appeared in the wake of World War I. They had little interest in political and economic problems.

8.　**(C)**　Most Americans welcomed the economic growth and prosperity of the mid-1920s. However, some found the collapse of Progressivism, the subsequent dominance of materialistic consumerism, laissez-faire capitalism with its greed, corruption, and conspicuous consumption, as well as the emphasis on social conformity and dearth of spirituality to be morally repugnant. This repugnance and cynicism regarding America's social framework were captured most poignantly in the works of several young American authors. F. Scott Fitzgerald, H.L. Mencken, Ernest Hemingway, and Sinclair Lewis wrote stories of heroes as flawed as the villains they sought to conquer. Their works raised questions about traditional assumptions of right and wrong and often left those questions unanswered. They painted unsettling pictures of American society, frequently with a sharply critical, sometimes satirical portrayal of American hypocrisy and decadence.

Their unsettling works, with the inherent crying out at the loss of ideals, values, and purpose as well as the interwoven criticism of the current dominance of materialism, led critics and historians to label them the "Lost Generation." A whole generation of young writers faced with what they believed to be a spiritually lost America desperately needing to find new and meaningful goals and values. These writers' works attempted to point out the folly of 1920s America and rekindle the idealism and sense of deeper purpose they felt necessary for America to live up to its potential for all its citizens.

9.   **(B)**   The National Origins Act of 1924 was passed through Congress by a wave of anti-immigrant fervor sweeping the country in the 1920s. The act restricted total immigration to under 200,000 per year, with the groups arriving to be based on a quota system determined from the 1890 American census of ethnic groups. This measure was directed against immigrants from Southern and Eastern Europe, as well as Asia, and in support of immigrants from the British Isles. The federal census is established by the Constitution of 1788, and there is no law banning naturalized citizens from holding public office, save for the presidency. Canadian-American relations were not part of this act, nor were passport requirements.

10.   **(B)**   The "flapper" was the new liberated American woman of the 1920s who drew attention because of her clothing styles and public behavior such as smoking in public. "Rosie the Riveter" was the symbol of American women who entered the field of manual labor during World War II to support the war effort. The creation of NOW took place in 1966, while the Supreme Court's decision on abortion in *Roe v. Wade* was handed down in 1973.

11.   **(B)**   Warren Harding's administration was plagued by scandals. While Harding was never accused of being corrupt himself, he was in many ways similar to President Grant in that he surrounded himself with scoundrels who were more than willing to take advantage of his loyalties. He once remarked to the effect that it wasn't his enemies giving his presidency problems, it was his friends. Until Richard Nixon and the Watergate affair, Harding's administration had the ignoble honor, according to many historians, of being the most corrupt administration in American history. Most notable was the Teapot Dome scandal, which led to Harding's secretary of the interior, Albert Fall, spending a year in jail and resigning in disgrace. To that time, Fall's removal from office made him the highest ranking government official ever forced to resign because of criminal activity. Throughout it all, Harding remained personally popular until his un-

timely death in August 1923. The scandals then served to help Harding's successor, Calvin Coolidge, by allowing Coolidge to claim that he was cleaning up the corruption of Harding's administration.

Of the remaining choices, Harding was not strongly interested in conservationism (A) and did little to promote it during his administration. While Harding himself was seen as having integrity, the scandals plaguing his administration effectively removed any chance that people would believe his administration had any. Finally, his pro-business domestic policies and the movement toward isolationism during his presidency were opposite the internationalism (E) and Progressivism (D) of his predecessor, Woodrow Wilson.

12.   **(B)**   The Scopes "Monkey Trial" was instigated when in 1925 a Dayton, Tennessee biology teacher, John Scopes, challenged a state law prohibiting the teaching of evolution. His trial that summer became a national news story as the state brought in former Secretary of State William Jennings Bryan as an expert witness. The defense was led by well-known trial lawyer Clarence Darrow. The case took on a circus atmosphere with vendors and crowds of reporters milling about the courtroom and the surrounding environs.

Bryan's unswerving defense of the literal truth of the Bible was attacked as foolish and ignorant. He was made a laughingstock in the national press. Despite the fact that Scopes admitted breaking the law and was found guilty, defense attorneys claimed victory in that they had pointed out the intolerance of religious fundamentalism and showed it to be out of place in modern society.

Observers of the trial saw it to be a clash between reactionary social elements trying to resist the onslaught of changing values, life-styles, and technology by desperately clinging to antiquated belief systems, and modernists trying to replace traditional thought with newer secular ideas based on individualism and supported by scientific evidence. While the fundamentalists won the verdict, it was a Pyrrhic victory in that the trial painted them in such a bad light that they lost ground in their efforts to sway society from becoming increasingly secular.

13.   **(E)**   T.S. Eliot authored "The Waste Land," his epic poem on the vacuum of modern life in America, in 1922.

14.   **(A)**   Sinclair Lewis authored *Main Street,* the classic novel on the materialism invading small town America, in 1920.

15.   **(B)**   John Dos Passos completed his famous U.S.A. trilogy with the publication of *The Big Money* in 1931. Dos Passos focused on the increased class, ethnic, and racial biases in America.

16.   **(C)**   Charlotte Perkins Gilman was a late nineteenth century feminist author who compared the life of a mental patient with the confinement of a housewife in "The Yellow Wallpaper" in 1885.

17.   **(D)**   F. Scott Fitzgerald published *The Great Gatsby* in 1925 as a state-

ment of the loss of direction for America's post-World War I society.

18.   **(C)**   Next to the Watergate scandal, the Teapot Dome scandal of the Harding administration is the biggest political scandal in American history. Under the Harding presidency, the secretary of the treasury, Herbert Falls, secretly leased oil reserves to Harry Sinclair of the Sinclair Oil Company, who refined the petroleum for his company. Secretary Fall pleaded guilty to corruption charges and the lands were returned to the United States government. The code name for the atomic bomb project in World War II was the Manhattan Project. The Ashcan School is the school of artistic realism that flourished in the 1920s.

19.   **(A)**   Although the Woman's party advocated the Equal Rights Amendment it did not attain passage. The nineteenth Amendment gave women the right to vote in national elections for the first time in 1920. An increasing number of jobs were available for women in both industries and offices. Devices such as washing machines and vacuum cleaners made housework easier. And women such as the "flappers" rejected older social conventions in favor of such things as lipstick and bobbed hair.

20.   **(E)**   By establishing quotas based on a percentage of a national group living in the United States in 1890, the Johnson Act effectively favored Northern Europeans and discriminated against the "New Immigration."

21.   **(D)**   The Immigration Acts of 1921 and 1924 were a watershed in immigration law because they were the first to set limits on the immigration of certain groups including natives of Eastern Europe, Africa, Asia, and Oceania. Qualitative determinants (C), such as fitness of health and character, had previously been the determinants of immigration levels. Under the laws of 1921 and 1924, however, the overall quota of immigrants was to be 150,000 by 1927, and quotas for individual groups were to be set at the percentage of the 150,000 figure that each group constituted in the total population. Western Hemisphere immigrants, including Mexicans and Canadians (A), were, however, exempt from these quotas; thus the actual immigration figures of these years regularly exceeds 150,000. The McCarran-Walter Act of 1952 (E) simplified the quota formula so that the limit was one-sixth of one percent of the population, which usually amounted to about 160,000. In 1965, the United States began to admit nuclear relatives of citizens, returning resident aliens, certain former citizens, and families of Western Hemisphere countries as "special immigrants" (B), who were exempt from numerical ceilings.

22.   **(D)**   Sinclair Lewis depicted small-town America as dreary, prejudiced and vulgar, rather than in any of the more traditional and positive ways reflected in the other answer choices.

23.   **(E)**   Despite friction with Britain over oil rights, the Harding and Coolidge administrations apparently preferred Middle Eastern lands to remain in the hands

of European powers, and secured such rights via the negotiations of Secretary of State Charles Evans Hughes. The United States generally took an "isolationist" line toward European political conflicts, such as the Ruhr Crisis, during this time (B). But they also had to contend with Allied war debts (D), which they did not forgive, and were slow to restructure. In the Five-Power Naval Treaty of 1921–1922, the United States negotiated naval parity with Britain and superiority to Japan (C) based on a 5-5-3 ratio. The Coolidge years are also notorious for armed intervention and occupation of the Dominican Republic, Haiti, Mexico, and Nicaragua (A) at various times.

24.   **(A)**   Georgia O'Keeffe, Thomas Hart Benton, and Edward Hopper were all American painters of the 1920s (A). This was the age of jazz (B) and of skyscrapers (D). Georgia O'Keeffe was known for her abstract paintings of flowers and animal skulls against the background of the New Mexico desert (C).

25.   **(A)**   During his second term, Franklin Roosevelt decided to ask Congress to shift the balance on the Supreme Court to pro-New Deal justices. He thinly disguised his plan by making it part of a general reorganization of the judiciary. Roosevelt's plan provided for the retirement of Supreme Court justices at the age of 70 with full pay. If a justice chose not to retire, the president was to appoint an additional justice, up to a maximum of six, to ease the work load for the aged justices who remained on the court. Congress failed to pass Roosevelt's plan.

1920–1929
REVIEW

1. ECONOMIC ADVANCES AND SOCIAL TENSIONS

The Recession of 1920–1921

The United States experienced a severe recession from mid-1920 until the end of 1921. Europe returned to normal and reduced its purchases in America, and domestic demand for goods not available in wartime was filled. Prices fell, and unemployment exceeded 12 percent in 1921.

Prosperity and Industrial Productivity

The economy improved rapidly in 1922 and continued to be strong until 1929. Improved industrial efficiency which resulted in lower prices for goods was primarily responsible. Manufacturing output increased about 65 percent, and productivity, or output per hour of work, increased about 40 percent. The number of industrial workers actually decreased from 9 million to 8.8 million during the decade. The increased productivity resulted from improved machinery, which in turn came about for several reasons. Industry changed from steam to electric power, allowing the design of more intricate machines which replaced the work of human hands. By 1929, 70 percent of industrial power came from electricity. The moving assembly line, first introduced by Henry Ford in the automobile industry in 1913 and 1914, was widely adopted. Scientific management, exemplified by the time and motion studies pioneered by Frederick W. Taylor before the war, led to more efficient use of workers and lower labor costs. Larger firms began, for the first time, to fund major research and development activities to find new and improved products, reduce production costs, utilize by-products, and the like.

The Automobile

The principal driving force of the economy of the 1920s was the automobile. There were 8,131,522 motor vehicles registered in the United States in 1920, and 26,704,825 in 1929. Annual output of automobiles reached 3.6 million in 1923 and remained at about that level throughout the decade. By 1925 the price of a Ford Model T had been reduced to $290, less than three-months pay for an average worker. Ford plants produced 9,000 Model Ts per day, and Henry Ford cleared about $25,000 a day throughout the decade. Automobile manufacturing stimulated supporting industries, such as steel, rubber, and glass, as well as gasoline refining and highway construction. It was during the 1920s that the United States became a nation of paved roads. Mileage of paved roads increased from 387,000 miles in 1921, most of which was in urban areas, to 662,000 in 1929. Highway construction costs averaged over one billion dollars a year in the late 1920s, in part due to the Federal Highway Act of 1916 which started the federal highway system and gave matching funds to the states for construction. One estimate stated that the automobile industry directly or indirectly employed 3.7 million people in 1929.

Other Leading Industries

The electrical industry also expanded rapidly during the 1920s. The demand for power for industrial machinery as well as for business and some lighting increased dramatically, and a host of electrical appliances such as stoves, vacuum cleaners, refrigerators, toasters, and radios became available. About two-thirds of American homes had electricity by 1929, leaving only those in rural areas without it. Home and business construction also experienced a boom from 1922 until 1928. Other large industries which grew rapidly were chemicals and printing. The movie industry expanded rapidly, especially after the introduction of sound films, and employed about 325,000 people by 1930. New industries which began in the period were radio and commercial aviation.

Consumer Credit and Advertising

Unlike earlier boom periods which had involved large expenditures for capital investments such as railroads and factories, the prosperity of the 1920s depended heavily on the sale of consumer products. Purchases of "big ticket" items such as automobiles, refrigerators, and furniture were made possible by installment or time payment credit. The idea was not new, but the availability of consumer credit expanded tremendously during the 1920s. Consumer interest and demand was spurred by the great increase in professional advertising using newspapers, magazines, radio, billboards, and other media. By 1929 advertising expenditures reached $3.4 billion, more than was spent on education at all levels.

The Dominance of Big Business

There was a trend toward corporate consolidation during the 1920s. By 1929 the 200 largest corporations held 49 percent of the corporate wealth and received 43 percent of corporate income. The top five percent of the corporations in the nation received about 85 percent of the corporate income. Corporate profits and dividends increased about 65 percent during the decade. In most fields an oligopoly of two to four firms dominated, exemplified by the automobile industry where Ford, General Motors, and Chrysler produced 83 percent of the vehicles in 1929. Firms in many fields formed trade associations which represented their interests to the public and the government, and which claimed to stabilize each industry. Government regulatory agencies such as the Federal Trade Commission and the Interstate Commerce Commission were passive and generally controlled by persons from the business world. The public generally accepted the situation and viewed the businessmen with respect. Illustrating the attitudes of the time, *The Man Nobody Knows*, a book by advertising executive Bruce Barton published in 1925, became a best-seller. It described Jesus as the founder of modern business and his apostles as an exemplary business management team.

Banking and Finance

As with other corporations, there was a trend toward bank consolidation. Bank assets increased about 66 percent from 1919 to 1929. There was a growth in branch banking, and in 1929 the 3.2 percent of the banks with branch operations controlled 46 percent of the banking resources. Because corporations were raising much of their money through the sale of stocks and bonds, the demand for business loans declined. Commercial banks then put more of their funds into real estate loans, loans to brokers against stocks and bonds, and the purchase of stocks and bonds themselves. By doing so they made themselves vulnerable to economic disaster when the depression began in late 1929. Even during the prosperous 1920s, 5,714 banks failed, most of them in rural areas or in Florida. Banks in operation in 1929 numbered 25,568.

Labor

The National Association of Manufacturers and its state affiliates began a drive in 1920 to restore the "open shop" or nonunion workplace. The alternative used was "welfare capitalism" whereby the firm sought to provide job satisfaction so that the workers would not want a union. Company-sponsored pension and insurance plans, stock purchase plans, efforts to insure worker safety and comfort, social and sporting events, and company magazines were undertaken. Company unions, designed to give workers some voice with management under company control, were organized by 317 firms. The American Federation of Labor and other unions, which had prospered during World War I, found themselves on the defensive. Leaders, especially William Green, president of the American Federation of Labor after 1924, were conservative and nonaggressive. Union membership dropped about 20 percent from five million to about four million during the decade. The most violent labor confrontations occurred in the mining and southern textile industries. The United Mine Workers of America, headed by John L. Lewis, was involved in bitter strikes in Pennsylvania, West Virginia, Kentucky, and Illinois, but by 1929 had lost most of its power. The United Textile Workers failed to organize southern textile workers in a campaign from 1927 to 1929, but violent strikes occurred in Tennessee, North Carolina, and Virginia.

The Farm Problem

Farmers did not share in the prosperity of the twenties. Farm prices had been high during World War I because of European demand and government price fixing. By 1920 the European demand dropped considerably, and farm prices were determined by a free market. Farm income dropped from $10 billion annually in 1919 to about $4 billion in 1921, and then leveled off at about $7 billion a year from 1923 through 1929. During the same period, farm expenses rose with the cost of more sophisticated machinery and a greater use of chemical fertilizers.

QUESTION

What fueled the economic boom of the 1920s?

EXPLANATION

The sale of consumer goods was an important stimulus to the economy in the 1920s. Consumer purchases were financed by credit. Consumer credit expanded during the 1920s. In addition, consumer purchases were stimulated by advertising. Another factor in the growth of consumer purchases were efficient techniques in manufacturing that made products less expensive and more widely available.

American Society in the 1920s

Population

During the 1920s the population of the United States increased by 16.1 percent from 105,710,620 in 1920 to 122,775,046 in 1930, a slower percentage of growth than in previous decades. The birthrate was also lower than in former times, dropping from 27.7 per 100,000 in 1920 to 21.3 per 100,000 in 1930. About 88 percent of the people were white.

Urbanization

In 1920 for the first time a majority of Americans, 51 percent, lived in an urban place with a population of 2,500 or more. By 1930 the figure had increased to 56 percent. In terms of Standard Metropolitan Areas, which are defined as areas with central cities of at least 50,000 in population, 44 percent of the people lived in an SMA in 1920 and 50 percent in 1930. Farm residents dropped from 26 percent of the total population in 1920 to 21 percent in 1930. A new phenomenon of the 1920s was the tremendous growth of suburbs and satellite cities, which grew more rapidly than the central cities. Streetcars, commuter railroads, and automobiles contributed to the process, as well as the easy availability of financing for home construction. The suburbs had once been the domain of the wealthy, but the technology of the twenties opened them to working-class families.

The Standard of Living

Improved technology and urbanization led to a sharp rise in the standard of living. Urban living improved access to electricity, natural gas, telephones, and piped water. Two-thirds of American homes had electricity by 1929. The use of indoor plumbing, hot water, and central heating increased dramatically. Conveniences such as electric stoves, vacuum cleaners, refrigerators, washing machines, toasters, and irons made life less burdensome. Improved machinery produced better-fitting and more comfortable ready-made clothing and shoes. Diet improved as the consumption of fresh vegetables increased 45 percent and canned vegetables 35 percent. Sales of citrus fruit and canned fruit were also up. Correspondingly, per capita consumption of wheat, corn, and potatoes fell. Automobiles, radios, phonographs, and commercial entertainment added to the enjoyment of life. Yet enjoyment of the new standard of living was uneven. The one-third of the households which still did not have electricity in 1929 lacked access to many of the new products. For those who had access, the new standard of living required more money than had been necessary in former times. Despite heavy sales of appliances, by 1929 only 25 percent of American families had vacuum cleaners, and only 20 percent had electric toasters. The real income of workers increased about 11 percent during the decade, but others suffered a decline in real income, including farmers who still comprised about one-fourth of the population. It is estimated that the bottom 93 percent of the population had an average increase in real income of six percent during the 1920s. In 1929 about 12 million families, or 43 percent of the total, had annual incomes under $1,500, which was considered by many to be the poverty line. About 20 million families, or 72 percent, had incomes under $2,500, the family income deemed necessary for a decent standard of living with reasonable comforts.

The Sexual Revolution

Traditional American moral standards regarding premarital sex and marital fidelity were widely questioned for the first time during the 1920s. There was a popular misunderstanding by people who had not read his works that Sigmund Freud had advocated sexual promiscuity. Movies, novels, and magazine stories were more sexually explicit and sensational. The "flaming youth" of the "Jazz Age" emphasized sexual promiscuity and drinking, as well as new forms of dancing considered erotic by the older generation. The automobile, by giving people mobility and privacy, was generally considered to have contributed to sexual license. Journalists wrote about "flappers," young women who were independent, assertive, and promiscuous. Birth control, though illegal, was promoted by Margaret Sanger and others, and was widely accepted. The sexual revolution occurred mostly among some urban dwellers, middle-class people, and students, who were an economically select group at the time. Many continued to adhere to the old ways. Compared with the period from 1960 to the present, it was a relatively conservative time.

Women

Many feminists believed that the passage of the Nineteenth Amendment in 1920 providing woman suffrage would solve all problems for women. When it became apparent that women did not vote as a block, political leaders gave little additional attention to the special concerns of women. The sexual revolution brought some emancipation. Women adopted less bulky clothing with short skirts and bare arms and necks. They could smoke and socialize with men in public more freely than before. Birth control was more acceptable. Divorce laws were liberalized in many states at the insistence of women. In 1920 there was one divorce for every 7.5 marriages. By 1929 the ratio was 1 in 6. The number of employed women rose from 8.4 million in 1920 to 10.6 million in 1929, but the total work force increased in about the same proportion. Black and foreign-born women comprised 57 percent of the female work force, and domestic service was the largest job category. Most other women workers were in traditional female occupations such as secretarial and clerical work, retail sales, teaching, and nursing. Rates of pay were below those for men. Most women still pursued the traditional role of housewife and mother, and society accepted that as the norm.

Blacks

The migration of Southern rural blacks to the cities continued, with about 1.5 million moving during the 1920s. By 1930 about 20 percent of American blacks lived in the North, with the largest concentrations in New York, Chicago, and Philadelphia. While they were generally better off economically in the cities than they had been as tenant farmers, they generally held low-paying jobs and were confined to segregated areas of the cities. The Harlem section of New York City, with a black population of 73,000 in 1920 and 165,000 in 1930, was the largest black urban community, and became the center for black writers, musicians, and intellectuals. Blacks throughout the country developed jazz and blues as music forms which enjoyed widespread popularity. W. E. B. DuBois, the editor of *The Crisis*, continued to call for integration and to attack segregation despite his disappointment with the lack of progress after World War I. The National Association for the Advancement of Colored People was a more conservative but active voice for civil rights, and the National Urban League concentrated on employment and economic advancement. Lynchings continued in the South, and the anti-black activities of the Ku Klux Klan will be mentioned under Social Conflicts below.

Marcus Garvey and the UNIA

A native of Jamaica, Marcus Garvey founded the Universal Negro Improvement Association there in 1914 and moved to New York in 1916. He advocated black racial pride and separatism rather than integration and a return of blacks to Africa. Some of his ideas soon alienated the older black organizations. He developed a large following, especially among Southern blacks, but his claim of six million members in 1923 may be inflated. An advocate of black economic self-sufficiency, he urged his followers to buy only from blacks, and founded a chain of businesses, including grocery stores, restaurants, and laundries. In 1921 he proclaimed himself the provisional president of an African empire and sold stock in the Black Star Steamship Line which would take migrants to Africa. The line went bankrupt in 1923. Garvey was convicted and imprisoned for mail fraud in the sale of the line's stock, and then deported. His legacy was an emphasis on black pride and self-respect.

Mexicans and Puerto Ricans

Mexicans had long migrated to the southwestern part of the United States as agricultural laborers, but in the 1920s they began to settle in cities such as Los Angeles, San Antonio, and Denver. Like other immigrants, they held low-paying jobs and lived in poor neighborhoods, called barrios. The 1920s also saw the first large migration of Puerto Ricans to the mainland, mostly to New York City. There they were employed in manufacturing, in service industries such as restaurants, and in domestic work. They lived in barrios in Brooklyn and Manhattan.

Education

Free elementary education was available to most students in 1920, except for many black children. Growth of elementary schools in the 1920s reflected population growth and the addition of kindergartens. High school education became more available, and the number of public secondary schools doubled from 2.2 million in 1920 to 4.4 million in 1930. High school instruction shifted from an emphasis on college preparation to include vocational education, which was funded in part by the Smith-Hughes Act of 1917 which gave federal funds for agricultural and technical studies. There was also a substantial growth in enrollment in higher education from 600,000 in 1920 to 1.1 million in 1930.

Religion

Church and synagogue membership increased more rapidly than the population during the 1920s despite much religious tension and conflict. Most Protestants had been divided North and South since before the Civil War. By the 1920s, there was another major division between the modernists who accommodated their thinking with modern biblical criticism and evolution, and fundamentalists who stressed the literal truth of the Bible and creationism. There was also division on social issues such as support of labor. The only issue which united most Protestants, except Lutherans, was prohibition. The Roman Catholic Church and Jewish congregations were assimilating the large number of immigrants who had arrived prior to 1922. They also found themselves under attack from the Ku Klux Klan and the immigration restrictions.

Popular Culture

The trend whereby entertainment shifted from the home and small social groups to commercial profit-making activities had begun in the late nineteenth century and reached maturity in the 1920s. Spending for entertainment in 1929 was $4.3 billion. The movies attracted the most consumer interest and generated the most money. Movie attendance averaged 40 million a week in 1922 and 90 million a week in 1929. Introduction of sound with *The Jazz Singer* in 1927 generated even more interest. Stars like Douglas Fairbanks, Gloria Swanson, Rudolph Valentino, Clara Bow, and Charlie Chaplin were tremendously popular. Americans spent ten times more on movies than on all sports, the next attraction in popularity. It was called the golden age of major-league baseball, with an attendance increase of over 50 percent during the decade. Millions followed the exploits of George Herman "Babe" Ruth and other stars. Boxing was popular and made Jack Dempsey and others famous. College football began to attract attention with Knute Rockne coaching at Notre Dame and Harold "Red" Grange playing for the University of Illinois. When Grange signed with the Chicago Bears in 1926, professional football began to grow in popularity. Commercial radio began when station KDKA in Pittsburgh broadcasted the election results in November 1920. By 1929 over ten million families, over one-third of the number of families in the United States, had radios. National network broadcasting began when the National Broadcasting Company was organized in 1926, followed by the Columbia Broadcasting System in 1927. Radio was free entertainment, paid for by advertising. Despite the many new diversions, Americans continued to read, and millions of popular magazines were sold each week. Popular books of the period included the Tarzan series and Zane Grey's Westerns, as well as literary works, some of which are mentioned below.

Literary Trends

Many talented writers of the 1920s were disgusted with the hypocrisy and materialism of contemporary American society, and expressed their concern in their works. Often called the "Lost Generation," many of them, such as novelists Ernest Hemingway and F. Scott Fitzgerald and poets Ezra Pound and T.S. Eliot, moved to Europe. Typical authors and works include Ernest Hemingway's *The Sun Also Rises* (1926) and *A Farewell to Arms* (1929); Sinclair Lewis' *Babbitt* (1922), *Arrowsmith* (1925), and *Elmer Gantry* (1927); F. Scott Fitzgerald's *The Great Gatsby* (1925) and *Tender Is the Night* (1929); John Dos Passos' *Three Soldiers* (1921); and Thomas Wolfe's *Look Homeward, Angel* (1929). H. L. Mencken, a journalist who began publication of the *American Mercury* magazine in 1922, ceaselessly and vitriolicly attacked the "booboisie," as he called middle-class America, but his literary talent did not match that of the leaders of the period.

QUESTION

What values did the "Lost Generation" of writers represent?

EXPLANATION

The "Lost Generation" writers, including F. Scott Fitzgerald, Ernest Hemingway, Ezra Pound, T.S. Eliot, and Sinclair Lewis, wrote novels critical of mainstream America. They found middle-class life hypocritical and materialistic, devoid of meaning. They believed that society rewarded conformity, and this attitude led to bigotry. They often found the intellectual climate of the U.S. stifling, and some went to live in Europe to find a more fulfilling artistic and intellectual environment.

Social Conflicts

A Conflict of Values

The rapid technological changes represented by the automobile, the revolution in morals, and the rapid urbanization with many immigrants and blacks inhabiting the growing cities brought a strong reaction from white Protestant Americans of older stock who saw their traditional values gravely threatened. In many ways their concerns continued the emotions of wartime hysteria and the Red Scare. The traditionalists were largely residents of rural areas and small towns, and the clash of farm values with those of an industrial society of urban workers was evident. The conflict is often called a rural-urban conflict, and to a great extent it was, but some think the lines of division were not that neat. The traditionalist backlash against modern urban industrial society expressed itself primarily through intolerance.

The Ku Klux Klan

On Thanksgiving Day in 1915 the Knights of the Ku Klux Klan, modeled on the organization of the same name in the 1860s and 1870s, was founded near Atlanta by William J. Simmons. Its purpose was to intimidate blacks who were experiencing an apparent rise in status during World War I. The Klan remained small until 1920 when two advertising experts, Edward Y. Clark and Elizabeth Tyler, were hired by the leadership. Clark and Tyler used modern advertising to recruit members, charged a $10 initiation fee of which they received $2.50, and made additional money from the sale of regalia and emblems. By 1923 the Klan had about five million members throughout the nation. The largest concentrations of members were in the South, the Southwest, the Midwest, California, and Oregon. The use of white hoods, masks, and robes, and the secret ritual and jargon, seemed to appeal mostly to lower middle-class men in towns and small cities. The Klan stood for "100 percent pure Americanism" to preserve "native, white, Protestant supremacy." It opposed blacks and Catholics primarily. In addition, Jews, Mexicans, Orientals, and foreigners were often its targets. It also attacked bootleggers, drunkards, gamblers, and adulterers for violating moral standards. The Klan's methods of repression included cross burnings, tar and featherings, kidnappings, lynchings, and burnings. The Klan was not a political party, but it endorsed and opposed candidates, and exerted considerable control over elections and politicians in at least nine states. The Klan began to decline after 1925 when it was hit by scandals, especially the murder conviction of Indiana Grand Dragon David Stephenson. The main reason for its decline was the staunch opposition of courageous editors, politicians, and other public figures who exposed its lawlessness and terrorism in the face of great personal danger of violence. Many historians see the Klan as the American expression of fascism which was making headway in Italy, Germany, and other European nations during the twenties.

Immigration Restriction

There had been calls for immigration restriction since the late nineteenth century. Labor leaders believed that immigrants depressed wages and impeded unionization. Some Progressives believed that they created social problems. In June 1917 Congress, over Wilson's veto, had imposed a literacy test for immigrants and excluded many Asian nationalists. During World War I and the Red Scare, almost all immigrants were considered radicals and Communists, and the tradition was quickly picked up by the Klan. With bad economic conditions in postwar Europe, over 1.3 million came to the United States during the three years from 1919 through 1921. As in the period before the war, they were mostly from south and east Europe and mostly Catholics and Jews, the groups most despised by nativist Americans. In 1921 Congress quickly passed the Emergency Quota Act which limited immigration by nation to three percent of the number of foreign-born persons from that nation in the United States in 1910. In practice, the law admitted about as many as wanted to come from such nations as Britain, Ireland, and Germany, while severely restricting Italians, Greeks, Poles, and east European Jews. It became effective in 1922 and reduced the number of immigrants annually to about 40 percent of the 1921 total. Congress then passed the National Origins Act of 1924 which set the quotas at two percent of the number of foreign-born persons of that nationality in the United States in 1890, excluded all Orientals, and imposed an annual maximum of 164,000.

Immigration from Western Hemisphere nations, including Canada and Mexico, was not limited. The law further reduced the number of south and east Europeans, and cut the annual immigration to 20 percent of the 1921 figure. In 1927 the annual maximum was reduced to 150,000. The quotas were not fully calculated and implemented until 1929. Objections to the law were not aimed at the idea of restriction, but at the designation of certain nationalities and religious groups as undesirable. The law was resented by such groups as Italian- and Polish-Americans.

Prohibition

The Eighteenth Amendment which prohibited the manufacture, sale, or transportation of intoxicating liquors took effect in January 1920. It was implemented by the Volstead Act of October 1919 which defined intoxicating beverages as containing one-half of one percent alcohol by volume and imposed criminal penalties for violations. Many states had authorized the sale of light beer, believing that it was not covered by the amendment, but Anti-Saloon League lobbyists pushed through the Volstead Act. Many historians believe that prohibition of hard liquor might have been successful if light wine and beer had been allowed. As things turned out, the inexpensive light beverages were less available while expensive illegal hard liquor was readily available. Prohibition was enforceable only if many people in the society accepted and supported it. Enforcement was reasonably effective in some rural Southern and Midwestern states which had been dry before the amendment. In urban areas where both foreign-born and native citizens often believed that their liberty had been infringed upon, neither the public nor their elected officials were interested in enforcement. Speakeasies, supposedly secret bars operated by bootleggers, replaced the saloons. Smuggled liquor flowed across the boundaries and coastlines of the nation, and the manufacture of "bathtub gin" and similar beverages was undertaken by thousands. Organized crime, which previously had been involved mainly with prostitution and gambling, grew tremendously to meet the demand. Al Capone of Chicago was perhaps the most famous of the bootlegging gangsters. The automobile was used both to transport liquor and to take customers to speakeasies. Women, who had not gone to saloons in the pre-prohibition period, frequented speakeasies and began to drink in public. By the mid-1920s, the nation was badly divided on the prohibition issue. Support continued from rural areas and almost all Republican officeholders. The Democrats were divided between the urban Northerners who advocated repeal, and rural, especially Southern, Democrats who supported prohibition. Some people who originally favored prohibition changed their views because of the public hypocrisy and criminal activity which it caused.

Creationism and the Scopes Trial

Fundamentalist Protestants, under the leadership of William Jennings Bryan, began a campaign in 1921 to prohibit the teaching of evolution in the schools, and thus protect belief in the literal biblical account of creation. The idea was especially well-received in the South. In 1925 the Tennessee legislature passed a law which forbade any teacher in the state's schools or colleges to teach evolution. The American Civil Liberties Union found a young high school biology teacher, John Thomas Scopes, who was willing to bring about a test case by breaking the law. Scopes was tried in Dayton, Tennessee, in July 1925. Bryan came to assist the prosecution, and Chicago trial lawyer Clarence Darrow defended Scopes. The trial attracted national attention through newspaper and radio coverage. The judge refused to allow expert testimony, so the trial was a duel of words between Darrow and Bryan. As was expected, Scopes was convicted and fined $100. Bryan died of exhaustion a few days after the trial. Both sides claimed a moral victory. The anti-evolution crusaders continued their efforts and secured enactment of a statute in Mississippi in 1926. They failed after a bitter fight in North Carolina in 1927, and in several other states until Arkansas in 1928 passed an anti-evolution law by use of the initiative.

Sacco and Vanzetti

On April 15, 1920, two unidentified gunmen robbed a shoe factory and killed two men in South Braintree, Massachusetts. Nicola Sacco and Bartolomeo Vanzetti, Italian immigrants and admitted anarchists, were tried for the murders. Judge Webster Thayer clearly favored the prosecution, which based its case on the political radicalism of the defendants. After they were convicted and sentenced to death in July 1921, there was much protest in the United States and in Europe that they had not received a fair trial. After six years of delays, they were executed on August 23, 1927. A debate on their innocence and the possible perversion of American justice continued long afterward. The pair were ultimately vindicated 50 years later, in 1977, by Gov. Michael Dukakis.

Drill 1: Economic Advances and Social Tensions

1. The unbalanced distribution of income that characterized the 1920s led to which of the following consequences?

    (A) Inability of people to buy all the consumer goods that were being produced

    (B) A reduction in the percentage of national income going to the wealthiest five percent of the population

    (C) A major increase in wages relative to the increase of corporate profits

    (D) A decrease in stock purchases "on the margin"

    (E) An increase in the building of new houses and sales of automobiles after 1925

2. Which of the following words best describes the spirit of American intellectuals in the 1920s?

    (A) Alienation   (B) Complacency

    (C) Romanticism   (D) Patriotism

    (E) Pietism

3. Who among the following appealed to black pride and urged separation of the races?

    (A) Paul Robeson   (B) A. Philip Randolph

‹(C) Marcus Garvey   (D) Claude McKay

(E) Langston Hughes

4. *Babbit*, one of Sinclair Lewis' earlier novels, depicted the American businessman as

(A) a hard worker, willing to sacrifice social life for the sake of his buiness.

(B) a man of weak character hiding behind a facade of propriety.

(C) an unfeeling powerbroker, willing to do anything to get ahead.

(D) a heroic figure who embodied the true strength of the American character.

(E) None of the above.

5. American art of the 1920's, like that of Georgia O'Keefe and Edward Hopper was characterized by

(A) abstract expression of the hardships endured during World War I.

(B) stark objectivism embodying the American sense of individuality in cityscapes.

(C) realistic images of the American cultural landscape expresed with soft lines and colors.

(D) surreal, nightmarish images of turmoil and despair.

(E) strong, vivid colors.

6. H. L. Mencken, Ernest Hemingway, and F. Scott Fitzgerald were all

(A) classical musicians of the 1920s.

(B) American expatriates living in Paris during the 1920s.

(C) American painters of the 1920s.

‹(D) American writers of the 1920s.

(E) prominent actors in the silent movies of the 1920s.

7. The music most popular and most characteristic of American culture in the 1920s was

(A) an American modification of the traditional classical European style.

(B) an early form of rock 'n roll.

(C) based on old Negro spirituals.

(D) classically romantic.

‹(E) jazz.

8. Which of the following were prominent members of the Harlem Renaissance literary movement?

    I.   Countee Cullen

    II.   James Baldwin

    III. Langston Hughes

    IV.   Alain Locke

    V.   Zora Neale Hurston

    (A) I and III

    (B) I, II, and III

    (C) I, III, and IV

    (D) I, III, IV, and V

    (E) III and IV

9. All of the following were characteristic of the 1920s EXCEPT

    (A) voting rights for women.

    (B) prohibition and bootlegging.

    (C) consumerism and easy credit.

    (D) Progressivist reform and union growth.

    (E) Ku Klux Klan power and popularity.

10. The combination of European musical influences with African musical influences came together in 1890s New Orleans to form a new distinctly American musical style called

    (A) gospel.

    (B) jazz.

    (C) folk.

    (D) country.

    (E) blues.

2. GOVERNMENT AND POLITICS

The Harding Administration

Warren G. Harding

Harding was a handsome and amiable man of limited intellectual and organizational abilities. He had spent much of his life as the publisher of a newspaper in the small city of Marion, Ohio. He recognized his limitations, but hoped to be a much-loved president. He showed compassion by pardoning socialist Eugene V. Debs for his conviction under the Espionage Act and inviting him to dinner at the White House. He also persuaded U.S. Steel to give workers the eight-hour day. A convivial man, he liked to drink and play poker with his friends, and kept the White House stocked with bootleg liquor despite prohibition. He was accused of keeping a mistress, Nan Britton. His economic philosophy was conservative.

The Cabinet and Government Appointments

Harding appointed some outstanding persons to his cabinet, including Secretary of State Charles Evans Hughes, a former Supreme Court justice and presidential candidate; Secretary of the Treasury Andrew Mellon, a Pittsburgh aluminum and banking magnate and reportedly the richest man in America; and Secretary of Commerce Herbert Hoover, a dynamic multimillionaire mine owner and famous for wartime relief efforts. Less impressive was his appointment of his cronies Albert B. Fall as secretary of the interior and Harry M. Daugherty as attorney general. Other cronies, some dishonest, were appointed to other government posts.

Tax Reduction

Mellon believed in low taxes and government economy to free the rich from "oppressive" taxes and thus encourage investment. The farm bloc of Midwestern Republicans and Southern Democrats in Congress prevented cuts in the higher tax brackets as great as Mellon recommended. The Revenue Acts of 1921 and 1924 cut the maximum tax rates to 50 percent and then to 40 percent. Taxes in lower brackets were also reduced, but inheritance and corporate income taxes were retained. Despite the cuts, Mellon was able to reduce the federal debt by an average of $500 million a year.

The Fordney-McCumber Tariff

Mellon sought substantial increases in the tariffs, but again there was a compromise with the farm bloc. The Fordney-McCumber Tariff of September 1922 imposed high rates on farm products and protected such infant industries as rayon, china, toys, and chemicals. Most other items received moderate protection, and a few items including farm equipment were duty-free. The president could raise or lower rates to a limit of 50 percent on recommendation of the Tariff Commission. The average rate was about 33 percent, compared with about 26 percent under the previous tariff.

The Budget

As a result of the Budget and Accounting Act of 1921, the federal government had a unified budget for the first time. The law also provided for a director of the budget to assist in its preparation, and a comptroller general to audit government accounts.

The Harding Scandals

Harding apparently was completely honest, but several of his friends whom he appointed to office became involved in major financial scandals. Most of the information about the scandals did not become public knowledge until after Harding's death.

The "Teapot Dome" Scandal began when Secretary of the Interior Albert B. Fall in 1921 secured the transfer of several naval oil reserves to his jurisdiction. In 1922 he secretly leased reserves at Teapot Dome in Wyoming to Harry F. Sinclair of Monmouth Oil and at Elk Hills in California to Edward Doheny of Pan-American Petroleum. A Senate investigation later revealed that Sinclair had given Fall $305,000 in cash and bonds and a herd of cattle, while Doheny had given him a $100,000 unsecured loan. Sinclair and Doheny were acquitted in 1927 of charges of defrauding the government, but in 1929 Fall was convicted, fined, and imprisoned for bribery.

Another scandal involved Charles R. Forbes, appointed by Harding to head the new Veterans' Bureau. He seemed energetic and efficient in operating the new hospitals and services for veterans. It was later estimated that he had stolen or squandered about $250 million in bureau funds.

Scandal also tainted Attorney General Daugherty who, through his intimate friend Jesse Smith, took bribes from bootleggers, income tax evaders, and others in return for protection from prosecution. When the scandal began to come to light, Smith committed suicide in Daugherty's Washington apartment in May 1923. There was also evidence that Daugherty received money for using his influence in returning the American Metal Company, seized by the government during the war, to its German owners.

Depressed by the first news of the scandals, Harding left in June 1923 for an extended trip including a tour of Alaska. On his return to California, he died suddenly in San Francisco on August 2, 1923, apparently of a heart attack. Rumors of foul play or suicide persisted for years.

Coolidge Becomes President

Vice President Calvin Coolidge became president to complete Harding's term. As the scandals of the deceased president's administration came to light, Coolidge was able to avoid responsibility for them. He had a reputation for honesty, although he did not remove Daugherty from the cabinet until March 1924.

THE ELECTION OF 1924

Progressive Republican insurgents failed to capture the convention. Calvin Coolidge was nominated on the first ballot with Charles G. Dawes as his running mate. The platform endorsed business development, low taxes, and rigid economy in government. The party stood on its record of economic growth and prosperity since 1922.

The Democratic party had an opportunity to draw farmers and labor into a new progressive coalition. An attractive Democratic candidate would have had a good chance against the bland Coolidge and the Harding scandals. Instead, two wings of the party battled to exhaustion at the convention. The Eastern wing, led by Governor Alfred E. Smith of New York, wanted the platform to favor repeal of prohibition and to condemn the Ku Klux Klan. Southern and Western delegates, led by William G. McAdoo and William Jennings Bryan, narrowly defeated both proposals. Smith and McAdoo contested for 103 ballots with neither receiving the two-thirds necessary for nomination. John W. Davis, a conservative Wall Street lawyer, was finally chosen as a dark horse with Charles W. Bryan, brother of William Jennings, as the vice presidential candidate. The platform favored a lower tariff, but otherwise was similar to the Republican document.

Robert M. LaFollette, after failing in a bid for the Republican nomination, formed a new Progressive party with support from Midwest farm groups, socialists, and the American Federation of Labor. The platform attacked monopolies, and called for the nationalization of railroads, the direct election of the president, and other reforms.

Neither Coolidge nor Davis were active or effective campaigners. Republican publicity concentrated on attacking LaFollette as a Communist. LaFollette campaigned vigorously, but he lacked money and was disliked by many for his 1917 opposition to entrance into World War I.

Coolidge received 15,725,016 votes and 382 electoral votes, more than his two opponents combined. Davis received 8,385,586 votes and 136 electoral votes, while LaFollette had 4,822,856 votes and 13 electoral votes from his home state of Wisconsin.

QUESTION

Why did the Democrats fail to win the election of 1924, following a series of Republican scandals?

EXPLANATION

1924 presented a good opportunity for the Democrats to capture the White House. Calvin Coolidge was not a dynamic candidate, and the Republican party had been tainted by the scandals of the Harding administration. However, the two main Democratic factions, farm and labor, could not come to an agreement on a candidate or on major platform planks. The party nominated a little known candidate for president, John Davis. Its party platform did not differ significantly from the Republican platform, except in calling for a lower tariff.

The Coolidge Administration

Calvin Coolidge

Coolidge was a dour and taciturn man. Born in Vermont, his adult life and political career were spent in Massachusetts. "The business of the United States is business," he proclaimed, and "the man who builds a factory builds a temple." His philosophy of life was stated in the remark that "four-fifths of all our troubles in this world would disappear if only we would sit down and keep still." Liberal political commentator Walter Lippmann wrote that "Mr. Coolidge's genius for inactivity is developed to a very high point." He intentionally provided no presidential leadership.

The McNary-Haugen Bill

In 1921 George Peek and Hugh S. Johnson, farm machinery manufacturers in Illinois, developed a plan to raise prices for basic farm products. The government would buy and resell in the domestic market a commodity such as wheat at the world price plus the tariff. The surplus would be sold abroad at the world price, and the difference made up by an equalization fee on all farmers in proportion to the amount of the commodity they had sold. When farm conditions did not improve, the idea was incorporated in the McNary-Haugen Bill which passed Congress in 1927 and 1928, but was vetoed both times by Coolidge. The plan was a forerunner of the agricultural programs of the 1930s.

Muscle Shoals

During World War I the government had constructed a dam and two nitrate plants on the Tennessee River at Muscle Shoals, Alabama. In 1925 Senator George W. Norris of Nebraska led the defeat of a plan to lease the property to private business, but his proposal for government operation was vetoed by Coolidge in 1928. The facility was to become the nucleus of the Tennessee Valley Authority in the 1930s.

Veterans' Bonus

Legislation to give veterans of World War I 20-year endowment policies with values based on their length of service was passed over Coolidge's veto in 1924.

The Revenue Act of 1926

Mellon's tax policies were finally implemented by this law which reduced the basic income tax, cut the surtax to a maximum of 20 percent, abolished the gift tax, and cut the estate tax in half.

The Election of 1928

The Republicans

Coolidge did not seek another term, and the convention quickly nominated Herbert Hoover, the secretary of commerce, for president, and Charles Curtis as his running mate. The platform endorsed the policies of the Harding and Coolidge administrations.

The Democrats

Governor Alfred E. Smith of New York, a Catholic and an anti-prohibitionist, controlled most of the non-Southern delegations. Southerners supported his nomination with the understanding that the platform would not advocate repeal of prohibition. Senator Joseph T. Robinson of Arkansas, a Protestant and a prohibitionist, was the vice-presidential candidate. The platform differed little from the Republican, except in advocating lower tariffs.

The Campaign

Hoover asserted that Republican policies would end poverty in the country. Smith was also economically conservative, but he attacked prohibition and bigotry. He was met in the South by a massive campaign headed by Bishop James Cannon, Jr., of the Methodist Episcopal Church South, attacking him as a Catholic and a wet.

The Election

Hoover received 21,392,190 votes and 444 electoral votes, carrying all of the North except Massachusetts and Rhode Island, and seven states in the solid South. Smith had 15,016,443 votes for 87 electoral votes in eight states.

Foreign Policy in the Twenties

The Washington Conference

At the invitation of Secretary of State Charles Evans Hughes, representatives of the United States, Great Britain, France, Japan, Italy, China, the Netherlands, Belgium, and Portugal met in Washington in August 1921 to discuss naval limitations and Asian affairs. Three treaties resulted from the conference.

The Five Power Pact or Treaty, signed in February 1922, committed the United States, Britain, Japan, France, and Italy to end new construction of capital naval vessels, to scrap some ships, and to maintain a ratio of 5:5:3:1.67:1.67 for tonnage of capital or major ships in order of the nations listed. Hughes did not realize that the treaty gave Japan naval supremacy in the Pacific.

The Nine Power Pact or Treaty was signed by all of the participants at the conference. It upheld the Open Door in China by binding the nations to respect the sovereignty, independence, and integrity of China.

The Four Power Pact or Treaty bound the United States, Great Britain, Japan, and France to respect each other's possessions in the Pacific, and to confer in the event of disputes or aggression in the area.

War Debts, Reparations, and International Finance

The United States had loaned the Allies about $7 billion during World War I and about $3.25 billion in the postwar period, and insisted on full payment of the debts. Meanwhile, Germany was to pay reparations to the Allies, but by 1923 Germany was bankrupt. The Dawes Plan, proposed by American banker Charles G. Dawes, was accepted in 1924. Under it, American banks made loans of $2.5 billion to Germany by 1930. Germany paid reparations of over $2 billion to the Allies during the same period, and the Allies paid about $2.6 billion to the United States on their war debts. The whole cycle was based on loans from American banks.

The Kellogg-Briand Pact

A group of American citizens campaigned during the 1920s for a treaty which would outlaw war. In 1927 the French foreign minister, Aristide Briand, proposed such a treaty with the United States. Frank B. Kellogg, Coolidge's secretary of state, countered by proposing that other nations be invited to sign. At Paris, in August 1928, almost all major nations signed the treaty which renounced war as an instrument of national policy. It outlawed only aggression, not self-defense, and had no enforcement provisions.

Latin America

American investment in Latin America almost doubled during the 1920s to $5.4 billion, and relations with most nations in the region improved. Coolidge removed the marines from Nicaragua in 1925, but a revolution erupted and the marines were returned. Revolutionary General Augusto Sandino fought against the marines until they were replaced by an American-trained national guard under Anastasio Somoza. The Somoza family ruled Nicaragua until 1979 when they were overthrown by revolutionaries called the Sandinistas.

The Great Depression: The Crash

Herbert Hoover, an Iowa farm boy and an orphan, graduated from Stanford University with a degree in mining engineering. He became a multimillionaire from mining and other investments around the world. After serving as the director of the Food Administration under Wilson, he became secretary of commerce under Harding and Coolidge. He believed that an associative economic system with voluntary cooperation of business and government would enable the United States to abolish poverty through continued economic growth.

Stock prices increased throughout the decade. The boom in prices and volume of sales was especially active after 1925, and was intensive during 1928-29. The Dow-Jones Industrial Average for the year 1924 was 120; for the month of September 1929 it was 381; and for the year 1932 it dropped to 41. Stocks were selling for more than 16 times their earnings in 1929, well above the rule of thumb of ten times their earnings.

Careful investors, realizing that stocks were overpriced, began to sell to take their profits. During October 1929 prices declined as more stock was sold. On "Black Thursday," October 24, 1929, almost 13 million shares were traded, a large number for that time, and prices fell precipitously. Investment banks tried to boost the market by buying, but on October 29, "Black Tuesday," the market fell about 40 points with 16.5 million shares traded. A long decline followed until early 1933, and with it, depression.

Drill 2: Government and Politics

1. Which of the following was an EXCEPTION to the isolationism that generally characterized American foreign policy in the 1920s?

    (A) The Washington Armament Conference

    (B) The Stimson Non-Recognition Doctrine

    (C) American membership in the World Court

    (D) The Dawes and Young Commissions

    (E) The Fordney-McCumber Tariff

2. At the time of his death, Warren G. Harding was

    (A) at the height of his popularity.

    (B) in the midst of a well-publicized scandal.

    (C) still popular but gradually losing his hold on the people.

    (D) one of the most unpopular presidents in U.S. history.

    (E) in serious danger of impeachment.

3. As president, Calvin Coolidge generally

    (A) favored large government building projects.

    (B) urged Congress to raise taxes.

    (C) kept government spending low and encouraged private business.

    (D) took an active role in pushing legislation through Congress.

    (E) argued that the protective tariff should be lowered in order to provide a more healthy economic environment.

4. Which of the following best describes the administrations of Warren Harding and Calvin Coolidge?

    (A) "The trusts must be broken!"

    (B) "The only thing we have to fear is fear itself!"

    (C) "The business of government is business!"

    (D) "The taste of empire is in the mouths of the people!"

    (E) "The world must be made safe for democracy!"

5. Which of the following factors led to the crash of the stock market in 1929?

    (A) The mass purchase of underpriced stocks

    (B) The selling off of overpriced stocks by investors

    (C) The election of Herbert Hoover

    (D) The passage of the Revenue Act of 1926

    (E) The accumulation of debt from World War I loans

1920–1929
DRILLS

ANSWER KEY

Drill 1—Economic Advances and Social Tensions

1. (A)   2. (A)   3. (C)   4. (B)   5. (C)
6. (D)   7. (E)   8. (D)   9. (D)   10. (B)

Drill 2—Government and Politics

1. (A)   2. (A)   3. (C)   4. (C)   5. (B)

GLOSSARY: 1920–1929

Big Ticket Items
Large, expensive consumer items such as automobiles, refrigerators, and furniture.

Black Tuesday
October 29, 1929, the stock market fell about 40 points with 16.5 million shares traded.

Creationism
Belief in the biblical account of the origin of the universe and life on earth.

Flappers
Young women who were independent, assertive, and promiscuous.

Installment Credit
Purchasing expensive goods by making monthly payments.

Lost Generation
Young writers of the 1920s who were dissatisfied with the hypocrisy and materialism of contemporary American society.

Oligopoly
A situation when three or four firms dominate an industry.

Open Shop
A nonunion workplace.

Standard Metropolitan Area
An area with a central city of at least 50,000 in population.

Welfare Capitalism
A system where a firm provides job satisfaction so workers would not see the need for a union.

CHAPTER 12

1929–1941

THE GREAT DEPRESSION AND THE NEW DEAL

➤ Diagnostic Test
➤ 1929–1941 Review & Drills
➤ Glossary

1929-1941
DIAGNOSTIC TEST

1. (A) (B) (C) (D) (E)
2. (A) (B) (C) (D) (E)
3. (A) (B) (C) (D) (E)
4. (A) (B) (C) (D) (E)
5. (A) (B) (C) (D) (E)
6. (A) (B) (C) (D) (E)
7. (A) (B) (C) (D) (E)
8. (A) (B) (C) (D) (E)
9. (A) (B) (C) (D) (E)
10. (A) (B) (C) (D) (E)
11. (A) (B) (C) (D) (E)
12. (A) (B) (C) (D) (E)
13. (A) (B) (C) (D) (E)
14. (A) (B) (C) (D) (E)
15. (A) (B) (C) (D) (E)
16. (A) (B) (C) (D) (E)
17. (A) (B) (C) (D) (E)
18. (A) (B) (C) (D) (E)
19. (A) (B) (C) (D) (E)
20. (A) (B) (C) (D) (E)

1929–1941
DIAGNOSTIC TEST

This diagnostic test is designed to help you determine your strengths and weaknesses in your knowledge of the Great Depression and the New Deal (1929–1941). Follow the directions and check your answers.

Study this chapter for the following tests:
AP U.S. History, CLEP General, CLEP United States History I,
GED, Praxis Specialty Area, SAT: United States History

---

20 Questions

DIRECTIONS: Choose the correct answer for each of the following questions. Fill in each answer on the answer sheet.

1. Which of the following does NOT describe Franklin D. Roosevelt's New Deal or its consequences?

   (A) New Deal policies were often inconsistent.

   (B) The New Deal created a large federal bureaucracy without central control.

   (C) The New Deal set up public works projects to help the unemployed and provided direct relief to the unemployed.

   (D) The New Deal gave Americans greater economic security than they had known before.   *FDIC*

   - (E) The New Deal weakened the position of workers in relationship to employers.   *Wagner Act*

2. The Social Security program of 1935 provided which of the following?

   (A) Federally administered unemployment insurance

   - (B) Old age pensions paid for by taxes on employers and workers

   (C) Unemployment insurance administered by the federal government

   (D) Old age pensions paid for by taxes on employees

   (E) Federally administered assistance to the blind and disabled

   Medicaid – 1960's

505

3.   Which of the following gave people jobs building such things as schools, airports, and roads?

   (A)   Civilian Conservation Corps

 • (B)   Civil Works Administration

   (C)   Agricultural Adjustment Administration

   (D)   National Industrial Recovery Administration

   (E)   Tennessee Valley Authority

4.   The effect of the neutrality acts of 1935–1937 was to

   (A)   halt all trade between the U.S. and belligerent nations.

 • (B)   encourage aggressor nations because they knew in advance that the U.S. would not become involved.

   (C)   prevent United States involvement in European wars.

   (D)   encourage trade between the United States and belligerent nations.

   (E)   encourage peaceful settlement of problems between potentially belligerent nations.

purpose

5.   The "Bonus army" of 1932 called for which of the following?

   (A)   A pension for all citizens over 65

   (B)   Relief money for the unemployed

   (C)   The establishment of the Social Security system

 • (D)   A $1,000 payment for World War I veterans

   (E)   The creation of an unemployment insurance system

6.   Franklin Roosevelt's solution to the banking crisis included all of the following EXCEPT

   (A)   a "fireside chat" to assure the public of the soundness of banks.

   (B)   establishment of federally backed insurance on bank deposits. *F2x C*

 • (C)   government ownership of unsound banks. *Not This far*

   (D)   providing additional funds for banks from the RFC and the Federal Reserve.

   (E)   separating commercial banks from investment banks.

   Glass Steagan

7.   President Franklin Roosevelt's "court-packing plan" called for

 • (A)   the addition of up to six new justices if present justices over the age of 70 did not retire.

(B) the immediate and mandatory removal of all Supreme Court justices over the age of 70.

(C) the immediate and mandatory removal of all Supreme Court justices who voted against New Deal legislation.

(D) the addition of up to 15 new justices if present justices over the age of 70 did not retire.

(E) the mandatory retirement of justices over the age of 70 combined with the subsequent expansion of the Court to 15 members.

8. At the time the Second World War began in Europe, the general mood in the United States with regard to the war was

(A) determination not to become involved.

(B) eagerness to aid Great Britain by all means short of war.

(C) dissatisfaction with Roosevelt for failing to take the U.S. into the war immediately.

(D) mildly favorable to Germany.

(E) relief that the uncertainty of waiting was finally over.

9. All of the following statements about the Civilian Conservation Corps are true EXCEPT

(A) its members lived in camps, wore uniforms, and were under semi-military discipline.

(B) it engaged in such projects as preventing soil erosion and impounding lakes.

(C) it eventually came to employ over one-third of the American work force.

(D) it provided that some of the workers' pay should be sent home to their families.

(E) it was part of President Franklin D. Roosevelt's New Deal.

10. In personally taking over the task of setting the dollar amount the government would pay for gold, Franklin Roosevelt's announced purpose was to

(A) maintain the value of the dollar at a constant level.

(B) prevent inflation.

(C) prevent a run on the banks, which would be likely to deplete the nation's gold supply dangerously.

(D) manipulate the price of gold so as to raise prices.

(E)   revise the value of the dollar so as to force prices down to affordable levels in America's depressed economy.

11.   The underlying issue that led to the outbreak of war between the United States and Japan in 1941 was

(A)   Japanese aid to the Germans in their war against Britain.

(B)   U.S. desire to annex various Pacific islands held by Japan.

(C)   Japanese desire to annex the Aleutian Islands.

· (D)   Japanese desire to annex large portions of China.

(E)   American resentment of Japanese trading policies and trade surpluses.

12.   The Smoot-Hawley Tariffs and other protectionist trade measures had the long-term effect of

(A)   improving the competitiveness of U.S. industry in foreign markets.

(B)   improving U.S. economic strength in the long-term, although short-term economic performance was weakened.

(C)   making little difference in the economies of Europe and the U.S.

· (D)   sparking retaliatory measures from Europe which weakened both their economies and ours.

(E)   providing European leaders with the incentive to finally put their differences aside and form an economic confederation, which would eventually evolve into the European Common Market.

13.   The economic theory that relies upon large scale government intervention in the economy to stimulate investment and consumption is known as

(A)   monetarist.   · (B)   Keynesian economics.

(C)   supply-side economics.   (D)   classical economics.

(E)   laissez-faire.

14.   A major cause of the Great Depression was

· (A)   the stock market crash.

(B)   reliance upon a single metallic base for currency.

(C)   the inability of wages to keep pace with production increases.

(D)   the inability of production to keep pace with wage increases.

(E)   federal budget increases during the New Deal.

15. All of the following were outspoken critics of the New Deal EXCEPT

    (A) Francis Townsend.   (B) Huey Long.

    (C) Father Charles Coughlin.   (D) Frances Perkins.

    (E) Upton Sinclair.

16. The National Labor Relations Act (1935) aided the labor movement by

    (A) legalizing labor organizations.   *Started in 19ᵗʰ century*

    (B) establishing government mediation in labor disputes. *TR – 1902*

    (C) outlawing establishment of company unions.

    (D) creating the National Labor Relations Board.

    (E) guaranteeing the right of collective bargaining. *Wagner Act*

17. Who is the only president to have served more than two terms?

    (A) George Washington   (B) Andrew Jackson

    (C) Grover Cleveland   (D) Franklin D. Roosevelt *1932 – 1945*

    (E) Dwight D. Eisenhower

18. In 1937 the United States joined Great Britain and France by not intervening in a civil war in what European country?

    (A) Czechoslovakia   (B) Poland

    (C) Greece   (D) Spain

    (E) Hungary

19. Which of the following has NOT been identified as a cause of the Great Depression of the 1930s?

    (A) The high tariffs of the United States

    (B) Uneven distribution of income   *Yes – 1920s*

    (C) The increasing strength of organized labor

    (D) Excessive borrowing of money

    (E) Worldwide dislocation of trade during and after World War I

20. Which of the following did NOT follow the Montevideo Pact (1933) in which the United States agreed not to interfere in the internal or external affairs of its neighbors?

    (A) Cancellation of the Platt Amendment

    (B) Withdrawal of American troops from Nicaragua

    (C)   Removal of American troops from Haiti

    (D)   Ending control over customs houses of the Dominican Republic

    (E)   Giving up the American right to intervene in the affairs of Panama

1929–1941
DIAGNOSTIC TEST

ANSWER KEY

1.	(E)	5.	(D)	9.	(C)	13.	(B)	17.	(D)
2.	(B)	6.	(C)	10.	(D)	14.	(C)	18.	(D)
3.	(B)	7.	(A)	11.	(D)	15.	(D)	19.	(C)
4.	(B)	8.	(A)	12.	(D)	16.	(E)	20.	(B)

DETAILED EXPLANATIONS
OF ANSWERS

1.   **(E)**   The New Deal years strengthened the position of the worker through such legislation as the Wagner Act (1936), which gave unions a strong legal basis, and the Fair Labor Standards Act (1938), which established a minimum wage.

2.   **(B)**   The Social Security Act of 1935 set up an old age pension fund paid for by taxes on both employers and employees. It also set up state administered unemployment insurance and assistance to the blind and disabled.

3.   **(B)**   The Civil Works Administration, established in 1933, hired people to work on various government construction projects. The Civilian Conservation Corps hired young men to work in conservation and related projects. The AAA and NIRA attempted to address structural problems in agriculture and industry. The TVA administered the building and operation of dams in the Tennessee Valley.

4.   **(B)**   The neutrality acts encouraged such aggressor nations as Italy and Germany because they knew in advance that the U.S. would not help the other side.

5.   **(D)**   The "Bonus army" marched on Washington to demand early payment of a promised $1,000 bonus for WWI veterans. Social Security and unemployment insurance did not become national issues until the Franklin D. Roosevelt administration.

6.   **(C)**   While Roosevelt's solution to the banking crisis did increase federal regulation of the banking industry, it did not go so far as to actually own banks. Banks remained in private hands. The "fireside chat" was a radio broadcast where the president assured Americans that the banks were safe. Roosevelt also established the Federal Deposit Insurance Corporation, through the Glass-Steagall Act which also separated commercial banks from investment banks. He also authorized more funds from banks from the Federal Reserve.

7.   **(A)**   Roosevelt's court-packing plan called for the addition of up to six new justices if present justices over the age of 70 did not retire. While this would raise the *total* number of justices to 15, it is not to be confused with *adding* 15 new justices (D). Also, if those justices currently over 70 years of age did retire, no new justices would be added; and the Supreme Court would continue to have nine, not 15 (E), members. Retirement of the justices was to be voluntary rather than mandatory (B), and while the general purpose was to remove or decrease the

influence of justices who opposed the New Deal, political considerations, of course, prevented its being stated in those terms (C).

8.   **(A)**   At the beginning of the Second World War in Europe, Americans were generally determined not to become involved. The public was by no means relieved (E), nor desirous that Roosevelt should take the U.S. into the war (C), but at no time favorable to Germany (D). Desire to aid Britain came only later (B).

9.   **(C)**   The Civilian Conservation Corps never employed anywhere near one-third of the U.S. work force, but it was part of FDR's New Deal (E). Its workers did live in camps under semi-military discipline (A) and work on such projects as preventing soil erosion (B), and it did provide that some of the workers' pay be sent home to help their families.

10.   **(D)**   Roosevelt wanted to manipulate the dollar amount the government would pay for gold in order to raise prices, since it was believed this would relieve the depression. Since Roosevelt had already made it impossible for Americans to own gold, there could be no run on the banks by people wanting to get it (C). Maintaining the dollar's value at a constant level (A), preventing inflation (B), or lowering prices (E) were all just the opposite of what Roosevelt hoped to accomplish.

11.   **(D)**   The basic issue in the coming of war between the U.S. and Japan in 1941 was Japan's desire to annex large portions of China. The Japanese were not yet aiding the Germans in their war against Britain (A) and did not desire to annex the Aleutians (C)—although during the course of the war they did attack and occupy a couple of them. The U.S. did not desire the Japanese-held islands in the Pacific (B), although during the war it wound up taking a great many of them. American resentment of Japanese trading policies (E) characterizes more the last quarter of the twentieth century.

12.   **(D)**   The Smoot-Hawley Tariffs were enacted in 1930, a time when the world economy had already been badly weakened and was still collapsing. These protectionist measures protected a few powerful industries but at high cost. Europeans called the measures an "economic declaration of war" and responded with their own retaliatory tariffs. What few jobs the Smoot-Hawley Tariffs initially saved were far outnumbered by the other jobs lost when European tariffs took effect. Additionally, Europeans now could not sell their goods to Americans, because of the high tariffs, and thus could not earn the money they needed to buy American products. At a time when trading doors needed to be opened wide and international trade needed to be expanded, Smoot-Hawley had the effect of closing those doors and stifling what little was left of international trade between Europe and the United States.

13. **(B)** It is Keynesian economics that recognizes the government as one of three major forces acting upon an economy. (The other two forces are investment and consumption.) Keynesian economics was adopted by President Franklin Roosevelt in modest forms during the 1930s in an effort to stimulate the stagnated American economy. To one degree or another, American presidents followed Keynesian policies continuously until 1981, when President Reagan abandoned Keynesian policies for an economic policy labeled supply-side or monetarist. By focusing on inflation, supply-siders advocate limited government involvement in the economy with regard to the money supply. Both classical economics and laissez-faire doctrines establish minimal governmental economic activity. Thus, among the theories listed, it was only the policies of the British economist John Maynard Keynes who, in 1929, advanced the view of large-scale government deficit spending to artificially prime an economy.

14. **(C)** The problems that caused the Great Depression were structural in nature and stemmed primarily from the fact that wage increases simply did not keep pace with industrial output in the 1920s. As a result, consumption declined and businesses began to build up inventories. The result was increased layoffs of workers and further declines in consumer spending. Finally, the stock market crash of 1929 signaled the house of cards that was the American economy. The stock market crash was a symptom and not a cause of the Great Depression. The New Deal was erected in reaction to the Depression and the issuance of more money in the economy would only have helped if the inflated currency had found its way to the American consumer.

15. **(D)** Frances Perkins was Roosevelt's longtime secretary of labor and supporter of the New Deal programs. Francis Townsend attacked Roosevelt's First New Deal in 1935 for not being radical enough of a change and not helping the destitute and downtrodden. Huey Long and Upton Sinclair both attacked Roosevelt from the left for ignoring the American farmer and worker under the New Deal. Father Coughlin attacked Roosevelt from both the left and the right on his popular radio shows until Coughlin's severe anti-Semitism forced him from the airwaves.

16. **(E)** The National Labor Relations Act, or Wagner Act, of 1935 reaffirmed the right of collective bargaining which had first appeared in Section 7a of the National Industrial Recovery Act of 1933. Franklin Roosevelt had created the National Labor Relations Board in 1934; the National Labor Relations Act made this board a permanent body.

17. **(D)** Franklin D. Roosevelt was elected to four terms, although he died in 1945, the first year of his fourth term. Washington, Jackson, Cleveland, and Eisenhower all served two terms; Cleveland's terms, however, were not consecutive.

18.   **(D)**   Congress in 1937 banned all shipments of war materials to either side in the Spanish Civil War.

19.   **(C)**   During the 1920s, organized labor lost strength after 1920 which contributed to the uneven distribution of income. The Fordney-McCumber Tariff of 1922 once again introduced high tariffs, which contributed to the inability of worldwide trade to get back on track. Both consumer products and stock were widely purchased on credit. Farmers, among other groups, never participated in the prosperity of the 1920s.

20.   **(B)**   The U.S. withdrew its troops from Nicaragua, sent there for a second time in 1926, in 1933. The U.S. cancelled the Platt Amendment and removed its troops from Haiti in 1934, gradually ended its control over Dominican Republic customs houses in the mid-1930s, and in 1936 gave up its right to intervene in Panama.

1929–1941
REVIEW

1. THE GREAT DEPRESSION

Reasons for the Depression

A stock market crash does not mean that a depression must follow. A similar crash in October 1987 did not lead to depression. In 1929 a complex interaction of many factors caused the decline of the economy.

Many people had bought stock on a margin of ten percent, meaning that they had borrowed 90 percent of the purchase through a broker's loan, and put up the stock as collateral. Broker's loans totaled $8.5 billion in 1929, compared with $3.5 billion in 1926. When the price of a stock fell more than ten percent, the lender sold the stock for whatever it would bring and thus further depressed prices. The forced sales brought great losses to the banks and businesses which had financed the broker's loans, as well as to the investors.

There were already signs of recession before the market crash in 1929. Because the gathering and processing of statistics was not as advanced then as now, some factors were not so obvious to people at the time. The farm economy, which involved almost 25 percent of the population, had been depressed throughout the decade. Coal, railroads, and New England textiles had not been prosperous. After 1927 new construction declined and auto sales began to sag. Many workers had been laid off before the crash of 1929.

Many scholars believe that there was a problem of underconsumption, meaning that ordinary workers and farmers, after using their consumer credit, did not have enough money to keep buying the products which were being produced. One estimate says that the income of the top one percent of the population increased at least 75 percent during the decade, while that of the bottom 93 percent increased only six percent. The process continued after the depression began. After the stock market crash, people were conservative and saved their money, thus reducing the demand for goods. As demand decreased, workers were laid off or had wage reductions, further reducing their purchasing power and bringing another decrease in demand.

With the decline in the economy, Americans had less money for foreign loans and bought fewer imported products. That meant that foreign governments and individuals were not able to pay their debts in the United States. The whole reparations and war debts structure collapsed. American exports dropped, further hurting the domestic economy. The depression eventually spread throughout the world.

Economic Effects of the Depression

During the early months of the depression most people thought it was just an adjustment in the business cycle which would soon be over. Hoover repeatedly assured the public that prosperity was just around the corner. As time went on, the worst depression in American history set in, reaching its bottom point in early 1932. The gross national product fell from $104.6 billion in 1929 to $56.1 billion in 1933. Unemployment reached about 13 million in 1933, or about 25 percent of the labor force excluding farmers. National income dropped 54 percent from $87.8 billion to $40.2 billion. Labor income fell about 41 percent, while farm income dropped 55 percent from $11.9 billion to $5.3 billion. Industrial production dropped about 51 percent. The banking system suffered as 5,761 banks, over 22 percent of the total, failed by the end of 1932.

The Human Dimension of the Depression

As the depression grew worse, more and more people lost their jobs or had their wages reduced. Many were unable to continue credit payments on homes, automobiles, and other possessions, and lost them. Families doubled up in houses and apartments. Both the marriage rate and the birth rate declined as people put off family formation. Hundreds of thousands became homeless and lived in groups of makeshift shacks called Hoovervilles in empty spaces around cities. Others traveled the country by foot and boxcar seeking food and work. State and local government agencies and private charities were overwhelmed in their attempts to care for those in need, although public and private soup kitchens and soup lines were set up throughout the nation. Malnutrition was widespread but few died of starvation, perhaps because malnourished people are susceptible to many fatal diseases.

HOOVER'S DEPRESSION POLICIES

The Agricultural Marketing Act

Passed in June 1929 before the market crash, this law proposed by the president created the Federal Farm Board with a revolving fund of $500 million to lend the agricultural cooperatives to buy commodities such as wheat and cotton, and hold them for higher prices. Until 1931 it did keep agricultural prices above the world level. Then world prices plummeted, the board's funds ran out, and there was no period of higher prices in which the cooperatives could sell their stored commodities.

The Hawley-Smoot Tariff

This law, passed in June 1930, raised duties on both agricultural and manufactured imports. It did nothing of significance to improve the economy, and historians argue over whether or not it contributed to the spread of the international depression.

Voluntarism

Hoover believed that voluntary cooperation would enable the country to weather the depression. He held meetings with business leaders at which he urged them to avoid layoffs of workers and wage cuts, and he secured no-strike pledges from labor leaders. He urged all citizens to contribute to charities to help alleviate the suffering. While people were generous, private charity could not begin to meet the needs.

Public Works

In 1930 Congress appropriated $750 million for public buildings, river and harbor improvements, and highway construction in an effort to stimulate employment.

The Reconstruction Finance Corporation

Chartered by Congress in 1932, the RFC had an appropriation of $500 million and authority to borrow $1.5 billion for loans to railroads, banks, and other financial institutions. It prevented the failure of basic firms on which many other elements of the economy depended, but was criticized by some as relief for the rich.

The Federal Home Loan Bank Act

This law, passed in July 1932, created home loan banks with a capital of $125 million to make loans to building and loan associations, savings banks, and insurance companies to help them avoid foreclosures on homes.

Relief

Hoover staunchly opposed the use of federal funds for relief for the needy. In July 1932 he vetoed the Garner-Wagner Bill which would have appropriated funds for relief. He did compromise by approving legislation authorizing the RFC to lend $300 million to the states for relief, and to make loans to states and cities for self-liquidating public works.

The Bonus Army

The Bonus Expeditionary Force, which took its name from the American Expeditionary Force of World War I, was a group of about 14,000 unemployed veterans who went to Washington in the summer of 1932 to lobby Congress for immediate payment of the bonus which had been approved in 1926 for payment in 1945. At Hoover's insistence, the Senate did not pass the bonus bill, and about half of the BEF accepted a congressional offer of transportation home. The remaining 5,000–6,000, many with wives and children, continued to live in shanties along the Anacostia River and to lobby for their cause. After two veterans were killed in a clash with the police, Hoover, calling them insurrectionists and Communists, ordered the army to remove them. On July 28, 1932 General Douglas MacArthur, the army chief of staff, assisted by Majors Dwight D. Eisenhower and George S. Patton, personally commanded the removal operation. With machine guns, tanks, cavalry, infantry with fixed bayonets, and tear gas, MacArthur drove the veterans from Washington and burned their camp.

The Farm Holiday Association

Centered in Iowa, the association, headed by Milo Reno and others, called a farm strike in August 1932. They urged farmers not to take their products to market in an effort to raise farm prices. The picketing of markets led to violence, and the strike collapsed.

QUESTION

> Why were tariffs ineffective in fighting the depression?

EXPLANATION

Tariffs did little to help the economy, and some historians believe that tariffs might have made the economy worse. This was because one cause of the depression was underconsumption. Tariffs make goods more expensive, and therefore discourage consumption. In addition, tariffs imposed by the U.S. on imported goods led to other nations imposing tariffs on goods exported from the U.S., further depressing the market for U.S. goods purchased abroad.

QUESTION

> What policy did Hoover propose to relieve the suffering of the needy during the depression?

EXPLANATION

Hoover opposed using any federal funds to relieve the needy. In fact, with the exception of some public works projects, Hoover's relief efforts were aimed at preventing banks and other corporations from collapsing during the depression. For relief of individual citizens, Hoover thought that voluntary cooperation would stem the suffering. He urged business leaders to avoid layoffs and wage cuts. For those unemployed, he urged American citizens to contribute to charities that provided for relief to the needy.

The Election of 1932

At the Republican convention in Chicago, Hoover was nominated on the first ballot. The platform called for a continuation of his depression policies.

Franklin D. Roosevelt, the popular Democratic governor of New York, gained the support of many Southern and Western delegates through the efforts of his managers, Louis Howe and James Farley. When the convention opened in Chicago, he had a majority of delegates, but not the necessary two-thirds for nomination. House Speaker John Nance Garner, a favorite son candidate from Texas, threw support to Roosevelt, who was nominated on the fourth ballot. Garner then became the vice presidential candidate. Roosevelt took the unprecedented step of flying to the convention to accept the nomination in person, declaring that he pledged a "new deal" for the American people. The platform called for the repeal of prohibition, government aid for the unemployed, and a 25 percent cut in government spending.

Hoover declared that he would lead the nation to prosperity with higher tariffs and the maintenance of the gold standard. He warned that the election of Roosevelt would lead to grass growing in the streets of the cities and towns of America. Roosevelt called for "bold, persistent experimentation," and expressed his concern for the "forgotten man" at the bottom of the economic heap, but he did not give a clear picture of what he intended to do. Roosevelt had a broad smile and amiable disposition which attracted many people, while Hoover was aloof and cold in his personal style.

Roosevelt received 22,809,638 votes for 57.3 percent of the total, and 472 electoral votes, carrying all but six Northeastern states. Hoover had 15,758,901 votes and 59 electoral votes. Despite the hard times, Norman Thomas, the Socialist candidate, received only 881,951 votes. The Democrats also captured the Senate and increased their majority in the House.

Drill 1: The Great Depression

1. All of the following are true of Hoover's response to the Great Depression EXCEPT

   (A) he at first stressed the desirability of localism and private initiative rather than government intervention.

   (B) he saw the depression as akin to an act of nature, about which nothing could be done except to ride it out.

   (C) he urged the nation's business leaders to maintain wages and full employment.

   (D) his strategy for ending the depression was a failure.

   (E) he was not able to avoid increasing unpopularity.

2. In his inaugural address, Franklin D. Roosevelt said that if Congress did not pass the laws he believed it should, he would

   (A) accept this decision as the will of the people.

   (B) allow the nation to suffer the consequences of congressional stubbornness.

   (C) seek wartime emergency powers to carry out the measures himself.

   (D) hold an unprecedented national referendum.

   (E) call on the American people to place pressure on their representatives in Congress.

3. In order to deal with the crisis in banking at the time of his inauguration, Franklin Roosevelt

   (A) drastically curtailed government spending and cut taxes.

   · (B) declared a four-day "banking holiday" and prohibited the export of money.

   (C) urged Congress to pass legislation banning fractional reserve banking and holding bank trustees responsible for all deposits.

   (D) announced a multi-billion dollar federal bailout package.

   (E) announced the nationalization of all banks with over $100 million in total assets.

4. Herbert Hoover's Reconstruction Finance Corporation of 1932 did which of the following?

   (A) Gave direct federal relief to the unemployed

   (B) Financed major public-works programs such as Boulder Dam

   (C) Lent money to banks which in turn would lend it to businesses

   (D) Hired unemployed men to perform unskilled labor for the government

   (E) Reorganized the banking system and established deposit requirements

5. The 1932 demonstration known as the "Bonus March" involved

   (A) farmers disgruntled about low prices for meat, grain, and dairy products.

   (B) homeless persons building shantytowns near Washington, D.C.

   (C) Japanese-Americans protesting forced relocation from the West Coast.

   (D) World War I veterans demanding financial aid from the federal government.

   (E) migrant farm workers seeking employment in California.

6. In *The Grapes of Wrath* author John Steinbeck attempted to show

    (A) the plight of a poor young country girl in the big city.

    (B) that increasing material progress was creating increasing poverty.

    (C) his view of a future socialist utopia.

    (D) the plight of a family of poor Oklahomans seeking work in California during the depression.

    (E) the hollowness of the 1920s.

7. What was the OVERALL U.S. unemployment rate during the worst periods of the depression?

    (A) 10%   (B) 25%

    (C) 40%   (D) 60%

    (E) 90%

8. All of the following contributed to the Great Depression EXCEPT

    (A) excessive stocks and securities speculation.

    (B) protectionist trade measures.

    (C) huge farm debts resulting from collapsed crop prices.

    (D) lack of credit to help consumers sustain economic growth.

    (E) an imbalance of distribution of wealth in which the rich controlled far too much of the available income.

9. When the Great Depression hit, what action did President Hoover take to deal with it?

    (A) He began a massive program of deficit spending to pump money into the economy and create thousands of public works jobs for the unemployed.

    (B) He began a program of strict regulation of banks and industry to insure that the abuses which caused the depression could never again happen.

    (C) He borrowed money from Europe to finance our national debt and get U.S. industry back on its feet again.

    (D) He immediately lowered tariffs and removed other protectionist trade measures in an effort to rebuild the shattered world economy.

    (E) He took no meaningful actions until it was too late, believing that private enterprise would put the country out of the depression.

10. The "Bonus army" was

   (A) the nickname given to black army volunteers during the Civil War.

   (B) Japanese-American victims of relocation camps in World War II

   (C) a 1932 protest group against Herbert Hoover's economic policies.

   (D) an American volunteer cavalry unit during the Spanish-American War.

   (E) Vietnam War veterans.

2. THE FIRST AND SECOND NEW DEALS

Franklin D. Roosevelt

The heir of a wealthy family and a fifth cousin of Theodore Roosevelt, Franklin was born in 1882 on the family estate at Hyde Park, New York, graduated from Harvard and the Columbia Law School, married his distant cousin Anna Eleanor Roosevelt in 1905, and practiced law in New York City. He entered state politics, then served as assistant secretary of the navy under Wilson, and was the Democratic vice presidential candidate in 1920. In 1921 he suffered an attack of polio which left him paralyzed for several years and on crutches or in a wheelchair for the rest of his life. In 1928 he was elected governor of New York to succeed Al Smith and was reelected in 1930. As governor, his depression programs for the unemployed, public works, aid to farmers, and conservation attracted national attention.

The Cabinet

Important cabinet appointments included Senator Cordell Hull of Tennessee as secretary of state; Henry A. Wallace as secretary of agriculture; Harold L. Ickes as secretary of the interior; Frances Perkins, a New York social worker, as secretary of labor and the first woman appointed to a cabinet post; and James A. Farley, Roosevelt's political manager, as postmaster general.

The Brain Trust

Roosevelt's inner circle of unofficial advisors, first assembled during the campaign, was more influential than the cabinet. Prominent in it were agricultural economist Rexford G. Tugwell, political scientist Raymond Moley, lawyer Adolph A. Berle, Jr., the originators of the McNary-Haugen Bill—Hugh S. Johnson and George Peek—and Roosevelt's personal political advisor Louis Howe.

The New Deal Program

Roosevelt did not have a developed plan of action when he took office. He intended to experiment and to find that which worked. As a result, many programs overlapped or contradicted others, and were changed or dropped if they did not work.

Repeal of Prohibition

In February 1933, before Roosevelt took office, Congress passed the Twenty-first Amendment to repeal prohibition, and sent it to the states. In March the new Congress legalized light beer. The amendment was ratified by the states and took effect in December 1933.

The Banking Crisis

In February 1933, as the inauguration approached, a severe banking crisis developed. Banks could not collect their loans or meet the demands of their depositors for withdrawals, and runs occurred on many banks. Eventually, banks in 38 states were closed by the state governments, and the remainder were open for only limited operations. An additional 5,190 banks failed in 1933, bringing the depression total to 10,951.

The Inaugural Address

When Roosevelt was inaugurated on March 4, 1933, the American economic system seemed to be on the verge of collapse. Roosevelt assured the nation that "the only thing we have to fear is fear itself," called for a special session of Congress to convene on March 9, and asked for "broad executive powers to wage war against the emergency." Two days later, he closed all banks, and forbade the export of gold or the redemption of currency in gold.

Legislation of the First New Deal

The Hundred Days and the First New Deal

The special session of Congress, from March 9 to June 16, 1933, passed a great body of legislation which has left a lasting mark on the nation, and the period has been referred to ever since as the "Hundred Days." Over the next two years legislation was added, but the basic recovery plan of the Hundred Days remained in operation. Hence, the period from 1933 to 1935 is called the First New Deal. A new wave of programs beginning in 1935 is called the Second New Deal. The distinction was not known at the time, but is a device of historians to differentiate between two stages in Roosevelt's administration.

Economic Legislation of the Hundred Days

The banking crisis was the most immediate problem facing Roosevelt and the Congress. A series of laws was passed to deal with the crisis and to reform the American economic system.

The Emergency Banking Relief Act was passed on March 9, the first day of the special session. The law provided additional funds for banks from the RFC and the Federal Reserve, allowed the Treasury to open sound banks after ten days and to merge or liquidate unsound ones, and forbade the hoarding or export of gold. Roosevelt on March 12 assured the public of the soundness of the banks in the first of many "fireside chats," or radio addresses. People believed him and most banks were soon open with more deposits than withdrawals.

The Banking Act of 1933, or the Glass-Steagall Act, established the Federal Deposit Insurance Corporation (FDIC) to insure individual deposits in commercial banks, and separated commercial banking from the more speculative activity of investment banking.

The Truth-in-Securities Act required that full information about stocks and bonds be provided by brokers and others to potential purchasers.

The Home Owners Loan Corporation (HOLC) had authority to borrow money to refinance home mortgages and thus prevent foreclosures. Eventually, it lent over $3 billion to over one million home owners.

Gold was taken out of circulation following the president's order of March 6, and the nation went off the gold standard. Eventually, on January 31, 1934, the value of the dollar was set at $35 per ounce of gold, 59 percent of its former value. The object of the devaluation was to raise prices and help American exports.

Later Economic Legislation of the First New Deal

The Securities and Exchange Commission was created in 1934 to supervise stock exchanges and to punish fraud in securities trading.

The Federal Housing Administration (FHA) was created by Congress in 1934 to insure long-term, low-interest mortgages for home construction and repair.

Relief and Employment Programs of the Hundred Days

These programs were intended to provide temporary relief for people in need and to be disbanded when the economy improved.

The Federal Emergency Relief Act appropriated $500 million for aid to the poor to be distributed by state and local governments. Half of the funds were to be distributed on a one to three matching basis with the states. It also established the Federal Emergency Relief Administration under Harry Hopkins. Additional appropriations were made many times later.

The Civilian Conservation Corps enrolled 250,000 young men ages 18 to 24 from families on relief to go to camps where they worked on flood control, soil conservation, and forest projects under the direction of the War Department. A small monthly payment was made to the family of each member. By the end of the decade, 2.75 million young men had served in the corps.

The Public Works Administration, under Secretary of the Interior Harold Ickes, had $3.3 billion to distribute to state and local governments for building projects such as schools, highways, and hospitals. The object was to "prime the pump" of the economy by creating construction jobs. Additional money was appropriated later.

Later Relief Efforts

After the Hundred Days, in November 1933, Roosevelt established the Civil Works Administration under Harry Hopkins with $400 million from the Public Works Administration to hire four million unemployed workers. The temporary and make-shift nature of the jobs, such as sweeping streets, brought much criticism, and the experiment was terminated in April 1934.

Agricultural Programs of the Hundred Days

The Agricultural Adjustment Act of 1933 created the Agricultural Adjustment Administration (AAA) which was headed by George Peek. It sought to return farm prices to parity with those of the 1909 to 1914 period. Farmers agreed to reduce production of principal farm commodities and were paid a subsidy in return. The money came from a tax on the processing of the commodities. Farm prices increased, but tenants and sharecroppers were hurt when owners took land out of cultivation. The law was declared unconstitutional in January 1936 on the grounds that the processing tax was not constitutional.

The Federal Farm Loan Act consolidated all farm credit programs into the Farm Credit Administration to make low-interest loans for farm mortgages and other agricultural purposes.

Later Agricultural Programs

The Commodity Credit Corporation was established in October 1933 by the AAA to make loans to corn and cotton farmers against their crops so that they could hold them for higher prices.

The Frazier-Lemke Farm Bankruptcy Act of 1934 allowed farmers to defer foreclosure on their land while they obtained new financing and helped them to recover property already lost through easy financing.

The National Industrial Recovery Act

This law, passed on June 16, 1933, the last day of the Hundred Days, was viewed as the cornerstone of the recovery program. It sought to stabilize the economy by preventing extreme competition, labor-management conflicts, and overproduction. A board composed of industrial and labor leaders in each industry or business drew up a code for that industry which set minimum prices, minimum wages, maximum work hours, production limits, and quotas. The antitrust laws were temporarily suspended. The approach was based on the idea of many economists at the time that a mature industrial economy produced more goods than could be consumed, and that it would be necessary to create a relative shortage of goods in order to raise prices and restore prosperity. The idea was proved wrong by the expansion of consumer goods after World War II. Section 7a of the law also provided that workers had the right to join unions and to bargain collectively. The National Recovery Administration (NRA) was created under the leadership of Hugh S. Johnson to enforce the law and generate public enthusiasm for it. In May 1935 the law was declared unconstitutional in the case of *Schechter v. United States*, on the grounds that Congress had delegated legislative authority to the code-makers, and that Schechter, who slaughtered chickens in New York, was not engaged in interstate commerce. It was argued later that the NRA had unintentionally aided big firms to the detriment of smaller ones because the representatives of the larger firms tended to dominate the code-making process. It was generally unsuccessful in stabilizing small businesses, such as retail stores, and was on the point of collapse when it was declared unconstitutional.

The Tennessee Valley Authority

Different from the other legislation of the Hundred Days which addressed immediate problems of the depression, the TVA, a public corporation under a three-member board, was proposed by Roosevelt as the first major experiment in regional public planning. Starting from the nucleus of the government's Muscle Shoals property on the Tennessee River, the TVA built 20 dams in an area of 40,000 square miles to stop flooding and soil erosion, improve navigation, and generate hydroelectric power. It also manufactured nitrates for fertilizer, conducted demonstration projects for farmers, engaged in reforestation, and attempted to rehabilitate the whole area. It was fought unsuccessfully in the courts by private power companies. Roosevelt believed that it would serve as a yardstick to measure the true cost of providing electric power.

Effects of the First New Deal

The economy improved but did not get well between 1933 and 1935. The gross national product rose from $74.2 billion in 1933 to $91.4 billion in 1935. Manufacturing salaries and wages increased from $6.24 billion in 1933 to over $9.5 billion in 1935, with average weekly earnings going from $16.73 to $20.13. Farm income rose from $1.9 billion in 1933 to $4.6 billion in 1935. The money supply, as currency and demand deposits, grew from $19.2 billion to $25.2 billion. Unemployment dropped from about 25 percent of nonfarm workers in 1933 to about 20.1 percent, or 10.6 million, in 1935. While the figure had improved, it was a long way from the 3.2 percent of pre-depression 1929, and suffering as a result of unemployment was still a major problem.

Criticism of the New Deal

The partial economic recovery brought about by the first New Deal provoked criticism from the right for doing too much, and from the left for doing too little. Conservatives and businessmen criticized the deficit financing, which accounted for about half of the federal budget, federal spending for relief, and government regulation of business. They frequently charged that the New Deal was Socialist or Communist in form, and some conservative writers labeled the wealthy Roosevelt "a traitor to his class." People on the lower end of the economic scale thought that the New Deal, especially the NRA, was too favorable to big business. Small business people and union members complained that the NRA codes gave control of industry to the big firms, while farmers complained that the NRA set prices too high. The elderly thought that nothing had been done to help them. Several million people who were or had been tenant farmers or sharecroppers were badly hurt. When the AAA paid farmers to take land out of production, the landowners took the money while the tenants and sharecroppers lost their livelihood. Several opposition organizations and persons were particularly active in opposing Roosevelt's policies.

The American Liberty League was formed in 1934 by conservatives to defend business interests and promote the open shop. While many of its members were Republicans and it was financed primarily by the Du Pont family, it also attracted conservative Democrats like Alfred E. Smith and John W. Davis. It supported conservative congressional candidates of both parties in the election of 1934 with little success.

The Old Age Revolving Pension Plan was advanced by Dr. Francis E. Townsend, a retired California physician. The plan proposed that every retired person over 60 receive a pension of $200 a month, about double the average worker's salary, with the requirement that the money be spent within the month. The plan would be funded by a national gross sales tax. Townsend claimed that it would end the depression by putting money into circulation, but economists thought it fiscally impossible. Some three to five million older Americans joined Townsend Clubs.

The Share Our Wealth Society was founded in 1934 by Senator Huey "The Kingfish" Long of Louisiana. Long was a populist demagogue who was elected governor of Louisiana in 1928, established a practical dictatorship over the state, and moved to the United States Senate in 1930. He supported Roosevelt in 1932, but then broke with him, calling him a tool of Wall Street for not doing more to combat the depression. Long called for the confiscation of all fortunes over $5 million and a tax of 100 percent on annual incomes over one million. With the money the government would provide subsidies so that every family would have a "homestead" of house, car, and furnishings worth at least $5,000, a minimum annual income of $2,000, and free college education for those who wanted it. His slogan was "Every Man a King." Long talked of running for president in 1936 and published a book entitled *My First Days in the White House*. His society had over five million members when he was assassinated on the steps of the Louisiana Capitol on September 8, 1935. The Reverend Gerald L.K. Smith appointed himself Long's successor as head of the society, but he lacked Long's ability.

The National Union for Social Justice was headed by Father Charles E. Coughlin, a Catholic priest in Royal Oak, Michigan, who had a weekly radio program. Beginning as a religious broadcast in 1926, Coughlin turned to politics and finance, and attracted an audience of millions of many faiths He supported Roosevelt in 1932, but then turned against him. He advocated an inflationary currency and was anti-Semitic, but beyond that his fascist-like program was not clearly defined.

QUESTION

> How could one characterize the opposition of the New Deal from the political left?

EXPLANATION

Whether one considers them "populists" or "demagogues," the opposition to the New Deal from the left attacked it for not going far enough. Dr. Francis E. Townsend, Huey Long, and Father Charles Coughlin all agitated for direct cash payments to different constituencies. They argued that getting more cash into the hands of American citizens would end the depression. The ideas for financing these plans were usually vague, involving new taxes, often on the very wealthy.

The Second New Deal Begins

With millions of Democratic voters under the sway of Townsend, Long, and Coughlin, with the destruction of the NRA by the Supreme Court imminent, and with the election of 1936 approaching the next year, Roosevelt began to push through a series of new programs in the spring of 1935. Much of the legislation was passed during the summer of 1935, a period sometimes called the Second Hundred Days.

Legislation and Programs of the Second New Deal

The Works Progress Administration (WPA) was started in May 1935 following the passage of the Emergency Relief Appropriations Act of April 1935. Headed by Harry Hopkins, the WPA employed people from the relief rolls for 30 hours of work a week at pay double the relief payment but less than private employment. There was not enough money to hire all of the unemployed, and the numbers varied from time to time, but an average of 2.1 million people per month were employed. By the end of the program in 1941, 8.5 million people had worked at some time for the WPA at a total cost of $11.4 billion. Most of the projects undertaken were in construction. The WPA built hundreds of thousands of miles of streets and roads, and thousands of schools, hospitals, parks, airports, playgrounds, and other facilities. Hand work was emphasized so that the money would go for pay rather than equipment, provoking much criticism for inefficiency. Unemployed artists painted murals in public buildings; actors, musicians, and dancers performed in poor neighborhoods; and writers compiled guide books and local histories.

The National Youth Administration (NYA) was established as part of the WPA in June 1935 to provide part-time jobs for high school and college students to enable them to stay in school, and to help young adults not in school to find jobs.

The Rural Electrification Administration (REA) was created in May 1935 to provide loans and WPA labor to electric cooperatives to build lines into rural areas not served by private companies.

The Resettlement Administration (RA) was created in the Agriculture Department in May 1935 under Rexford Tugwell. It relocated destitute families from seemingly hopeless situations to new rural homestead communities or to suburban greenbelt towns.

The National Labor Relations or Wagner Act was passed in May 1935 to replace the provisions of Section 7a of the NIRA. It reaffirmed labor's right to unionize, prohibited unfair labor practices, and created the National Labor Relations Board (NLRB) to oversee and insure fairness in labor-management relations.

The Social Security Act was passed in August 1935. It established a retirement plan for persons over age 65 funded by a tax on wages paid equally by employee and employer. The first benefits, ranging from $10 to $85 per month, were paid in 1942. Another provision of the act had the effect of forcing the states to initiate unemployment insurance programs. It imposed a payroll tax on employers which went to the state if it had an insurance program, and to the federal government if it did not. The act also provided matching funds to the states for aid to the blind, handicapped, and dependent children, and for public health services. The American Social Security system was limited compared with those of other industrialized nations, and millions of workers were not covered by it. Nonetheless, it marked a major change in American policy.

The Banking Act of 1935 created a strong central Board of Governors of the Federal Reserve System with broad powers over the operations of the regional banks.

The Public Utility Holding Company or Wheeler-Rayburn Act of 1935 empowered the Securities and Exchange Commission to restrict public utility holding companies to one natural region and to eliminate duplicate holding companies. The Federal Power Commission was created to regulate interstate electrical power rates and activities, and the Federal Trade Commission received the same kind of power over the natural gas companies.

The Revenue Act of 1935 increased income taxes on higher incomes, and also inheritance, large gift, and capital gains taxes.

The Motor Carrier Act of 1935 extended the regulatory authority of the Interstate Commerce Commission to cover interstate trucking lines.

The Election of 1936

At the Democratic convention in Philadelphia in June, Roosevelt and Garner were renominated by acclamation on the first ballot. The convention also ended the requirement for a two-thirds vote for nomination. The platform promised an expanded farm program, labor legislation, more rural electrification and public housing, and enforcement of the antitrust laws. In his acceptance speech, Roosevelt declared that "this generation of Americans has a rendezvous with destiny." He further proclaimed that he and the American people were fighting for democracy and capitalism against the "economic royalists," business people he charged with seeking only their own power and wealth, and opposing the New Deal.

Governor Alfred M. Landon of Kansas, a former Progressive supporter of Theodore Roosevelt, was nominated on the first ballot at the Republican convention in Cleveland in June. Frank Knox, a Chicago newspaper publisher, was chosen as his running mate. The platform criticized the New Deal for operating under unconstitutional laws, and called for a balanced budget, higher tariffs, and lower corporate taxes. It did not call for the repeal of all New Deal legislation, and promised better and less expensive relief, farm, and labor programs. In effect, Landon and the Republicans were saying that they would do about the same thing, but do it better.

Dr. Francis Townsend, Father Charles Coughlin, and the Reverend Gerald L.K. Smith, Long's successor in the Share Our Wealth Society, organized the Union party to oppose Roosevelt. The nominee was Congressman William Lemke of North Dakota, an advocate of radical farm legislation but a bland campaigner. Vicious attacks by Smith and Coughlin on Roosevelt brought a backlash against them, and American Catholic leaders denounced Coughlin.

Roosevelt carried all of the states except Maine and Vermont with 27,757,333 votes, or 60.8 percent of the total, and 523 electoral votes. Landon received 16,684,231 votes and eight electoral votes. Lemke had 891,858 votes for 1.9 percent of the total. Norman Thomas, the Socialist candidate, received 187,000 votes, only 21 percent of the 881,951 votes he received in 1932.

Roosevelt had put together a coalition of followers who made the Democratic party the majority party in the nation for the first time since the Civil War. While retaining the Democratic base in the solid South and among white ethnics in the big cities, Roosevelt also received strong support from Midwestern farmers. Two groups which made a dramatic shift into the Democratic ranks were union workers and blacks. Unions took an active political role for the first time since 1924, providing both campaign funds and votes. Blacks had traditionally been Republican since emancipation, but by 1936 about three-fourths of the black voters, who lived mainly in the Northern cities, had shifted into the Democratic party.

QUESTION

What was the impact of the coalition that supported Roosevelt in 1932 and 1936 on the Democratic party?

EXPLANATION

The "New Deal Coalition" included the traditional Democratic base of Southerners and Northern white ethnics. It also included Midwestern farmers, building on the remnants of the old Populist party. African-Americans and Labor switched to the Democratic party in large numbers. This coalition remained intact for several decades, making it the majority party.

The Last Years of the New Deal

Court Packing

Frustrated by a conservative Supreme Court which had overturned much of his New Deal legislation, Roosevelt, after receiving his overwhelming mandate in the election of 1936, decided to curb the power of the court. In doing so, he overestimated his own political power and underestimated the force of tradition. In February 1937 he proposed to Congress the Judicial Reorganization Bill which would allow the president to name a new federal judge for each judge who did not retire by the age of 70 1/2. The appointments would be limited to a maximum of 50, with no more than six added to the Supreme Court. At the time, six justices were over the proposed age limit. Roosevelt cited a slowing of the judicial process due to the infirmity of the incumbents and the need for a modern outlook. The president was astonished by the wave of opposition from Democrats and Republicans alike, and uncharacteristically refused to compromise. In doing so, he not only lost the bill but he lost control of the Democratic Congress which he had dominated since 1933. Nonetheless, the Court changed its position as Chief Justice Charles Evans Hughes and Justice Owen Roberts began to vote with the more liberal members. The National Labor Relations Act was upheld in March 1937, and the Social Security Act in April. In June a conservative justice retired, and Roosevelt had the opportunity to make an appointment.

The Recession of 1937–1938

Most economic indicators rose sharply between 1935 and 1937. The gross national product had recovered to the 1930 level, and unemployment, if WPA workers were considered employed, had fallen to 9.2 percent. Average yearly earnings of the employed had risen from $1,195 in 1935 to $1,341 in 1937, and average hourly manufacturing earnings from 55 cents to 62 cents. During the same period there were huge federal deficits. In fiscal 1936, for example, there was a deficit of $4.4 billion in a budget of $8.5 billion. Roosevelt decided that the recovery was sufficient to warrant a reduction in relief programs and a move toward a balanced budget. The budget for fiscal 1938, from July 1937 to June 1938, was reduced to $6.8 billion, with the WPA experiencing the largest cut. During the winter of 1937–1938, the economy slipped rapidly and unemployment rose to 12.5 percent. In April 1938 Roosevelt requested and received from

Congress an emergency appropriation of about $3 billion for the WPA, as well as increases for public works and other programs. In July 1938 the economy began to recover, and it regained the 1937 levels in 1939.

Legislation of the Late New Deal

With the threat of adverse Supreme Court rulings removed, Roosevelt rounded out his program during the late 1930s.

The Bankhead-Jones Farm Tenancy Act, passed in July 1937, created the Farm Security Administration (FSA) to replace the Resettlement Administration. The FSA continued the homestead projects, and loaned money to farmers to purchase farms, lease land, and buy equipment. It also set up camps for migrant workers and established rural health care programs.

The National Housing or Wagner-Steagall Act, passed in September 1937, established the United States Housing Authority (USHA) which could borrow money to lend to local agencies for public housing projects. By 1941 it had loaned $750 million for 511 projects.

The Second Agricultural Adjustment Act of February 1938 appropriated funds for soil conservation payments to farmers who would remove land from production. The law also empowered the Agriculture Department to impose market quotas to prevent surpluses in cotton, wheat, corn, tobacco, and rice if two-thirds of the farmers producing that commodity agreed.

The Fair Labor Standards Act, popularly called the minimum wage law, was passed in June 1938. It provided for a minimum wage of 25 cents an hour which would gradually rise to 40 cents, and a gradual reduction to a work week of 40 hours, with time-and-a-half for overtime. Workers in small businesses and in public and nonprofit employment were not covered. The law also prohibited the shipment in interstate commerce of manufactured goods on which children under 16 worked.

Drill 2: The First and Second New Deals

1. Which of the following critics of the New Deal advocated a "Share-the-Wealth" program?

    (A) Huey Long   (B) Frances Townsend

    (C) Charles E. Coughlin   (D) William Lemke

    (E) Alfred Landon

2. Franklin D. Roosevelt's New Deal program contained all of the following EXCEPT

    (A) the attempt to raise farm prices by paying farmers not to plant.

(B) the attempt to encourage cooperation within industries so as to raise prices generally.

(C) the attempt to invigorate the economy by lowering tariff barriers.

· (D) effectively eliminating the gold standard as it had previously existed.

(E) the attempt to restore confidence in the banking system.

3. Who was the first woman to serve as a cabinet member?

    (A) Jane Addams   (B) Lillian Wald

    (C) Sandra Day O'Connor   (D) Betty Friedan

    · (E) Frances Perkins

4. The Tennessee Valley Authority did all of the following EXCEPT

    (A) provide flood control.

    (B) provide low-cost electric power.

    (C) discourage private industry from moving into the valley.

    (D) manufacture fertilizer.

    (E) raise the average income of those living in the area.

5. "The only thing we have to fear is fear itself." This statement is from

    (A) Woodrow Wilson's 1917 message to Congress asking for a declaration of war against Germany.

    (B) a speech by President Herbert Hoover two weeks after the October 1929 stock market crash.

    (C) Franklin D. Roosevelt's first inaugural address.

    (D) Franklin D. Roosevelt's message to Congress asking for a declaration of war against Japan, December 8, 1941.

    (E) Harry S. Truman's announcement of the dropping of the atomic bomb on Hiroshima.

6. All of the following were New Deal reforms EXCEPT

    (A) the National Industrial Recovery Act.

    (B) the Tennessee Valley Authority.

    (C) the Reconstruction Finance Corporation.

    (D) the Agricultural Adjustment Act.

    (E) the Works Progress Administration.

7. All of the following New Deal agencies were created during the Great Depression to provide jobs for the unemployed EXCEPT

   (A) Farm Security Administration (FSA).

   (B) Civil Works Administration (CWA).

   (C) Civilian Conservation Corps (CCC).

   (D) Works Progress Administration (WPA).

   (E) National Youth Administration (NYA).

8. The following were all measures of the First New Deal EXCEPT

   (A) the Tennessee Valley Authority.

   (B) the bank holiday.

   (C) the Securities and Exchange Commission.

   (D) Social Security.

   (E) the Civilian Conservation Corps.

9. The recession of 1937 was primarily caused by

   (A) overextension of easy credit and high inflation.

   (B) excess business speculation in the rebounding stock market.

   (C) failure of New Deal programs to effectively lower unemployment and restore faith in the economy.

   (D) overregulation of key national industries, resulting in massive layoffs.

   (E) premature tightening of credit and cutbacks in spending for "New Deal" programs.

10. The philosophy behind the New Deal was primarily to

   (A) restore the laissez-faire capitalism which had worked so well in the early 1920s.

   (B) eliminate the massive federal deficit which had led to the Great Depression by mandating a balanced federal budget.

   (C) establish a Socialist system in which government would take over private industry, set all prices, and guarantee employment for workers.

   (D) cut down the size of government, which had become a massive drain on the nation's economy, and return more power to the states so they could each deal with their specific economic problems in their own way.

   (E) expand the role of the federal government in providing jobs, relief for the unemployed, better wages, and regulation of industry to control the abuses of the past which had led to the current depression.

3. SOCIAL DIMENSIONS OF THE NEW DEAL ERA

Blacks and the New Deal

Blacks suffered more than other people from the depression. Unemployment rates were much higher than for the general population, and before 1933 they were often excluded from state and local relief efforts. Blacks did benefit from many New Deal relief programs, but about 40 percent of black workers were sharecroppers or tenants who suffered from the provisions of the first Agricultural Adjustment Act. Roosevelt seems to have given little thought to the special problems of black people, and he was afraid to endorse legislation such as an anti-lynching bill for fear of alienating the Southern wing of the Democratic party. Eleanor Roosevelt and Harold Ickes strongly supported civil rights, and a "Black Cabinet" of advisors was assembled in the Interior Department. More blacks were appointed to government positions by Roosevelt than ever before, but the number was still small. When government military contracts began to flow in 1941, A. Philip Randolph, the president of the Brotherhood of Sleeping Car Porters, proposed a black march on Washington to demand equal access to defense jobs. To forestall such an action, Roosevelt issued an executive order on June 25, 1941 establishing the Fair Employment Practices Committee to insure consideration for minorities in defense employment.

Native Americans and the New Deal

John Collier, the commissioner of the Bureau of Indian Affairs, persuaded Congress to repeal the Dawes Act of 1887 by passing the Indian Reorganization Act of 1934. The law restored tribal ownership of lands, recognized tribal constitutions and government, and provided loans to tribes for economic development. Collier also secured the creation of the Indian Emergency Conservation Program, an Indian CCC for projects on the reservations. In addition, he helped Indians secure entry into the WPA, NYA, and other programs.

Mexican-Americans and the New Deal

Mexican-Americans benefited the least from the New Deal, for few programs covered them. Farm owners turned against them as farm workers after they attempted to form a union between 1933 and 1936. By 1940 most had been replaced by whites dispossessed by the depression. Many returned to Mexico, and the Mexican-American population dropped almost 40 percent from 1930 to 1940.

Women During the New Deal

The burden of the depression fell on women as much or more as it did on men. Wives and mothers found themselves responsible for stretching meager budgets by preparing inexpensive meals, patching old clothing, and the like.

"Making do" became a slogan of the period. In addition, more women had to supplement or provide the family income by going to work. In 1930 there were 10.5 million working women comprising 29 percent of the work force. By 1940 the figures had grown to over 13 million and 35 percent. There was much criticism of working women based on the idea that they deprived men of jobs. Male job losses were greatest in heavy industry such as factories and mills, while areas of female employment such as retail sales were not hit as hard. Unemployed men seldom sought jobs in the traditional women's fields.

QUESTION

How did African-Americans benefit from the New Deal?

EXPLANATION

There were few, if any, New Deal programs designed to specifically help African-Americans. Relief programs did help African-Americans as well as whites. Eleanor Roosevelt favored civil rights, and more African-Americans were appointed to government positions. But Roosevelt was concerned with alienating the Southern wing of the Democratic party, and was cautious in working to improve the status of African-Americans.

Labor Unions

Unions During the First New Deal

Labor unions had lost members and influence during the twenties, and slipped further during the economic decline of 1929 to 1933. The National Industrial Recovery Act gave them new hope when Section 7a guaranteed the right to unionize, and during 1933 about 1.5 million new members joined unions. It soon became clear that enforcement of the industrial codes by the NRA was ineffective, and labor leaders began to call it the "National Run Around." As a result, in 1934 there were many strikes, sometimes violent, including a general strike in San Francisco involving about 125,000 workers.

Craft versus Industrial Unions

The passage of the National Labor Relations or Wagner Act in 1935 resulted in a massive growth of union membership, but only at the expense of bitter conflict within the labor movement. The American Federation of Labor was made up primarily of craft unions. Some leaders, especially John L. Lewis, the dynamic president of the United Mine Workers, wanted to unionize the mass production industries, such as automobiles and rubber, with industrial unions. In 1934 the AFL convention authorized such unions, but the older unions continued to try to organize workers in those industries by crafts. In November 1935 Lewis and others established the Committee for Industrial Organization to unionize basic industries, presumably within the AFL. President William Green of the AFL ordered the CIO to disband in January 1936. When the rebels refused, they were expelled by the AFL executive council in March 1937. The insurgents then reorganized the CIO as the independent Congress of Industrial Organizations to be composed of industrial unions.

Growth of the CIO

During its organizational period, the CIO sought to initiate several industrial unions, particularly in the steel, auto, rubber, and radio industries. In late 1936 and early 1937 it used a tactic called the sit-down strike, with the strikers occupying the workplace to prevent any production. There were 477 sit-down strikes involving about 400,000 workers. The largest was in the General Motors plant in Flint, Michigan, as the union sought recognition by that firm. In February 1937 General Motors recognized the United Auto Workers as the bargaining agent for its 400,000 workers. When the CIO established its independence in March 1937, it already had 1.8 million members, and it reached a membership of 3.75 million six months later. The AFL had about 3.4 million members at that time. By the end of 1941 the CIO had about 5 million members, the AFL about 4.6 million, and other unions about one million. Union members comprised about 11.5 percent of the work force in 1933, and 28.2 percent in 1941.

Cultural Trends of the 1930s

Literary Developments

The writers and intellectuals who had expressed disdain for the middle-class materialism of the 1920s found it even more difficult to deal with the meaning of the crushing poverty in America and the rise of fascism in Europe during the 1930s. Some turned to Communism, including the 53 writers who signed an open letter endorsing the Communist presidential candidate in 1932. Some turned to proletarian novels, such as Jack Conroy in *The Disinherited* (1933) and Robert Cantwell in *The Land of Plenty* (1934). Ernest Hemingway seemed to have lost his direction in *Winner Take All* (1933) and *The Green Hills of Africa* (1935), but in *To Have and Have Not* (1937), a strike novel, he turned to social realism, and *For Whom the Bell Tolls* (1941) expressed his concern about fascism. Sinclair Lewis also dealt with fascism in *It Can't Happen Here* (1935), but did not show the power of his works of the 1920s. John Dos Passos depicted what he saw as the disintegration of American life from 1900 to 1929 in his trilogy *U.S.A.* (1930–1936).William Faulkner sought values in Southern life in *Light in August* (1932), *Absalom! Absalom!* (1936), and *The Unvanquished* (1938). The endurance of the human spirit and personal survival were depicted in James T. Farrell's trilogy *Studs Lonigan* (1936) about the struggles of lower-middle-class Irish Catholics in Chicago, Erskine Caldwell's *Tobacco Road* (1932) about impoverished

Georgia sharecroppers, and John Steinbeck's *The Grapes of Wrath* (1939) about "Okies" migrating from the dust bowl to California in the midst of the depression.

Popular Culture

The depression greatly reduced the amount of disposable income available for recreation and entertainment. There was an increase in games and sports among family groups and friends. The WPA and the CCC constructed thousands of playgrounds, playing fields, picnic areas, and the like for public use. Roosevelt and Harry Hopkins, the director of the WPA, hoped to develop a mass appreciation of culture through the WPA murals in public buildings, with traveling plays, concerts, and exhibits, and with community arts centers. Beyond some revival of handicrafts, it is doubtful that the program had much effect.

Radio was the favorite form of daily entertainment during the depression because, after the initial investment in the receiving set, it was free. By 1938, Americans owned 40 million radios. Radio provided comedy and mystery shows, music, sports, and news. One survey showed that radio tended to make Americans more uniform in their attitudes, taste, speech, and humor.

When it came to entertainment outside the home, the movies were king. By 1939 about 65 percent of the people went to the movies at least once a week. The movie industry was one of the few which did not suffer financially from the depression. Movies were the great means of escape, providing release from the pressures of the depression by transporting people to a make-believe world of beauty, mystery, or excitement. Spectacular musicals with dozens of dancers and singers, such as *Broadway Melody* of 1936, were popular. The dance team of Fred Astaire and Ginger Rogers thrilled millions in *Flying Down to Rio* and *Shall We Dance?* Shirley Temple charmed the public as their favorite child star. Judy Garland rose to stardom in *The Wizard of Oz*, while animated films like *Snow White* appealed to children of all ages. People enjoyed the triumph of justice and decency in *Mr. Smith Goes to Washington* and *You Can't Take It With You* with Jimmy Stewart. Dozens of light comedies starred such favorites as Cary Grant, Katharine Hepburn, Clark Gable, and Rosalind Russell, while Errol Flynn played in such larger-than-life roles as Robin Hood. A different kind of escape was found in gangster movies with Edward G. Robinson, James Cagney, or George Raft. Near the end of the decade *Gone With the Wind*, released in 1939 starring Clark Gable and Vivien Leigh, became a timeless classic, while *The Grapes of Wrath* in 1940 commented on the depression itself.

The popular music of the decade was swing, and the big bands of Duke Ellington, Benny Goodman, Glenn Miller, Tommy Dorsey, and Harry James vied for public favor. The leading popular singer was Bing Crosby. City blacks refined the country blues to city blues, and interracial audiences enjoyed both city blues and jazz. Black musicians were increasingly accepted by white audiences.

Comic strips existed before the thirties, but they became a standard newspaper feature as well as a source of comic books during the decade. "Dick Tracy" began his war on crime in 1931, and was assisted by "Superman" after 1938. "Tarzan" began to swing through the cartoon jungles in 1929, and "Buck Rogers" began the exploration of space in 1930.

Drill 3: Social Dimensions of the New Deal Era

1. All of the following literary works dealt with the effects of the depression in the 1930s EXCEPT

    (A) *The Sun Also Rises.* (B) *The Grapes of Wrath.*

    (C) *Studs Lonigan Trilogy.* (D) *U.S.A. Trilogy.*

    (E) *Tobacco Road.*

2. The Wagner Act of 1935 helped which of the following groups?

    (A) Labor (B) Businessmen

    (C) Farmers (D) Veterans

    (E) Home owners

3. In what election did blacks begin to overwhelmingly support the Democratic party?

    (A) 1928 (B) 1932

    (C) 1936 (D) 1948

    (E) 1960

4. The Indian Reorganization Act of 1934 sought to

    (A) end federal subsidies to landless Indian tribes and force them to support themselves.

    (B) prohibit the division of tribal lands into allotments and allowed Indians to resume using their own tribal languages and rituals on their lands.

    (C) requisition desirable land from Indian tribes and force those tribes to relocate on smaller jointly occupied reservations, in which several tribes would reside, intermingle, and share the same land.

    (D) break up tribal reservations into individual allotments of land that could be occupied by Indians or purchased by whites.

    (E) prohibit Indians from using tribal languages or practicing ancient tribal religions on government reservations.

5. Fearing the U.S. Supreme Court would find much of his second term "New Deal" legislation unconstitutional, as it had done for much of the "New Deal" legislation passed during his first term, Franklin Roosevelt responded by

(A) withdrawing the proposed legislation.

(B) ignoring the court's rulings.

(C) stripping the court of its power.

(D) threatening to increase the number of justices.

(E) offering bribes to seven of the nine justices.

4. NEW DEAL DIPLOMACY AND THE ROAD TO WAR

The Good Neighbor Policy

Roosevelt and Secretary of State Cordell Hull continued the policies of their predecessors in endeavoring to improve relations with Latin American nations, and formalized their position by calling it the Good Neighbor Policy.

Nonintervention

At the Montevideo Conference of American Nations in December of 1933, the United States renounced the right of intervention in the internal affairs of Latin American countries. In 1936 in the Buenos Aires Convention, the United States further agreed to submit all American disputes to arbitration. Accordingly, the marines were removed from Haiti, Nicaragua, and the Dominican Republic by 1934. The Haitian protectorate treaty was allowed to expire in 1936, the right of intervention in Panama was ended by treaty in 1936, and the receivership of the finances of the Dominican Republic ended in 1941.

Cuba

The United States did not intervene in the Cuban revolution in the spring of 1933, but it did back a coup by Fulgentio Batista to overthrow the liberal regime of Ramon Grau San Martin in 1934. Batista was given a favorable sugar import status for Cuba in return for establishing a conservative administration. In May 1934 the United States abrogated its Platt Amendment rights in Cuba except for control of the Guantanamo Naval Base.

Mexico

The government of Lazaro Cardenas began to expropriate American property, including oil holdings, in 1934. Despite calls for intervention, Roosevelt insisted only on compensation. A joint commission worked out a settlement which was formally concluded on November 19, 1941.

The London Economic Conference

An international conference in London in June 1933 tried to obtain tariff reduction and currency stabilization for the industrialized nations. Roosevelt would not agree to peg the value of the dollar to other currencies because he feared that it might impede his recovery efforts. The conference failed for lack of American cooperation.

Recognition of Russia

The United States had not had diplomatic relations with the Union of Soviet Socialist Republics since it was established after the 1917 revolution. In an effort to open trade with Russia, mutual recognition was negotiated in November 1933. The financial results were disappointing.

Philippine Independence

The Tydings-McDuffie Act of March 1934 forced the Philippines to become independent on July 4, 1946, rather than granting the dominion status which the Filipinos had requested.

The Reciprocal Trade Agreement Act

This law, the idea of Cordell Hull, was passed in June 1934. It allowed the president to negotiate agreements which could vary from the rates of the Hawley-Smoot Tariff up to 50 percent. By 1936 lower rates had been negotiated with 13 nations, and by 1941 almost two-thirds of all American foreign trade was covered by agreements.

United States Neutrality Legislation

Belief that the United States should stay out of foreign wars and problems began in the 1920s and grew in the 1930s. It was fed by House and Senate investigations of arms traffic and the munitions industry in 1933 and 1934, especially an examination of profiteering by bankers and munitions makers in drawing the United States into World War I by Senator Gerald Nye of North Dakota. Books of revisionist history which asserted that Germany had not been responsible for World War I and that the United States had been misled were also influential during the 1930s. A Gallup poll in April 1937 showed that almost two-thirds of those responding thought that American entry into World War I had been a mistake. Such feelings were strongest in the Midwest and among Republicans, but were found in all areas and across the political spectrum. Leading isolationists included Congressman Hamilton Fish of New York, Senator William Borah of Idaho, and Senator George Norris of Nebraska, all Republicans. Pacifist movements, such as the Fellowship of Christian Reconciliation, were influential among college and high school students and the clergy.

The Johnson Act of 1934

When European nations stopped payment on World War I debts to the United States, this law prohibited any nation in default from selling securities to any American citizen or corporation.

The Neutrality Acts of 1935

Isolationist sentiment prompted Senator Key Pittman, a Nevada Democrat, to propose these laws. Roosevelt would have preferred more presidential flexibility, but Congress wanted to avoid flexibility and the mistakes of World War I. The laws provided that, on outbreak of war between foreign nations, all exports of American arms and munitions to them would be embargoed for six months. In addition, American ships were prohibited from carrying arms to any belligerent, and the president was to warn American citizens not to travel on belligerent ships.

The Neutrality Acts of 1936

The laws gave the president authority to determine when a state of war existed, and prohibited any loans or credits to belligerents.

The Neutrality Acts of 1937

The laws gave the president authority to determine if a civil war was a threat to world peace and covered by the Neutrality Acts, prohibited all arms sales to belligerents, and allowed the cash-and-carry sale of nonmilitary goods to belligerents.

Threats to World Order

The Manchurian Crisis

In September 1931 the Japanese army invaded and seized the Chinese province of Manchuria. The action violated the Nine Power Pact and the Kellogg-Briand Pact. When the League of Nations sought consideration of some action against Japan, Hoover refused to consider either economic or military sanctions. The only American action was to refuse recognition of the action or the puppet state of Manchukuo which the Japanese created.

Ethiopia

Following a border skirmish between Italian and Ethiopian troops, the Italian army of Fascist dictator Benito Mussolini invaded Ethiopia from neighboring Italian colonies in October 1935. The League of Nations failed to take effective action, the United States looked on, and Ethiopia fell in May 1936.

Occupation of the Rhineland

In defiance of the Versailles Treaty, Nazi dictator Adolph Hitler sent his German army into the demilitarized Rhineland in March 1936.

The Spanish Civil War (1936–1939)

The Spanish Civil War began in 1936 following an election victory by a popular front of republican and radical parties. Right-wing generals, led by Franscisco Franco, began a military revolt. The United States, Britain, and France remained neutral, despite the participation of German and Italian military units aiding Franco and the Fascist forces. The USSR, as well as volunteers from the United States and other countries, fought with the anti-Fascists, but were defeated in 1939.

The Rome-Berlin Axis

Germany and Italy, under Hitler and Mussolini, formed an alliance called the Rome-Berlin Axis on October 25, 1936.

The Sino-Japanese War

The Japanese launched a full-scale invasion of China in July 1937. When Japanese planes sank the American Gunboat *Panay* and three Standard Oil tankers on the Yangtze River in December 1937, the United States accepted a Japanese apology and damage payments while the American public called for the withdrawal of all American forces from China.

The "Quarantine the Aggressor" Speech

In a speech in Chicago in October 1937 Roosevelt proposed that the democracies unite to quarantine the aggressor nations. When public opinion did not pick up the idea, he did not press the issue.

German Expansion

Hitler brought about a union of Germany and Austria in March 1938, took the German-speaking Sudetenland from Czechoslovakia in September 1938, and occupied the rest of Czechoslovakia in March 1939.

The Invasion of Poland and the Beginning of World War II

On August 24, 1939 Germany signed a nonaggression pact with Russia which contained a secret provision to divide Poland between them. German forces then invaded Poland on September 1, 1939. Britain and France declared war on Germany on September 3 because of their treaties with Poland. By the end of September Poland had been dismembered by Germany and Russia, but the war continued in the west along the French-German border.

The American Response to the War in Europe

Preparedness

Even before the outbreak of World War II, Roosevelt began a preparedness program to improve American defenses. In May 1938 he requested and received a naval construction appropriation of about $1 billion. In October, Congress provided an additional $300 million for defense, and in January 1939 a regular defense appropriation of $1.3 billion with an added $525 million for equipment, especially airplanes. Defense spending increased after the outbreak of war. In August 1939 Roosevelt created the War Resources Board to develop a plan for industrial mobilization in the event of war. The next month he established the Office of Emergency Management in the White House to centralize mobilization activities.

The Neutrality Act of 1939

Roosevelt officially proclaimed the neutrality of the United States on September 5, 1939. He then called Congress into special session on September 21 and urged it to allow the cash-and-carry sale of arms. Despite opposition from isolationists, the Democratic Congress, in a vote that followed party lines, passed a new Neutrality Act in November. It allowed the cash-and-carry sale of arms and short-term loans to belligerents, but forbade American ships to trade with belligerents or Americans to travel on belligerent ships. The new law was helpful to the Allies because they controlled the Atlantic.

Changing American Attitudes

Hitler's armies invaded and quickly conquered Denmark and Norway in April 1940. In May, German forces swept through the Netherlands, Belgium, Luxembourg, and France. The British were driven from the continent, and France surrendered on June 22. Almost all Americans recognized Germany as a threat. They divided on whether to aid Britain or to concentrate on the defense of America. The Committee to Defend America by Aiding the Allies was formed in May 1940, and the America First Committee, which opposed involvement, was incorporated in September 1940.

Greenland

In April 1940 Roosevelt declared that Greenland, a possession of conquered Denmark, was covered by the Monroe Doctrine, and he supplied military assistance to set up a coastal patrol there.

Defense Mobilization

In May 1940 Roosevelt appointed a Council of National Defense chaired by William S. Knudson, the president of General Motors, to direct defense production and especially to build 50,000 planes. The council was soon awarding defense contracts at the rate of $1.5 billion a month. The Office of Production Management was created to allocate scarce materials, and the Office of Price Administration was established to prevent inflation and protect consumers. In June, Roosevelt made Republicans Henry L. Stimson and Frank Kellogg secretaries of war and navy, partly as an attempt to secure bipartisan support.

Selective Service

Congress approved the nation's first peacetime draft, the Selective Service and Training Act, in September 1940. Men 21 to 35 were registered, and many were called for one year of military training.

Destroyers for Bases

Roosevelt had determined that to aid Britain in every way possible was the best way to avoid war with Germany. He ordered the army and navy to turn over all available weapons and munitions to private dealers for resale to Britain. In September 1940 he signed an agreement to give Britain 50 American destroyers in return for a 99-year lease on air and naval bases in British territories in Newfoundland, Bermuda, and the Caribbean.

The Election of 1940

Passing over their isolationist frontrunners, Senator Robert A. Taft of Ohio and New York attorney Thomas E. Dewey, the Republicans nominated Wendell L. Willkie of Indiana, a dark horse candidate. Willkie was a liberal Republican who had been a Democrat most of his life, and the head of an electric utility holding company which had fought against the TVA. The platform supported a strong defense program, but severely criticized the New Deal domestic policies.

Roosevelt did not reveal his intentions regarding a third term, but he neither endorsed another candidate nor discouraged his supporters. When the convention came in July, he sent a message to the Democratic National Committee implying that he would accept the nomination for a third time if it were offered. He was then nominated on the first ballot, breaking a tradition which had existed since the time of Washington. Only with difficulty did Roosevelt's managers persuade the delegates to accept his choice of vice president, Secretary of Agriculture Henry A. Wallace, to succeed Garner. The platform endorsed the foreign and domestic policies of the administration.

Willkie's basic agreement with Roosevelt's foreign policy made it difficult for him to campaign. Willkie had a folksy approach which appealed to many voters, but he first attacked Roosevelt for the slowness of the defense program, and then, late in the campaign, called him a warmonger. Roosevelt, who lost the support of many Democrats, including his advisor James Farley, over the third term issue, campaigned very little. When Willkie began to gain on the warmongering issue, Roosevelt declared on October 30 that "your boys are not going to be sent into any foreign wars."

Roosevelt won by a much narrower margin than in 1936, with 27,243,466 votes, 54.7 percent, and 449 electoral votes. Willkie received 22,304,755 votes and 82 electoral votes. Socialist Norman Thomas had 100,264 votes, and Communist Earl Browder received 48,579.

American Involvement with the European War

The Lend-Lease Act

The British were rapidly exhausting their cash reserves with which to buy American goods. In January 1941 Roosevelt proposed that the United States provide supplies to be paid for in goods and services after the war. The Lend-Lease Act was passed by Congress and signed on March 11, 1941, and the first appropriation of $7 billion was provided. In effect, the law changed the United States from a neutral to a nonbelligerent on the Allied side.

The Patrol of the Western Atlantic

The Germans stepped up their submarine warfare in the Atlantic to prevent the flow of American supplies to Britain. In April 1941 Roosevelt started the American Neutrality Patrol. The American navy would search out but not attack German submarines in the western half of the Atlantic, and warn British vessels of their location.

Greenland

In April 1941, United States forces occupied Greenland and in May the president declared a state of unlimited national emergency.

Occupation of Iceland

American marines occupied Iceland, a Danish possession, in July 1941 to protect it from seizure by Germany. The American navy began to convoy American and Icelandic ships between the United States and Iceland.

The Atlantic Charter

On August 9, 1941 Roosevelt and Winston Churchill, the British prime minister, met for the first time on a British battleship off Newfoundland. This meeting resulted in the Atlantic Charter, signed on board the U.S. cruiser *Augusta* on August 10, 1941, which described a postwar world based on self-determination for all nations. It also endorsed the principles of freedom of speech and religion and freedom from want and fear, which Roosevelt had proposed as the Four Freedoms earlier that year.

Aid to Russia

Germany invaded Russia in June 1941, and in November the United States extended lend-lease assistance to the Russians.

The Shoot-on-Sight Order

The American destroyer *Greer* was attacked by a German submarine near Iceland on September 4, 1941. Roosevelt ordered the American military forces to shoot on sight at any German or Italian vessel in the patrol zone. An undeclared naval war had begun. The American destroyer *Kearny* was attacked by a submarine on October 16, and the destroyer *Reuben James* was sunk on October 30, with 115 lives lost. In November, Congress authorized the arming of merchant ships.

The Road to Pearl Harbor

Following their invasion of China in 1937, the Japanese began to speak of the Greater East Asia Co-Prosperity Sphere, a Japanese empire of undefined boundaries in east Asia and the western Pacific. Accordingly, they forced out American and other business interests from occupied China, declaring that the Open Door policy had ended. Roosevelt responded by lending money to China and requesting American aircraft manufacturers not to sell to Japan.

Following the fall of France, a new and more militant Japanese government in July 1940 obtained from the German-controlled Vichy French government the right to build air bases and to station troops in northern French Indochina. The United States, fearing that the step would lead to further expansion, responded in late July by placing an embargo on the export of aviation gasoline, lubricants, and scrap iron and steel to Japan, and by granting an additional loan to China. In December the embargo was extended to include iron ore and pig iron, some chemicals, machine tools, and other products.

Japan joined with Germany and Italy to form the Rome-Berlin-Tokyo Axis on September 27, 1940 when it signed the Tripartite Pact or Triple Alliance with the other Axis powers.

In July 1941 Japan extracted a new concession from Vichy France by obtaining military control of southern Indochina. Roosevelt reacted by freezing Japanese funds in the United States, closing the Panama Canal to Japan, activating the Philippine militia, and placing an embargo on the export of oil and other vital products to Japan.

Negotiations to end the impasse between the United States and Japan were conducted in Washington between Secretary Hull and Japanese Ambassador Kichisaburo Nomura. Hull demanded that Japan withdraw from Indochina and China, promise not to attack any other area in the western Pacific, and withdraw from the Tripartite Pact in return for the reopening of American trade. The Japanese offered to withdraw from Indochina when the Chinese war was satisfactorily settled, to promise no further expansion, and to agree to ignore any obligation under the Tripartite Pact to go to war if the United States entered a defensive war with Germany. Hull refused to compromise.

The Japanese proposed in August 1941 that Roosevelt meet personally with the Japanese prime minister, Prince Konoye, in an effort to resolve their differences. Such an action might have strengthened the position of Japanese moderates, but Roosevelt replied in September that he would do so only if Japan agreed to leave China. No meeting was held.

In October 1941 a new military cabinet headed by General Hideki Tojo took control of Japan. The Japanese secretly decided to make a final effort to negotiate, and to go to war if no solution was found by November 25. A new round of talks followed in Washington, but neither side would make a substantive change in its position, and on November 26, Hull repeated the American demand that the Japanese remove all their forces from China and Indochina immediately. The Japanese gave final approval on December 1 for an attack on the United States.

The Japanese planned a major offensive to take the Dutch East Indies, Malaya, and the Philippines in order to obtain the oil, metals, and other raw materials which they needed. At the same time they would attack Pearl Harbor in Hawaii to destroy the American Pacific fleet to keep it from interfering with their plans.

The United States had broken the Japanese diplomatic codes, and knew that trouble was imminent. Between December 1 and December 6, 1941, it became clear to administration leaders that Japanese task forces were being ordered into battle. American commanders in the Pacific were warned of possible aggressive action there, but not forcefully. Apparently, most American leaders thought that Japan would attack the Dutch East Indies and Malaya, but would avoid American territory so as not to provoke action by the United States. Some argue that Roosevelt wanted to let the Japanese attack so that the American people would be squarely behind the war.

The Pearl Harbor Attack

At 7:55 A.M. on Sunday, December 7, 1941 the first wave of Japanese carrier-based planes attacked the American fleet in Pearl Harbor. A second wave followed at 8:50 A.M. American defensive action was almost nil, but by the second wave a few antiaircraft batteries were operating and a few Army planes from another base in Hawaii engaged the enemy. The United States suffered the loss of two battleships sunk, six damaged and out of action, three cruisers and three destroyers sunk or damaged, and a number of lesser vessels destroyed or damaged. All of the 150 aircraft at Pearl Harbor were destroyed on the ground. Worst of all, 2,323 American servicemen were killed and about 1,100 wounded. The Japanese lost 29 planes, five midget submarines, and one fleet submarine.

The Declaration of War

On December 8, 1941, Roosevelt told a joint session of Congress that the day before had been a "date that would live in infamy." Congress declared war on Japan with one dissenting vote. On December 11, Germany and Italy declared war on the United States.

QUESTION

> Why did Japan attack the United States at Pearl Harbor?

EXPLANATION

Japan wanted to expand its influence throughout the Pacific. To this end, they invaded China, and prohibited U.S. business from activity there. Japan also formed an alliance with Italy and Germany. The U.S. imposed sanctions on Japan to prevent them from expanding further. The U.S. demanded that Japan withdraw from Indochina and China, but Japan refused and no compromise could be reached. Because of the sanctions, Japan needed to control more territory to acquire raw materials. They attacked the U.S. fleet at Pearl Harbor in order to prevent the U.S. from interfering with their plans.

Drill 4: New Deal Diplomacy and the Road to War

1. The United States began mobilizing for war after September 1939 through which of the following?

    (A) The Neutrality Act of 1939

    (B) The Selective Service Acts of 1940 and 1941

    (C) The establishment of Lend-Lease in 1941

    (D) The Declaration of Panama

    (E) The exchange of American destroyers for British naval bases in the Caribbean

2. Prior to declaring war in December 1941, the United States became an unofficial enemy of Germany and Italy through all of the following EXCEPT

    (A) American ships convoyed British shipping across the Atlantic.

    (B) the U.S. imprisoned German and Italian seamen.

    (C) the U.S. froze all Axis-held property within its borders.

(D)   the U.S. occupied Greenland and Iceland.

(E)   American and British merchant and warships were repaired in American shipyards.

3.   All of the following were steps taken by the United States to aid Great Britain prior to U.S. entry into World War II EXCEPT

(A)   the sale of 50 destroyers to the British in exchange for 99-year leases on certain overseas naval bases.

(B)   gradual assumption by the U.S. Navy of an increasing role in patrolling the Atlantic against German submarines.

(C)   institution of the Lend-Lease program for providing war supplies to Britain beyond its ability to pay.

(D)   the stationing of U.S. Marines in Scotland to protect it against possible German invasion.

(E)   the institution of the cash-and-carry system, allowing Britain to purchase war supplies in the United States provided they were paid for in cash.

4.   At the time of the Japanese attack on Pearl Harbor, the United States found itself

(A)   partially prepared by over a year of the nation's first peacetime draft.

(B)   fully prepared through complete mobilization and training beginning at the outbreak of the war in Europe.

(C)   almost completely unprepared, with one of the smallest armies in the world.

(D)   with a large and modern navy but an army of under 100,000 men.

(E)   with a large but untrained army of conscripts called up within the past six weeks.

5.   The purpose of Franklin D. Roosevelt's "Four Freedoms" speech was to

(A)   obtain a congressional declaration of war against Germany.

(B)   gain support for his Lend-Lease program.

(C)   obtain a congressional declaration of war against Japan.

(D)   assert complete American neutrality in the war in Europe.

(E)   set forth the terms under which Germany's surrender would be accepted.

1929–1941
DRILLS

ANSWER KEY

Drill 1—The Great Depression

1. (B)	2. (C)	3. (B)	4. (C)	5. (D)
6. (D)	7. (B)	8. (D)	9. (E)	10. (C)

Drill 2—The First and Second New Deals

1. (A)	2. (C)	3. (E)	4. (C)	5. (C)
6. (C)	7. (A)	8. (D)	9. (E)	10. (E)

Drill 3—Social Dimensions of the New Deal Era

1. (A)	2. (A)	3. (C)	4. (B)	5. (D)

Drill 4—New Deal Diplomacy and the Road to War

1. (B)	2. (D)	3. (D)	4. (A)	5. (B)

GLOSSARY: 1929–1941

Economic Royalists

Business people Roosevelt charged with seeking only their own power and wealth by opposing the New Deal.

Hoovervilles

Empty spaces around cities where the homeless would set up makeshift shacks to live in.

Hundred Days

The period immediately following Roosevelt's inauguration during which Congress passed the most important legislation of the New Deal.

Isolationism

The belief that the United States should stay out of foreign wars and problems.

Margin Trading

Purchasing stock by borrowing 90 percent of the purchase through a broker's loan, and putting up the stock as collateral.

New Deal

Roosevelt's plan for coping with the depression. It included both social programs as well as regulations on businesses.

Underconsumption

An economic situation that occurs when ordinary farmers and workers do not have money to continue purchasing products.

CHAPTER 13

1941–1960

WORLD WAR II AND THE POSTWAR ERA

➤ Diagnostic Test
➤ 1941–1960 Review & Drills
➤ Glossary

1941-1960
DIAGNOSTIC TEST

1. Ⓐ Ⓑ Ⓒ Ⓓ Ⓔ
2. Ⓐ Ⓑ Ⓒ Ⓓ Ⓔ
3. Ⓐ Ⓑ Ⓒ Ⓓ Ⓔ
4. Ⓐ Ⓑ Ⓒ Ⓓ Ⓔ
5. Ⓐ Ⓑ Ⓒ Ⓓ Ⓔ
6. Ⓐ Ⓑ Ⓒ Ⓓ Ⓔ
7. Ⓐ Ⓑ Ⓒ Ⓓ Ⓔ
8. Ⓐ Ⓑ Ⓒ Ⓓ Ⓔ
9. Ⓐ Ⓑ Ⓒ Ⓓ Ⓔ
10. Ⓐ Ⓑ Ⓒ Ⓓ Ⓔ
11. Ⓐ Ⓑ Ⓒ Ⓓ Ⓔ
12. Ⓐ Ⓑ Ⓒ Ⓓ Ⓔ
13. Ⓐ Ⓑ Ⓒ Ⓓ Ⓔ
14. Ⓐ Ⓑ Ⓒ Ⓓ Ⓔ
15. Ⓐ Ⓑ Ⓒ Ⓓ Ⓔ
16. Ⓐ Ⓑ Ⓒ Ⓓ Ⓔ
17. Ⓐ Ⓑ Ⓒ Ⓓ Ⓔ
18. Ⓐ Ⓑ Ⓒ Ⓓ Ⓔ

19. Ⓐ Ⓑ Ⓒ Ⓓ Ⓔ
20. Ⓐ Ⓑ Ⓒ Ⓓ Ⓔ
21. Ⓐ Ⓑ Ⓒ Ⓓ Ⓔ
22. Ⓐ Ⓑ Ⓒ Ⓓ Ⓔ
23. Ⓐ Ⓑ Ⓒ Ⓓ Ⓔ
24. Ⓐ Ⓑ Ⓒ Ⓓ Ⓔ
25. Ⓐ Ⓑ Ⓒ Ⓓ Ⓔ
26. Ⓐ Ⓑ Ⓒ Ⓓ Ⓔ
27. Ⓐ Ⓑ Ⓒ Ⓓ Ⓔ
28. Ⓐ Ⓑ Ⓒ Ⓓ Ⓔ
29. Ⓐ Ⓑ Ⓒ Ⓓ Ⓔ
30. Ⓐ Ⓑ Ⓒ Ⓓ Ⓔ
31. Ⓐ Ⓑ Ⓒ Ⓓ Ⓔ
32. Ⓐ Ⓑ Ⓒ Ⓓ Ⓔ
33. Ⓐ Ⓑ Ⓒ Ⓓ Ⓔ
34. Ⓐ Ⓑ Ⓒ Ⓓ Ⓔ
35. Ⓐ Ⓑ Ⓒ Ⓓ Ⓔ

1941–1960
DIAGNOSTIC TEST

This diagnostic test is designed to help you determine your strengths and weaknesses in your knowledge of World War II and the Postwar Era (1941–1960). Follow the directions and check your answers.

Study this chapter for the following tests:
AP U.S. History, CLEP General, CLEP United States History I,
GED, Praxis Specialty Area, SAT: United States History

---

35 Questions

DIRECTIONS: Choose the correct answer for each of the following questions. Fill in each answer on the answer sheet.

1. The Korean War is associated with all of the following EXCEPT

   (A) the Yalu River.

   (B) the 38th parallel.

   (C) the Truman-MacArthur controversy.

   (D) the United Nations.

   (E) "Total Victory."

2. Martin Luther King emerged as a civil rights leader during which of the following events?

   (A) The 1957 desegregation of the Little Rock schools

   (B) The Greensboro, N.C., sit-ins of 1960

   (C) The Montgomery Bus Boycott of 1956

   (D) The 1941 March on Washington

   (E) *Brown v. Topeka Board of Education* (1954)

3. After World War II, the United States sought to strengthen Western Europe through all of the following EXCEPT

   (A) the establishment of NATO.

(B)   The Lend-Lease Act.

(C)   the establishment of West Germany.

(D)   the Marshall Plan.

(E)   the Berlin airlift.

4.   Which of the following statements is correct about the case of Whitaker Chambers and Alger Hiss? *1948*

(A)   Hiss accused Chambers, an important mid-ranking government official, of being a Communist spy.

(B)   The case gained national attention through the involvement of Senator Joseph R. McCarthy.

(C)   Hiss was convicted of perjury for denying under oath that he had been a Communist agent.

(D)   The case marked the beginning of American concern about Communist subversion.

(E)   Chambers denied ever having had any involvement with the Communist party.

5.   As U.S. troops suffered a series of defeats during the early months of the Second World War in the Pacific, General Douglas MacArthur promised

(A)   to hold Australia.

(B)   to hold the Philippines.

(C)   to recapture Wake Island.

(D)   to hold Japanese generals personally responsible for the atrocities committed by their troops.

(E)   to return to the Philippines.

6.   The essential element of the policy of containment was

(A)   a commitment to rolling back Communism.

(B)   a commitment to working with the Soviet Union.

(C)   a rejection of involvement in affairs outside the Western Hemisphere.

(D)   a commitment to fight a defensive war against the Japanese while taking the offensive against Germany.

(E)   a commitment to holding Communism within the Soviet Union and Eastern Europe.

7. The Twenty-second Amendment to the Constitution did which of the following?

    (A) Established prohibition

    (B) Repealed prohibition

    (C) Gave women the right to vote

    (D) Limited the president to two terms

    (E) Gave Congress the power to enact an income tax

8. The Neutrality Act of 1939 enabled the United States to

    (A) sell military and nonmilitary goods on credit to belligerent nations and transport them on American ships.

    (B) sell military and nonmilitary goods for cash to belligerent nations and transport them on American ships.

    (C) sell military and nonmilitary goods on credit to belligerent nations if transported on another nation's ships.

    (D) sell only nonmilitary goods for cash to belligerent nations if transported on another nation's ships.

    (E) sell nonmilitary and military goods for cash to belligerent nations if transported on another nation's ships.

9. Which of the following was NOT a major diplomatic conference during World War II?

    (A) Yalta   (B) Versailles

    (C) Teheran   (D) Casablanca

    (E) Potsdam

10. In 1960 which of the following contributed most directly to Soviet leader Nikita Khrushchev's cancellation of a scheduled summit meeting with President Dwight Eisenhower?

    (A) The rise to power of Fidel Castro in Cuba

    (B) The failure, at the Bay of Pigs, of a U.S.-sponsored attempt to oust Castro

    (C) The sending of U.S. troops to Lebanon

    (D) The downing of an American U-2 spy plane over the Soviet Union

    (E) The success of the Soviet space program in launching the Sputnik satellite

11. All of the following statements about the Taft-Hartley Act are true EX-
    CEPT

    - (A) it had long been the goal of a number of large labor unions.

    (B) it allowed the president to call an eight-day cooling-off period to delay
        any strike that might endanger national safety or health.

    (C) it outlawed the closed shop.

    (D) it was backed by congressional Republicans.

    (E) it was vetoed by President Truman.

12. In the Second World War the Allied strategy, agreed upon by the U.S. and
    Great Britain, was to

    (A) concentrate on defeating Japan first before turning on Germany.

    (B) divide all resources equally between the war against Japan and that
        against Germany.

    (C) fight only against Japan, leaving the Russians to fight Germany alone.

    (D) take a passive role and limit operations to reacting to Axis moves.

    (E) concentrate on defeating Germany first before turning on Japan.

13. The Marshall Plan was

    (A) a strategy for defeating Germany.

    (B) a strategy for defeating Japan.

    (C) an American economic aid program for Europe.

    (D) an American commitment to give military and economic aid to any
        nation resisting Communist aggression.

    (E) a civil-defense plan for surviving a Soviet nuclear strike.

14. Which of the following statements is NOT true of the 1947 Taft-Hartley
    Act?

    (A) It made the "closed shop" illegal.

    (B) It established an 80-day cooling-off period for delaying strikes in key
        industries.

    (C) It banned the practice of forcing newly hired employees to join a
        union.

    (D) It prohibited secondary boycotts.

    (E) It required the administration of an anti-Communist oath to union
        officials.

15. Which of the following novels deals LEAST with World War II and its issues?

(A) Norman Mailer's *The Naked and the Dead*

(B) Saul Bellow's *Herzog*

(C) James Jones's *From Here to Eternity*

(D) Thomas Pynchon's *Gravity's Rainbow*

(E) Joseph Heller's *Catch-22*

16. What event triggered President Truman to announce the Truman Doctrine?

(A) The overthrow of the Czechoslovakian government by Soviet Communists

(B) Russian actions in Iran

(C) The Greek Civil War

(D) The Hungarian Revolution

(E) The Korean War

17. What prevented Hitler from defeating the Allied invasion at Normandy in 1944?

(A) Hitler's forces were, by then, so weak that he couldn't have defeated the Allied landing force no matter what he tried to do.

(B) The Allies led Hitler to believe that there wasn't going to be an invasion until 1945, so when the invasion took place, Hitler refused to react to it because he thought it was just an Allied "raid" of no real importance. He didn't realize his mistake until it was too late.

(C) Hitler was so insane by the time of the invasion that he was totally incapable of making any rational decisions, and his generals made no real effort to convince him to stop the invasion on the beaches.

(D) The Allies deceived Hitler into believing that the real invasion was to take place at Pas de Calais. When Allied troops landed at Normandy, Hitler thought it was a feint, and kept his best troops at Pas de Calais. He didn't realize his mistake until it was too late.

(E) Hitler thought that by letting the Allies land unopposed, he might be able to negotiate a peace treaty with Britain and the U.S., allowing him to send all his forces to the Russian front to defeat Russia.

18. The wartime conference in which Stalin, Churchill, and Roosevelt laid out plans for postwar Europe, allowing Eastern Europe to fall under the Russian "sphere of influence" while Western Europe would be under British and American influence, was the _____ conference.

Feb '45   *July* *Truman*

- (A) Yalta
- (B) Potsdam
- (C) Casablanca
- (D) Teheran
- (E) Geneva

19. What was the name of the U.S.-sponsored economic aid plan designed to rebuild Europe after WW II had ended?

- (A) The Marshall Plan
- (B) The Atlantic Charter
- (C) The Schleifen Plan
- (D) The Eisenhower Doctrine
- (E) The Truman Doctrine

20. What event, in 1957, caused a near panic among U.S. leaders and led to a massive increase in spending for science programs, etc., in U.S. schools and research institutions?

- (A) The revelation of huge Soviet stockpiles of deadly chemical weapons to be used in any future confrontation with the United States
- (B) The launching of Sputnik by the Soviet Union
- (C) The detonation of a hydrogen bomb by the Soviet Union   *we had it first*
- (D) The development of the microprocessor by the Soviet Union
- (E) Soviet Premier Nikita Khrushchev's promise to "bury" the West

21. The 49th state admitted into the Union was

- (A) Arizona.
- (B) Alaska.
- (C) Hawaii.
- (D) Puerto Rico.
- (E) the Virgin Islands.

22. A "closed shop" requires workers to

- (A) receive national security clearance.
- (B) promise not to join a union.
- (C) join a union to secure a job.
- (D) receive their pay in cash.
- (E) apply for unemployment benefits.

23. Place the following events of World War II in the correct order in which they occurred.

1. the attack on Pearl Harbor
2. the German invasion of the Soviet Union

3. the D-Day Invasion

4. the dropping of the atomic bomb on Hiroshima

(A) 1–3–2–4   (B) 2–3–1–4

(C) 2–1–4–3   (D) 2–1–3–4

(E) 3–2–1–4

24. The Soviet Union's launching of Sputnik in 1957 immediately led to

(A) an easing of U.S.-U.S.S.R. tensions.

(B) massive federal aid to American higher education.

(C) the Suez Crisis.

(D) the Geneva Summit's endorsement of Open Skies.

(E) the U-2 incident.

25. McCarthyism refers to

(A) the illegal practice of redistricting to favor the political party in power.

(B) the hysterical search for Communists and their sympathizers in American government.

(C) the post-World War II economic recovery programs for Western Europe.

(D) corrupt urban politicians.

(E) the United States policy toward Latin America in the 1950s.

26. The Japanese surprise attack on Pearl Harbor succeeded for all of the following reasons EXCEPT

(A) a conspiracy by the United States government to let the Japanese attack Pearl Harbor by surprise so America would have a legitimate excuse to enter World War II.

(B) commanders at Pearl Harbor were convinced that the only real threat to the base was from local saboteurs, not a Japanese naval attack.

(C) a message ordering the base on maximum war alert was sent via commercial telegraph rather than military cable and did not arrive until the day after the attack.

(D) Americans did not believe the Japanese would dare attempt such a risky attack, and did not believe the Japanese COULD pull it off if they tried.

(E) interservice rivalry effectively kept the military intelligence services from sharing and coordinating the information they had collected which could have allowed them to anticipate the Pearl Harbor attack.

27. In 1956, Egypt nationalized the Suez Canal primarily to

    (A) block Israeli usage of the Canal.

    (B) use it to blackmail Western nations into backing off on their political support for Israel.

    (C) fund the construction of the Aswan Dam after America had withdrawn its funding offer.

    (D) open it to use by Egypt's ally, the Soviet Union.

    (E) fund the building of Egypt's military forces for a planned attack against Israel in 1957.

28. The British and French policy of appeasement toward Mussolini and Hitler

    (A) curtailed Hitler's expansionism until the policy was abandoned by both the British and French during the Sudetenland crisis.

    (B) bought time for the British and French to effectively rebuild their militaries so they would be better able to confront Hitler when they were militarily ready.

    (C) convinced Hitler that both Britain and France were spineless and led him to accelerate the rate of German expansion.

    (D) forced Hitler to temporarily slow down his expansion plans so he could avoid being portrayed as a blatant aggressor in the face of French and British passivity and humanitarianism.

    (E) created temporary divisions between Mussolini who wanted to attack the British and French immediately and Hitler who wanted to wait until he had an excuse to make his aggression look justified.

29. What was the main goal of the Truman Doctrine?

    (A) Enforcement of the "Domino Theory"

    (B) Containment of Communism

    (C) Ending nationalistic revolts in American territories and colonies

    (D) Elimination of Communism

    (E) Rebuilding Western Europe after World War II

30. In 1948, what city did the U.S., Britain, and France have to keep supplied for over 300 days in a massive airlift due to the Soviets cutting off all land-based supply routes in an effort to drive the Westerners out of the city?

    (A) Helsinki   (B) Warsaw

    (C) Bonn   (D) Berlin

    (E) Prague

31. Which of the following was the MAJOR reason Truman used to justify his decision to drop the atomic bomb on Hiroshima in August 1945?

   •(A) He felt it would shorten the war and eliminate the need for an invasion of Japan.

   (B) He felt it would end up saving Japanese civilian lives, when compared to the casualties expected from an invasion of Japan.

   (C) He wanted to send a strong warning message to the Russians to watch their step in the Pacific after Japan was defeated.

   (D) He believed it would be an appropriate revenge for the Japanese attack on Pearl Harbor.

   (E) Once the bomb was completed, Truman felt he had to use it in order to justify the huge investments in time, resources, scientific expertise, and expense involved in developing it.

32. The Taft-Hartley Labor Act of 1947 had the effect of *PATCO*

   (A) prohibiting strikes by government employees.

   (B) granting railroad workers the right to strike and to organize unions.

   (C) extending the right to strike and to organize unions, previously allowed to railroad workers only, to all workers.

   (D) allowing unions to force management into binding arbitration when contract negotiations broke down.

   -(E) forbidding unions from closing shops to nonunion employees.

33. Where did MacArthur land his forces behind North Korean lines in an effort to trap the North Korean Army and quickly win the Korean War?

   (A) Pusan   (B) Seoul

   (C) Inchon   (D) Pan Mun Jong

   (E) Pyong Yang

34. The largest battle ever fought, which historians consider the turning point of World War II in Europe, was the battle of

   •(A) Stalingrad.   (B) Leningrad.

   (C) Normandy. *D-Day*   (D) Kiev.

   (E) the Bulge.

35. The Atlantic Charter

   •(A) set collective war strategy and long-term war goals for Britain and the United States.

   (B) guaranteed American neutrality in World War II as long as American warships stayed out of British territorial waters.

   (C) pledged South and Central American neutrality after Germany and Japan declared war on the United States.

   (D) provided Britain with 50 World War I vintage American destroyers in return for American control of British military bases in the Caribbean and the Mid-Atlantic.

   (E) repealed the American arms embargo and allowed Britain and France to buy American war materials on a cash-and-carry basis.

1941–1960
DIAGNOSTIC TEST

ANSWER KEY

1. (E)	8. (E)	15. (B)	22. (C)	29. (B)
2. (C)	9. (B)	16. (C)	23. (D)	30. (D)
3. (B)	10. (D)	17. (D)	24. (B)	31. (A)
4. (C)	11. (A)	18. (A)	25. (B)	32. (E)
5. (E)	12. (E)	19. (A)	26. (A)	33. (C)
6. (E)	13. (C)	20. (B)	27. (C)	34. (A)
7. (D)	14. (C)	21. (B)	28. (C)	35. (A)

DETAILED EXPLANATIONS
OF ANSWERS

1.　**(E)**　Instead of pursuing total victory, the United States sought limited objectives under the auspices of the United Nations. General MacArthur publicly disagreed with President Truman over restoring South Korea's hegemony to the 38th parallel. Instead, he wanted to unite Korea by driving north to the Yalu River.

2.　**(C)**　Martin Luther King organized the Montgomery Bus Boycott of 1956. The 1941 March on Washington was organized by A. Philip Randolph, but never took place. King participated in the 1963 March on Washington. He was not directly connected with *Brown v. Topeka Board of Education*, desegregation of the public schools in Little Rock, or the sit-ins in Greensboro, North Carolina.

3.　**(B)**　Lend-Lease was begun in 1941 to help in the fight against Germany. The Marshall Plan was created in 1947. West Germany was created in 1948 and was followed shortly by the Berlin Airlift. NATO was established in 1949.

4.　**(C)**　Hiss, a mid-ranking government official, was convicted of perjury for denying under oath that he had been a Communist agent, after being accused as such by admitted former Communist (E) Whitaker Chambers, not the other way around (A). The case gained national attention through the involvement of young Congressman Richard Nixon, not Senator Joseph R. McCarthy (B), and while it did increase American concern about Communist subversion, it was by no means the beginning of such concern (D).

5.　**(E)**　MacArthur's famous words with regard to the Philippines were, "I shall return"—and he did. It was already becoming clear that the Philippines could not be held at that time (B). Australia, of course, was held (A). Wake Island was not retaken (C) until after the Japanese surrender. In the end, some of the Japanese generals were held responsible for the atrocities committed.

6.　**(E)**　Containment, generally attributed to George F. Kennan, was the policy of holding communism within the Soviet Union and Eastern Europe. John Foster Dulles sought a more aggressive policy of "rolling back" Communism, while Richard Nixon sought to work with the Soviet Union through *détente*. Isolationism sought to avoid involvement in affairs outside the Western Hemisphere.

7.　**(D)**　In response to Franklin Roosevelt's four terms as president, the Twenty-second Amendment, passed in 1951, limited the president to two terms.

8.   **(E)**   According to the Neutrality Act of 1939, the U.S. could sell both military and nonmilitary goods on a "cash-and-carry" basis to belligerent nations.

9.   **(B)**   The conference at Versailles wrote the treaty ending World War I. Churchill and Roosevelt met at Casablanca in 1943; they were joined by Stalin later that year at Teheran. The "Big Three" also met at Yalta in 1945 and— Roosevelt being replaced by Truman—at Potsdam later that year.

10.   **(D)**   Khrushchev used the Soviet downing of the U-2 spy plane as a pretense to cancel the summit, thereby embarrassing Eisenhower. Castro had recently risen to power in Cuba (A), but the Bay of Pigs fiasco (B) was yet to come. Several years earlier, in unrelated incidents, the U.S. had sent troops into Lebanon (C), and the Soviet Union had launched Sputnik (E).

11.   **(A)**   The Taft-Hartley Act was definitely not sought but rather vehemently opposed by the labor unions. It did allow the president to call a cooling-off period (B), and it outlawed the closed shop (C). It was backed by Congressional Republicans (D), vetoed by President Truman (E), and passed over his veto.

12.   **(E)**   Allied strategy was to beat Germany first rather than the other way around (A) or an even division of resources (B).

13.   **(C)**   The Marshall Plan was an American economic aid program for Europe. The Truman Doctrine was the American commitment to help countries threatened by communism (D).

14.   **(C)**   The Taft-Hartley Act did not ban the practice known as the "union shop," by which newly hired employees are forced to join a union. It did make the "closed shop," in which only union members are hired, illegal (A), establish an 80-day cooling-off period for delaying strikes in key industries (B), prohibit secondary boycotts (D), and require that union officials take an anti-Communist oath (E). It also forbade such practices as employers collecting dues for the union, as well as jurisdictional strikes, featherbedding, and forced contributions to political campaigns.

15.   **(B)**   Saul Bellow's *Herzog* is a largely autobiographical novel about a college professor who suffers from bouts of paranoia. Mailer's *The Naked and the Dead* (A), about the members of an American infantry platoon invading a Japanese island; Jones's *From Here to Eternity* (C), about life in the army before the Japanese attack on Pearl Harbor; and Heller's *Catch-22* (E), about an enlisted man whose attempts to get himself declared insane backfire on him, are perhaps the most famous American postwar novels about the Second World War. Pynchon's *Gravity's Rainbow* (D) is a pessimistic, ambitious novel that begins at the end of World War II; the plot uses the V-2 rocket.

16.   **(C)**   In 1947, the British government told the American government that it could no longer afford the expense of economic and military aid to Greece and Turkey. At the time, both countries were locked in struggles against Communist insurgents. Greece was in virtual civil war and could not have won against Communist rebels without Western help. President Truman was determined that Greece should not be allowed to fall under Communist control. In response, he delivered a speech to Congress committing the United States to aid free people anywhere in the world in their struggle to preserve their freedom from foreign intervention or armed insurgents. This policy quickly became known as the Truman Doctrine. Congress approved aid to both Greece and Turkey, which both survived their respective Communist insurrections.

The aid to Greece and Turkey was just a first step in what became a massive aid program to non-Communist governments all over the world. Regrettably, many of the non-Communist governments receiving U.S. aid were led by brutal dictators every bit as evil as the Communist insurgents Truman wanted to suppress. American policy was so focused around Truman's effort to contain Communist expansion however, even brutal dictators were seen as preferable to Communists.

17.   **(D)**   The Allies set up an elaborate deception aimed at making Hitler believe that the invasion of France was intended for Pas de Calais, northeast of the actual invasion site at Normandy. Months before the invasion, General George Patton, whom the Germans considered to be the Americans' best field commander, was set up in a British estate and sent regular messages, in the open so the Germans would be sure to intercept them, related to a build-up for his "army," which existed only in the messages, to lead the invasion at Pas de Calais. The real armies were actually preparing for the assault at Normandy. On the night of the invasion, 10,000 miniature wooden dummies, sculpted to look like paratroopers and armed with automatically firing cap guns, were air-dropped in French fields inland from Pas de Calais. In the darkness they looked and sounded real, resulting in the German high command being deluged with reports of paratrooper landings in the Calais region. Additionally, Allied planes dropped "chaffe" over the region. Chaffe consisted of long thin strips of aluminum foil which, when air-dropped, would float in the upper atmosphere for hours. On German radar it looked like fleets of bombers flying over the Calais defenses.

Since Hitler had already convinced himself that Calais was the Allied invasion site, these Allied deceptions confirmed his beliefs. When the real invasion took place at Normandy, Hitler was convinced it was a diversion and refused to release his armored reserves from the Calais region until it was too late. Many military historians feel that had Hitler allowed his armored reserves to be used immediately, the Allies might have been thrown back into the Atlantic. With Hitler's succumbing to Allied deceptions at Calais whatever chance the Germans had of defeating the Normandy invasion was lost.

18.   **(A)**   The Yalta Conference took place in February 1945. At this time, the Allies could see victory approaching. American and British forces were lined

up along Germany's western border, and in the east, Russian forces were only 50 miles from Berlin and were preparing for a final assault on the German capital. The German Reich had only a few weeks of existence left. At Yalta, the major focus was to lay the foundations for postwar Europe. Bitter divisions existed between Stalin, Churchill, and Roosevelt. Churchill and Roosevelt wanted only limited Russian dominance over Poland and other areas of Eastern Europe. They also wanted only a temporary partitioning of Germany until Nazi influence could be eliminated. Stalin, however, felt slighted by previous Allied actions in Italy (in which he had been left out). He was determined to establish Eastern Europe as a Soviet "sphere of influence" by which Russia could surround itself with pro-Soviet governments from which there would be no danger of another invasion from the West. He also wanted a permanent partitioning of Germany and German reparations for the cost of fighting the war. Finally, he was determined to annex disputed territories along the Soviet border in Finland, Romania, and Poland, as well as all of the Baltic States.

In the end, Stalin got most of what he wanted. Since his soldiers already controlled Eastern Europe, there was not much the British or Americans could do, short of war with Russia, to deny Stalin's wishes in the region. In Germany, although partitioning was supposed to be temporary, Russian demands for a Communist-style government and Western demands for free elections resulted in the establishment of separate Eastern and Western governments in Germany. These governments operated as separate sovereign nations from the 1950s up until early 1990, when serious efforts at reunification finally began. While Britain and the United States refused to saddle Germany with reparations, the Soviets essentially got them by dismantling virtually every factory or piece of industrial equipment they could find and transporting it back to the Soviet Union.

19.   **(A)**   The Marshall Plan was conceived by Truman's secretary of state General George Marshall. After World War II, Europe was socially and economically devastated. Industries were destroyed. Farmers' fields were often too torn up from the war to cultivate. People were homeless and starving. The governments of Western Europe no longer had the resources to rebuild the cities and restore the economies to reasonable working order. There was a very real possibility that unless the economic situation in Western Europe was turned around, Communists would win control of several governments in free elections.

In addition, there was growing anti-American sentiment in Western Europe. America was viewed as big, fat, selfish, and lazy by many Europeans. They believed that America had the power to ease the poverty and pain being suffered by Europeans, but was too preoccupied with itself to do the job.

In response, in 1947 George Marshall conceived a massive economic aid plan to help Europe rebuild. The plan eventually resulted in more than $12.5 billion being given to Europe to finance reconstruction of the battered European infrastructure. With that money, the starvation problem eased, people were put back to work as new industries were built, and Communist opposition to the plan led to the collapse of Communist party support in many Western European countries. While the plan was not universally successful, it was one of the most innovative and well received policies ever conceived by the United States.

20.   **(B)**   The launching of Sputnik reverberated across the United States like nothing had since Pearl Harbor. After World War II Americans were taught to fear the Soviet Union through the glasses of the Cold War. However, one area of American-Soviet relations in which nearly all Americans felt more than secure was the superiority of American technology and American scientific know-how. Sure, the Russians had developed an atomic bomb and later a hydrogen bomb, but only after their spies had managed to steal plans from America. The inferiority of Soviet weapons was well known and widely joked about. Then came Sputnik, a little metal sphere which, when placed in orbit around the earth making it the world's first man-made orbital satellite, shook the world.

Suddenly, Soviet technological ineptitude was no longer a laughing matter. It became increasingly unhumorous when repeated American attempts to duplicate Sputnik failed miserably. American self-confidence was badly shaken. The quality of American science education was questioned, as was the moral fiber of the country. For the military, a new term suddenly blossomed into existence: Intercontinental Ballistic Missile (ICBM). If the Soviets could put a satellite into orbit, then it was no great leap for them to place a nuclear warhead on top of a missile and drop it right down Washington's collective throat. American Cold War fears intensified.

Using Sputnik as an excuse, Washington demanded and got increased funding for the military, particularly funding for missile research, as well as increased funding for education. Most of the education money was directed at colleges and universities and focused on mathematics and science education. It roused America from its complacency and led to a new wave of technical advances related to the influx of science-related funding.

21.   **(B)**   Alaska was admitted into the United States on January 3, 1959. Arizona was the 48th state and was admitted in 1912. Hawaii was the 50th state and was admitted eight months after Alaska, on August 21, 1959. Both Puerto Rico and the Virgin Islands are overseas possessions belonging to the United States. As of this date, neither has been admitted to statehood.

22.   **(C)**   The closed shop was one where a worker was required to join a union as a condition of receiving a job. This practice started in the late nineteenth century and continued until 1947 when the Taft-Hartley Act declared the closed shop illegal. This Act was passed by a Congress dominated by the Republican party over President Truman's veto. The act was designed by the Republicans to weaken the power of labor unions.

23.   **(D)**   The German invasion of the Soviet Union occurred in 1941. The attack on Pearl Harbor by the Japanese was in 1941; the D-Day Invasion of the Allies against Germany occurred in 1944; and the American bombing of Hiroshima took place in 1945.

24.   **(B)**   American reaction to the launching of the Soviet satellite Sputnik was immediate. Fearing that the United States had fallen behind the Soviets in scientific and mathematical research, a massive aid act was pushed through Congress to increase federal aid to higher education. The Geneva Summit took place in 1955 prior to the launching of Sputnik in 1957. The Suez Crisis occurred in 1956, while the U-2 incident involving the Soviet capture of an American spy plane occurred in 1960. Sputnik's launching led to heightened tensions globally for the U.S. and U.S.S.R.

25.   **(B)**   McCarthyism was the name attached to the domestic political situation in the early 1950s which involved the American search for Communists and their sympathizers in government offices. Named after Senator Joseph McCarthy of Wisconsin, the movement relied upon the Cold War fears of Americans and never resulted in the discovery of large numbers of Communists. The movement was brought to a close through the televised Army-McCarthy hearings in 1954 when Senator McCarthy repeatedly badgered witnesses in trying to uncover non-existent Communists in military command. The illegal practice of redistricting is referred to as gerrymandering. The post-World War II economic recovery programs for Western Europe were part of the Marshall Plan. A corrupt urban politician generally is called a "boss," and Eisenhower sought to re-establish Roosevelt's 1930s Good Neighbor policy toward Latin America.

26.   **(A)**   Pearl Harbor was the worst defeat ever suffered by the American Navy. To be caught as unprepared as the commanders at Pearl Harbor were was unbelievable to most Americans. American racism against the Japanese led many people to believe that the Japanese could never have pulled off their stunning raid without "inside help" of some sort. Suspicions immediately turned to Washington where Roosevelt's desire to bring America into World War II was well known. To these people, a conspiracy by Washington to let the Japanese get away with the attack, stirring up American anger and bringing America into the war, answered so many questions about the Japanese success that many felt it HAD to be the real reason Pearl Harbor had succeeded for the Japanese.

Evidence indicates that there was no plot. While American intelligence analysts knew the Japanese were about to attack somewhere, they did not know where. Since Japanese ships had been spotted sailing south, it was natural to assume that they were going to attack Southeast Asia or the Philippines, where British and American naval strength were too weak to effectively deter them. Military leaders sold themselves on this idea to the point that they ignored evidence indicating Pearl Harbor was also a target.

In addition, prejudice against the Japanese played a large role in the base being unprepared. Commanders at the base refused to focus on what the Japanese were capable of doing and instead focused on what seemed to make sense for them to do. To these commanders, a Japanese attack on Pearl Harbor was senseless. The odds against their fleet approaching Hawaii without being detected were slim. The risks involved with attacking the bulk of the American Pacific

Fleet, in its home harbor with the hundreds of defensive aircraft and antiaircraft guns, were so high that to Americans it seemed suicidal for the Japanese to attempt an attack. Americans felt that the Japanese wouldn't dare try it and ignored the fact that they had the capability to pull it off if they got lucky. Based on these assumptions, base commanders prepared only for the immediate threat of sabotage from local Japanese-Americans on Hawaii. They never seriously considered preparation for a full-scale Japanese assault, in spite of repeated war warnings from Washington, until the bombs actually began to fall.

While a message warning Pearl Harbor was sent before the attack, it was sent over commercial telegraph services rather than priority military lines. It did not arrive until after the attack, too late to make a difference. Some historians question if the telegram would have changed the result even if it had arrived on time, so convinced were Pearl's commanders that the Japanese wouldn't dare attack.

Finally, one of the major contributors to the belief in a government conspiracy was the amount of intelligence gathered before the attack which clearly indicated Pearl Harbor was at risk. In hindsight, the failure to effectively use this intelligence was shocking. Unfortunately, the intelligence was gathered in bits and pieces by several different intelligence agencies within the army and navy. At the time the two services didn't share their intelligence with each other, due to interservice rivalry and other logistical factors. As a result each intelligence service had only some of the necessary "bits" of information needed to piece the entire picture together. It was only AFTER the attack that all the intelligence was put together and the obviousness of Pearl Harbor as a target became clear.

27.   **(C)**   In 1956, Egypt was ruled by a popular, independent-minded nationalist named Gamal Abdel Nasser. Nasser was wary of becoming embroiled in the Cold War confrontation of the two superpowers. He quite properly feared that aligning with either power would put him in a position of being used as a pawn in the superpower struggle. Accordingly, Nasser pioneered a movement toward nonalignment by Third-World countries in Africa and Asia. Nasser was faced with a problem of his own, though. He wanted to build a large hydroelectric dam on the Nile River at Aswan to provide Egypt with the electric power it needed to expand industrially. Egypt did not have the funds to build the project on its own and turned to the most obvious choice for obtaining financial aid on the project, the United States.

Eisenhower's secretary of state, John Foster Dulles, did not believe in Third-World nonalignment. He attempted to link financing of the dam with Egyptian military and political commitments to the United States. When Nasser balked and demanded to maintain neutrality, Dulles basically responded that neutrality was impossible, either Nasser was pro-American or pro-Soviet. Since Nasser wouldn't make commitments to the United States, he must be pro-Soviet. Upon this reasoning, Dulles withdrew American funding for the project.

Denied American funding, Nasser responded by nationalizing the hugely profitable Suez Canal, hoping to use its profits to fund the dam. The canal had been under joint British/French control, and they were more than a little upset when Nasser took control of it from them. They responded by joining with the Israelis in a joint military invasion of Egypt in which they seized back the canal, sparking a major international crisis. Although Eisenhower and Dulles did not care for Nasser's nonalignment policies, they were outraged at the British/French/Israeli invasion of Egypt. They were especially outraged that they invaded without forewarning the United States. For one of the few times in the 1950s, the United States joined with the Soviet Union in condemning the action. Eventually, the British, French, and Israelis backed down. Nasser did get assistance for the dam, but that assistance came from the Soviet Union, not from the United States.

28.　**(C)**　The British and French engaged in their policy of appeasement in a desperate effort to avoid a war neither of them wanted. France had become extremely pacifistic since World War I and wanted to avoid a war at all costs. Britain did not want to get dragged into another war if it could be avoided, particularly a French-German war. The appeasement policy was first seen with Mussolini's invasion of Ethiopia. Although the invasion was a clear-cut case of aggression, neither Britain nor France took significant action, fearing that if they ostracized Mussolini they would drive him into the waiting arms of Adolph Hitler. Hitler watched Mussolini "get away" with Ethiopia, and immediately began to accelerate his own plans for expansion, negating the Versailles Treaty that same year and sending German soldiers into the supposedly demilitarized Rhineland the next. France refused to act alone, and Britain refused to go to war for France over the Rhineland.

Having gotten away with this, Hitler turned next to Austria. When German soldiers entered Austria, Italy—which was now Germany's partner—refused to intervene. France protested but wouldn't act alone, and Britain protested but refused to interfere. The British and French both hoped that by letting Hitler get what he wanted now—and everything he had done thus far could be rationalized as correcting the wrongs imposed on Germany by the Versailles Treaty—he would be satisfied and cease his expansionism. Regrettably, the more Hitler got away with the more it whetted his appetite for increased expansion.

The appeasement policy peaked with the French/British sellout of the Sudetenland to Germany in return for promises from Hitler that if he got the Sudetenland he would leave the remainder of Czechoslovakia alone and would make no new territorial demands. It was a humiliating agreement for France, because it meant reneging on a defense treaty they had signed with Czechoslovakia. It also left the Czechs completely unable to defend what remained of their territory. Although it was politically costly to the French, the British, who wanted no part in a war over Czechoslovakia, celebrated the Munich Agreement and Prime Minister Neville Chamberlain returned to England proclaiming "peace for our time." When Hitler's forces occupied the remainder of Czechoslovakia fewer than six months later, and then began making demands for territorial concessions from Poland, it was clear that appeasement had failed.

Today, the word appeasement is almost synonymous with a sellout because of its association with the selling-out of Sudetenland Czechs to appease Hitler and keep Britain and France out of war. The long-term effect of the policy had been only to increase Hitler's appetite and increase the pace at which he attempted to expand Nazi Germany.

29.   **(B)**   The main goal of the Truman Doctrine was the containment of Communist expansion beyond those areas already under Communist control. The Truman Doctrine was the result of requests for American aid to the Turkish and Greek governments, both of which were fighting Communist insurgencies. Truman, instead of just requesting aid for Turkey and Greece, responded with a general policy statement declaring American intent to aid free people everywhere in their efforts to protect themselves from internal Communist uprisings or external pressure from Communist countries. Truman's "doctrine" did not extend to attempting to eliminate Communist governments where they already held power. It just promised to help countries resist communist expansion to non-Communist countries. It committed the United States to an expensive long-term policy of propping up non-Communist governments even when those governments were more brutal than the Communists attempting to oust them. It placed the United States in the position of leader of the "free world" but guaranteed greater future tensions with the Soviet Union

The Truman Doctrine also did not seek to enforce the Domino Theory. The Domino Theory did not exist in the 1940s. It came into existence as a rationale for American involvement in Vietnam. According to the Domino Theory, the war in Vietnam was the beginning of a massive Communist effort to expand control into Southeast Asia. If Vietnam fell, according to this theory, then Cambodia, Laos, Burma, and Thailand would all fall shortly afterwards, like a row of dominoes. Current evidence provides little support for this theory.

30.   **(D)**   In post-World War II Europe, Berlin was a headache for both the United States and the Soviet Union. The city was jointly occupied by the French, British, Americans, and the Soviets. It was situated about 100 miles inside the Soviet zone of occupation in eastern Germany. For the Western Allies, Berlin was a headache because in the event of Soviet aggression the city was virtually indefensible. It was also vulnerable to supply cutoffs because all its supplies had to be transported through Russian-controlled East Germany. At the same time, a Western pullout from the city was politically unacceptable in the supercharged Cold War atmosphere of the time.

Berlin was a headache for the Russians because it sat right in the middle of their occupation zone in eastern Germany. It provided the Americans with an ideal observation post from which to monitor Soviet troop movements. It also sat on one of the main supply routes needed by Soviet forces if they were forced to fight the Western Allies. Soviet leaders called it a "bone in the throat" of Russia.

In June 1948, Stalin decided to drive the Westerners permanently out of Berlin. Rather than force the issue by starting a war, Stalin decided to blockade the city, cutting off its land supply routes. In this way, if a war started, the undermanned forces of the Western Allies would have to start it. Stalin knew the

Allies' conventional military forces were not capable of winning a war at this time against Soviet forces in Germany. He also doubted that Truman would initiate a nuclear war over Berlin. Without resorting to war, there seemed to be no way for the West to maintain its forces in western Berlin. Stalin also hoped to pressure the West Germans and the Americans into ceasing their efforts to create a separate sovereign state of West Germany. If nothing else, cutting off Berlin might force a compromise which would prevent a new West German state.

While Stalin's blockade was capable of closing the highways and railroads into the city, the World War II agreements regarding the occupation of Berlin had given the Allies use of air space on several approaches to Berlin. Stalin could not blockade this air space without himself resorting to war, which he did not want to do. With this loophole in mind, President Truman initiated a massive airlift to keep the city supplied. For 11 months the planes flew back and forth supplying the beleaguered Berliners. While the Berliners did not live well, they survived. When it became apparent that Truman would maintain the airlift no matter how long it took, Stalin decided the cost to the Soviets' international image wasn't worth it and he ordered the blockade lifted.

The blockade backfired on Stalin in an additional manner. Rather than forcing a compromise on the issue of a West German state, the blockade unified West Germans more than ever and convinced the Americans even further of the need for a strong, independent West Germany. The Federal Republic of Germany was the result. It was founded in May, 1949 within two weeks of Stalin lifting the Berlin blockade.

31.   **(A)**   While each of the choices was a factor in Truman's decision to drop the atomic bomb, the major factor was Truman's belief that it would shorten the war and save lives. Germany had already surrendered, and Americans wanted the war to end. Thus far, the Japanese had been fighting fanatically, usually to the last man, to defend the islands approaching Japan itself. Casualties had been heavy for both sides. It looked as if the only way the Japanese would surrender was through an all-out invasion of the Japanese home islands. Given the ferocity of Japanese defenses of the outlying islands, predictions of casualties ranged up to 2 million Americans dead and 10 million Japanese dead in an all-out invasion. Given that the United States had lost only 300,000 dead throughout the entire war thus far, 2 million dead American servicemen was a politically unacceptable cost to Truman if it could possibly be avoided. The atomic bomb gave him a tool to avoid that cost. Predictions also emphasized that the invasion could take from one to four more years to eliminate major centers of Japanese resistance, and the United States could face a protracted struggle against Japanese partisans. A Japanese surrender before a full-scale invasion could prevent this. Again, the atomic bomb gave Truman a tool to avoid an invasion. Therefore, if it worked it would shorten the war and save American lives.

32.   **(E)**   The Taft-Hartley Labor Act of 1947 reflected the culmination of increasing public and government disaffection with labor unions. A series of strikes in the steel industries, coal mines, automobile factories, and the railroads

had left Truman and many others feeling that unions were acting beyond the legitimate interests of workers and were engaging in actions which could endanger the nation. Truman led the attack with calls for laws giving the government greater authority to control striking unions and punish their members.

In the 1946 election, conservative Republicans gained control of Congress. They were even more anti-union than Truman. Led by Republican Robert Taft, conservatives passed the Taft-Hartley Act over the veto of President Truman, who felt that it went too far in controlling unions. The law prohibited unions from running "closed shops" in which workers had to join the union to keep their jobs. It also gave the president the power to call for a "cooling off " period in strikes which threatened the national security. It forced union leaders to sign affidavits certifying they were not Communists. Finally, it reduced the ability of unions to actively participate in elections by restricting union contributions to election campaigns.

33.   **(C)**   In September 1950, United Nations forces were trapped within a small defensive perimeter outside the South Korean port of Pusan. United Nations forces were not powerful enough to break through North Korean lines without heavy casualties. North Korean forces were not powerful enough to break through U.N. lines. The war had ground to a bloody stalemate. However, Korea is a long, narrow peninsula, and North Korea did not have enough troops to defend the Pusan perimeter and the entire Korean coastline behind their lines. The North Koreans also had no significant naval forces to protect the coastline.

General MacArthur understood this and decided to use superior American naval forces to American advantage. Assembling a force of warships and transports, MacArthur ordered an amphibious assault on the port of Inchon, a few miles from the occupied South Korean capital of Seoul, both of which lay just south of the original border between North and South Korea. While the Koreans expected that MacArthur might attempt an amphibious assault behind their lines, they did not expect it so far north. They also did not expect the assault to be so successful. The North Koreans were quickly faced with a decision to retreat or face the loss of their entire army. They attempted to retreat, but continually harassed by American air, naval, and ground forces, the retreat quickly turned into a rout. When they crossed the border only 15 percent of their original force remained. In one stroke, MacArthur had turned a stalemate into a decisive victory.

From here, MacArthur moved U.N. forces across the border into North Korea. This move led eventually to Chinese involvement and the long and bloody standoff which ensued. But at least the Inchon landings insured that the war would be fought near the original border rather than on the South Korean coast.

34.   **(A)**   Stalingrad marked the end of effective German offensive operations in World War II. Until Stalingrad, the Germans had held the initiative throughout most of the Russian campaign. The Russian counteroffensives at Stalingrad not only seized the initiative from Germany but annihilated an entire German army in

addition to destroying German allied forces from Hungary, Romania, and Italy. The total Axis casualties in the Stalingrad campaign exceeded 800,000 men. By comparison, the Soviets are estimated to have lost over 1.2 million men. While the Soviets lost more men, they had three times the manpower available to Germany. In other words, Russia could afford to absorb such losses, Germany couldn't. After Stalingrad, the Germans found themselves on the defensive, steadily conceding ground to the advancing Soviet armies. It was a disaster from which the Germans never recovered. Often, the importance of this Russian victory is overlooked by Americans because our history books focus so much on the American contribution to the war. It is important to note, however, that the Soviets lost more men killed in the battle of Stalingrad than the Americans lost in the entire war! Eight out of ten Germans who were killed in World War II were killed fighting Russians, so the Soviet contribution to the war effort cannot be ignored. After Stalingrad, so many German soldiers were tied down on the Russian front, the Germans were never able to effectively respond to Allied moves in Africa, Italy, or France. Thus, Stalingrad was in many ways the turning point of World War II in Europe.

35. **(A)** The Atlantic Charter was the end product of a meeting between Winston Churchill and Franklin Roosevelt in August 1941 aboard the American *Augusta* off the coast of Newfoundland, Canada. The document pledged Britain and the United States to mutual cooperation in working for the defeat of Hitler. This was significant because America was still officially neutral, but Roosevelt's signature of the Atlantic Charter made the United States and Britain de facto allies. Roosevelt was convinced that it was now just a matter of time before the United States would have to fight Hitler's Germany, and he was determined not to let the British fall before the United States could become fully engaged. The Atlantic Charter cemented these beliefs and laid out long-term military and political goals in a combined Anglo-American war effort. The Charter was the foundation of the extremely successful coordination of operations between the two countries for the remainder of the war.

It did not exchange American destroyers for British bases. Nor did it repeal the Neutrality Acts and allow cash-and-carry sales of arms to Britain. The destroyers for bases exchange had taken place in 1940. Cash-and-carry had been surplanted by Lend-Lease five months previously.

1941–1960
REVIEW

1. DECLARED WAR BEGINS

Declaration of War

On December 8, Congress declared war on Japan. Three days later the Axis powers, Germany and Italy, declared war on the United States. Great Britain and the United States then established the Combined Chiefs of Staff, headquartered in Washington, to direct Anglo-American military operations.

Declaration of the United Nations

On January 1, 1942, representatives of 26 nations met in Washington, D.C., and signed the Declaration of the United Nations, pledging themselves to the principles of the Atlantic Charter and promising not to make a separate peace with their common enemies.

The Home Front

The WPB was established in 1942 by President Franklin D. Roosevelt for the purpose of regulating the use of raw materials.

In April 1942, the General Maximum Price Regulation Act froze prices and extended rationing. In April 1943, prices, wages, and salaries were all frozen.

The Revenue Act of 1942 extended the income tax to the majority of the population. Payroll deduction for the income tax began in 1944.

Social Changes

Rural areas lost population while coastal areas increased rapidly. Women entered the work force in increasing numbers. Blacks moved from the rural South to northern and western cities with racial tensions often resulting, most notably in the June 1943 racial riot in Detroit.

Smith-Connolly Act

Passed in 1943, the Smith-Connolly Antistrike Act authorized government seizure of a plant or mine idled by a strike if the war effort was impeded. It expired in 1947.

Korematsu v. United States

In 1944 the Supreme Court upheld President Roosevelt's 1942 order that

Issei (Japanese-Americans who had immigrated from Japan) and Nisei (native born Japanese-Americans) be relocated to concentration camps. The camps were closed in March 1946.

Smith v. Allwright

In 1944 the Supreme Court struck down the Texas primary elections, which were restricted to whites, for violating the Fifteenth Amendment.

Presidential Election of 1944

President Franklin D. Roosevelt, together with new vice presidential candidate Harry S. Truman of Missouri, defeated his Republican opponent, Governor Thomas Dewey of New York.

Death of Roosevelt

Roosevelt died on April 12, 1945, at Warm Springs, Georgia. Harry S. Truman became president.

QUESTION

What large-scale social transformations were caused by World War II?

EXPLANATION

During World War II, women entered the work force in large numbers to replace the men who had entered military service, often in jobs previously thought beyond their physical abilities. Urbanization accelerated, and African-Americans migrated to northern cities in increasing numbers. These social changes would have a lasting impact on the social structure of the United States.

The North African and European Theaters

Nearly 400 ships were lost in American waters of the Atlantic to German submarines between January and June 1942.

The United States joined in the bombing of the European continent in July 1942. Bombing increased during 1943 and 1944 and lasted to the end of the war.

The Allied army under Dwight D. Eisenhower attacked French North Africa in November 1942. The French surrendered.

In the Battle of Kassarine Pass, February 1943, North Africa, the Allied army met General Erwin Rommel's Africa Korps. Although the battle is variously interpreted as a standoff or a defeat for the U.S., Rommel's forces were soon trapped by the British moving in from Egypt. In May 1943, Rommel's Africa Korps surrendered.

Allied armies under George S. Patton invaded Sicily from Africa in July

1943 and gained control by mid-August. Moving from Sicily, the Allied armies invaded the Italian mainland in September. Benito Mussolini had already fallen from power and his successor, Marshal Pietro Badoglio, surrendered. The Germans, however, put up a stiff resistance with the result that Rome did not fall until June 1944.

In March 1944, the Soviet Union began pushing into Eastern Europe.

On "D-Day," June 6, 1944, Allied armies under Dwight D. Eisenhower, now commander in chief of Supreme Headquarters, Allied Expeditionary Forces, began an invasion of Normandy, France. Allied armies under General Omar Bradley took the transportation hub of St. Lo, France in July.

Allied armies liberated Paris in August. By mid-September they had arrived at the Rhine, on the edge of Germany.

Beginning December 16, 1944, at the Battle of the Bulge, the Germans counter-attacked, driving the Allies back about 50 miles into Belgium. By January the Allies were once more advancing toward Germany.

The Allies crossed the Rhine in March 1945. In the last week of April, Eisenhower's forces met the Soviet army at the Elbe.

On May 7, 1945, Germany surrendered.

The Pacific Theater

By the end of December 1941, Guam, Wake Island, the Gilbert Islands, and Hong Kong had fallen to the Japanese. In January 1942, Raboul, New Britain fell, followed in February by Singapore and Java, and in March by Rangoon, Burma.

The U.S. air raids on Tokyo in April 1942 were militarily inconsequential but they raised Allied morale.

U.S. forces surrendered at Corregidor, Philippines, on May 6, 1942.

In the Battle of the Coral Sea, May 7–8, 1942 (northeast of Australia, south of New Guinea and the Solomon Islands), planes from the American carriers *Lexington* and *Yorktown* forced Japanese troop transports to turn back from attacking Port Moresby. The battle stopped the Japanese advance on Australia.

At the Battle of Midway, June 4–7, 1942, American air power destroyed four Japanese carriers and about 300 planes while the U.S. lost the carrier *Yorktown* and one destroyer. The battle proved to be the turning point in the Pacific.

A series of land, sea, and air battles took place around Guadalcanal in the Solomon Islands from August 1942 to February 1943, stopping the Japanese.

The Allied strategy of island hopping, begun in 1943, sought to neutralize Japanese strongholds with air and sea power and then move on. General Douglas MacArthur commanded the land forces moving from New Guinea toward the Philippines, while Admiral Chester W. Nimitz directed the naval attack on important Japanese islands in the central Pacific.

U.S. forces advanced into the Gilberts (November 1943), the Marshalls (January 1944), and the Marianas (June 1944).

In the Battle of the Philippine Sea, June 19-20, 1944, the Japanese lost three carriers, two submarines, and over 300 planes while the Americans lost 17 planes.

After the American capture of the Marianas, General Tojo resigned as premier of Japan.

The Battle of Leyte Gulf, October 25, 1944, involved three major engagements that resulted in Japan's loss of most of its remaining naval power. It also brought the first use of the Japanese *kamikaze* or suicide attacks by Japanese pilots who crashed into American carriers.

Forces under General Douglas MacArthur liberated Manila in March 1945.

Between April and June 1945, in the battle for Okinawa, nearly 50,000 American casualties resulted from the fierce fighting which virtually destroyed Japan's remaining defenses.

The Atomic Bomb

The Manhattan Engineering District was established by the army engineers in August 1942 for the purpose of developing an atomic bomb (it eventually became known as the Manhattan Project). J. Robert Oppenheimer directed the design and construction of a transportable atomic bomb at Los Alamos, New Mexico.

On December 2, 1942, Enrico Fermi and his colleagues at the University of Chicago produced the first atomic chain reaction.

On July 16, 1945, the first atomic bomb was exploded at Alamogordo, New Mexico.

The *Enola Gay* dropped an atomic bomb on Hiroshima, Japan, on August 6, 1945, killing about 78,000 persons and injuring 100,000 more. On August 9, a second bomb was dropped on Nagasaki, Japan.

On August 8, 1945, the Soviet Union entered the war against Japan.

Japan surrendered on August 14, 1945. The formal surrender was signed on September 2, 1945.

QUESTION

What was the Manhattan Project and what was its significance?

EXPLANATION

The Manhattan Project was the name for the secret program to design an atomic bomb. The project was successful, and two bombs were dropped on Japan. This led to the surrender of Japan, and also introduced atomic warfare to the world.

Diplomacy

Casablanca Conference

On January 14–25, 1943, Franklin D. Roosevelt and Winston Churchill, prime minister of Great Britain, declared a policy of unconditional surrender for "all enemies."

Moscow Conference

In October 1943, Secretary of State Cordell Hull obtained Soviet agreement to enter the war against Japan after Germany was defeated and to participate in a world organization after the war was over.

Declaration of Cairo

Issued on December 1, 1943 after Roosevelt met with General Chiang Kai-shek in Cairo from November 22 to 26, the Declaration of Cairo called for Japan's unconditional surrender and stated that all Chinese territories occupied by Japan would be returned to China and that Korea would be free and independent.

Teheran Conference

The first "Big Three" (Roosevelt, Churchill, and Stalin) conference, met at Casablanca from November 28 to December 1, 1943. Stalin reaffirmed the Soviet commitment to enter the war against Japan and discussed coordination of the Soviet offensive with the Allied invasion of France.

Yalta Conference

On February 4–11, 1945, the "Big Three" met to discuss post-war Europe. Stalin said that the Soviet Union would enter the Pacific war within three months after Germany surrendered and agreed to the "Declaration of Liberated Europe" which called for free elections. They called for a conference on world organization, to meet in the U.S. beginning on April 25, 1945 and agreed that the Soviets would have three votes in the General Assembly and that the U.S., Great Britain, the Soviet Union, France, and China would be permanent members of the Security Council. Germany was divided into occupation zones, and a coalition government of Communists and non-Communists was agreed to for Poland. Roosevelt accepted Soviet control of Outer Mongolia, the Kurile Islands, the southern half of Sakhalin Island, Port Arthur (Darien), and participation in the operation of the Manchurian railroads.

Potsdam Conference

From July 1 to August 2, 1945, Truman, Stalin, and Clement Atlee (who during the conference replaced Churchill as prime minister of Great Britain) met at Potsdam. During the conference, Truman ordered the dropping of the atomic bomb on Japan. The conference disagreed on most major issues but did establish a Council of Foreign Ministers to draft peace treaties for the Balkans. Approval was also given to the concept of war-crimes trials and the demilitarization and denazification of Germany.

Drill 1: Declared War Begins

1. Which of the following is NOT associated with the atomic bomb?

   (A) Manhattan Project   (B) J. Robert Oppenheimer

   (C) General Billy Mitchell   (D) Nagasaki and Hiroshima

   (E) Los Alamos, New Mexico

2. During World War II, which of the following served as an American commander in the Pacific Theater?

   (A) George S. Patton, Jr.   (B) Douglas MacArthur

   (C) Dwight D. Eisenhower   (D) Omar Bradley

   (E) Bernard Montgomery

3. During the Second World War, Soviet leader Joseph Stalin constantly urged that U.S. and British forces should

   (A) open a "Second Front" by landing troops in the Balkans and advancing toward Vienna.

   (B) open a "Second Front" by driving the Germans out of North Africa and subsequently moving into Italy.

   (C) transfer large numbers of troops to join the Soviets in facing the Germans from the east.

   (D) join the Soviet Union in its war against Japan.

   (E) open a "Second Front" by landing troops in France and driving toward Germany from the west.

4. Which of the following was NOT agreed upon at the Potsdam Conference?

   (A) The concept of war-crimes trials

   (B) The demilitarization of Germany

   (C) The replacement of Churchill as prime minister of Great Britain

   (D) The dropping of the atomic bomb on Japan

   (E) The establishment of a Council of Foreign Ministers to draft peace treaties for the Balkans.

5. At the Casablanca Conference in January 1943, President Franklin Roosevelt and British Prime Minister Winston Churchill agreed

   (A) to concentrate on beating the Germans first before dealing with the Japanese.

    (B)   to shift Allied efforts from the European to the Pacific Theater of the war.

    (C)   to demand unconditional surrender of the Axis powers.

    (D)   to grant a general amnesty to Axis leaders who would surrender.

    (E)   to land troops in France in the summer of 1943.

6.   The Axis alliance of World War II included which of the following?

    (A)   Soviet Union, Germany, Italy

    (B)   Soviet Union, Germany, Japan

    (C)   France, Germany, Italy

    (D)   Germany, Italy, Japan

    (E)   France, Germany, Japan

7.   The Yalta Conference of February 1945 was a meeting of the leaders of

    (A)   the U.S., Great Britain, Canada, and Australia.

    (B)   the U.S., Great Britain, the Soviet Union, and China.

    (C)   the U.S., Great Britain, the Soviet Union, and France.

    (D)   the U.S., the Soviet Union, and China.

    (E)   the U.S., the Soviet Union, and Great Britain.

8.   The 1944 Dumbarton Oaks Conference involved primarily

    (A)   the trial and punishment of Nazi war criminals.

    (B)   the decision on whether or not to use the atomic bomb.

    (C)   startling revelations of the Nazi atrocities against Jews.

    (D)   American plans for redrawing the map of Eastern Europe.

    (E)   the formation of the United Nations.

9.   In order to prevent the effects of inflation during the Second World War, the federal government

    (A)   raised taxes so as to prevent deficit spending.

    (B)   financed spending deficits only through the sale of war bonds to the public.

    (C)   endeavored to intervene in the civilian economy as little as possible.

    (D)   imposed wage and price controls.

    (E)   endeavored to boost its gold reserves.

10. The battle that marked the shift of power in the naval struggle between the United States and Japan in World War II was

(A) Leyte Gulf.

(B) Guadalcanal.

(C) Pearl Harbor.

(D) Coral Sea.

(E) Midway.

2. THE COLD WAR

Failure of U.S.–Soviet Cooperation

By the end of 1945 the Soviet Union controlled most of Eastern Europe, Outer Mongolia, parts of Manchuria, Northern Korea, the Kurile Islands, and Sakhalin Island. In 1946–47 it took over Poland, Hungary, Romania, and Bulgaria.

Iron Curtain

In a speech in Fulton, Missouri in 1946, Winston Churchill stated that an Iron Curtain had been spread across Europe separating the democratic from the authoritarian Communist states.

Containment

In 1946, career diplomat and Soviet expert George F. Kennan warned that the Soviet Union had no intention of living peacefully with the United States. The next year, in July 1947, he wrote an anonymous article for Foreign Affairs in which he called for a counter-force to Soviet pressures for the purpose of "containing" Communism.

Truman Doctrine

In February 1947 Great Britain notified the United States that it could no longer aid the Greek government in its war against Communist insurgents. The next month President Harry S. Truman asked Congress for $400 million in military and economic aid for Greece and Turkey. He argued in what became known as the Truman Doctrine that the United States must support free peoples who were resisting Communist domination.

Marshall Plan

Secretary of State George C. Marshall proposed in June 1947 that the United States provide economic aid to help rebuild Europe. Meeting in July, representatives of the European nations agreed on a recovery program jointly financed by the United States and the European countries. The following March, Congress passed the European Recovery Program, popularly known as the Marshall Plan, providing more than $12 billion in aid.

Czechoslovakia

In February 1948 the Soviets sponsored a *coup d'état* in Czechoslovakia, thereby extending communism in Europe.

Berlin Crisis

After the United States, France, and Great Britain announced plans to create a West German Republic out of their German zones, the Soviet Union in June 1948 blocked surface access to Berlin. The U.S. then instituted an airlift to transport supplies to the city until the Soviets lifted their blockade in May 1949.

NATO

In April 1949 the North Atlantic Treaty Organization was signed by the United States, Great Britain, France, Italy, Belgium, the Netherlands, Luxembourg, Denmark, Norway, Portugal, Iceland, and Canada. The signatories pledged that an attack against one would be considered an attack against all. Greece and Turkey joined the alliance in 1952 and West Germany in 1954. The Soviets formed the Warsaw Treaty Organization in 1955 to counteract NATO.

Atomic Bomb

The Soviet Union exploded an atomic device in September 1949.

QUESTION

Briefly explain Truman's foreign policy of "containment."

EXPLANATION

"Containment" referred to the policy of preventing the spread of Communism beyond where it had already been established. The Truman Doctrine was the outcome of this policy, which stated that the U.S. would aid any country resisting Communist insurgencies. Aid was granted to Greece and Turkey in 1947. Later, the policy would involve the commitment of U.S. troops to Korea.

International Cooperation

Bretton Woods, New Hampshire

Representatives from Europe and the United States at a conference held July 1–22, 1944 signed agreements for an international bank and a world monetary fund to stabilize international currencies and rebuild the economies of war-torn nations.

Yalta Conference

In February 1945, Roosevelt, Churchill, and Stalin called for a conference on world organization to meet in April 1945 in the United States.

United Nations

From April to June 1945, representatives from 50 countries met in San Francisco to establish the United Nations. The U.N. charter created a General Assembly composed of all member nations which would act as the ultimate policy-making body. A Security Council, made up of 11 members, including the United States, Great Britain, France, the Soviet Union, and China as permanent members and six additional nations elected by the General Assembly for two-year terms, would be responsible for settling disputes among U.N. member nations.

Containment in Asia

Japan

General Douglas MacArthur headed a four-power Allied Control Council which governed Japan, allowing it to develop economically and politically.

China

Between 1945 and 1948 the United States gave over $2 billion in aid to the Nationalist Chinese under Chiang Kai-shek and sent George C. Marshall to settle the conflict between Chiang's Nationalists and Mao Tse-tung's Communists. In 1949, however, Mao defeated Chiang and forced the Nationalists to flee to Formosa (Taiwan). Mao established the People's Republic of China on the mainland.

Korean War

On June 25, 1950 North Korea invaded South Korea. President Truman committed U.S. forces commanded by General MacArthur but under United Nations auspices. By October, the U.N. (mostly American) had driven north of the 38th parallel which divided North and South Korea. Chinese troops attacked MacArthur's forces on November 26, pushing them south of the 38th parallel, but by spring 1951, the U.N. forces had recovered their offensive. MacArthur called for a naval blockade of China and bombing north of the Yalu River, criticizing the president for fighting a limited war. In April 1951 Truman removed MacArthur from command.

Armistice talks began with North Korea in the summer of 1951. In June

1953 an armistice was signed leaving Korea divided along virtually the same boundary that had existed prior to the war.

Eisenhower-Dulles Foreign Policy

John Foster Dulles

Dwight D. Eisenhower, elected president in 1952, chose John Foster Dulles as secretary of state. Dulles talked of a more aggressive foreign policy, calling for "massive retaliation" and "liberation" rather than containment. He wished to emphasize nuclear deterrents rather than conventional armed forces. Dulles served as secretary of state until ill-health forced him to resign in April 1959. Christian A. Herter took his place.

Hydrogen Bomb

The U.S. exploded its first hydrogen bomb in November 1952 while the Soviets followed with theirs in August 1953.

Soviet Change of Power

Josef Stalin died in March 1953. After an internal power struggle that lasted until 1955, Nikita Khrushchev emerged as the Soviet leader. He talked of both "burying" capitalism and "peaceful coexistence."

Asia

In 1954 the French asked the U.S. to commit air forces to rescue French forces at Dien Bien Phu, Vietnam, besieged by the nationalist forces led by Ho Chi Minh, but Eisenhower refused. In May 1954 Dien Bien Phu surrendered.

Geneva Accords

France, Great Britain, the Soviet Union, and China signed the Geneva Accords in July 1954, dividing Vietnam along the 17th parallel. The North would be under Ho Chi Minh and the South under Emperor Bao Dai. Elections were scheduled for 1956 to unify the country, but Ngo Dinh Diem overthrew Bao Dai and prevented the elections from taking place. The United States supplied economic aid to South Vietnam.

Southeast Asia Treaty Organization

Dulles attempted to establish a Southeast Asia Treaty Organization parallel to NATO but was able to obtain only the Philippine Republic, Thailand, and Pakistan as signatories in September 1954.

Quemoy and Matsu

The small islands of Quemoy and Matsu off the coast of China were occupied by the Nationalist Chinese under Chiang Kai-shek but claimed by the People's Republic of China. In 1955, after the mainland Chinese began shelling these islands, Eisenhower obtained authorization from Congress to defend Formosa (Taiwan) and related areas.

Middle East—The Suez Canal Crisis

The United States had agreed to lend money to Egypt, under the leadership of Colonel Gamal Abdel Nasser, to build the Aswan Dam but refused to give arms. Nasser then drifted toward the Soviet Union and in 1956 established diplomatic relations with the People's Republic of China. In July 1956 the U.S. withdrew its loan to Egypt. In response, Nasser nationalized the Suez Canal. France, Great Britain, and Israel then attacked Egypt, but Eisenhower demanded that they pull out. On November 6 a cease-fire was announced.

Eisenhower Doctrine

President Eisenhower announced in January 1957 that the U.S. was prepared to use armed force in the Middle East against Communist aggression. Under this doctrine, U.S. marines entered Beirut, Lebanon in July 1958 to promote political stability during a change of governments. The marines left in October.

Summit Conference with the Soviet Union

In July 1955 President Eisenhower met in Geneva with Anthony Eden, prime minister of Great Britain; Edgar Faure, premier of France; and Nikita Khrushchev and Nikolai Bulganin, at the time co-leaders of the Soviet Union. They discussed disarmament and reunification of Germany but made no agreements.

Atomic Weapons Test Suspension

Eisenhower and Khrushchev voluntarily suspended atmospheric tests of atomic weapons in October 1958.

Soviet-American Visitations

Vice President Richard M. Nixon visited the Soviet Union, and Soviet Vice-Premier Anastas I. Mikoyan came to the United States in the summer of 1959. In September Premier Khrushchev toured the United States and agreed to another summit meeting.

U-2 Incident

On May 1, 1960 an American U-2 spy plane was shot down over the Soviet

Union and pilot Francis Gary Powers was captured. Eisenhower ultimately took responsibility for the spy plane, and Khrushchev angrily called off the Paris summit conference which was to take place in a few days.

Latin America

The U.S. supported the overthrow of President Jacobo Arbenz Guzman of Guatemala in 1954, because he began accepting arms from the Soviet Union.

Vice President Nixon had to call off an eight nation goodwill tour of Latin America after meeting hostile mobs in Venezuela and Peru in 1958.

In January 1959 Fidel Castro overthrew Fulgencio Batista, dictator of Cuba. Castro soon began criticizing the United States and moved closer to the Soviet Union, signing a trade agreement with the Soviets in February 1960. The United States prohibited the importation of Cuban sugar in October 1960 and broke off diplomatic relations in January 1961.

QUESTION

Why was the U.S.-Soviet conflict referred to as the "Cold War"?

EXPLANATION

During the "Cold War," U.S. and. Soviet troops rarely, if ever, confronted one another directly. Instead, the conflict was conducted through diplomacy, continued arms build ups, military aid to "client nations," and limited engagement of troops in disputed areas. A state of war never existed between the U.S. and the Soviet Union, and both nations maintained diplomatic relations throughout this period.

Drill 2: The Cold War

1. John Foster Dulles' negotiations of the SEATO and CENTO defense pacts in the 1950s were an example of what policy?

    (A) Liberation

    (B) Brinksmanship

    (C) Massive Retaliation

    (D) Containment

    (E) Peaceful Coexistence

2. Which of the following was NOT involved in the anti-Communist crusade of the 1940s and 1950s?

   (A) A. Mitchell Palmer   (B) Richard M. Nixon

   (C) Whitaker Chambers   (D) Joseph R. McCarthy

   (E) House Un-American Activities Committee

3. The Berlin Airlift was America's response to

   (A) the Soviet blockade of West Berlin from land communication with the rest of the western zone.

   (B) the acute wartime destruction of roads and railroads, making land transport almost impossible.

   (C) the unusually severe winter of 1947.

   (D) a widespread work stoppage by German transportation workers in protest of the allied occupation of Germany.

   (E) the increased need for flu vaccine in the midst of a serious epidemic.

4. At the beginning of the Cold War, U.S. policy toward the Soviet Union tended to follow the ideas of George F. Kennan, that is

   (A) an isolationist policy that took no notice of Soviet expansionism.

   (B) an aggressive policy of rolling back the gains already made by the Soviet Union.

   (C) active aid to nationalist movements attempting to throw off Soviet domination.

   (D) strict enforcement of the Monroe Doctrine with regard to Soviet expansionism in the Western Hemisphere.

   (E) a policy of containment of Soviet expansionist tendencies.

5. According to the U.S. State Department, China fell to Communism in 1949 because of which of the following?

   (A) Inadequate American aid to Chiang Kai-shek

   (B) Communist influence within the U.S. government

   (C) Soviet development of the atomic bomb

   (D) The incompetence and corruption of Chiang Kai-shek's government

   (E) The poor advice of General Joseph Stillwell, U.S. commander in China during World War II

6. Which of the following events led to the cancellation of the 1960 Paris Summit?

   (A) The U.S. involvement in Korea

   (B) The U-2 incident

   (C) The Suez Canal crisis

   (D) The declaration of the Eisenhower Doctrine

   (E) The explosion of the first hydrogen bomb by the U.S.

7. The purpose of the Truman Doctrine was to

   (A) aid the economic recovery of war-torn Europe.

   (B) prevent European meddling in the affairs of South American countries.

   (C) aid countries that were the targets of Communist expansionism.

   (D) reduce the dependence of the European economy on overseas empires.

   (E) expand the Monroe Doctrine to include Eastern Asia.

8. The Truman Doctrine was issued in response to

   (A) the threat of Communist expansion in Greece and Turkey.

   (B) the devastated economic condition of postwar Europe.

   (C) the threat presented by the Red Army in Central Europe.

   (D) the Communist North Korean invasion of South Korea.

   (E) the Communist threat to South Vietnam.

9. Which of the following led President Truman to remove MacArthur from command in Korea?

   (A) Heavy U.S. casualties

   (B) The threat of Japanese involvement

   (C) MacArthur's desire to use the atomic bomb on North Korea

   (D) Truman's belief that MacArthur's war strategy was too conservative

   (E) MacArthur's wish for a naval blockade of China and bombing north of the Yalu River

10. The Korean War was fought to

    (A) stop an invasion of North Korea by the Communist-led South.

    (B) end U.S. imperialism in Southeast Asia.

    (C) stop an invasion of South Korea by Japan.

(D)   eliminate taxation without representation in South Korea.

(E)   stop an invasion of South Korea by the Communist-led North.

3.   THE POLITICS OF AFFLUENCE

Truman Becomes President

Harry S. Truman, formerly a senator from Missouri and vice president of the United States, became president on April 12, 1945. In September 1945 he proposed a liberal legislative program, including expansion of unemployment insurance, extension of the Employment Service, a higher minimum wage, a permanent Fair Employment Practices Commission, slum clearance, low rent housing, regional TVA-type programs, and a public works program, but was unable to put it through Congress.

Employment Act of 1946

This act established a three member Council of Economic Advisors to evaluate the economy and advise the president and set up a Congressional Joint Committee on the Economic Report. The act declared that the government was committed to maintaining maximum employment.

Atomic Energy

Congress created the Atomic Energy Commission in 1946, establishing civilian control over nuclear development and giving the president sole authority over the use of atomic weapons in warfare.

Price Controls

Truman vetoed a weak price control bill passed by Congress, thereby ending the wartime price control program. When prices quickly increased about 6 percent, Congress passed another bill in July 1946. Although Truman signed this bill, he used its powers inconsistently, especially when—bowing to pressure—he ended price controls on beef. In late 1946, he lifted controls on all items except rents, sugar, and rice.

Labor

In early 1946, the United Auto Workers, under Walter Reuther, struck General Motors, and steelworkers, under Philip Murray, struck U.S. Steel, demanding wage increases. Truman suggested an 18 cents-per-hour wage increase and in February allowed U.S. Steel to raise prices to cover the increase. This formula became the basis for settlements in other industries. After John L. Lewis's United Mine Workers struck in April 1946, Truman ordered the government to take over the mines and then accepted the union's demands, which included safety and health and welfare benefits. The president averted a railway strike by seizing the railroads and threatening to draft strikers into the army.

Demobilization

By 1947 the total armed forces had been cut to 1.5 million. The army fell to 600,000 from a WW II peak of 8 million. The Serviceman's Readjustment Act (G.I. Bill of Rights) of 1944, provided $13 billion in aid ranging from education to housing.

Taft-Hartley Act

The Republicans, who had gained control of Congress as a result of the 1946 elections, sought to control the power of the unions through the Taft-Hartley Act, passed in 1947. This act made the "closed shop" illegal; labor unions could no longer force employers to hire only union members although it allowed the "union shop" in which newly hired employees were required to join the union. It established a 60-day cooling-off period for strikers in key industries; ended the practice of employers collecting dues for unions; forbade such actions as secondary boycotts, jurisdictional strikes, featherbedding, and contributing to political campaigns; and required an anti-Communist oath of union officials. The act slowed down efforts to unionize the South and by 1954, 15 states had passed "right to work" laws, forbidding the "union shop."

Reorganization of Armed Forces

In 1947 Congress passed the National Security Act creating a National Military Establishment, National Security Council, Joint Chiefs of Staff, and Central Intelligence Agency (CIA). Together these organizations were intended to coordinate the armed forces and intelligence services.

Government Reorganization

Truman in 1947 appointed former President Herbert Hoover to head a Commission on Organization of the Executive Branch. The Commission's 1949 report led to the Organization Act of 1949 which allowed the president to make organizational changes subject to congressional veto.

Civil Rights

In 1946 Truman appointed the President's Committee on Civil Rights, which a year later produced its report *To Secure These Rights*. The report called for the elimination of all aspects of segregation. In 1948 the president banned racial discrimination in federal government hiring practices and ordered desegregation of the armed forces.

Presidential Succession

The Presidential Succession Act of 1947 placed the speaker of the House and the president *pro tempore* of the Senate ahead of the secretary of state and after the vice president in the line of succession. The Twenty-second Amendment to the Constitution, ratified in 1951, limited the president to two terms.

Election of 1948

Truman was the Democratic nominee, but the Democrats were split by the States' Rights Democratic party (Dixiecrats) which nominated Governor Strom Thurmond of South Carolina and the Progressive party which nominated former Vice President Henry Wallace. The Republicans nominated Governor Thomas E. Dewey of New York. After traveling widely and attacking the "do-nothing Congress," Truman won a surprise victory.

The Fair Deal

The Fair Deal Program

Truman sought to enlarge and extend the New Deal. He proposed increasing the minimum wage, extending Social Security to more people, maintaining rent controls, clearing slums and building public housing, and providing more money to TVA, rural electrification, and farm housing. He also introduced bills dealing with civil rights, national health insurance, federal aid to education, and repeal of the Taft-Hartley Act. A coalition of Republicans and Southern Democrats prevented little more than the maintenance of existing programs.

Farm Policy

Because of improvements in agriculture, overproduction continued to be a problem. Secretary of Agriculture Charles F. Brannan proposed a program of continued price supports for storable crops and guaranteed minimum incomes to farmers of perishable crops. It was defeated in Congress and surpluses continued to pile up.

Anti-Communism

Smith Act

The Smith Act of 1940, which made it illegal to advocate the overthrow of the government by force or to belong to an organization advocating such a position, was used by the Truman administration to jail leaders of the American Communist party.

Loyalty Review Board

In response to criticism, particularly from the House Committee on Un-American Activities, that his administration was "soft on Communism," Truman established this board in 1947 to review government employees.

The Hiss Case

In 1948 Whittaker Chambers, formerly a Communist and now an editor of *Time*, charged Alger Hiss, a former State Department official and currently president of the Carnegie Endowment for International Peace, with having been a Communist who supplied classified American documents to the Soviet Union. In 1950 Hiss was convicted of perjury, the statute of limitations on his alleged spying having run out.

McCarran Internal Security Act

Passed in 1950, this act required communist-front organizations to register with the attorney general and prevented their members from defense work and travel abroad. It was passed over Truman's veto.

Rosenberg Case

In 1950 Julius and Ethel Rosenberg, as well as Harry Gold, were charged with giving atomic secrets to the Soviet Union. The Rosenbergs were convicted and executed in 1953.

Joseph McCarthy

On February 9, 1950 Senator Joseph R. McCarthy of Wisconsin stated that he had a list of known Communists who were working in the State Department. He later expanded his attacks to diplomats and scholars and contributed to the electoral defeat of two senators. After making charges against the army, he was censured by the Senate in 1954 and died in 1957.

QUESTION

How did the government deal with the supposed threat of Communists in the United States?

EXPLANATION

The activities of Senator Joseph McCarthy and the House Committee on Un-American Activities are well known. They worked to expose alleged Communists in many areas of American life, including within the government itself. Several laws were enacted to prosecute Communists, including the Smith Act, which made it illegal to advocate the overthrow of the government by force, or to belong to an organization that advocated such a position. The McCarran Internal Security Act required Communist front organizations to register with the attorney general and prevented their members from defense work and travel abroad.

Eisenhower's Dynamic Conservatism

1952 Election

The Republicans nominated Dwight D. Eisenhower, most recently NATO commander, for the presidency and Richard M. Nixon, senator from California, for the vice presidency. The Democrats nominated Governor Adlai E. Stevenson of Illinois for president. Eisenhower won by a landslide; for the first time since Reconstruction, the Republicans won some Southern states.

Conservatism

Eisenhower sought to balance the budget and lower taxes but did not attempt to roll back existing social and economic legislation. Eisenhower first described his policy as "dynamic conservatism" and then as "progressive moderation." The administration abolished the Reconstruction Finance Corporation, ended wage and price controls, and reduced farm price supports. It cut the budget and in 1954 lowered tax rates for corporations and individuals with high incomes; an economic slump, however, made balancing the budget difficult.

Social Legislation

Social Security was extended in 1954 and 1956 to an additional 10 million people, including professionals, domestic and clerical workers, farm workers, and members of the armed services. In 1959 benefits were increased 7 percent. In 1955 the minimum wage was raised from 75 cents to $1.00 an hour.

Public Power

Opposed to the expansion of TVA, the Eisenhower administration supported a plan to have a privately owned power plant (called Dixon-Yates) built to supply electricity to Memphis, Tennessee. After two years of controversy and discovery that the government consultant would financially benefit from Dixon-Yates, the administration turned to a municipally owned power plant. The Idaho Power Company won the right to build three small dams on the Snake River rather than the federal government establishing a single large dam at Hell's Canyon. The Atomic Energy Act of 1954 allowed the construction of private nuclear power plants under Atomic Energy Commission license and oversight.

Farm Policy

The Rural Electrification Administration announced in 1960 that 97 percent of American farms had electricity. In 1954 the government began financing the export of farm surpluses in exchange for foreign currencies and later provided surpluses free to needy nations, as milk to school children, and to the poor in exchange for governmentally issued food stamps.

Public Works

In 1954 Eisenhower obtained congressional approval for joint Canadian-U.S. construction of the St. Lawrence Seaway, giving ocean-going vessels access to the Great Lakes. In 1956 Congress authorized construction of the Interstate Highway System, with the federal government supplying 90 percent of the cost and the states 10 percent. The program further undermined the American railroad system.

Supreme Court

Eisenhower appointed Earl Warren, formerly governor of California, chief justice of the Supreme Court in 1953. That same year he appointed William J. Brennan associate justice. Although originally perceived as conservatives, both justices used the court as an agency of social and political change.

Election of 1956

The 1956 election once again pitted Eisenhower against Stevenson. The president won easily, carrying all but seven states.

Space and Technology

The launching of the Soviet space satellite Sputnik on October 4, 1957 created fear that America was falling behind technologically. Although the U.S. launched Explorer I on January 31, 1958 the concern continued. In 1958 Congress established the National Aeronautics and Space Administration (NASA) to coordinate research and development and the National Defense Education Act to provide grants and loans for education.

Sherman Adams Scandal

In 1958 the White House chief of staff resigned after it was revealed that he had received a fur coat and an Oriental rug in return for helping a Boston industrialist deal with the federal bureaucracy.

Labor

The Landrum-Griffen Labor Management Act of 1959 sought to control unfair union practices by establishing such rules as penalties for misuse of funds.

New States

On January 3, 1959 Alaska became the 49th state and on August 21, 1959 Hawaii became the 50th.

Civil Rights

Initial Eisenhower Actions

Eisenhower completed the formal integration of the armed forces, desegregated public services in Washington, D.C., naval yards, and veteran's hospitals, and appointed a Civil Rights Commission.

Legal Background to Brown

In *Ada Lois Sipuel v. Board of Regents* (1948) and *Sweatt v. Painter* (1950), the Supreme Court ruled that blacks must be allowed to attend integrated law schools in Oklahoma and Texas.

Brown v. Board of Education of Topeka

In this 1954 case, NAACP lawyer Thurgood Marshall challenged the doctrine of "separate but equal" (*Plessy v. Ferguson,* 1896). The Court declared that separate educational facilities were inherently unequal. In 1955 the Court ordered states to integrate "with all deliberate speed."

Southern Reaction to Brown

Although at first the South reacted cautiously, by 1955 there were calls for "massive resistance," and White Citizens Councils emerged to spearhead the resistance. State legislatures used a number of tactics to get around *Brown*. By the end of 1956 desegregation of the schools had advanced very little.

Little Rock

Although he did not personally support the Supreme Court decision, Eisenhower sent 10,000 National Guardsmen and 1,000 paratroopers to Little Rock, Arkansas to control mobs and enable blacks to enroll at Central High in September 1957. A small force of soldiers was stationed at the school throughout the year.

Emergence of Nonviolence

On December 11, 1955 in Montgomery, Alabama, Rosa Parks, a black woman, refused to give up her seat to a white and was arrested. Under the leadership of Martin Luther King, a black pastor, blacks in Montgomery organized a bus boycott that lasted for a year, until in December 1956 the Supreme Court refused to review a lower court ruling that stated that separate but equal was no longer legal.

Civil Rights Acts

Eisenhower proposed the Civil Rights Act of 1957 which established a permanent Civil Rights Commission and a Civil Rights Division of the Justice

Department which was empowered to prevent interference with the right to vote. The Civil Rights Act of 1960 gave the federal courts power to register black voters.

Ending "Massive Resistance"

In 1959 state and federal courts nullified Virginia laws which prevented state funds from going to integrated schools. This proved to be the beginning of the end for "massive resistance."

Sit-Ins

In February 1960 four black students staged a sit-in at a Woolworth lunch counter in Greensboro, North Carolina. This inspired sit-ins elsewhere in the South and led to the formation of the Student Nonviolent Coordinating Committee (SNCC).

The Election of 1960

Vice President Richard M. Nixon won the Republican presidential nomination while the Democrats nominated Senator John F. Kennedy for the presidency with Lyndon B. Johnson, majority leader of the Senate, as his running mate.

Kennedy's Catholicism was a major issue until, on September 12, Kennedy told a gathering of Protestant ministers that he accepted separation of church and state and that Catholic leaders would not tell him how to act as president.

A series of televised debates between Kennedy and Nixon helped create a positive image for Kennedy and may have been a turning point in the election.

Kennedy won the election by slightly over 100,000 popular votes and 94 electoral votes, based on majorities in New England, the Middle Atlantic, and the South.

Society and Culture

Gross National Product

The GNP almost doubled between 1945 and 1960, growing at an annual rate of 3.2 percent from 1950 to 1960. Inflation, meanwhile, remained under 2 percent annually throughout the 1950s. Defense spending was the most important stimulant and military-related research helped create or expand the new industries of chemicals, electronics, and aviation. The U.S. had a virtual monopoly over international trade, because of the devastation of the World War. Technological innovations contributed to productivity, which jumped 35 percent between 1945 and 1955. After depression and war, Americans had a great desire to consume. Between 1945 and 1960 the American population grew by nearly 30 percent, which contributed greatly to consumer demand.

Consumption Pattern

Home ownership grew by 50 percent between 1945 and 1960. These new homes required such appliances as refrigerators and washing machines, but the most popular product was the television, which increased from 7,000 sets in 1946 to 50 million sets in 1960. *TV Guide* became the fastest growing magazine, and advertising found the TV medium especially powerful. Consumer credit increased 800 percent between 1945 and 1957 while the rate of savings dropped to about 5 percent of income. The number of shopping centers rose from eight in 1945 to 3,840 in 1960. Teenagers became an increasingly important consumer group, making—among other things—a major industry of rock 'n' roll music, with Elvis Presley as its first star, by the mid-1950s.

Demographic Trends

Population Growth

In the 1950s population grew by over 28 million, 97 percent of which was in urban and suburban areas. The average life expectancy increased from 66 in 1955 to 71 in 1970. Dr. Benjamin Spock's *The Commonsense Book of Baby and Child Care* sold an average of one million copies a year between 1946 and 1960.

The Sun Belt

Aided by use of air conditioning, Florida, the Southwest, and California grew rapidly, with California becoming the most populous state by 1963. The Northeast, however, remained the most densely populated area.

Suburbs

The suburbs grew six times faster than the cities in the 1950s. William Levitt pioneered the mass-produced housing development when he built 10,600 houses (Levittown) on Long Island in 1947, a pattern followed widely elsewhere in the country. The Federal Housing Administration helped builders by insuring up to 95 percent of a loan and buyers by insuring their mortgages. Car production increased from 2 million in 1946 to 8 million in 1955, which further encouraged the development of suburbia. As blacks moved into the Northern and Midwestern cities, whites moved to the suburbs, a process dubbed "white flight." About 20 percent of the population moved their residence each year.

Middle Class

The number of American families that were classified as middle class changed from 5.1 million in 1947 to more than 12 million by the early 1960s.

Jobs

The number of farm workers dropped from 9 million to 5.2 million between 1940 and 1960. By 1960 more Americans held white-collar than blue-collar jobs.

Conformity and Security

Corporate Employment

Employees tended to work for larger organizations. By 1960, 38 percent of the work force was employed by organizations with over 500 employees. Such environments encouraged the managerial personality and corporate cooperation rather than individualism.

Homogeneity

Observers found the expansion of the middle class an explanation for emphasis on conformity. David Riesman argued in *The Lonely Crowd* (1950) that Americans were moving from an inner-directed to an outer-directed orientation. William Whyte's *The Organization Man* (1956) saw corporate culture as emphasizing the group rather than the individual. Sloan Wilson's *The Man in the Grey Flannel Suit* (1955) expressed similar concerns in fictional form.

Leisure

The standard work week shrank from six to five days. Television became the dominant cultural medium, with over 530 stations by 1961. Books, especially as paperbacks, increased in sales annually.

Women

A cult of feminine domesticity re-emerged after World War II. Marynia Farnham and Ferdinand Lundberg published *Modern Woman: The Lost Sex* in 1947, suggesting that science supported the idea that women could only find fulfillment in domesticity. Countless magazine articles also promoted the concept that a woman's place was in the home.

Religion

From 1940, when less than half the population belonged to a church, membership rose to over 65 percent by 1960. Catholic Bishop Fulton J. Sheen had a popular weekly television show, "Life Worth Living," while Baptist evangelist Billy Graham held huge crusades. Norman Vincent Peale best represented the tendency of religion to emphasize reassurance with his bestseller *The Power of Positive Thinking* (1952). Critics noted the shallowness of this religion. Will Herberg in *Protestant-Catholic-Jew* (1955) said that popular religiosity lacked conviction and commitment. Reinhold Niebuhr, the leading neo-orthodox theologian, criticized the self-centeredness of popular religion and its failure to recognize the reality of sin.

QUESTION

What was the state of the economy between 1945 and 1960?

EXPLANATION

The economy experienced unprecedented growth during this period, with the Gross National Product almost doubling during this period. Several factors contributed to this growth. Defense spending remained high because of the Cold War. American goods were needed in very large numbers during the rebuilding of Europe and Asia. American population grew, fueled by the "baby boom." Finally, following the depression and World War II, Americans were eager to purchase consumer goods.

Seeds of Rebellion

Intellectuals

Intellectuals became increasingly critical of American life. John Kenneth Galbraith in *The Affluent Society* (1958) argued that the public sector was underfunded. John Keats's *The Crack in the Picture Window* (1956) criticized the homogeneity of suburban life in the new mass-produced communities. The adequacy of American education was questioned by James B. Conant in *The American High School Today* (1959).

Theater and Fiction

Arthur Miller's *Death of a Salesman* (1949) explored the theme of the loneliness of the other-directed person. Novels also took up the conflict between the individual and mass society. Notable works included J.D. Salinger's *The Catcher in the Rye* (1951), James Jones's *From Here to Eternity* (1951), Joseph Heller's *Catch-22* (1955), Saul Bellow's *The Adventures of Augie March* (1953), and John Updike's *Rabbit, Run* (1960).

Art

Painter Edward Hopper portrayed isolated, anonymous individuals. Jackson Pollock, Robert Motherwell, Willem de Kooning, Arshile Gorky, and Mark Rothko were among the leaders in abstract expressionism, in which they attempted spontaneous expression of their subjectivity.

The Beats

The Beats were a group of young men alienated by twentieth-century life. Their movement began in Greenwich Village, New York, with the friendship of

Allen Ginsburg, Jack Kerouac, William Burroughs, and Neal Cassady. They emphasized alcohol, drugs, sex, jazz, Buddhism, and a restless vagabond life, all of which were vehicles for their subjectivity. Ginsberg's long poem "Howl" (1956) and Kerouac's novel *On the Road* (1957) were among their more important literary works.

Drill 3: The Politics of Affluence

1. All of the following statements about the 1950s in America are true EXCEPT

    (A) there were some improvements in the areas of civil rights and integration.

    (B) Americans moved increasingly to the suburbs.

    (C) more Americans owned automobiles than at any time before.

    (D) Americans had fewer children than at any time since the Civil War.

    (E) Americans' standard of living improved steadily.

2. Which of the following contributed to Harry Truman's victory in the presidential election of 1948?

    (A) Emergence of the "Dixiecrat" party

    (B) Democratic Party opposition to civil rights legislation

    (C) Labor union support for Truman

    (D) The candidacy of Henry Wallace

    (E) The "solid South"

3. As president, Dwight D. Eisenhower gave the LEAST support to which of the following?

    (A) St. Lawrence Seaway

    (B) Civil rights for blacks

    (C) Extension of Social Security

    (D) Creation of the interstate highway system

    (E) Reduction of military expenditures

4. Which of the following statements is correct about the case of Julius and Ethel Rosenberg?

    (A) They were accused of giving atomic secrets to Germany during World War II.

(B) They were exposed as spies by former Communist agent Whitaker Chambers.

(C) They were convicted of espionage, condemned, and electrocuted.

(D) They were convicted but were later pardoned by President Eisenhower because public opinion did not favor harsh treatment of accused Communist spies.

(E) They confessed to having carried out espionage on behalf of the Soviet Union.

5. The growth of suburbs during the 1950s resulted in which of the following?

(A) A loss of white population in the central cities

(B) A growing dependence on public transportation

(C) A reduction in the migration of blacks to the cities

(D) A decline in automobile sales

(E) A rejection of mass-produced housing

1941–1960

DRILLS

ANSWER KEY

Drill 1—Declared War Begins

1. (C)	2. (B)	3. (E)	4. (C)	5. (C)
6. (D)	7. (E)	8. (E)	9. (D)	10. (E)

Drill 2—The Cold War

1. (D)	2. (A)	3. (A)	4. (E)	5. (D)
6. (B)	7. (C)	8. (A)	9. (E)	10. (E)

Drill 3—The Politics of Affluence

1. (D)	2. (C)	3. (B)	4. (C)	5. (A)

GLOSSARY: 1941–1960

Alienation
> The condition of being isolated or separated from mainstream society.

Big Three
> The leaders of the major Allied powers, Roosevelt, Churchill, and Stalin.

Containment
> A strategy that called for containing communism and preventing it from spreading further.

Dixiecrats
> Southern Democrats who opposed Truman due to his support of civil rights. They nominated Strom Thurmond as their presidential candidate in 1948.

Manhattan Project
> The project to design and construct a portable atomic bomb.

Marshall Plan
> The European Recovery Program providing more than $12 billion in aid to rebuild Europe.

NATO
> The North Atlantic Treaty Organization, which pledged that an attack against one member was an attack against all.

Truman Doctrine
> President Truman stated that the United States must support free peoples who were resisting Communist domination.

White Flight
> The migration of whites from cities to suburbs as blacks migrated to northern cities.

CHAPTER 14

1960–1972
THE NEW FRONTIER, VIETNAM, AND SOCIAL UPHEAVAL

➤ Diagnostic Test
➤ 1960–1972 Review & Drills
➤ Glossary

1960-1972
DIAGNOSTIC TEST

1. Ⓐ Ⓑ Ⓒ Ⓓ Ⓔ
2. Ⓐ Ⓑ Ⓒ Ⓓ Ⓔ
3. Ⓐ Ⓑ Ⓒ Ⓓ Ⓔ
4. Ⓐ Ⓑ Ⓒ Ⓓ Ⓔ
5. Ⓐ Ⓑ Ⓒ Ⓓ Ⓔ
6. Ⓐ Ⓑ Ⓒ Ⓓ Ⓔ
7. Ⓐ Ⓑ Ⓒ Ⓓ Ⓔ
8. Ⓐ Ⓑ Ⓒ Ⓓ Ⓔ
9. Ⓐ Ⓑ Ⓒ Ⓓ Ⓔ
10. Ⓐ Ⓑ Ⓒ Ⓓ Ⓔ
11. Ⓐ Ⓑ Ⓒ Ⓓ Ⓔ
12. Ⓐ Ⓑ Ⓒ Ⓓ Ⓔ
13. Ⓐ Ⓑ Ⓒ Ⓓ Ⓔ
14. Ⓐ Ⓑ Ⓒ Ⓓ Ⓔ
15. Ⓐ Ⓑ Ⓒ Ⓓ Ⓔ
16. Ⓐ Ⓑ Ⓒ Ⓓ Ⓔ
17. Ⓐ Ⓑ Ⓒ Ⓓ Ⓔ
18. Ⓐ Ⓑ Ⓒ Ⓓ Ⓔ
19. Ⓐ Ⓑ Ⓒ Ⓓ Ⓔ
20. Ⓐ Ⓑ Ⓒ Ⓓ Ⓔ
21. Ⓐ Ⓑ Ⓒ Ⓓ Ⓔ
22. Ⓐ Ⓑ Ⓒ Ⓓ Ⓔ
23. Ⓐ Ⓑ Ⓒ Ⓓ Ⓔ
24. Ⓐ Ⓑ Ⓒ Ⓓ Ⓔ
25. Ⓐ Ⓑ Ⓒ Ⓓ Ⓔ

1960–1972
DIAGNOSTIC TEST

This diagnostic test is designed to help you determine your strengths and weaknesses in your knowledge of the New Frontier, Vietnam, and Social Upheaval (1960–1972). Follow the directions and check your answers.

Study this chapter for the following tests:
AP U.S. History, CLEP General, CLEP United States History I,
GED, Praxis Specialty Area, SAT: United States History

---

25 Questions

DIRECTIONS: Choose the correct answer for each of the following questions. Fill in each answer on the answer sheet.

1. The Twenty-fifth Amendment to the Constitution provides for which of the following?

   (A) Filling the office of vice president between elections

   (B) Lowering the voting age to 18   26

   (C) Equal rights for women — ERA failed

   (D) Prohibition of the poll tax   24

   (E) Limiting presidential terms to two   22

2. A government-sponsored healthcare program for people over 65 was passed during whose presidential administration?

   (A) Harry S. Truman   (B) Dwight D. Eisenhower

   (C) John F. Kennedy   (D) Lyndon B. Johnson   Medicare

   (E) Richard M. Nixon

3. Which of the following best describes black Americans after 1965?

   (A) They called for an end to legalized segregation.

   (B) They called for voting rights legislation.

   post voting rights
   & Civil Rights
   Acts

(C) They sought to end discrimination in the North and improve their economic condition.

extreme solutions

(D) They rejected integration in favor of black separatism.

(E) They rejected nonviolence in favor of force.

4. Which of the following best characterizes the methods of Martin Luther King, Jr.?

    (A) Nonviolent defiance of segregation

    (B) Armed violence against police and troops

    (C) Patience while developing the skills that would make blacks economically successful and gain them the respect of whites

    (D) A series of petitions to Congress calling for correction of racial abuses

    (E) A series of speaking engagements in Northern cities in hopes of pressuring Congress to take action

5. Which of the following best describes the agreement that ended the 1962 Cuban Missile Crisis?

    (A) The Soviet Union agreed not to station troops in Cuba, and the United States agreed not to invade Cuba.

    (B) The Soviet Union agreed to withdraw its missiles from Cuba, and the United States agreed not to invade Cuba.

    (C) The Soviet Union agreed not to invade Turkey, and the United States agreed not to invade Cuba.

    (D) The Soviet Union agreed to withdraw its missiles from Cuba, and the United States agreed not to invade Turkey.

    (E) The Soviet Union agreed to withdraw its missiles from Cuba, and the United States agreed to withdraw its missiles from Western Europe.

6. The term "Long Hot Summers" refers to

    Woodstock 1969

    (A) major outdoor rock concerts during the late 1960s and early 1970s.

    (B) major Communist offensives against U.S. troops in Vietnam.

    Martin

    (C) protests held in large American cities against the Vietnam War.

    (D) a series of warmer-than-usual summers during the 1950s, leading to speculation about climatic change.

    (E) race riots in large American cities during the 1960s.

7. All of the following characterized the youth culture of the 1960s EXCEPT

   (A) use of drugs as a way of finding meaning in life.

   (B) popularity of such groups as the Beatles.

   (C) changing standards of sexual morality.

   (D) desire to spread American imperialism.

   (E) the "Hippie" life-style and manner of dress.

8. Each of the following expanded the right to vote in some way EXCEPT

   (A) the Twenty-third Amendment to the Constitution.

   (B) the Twenty-fourth Amendment to the Constitution.

   (C) *Gideon v. Wainright* (1963).

   (D) *Westberry v. Sanders* (1964).

   (E) the Voting Rights Act (1964).

9. Which of the following was the most important factor in John F. Kennedy's 1960 presidential election victory over Richard Nixon?

   (A) Americans' deep and growing dissatisfaction with the Eisenhower administration

   (B) Revelations of corrupt activities on the part of Nixon

   (C) Kennedy's better showing in nationally televised debates

   (D) Kennedy's long record of administrative experience as governor of Massachusetts

   (E) Nixon's failure to serve in the armed forces during the Second World War

10. After concluding its investigation of the assassination of President John F. Kennedy, the Warren Commission announced its finding that

   (A) Lee Harvey Oswald acted alone in assassinating the president.

   (B) Oswald was assisted by two other marksmen on the "grassy knoll" in front of the presidential motorcade.

   (C) Oswald had been the only gunman but was part of a widespread conspiracy.

   (D) Oswald, in fact, had nothing to do with the assassination.

   (E) the true facts of the assassination and any possible conspiracy involved with it will probably never be known.

11. Which of the following gave the president the most power in directing American foreign policy during the post-World War II era?

(A) The Tonkin Gulf Resolution *Closest to declaration of war*

(B) The Civil Rights Act of 1964

(C) The Boland Amendments of 1982 and 1984

(D) The War Powers Act *limited*

(E) The Good Neighbor Policy *earlier*

12. Which of the following are decisions of the Warren Court?

I. *Edwards v. Aguillard*

II. *Reynolds v. Sims*

III. *Miranda v. State of Arizona*

IV. *Roe v. Wade*

V. *Watkins v. United States*

(A) I and II   (B) II, III, and IV

(C) I, IV, and V   (D) II, III, and V

(E) II, III, IV, and V

13. The Civil Rights Act of 1964 accomplished all of the following EXCEPT

(A) barring racial discrimination in public hotels.

(B) authorizing the attorney general to bring suit to desegregate the public schools.

(C) outlawing discriminatory employment practices.

(D) barring racial discrimination in restaurants.

(E) outlawing literacy tests used to prevent citizens from voting. *Voting Rights Act*

14. Betty Friedan wrote which book?

(A) *Silent Spring* *Rachel Carson DDT + other pesticides*

(B) *Modern Women: The Lost Sex*

(C) *In Cold Blood* *Truman Capote*

(D) *The Feminine Mystique*

(E) *The Other America*

15. Earl Clarence Gideon earned fame in 1963 by

    (A) being the first American to orbit Earth. *John Glenn*

    - (B) establishing the accused's right to legal counsel in all criminal cases.

    (C) being impeached from the Supreme Court.

    (D) authoring *Catch-22*.

    (E) breaking Babe Ruth's home run record.

16. What event made Kennedy a national hero in 1962 due to the way in which people believed he successfully stood up to the Russians?

    (A) The Berlin Blockade

    (B) The Berlin Wall Crisis

    (C) The Pueblo incident

    - (D) The Cuban Missile Crisis

    (E) The Gulf of Tonkin incident

X. What specific disagreement took a full year to rectify before peace negotiations actually began to end the Vietnam War?

    (A) The city in which the negotiations would be held *Paris*

    (B) The governments which would be allowed to attend the negotiations

    - (C) The shape of the negotiating table

    (D) The actual border between North and South Vietnam

    (E) The participation of representatives from the People's Republic of China as moderators of the negotiations

18. The popular press's nickname for the White House during John Kennedy's administration was

    (A) South Boston.   (B) Valhalla.

    - (C) Camelot.   (D) Shangri-La. *— original name for Camp David*

    (E) Tara. *Gone with the Wind*

19. What incident led to Lyndon Johnson escalating American involvement in Vietnam by sending more than 550,000 American soldiers to actively fight the Viet Cong and the North Vietnamese?

    (A) The Mayaguez Affair   (B) The Pueblo Incident

    - (C) The Gulf of Tonkin incident (D) The attack on Khe Sahn
        1964

    - (E) The Tet Offensive
        1968 — turning point
        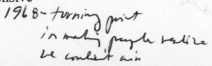

20. What effect did the Tet Offensive have on President Lyndon Johnson?

    (A) It gave him an excuse to escalate the war even further.

    (B) It united Americans even more against the North Vietnamese and bolstered (strengthened) Johnson's campaign for re-election.

    (C) It had little, if any effect on Johnson or his handling of the war.

    (D) It caused him to withdraw from the 1968 presidential race and led Americans to lose faith in American policies in Vietnam.

    (E) It forced him to send Henry Kissinger to negotiate with the North Vietnamese.

21. The "baby boomers" refer to those Americans who were

    (A) disenchanted with the United States in the aftermath of World War I.

    (B) born in the immediate aftermath of World War II.

    (C) anti-Eisenhower in the election of 1956.

    (D) veterans of World War II.

    (E) the first seven astronauts.

22. The liberal views of the Earl Warren court are displayed in all of the following Supreme Court decisions EXCEPT

    (A) *Baker v. Carr.*

    (B) *Roe v. Wade.*

    (C) *Brown v. The Topeka Board of Education.*

    (D) *Miranda v. Arizona.*

    (E) *Engel v. Vitale.*

23. The first black appointed to the United States Supreme Court was

    (A) Warren Burger.   (B) Earl Warren.

    (C) William Rehnquist.   (D) Thurgood Marshall.

    (E) Sandra Day O'Connor.

24. Modeled after the New Deal, Lyndon Johnson's Great Society Program included all of the following EXCEPT

    (A) Medicare.   (B) the Fair Housing Act.

    (C) the Voting Rights Act.   (D) Project Head Start.

    (E) the Department of Energy.

25. The Cuban Missile Crisis of 1962 resulted in

    (A) Soviet deployment of offensive nuclear missiles in Cuba.

    (B) the closing of the American naval base in Cuba.

    (C) Fidel Castro coming to power.

    (D) an American pledge not to invade Cuba.

    (E) increased American reliance on the policy of brinkmanship.

1960–1972
DIAGNOSTIC TEST

ANSWER KEY

1.	(A)	6.	(E)	11.	(A)	16.	(D)	21.	(B)
2.	(D)	7.	(D)	12.	(D)	17.	(C)	22.	(B)
3.	(C)	8.	(C)	13.	(E)	18.	(C)	23.	(D)
4.	(A)	9.	(C)	14.	(D)	19.	(C)	24.	(E)
5.	(B)	10.	(A)	15.	(B)	20.	(D)	25.	(D)

DETAILED EXPLANATIONS
OF ANSWERS

1.   **(A)**   The Twenty-fifth Amendment provided for filling the office of vice president between elections. The Twenty-sixth Amendment lowered the voting age to 18, the 24th Amendment prohibited the poll tax, and the Twenty-second Amendment limited presidential terms to two for any one individual. The Equal Rights Amendment was not ratified.

2.   **(D)**   Medicare and Medicaid were passed in 1965 during Johnson's presidency. Harry Truman had first proposed a national health insurance program in the 1940s but was unable to gain congressional approval.

3.   **(C)**   After passage of the Civil Rights Act of 1964 and the Voting Rights Act of 1965, blacks turned their attention to ending discrimination in the North and improving their economic situation. Although some advocated separatism and use of force, most blacks rejected these approaches.

4.   **(A)**   Martin Luther King's methods were characterized by nonviolent defiance of segregation. While King and/or his supporters might make speeches (E) or send petitions (D), civil disobedience gave his movement its urgency. Patience while developing the skills that would make blacks economically successful and gain them the respect of whites was the advice of late nineteenth century black leader Booker T. Washington, while armed violence was called for by King's more radical contemporaries of the 1960s.

5.   **(B)**   The agreement ending the Cuban Missile Crisis called for the Soviet Union to withdraw its missiles from Cuba while the United States agreed not to overthrow Castro's regime there. Turkey pertained to the matter in that the Soviets objected to U.S. missiles there, but it was not included in the agreement (C) and (D). The agreement also said nothing with regard to Soviet troops in Cuba (A) or U.S. missiles in Europe (E).

6.   **(E)**   The "Long Hot Summers" were filled with race rioting in America's large cities during the 1960s. Major outdoor rock concerts (A), such as the 1969 Woodstock concert, did occur during these years. The large Communist offensives against U.S. troops in Vietnam (B) went by the name Tet. The protests (C) which were many, were called anti-war protests. Concern about warm summer weather and the possibility of climatic change (D) was a phenomenon of the late 1980s.

7.   **(D)**   The youth culture of the 1960s definitely did not approve of what it considered American imperialism. It did, however, use drugs in an attempt to find meaning in life (A), enjoy the music of such groups as the Beatles (B), reject

the previous standards of sexual morality (C), and adopt the "Hippie" life-style and dress (E).

8.   **(C)**   *Gideon v. Wainright* guaranteed the right of a lawyer to persons charged with a serious crime. The Twenty-third Amendment gave voting rights in presidential elections to the District of Columbia. The Twenty-fourth Amendment prohibited the poll tax. *Westberry v. Sanders* established the principle of one person one vote; and the Voting Rights Act prohibited the use of literacy tests in voting.

9.   **(C)**   Kennedy came off looking better in the televised debates. Americans were perhaps somewhat bored with Eisenhower, though not deeply dissatisfied (A). There were no revelations of corruption on Nixon's part during this election (B) though there were during his 1952 run for vice president and his 1972 run for re-election as president. Kennedy had never been governor of Massachusetts and was short of administrative experience (D). Nixon, like Kennedy, had served in the navy during World War II (E), though without achieving the fame Kennedy had gained on the PT-109.

10.   **(A)**   The Warren Commission held that Oswald acted alone. Many since then, however, have suggested that Oswald was part of a large conspiracy (C) and that he was aided by marksmen on a "grassy knoll" (B). Some have indeed gone so far as to suggest that Oswald had nothing to do with the assassination (D). In fact there are very few allegations, however bizarre, that have not been made about the Kennedy assassination, and, not surprisingly, many Americans seem to believe that the true facts of the matter will probably never be known (E).

11.   **(A)**   The Tonkin Gulf Resolution of 1964, which granted President Johnson vast powers in pursuing the Vietnam War, best exemplifies the post-World War II trend toward executive-directed foreign policy in which Congress plays only a small role. The Civil Rights Act (B), while it enhanced the reputation of President Johnson, was an act of domestic, not foreign, policy. Both the Boland Amendments (C), which forbade the president from providing monetary aid to overthrow the Nicaraguan government and the War Powers Act of 1973 (D), which limited the president's war-making powers to 60 days without congressional approval, represent congressional attempts to curtail executive foreign policy-making power. The Good Neighbor Policy (E) was a complex set of initiatives toward Latin American nations that was part of Franklin D. Roosevelt's foreign policy.

12.   **(D)**   *Miranda v. State of Arizona* (III) is probably the most well known of the Warren Court's decisions; it ruled that police must inform suspects of their rights to silence and counsel before questioning them. *Reynolds v. Sims* (II), also known as the "one man, one vote" decision, dictated that representation in state legislatures must be based on population, not area. *Watkins v. United States* (V)

upheld the Fifth Amendment right of a witness to refuse to testify before a congressional committee, even if the committee was investigating subversive activities. *Roe v. Wade* (IV), which declared abortion legal on the basis of a "zone of privacy" implied by several amendments in the Bill of Rights, was a Burger Court decision of 1973. *Edwards v. Aguillard* (I) was a Rehnquist Court decision of 1988, prohibiting the state of Louisiana from requiring its schools to give a "balanced treatment" of "creation science" and evolution on the grounds that such a requirement advanced religious teachings in violation of the First Amendment.

13. **(E)** The ending of literacy tests to bar minority groups from voting was brought about by the Voting Rights Act of 1965 and not the Civil Rights Act of 1964. The main focus of the Civil Rights Act was to bar racial discrimination in public areas and in the hiring systems of companies, and to hasten the desegregation of public schools. The act was a hallmark of President Johnson's Great Society of the 1960s. Both acts were renewed by President Reagan in 1989.

14. **(D)** Betty Friedan wrote *The Feminine Mystique* (1963) which argued that the life of middle-class women did not allow them to use or develop their abilities. It is considered one of the important catalysts of the feminist movement of the 1960s.

15. **(B)** Earl Gideon earned fame in American civil liberties by being the defendant in the case that led to the Supreme Court's ruling in 1963 that the accused has a right to legal counsel in all criminal cases. Prior to this ruling, free legal counsel was supplied to the accused usually only in cases that were capital offenses.

16. **(D)** The Cuban Missile Crisis was the ultimate test of John Kennedy's administration. It brought the two superpowers closer to nuclear war than they had ever been before, or have ever been since. Until the Cuban Missile Crisis, Kennedy's attempts to confront Soviet moves had been largely ineffectual. He had been badly humiliated in the Bay of Pigs debacle. This was followed by a failed summit in which Soviet Premier Khrushchev totally dominated the proceedings. Then there was the building of the Berlin Wall, which occurred while Kennedy and his family were vacationing in Massachusetts. By the time Kennedy returned to Washington, the wall was already being installed and the White House found itself with no options but verbal protestations. Again, the president looked weak and unprepared.

With the discovery of construction of nuclear missile bases in Cuba, Kennedy knew he had to act decisively or face total loss of credibility in dealing with the Soviets. The Soviets and Cubans had been emboldened to attempt constructing these bases precisely because of Kennedy's previous, and ineffectual, efforts to oust Castro from Cuba, and Khrushchev's belief that Kennedy was a weak and inexperienced foe. Kennedy's challenge was to eliminate the bases without sparking a full-scale war.

The majority of Kennedy's advisors recommended military strikes against Cuba. Kennedy feared this would spark Soviet retaliation against American allies in Europe or against Turkey. Other advisors recommended direct talks with the Soviets. Kennedy feared that such talks would be used by the Soviets to stall for time until the missile bases were completed. Then it would be impossible to remove the missiles. Finally, Kennedy settled on a naval blockade to prevent Cuba from receiving the materials they needed to complete the missile sites. While technically, a naval blockade is an act of war, it is still a nonviolent act that in this case forced the Soviets to make the next move. New evidence indicates that the Soviets came much closer to going to war than was previously thought. They sent their ships right up to the blockade, and they had submarines in position to attack American ships enforcing the blockade. Kennedy held firm. The Soviet ships were turned back, without violence. Faced with the decision of starting a full-scale war or backing down, and faced with a five to one American superiority in nuclear warheads, Khrushchev backed down. Kennedy was hailed as a hero and many historians view this crisis as the high point of Kennedy's presidency. What was not publicized is that while the press was focusing on the success of the naval blockade, behind the scenes Kennedy made promises to stay out of Cuba and to remove American nuclear missiles from Turkey. It was these pledges more than the highly publicized blockade that led to the Russian withdrawal of their missiles from Cuba.

17.   **(C)**   When peace negotiations began in 1969 in Paris between the United States and the North Vietnamese, it was already clear in the minds of the Vietnamese that America wanted to get out of Vietnam. Thus, their strategy was to stall the talks as long as possible, giving as little as possible, and hoping that further American discouragement would result in the United States withdrawing on North Vietnamese terms.

On the other side, American negotiators were determined to insure that the peace talks did not leave an image of North Vietnamese domination and American impotence. The result was that neither side was willing to compromise on even the most simple issues in the first years of the talks. The most blatant example of this was the dispute about the shape of the table at which all sides would sit to negotiate the peace. The North Vietnamese demanded a round table, and the Americans demanded a rectangular table. Neither side would compromise and the peace talks could not seriously begin until a compromise was reached. It took a year of haggling before both sides finally agreed to an oval shaped table. While this issue was certainly not the most important issue discussed at the peace talks, it is symbolic of the attitude both sides brought to the talks and helps explain why it took until 1973 to finally reach an agreement.

18.   **(C)**   John F. Kennedy was one of the most romanticized presidents in American history. The youngest president ever elected, handsome, bright, witty, with a storybook family, it was easy to make him bigger than life. He had an easygoing charm that endeared him to millions, and his television press conferences—the first regularly scheduled television press conferences, were both en-

lightening and entertaining. He inspired the nation with his idealism and energy.

When Kennedy became president, he brought in a new generation of young, intellectual, and dedicated advisors who sought to correct the wrongs in America. The press labelled Kennedy's appointees the "best and the brightest." With the attractive young president and his lovely wife presiding over this entourage of bright young intellectuals, the press quickly drew comparisons to a young King Arthur and his knights of the round table. The popular press quickly picked up on this analogy, and the White House was immediately dubbed "Camelot." This myth of the Kennedy White House as Camelot continued and even grew somewhat after his assassination. With America bogged down in Vietnam and race riots at home, the Kennedy years were looked back on nostalgically by many Americans as a time of happiness and unbounded idealism. The reality was never as good as the memory, but the Kennedy/Camelot analogy remains a signature of his tragically brief presidency.

19.   **(C)**   In the summer of 1964, the war between North and South Vietnam was not going well for the American-backed South. Corrupt government leaders, poorly trained and motivated soldiers, and a lack of support from the people left the South Vietnamese government in precarious straits. While the United States publicly admitted to having advisors in Vietnam, in reality these "advisors" had been actively engaged in combat missions for almost three years. American intelligence estimates indicated that South Vietnam would not survive without increased American involvement in the war. The United States either had to pull out of Vietnam or expand the war. President Johnson reluctantly decided to expand American involvement in the war.

This expansion was dramatically increased following an incident in which an American warship, operating in international wars off the coast of North Vietnam in the Gulf of Tonkin, was attacked by North Vietnamese patrol boats. A second, but never confirmed, attack was reported soon after. Based on these attacks, President Johnson went to Congress to request authority to take whatever measures necessary to repel attacks against American forces. The Tonkin Gulf Resolution, as it was called, passed unanimously in the House and nearly unanimously in the Senate. Johnson used this resolution as a "carte blanche" to do whatever he felt was necessary to defeat the North Vietnamese. This led to increased bombing of North Vietnam and increased numbers of American soldiers fighting in South Vietnam. By 1968, the number of Americans stationed in South Vietnam approached 550,000. All of this expansion can be traced back to the Gulf of Tonkin Incident and the Tonkin Gulf Resolution which followed. While the war probably would have been expanded anyway, this incident provided the excuse and the congressional backing Johnson needed to expand the war in 1964.

20.   **(D)**   Up until the Tet Offensive, Lyndon Johnson's advisors assured him that with more soldiers and more weapons, the war in Vietnam could be won. While there was rising unrest at home, most Americans still backed Johnson and

American involvement in Vietnam. When the North Vietnamese launched their massive Tet assaults in 1968, any hope for a victory in Vietnam disappeared. While Tet was a military disaster for the North Vietnamese, the fact that they had been able to amass such a sizable assault force and had successfully launched the offensive at all, called into question everything America had done in Vietnam for the last four years.

With Tet, Johnson's advisors told him that the war could not be won even if another quarter of a million American soldiers were sent to Vietnam. Congress, the press, and the American people all began attacking American Vietnam policy with a vigor never before seen. Protests, which had previously attracted limited numbers of students and political radicals, now exploded into sometimes violent confrontations with police and national guardsmen and involved hundreds of thousands of "mainstream" Americans. Johnson was psychologically exhausted and emotionally beaten. Seeing his war policy in shambles, he withdrew from the election campaign and requested peace talks with the North Vietnamese. Support for American involvement in Vietnam dissolved, and the government began looking for a respectable way out as reflected in Richard Nixon's 1968 campaign pledge to obtain "peace with honor."

21.　**(B)**　The "baby boomers" are that generation of Americans born in the immediate aftermath of World War II (1945–1952). This generation of Americans are the result of a sudden demographic rise after the war when returning soldiers began to raise families with their wives. Baby boomers are considered among the most competitive and achievement-oriented generations, and were deeply responsible for the creation of the counterculture/"hippie" movement of the 1960s. Those Americans disenchanted with the United States after World War I are called "The Lost Generation," while World War II veterans went by the label "G.I.'s" during the war.

22.　**(B)**　The *Roe v. Wade* decision on abortion was handled by the Burger Court and not the Warren Court. Chief Justice Earl Warren stepped down from the Supreme Court in 1969 (Warren Court, 1954–1969) after rendering his decisions on protecting the rights of the accused in *Miranda* (1966); prohibiting state sponsored school prayer in *Engel* (1962); declaring segregation illegal in public schools *Brown* (1954); the one person, one vote principle in state apportionment of legislative districts in *Baker* (1966). Warren Burger was named chief justice of the Court by President Nixon in 1969 and resigned in 1986; President Ronald Reagan replaced him with William Rehnquist.

23.　**(D)**　Thurgood Marshall was the first black appointed to the U.S. Supreme Court in 1967 by President Johnson. Sandra Day O'Connor was the first woman appointed in 1981 by President Reagan. Burger was the chief justice appointed by Nixon in 1969, and Warren was appointed chief justice by Eisenhower in 1954. Rehnquist was first appointed to the Court in 1971 by President Nixon and named chief justice by Reagan in 1986.

24.   **(E)**   The Cabinet post of secretary of energy was created in 1977 by President Carter with James Schlesinger as its head. The department was created by Carter in response to the mounting energy crisis in America. President Johnson's Great Society Program included Medicare for the sick and disabled; a Fair Housing Act to end residential segregation; a Voting Rights Act to end the use of the literacy test against blacks who were seeking to vote in the South; and Project Headstart for nursery age children of low income families. All these programs were created in 1964–1965 by President Johnson as part of his war on racism and poverty.

25.   **(D)**   In 1962, the United States and the Soviet Union nearly engaged in nuclear war over the Soviet placement of offensive nuclear weapons in Cuba. The Soviets began placing the missiles in 1962 in reaction to the United States supported abortive invasion of Cuba in 1961 at the Bay of Pigs. With the discovery of the missiles, the United States established a naval blockade of Cuba and narrowly averted a nuclear war when President Kennedy agreed to a pact with Khruschev: the Soviets would remove the missiles if the United States pledged never to support an invasion of Cuba. Fidel Castro has been Cuba's leader since 1957 when his Communist guerrilla forces overthrew Batista. The U.S. continued to operate its naval base in Cuba through the 1980s. Finally, President Kennedy proved less enamored with the policy of brinkmanship after the missile crisis.

1960–1972
REVIEW

1. KENNEDY'S "NEW FRONTIER" AND THE LIBERAL REVIVAL

Legislative Failures

Kennedy was unable to get much of his program through Congress because of the alliance of Republicans and Southern Democrats. He proposed plans for federal aid to education, urban renewal, medical care for the aged, reductions in personal and corporate income taxes, and the creation of a Department of Urban Affairs. None of these proposals passed.

Minimum Wage

Kennedy gained congressional approval for raising the minimum wage from $1.00 to $1.25 an hour and extending it to 3 million more workers.

Area Redevelopment Act

The Area Redevelopment Act of 1961 made available nearly $400 million in loans to "distressed areas."

Housing Act

The 1961 Housing Act provided nearly $5 billion over four years for the preservation of open urban spaces, development of mass transit, and the construction of middle-class housing.

Steel Prices

In 1961 Kennedy "jawboned" the steel industry into overturning a price increase after having encouraged labor to lower its wage demands.

Civil Rights

Freedom Riders

In May 1961, blacks and whites, sponsored by the Congress on Racial Equality, boarded buses in Washington, D.C., traveling across the South to New Orleans to test federal enforcement of regulations prohibiting discrimination.

They met violence in Alabama but continued to New Orleans. Others came into the South to test the segregation laws.

Justice Department

The Justice Department, under Attorney General Robert F. Kennedy, began to push civil rights, including desegregation of interstate transportation in the South, integration of schools, and oversight of elections.

Mississippi

In the fall of 1962 President Kennedy called the Mississippi National Guard to federal duty to enable a black, James Meredith, to enroll at the University of Mississippi.

March on Washington

Kennedy presented a comprehensive civil rights bill to Congress in 1963. It banned racial discrimination in public accommodations, gave the attorney general power to bring suits in behalf of individuals for school integration, and withheld federal funds from state administered programs that practiced discrimination. With the bill held up in Congress, 200,000 people marched, demonstrating on its behalf on August 28, 1963 in Washington, D.C. Martin Luther King gave his "I Have a Dream" speech.

QUESTION

> What progress was made on civil rights during the Kennedy administration?

EXPLANATION

The progress of civil rights during the early sixties was limited, but significant. The Kennedy administration worked to further the desegregation of schools, including using the Mississippi National Guard to desegregate the University of Mississippi. African-Americans continued to demand an end to desegregation, but Kennedy's bills to prohibit racial desegregation were stalled in Congress. These bills would not pass until after Kennedy was assassinated.

The Cold War Continues

Bay of Pigs

Under Eisenhower, the Central Intelligence Agency had begun training some 2,000 men for an invasion of Cuba to overthrow Fidel Castro, the left-leaning revolutionary who had taken power in 1959. On April 19, 1961 this force invaded at the Bay of Pigs but was pinned down and forced to surrender. Some 1,200 men were captured.

Berlin Wall

After a confrontation between Kennedy and Khrushchev in Berlin, Kennedy called up reserve and National Guard units and asked for an increase in defense funds. In August 1961 Khrushchev in response closed the border between East and West Berlin and ordered the erection of the Berlin Wall.

Nuclear Testing

The Soviet Union began testing of nuclear weapons in September 1961. Kennedy then authorized resumption of underground testing by the U.S.

Cuban Missile Crisis

On October 14, 1962 a U-2 reconnaissance plane brought photographic evidence that missile sites were being built in Cuba. Kennedy, on October 22, announced a blockade of Cuba and called on Khrushchev to dismantle the missile bases and remove all weapons capable of attacking the U.S. from Cuba. Six days later Khrushchev backed down, withdrew the missiles, and Kennedy lifted the blockade. The U.S. promised not to invade Cuba, and removed missiles from bases in Turkey, claiming they had planned to do so anyway.

Afterwards, a "hot line" telephone connection was established between the White House and the Kremlin to effect quick communication in threatening situations.

Nuclear Test Ban

In July 1963, a treaty banning the atmospheric testing of nuclear weapons was signed by all the major powers except France and China.

Alliance for Progress

In 1961 Kennedy announced the Alliance for Progress, which would provide $20 million in aid to Latin America.

Peace Corps

The Peace Corps, established in 1961, sent young volunteers to Third World countries to contribute their skills in locally sponsored projects.

Johnson and the Great Society

Kennedy Assassination

On November 22, 1963, Kennedy was assassinated by Lee Harvey Oswald in Dallas, Texas. Jack Ruby, a nightclub owner, killed Oswald two days later. Conspiracy theories emerged. Chief Justice Earl Warren led an investigation of the murder and concluded that Oswald had acted alone, but questions continued.

Lyndon Johnson

Succeeding Kennedy, Johnson had extensive experience in both the House and Senate and, as a Texan, was the first Southerner to serve as president since Woodrow Wilson. He pushed hard for Kennedy's programs, which were languishing in Congress.

Tax Cut

A tax cut of over $10 billion passed Congress in 1964 and an economic boom resulted.

Civil Rights Act

The 1964 Civil Rights Act outlawed racial discrimination by employers and unions, created the Equal Employment Opportunity Commission to enforce the law, and eliminated the remaining restrictions on black voting.

Economic Opportunity Act

Michael Harrington's *The Other America* (1962) showed that 20 to 25 percent of American families were living below the governmentally defined poverty line. This poverty was created by increased numbers of old and young, job displacement produced by advancing technology, and regions bypassed by economic development. The Economic Opportunity Act of 1964 sought to address these problems by establishing a Job Corps, community action programs, educational programs, work-study programs, job training, loans for small businesses and farmers, and Volunteers in Service to America (VISTA), a "domestic peace corps." The Office of Economic Opportunity administered many of these programs.

Election of 1964

Lyndon Johnson was nominated for president by the Democrats with Senator Hubert H. Humphrey of Minnesota for vice president. The Republicans nominated Senator Barry Goldwater, a conservative from Arizona. Johnson won over 61 percent of the popular vote and could now launch his own "Great Society" program.

Health Care

The Medicare Act of 1965 combined hospital insurance for retired people with a voluntary plan to cover physician's bills. Medicaid provided grants to states to help the poor below retirement age.

Education

In 1965 the Elementary and Secondary Education Act provided $1.5 billion to school districts to improve the education of poor people. Head Start prepared educationally disadvantaged children for elementary school.

Immigration

The Immigration Act of 1965 discontinued the national origin system, basing immigration instead on such things as skills and need for political asylum.

Cities

The 1965 Housing and Urban Development Act provided 240,000 housing units and $2.9 billion for urban renewal. The Department of Housing and Urban Affairs was established in 1966, and rent supplements for low income families also became available.

Appalachia

The Appalachian Regional Development Act of 1966 provided $1.1 billion for isolated mountain areas.

Space

Fulfilling a goal established by Kennedy, Neil Armstrong and Edwin Aldrin on July 20, 1969 became the first humans to walk on the moon.

Emergence of Black Power

Voting Rights

In 1965, Martin Luther King announced a voter registration drive. With help from the federal courts, he dramatized his effort by leading a march from Selma to Montgomery, Alabama between March 21 and 25. The Voting Rights Act of 1965 authorized the attorney general to appoint officials to register voters.

Racial Riots

70 percent of American blacks lived in central city ghettoes. It did not appear that the tactics used in the South would help them. Frustration built up. In August 1965 Watts, an area of Los Angeles, erupted in riot. Over 15,000 National

Guardsmen were brought in; 34 people were killed, 850 wounded, and 3,100 arrested. Property damage reached nearly $200 million. In 1966 New York and Chicago experienced riots and the following year there were riots in Newark and Detroit. The Kerner Commission, appointed to investigate the riots, concluded that they were directed at a social system that prevented blacks from getting good jobs and crowded them into ghettoes.

Black Power

Stokely Carmichael, chairman of SNCC, by 1964 was unwilling to work with white civil rights activists. In 1966 he called for the civil rights movements to be "black-staffed, black-controlled, and black-financed." Later he moved on to the Black Panthers, self-styled urban revolutionaries based in Oakland, California. Other leaders such as H. Rap Brown also called for Black Power.

King Assassination

On April 4, 1968 Martin Luther King was assassinated in Memphis by James Earl Ray. Riots in over 100 cities followed.

Black Officials

Despite the rising tide of violence, the number of blacks achieving elected and appointed office increased. Among the more prominent were Associate Justice of the Supreme Court Thurgood Marshall, Secretary of Housing and Urban Affairs Robert Weaver, and Senator Edward W. Brooke.

Other Minority Activism

Hispanics

The number of Hispanics grew from 3 million in 1960 to 9 million in 1970 to 20 million in 1980. They were made up of Mexican-Americans (Chicanos) in California and the Southwest, Puerto Ricans in the Northeast, and Cubans in Florida.

United Farm Workers

Cesar Chavez founded the United Farm Workers' Organizing Committee to unionize Mexican-American farm laborers. He turned a grape pickers strike in Delano, California into a national campaign for attacking the structure of the migrant labor system through a boycott of grapes. The UFW gained recognition from the grape growers in 1970.

Native Americans

The American Indian Movement (AIM) was founded in 1968. While at first it staged sit-ins to dramatize Indian demands, by the early 1970s it was turning to the courts.

The "New Left"

Demographic Origins

By the mid-1960s the majority of Americans were under age 30. College enrollments increased fourfold between 1945 and 1970. Universities became multiversities, often perceived as bureaucracies indifferent to student needs.

Students for a Democratic Society

SDS was organized by Tom Hayden and Al Haber of the University of Michigan in 1960. Hayden's Port Huron Statement (1962) called for "participatory democracy." SDS drew much of its ideology from the writings of C. Wright Mills, Paul Goodman, and Herbert Marcuse.

Free Speech Movement

Students at the University of California, Berkeley staged sit-ins in 1964 to protest the prohibition of political canvassing on campus. Led by Mario Savio, the movement changed from emphasizing student rights to criticizing the bureaucracy of American society. In December police broke up a sit-in; protests spread to other campuses.

Vietnam

Student protests began focusing on the Vietnam War. In the spring of 1967, 500,000 gathered in Central Park in New York City to protest the war, many burning their draft cards. SDS became more militant, willing to use violence and turning to Lenin for its ideology. More than 200 large campus demonstrations took place in the spring, culminating in the occupation of buildings at Columbia University to protest the University's involvement in military research and relations with minority groups. Police wielding clubs eventually broke up the demonstration. In August thousands gathered in Chicago to protest the war during the Democratic convention. Although police violence against the demonstrators aroused anger, the anti-war movement began to split between those favoring violence and those opposed to it.

Beginning in 1968, SDS began breaking up into rival factions. After the more radical factions began using bombs, Tom Hayden left the group. By the early 1970s the "New Left" had lost political influence, having abandoned its original commitment to democracy and nonviolence.

QUESTION

What did the "New Left" of the 1960s stand for?

EXPLANATION

The "New Left," a term credited to C. Wright Mills, emerged from the civil rights movement. Adherents of the movement originally sought "participatory democracy," arguing that government bureaucracies and large corporations worked together to minimize real democratic impact at the grass roots. The movement grew rapidly as college students across the country began to stage demonstrations protesting U.S. involvement in Southeast Asia.

The Counterculture

Origins

Like the "New Left," the founders of the counterculture were alienated by bureaucracy, materialism, and the Vietnam War, but they turned away from politics in favor of an alternative society. In many respects, they were heirs of the Beats, who had expressed broad disillusionment with the Cold War.

Counterculture Expression

Many young people formed urban communes in such places as San Francisco's Haight-Ashbury district or in rural areas. "Hippies," as they were called, experimented with Eastern religions, drugs, and sex, but most were unable to establish a self-sustaining life-style. Leading spokesmen included Timothy Leary, Theodore Roszak, and Charles Reich.

Woodstock

Rock music was a major element of the counterculture. The Woodstock Music Festival, held in August 1969 in upstate New York featured such musicians as Joan Baez, Jimi Hendrix, and Santana and offered an opportunity for unrestrained drug use and sex. In contrast to the joy of Woodstock was the slaying, in full view of the audience, of a concertgoer a few months later at the Altamont Speedway in California. By the early 1970s the counterculture was shrinking, either as the victim of its own excesses or by way of absorption into the mainstream.

Women's Liberation

Betty Friedan

In *The Feminine Mystique* (1963) Betty Friedan argued that middle-class society stifled women and did not allow them to use their individual talents. She attacked the cult of domesticity.

National Organization for Women

Friedan and other feminists founded the National Organization for Women (NOW) in 1966, calling for equal employment opportunities and equal pay. In 1967 NOW advocated an Equal Rights Amendment to the Constitution, changes in divorce laws, and legalization of abortion. In 1972 the federal government required colleges receiving federal funds to establish "affirmative action" programs for women to ensure equal opportunity, and the following year the Supreme Court legalized abortion in *Roe v. Wade*.

Problems

The women's movement was largely limited to the middle class. The Equal Rights Amendment failed to pass, and abortion rights stirred up a counter "right-to-life" movement.

The Sexual Revolution

In 1948 Alfred C. Kinsey published pioneering research indicating widespread variation in sexual practices. In the 1960s new methods of birth control, particularly the "pill," and antibiotics encouraged freer sexual practices and challenges to traditional taboos against premarital sex.

Gay and Lesbian rights activists emerged in the 1960s and 1970s, particularly after a 1969 police raid on the Stonewall Inn, an establishment frequented by homosexuals in New York City's Greenwich Village.

Cultural Expressions

American films achieved a higher level of maturity. *Who's Afraid of Virginia Woolf* (1966) and *The Graduate* (1967) questioned dominant social values. *Dr. Strangelove* (1964) satirized the military establishment while *Bonnie and Clyde* (1969) glorified two bank robbers. *Easy Rider* (1969) portrayed the counterculture. The dehumanizing aspects of technology were featured in *2001: A Space Odyssey* (1968).

In literature, Truman Capote's *In Cold Blood* (1965), Norman Mailer's *Armies of the Night* (1968), and Tom Wolfe's *Electric Kool-Aid Acid Test* (1968) combined factual and fictional elements.

Pop artists such as Andy Warhol, Roy Lichtenstein, and Claes Oldenburg drew their subjects out of such elements of popular culture as advertising, comics, and hamburgers.

Much theater became experimental as exemplified by the San Francisco Mime Troupe. Some plays, including Barbara Garson's *MacBird* (1966) and Arthur Kopit's *Indians* (1969) took an explicitly radical political stance.

Vietnam

Background

After the French defeat in 1954, the United States sent military advisors to South Vietnam to aid the government of Ngo Dinh Diem. The pro-Communist Vietcong forces gradually grew in strength, partly because Diem failed to follow through on promised reforms. They received support from North Vietnam, the Soviet Union, and China. The U.S. government supported a successful military coup against Diem in the fall of 1963. The number of U.S. military advisors increased from 2,000 in 1961 to 16,000 at the time of John F. Kennedy's death.

Escalation

In August 1964—after claiming that North Vietnamese gunboats had fired on American destroyers in the Gulf of Tonkin—Lyndon Johnson pushed the Gulf of Tonkin Resolution through Congress which authorized him to use military force in Vietnam. After a February 1965 attack by the Vietcong on Pleiku, Johnson ordered operation "Rolling Thunder," the first sustained bombing of North Vietnam. Johnson then sent combat troops to South Vietnam; under the leadership of General William C. Westmoreland, they conducted search and destroy operations. The number of troops increased to 184,000 in 1965; 385,000 in 1966; 485,000 in 1967, and 538,000 in 1968. Increases in the number of American troops were met by increases in the number of North Vietnamese fighting with the Vietcong and increased aid from the Soviet Union and China.

Defense of American Policy

"Hawks" defended the president's policy and, drawing on containment theory, said that the nation had the responsibility to resist aggression. Secretary of State Dean Rusk became a major spokesman for the domino theory, which justified government policy by analogy with England's and France's failure to stop Hitler prior to 1939. If Vietnam should fall, it was said, all Southeast Asia would eventually go. The administration stressed the U.S. willingness to negotiate the withdrawal of all "foreign" forces from the war.

Opposition

Opposition began quickly, with "teach-ins" at the University of Michigan in 1965, and a 1966 congressional investigation led by Senator J. William Fulbright.

Antiwar demonstrations were gaining large crowds by 1967. "Doves" argued that the war was a civil war in which the U.S. should not meddle. They said that the South Vietnamese regimes were not democratic, and opposed large-scale aerial bombings, use of chemical weapons, and the killing of civilians. "Doves" rejected the domino theory, pointing to the growing losses of American life (over 40,000 by 1970), and the economic cost of the war.

Tet Offensive

On January 31, 1968, the first day of the Vietnamese new year (Tet), the Vietcong attacked numerous cities and towns, American bases, and even Saigon. Although they suffered large losses, the Vietcong won a psychological victory as American opinion began turning against the war.

Election of 1968

In November 1967, Senator Eugene McCarthy of Minnesota announced his candidacy for the 1968 Democratic presidential nomination, running on the issue of opposition to the war. In February, McCarthy won 42 percent of the Democratic vote in the New Hampshire primary, compared with Johnson's 48 percent. Robert F. Kennedy then announced his candidacy for the Democratic presidential nomination.

Lyndon Johnson withdrew his candidacy on March 31, 1968 and Vice President Hubert H. Humphrey took his place as a candidate for the Democratic nomination.

After winning the California primary over McCarthy, Robert Kennedy was assassinated by Sirhan Sirhan, a young Palestinian. This event assured Humphrey's nomination.

The Republicans nominated Richard M. Nixon, who chose Spiro T. Agnew, Governor of Maryland, as his running mate in order to appeal to Southern voters. Governor George C. Wallace of Alabama ran for the presidency under the banner of the American Independent party, appealing to fears generated by protestors and big government. The Democrats nominated Humphrey at their convention in Chicago, while outside the convention hall police and anti-war activists clashed.

Johnson suspended air attacks on North Vietnam shortly before the election. Nonetheless, Nixon, who emphasized stability and order, defeated Humphrey by a margin of 1 percent. Wallace's 13.5 percent was the best showing by a third party candidate since 1924.

Drill 1: Kennedy's "New Frontier" and the Liberal Revival

1. Which of the following is true of the Tonkin Gulf incident?

   (A) The Tonkin Gulf incident involved a clash of U.S. and Soviet warships.

   (B) In the Tonkin Gulf incident, two North Vietnamese fighter-bombers were shot down as they neared U.S. Navy ships.

   (C) The Tonkin Gulf incident involved the seizure, by North Vietnam, of a U.S. Navy intelligence ship in international waters.

   (D) The Tonkin Gulf incident led to major U.S. involvement in the Vietnam War.

   (E) In the Tonkin Gulf incident, a U.S. Navy destroyer was damaged by a guided missile fired by a North Vietnamese plane.

2. The Bay of Pigs incident involved

   (A) the presence of Soviet nuclear missiles in Cuba.

   (B) a CIA plot to overthrow Chilean leader Salvador Allende.

   (C) a confrontation between U.S. and Soviet troops in Europe.

   (D) a clash between a U.S. Navy destroyer and North Vietnamese patrol boats.

   (E) a U.S.-sponsored attempt by free Cubans to overthrow Communist dictator Fidel Castro.

3. The Vietnam War ultimately had its roots in which of the following?

   (A) French colonialism

   (B) The Japanese invasion of Southeast Asia

   (C) The Korean War

   (D) The Geneva Accords

   (E) The Gulf of Tonkin Resolution

4. All of the following events took place during the Kennedy administration EXCEPT

   (A) the Bay of Pigs invasion.

   (B) the building of the Berlin Wall.

(C) a limited test ban treaty signed by the United States, the Soviet Union, and Great Britain.

(D) the Cuban missile crisis.

(E) the U-2 incident.

5. In 1968 who challenged President Lyndon Johnson in the New Hampshire primary, ultimately forcing him to withdraw from the presidential race?

(A) Hubert H. Humphrey   (B) Robert Kennedy

(C) Edmund Muskie   (D) Eugene McCarthy

(E) George C. Wallace

6. In 1968, Vietcong guerrillas and North Vietnamese regulars launched a massive series of attacks which failed militarily, but succeeded in ending U.S. fantasies about an early end to the Vietnam War. This episode of the war became known as the

(A) Pleiku Offensive.   (B) NLF Offensive.

(C) Gulf of Tonkin incident.   (D) Battle of Khe Sahn.

(E) Tet Offensive.

7. All of the following were legislative failures of the Kennedy Administration EXCEPT

(A) urban renewal.

(B) raising of the minimum wage.

(C) federal aid to education.

(D) medical care for the aged.

(E) tax reductions.

8. The 1968 Tet Offensive

(A) was depicted in the American news media as a major victory for U.S. forces.

(B) was a military victory for the Communist North Vietnamese forces.

(C) brought an immediate end to the Vietnam War.

(D) led to the belief in the United States that the Vietnam War was unwinnable.

(E) had little appreciable effect on the course of the Vietnam War.

9. The Bay of Pigs Affair had what effect on John Kennedy's presidency?

   (A) It made Kennedy a national hero for his tough, uncompromising stand against Castro and Communist Cuba.

   (B) It forced Soviet Premier Khrushchev to schedule an early summit meeting with Kennedy to avoid future American-Soviet confrontations.

   (C) It had virtually no effect on Kennedy's presidency, as it was kept secret until after Kennedy's assassination.

   (D) It forced Kennedy to allow Soviet occupation of military bases in Cuba.

   (E) It was a major embarrassment to Kennedy's administration and led to further crises in American-Cuban relations.

10. Lyndon Johnson's "Great Society" program was aimed primarily at

    (A) spurring advances in American science and technical education and increasing funding to high-tech research facilities.

    (B) sending American volunteers to impoverished foreign nations to help educate their people and build their economic base.

    (C) securing civil rights for all Americans and eliminating poverty.

    (D) providing minimum wage jobs for all unemployed Americans and shifting tax dollars from the military to the civilian sector of the economy.

    (E) retraining adults who had dropped out of school and increasing the number of Americans who attended college.

2. THE NIXON CONSERVATIVE REACTION

Civil Rights

The Nixon administration sought to block renewal of the Voting Rights Act and delay implementation of court ordered school desegregation in Mississippi. After the Supreme Court ordered busing of students in 1971 to achieve school desegregation, the administration proposed an anti-busing bill which was blocked in Congress.

Supreme Court

In 1969 Nixon appointed Warren E. Burger, a conservative, as chief justice but ran into opposition with the nomination of Southerners Clement F. Haynesworth, Jr. and G. Harold Carswell. After these nominations were defeated, he nominated Harry A. Blackmun, who received Senate approval. He later appointed Lewis F. Powell, Jr. and William Rehnquist as associate justices. Although more conservative than the Warren Court, the Burger Court did declare the death penalty, as used at the time, as unconstitutional in 1972 and struck down state anti-abortion legislation in 1973.

Revenue Sharing

The heart of Nixon's "New Federalism," a five-year plan to distribute $30 billion of federal revenues to the states was passed by Congress in 1972.

Welfare

Nixon proposed that the bulk of welfare payments be shifted to the states and that a "minimum income" be established for poor families, but did not push the program through Congress.

Congressional Legislation

Congress passed bills giving 18-year-olds the right to vote (1970), increasing Social Security benefits and funding for food stamps (1970), the Occupational Safety and Health Act (1970), the Clean Air Act (1970), acts to control water pollution (1970, 1972), and the Federal Election Campaign Act (1972). None were supported by the Nixon administration.

Economic Problems and Policy

Unemployment climbed to 6 percent in 1970, real gross national product declined in 1970, and in 1971 the U.S. experienced a trade deficit. Inflation reached 12 percent by 1974. These problems resulted from federal deficits in the 1960s, international competition, and rising energy costs.

In 1969, Nixon cut spending and raised taxes. He then encouraged the Federal Reserve Board to raise interest rates. The economy worsened. In 1970 Congress gave the president the power to regulate prices and wages. Nixon used this power in August 1971 by announcing a 90-day price and wage freeze and taking the U.S. off the gold standard. At the end of the 90 days, he established mandatory guidelines for wage and price increases. Finally, in 1973 he turned to voluntary wage and price controls except on health care, food, and construction. When inflation increased rapidly, Nixon cut back on government expenditures, refusing to spend (impound) funds already appropriated by Congress.

QUESTION

What unique set of economic difficulties did the U.S. experience in the early 1970s?

EXPLANATION

During the early 1970s, high inflation combined with high unemployment occurred at the same time. Economists referred to this phenomenon as "stagflation." The gross national product declined, while costs increased. These problems were caused by deficit spending, rising energy costs, and a trade deficit, where the U.S. was importing more goods than it was exporting.

Vietnamization

Nixon first proposed that all non-South Vietnamese troops be withdrawn in phases and that an internationally supervised election be held in South Vietnam. The North Vietnamese rejected this plan.

The president then turned to "Vietnamization," the effort to build up South Vietnamese forces while withdrawing American troops. In 1969 Nixon reduced American troop strength by 60,000, but at the same time ordered the bombing of Cambodia, a neutral country.

Protests

Two Moratorium Days in 1969 brought out several hundred thousand protesters, and reports of an American massacre of Vietnamese at My Lai reignited controversy over the nature of the war, but Nixon continued to defend his policy. Troop withdrawals continued and a lottery system was instituted in 1970 to make the draft more equitable. In 1973 Nixon abolished the draft and established an all-volunteer army.

Cambodia

In April 1970, Nixon announced that Vietnamization was succeeding and that another 150,000 American troops would be out of Vietnam by the end of the year. A few days later, he sent troops into Cambodia to clear out Vietcong sanctuaries and resumed bombing of North Vietnam.

Kent State

Protests against escalation of the war were especially strong on college campuses. During a May 1970 demonstration at Kent State University in Ohio, the National Guard opened fire on protesters, killing four students. Soon after, two black students were killed by a Mississippi state policeman at Jackson State University. Several hundred colleges were soon closed down by student strikes as moderates joined the radicals. Congress repealed the Gulf of Tonkin Resolution.

Pentagon Papers

The publication in 1971 of classified Defense Department documents, called *The Pentagon Papers*, revealed that the government had misled the Congress and the American people regarding its intentions in Vietnam during the mid-1960s.

Mining

Nixon drew American forces back from Cambodia but increased bombing. In March 1972, after stepped-up aggression from the North, Nixon ordered the mining of Haiphong and other northern ports.

End of U.S. Involvement

In the summer of 1972, negotiations between the U.S. and North Vietnam began in Paris. A draft agreement was developed by October which included a cease-fire, return of American prisoners of war, and withdrawal of U.S. forces from Vietnam. A few days before the 1972 presidential election, Henry Kissinger, the president's national security advisor, announced that "peace was at hand."

Bombing is Resumed

Nixon resumed bombing of North Vietnam in December 1972, claiming that the North Vietnamese were not bargaining in good faith. In January 1973 the opponents reached a settlement in which the North Vietnamese retained control over large areas of the South and agreed to release American prisoners of war within 60 days. After the prisoners were released, the U.S. would withdraw its remaining troops. Nearly 60,000 Americans had been killed and 300,000 more were wounded, while the war had cost Americans $109 billion. On March 29, 1973 the last American combat troops left South Vietnam.

Foreign Policy

China

With his National Security Advisor Henry Kissinger, Nixon took some bold diplomatic initiatives. Kissinger traveled to China and the Soviet Union for secret sessions to plan summit meetings with the Communists. In February 1972, Nixon and Kissinger went to China to meet with Mao Tse-tung and his associates. The U.S. agreed to support China's admission to the United Nations and to pursue economic and cultural exchanges. These decisions ended the refusal of the U.S. to accept the Chinese revolution.

Soviet Union

At a May 1972 meeting with the Soviets, a Strategic Arms Limitation Treaty (SALT) was signed. The signatories agreed to stop making nuclear ballistic missiles and to reduce the number of antiballistic missiles to 200 for each power.

Détente

Nixon and Kissinger called their policy *détente*, a French term which meant a relaxation in the tensions between two governments. The policy sought to establish rules to govern the rivalry between the U.S. and China and the Soviet Union. The agreements were significant in part because they were made before the U.S. withdrew from Vietnam.

Middle East

Following the Arab-Israeli war of 1973, the Arab states established an oil boycott to push the Western nations into forcing Israel to withdraw from lands controlled since the "six day" war of 1967. Kissinger, now secretary of state, negotiated the withdrawal of Israel from some of the lands and the Arabs lifted their boycott. The Organization of Petroleum Exporting Countries (OPEC)—Venezuela, Saudi Arabia, Kuwait, Iraq, and Iran—then raised the price of oil from about $3.00 to $11.65 a barrel. U.S. gas prices doubled and inflation shot above 10 percent.

Election of 1972

The Democrats nominated Senator George McGovern of South Dakota for president and Senator Thomas Eagleton for vice president. After the press revealed that Eagleton had previously been treated for psychological problems, McGovern eventually forced him off the ticket, replacing him with Sargent Shriver. McGovern was also hampered by a party divided over the war and social policies as well as his own relative radicalism.

Wallace ran once again as the American Independent party candidate but was shot on May 15 and left paralyzed below the waist.

Richard M. Nixon and Spiro T. Agnew, who had been renominated by the Republicans, won a land-slide victory, 521 to 17 electoral votes. Nixon now appeared as one of the most powerful presidents in American history.

Drill 2: The Nixon Conservative Reaction

1. Antiwar protests became more intense in the early 1970s because

    (A) Richard Nixon turned to a policy of Vietnamization.

    (B) Congress voted to repeal the Gulf of Tonkin Resolution.

    (C) Richard Nixon extended the war into Cambodia.

    (D) Attorney General John Mitchell placed FBI and CIA spies within the protest movement.

    (E) the United States had rejected holding peace talks with the North Vietnamese.

2. All of the following were associated with the women's rights movement of the 1960s and 1970s EXCEPT

    (A) Betty Friedan.

    (B) the National Organization for Women.

    (C) the Seneca Falls Convention.

    (D) the Equal Rights Amendment.

    (E) abortion rights.

3.   The Nixon-Kissinger policy of *détente* took into account all of the following "ambiguous tendencies" in international affairs EXCEPT

    (A) rivalries within international communism.

    (B) the achievement of Soviet military parity.

    (C) Soviet frustration with negotiated settlements.

    (D) the emergence of a Soviet industrial economy.

    (E) Soviet expansion into the Third World.

4.   All of the following groups were involved in protest movements during the 1960s EXCEPT

    (A) blacks.   (B) Hispanics.

    (C) Chinese-Americans.   (D) women.

    (E) American Indians.

5.   Which of the following statements is true of the SALT I treaty?

    (A) It brought sharp reductions in the number of ballistic missiles in both the U.S. and Soviet arsenals.

    (B) It was intended to encourage the deployment of defensive rather than offensive strategic weapons.

    (C) It indicated U.S. acceptance of the concept of Mutual Assured Destruction.

    (D) It was never ratified by the U.S. Senate.

    (E) It created basic equality in the number of ballistic missiles on each side.

1960–1972
DRILLS

ANSWER KEY

Drill 1—Kennedy's "New Frontier" and the Liberal Revival

| 1. | (D) | 2. | (E) | 3. | (A) | 4. | (E) | 5. | (D) |
| 6. | (E) | 7. | (B) | 8. | (D) | 9. | (E) | 10. | (C) |

Drill 2—The Nixon Conservative Reaction

| 1. | (C) | 2. | (C) | 3. | (C) | 4. | (C) | 5. | (C) |

GLOSSARY: 1960–1972

Counterculture

Young people alienated by bureaucracy, materialism, and the Vietnam War, who attempted to create alternative societies.

Détente

A French term which meant a relaxation in tensions between two governments.

Domino Theory

A justification for American involvement in Vietnam, claiming that if Vietnam fell to the Communists, all of Southeast Asia would fall.

Doves

Those who favored withdrawal from the Vietnam War.

Great Society

Lyndon Johnson's program of social reform, including federal assistance in housing, education, and health.

Hawks

Those who favored continued involvement in the Vietnam War.

Hippies

Young people who experimented with Eastern religions, recreational drugs, and sex.

New Left

Young radicals of the 1960s who centered their political activities in and around college and university campuses. Strategies often involved protests, demonstrations, and sit-ins.

Vietcong

The pro-Communist Vietnamese forces.

Vietnamization

The effort to build up South Vietnamese troops while withdrawing American troops.

CHAPTER 15

1972–2001

WATERGATE AND THE NEW CONSERVATISM

➤ Diagnostic Test
➤ 1972–2001 Review & Drills
➤ Glossary

1972-2001
DIAGNOSTIC TEST

1. Ⓐ Ⓑ Ⓒ Ⓓ Ⓔ
2. Ⓐ Ⓑ Ⓒ Ⓓ Ⓔ
3. Ⓐ Ⓑ Ⓒ Ⓓ Ⓔ
4. Ⓐ Ⓑ Ⓒ Ⓓ Ⓔ
5. Ⓐ Ⓑ Ⓒ Ⓓ Ⓔ
6. Ⓐ Ⓑ Ⓒ Ⓓ Ⓔ
7. Ⓐ Ⓑ Ⓒ Ⓓ Ⓔ
8. Ⓐ Ⓑ Ⓒ Ⓓ Ⓔ
9. Ⓐ Ⓑ Ⓒ Ⓓ Ⓔ
10. Ⓐ Ⓑ Ⓒ Ⓓ Ⓔ
11. Ⓐ Ⓑ Ⓒ Ⓓ Ⓔ
12. Ⓐ Ⓑ Ⓒ Ⓓ Ⓔ
13. Ⓐ Ⓑ Ⓒ Ⓓ Ⓔ
14. Ⓐ Ⓑ Ⓒ Ⓓ Ⓔ
15. Ⓐ Ⓑ Ⓒ Ⓓ Ⓔ
16. Ⓐ Ⓑ Ⓒ Ⓓ Ⓔ
17. Ⓐ Ⓑ Ⓒ Ⓓ Ⓔ
18. Ⓐ Ⓑ Ⓒ Ⓓ Ⓔ
19. Ⓐ Ⓑ Ⓒ Ⓓ Ⓔ
20. Ⓐ Ⓑ Ⓒ Ⓓ Ⓔ

1972–2001
DIAGNOSTIC TEST

This diagnostic test is designed to help you determine your strengths and weaknesses in your knowledge of Watergate and the New Conservatism (1972–2001). Follow the directions and check your answers.

Study this chapter for the following tests:
AP U.S. History, CLEP General, CLEP United States History I,
GED, Praxis Specialty Area, SAT: United States History

---

20 Questions

DIRECTIONS: Choose the correct answer for each of the following questions. Fill in each answer on the answer sheet.

1. What Supreme Court decision stated that state laws prohibiting abortion violated women's rights?

   (A) *Miranda v. Arizona*   (B) *Roe v. Wade*

   (C) *Gideon v. Wainright*   (D) *Escobedo v. Illinois*

   (E) *Mapp v. Ohio*

2. What vice-president, charged with accepting bribes and kickbacks while he was a county executive, pleaded *nolo contendre* to tax evasion charges and resigned from office?

   (A) Walter Mondale   (B) Spiro T. Agnew

   (C) John D. Calhoun   (D) Nelson Rockefeller

   (E) Richard M. Nixon

3. The "Saturday Night Massacre" refers to

   (A) Nixon's firing of Watergate special prosecutor Archibald Cox and his staff in October 1973.

   (B) the bombing of the Marine Corps barracks in Lebanon by a suicide truck bomber in October 1983.

(C) Reagan's bombing of military bases in Libya in April 1986.

(D) Oliver North's destruction of files related to the Iran-Contra scandal, the day before his office was searched by the FBI.

(E) the slaughter of Vietnamese villagers in My Lai by American soldiers under the command of Lt. William Calley.

4. The term *détente* refers to

    (A) easing of tensions between the United States and the Soviet Union.

    (B) the Russian term for "Cold War."

    (C) United States relations with Latin America in the 1960s.

    (D) Nixon's invasion of Cambodia.

    (E) Kennedy's strategy during the Berlin airlift.

5. The two *Washington Post* reporters who "broke" the Watergate scandal to the American public were

    (A) Cronkite-Rather.   (B) Hearst-Pulitzer.

    (C) Ervin-Baker.   (D) Woodward-Bernstein.

    (E) Liddy-Dean.

"THE WINNER!"

GENE BASSET / *Scripps-Howard Newspapers*

6. This cartoon of 1978 depicts the Supreme Court's decision in *Bakke v. The Regents of the University of California* as

    (A) ending affirmative action programs based on race.

(B)   ending debate on issues of reverse discrimination.

'(C)   ambiguous on the issue of affirmative action programs and the issue of reverse discrimination.

(D)   a clear statement on race relations.

(E)   a racist backlash against minority quota systems.

7.   President Jimmy Carter achieved major success in dealing with

(A)   inflation.   (B)   the Iranian hostage crisis.

(C)   the energy crisis.   ·(D)   Middle East peace.

(E)   unemployment.

8.   The Iran-Contra affair upset most Americans because it involved

(A)   illegal support for the Contra rebels in Nicaragua.

(B)   illegal support for government backed "death squads" in El Salvador.

·(C)   a cover-up similar to, and to some extent worse than, the Watergate affair.

(D)   trading arms to Iran for release of American hostages.

(E)   providing funding for Contra rebels to be trained by Iranians in terrorist tactics to be used against the Nicaraguan government.

9.   The Watergate scandal led to Richard Nixon's downfall primarily because

(A)   of his role in planning and coordinating the Watergate break-in and other illegal campaign activity.

(B)   the press, the Democrats, and some liberal Republicans united to rid themselves of Nixon and his conservative philosophy.

(C)   he was already so unpopular because of his Vietnam War policies that virtually anything he did wrong would have been used as an excuse to remove him from office.

. (D)   of his role in directing the cover-up of the Watergate affair.

(E)   of his involvement with organized crime in carrying out political "dirty tricks" against his Democratic opponent, George McGovern.

10.   President Carter's administration had its greatest difficulties with its

(A)   Central American policy.   (B)   energy conservation policy.

(C)   land conservation policy.   (D)   Middle East policy.

. (E)   economic policy.

11. In the 1980 census, the total American population was

    (A) 130 million.   (B) 180 million.

    ·(C) 226 million.   (D) 307 million.

    (E) 435 million.

12. During his second term, President Reagan faced his gravest foreign policy challenge from Congress over his support for

    (A) the Sandinistas.   · (B) the *contras.*

    (C) the MX missile system. (D) Iraq.

    (E) Margaret Thatcher.

13. Between 1940 and 1979 from what areas did the largest percentage of immigrants to the United States come?

    (A) Asia   (B) Canada

    (C) Great Britain   · (D) Latin America

    (E) Germany

14. Who is the only president to have served by appointment rather than election?

    (A) Andrew Johnson   (B) Chester A. Arthur

    (C) John Tyler   (D) Gerald Ford

    (E) Lyndon Johnson

15. From Nixon to Reagan, American presidents used all of the following policies to combat inflation EXCEPT

    (A) mandatory wage and price controls.

    (B) voluntary wage and price controls.

    (C) cuts in federal spending.

    (D) tax increases.

    (E) tightening of credit.

16. The 1979 accident at the Three Mile Island power plant involved what energy source?

    (A) Coal   (B) Hydroelectricity

    (C) Natural gas   (D) Geothermal

    · (E) Nuclear

17. What was the name of the agreement that lifted most trade barriers between the United States, Canada, and Mexico?

    (A) SALT   (B) START

    (C) SDI   • (D) NAFTA

    (E) The Gulf of Tonkin Resolution

18. The first woman to serve as a member of the Supreme Court was

    , (A) Sandra Day O'Connor.   (B) Nancy Kassebaum.

    (C) Barbara Jordan.   (D) Ella Grasso.

    (E) Jane Byrne.

19. Jimmy Carter's major foreign policy accomplishment was

    (A) the release of hostages by Iran.

    (B) the Panama Canal treaties.

    • (C) a peace treaty between Egypt and Israel.

    (D) withdrawal of Soviet troops from Afghanistan.

    (E) reduction of Soviet influence in Africa.

20. The issue that most influenced voters in choosing Bill Clinton over President Bush in 1992 was

    (A) the aftermath of the Persian Gulf War.

    • (B) the condition of the U.S. economy.

    (C) U.N. relief efforts in Somalia.

    (D) reports of ethnic cleansing in the former Yugoslavia.

    (E) the breakup of the Soviet Union.

1972–2001
DIAGNOSTIC TEST

ANSWER KEY

1. (B)	5. (D)	9. (D)	13. (D)	17. (D)
2. (B)	6. (C)	10. (E)	14. (D)	18. (A)
3. (A)	7. (D)	11. (C)	15. (D)	19. (C)
4. (A)	8. (C)	12. (B)	16. (E)	20. (B)

DETAILED EXPLANATIONS
OF ANSWERS

1.   **(B)**   In *Roe v. Wade* (1973) the Court held that state laws barring abortions violated the rights of women. *Miranda v. Arizona* (1966), *Gideon v. Wainright* (1963), *Escobedo v. Illinois* (1964), and *Mapp v. Ohio* (1961) all involved the rights of the accused.

2.   **(B)**   Vice-President Spiro T. Agnew was accused of income tax fraud and of having accepted bribes while county executive of Baltimore County and governor of Maryland. Agnew pleaded *nolo contendre* to these charges and resigned as vice-president.

3.   **(A)**   When stories of White House involvement in the Watergate break-in began surfacing in 1973, President Richard Nixon came under increasing pressure to formally investigate the entire affair. Nixon denied any involvement in the Watergate caper, but during the trial of one of the Watergate burglars, a White House aid revealed that Nixon had a taping system which had recorded virtually all conversations in the oval office during the period in question. Investigators demanded the tapes. Nixon refused on the grounds of "executive privilege." Investigators smelled a cover-up.

 To quiet his critics, Nixon appointed a special prosecutor, Archibald Cox, to investigate any White House involvement in Watergate. Cox also requested the tapes. When Nixon refused, Cox went to court to obtain a court order forcing Nixon to relinquish the tapes. When Nixon realized what Cox had done and also realized that Cox might succeed in getting the court order, he ordered Cox to be fired. Nixon's attorney general and his assistant both refused to carry out the order. Instead, they resigned in protest. Nixon finally got another Justice Department official to carry out the order. Cox and his staff were duly fired on Saturday night, October 20, 1973, thus the name "Saturday Night Massacre."

 The press, the public, Nixon's political opposition, and even some of his supporters were outraged. The demand for continued investigation forced Nixon to name a new special prosecutor, Leon Jaworski. Jaworski also sought, and eventually got, custody of the complete tapes and those tapes proved to be the "smoking gun" which ruined the little credibility Nixon had left and finished his presidency.

4.   **(A)**   *Détente* was the foreign policy of the Nixon administration toward the Soviet Union in the early 1970s. Through the efforts of Henry Kissinger, secretary of state, *détente* sought to ease tensions with the Soviet Union through a series of arrangements based upon "realpolitik." Although relations did improve under this strategy, the Cold War clash between the world's superpowers continued throughout the decade. *Détente* did, however, move American foreign policy

away from a reliance on force in dealing with the Soviet Union and to recognize China in 1971. The first SALT (Strategic Arms Limitation Treaty) treaty reducing nuclear weapons between the United States and the Soviet Union in over a decade was also signed in 1972.

5.   **(D)**   Bob Woodward and Carl Bernstein were the two *Washington Post* reporters who painstakingly tracked down the Watergate scandal for the American public. Their investigative journalism eventually led to the resignation of President Nixon in 1974 and the criminal indictments of most of his top advisors owing to violations of various campaign laws and obstruction of justice charges. Gordon Liddy and John Dean were two of Nixon's indicted aides, while Sam Ervin and Howard Baker were the two U.S. Senators heading the Senate Investigative Hearings into the Watergate Affair. William Randolph Hearst and Joseph Pulitzer were New York newspaper editors in the late nineteenth century who created "yellow journalism." Walter Cronkite and Dan Rather were CBS News reporters.

6.   **(C)**   By declaring both parties the winner in the Bakke case, the Supreme Court left the American public confused on the issues of reverse discrimination and affirmative action. The cartoonist captures this sentiment well with this image of a boxing match ending not in a draw, but double winners.

7.   **(D)**   During his presidency, Jimmy Carter (1977–1981) was beset by a seemingly endless series of crises. His policies to combat inflation proved ineffective and ultimately led to the election of the Republican party's Ronald Reagan in 1980. In addition, Carter was unable to effectively combat soaring rates of unemployment (giving rise to the notion of "stagflation," high unemployment combined with rapid inflation) or the continuing energy crisis. His gravest crisis was in foreign affairs when in 1979 Iran seized 53 American hostages who were not released until Reagan's inauguration in 1981. The one shining moment for President Carter occurred in 1978 when he negotiated a peace accord between Egypt (Anwar Sadat) and Israel (Menachem Begin) known as the Camp David Accords. Both Begin and Sadat won the Nobel Prize for Peace for their efforts.

8.   **(C)**   Most Americans were angered about the Iran-Contra affair not because of the illegal funding of the Contra rebels in Nicaragua, but because of the shipment of arms to Iran for Iranian help in releasing American hostages in Lebanon. Despite the fact that the support for the Contra rebels involved direct violations of Congressional restrictions, which was a more serious legal concern than shipping arms to Iran, Congress had changed its rules several times regarding aid to the Contras and many Americans felt they should be supported, regardless of what Congress said.

This is not to say that Americans were not upset by the illegal aid to the Contras. Many Americans opposed any aid to the Contras and to find out it had been done illegally by members of the government outraged many. But the level of rage and the number of people outraged did not come close to matching the anger felt over the "arms for hostages" aspects of the affair.

9. **(D)** What got Nixon into trouble was his involvement in covering up White House involvement with the entire Watergate Affair. What began as a second-rate burglary by a group of unknowns became a national scandal when the burglars' connections with the White House became public. Nixon actively involved himself in trying to prevent White House involvement in Watergate from reaching the public, and it was this effort that ruined his presidency.

Had Nixon admitted White House involvement from the beginning, firing those involved and making a public apology for the "excesses" of his underlings, he probably would have completed a successful second term. However, he and his advisors felt that the damage from Watergate could be contained if White House involvement was kept secret. Documents were shredded, records were changed, people were paid off, and Nixon was involved every step of the way. When the press finally began unraveling the mystery, Nixon continued to deny involvement and continued the cover-up. When it was revealed that the White House had a taping system which had recorded Nixon's conversations during the period in question, Nixon refused to release the tapes. Eventually, in April 1974, under increasing pressure and surrounded by growing stacks of incriminating evidence, Nixon released edited versions of the tapes. This move sparked even more controversy because the edited portions of the tapes included suspicious gaps where crucial conversations should have been.

Finally, under Supreme Court order, Nixon handed over unedited tapes which, combined with the other evidence, confirmed Nixon's involvement in a massive, illegal cover-up of the Watergate Affair. Nixon, facing impeachment, was forced to resign in disgrace. Later, he was pardoned by his successor, Gerald Ford.

10. **(E)** While many people would argue, because of the highly publicized hostage crisis, that Carter's greatest difficulties were with his Middle East policy, the Camp David Accords, which many consider Carter's greatest success, were a central part of those policies. Carter's Central American policies, while some-what criticized at home, were considered successful by most Central American experts. The Panama Canal Treaty and other Carter policies focused on human rights, earning him tremendous respect among Central and South American leaders.

Domestically, Carter's greatest successes were in the areas of energy and land conservation. Carter was determined to develop new alternative sources of energy to free the United States from dependence on foreign oil. He was also a naturalist determined to protect the environment. His funding of alternative fuels research and of the Environmental Protection Agency were positive moves of which most Americans approved.

Carter's biggest failure was in economic policy. While it can be argued that many of the economic calamities that befell Carter were not entirely his fault, as many of the country's economic difficulties can be traced back to Nixon's and Johnson's policies, Carter still failed to effectively deal with them. Carter was determined to cut federal spending and reduce the federal deficit in an effort to control rising inflation. Unfortunately, his policies resulted in increasing unemployment, higher interest rates, and continued inflation. By 1979 the prime lending rate reached a historic high of 20 percent. Home mortgage rates reached 16 percent in many areas, putting many people out of the home buying market and sending the housing industry into a tailspin. Unemployment rose to over 7.5 percent, and inflation was approaching 14 percent annually.

Carter's political opponents created a new measuring standard called the "misery index" to rate how poorly the nation's economy was doing. None of Carter's efforts seemed to affect the downwardly spiraling economy. When the Iran hostage crisis hit, Carter's presidency was already in ruins. Carter's failure to free the Iran hostages simply added to the public perception of his ineptitude and was symbolic of the collapse of his leadership. While people remember the hostage crisis, had the nation's economy been relatively healthy, Carter's image would have probably been much different. People might have been more willing to see the hostage crisis as not being his fault. With the economy in shambles, it was easy to add the hostage crisis as one more thing to blame on Carter's incompetence.

11. **(C)** In 1980 the total American population stood at 226,504,825. The population figure of 130 million was the population in 1940, while 180 million was the approximate population in 1960.

12. **(B)** Throughout his second term in office, President Reagan faced repeated challenges from Congress regarding his support of the Nicaraguan rebels, called the Contras. Reagan continued to support the Contras against the Communist regime of the Sandinistas under the leadership of Daniel Ortega. Congressional restrictions on Contra aid led some members of the Reagan administration to devise the scheme of "arms for hostages" deals to indirectly provide Contra military aid from the sale of weapons to Iran. President Reagan escaped any direct involvement in this Iran-Contra affair, while junior members of the National Security Agency, such as Oliver North and Richard Poindexter, were indicted as co-conspirators for violating the Congressional statutes in question. Iran-Contra by far proved to be President Reagan's worst foreign policy crisis.

13. **(D)** Latin America, together with the West Indies, provided nearly 34% of the immigrants to the United States. Eighteen percent of the immigrants came from Asia, 10% from Canada, 6% from Great Britain, and 9% from Germany.

14. **(D)** Under the provisions of the Twenty-fifth Amendment, Gerald Ford was appointed vice president by Richard Nixon upon the resignation of Spiro Agnew from the vice presidency in 1973. Ford became president when Nixon resigned the presidency in 1974. Ford in turn appointed Nelson Rockefeller as vice president.

15. **(D)** Lyndon Johnson put in a tax increase that took effect about the time that Richard Nixon took office. Nixon cut federal spending and encouraged the Federal Reserve to follow a "tight money" policy. He also used both mandatory and voluntary wage and price controls. Gerald Ford cut government spending. Carter increased government spending, cut taxes, and called for voluntary wage and price controls. Reagan reduced government spending and instituted a tax cut. The Federal Reserve at the same time followed a tight money policy. The tax cuts of Ford, Carter, and Reagan were attempts to break the back of "stagflation," a combination of a stagnant economy and inflation.

16. **(E)** The Three Mile Island, Pennsylvania, nuclear reactor sustained damage to its reactor core. Technicians were able to bring the reactor under control before a meltdown occurred.

17. **(D)** From the protests of organized labor and presidential candidates Pat Buchanan and Ross Perot to the ringing endorsement of most Republicans and large business interests, NAFTA, the North American Free Trade Agreement was widely debated in the months leading up to Congress's passage in November 1993. NAFTA, which is to be phased in over 15 years, went into effect in January 1994, one year into Clinton's first term. SALT (A), the Strategic Arms Limitation Talks, and START (B), the Strategic Arms Reduction Talks, were negotiations between the U.S. and the Soviet Union that focused on controlling nuclear arms. The Gulf of Tonkin Resolution authorized President Johnson to take measures necessary to "maintain peace" in the wake of North Vietnam's reported torpedo attacks against U.S. destroyers in the Gulf of Tonkin in 1964. SDI (C), the Strategic Defense Initiative, or "Star Wars," as it came to be known, was President Reagan's idea for a space-based missile defense system.

18. **(A)** Sandra Day O'Connor was appointed to the Supreme Court by Ronald Reagan in 1981. Nancy Kassebaum and Barbara Jordan served in Congress, Ella Grasso was governor of Connecticut, and Jane Byrne mayor of Chicago.

19. **(C)** Although Carter was successful in obtaining congressional passage of the Panama Canal Treaty in 1978, his major triumph was the treaty between Egypt and Israel in 1979. Carter was unable to obtain the release of the hostages by Iran—as it turns out, they were released within minutes of his leaving office—nor was he successful in obtaining the withdrawal of Soviet troops from Afghanistan, or a reduction in Soviet influence in Africa.

20. **(B)** Opinion polls showed that the election's outcome came down overwhelmingly to the widespread perception that the economy had sagged on President Bush's watch. The unemployment rate had climbed to 7.8 percent, an eight-year high, and GNP growth was averaging an anemic 0.5%. Combine those factors with the Clinton campaign's relentless pounding of economic themes and you have a strategy and set of circumstances that put Clinton in the White House.

1972–2001
REVIEW

1. WATERGATE, FORD, AND CARTER

Watergate

What became known as the Watergate crisis began during the 1972 presidential campaign. Early on the morning of June 17, James McCord, a security officer for the Committee for the Re-election of the President, and four other men broke into Democratic headquarters at the Watergate apartment complex in Washington, D.C., and were caught while going through files and installing electronic eavesdropping devices. On June 22, Nixon announced that the administration was in no way involved in the burglary attempt.

The trial of the burglars began in early 1973, with all but McCord, who was convicted, pleading guilty. Before sentencing, McCord wrote a letter to Judge John J. Sirica arguing that high Republican officials had known in advance about the burglary and that perjury had been committed at the trial.

Soon Jeb Stuart Magruder, head of the Nixon re-election committee, and John W. Dean, Nixon's attorney, stated that they had been involved. Dean testified before a Senate Watergate investigating committee that Nixon had been involved in covering up the incident. Over the next several months, extensive involvement of the administration, including payment of "hush" money to the burglars, destruction of FBI records, forgery of documents, and wiretapping, was revealed. Dean was fired and H.R. Haldeman and John Ehrlichman, who headed the White House staff, and Attorney General Richard Kleindienst, resigned. Nixon claimed that he had not personally been involved in the cover-up but refused, on the grounds of executive privilege, to allow investigation of White House documents.

Under considerable pressure, Nixon agreed to the appointment of a special prosecutor, Archibald Cox of Harvard Law School. When Cox obtained a subpoena for tape recordings of White House conversations (whose existence had been revealed during the Senate hearings)—and the administration lost an appeal in the appellate court—Nixon ordered Elliot Richardson, now the attorney general, to fire Cox. Both Richardson and his subordinate, William Ruckelshaus, resigned, leaving Robert Bork, the solicitor general, to carry out the order. This "Saturday Night Massacre," which took place on October 20, 1973, sparked a storm of controversy. The House Judiciary Committee, headed by Peter Rodino of New Jersey, began looking into the possibility of impeachment. Nixon agreed to turn the tapes over to Judge Sirica and named Leon Jaworski as the new special prosecutor. But it soon became known that some of the tapes were missing and that a portion of another had been erased.

Vice President Spiro Agnew was accused of income tax fraud and having accepted bribes while a local official in Maryland. He resigned the vice presidency in October 1973, and was replaced by Congressman Gerald R. Ford of Michigan under provisions of the new Twenty-fifth Amendment.

Nixon was accused of paying almost no income taxes between 1969 and 1972, and of using public funds for improvements to his private residences in California and Florida. The IRS reviewed the president's tax return and assessed him nearly $500,000 in back taxes and interest.

In March 1974 a grand jury indicted Haldeman, Ehrlichman, former Attorney General John Mitchell, and four other White House aides and named Nixon an unindicted co-conspirator.

In April, Nixon released edited transcripts of the White House tapes, the contents of which led to further calls for his resignation. Jaworski subpoenaed 64 additional tapes, which Nixon refused to turn over, and the case went to the Supreme Court.

Meanwhile, the House Judiciary Committee televised its debate over impeachment, adopting three articles of impeachment. It charged the president with obstructing justice, misusing presidential power, and failing to obey the committee's subpoenas.

Before the House began to debate impeachment, the Supreme Court ordered the president to release the subpoenaed tapes to the special prosecutor. On August 5, Nixon, under pressure from his advisors, released the tape of June 23, 1972, to the public. This tape, recorded less than a week after the break-in, revealed that Nixon had used the CIA to keep the FBI from investigating the case. Nixon announced his resignation on August 8, 1974, to take effect at noon the following day. Gerald Ford then became president.

Congress responded to the Vietnam War and Watergate by enacting legislation intended to prevent such situations. The War Powers Act (1973) required congressional approval of any commitment of combat troops beyond 90 days. In 1974 Congress limited the amounts of contributions and expenditures in presidential campaigns. And it strengthened the 1966 Freedom of Information Act by requiring the government to act promptly when asked for information and to prove its case for classification when attempting to withhold information on grounds of national security.

QUESTION

How did the Watergate scandal threaten the checks and balances formula?

EXPLANATION

The heart of the Watergate scandal was the abuse of executive power. The Nixon administration itself was in charge of the Watergate investigation, and the White House worked to cover-up its activities. The White House was not held accountable for its actions. In addition, the House of Representatives received little cooperation from the White House in conducting its own investigation of the affair. The House indicted the president for obstructing justice, misusing presidential power, and failing to obey subpoenas. In order to prevent similar abuse in the future, Congress passed campaign reform and strengthened the Freedom of Information Act.

The Ford Presidency

Gerald Ford was in many respects the opposite of Nixon. Although a partisan Republican, he was well-liked and free from any hint of scandal. Ford almost immediately encountered controversy when in September 1974 he pardoned Nixon, who accepted the offer, although he admitted no wrongdoing and had not yet been charged with a crime.

The Economy

Ford also faced major economic problems which he approached somewhat inconsistently. Saying that inflation was the major problem, he called for voluntary restraints and asked citizens to wear WIN (Whip Inflation Now) buttons. The economy went into decline, unemployment reaching above 9 percent in 1975 and the federal deficit topping $60 billion the following year. Ford asked for tax cuts to stimulate business and argued against spending for social programs.

When New York City teetered on the brink of bankruptcy in 1975, Ford at first opposed federal aid, but he changed his mind when the Senate and House Banking Committees guaranteed the loans.

Vietnam

As North Vietnamese forces pushed back the South Vietnamese, Ford asked Congress to provide more arms for the South. Congress rejected the request and in April 1975 Saigon fell to the North Vietnamese.

The Mayaguez

On May 12, 1975, Cambodia, which had been taken over by Communists two weeks earlier, seized the American merchant ship *Mayaguez* in the Gulf of Siam. After demanding that the ship and crew be freed, Ford ordered a marine assault on Tang Island, where the ship had been taken. The ship and crew of 39 were released but 38 marines were killed.

Election of 1976

Ronald Reagan, formerly a movie actor and governor of California, opposed Ford for the Republican nomination, but Ford won by a slim margin. The Democrats nominated James Earl Carter, formerly governor of Georgia, who ran on the basis of his integrity and lack of Washington connections. Carter, with Walter Mondale, senator from Minnesota, as the vice presidential candidate, defeated Ford narrowly.

Carter's Moderate Liberalism

Carter, who wished to be called "Jimmy," sought to conduct the presidency on democratic and moral principles. However, his administration gained a reputation for proposing complex programs to Congress and then not continuing to support them through the legislative process.

The Economy

Carter approached economic problems inconsistently. Although during the campaign he had argued that inflation needed to be restrained, in 1977 he proposed a $50-per-person income tax rebate, but the idea ran into congressional resistance. In 1978 Carter proposed voluntary wage and price guidelines. Although somewhat successful, the guidelines did not apply to oil, housing, and food. Carter then named Paul A. Volcker as chairman of the Federal Reserve Board. Volcker tightened the money supply in order to reduce inflation, but this action caused interest rates to go even higher. High interest rates depressed sales of automobiles and houses which in turn increased unemployment. By 1980 unemployment stood at 7.5 percent, interest at 20 percent, and inflation at 12 percent.

Energy

Carter also approached energy problems inconsistently. Attempting to reduce America's growing dependence on foreign oil, in 1977 he proposed raising the tax on gasoline and taxing automobiles that used fuel inefficiently, among other things, but obtained only a gutted version of his bill. Near the end of his term, Carter proposed coupling deregulation of the price of American crude oil with a windfall profits tax, a program that pleased neither liberals nor conservatives. Energy problems were further exacerbated by a second fuel shortage which occurred in 1979.

Domestic Achievements

Carter offered amnesty to Americans who had fled the draft and gone to other countries during the Vietnam War. He established the Departments of Energy and Education and placed the civil service on a merit basis. He created a "superfund" for cleanup of chemical waste dumps, established controls over strip mining, and protected 100 million acres of Alaskan wilderness from development.

Carter's Foreign Policy

Human Rights

Carter sought to base foreign policy on human rights but was criticized for inconsistency and lack of attention to American interests.

Panama Canal

Carter negotiated a controversial treaty with Panama, affirmed by the Senate in 1978, that provided for the transfer of ownership of the canal to Panama in 1999, and guaranteed its neutrality.

China

Carter ended official recognition of Taiwan and in 1979 recognized the People's Republic of China. Conservatives called the decision a "sell-out."

SALT II

In 1979 the administration signed a second Strategic Arms Limitation Treaty (SALT II) with the Soviet Union. The treaty set a ceiling of 2,250 bombers and missiles for each side and established limits on warheads and new weapons systems. It never passed the Senate.

Camp David Accords

In 1978 Carter negotiated the Camp David Agreement between Israel and Egypt. Bringing Anwar Sadat, the president of Egypt, and Menachem Begin, prime minister of Israel, to Camp David for two weeks in September 1978, Carter sought to end the state of war that existed between the two countries. Israel promised to return occupied land in the Sinai to Egypt in exchange for Egyptian recognition, a process completed in 1982. An agreement to negotiate the Palestinian refugee problem proved ineffective.

Afghanistan

The policy of *détente* went into decline. Carter criticized Soviet restrictions on political freedom and reluctance to allow dissidents and Jews to emigrate. In December 1979 the Soviet Union invaded Afghanistan. Carter stopped shipments of grain and certain advanced technology to the Soviet Union, withdrew SALT II from the Senate, and barred Americans from competing in the 1980 summer Olympics held in Moscow.

The Iranian Crisis

In 1978 a revolution forced the Shah of Iran to flee the country, replacing him with a religious leader, Ayatollah Ruhollah Khomeini. Because the U.S. had supported the Shah with arms and money, the revolutionaries were strongly anti-American, calling the U.S. the "Great Satan."

After Carter allowed the exiled Shah to come to the U.S. for medical treatment in October 1979, some 400 Iranians broke into the American Embassy in Teheran on November 4, taking the occupants captive. They demanded that the Shah be returned to Iran for trial and that his wealth be confiscated and given to Iran. Carter rejected these demands; instead, he froze Iranian assets in the U.S. and established a trade embargo against Iran. He also appealed to the United

Nations and the World Court. The Iranians eventually freed the black and women hostages but retained 52 others. At first the crisis helped Carter politically as the nation rallied in support of the hostages.

The Shah, who now lived in Egypt, died in July 1980, but this had no effect on the hostage crisis.

In April 1980 Carter ordered a marine rescue attempt, but it collapsed after several helicopters broke down and another crashed, killing eight men. Secretary of State Cyrus Vance resigned in protest before the raid began, and Carter was widely criticized for the attempted raid.

The Election of 1980

Carter, whose standing in polls had dropped to about 25 percent in 1979, successfully withstood a challenge from Senator Edward M. Kennedy for the Democratic presidential nomination.

The Republicans nominated Ronald Reagan of California, who had narrowly lost the 1976 nomination and was the leading spokesman for American conservatism. Reagan chose George H. W. Bush, a New Englander transplanted to Texas and former CIA director, as his vice presidential candidate. One of Reagan's opponents, Congressman John Anderson of Illinois, continued his presidential campaign on a third-party ticket.

While Carter defended his record, Reagan called for reductions in government spending and taxes, said he would transfer more power from the federal government to the states, and advocated what were coming to be called traditional values—family, religion, hard work, and patriotism.

Although the election was regarded by many experts as "too close to call," Reagan won by a large electoral majority and the Republicans gained control of the Senate and increased their representation in the House.

After extensive negotiations with Iran, in which Algeria acted as an intermediary, Carter released Iranian assets and the hostages were freed on January 20, 1981, 444 days after being taken captive and on the day of Reagan's inauguration.

QUESTION

How did Ronald Reagan break apart the New Deal Democratic coalition?

EXPLANATION

Reagan's conservatism appealed to many factions of the New Deal coalition. Southern whites had been drifting away from the Democratic party since civil rights had become part of the Democratic agenda. When Reagan supported other conservative social issue positions, Southern whites voted Republican in increasing numbers. Other Americans supported Reagan's foreign policy, especially his strong stand against the Soviet Union. In addition, by the 1984 election, the economy was performing better than it had in years, and Reagan received credit for the economic expansion.

Social Trends

Minorities and Women

A two-tier black social structure was emerging that comprised a middle class and an "underclass" living in the ghettoes. Single-parent families, usually headed by females, grew disproportionately among the black underclass.

The Hispanic population grew 61 percent during the 1970s, many of whose number were "undocumented" immigrants who worked in low-paying service jobs.

The number of Asians—including Chinese, Japanese, Filipinos, Koreans, and Vietnamese—increased rapidly during the 1970s. Disciplined and hard working, many of them moved into the middle class in a single generation.

By 1978, 50 percent of all women over 16 were employed, up from 37 percent in 1965. Marriages dropped from 148 per thousand women in 1960 to 108 per thousand in 1980. Divorce climbed from 2.2 percent in 1960 to 5.2 percent in 1980. During the same years, births dropped from 24 per thousand to 14.8 per thousand.

The Equal Rights Amendment, approved by Congress in 1972, aroused opposition among traditionalists, led by Phyllis Schlafly, and fell three states short of the 38 states required for ratification.

Abortion

After the Supreme Court in *Roe v. Wade* (1973) legalized abortion during the first three months of pregnancy, conflict arose between "pro-choice" (those who wished to keep abortion legal) and "pro-life" (those who were anti-abortion) groups. The issue affected many local and state political campaigns.

Population Shift

Population was shifting from the Northeast to the "Sunbelt," represented by such states as Florida, Texas, Arizona, and California. When Congress was reapportioned following the 1980 census, these four states gained representation while New York, Illinois, Ohio, and Pennsylvania lost seats. The Sunbelt tended to be politically conservative.

Narcissism

In contrast to the social consciousness of the 1960s, the 1970s were often described as the time of the "me generation." Writers such as Tom Wolfe and Christopher Lasch described a "culture of narcissism," in which preoccupation with the self appeared in the popularity of personal fulfillment programs, health and exercise fads, and even religious cults.

Religion

During the 1970s the U.S. experienced a major revival of conservative Christianity, spread among both the fundamentalists and the more moderate evangelicals. A 1977 survey suggested that some 70 million Americans considered themselves "born-again" Christians, the most prominent of whom was President Jimmy Carter, a devout Baptist. Many of these Christians, led by Reverend Jerry Falwell's "Moral Majority," became politically active, favoring prayer and the teaching of creationism in the public schools, opposing abortion, pornography and the ERA, and supporting a strong national defense.

Drill 1: Nixon, Ford, and Carter

1. All of the following occurred under the Carter administration EXCEPT

    (A) the Camp David agreement between Israel and Egypt.

    (B) a treaty was made with Panama to transfer ownership of the Panama Canal to that country in 1999.

    (C) a bill was passed that successfully resolved the energy crisis.

    (D) a "superfund" was created to clean up chemical waste dumps.

    (E) a boycott of the 1980 summer Olympic games.

2. Henry Kissinger was involved in all of the following EXCEPT

    (A) *détente* with the Soviet Union.

    (B) the peace treaty between Egypt and Israel.

    (C) shuttle diplomacy in the Middle East.

    (D) Richard Nixon's visit to China.

    (E) peace talks with the North Vietnamese.

3. All of the following correctly describe Gerald Ford as president EXCEPT

    (A) he pardoned Richard Nixon.

    (B) he was the first president not elected to a national executive office.

    (C) he gave federal help when New York City faced bankruptcy.

    (D) he aided South Vietnam militarily when it was about to collapse.

    (E) he cut inflation from 12 percent to 6 percent.

4. The "Moral Majority" does NOT favor

    (A) prayer in public schools.

    (B) the ERA.

    (C) a strong national defense.

    (D) political activism.

    (E) the teaching of creationism in schools.

5. The American hostage crisis in Iran was precipitated by

    (A) the American government allowing the deposed Shah of Iran to come to the United States for cancer treatment.

    (B) Jimmy Carter's involvement in arranging the Camp David accords between the Egyptians and the Israelis.

    (C) American air strikes against Iran's ally, Libya.

    (D) American support for Israel's 1980 invasion of southern Lebanon.

    (E) American attempts to overthrow the newly emplaced government of Ayatollah Khomeini.

---

2. THE REAGAN YEARS

The Economy

An ideological though pragmatic conservative, Ronald Reagan acted quickly and forcefully to change the direction of government policy. He placed priority on cutting taxes. His approach was based on "supply-side" economics, the idea that if government left more money in the hands of the people, they would invest rather than spend the excess on consumer goods. The results would be greater production, more jobs, and greater prosperity, and thus more income for the government despite lower tax rates.

Reagan asked for a 30 percent tax cut and, despite fears of inflation on the part of Congress, in August 1983 obtained a 25 percent cut, spread over three years. The percentage was the same for everyone; hence, high income people received greater savings than middle and low income individuals. To encourage investment, capital gains, gift, and inheritance taxes were reduced and business taxes liberalized. Anyone with earned income was also allowed to invest up to $2,000 a year in an individual retirement account (IRA), deferring all taxes on both the principal and its earnings until retirement.

Congress passed the Budget Reconciliation Act in 1981, cutting $39 billion from domestic programs, including education, food stamps, public housing, and the National Endowments for the Arts and Humanities. Reagan said that he would maintain a "safety net" for the "truly needy," focusing aid on those unable to work because of disability or need for child care. While cutting domestic programs, Reagan increased the defense budget by $12 billion.

By December 1982 the economy was experiencing recession because of the Federal Reserve's "tight money" policy, with over 10 percent unemployment. From a deficit of $59 billion in 1980, the federal budget was running $195 billion in the red by 1983. The rate of inflation, however, helped by the lower demand for goods and services and an oversupply of oil as non-OPEC countries increased production, fell from a high of 12 percent in 1979 to 4 percent in 1984. The Federal Reserve Board then began to lower interest rates which, together with lower inflation and more spendable income because of lower taxes, resulted in more business activity. Unemployment fell to less than 8 percent.

Because of rising deficits, Reagan and Congress increased taxes in various ways. The 1982 Tax Equity and Fiscal Responsibility Act reversed some concessions made to business in 1981. Social Security benefits became taxable income in 1983. In 1984 the Deficit Reduction Act increased taxes by another $50 billion. But the deficit continued to increase.

Other Domestic Issues

Labor

The federally employed air traffic controllers entered an illegal strike in August 1981. After Reagan ordered them to return to work, and most refused to do so, the president then fired them, 11,400 in all, effectively destroying their union, and began training replacements. Reagan ended ongoing antitrust suits against International Business Machines and American Telephone and Telegraph, thereby fulfilling his promise to reduce government interference with business.

Assassination Attempt

John W. Hinckley shot Reagan in the chest on March 30, 1981. The president was seriously wounded but handled the incident with humor and made a swift recovery. His popularity increased, possibly helping his legislative program.

Women and Minorities

Although Reagan appointed Sandra Day O'Connor to the Supreme Court, his administration gave fewer of its appointments to women and minorities than had the Carter administration. The Reagan administration also opposed "equal pay for equal work" and renewal of the Voting Rights Act of 1965.

Problems with Appointed Officials

A number of Reagan appointees were accused of conflict of interest, including Anne Gorsuch Burford and Rita Lavelle of the Environmental Protection Agency, Edwin Meese, presidential advisor and later attorney general, and Michael Deaver, the deputy chief of staff. Ray Donovan, secretary of labor, was indicted but acquitted of charges that he had made payoffs to government officials while he was in private business. By the end of Reagan's term, more than 100 of his officials had been accused of questionable activities.

Asserting American Power Overseas

Soviet Union

Reagan took a hard line against the Soviet Union, calling it an "evil empire." He placed new cruise missiles in Europe, despite considerable opposition from Europeans.

Latin America

Reagan encouraged the opposition (*contras*) to the leftist Sandinista government of Nicaragua with arms, tactical support, and intelligence and supplied aid to the government of El Salvador in its struggles against left-wing rebels. In October 1983 the president also sent American troops into the Caribbean Island of Grenada to overthrow a newly established Cuban-backed regime.

Middle East

As the Lebanese government collapsed and fighting broke out between Christian and Islamic Lebanese in the wake of the 1982 Israeli invasion, Reagan sent American troops into Lebanon as part of an international peacekeeping force. Soon, however, Israel pulled out and the Americans came under continual shelling from the various Lebanese factions. In October 1983 a Moslem drove a truck filled with explosives into a building housing marines, killing 239. A few months later, Reagan removed all American troops from Lebanon.

Election of 1984

Walter Mondale, formerly a senator from Minnesota and vice president under Carter, won the Democratic nomination over Senator Gary Hart and Jesse Jackson, a black civil rights leader. Mondale chose Geraldine Ferraro, a congresswoman from New York, as his running mate. Mondale criticized Reagan for his budget deficits, high unemployment and interest rates, and reduction of spending on social services.

The Republicans renominated Ronald Reagan and George Bush. Reagan drew support from groups such as the Moral Majority, which opposed such cultural issues as abortion and homosexual rights and advocated government aid to private schools. Reagan appealed to other voters because of his strong stand against the Soviet Union and the lowering of inflation, interest rates, and unemployment. He defeated Mondale by gaining nearly 60 percent of the vote, breaking apart the Democratic coalition of industrial workers, farmers, and the poor that had existed since the days of Franklin Roosevelt. Only blacks as a block continued to vote Democratic. Reagan's success did not help Republicans in Congress, however, where they lost two seats in the Senate and gained little in the House.

Second Term Foreign Concerns

The Middle East

In October 1985 Arab terrorists seized the Italian cruise ship *Achille Lauro* in the Mediterranean, threatening to blow up the ship if 50 jailed Palestinians in Israel were not freed. They killed an elderly Jewish-American tourist and surrendered to Egyptian authorities on the condition that they be sent to Libya on an Egyptian airliner. Reagan ordered navy F-14 jets to intercept the airliner and force it to land in Italy, where the terrorists were jailed.

Reagan also challenged Muammar al-Qaddafi, the anti-American leader of Libya, by sending 6th Fleet ships within the Gulf of Sidra, which Qaddafi claimed. When Libyan gunboats challenged the American ships, American planes destroyed the gunboats and bombed installations on the Libyan shoreline. Soon after, a West German night club popular among American servicemen was bombed, killing a soldier and a civilian. Reagan, believing the bombing was ordered directly by Qaddafi, launched an air strike from Great Britain against Libyan bases in April 1986.

Soviet Union

After Mikhail S. Gorbachev became the premier of the Soviet Union in March 1985 and took an apparently more flexible approach toward both domestic and foreign affairs, Reagan softened his anti-Soviet stance. Nonetheless, although the Soviets said that they would continue to honor the unratified SALT II agreement, Reagan argued that they had not adhered to the pact and he sought to expand and modernize the American defense system.

Reagan concentrated on obtaining funding for the development of a computer-controlled strategic defense initiative system (SDI), popularly called "Star Wars" after the widely-seen movie, that would from outer space destroy enemy missiles. Congress balked, skeptical about the technological possibilities and fearing enormous costs.

SDI also appeared to prevent Reagan and Gorbachev from reaching an agreement on arms limitations at summit talks in 1985 and 1986. Finally, in December 1987, they signed an agreement eliminating medium-range missiles from Europe.

Iran-Contra

Near the end of 1986, a scandal arose involving William Casey, head of the CIA, Lieutenant Colonel Oliver North of the National Security Council, Admiral John Poindexter, national security advisor, and Robert McFarlane, former national security advisor. In 1985 and 1986, they had sold arms to the Iranians in hopes of encouraging them to use their influence in getting American hostages in Lebanon released. The profits from these sales were then diverted to the Nicaraguan *contras* in an attempt to get around congressional restrictions on funding the *contras*. The president was forced to appoint a special prosecutor and Congress held hearings on the affair in May 1987.

Nicaragua

The Reagan administration did not support a peace plan signed by five Central American nations in 1987, but the following year the Sandinistas and the *contras* agreed on a cease-fire.

Second Term Domestic Affairs

The Economy

The Tax Reform Act of 1986 lowered tax rates, changing the highest rate on personal income from 50 percent to 28 percent and corporate taxes from 46 percent to 34 percent. At the same time, it removed many tax shelters and tax credits. Six million low-income families did not have to pay any federal income tax at all. The law did away with the concept of progressive taxation, the requirement that the percentage of income paid as tax increased as income increased. Instead, over a two-year period it established two rates, 15 percent on incomes below $17,850 for individuals and $29,750 for families and 28 percent on incomes above these amounts. The tax system would no longer be used as an instrument of social policy.

Unemployment declined, reaching 6.6 percent in 1986, while inflation fell as low as 2.2 percent during the first quarter of that year. The stock market was bullish through mid-1987.

Falling oil prices hit the Texas economy particularly hard as well as other oil-producing states of the Southwest. The oil-producing countries had to cut back on their purchases of imports, which in turn hurt all manufacturing nations. American banks suffered when oil-related international loans went unpaid.

During the 1970s many farmers had borrowed, because of rising prices, to expand production. Between 1975 and 1983 farm mortgages increased from under $50 billion to over $112 billion while total indebtedness increased to $215 billion. With the general slowing of inflation and the decline of world agricultural prices, many American farmers began to descend into bankruptcy in the mid-1980s, often dragging the rural banks that had made them the loans into bankruptcy as well. Although it lifted the ban on wheat exports to the Soviet Union, the Reagan administration reduced price supports and opposed debt relief passed by Congress.

The federal deficit reached $179 billion in 1985 and about the same time the United States experienced trade deficits of more than $100 billion annually, partly because management and engineering skills had fallen behind Japan and Germany and partly because the U.S. provided an open market to foreign businesses. In the mid-1980s the United States became a debtor nation for the first time since World War I, owing more to foreigners than they owed to the U.S. Consumer debt also rose from $300 billion in 1980 to $500 billion in 1986.

Merging of companies, encouraged by the deregulation movement of Carter and Reagan as well as the emerging international economy, and fueled by funds released by new tax breaks, became a widespread phenomenon. Twenty-seven major companies, valued from $2.6 to $13.3 billion, merged between 1981 and 1986. Multinational corporations, which produced goods in many different countries, also began to characterize the economy.

On October 19, 1987 the Dow Jones stock market average dropped over 500 points. Between August 25 and October 20 the market lost over a trillion dollars in paper value. Fearing a recession, Congress in November 1987 reduced 1988 taxes by $30 billion.

NASA

The controversial SDI program was to be developed by the National Aeronautics and Space Administration (NASA) which had gained great prestige through its expeditions to the moon (1969–1972), Skylab orbiting space station program (1973–1974), and the space shuttle program (early 1981). The explosion of the shuttle Challenger soon after take-off on January 28, 1986, damaged NASA's credibility and reinforced doubts about the complex technology required for the SDI program.

Supreme Court

Reagan considerably reshaped the Court, replacing in 1986 Chief Justice Warren C. Burger with Associate Justice William H. Rehnquist, probably the most conservative member of the Court. Although failing in his nomination of Robert Bork for associate justice, Reagan also appointed other conservatives to the Court: Sandra Day O'Connor, Antonin Scalia, and Anthony Kennedy.

Drill 2: The Reagan Years

1. "Reaganomics" was based upon which of the following theories?

   (A) Cutting taxes would stimulate investment which would in turn increase employment and tax revenue.

   (B) Government must "prime" the economic pump by large expenditures in order to produce prosperity.

   (C) The United States was an undertaxed country where taxes must be increased substantially and the money spent on public needs.

   (D) The government must institute wage and price controls in order to control inflation.

   (E) The government must turn to tight controls on the money supply in order to cut inflation.

2. "Reaganomics" is most closely associated with

   (A) the "trickle down" theory.

   (B) the "controlled growth" theory.

   (C) the "bubble up" theory.

   (D) New Deal reform economics.

   (E) Fair Deal progressivist economics.

3. During the 1980s, neo-conservatives advocated all of the following positions EXCEPT

   (A) limited government.

   (B) traditional religious values.

   (C) reinvigorated patriotism.

   (D) decreased military spending.

   (E) restoration of the nuclear family.

4. A 1982 crisis over the War Power Resolution Act between Congress and President Reagan was narrowly averted when the president withdrew American ground forces from

   (A) Iran. (B) Grenada.

   (C) Lebanon. (D) Israel.

   (E) Libya.

5. The "Reagan Revolution" was launched through the budget of 1981 which

   (A) reduced government spending across all areas equally.

   (B) reduced government spending primarily in the domestic area.

   (C) reduced government spending primarily in the military arena.

   (D) increased personal income taxes.

   (E) increased corporate taxes.

3. THE BUSH AND CLINTON ADMINISTRATIONS

Election of 1988

After a sex scandal eliminated Senator Gary Hart from the race for the Democratic presidential nomination, Governor Michael Dukakis of Massachusetts emerged as the victor over his major challenger, the Rev. Jesse Jackson. He chose Senator Lloyd Bentsen of Texas as his vice presidential running mate.

Vice President George H. W. Bush, after a slow start in the primaries, won the Republican nomination. He chose Senator J. Danforth (Dan) Quayle of Indiana as his running mate. After starting behind in the polls, Bush soon caught up with Dukakis by emphasizing patriotism, defense, anti-crime, and a pledge for "no new taxes." The Dukakis campaign called for competence rather than ideology to rule the day but was unable to sustain any focus.

Bush easily defeated Dukakis, winning 40 states and 426 electoral votes, while Dukakis won only 10 states and 112 electoral votes. The Democrats gained one seat in the Senate, two seats in the House, and one governorship.

Bush Abandons Reaganomics

Soon after George H. W. Bush took office as president on January 20, 1989, the budget deficit for 1990 was estimated at $143 billion. With deficit estimates continuing to grow, Bush held a "budget summit" with Congressional leaders in May 1990, and his administration continued talks throughout the summer. In September the administration and Congress agreed to increase taxes on gasoline, tobacco, and alcohol, establish an excise tax on luxury items, and raise Medicare taxes. Cuts were also to be made in Medicare and other domestic programs. The 1991 deficit was now estimated to be over $290 billion. The following month Congress approved the plan, hoping to cut a cumulative amount of $500 billion from the deficit over the next five years. In a straight party vote, Republicans voting against and Democrats voting in favor, Congress in December transferred the power to decide whether new tax and spending proposals violated the deficit cutting agreement from the White House Office of Management and Budget to the Congressional Budget Office.

The Commission on Base Realignment and Closure proposed in December 1989 that 54 military bases be closed. In June 1990 Secretary of Defense Richard Cheney sent to Congress a five-year plan to cut military spending by 10 percent and the armed forces by 25 percent. The following April, Cheney recommended the closing of 43 domestic military bases plus many more abroad.

In May 1989, Bush vetoed an increase in the minimum wage from $3.35 to $4.55 an hour. But the following November, Bush signed an increase to $4.25 an hour, to become effective in 1991.

With the savings and loan industry in financial trouble in February 1989, largely because of bad real estate loans, Bush proposed to close or sell 350 institutions, to be paid for by the sale of government bonds. In July he signed a bill that created the Resolution Trust Corporation to oversee the closure and merging of S&Ls, and which provided $166 billion over 10 years to cover the bad debts. Estimates of the total costs of the debacle were over $300 billion.

The Gross National Product slowed from 4.4 percent in 1988 to 2.9 percent in 1989. Unemployment gradually began to increase, reaching 6.8 percent in March 1991, a three year high. Every sector of the economy, except for medical services, and all geographical areas experienced the slowdown. The "Big Three" automakers posted record losses and Pan American and Eastern Airlines entered bankruptcy proceedings. In September 1991 the Federal Reserve lowered the interest rate.

Other Domestic Issues Under Bush

Exxon Valdez

After the Exxon *Valdez* spilled more than 240,000 barrels of oil into Alaska's Prince William Sound in March 1989, the federal government ordered Exxon Corporation to develop a clean-up plan, which it carried out until the weather prevented them from continuing in September. The *Valdez* captain, Joseph Hazelwood, was found guilty of negligence the following year. Exxon Corporation, the State of Alaska, and the Justice Department of the Federal Government reached a settlement in October 1991 requiring Exxon to pay $1.025 billion in fines and restitution through the year 2001.

Congressional Ethics Violations

After the House Ethics Committee released a report charging that Speaker of the House Jim Wright had violated rules regulating acceptance of gifts and outside income, Wright resigned in May 1989. A short time later, the Democratic Whip Tony Coelho resigned because of alleged improper use of campaign funds.

Flag Burning

In May 1989 the Supreme Court ruled that the Constitution protected protesters who burned the United States flag. Bush denounced the decision and supported an amendment barring desecration of the flag. The amendment failed to pass Congress.

HUD Scandal

In July 1989 Secretary of Housing and Urban Development Jack Kemp revealed that the department had lost more than $2 billion under his predecessor, Samuel Pierce. A special prosecutor was named in February 1990 to investigate the case and the House held hearings on HUD during the next two months.

Medicare

In July 1988 the Medicare Catastrophic Coverage Act had placed a cap on fees Medicare patients paid to physicians and hospitals. After many senior citizens, particularly those represented by the American Association of Retired Persons (AARP), objected to the surtax that funded the program, Congress repealed the Act in November 1989.

Pollution

The Clean Air Act, passed in October 1990 and updating the 1970 law, mandated that the level of emissions was to be reduced 50 percent by the year 2000. Cleaner gasolines were to be developed, cities were to reduce ozone, and nitrogen oxide emissions were to be cut one-third.

Civil Rights

The Americans with Disabilities Act, passed in July 1990, barred discrimination against people with physical or mental disabilities. In October 1990 Bush vetoed the Civil Rights Act on the grounds that it established quotas, but a year later he accepted a slightly revised version that, among other things, required that employers in discrimination suits prove that their hiring practices are not discriminatory.

Supreme Court Appointments

Bush continued to reshape the Supreme Court in a conservative direction when, upon the retirement of Justice William J. Brennan, he successfully nominated Judge David Souter of the U.S. Court of Appeals in 1989. Two years later, Bush nominated a conservative black judge, Clarence Thomas, also of the U.S. Court of Appeals, upon the retirement of Justice Thurgood Marshall. Thomas's nomination stirred up opposition from the NAACP and other liberal groups which supported affirmative action and abortion rights. Dramatic charges of sexual harassment against Thomas from Anita Hill, a University of Oklahoma law professor, were revealed only days before the nomination was to go to the Senate, and provoked a reopening of Judiciary Committee hearings which were nationally televised. Nonetheless, Thomas narrowly won confirmation in October 1991.

Bush's Activist Foreign Policy

Panama

Since coming to office, the Bush administration had been concerned with Panamanian dictator Manuel Noriega because he allegedly provided an important link in the drug traffic between South America and the United States. After economic sanctions, diplomatic efforts, and an October 1989 coup failed to oust Noriega, Bush ordered 12,000 troops into Panama on December 20. The Americans installed a new government headed by Guillermo Endara, who had earlier apparently won a presidential election which was then nullified by Noriega. On January 3, 1990 Noriega surrendered to the Americans and was taken to the United States to stand trial on drug trafficking charges, a trial that began in September 1991. Twenty-three United States soldiers and three American civilians were killed in the operation. The Panamanians lost nearly 300 soldiers and more than 500 civilians.

Nicaragua

After years of civil war, Nicaragua held a presidential election in February 1990. Because of an economy largely destroyed by civil war and large financial debt to the United States, Violetta Barrios de Chamorro of the National Opposition Union defeated Daniel Ortega of the Sandinistas, thereby fulfilling a longstanding American objective. The United States lifted its economic sanctions in March and put together an economic aid package for Nicaragua. In September 1991, the Bush administration forgave Nicaragua most of its debt to the United States.

China

After the death in April 1989 of reformer Hu Yaobang, formerly general secretary and chairman of the Chinese Communist party, students began pro-democracy marches in Beijing. By the middle of May, more than one million people were gathering on Beijing's Tiananmen Square, and others elsewhere in China, calling for political reform. Martial law was imposed and in early June the army fired on the demonstrators. Estimates of the death toll in the wake of the nationwide crackdown on demonstrators ranged between 500 and 7,000. In July 1989, United States National Security Advisor Brent Scowcroft and Deputy Secretary of State Lawrence Eagleburger secretly met with Chinese leaders. When they again met the Chinese in December and revealed their earlier meeting, the Bush administration faced a storm of criticism for its policy of "constructive engagement" by opponents arguing that sanctions were needed. Although establishing sanctions to China in 1991 on high-technology satellite-part exports, Bush continued to support renewal of China's Most Favored Nation trading status.

Africa

To rescue American citizens threatened by civil war, Bush sent 230 marines into Liberia in August 1990, evacuating 125 people. South Africa in 1990 freed Nelson Mandela, the most famous leader of the African National Congress, after 28 years of imprisonment. South Africa then began moving away from Apartheid, and in 1991 Bush lifted economic sanctions imposed five years earlier. Mandela and his wife Winnie toured the U.S. in June 1990 to a tumultuous welcome, particularly from African-Americans. During their visit, they also addressed Congress.

Collapse of East European Communism

With the Soviet Union suffering severe economic problems, and Mikhail Gorbachev stating that he would not interfere in Poland's internal affairs, communism began to crumble in Eastern Europe. After years of effort by Solidarity, the non-Communist labor union, Poland became the first European nation to shift from communism. Through a democratic process, Solidarity overwhelmingly won the parliamentary elections in June 1989 and Tadeuiz Mazowiecki became premier the following August.

In August 1989 Hungary opened its borders with Austria. The following October, the Communists reorganized their party, calling it the Socialist party. Hungary then proclaimed itself a "Free Republic."

With thousands of East Germans passing through Hungary to Austria, after the opening of the borders in August 1989, Erich Honecker stepped down as head of state in October. On November 1, the government opened the border with Czechoslovakia and eight days later the Berlin Wall fell. On December 6, a non-Communist became head of state, followed on December 11 by large demonstrations demanding German reunification. Reunification took place in October 1990.

After anti-government demonstrations were forcibly broken up in Czechoslovakia in October 1989, changes took place in the Communist leadership the following month. Then, on December 8, the Communists agreed to relinquish power and Parliament elected Vaclav Havel, a playwright and anti-Communist leader, to the presidency on December 29.

When anti-government demonstrations in Romania were met by force in early December, portions of the military began joining the opposition which captured dictator Nicolae Ceausescu and his wife Elena, killing them on December 25, 1989. In May 1990 the National Salvation Front, made up of many former Communists, won the parliamentary elections.

In January 1990 the Bulgarian national assembly repealed the dominant role of the Communist party. A multi-party coalition government was formed the following December.

Albania opened its border with Greece and legalized religious worship in January 1990, and in July ousted hardliners from the government.

Amid the collapse of Communism in Eastern Europe, Bush met with Mikhail Gorbachev in Malta from December 1 through December 3, 1989; the two leaders appeared to agree that the Cold War was over. On May 30 and 31, 1990 Bush and Gorbachev met in Washington to discuss the possible reunification of Germany, and signed a trade treaty between the United States and the Soviet Union. The meeting of the two leaders in Helsinki on September 9 addressed strategies for the developing Persian Gulf crisis. At the meeting of the "Group of 7" nations (Canada, France, Germany, Italy, Japan, United Kingdom, and the United States) in July 1991, Gorbachev requested economic aid from the West. A short time later, on July 30 and 31, Bush met Gorbachev in Moscow where they signed the START treaty, which cut U.S. and Soviet nuclear arsenals by 30 percent, and pushed for Middle Eastern talks.

QUESTION

> What allowed for the disintegration of Soviet influence in Eastern Europe?

EXPLANATION

By 1988 the Soviet Union was experiencing a severe economic crisis. It could no longer afford to support Communist regimes in Eastern Europe. In addition, Gorbachev had been slowly liberalizing Soviet society, attempting to make it more modern. Anti-Communist sentiment had been building in these countries for some time, and free elections in Poland resulted in the defeat of the Communist party. This led to widespread demonstrations throughout Eastern Europe, and multi-party elections were held in many of these countries by 1990. In addition, East Germany re-united with West Germany in 1990.

Persian Gulf Crisis

Saddam Hussein of Iraq charged that Kuwait had conspired with the United States to keep oil prices low and began massing troops at the Iraq-Kuwait border.

On August 2, Iraq invaded Kuwait, an act that Bush denounced as "naked aggression." One day later 100,000 Iraqi soldiers were poised south of Kuwait City near the Saudi Arabian border. The United States quickly banned most trade with Iraq, froze Iraq's and Kuwait's assets in the United States, and sent aircraft carriers to the Persian Gulf. After the United Nations Security Council condemned the invasion, on August 6 Bush ordered the deployment of air, sea, and land forces to Saudi Arabia, dubbing the operation "Desert Shield." At the end of August there were 100,000 American soldiers in Saudi Arabia.

Bush encouraged Egypt to support American policy by forgiving Egypt its debt to the United States and obtaining pledges of financial support from Saudi Arabia, Kuwait, and Japan, among other nations, to help pay for the operation. On October 29, the Security Council warned Hussein that further actions might be taken if he did not withdraw from Kuwait. In November Bush ordered that U.S. forces be increased to more than 400,000. On November 29, the United Nations set January 15, 1991 as the deadline for Iraqi withdrawal from Kuwait.

On January 9, Iraq's foreign minister rejected a letter written by Bush to Hussein. Three days later, after an extensive debate, Congress authorized the use of force in the Gulf. On January 17, an international force including the United States, Great Britain, France, Italy, Saudi Arabia, and Kuwait launched an air and missile attack on Iraq and occupied Kuwait. The U.S. called the effort "Operation Desert Storm." Under the overall command of Army General H. Norman Schwarzkopf, the military effort emphasized high-technology weapons, including Patriot anti-missile missiles. Beginning on January 17, Iraq sent SCUD missiles into Israel in an effort to draw that country into the war and splinter the U.S.-Arabian coalition. On January 22 and 23, Hussein's forces set Kuwaiti oil fields on fire and spilled oil into the Gulf.

On February 23, the allied ground assault began. Four days later Bush announced that Kuwait was liberated and ordered offensive operations to cease. The United Nations established the terms for the cease-fire: Iraqi annexation of Kuwait to be rescinded, Iraq to accept liability for damages and return Kuwaiti property, Iraq to end all military actions and identify mines and booby traps, and Iraq to release captives.

On April 3, the Security Council approved a resolution to establish a permanent cease-fire; Iraq accepted U.N. terms on April 6. The next day the United States began airlifting food to Kurdish refugees on the Iraq-Turkey border who were fleeing the Kurdish rebellion against Hussein, a rebellion that was seemingly encouraged by Bush, who nonetheless refused to become militarily involved. The United States estimated that 100,000 Iraqis had been killed during the war while the Americans had lost about 115 lives.

On February 6, 1991, the United States had set out its postwar goals for the Middle East. These included regional arms control and security arrangements, international aid for reconstruction of Iraq and Kuwait, and resolution of the Israeli-Palestinian conflict. Immediately after cessation of the conflict, Secretary of State James Baker toured the Middle East attempting to promote a conference to address the problems of the region. After several more negotiating sessions, Saudi Arabia, Syria, Jordan, and Lebanon had accepted the United States proposal for an Arab-Israeli peace conference by the middle of July; Israel conditionally accepted in early August. Despite continuing conflict with Iraq, which kept the conference agreement tenuous, the nations met in Madrid, Spain, at the end of October. Bilateral talks in early November between Israel and the Arabs concentrated on procedural issues.

Breakup of the Soviet Union

Following the collapse of Communism in Eastern Europe, the Baltic republic of Lithuania, which had been taken over by the Soviet Union in 1939, declared its independence from the Soviet Union on March 11, 1990.

Two days later, on March 13, the Soviet Union removed the Communist monopoly of political power, allowing non-Communists to run for office. The process of liberalization went haltingly forward in the Soviet Union. Perhaps the most significant event was the election of Boris Yeltsin, who had left the Communist party, as president of the Russian republic on June 12, 1991.

On August 19, Soviet hard-liners attempted a coup to oust Gorbachev, but a combination of their inability to control communication with the outside world, a failure to quickly establish military control, and the resistance of Yeltsin, members of the military, and people in the streets of cities such as Moscow and Leningrad ended the coup on August 21, returning Gorbachev to power.

In the aftermath of the coup, much of the Communist structure came crashing down, including the prohibition of the Communist party in Russia. The remaining Baltic republics of Latvia and Estonia declared their independence, which was recognized by the United States several days after other nations had done so. Most of the other Soviet republics then followed suit in declaring their independence. The Bush administration wanted some form of central authority to remain in the Soviet Union; hence, it did not seriously consider recognizing the independence of any republics except the Baltics. Bush also resisted offering economic aid to the Soviet Union until it presented a radical economic reform plan to move toward a free market. However, humanitarian aid such as food was pledged in order to preserve stability during the winter.

In September 1991, Bush announced unilateral removal and destruction of ground-based tactical nuclear weapons in Europe and Asia, removal of nuclear-armed Tomahawk cruise missiles from surface ships and submarines, immediate destruction of intercontinental ballistic missiles covered by START, and an end to the 24-hour alert for strategic bombers that the U.S. had maintained for decades. Gorbachev responded the next month by announcing the immediate deactivation of intercontinental ballistic missiles covered by START, removal of all short-range missiles from Soviet ships, submarines, and aircraft, and destruction of all ground-based tactical nuclear weapons. He also said that the Soviet Union would reduce its forces by 700,000 troops, and he placed all long-range nuclear missiles under a single command. Gorbachev's hold on the presidency progressively weakened in the final months of 1991, with the reforms he had put in place taking on a life of their own. The dissolution of the U.S.S.R. led to his resignation in December, making way for Boris Yeltsin, who had headed popular resistance.

The Democrats Reclaim the White House

William Jefferson Clinton, governor of Arkansas, overcame several rivals to win the Democratic presidential nomination in 1992 and with his running mate, Senator Albert Gore of Tennessee, went on to win the White House. During the campaign, Clinton and independent candidate H. Ross Perot, a wealthy Texas businessman, emphasized jobs and the economy, while attacking the mounting federal debt. The incumbent, Bush, stressed traditional values and his foreign policy accomplishments. In the 1992 election, Clinton won 43 percent of the popular vote and 370 electoral votes, defeating Bush and Perot. Perot took 19 percent of the popular vote, but was unable to garner any electoral votes.

Clinton came to be dogged by a number of controversies, ranging from alleged ill-gotten gains in a complex Arkansas land deal (known as "Whitewater") to charges of sexual misconduct.

On the legislative front, Clinton was strongly rebuffed in an attempt during his first term to reform the nation's healthcare system. In the 1994 mid-term elections, in what Clinton himself considered a repudiation of his administration, the Republicans took both houses of Congress from the Democrats and voted in Newt Gingrich of Georgia, who aimed to shrink the federal government, as Speaker of the House.

Clinton was not without his successes, both on the legislative and diplomatic fronts. He signed a bill establishing a five-day waiting period for handgun purchases, and he signed a Crime Bill emphasizing community policing. He signed the Family Leave Bill, which required large companies to provide up to 12 weeks' unpaid leave to workers for family and medical emergencies. He also championed welfare reform (a central theme of his campaign), but made it clear that the legislation he signed into law in August 1996 radically overhauling FDR's welfare system disturbed him on two counts—its exclusion of legal immigrants from getting most federal benefits and its deep cut in federal outlays for food stamps; Clinton said these flaws could be repaired with further legislation. In foreign affairs, Clinton, with support from then-Minority Whip Gingrich, won congressional approval of the hotly debated North American Free Trade Agreement, which, as of January 1994, lifted most trade barriers with Mexico and Canada. Clinton sought to ease tensions between Israelis and Palestinians, and he helped bring together Itzhak Rabin, prime minister of Israel, and Yasir Arafat, chairman of the Palestine Liberation Organization, for a summit at the White House. Ultimately, the two Middle East leaders signed an accord in 1994 establishing Palestinian self-rule in the Gaza Strip and Jericho. In October 1994 Israel and Jordan signed a treaty to begin the process of establishing full diplomatic relations.

Clinton recaptured the Democratic nomination without a serious challenge, while longtime GOP Senator Robert Dole of Kansas, the Senate majority leader, had to overcome several opponents, but orchestrated a harmonious nominating convention with running mate Jack Kemp, a former New York congressman and Cabinet member. In November 1996, with most voters citing a healthy economy and the lack of an enticing alternative in Dole or the Reform Party's Perot, Clinton received 49 percent of the vote, becoming the first Democrat to be re-elected since FDR. The GOP retained control of both houses of Congress.

Clinton, intent on mirroring the diversity of America in his Cabinet appointments, chose Latinos Henry Cisneros (Housing and Urban Development) and Federico Peña (Transportation and, later, Energy), African-Americans Ron Brown (Commerce) and Mike Espy (Agriculture), and women, including the nation's first woman attorney general, Janet Reno, and Madeleine Albright, the first woman secretary of state in U.S. history (Albright succeeded Warren Christopher, who served through Clinton's first term). Brown and 34 others on a trade mission died when his Air Force plane crashed in Croatia in April 1996. Espy and Cisneros resigned under ethics clouds.

Impeachment and Acquittal

In December 1998 Clinton was impeached by the House and in January and February 1999 he was tried and acquitted by the Senate on charges that he had lied about an adulterous affair with a White House intern. The affair had been uncovered by independent counsel Kenneth Starr during the course of a long-running investigation into other matters, including the Whitewater real estate deal in Arkansas, which pre-dated the Clinton presidency.

The Election of 2000

The Democrats nominated Vice President Al Gore for president and Senator Joseph Lieberman for vice president. The Republican Party nominated Texas Governor George W. Bush (son of President George H. W. Bush). After some conflict, the Reform Party nominated Patrick Buchanan. The Green Party ran Ralph Nader. After one of the tightest presidential elections ever, highlighted by a withdrawn initial concession by Gore, a recount in Florida, and several court challenges, Bush was declared the winner.

Social and Cultural Developments

Terrorism Hits Home

Major symbols of U.S. economic and military might—the World Trade Center in New York and the Pentagon just outside Washington, D.C.—were attacked on September 11, 2001, when hijackers deliberately crashed commercial jetliners into the buildings, toppling the trade center's 110-story twin towers. Thousands died in the worst act of terrorism in American history. The prime suspect, said President Bush, was Saudi exile Osama bin Laden, the alleged mastermind of previous attacks on U.S. interests overseas. Terrorist attacks had continued to be a grim reality overseas through the 1980s and early 1990s, with Americans frequently targeted. Yet such incidents had come to be viewed as something the United States wouldn't have to face on its own soil—until February 26, 1993, when a terrorist bomb ripped through the underground parking garage of the World Trade Center, killing six people and injuring more than 1,000. Convicted and sentenced to 240 years each were four Islamic militants. On April 19, 1995, the Oklahoma City federal building was bombed, killing 168 people and injuring 500. Timothy James McVeigh, a gun enthusiast and member of the American militia movement who had expressed hatred toward the U.S. government and was aggrieved over its assault two years earlier on a self-proclaimed prophet's compound in Waco, Texas, was put to death for the crime in May 2001. A second defendant, Terry Nichols, was convicted on federal charges of conspiracy and involuntary manslaughter and sentenced to life in prison.

Crime and Drugs

George H. W. Bush had won the presidency in 1988 on a strong anti-crime message, crystallized in a controversial TV spot that demonized Willie Horton, an African-American inmate in the Massachusetts jail system who was released while then-presidential candidate Michael Dukakis was the Democratic governor. Bill Clinton co-opted the traditional Republican crime issue by pushing through legislation for more community policing, an approach that, together with aggressive central management, was credited for the plummeting crime rate in New York City, for example.

Between 1987 and 1997, the period spanning the Bush administration and Clinton's first term, the number of Americans in prison doubled, soaring from 800,000 to 1.6 million.

Drug abuse continued to be widespread, with cocaine becoming more readily available, particularly in a cheaper, stronger form called "crack."

Labor

Labor union strength continued to ebb in the 1990s, with the U.S. Department of Labor's Bureau of Labor Statistics reporting that union membership as a percent of wage and salary employment dropped to 14.5 percent in 1996, down from 14.9 percent in 1995. In 1983, union members made up 20.1 percent of the work force. Unions continued to be responsible for higher wages for their members: organized workers reported median weekly earnings of $615, as against a median of $462 for non-union workers, according to the bureau.

AIDS

In 1981 scientists announced the discovery of Acquired Immune Deficiency Syndrome (AIDS), which was especially prevalent among homosexual males and intravenous drug users. Widespread fear resulted, including upsurges in homophobia. The Food and Drug Administration responded to calls for fast-tracking evaluation of drugs by approving the drug AZT in February 1991. With the revelation that a Florida dentist had infected six patients, there were calls for mandatory testing of health care workers. Supporters of testing argued before a House hearing in September 1991 that testing should be regarded as a public health, rather than a civil rights, issue. In 1998 the federal Centers for Disease Control and Prevention estimated that between 400,000 and 650,000 Americans were HIV-positive, meaning that they had the virus that causes AIDS.

Families

More than half the married women in the United States continued to hold jobs outside the home. Nearly one out of every two marriages was ending in divorce, and there was an increase in the number of couples living together without the benefit of marriage, which contributed to a growing number of illegitimate births. So-called family values became a major theme in presidential politics.

Abortion

In a July 1989 decision, *Webster v. Reproductive Health Services*, the U.S. Supreme Court upheld a Missouri law prohibiting public employees from performing abortions, unless the mother's life is threatened. With this decision came a shift in focus on the abortion issue from the courts to the state legislatures. Pro-life (anti-abortion) forces moved in several states to restrict the availability of abortions, but their results were mixed. Florida rejected abortion restrictions in October 1989, the governor of Louisiana vetoed similar legislation nine months later, and in early 1991 Maryland adopted a liberal abortion law. In contrast, Utah and Pennsylvania enacted strict curbs on abortion during the same period. At the national level, Bush in October 1989 vetoed funding for Medicaid abortions. A pro-life demonstration was held in Washington in April 1990, and access to abortion clinics was blocked by Operation Rescue, a militant anti-abortion group, in 1991. Abortion clinics around the country continued to be the targets of protests and violence through the mid-'90s.

Censorship

The new conservatism revealed its cultural dimension in a controversy that erupted over the National Endowment for the Arts in September 1989. Criticism of photographer Robert Mapplethorpe's homoerotic and masochistic pictures, among other artworks which had been funded by the Endowment, led Senator Jesse Helms of North Carolina to propose that grants for "obscene or indecent" projects, or those derogatory of religion, be cut off. Although the proposal ultimately failed, it raised questions of the government's role as a sponsor of art in an increasingly pluralistic society. Meanwhile, in March 1990, the Recording Industry Association of America, in a move advocated by, among others, Tipper Gore, wife of Democratic Senator Al Gore (the man who would be elected vice president in 1992), agreed to place new uniform warning labels on recordings that contained potentially offensive language.

Crisis in Education

The National Commission on Excellence in Education, appointed in 1981, argued in "A Nation at Risk" that a "rising tide of mediocrity" characterized the nation's schools. In the wake of the report, many states instituted reforms, including higher teacher salaries, competency tests for teachers, and an increase in required subjects for high school graduation. In February 1990 the National Governors' Association adopted specific performance goals, stating that achievement tests should be given in grades four, eight, and twelve. As the millenium approached, signs began to emerge that the tide might be turning: a major global comparison found in June 1997 that America's 9- and 10-year-olds were among the world's best in science and also scored well above average in math.

Urban America Rebounds

The Economist reported in January 1998 that unemployment in the 50 biggest cities in America had fallen by a third over the prior four years, to about 6%. Rates for serious crime fell to their lowest in a generation. Cities such as New York—which just over two decades before had nearly gone bankrupt—and Los Angeles, victim of race riots and an earthquake during the early and mid-'90s, were "growing in both population and confidence." But as *The Economist* observed, "By the standards of Europe and Japan, [U.S. cities] still suffer appalling crime, yawning social disparities and remarkable underachievement in education."

The U.S. Counts Its People

The 2000 census counted 281,421,906 Americans, a 13.2% increase since the 1990 decennial enumeration. The state that saw the greatest numerical gain since the 1990 census was California, up 4,111,627, while Nevada had the highest percentage growth in population, climbing 66.3% (796,424 people) since the previous census.

Literary Trends

The 1980s and 1990s saw the emergence of writers who threw light on various, sometimes hidden facets of national life—from the immigrant experience as told by Amy Tan in *The Joy Luck Club* (1989) and Oscar Hijuelos in *The Mambo Kings Play Songs of Love* (1990) to Tom Wolfe's satirical take on greed and class and racial tensions in New York City in *The Bonfire of the Vanities* (1987). Toni Morrison's *Beloved* (1987) dramatized the African-American slave experience.

Drill 3: The Bush and Clinton Administrations

1.   The *Webster v. Reproductive Health Services* decision declared

  (A)   states could prohibit public employees from performing abortions unless the mother's life was threatened.

  (B)   Medicaid must provide funding for abortions.

  (C)   states may impose restrictions on abortion such as parental consent and a 24-hour waiting period.

  (D)   states may ban all abortions, except when the mother's life is in danger.

  (E)   the right to an abortion was guaranteed by the Constitution.

2.   The savings and loan crisis resulted in

  (A)   higher real estate prices in the Southwest.

  (B)   the creation of a corporation to manage the crisis.

  (C)   the end of federal insurance for bank deposits.

  (D)   wider use of "junk bonds" in financial markets.

  (E)   depositors losing all or most of their savings in these institutions.

3.   Who among the following was Clinton's second secretary of state?

(A) Sandra Day O'Connor   (B) Ann Richards

(C) James Baker   (D) Jeane Kirkpatrick

(E) Madeleine Albright

4. Nicolae Ceausescu was the dictator of which nation?

   (A) Poland   (B) Czechoslovakia

   (C) Hungary   (D) Romania

   (E) Yugoslavia

5. Which of the following was NOT an ally of the United States during the Gulf Crisis?

   (A) France   (B) Saudi Arabia

   (C) Japan   (D) Israel

   (E) Iran

1972–2001
DRILLS

ANSWER KEY

Drill 1—Nixon, Ford, and Carter

1. (C)   2. (B)   3. (D)   4. (B)   5. (A)

Drill 2—The Reagan Years

1. (A)   2. (A)   3. (D)   4. (C)   5. (B)

Drill 3—The Bush and Clinton Administrations

1. (A)   2. (B)   3. (E)   4. (D)   5. (E)

GLOSSARY: 1972–2001

AIDS
>Acquired Immune Deficiency Syndrome, a disease spread through sexual contact and the use of contaminated needles that weakens and destroys the immune system.

Contras
>Right wing guerrillas who fought the leftist Sandinista government of Nicaragua.

Crack
>An exceptionally powerful form of cocaine that is highly addictive.

Junk Bonds
>High-interest bonds with a low investment grade.

Misery Index
>A yardstick used by President Carter's critics to underscore the economy's poor performance.

Moral Majority
>Christian Conservatives, led by the Rev. Jerry Falwell, who favored prayer and teaching of creationism in public schools, opposed abortion, pornography, and the Equal Rights Amendment, and backed a strong national defense.

Pro-Choice Advocates
>Those who wish to keep abortion legal.

Pro-Life Advocates
>Those who wish to make abortion illegal.

Strategic Defense Initiative
>A defense system, using satellites to prevent enemy missiles from striking the United States.

Superfund
>A dedicated federal fund for toxic-waste site cleanups.

Supply-Side Economics
>An economic theory that says that if government policies leave more money in the hands of people, they will invest it and stimulate the economy.

CHAPTER 16

Mini Tests

MINI TEST 1

1. Ⓐ Ⓑ Ⓒ Ⓓ Ⓔ
2. Ⓐ Ⓑ Ⓒ Ⓓ Ⓔ
3. Ⓐ Ⓑ Ⓒ Ⓓ Ⓔ
4. Ⓐ Ⓑ Ⓒ Ⓓ Ⓔ
5. Ⓐ Ⓑ Ⓒ Ⓓ Ⓔ
6. Ⓐ Ⓑ Ⓒ Ⓓ Ⓔ
7. Ⓐ Ⓑ Ⓒ Ⓓ Ⓔ
8. Ⓐ Ⓑ Ⓒ Ⓓ Ⓔ
9. Ⓐ Ⓑ Ⓒ Ⓓ Ⓔ
10. Ⓐ Ⓑ Ⓒ Ⓓ Ⓔ
11. Ⓐ Ⓑ Ⓒ Ⓓ Ⓔ
12. Ⓐ Ⓑ Ⓒ Ⓓ Ⓔ
13. Ⓐ Ⓑ Ⓒ Ⓓ Ⓔ
14. Ⓐ Ⓑ Ⓒ Ⓓ Ⓔ
15. Ⓐ Ⓑ Ⓒ Ⓓ Ⓔ
16. Ⓐ Ⓑ Ⓒ Ⓓ Ⓔ
17. Ⓐ Ⓑ Ⓒ Ⓓ Ⓔ
18. Ⓐ Ⓑ Ⓒ Ⓓ Ⓔ
19. Ⓐ Ⓑ Ⓒ Ⓓ Ⓔ
20. Ⓐ Ⓑ Ⓒ Ⓓ Ⓔ
21. Ⓐ Ⓑ Ⓒ Ⓓ Ⓔ
22. Ⓐ Ⓑ Ⓒ Ⓓ Ⓔ
23. Ⓐ Ⓑ Ⓒ Ⓓ Ⓔ
24. Ⓐ Ⓑ Ⓒ Ⓓ Ⓔ
25. Ⓐ Ⓑ Ⓒ Ⓓ Ⓔ

MINI TEST 1

DIRECTIONS: Choose the correct answer for each of the 25 questions below.

1. The major effects of the Industrial Revolution of the late nineteenth century in the United States included all of the following EXCEPT

   (A) a rise in the overall standard of living.

   (B) an increase in massive labor disorders.

   (C) attempts by farmers to organize politically.

   (D) an equal distribution of national wealth.

   (E) a growing belief in the theory of survival of the fittest.

2. According to the terms of the Treaty of Tordesillas (1494), the lands of the Western Hemisphere were divided between

   (A) Spain and England.   (B) Portugal and France.

   (C) Portugal and Spain.   (D) England and Portugal.

   (E) France and England.

3. Urban growth in the United States between 1870 and 1900 was caused primarily by

   (A) the end of slavery and the migration of blacks to cities. *WW I*

   (B) industrialization.

   (C) immigration from Europe.

   (D) the invention of the mechanical elevator.

   (E) the expansion of railroads.

4. Which factor handicapped the growth of New France?

   (A) Poor relations with Native Americans

   (B) Lack of initiative in exploring new territory

   (C) The small population of French settlers

   (D) The dictatorial rule of governor-generals

   (E) The importation of indentured servants

5. All of the following are attributed to the Spanish conquistadores in the Americas EXCEPT

   (A) the exploration of North and South America.

   (B) the introduction of European diseases into Native American populations.

   (C) the conquest of Mexico and the destruction of the Aztec empire.

   . (D) the discovery of gold in North America.   *1840s - Gold RUSH*

   (E) the establishment of Spain's territorial claims to the America.

6. In the mid-1700s, England and France waged a full-scale war for control of North America. The disputed area in the French and Indian War was western Pennsylvania and

   (A) the Hudson Bay.   (B) the Ohio Valley.

   (C) the Hudson River.   (D) North Carolina.

   (E) the Mississippi River.

7. Alexander Hamilton, a leading Federalist, believed in all of the following EXCEPT

   (A) government stimulation of industrial development.

   (B) a broad interpretation of the Constitution.

   (C) the establishment of a national bank.

   (D) taxation to fund government programs.

   (E) limiting the role of the central government.

8. Jacob Riis' book *How the Other Half Lives* was

   (A) a fictional exposé of the meatpacking industry.

   (B) a detailed program for social reform.

   (C) a description of the life-styles of America's rich and famous.

   (D) a denunciation of machine politics in big city government.

   (E) a description of poverty, illness, and crime in the slums of New York City.

9. All of the following economic changes occurred during the Reagan administration EXCEPT

   (A) the concept of progressive taxation was removed from the federal income tax.

   (B) the federal deficit fell as a result of lower defense spending.

(C) the rate of inflation fell from about 12 percent to about 4 percent.

(D) the United States became a debtor nation for the first time since World War I.

(E) multinational corporations began to characterize the economy.

10. Before setting foot on land in the New World, the Pilgrims signed a document that established a foundation for orderly government based on the consent of the governed. This document was called

(A) the Fundamental Orders of Connecticut.

(B) the Act of Religious Toleration.

(C) the Mayflower Compact.

(D) the Navigation Acts.

(E) the Great Awakening.

11. Which of the following statements best describes the position of the "hawks" in the Vietnam War?

(A) Vietnam is vital to the security of the United States.

(B) The United States had to retaliate against the firing by North Vietnamese gunboats on American destroyers in the Gulf of Tonkin.

(C) In keeping with the policy of containment, the United States had the responsibility to resist Communist aggression against a non-Communist regime anywhere in the world.

(D) If Vietnam should turn Communist, the rest of Southeast Asia would eventually turn Communist also.

(E) The United States had never lost a war and should not quit in Vietnam.

12. The belief that the American nation was ordained to eventually expand all the way to the Pacific Ocean came to be known as

(A) transcendentalism.   (B) utopianism.

(C) Manifest Destiny.   (D) states' rights.

(E) abolitionism.

13. At the outbreak of the Civil War, the North's advantages included all of the following EXCEPT

(A) factories for the production of war goods.

(B) a large agricultural base.

(C) an extensive rail system.

(D) command of the navy.

(E) extensive manpower.

14. Which of the following inventors is correctly paired with his invention?

(A) Ottmar Mergenthaler: linotype machine

(B) Elisha Otis: plastics

(C) Thomas A. Edison: rayon

(D) Arthur Little: mechanical elevator

(E) Leo Baekeland: X-ray tube

15. During the 1960s and 1970s, many Americans moved

(A) from farms to cities.

(B) from the South to the North.

(C) from suburbs to cities.

(D) from the Northeast to the Sunbelt.

(E) west.

16. The Roosevelt Corollary to the Monroe Doctrine, enunciated by President Theodore Roosevelt in his annual message to Congress in May of 1904, was designed to

(A) provide massive aid to stabilize the governments of Latin America.

(B) prevent the French from building a canal across Central America to connect the Atlantic and Pacific Oceans.

•(C) justify the United States' intervention in the internal affairs of Western Hemisphere nations.

(D) cultivate friendship among Latin American nations.

(E) enable Latin American nations to forego payment of their debts to European powers.

17. Which of the following statements best describes a change in the position of women that occurred during World War I?

(A) Many women became active in the settlement-house movement.

(B) Women were barred from working in defense industries.

(C) Women obtained the right to vote in national elections.

(D) Women received equal pay for equal work.

(E) Many women organized to oppose the idea that their place was in the home.

18. America's dispute with British rule in the 1700s concerned

    (A) general search warrants issued against colonists.

    (B) taxation such as the Stamp Act of 1765.

    (C) the quartering of British troops in private homes.

    (D) the provision that royal officials accused of crimes could be tried away from the site of the crime.

    (E) All of the above.

19. The Puritans, fleeing religious persecution in England and desiring to set up a model Christian society, established a colony in 1630 in

    (A) Massachusetts Bay.   (B) Maryland.

    (C) the Carolinas.   (D) New York.

    (E) New Jersey.

20. The invention of the automobile had all the following results EXCEPT

    (A) the mileage of paved roads suitable for year-round driving increased.

    (B) industries such as steel, rubber, and glass expanded their operations.

    (C) railroads were forced out of business.

    (D) workers were able to live miles from their jobs, and suburbs began to grow more rapidly than the central cities.

    (E) sexual license increased.

21. Which of the following was a long-term result of the work performed by the CCC?

    (A) A decrease in unemployment

    (B) The lessening of soil erosion and flooding

    (C) An increase in people's income

    (D) A rehabilitation of inner-city neighborhoods

    (E) None of the above.

22. The purpose of the 1804 Lewis and Clark expedition was to

    (A) explore Florida.

    (B) seize the port of New Orleans.

    (C) explore the Mississippi River.

    (D) explore and map the Louisiana Purchase.

    (E) establish forts on the Pacific Coast.

23. The most popular form of entertainment during the Great Depression was

    (A) professional sports.   (B) radio.

    (C) television.   (D) motion pictures.

    (E) the theater.

24. The main strategy employed by the Allies in the Pacific theater during World War II was

    (A) the establishment of an embargo on the export of oil and other vital products to Japan.

    (B) the dropping of atomic bombs on Japan.

    (C) the use of kamikaze pilots.

    (D) the opening of a second front.

    (E) island hopping from one Japanese-held island to another.

25. The first ten amendments to the Constitution that guarantee certain individual rights are known as

    (A) the Supremacy Clause.

    (B) the Preamble.

    (C) the Bill of Rights.

    (D) the "Great Compromise."

    (E) the "Three-Fifths Compromise."

MINI TEST 1

ANSWER KEY

1. (D)	6. (B)	11. (C)	16. (C)	21. (B)
2. (C)	7. (E)	12. (C)	17. (C)	22. (D)
3. (B)	8. (E)	13. (B)	18. (E)	23. (D)
4. (C)	9. (B)	14. (A)	19. (A)	24. (E)
5. (D)	10. (C)	15. (D)	20. (C)	25. (C)

DETAILED EXPLANATIONS
OF ANSWERS

1. **(D)** The end of the Civil War saw a tremendous growth in America's industrial economy (A). But although the overall standard of living rose sharply, the increase primarily benefited factory owners and providers of financial services. Farmers suffered from currency deflation and railroad rate discrimination, while workers suffered from long hours, low wages, and dangerous working conditions. As a result, both groups tried to improve their lot through strikes and political protests (B) and (C). Factory owners and providers of financial services justified their ever-increasing share of the national wealth by arguing that they were naturally more competent than other people and therefore deserving of success (E). Thus, the correct answer is (D).

2. **(C)** Portugal and Spain divided the Western Hemisphere and the lands located there. As a result, Brazil came under Portuguese rule; all other lands became part of New Spain. England was not seriously involved in overseas exploration and settlement until the late 1500s, so (A), (D), and (E) are not correct. Jacques Cartier's expeditions for France did not begin until 1534 (B).

3. **(B)** The migration of blacks to cities from southern farms occurred primarily during and after World War I (A). Although some 11 million Europeans entered the United States during the 1870s, 1880s, and 1890s, that figure was dwarfed by an increase of 40 million in the urban population during the same period (C). Most newcomers to American cities came from American farms in order to obtain factory jobs. The invention of the mechanical elevator enabled skyscrapers to be built and thus changed the appearance of cities, but there would have been no demand for skyscrapers unless the urban population was growing rapidly (D). Similarly, although railroads carried people from rural to urban areas, the railroads were not the reason why people flocked to the cities (E).

4. **(C)** The French were less interested in establishing population centers in New France than they were in trapping and in trading with Native Americans, with whom they maintained generally good relations. French explorers boldly investigated the interior of the North American continent. The government of the mother country did not aggressively promote colonization in New France. The colonial officials in New France followed a relatively lax policy of supervision, and were interested primarily in the profits of the commercial enterprises (D). Since agriculture was never a major endeavor, indentured servants were not used extensively in the French settlements (E).

5. **(D)** While the Spanish did search for gold, they never found any deposits of note: Ponce de Leon explored Florida in search of gold; De Soto explored the southeastern part of North America; Coronado explored northward from what

is now Mexico into the present-day American Southwest. Cortes conquered Mexico with its advanced Aztec empire, and Pizzaro conquered the Incas of Peru, setting the stage for the exploration and conquest of South America and the conquest of Spanish claims to the lands of the Americas as far north as the central plains of North America and northern California (A), (C), and (E). Unfortunately, the Spaniards also unwittingly introduced smallpox, measles, and other European diseases for which the Native American populations had no immunity, and the resulting epidemics killed millions (B).

6. **(B)** The French and Indian War started in 1754 when the British attempted to drive the French from western Pennsylvania and the Ohio Valley where they had built a series of forts. The war spread to Europe and Asia. The British won and, as a result of the Treaty of Paris of 1763, gained all of North America east of the Mississippi including Spanish Florida. The war thus involved control over land jointly claimed or jointly occupied by French and English colonists. The English at Hudson's Bay (A) were trying to expand their trading activities into French territory, but the numbers involved were small. The valley of the Hudson River (C) had been claimed and occupied by the English since the 1660s, and North Carolina (D) had been an English colony since the 1670s, so French influence was non-existent. The Mississippi River (E) had been claimed and occupied by French trading companies since the 1670s, with no English presence. So the Ohio Valley was the only area where the two national groups actually clashed.

7. **(E)** Hamilton and the Federalists wanted a strong central government with broad powers. Jefferson and the Anti-Federalists wanted a central government that exercised a minimum of control and did not intrude in the lives of citizens. Thus Hamilton favored such policies as government stimulation of industrial development (A), the establishment of a national bank (C), and a tax structure to fund government programs (D). These programs required a broad interpretation of the Constitution (B), since they were not specifically permitted in the document.

8. **(E)** The fictional exposé of the meatpacking industry (A) was Upton Sinclair's *The Jungle*. The best known denunciation of big city machine politics (D) was Lincoln Steffens' *The Shame of the Cities*. Descriptions of the life-styles of America's rich and famous (C) became popular in the 1980s. Jacob Riis was a police reporter for the New York *Tribune* and later for the New York *Evening Sun*. His book *How the Other Half Lives* (1890) described New York's slum dwellings and the misery of lower-class urban life (E). The book aroused public demand for social reform but did not lay out a detailed program to accomplish this (B).

9. **(B)** President Ronald Reagan campaigned for office on a platform of lower taxes and government spending. Income tax changes in 1983 and 1986, while lowering overall rates, reduced the rates for upper-income families much

more than the rates for lower-income families (A). Although Reagan's budgets lowered government spending for social programs, they greatly increased government spending for defense. As a result, the federal budget deficit soared. Higher defense expenditures, combined with an increase in the nation's foreign trade deficits, changed the United States from a creditor to a debtor nation (D). Economists were unhappy about these results of Reaganomics, but they were pleased with the drop in the inflation rate (C). However, they tended to worry about the growth in multinational corporations (E), since such companies often tended to move jobs out of the United States to nations with lower wage scales.

10.   **(C)**   The Pilgrims signed the Mayflower Compact in 1620. This was the first *written* framework of government in what was to become the United States. The signers agreed to accept whatever form of government was established after landing. The Fundamental Orders of Connecticut (A) was the constitution adopted by the founders of Hartford in 1639, and was patterned after the government of Massachusetts Bay, which they had left in order to gain more religious freedom. The Navigation Acts (D) were trading regulations enacted by the English Parliament in 1660-1673, designed to tighten control over their colonial commerce, and they had no religious implications. The Great Awakening (E) was the religious revival which swept the American colonies in the 1740s, led by Jonathan Edward and others. The Act of Religious Toleration (B) was enacted by the Maryland assembly in 1649, and guaranteed the right to worship for all Christians, Catholic and Protestant.

11.   **(C)**   Few "hawks" argued that Vietnam was vital to the security of the United States (A). The country lay some 11,000 miles away and did not contain oil or other resources that the United States needed. The Tonkin Gulf incident was an excuse for Americanizing the Vietnam War rather than the reason why the war happened (B). The basic reason why people supported the Vietnam War was their belief that communism had to be contained. The United States, as one of the world's two superpowers (the other being the Soviet Union), was the only nation that could lead the struggle for containment (C). The domino theory, which held that if one nation turned Communist, its neighbors would eventually also turn Communist, developed out of the containment policy (D). Although many "hawks" argued that the United States had never lost a war, that was not the major reason why they supported America's role in Vietnam (E).

12.   **(C)**   Manifest Destiny became a reason for American expansionism in the 1800s. The term originated in the 1840s and was taken up by those desiring to secure the Oregon Territory, California, and Mexican lands in the Southwest. Transcendentalism (A) was the philosophical expression of the romantic movement in the pre-Civil War United States, as embraced by Emerson, Thoreau, and other literary figures. Utopianism (B) was another expression of romanticism which focused on the establishment of self-sufficient communities based on socialist formulas. Brook Farm and New Harmony are examples. States' rights (D) was the political doctrine sponsored by Southern leaders which claimed that the

individual states retained certain sovereign powers even as members of the Union, such as the right to nullify federal laws which they found offensive, and the right of secession if all other appeals failed. Abolitionism (E) was the movement which advocated the immediate and uncompensated freeing of the slaves.

13. **(B)** The South had the advantage of a large agricultural base which ultimately did very little to help it win against the North's military might, superior transportation system, navy, and extensive manpower. Although the North possessed farms sufficient to supply foodstuffs for it people, its primary advantages lay in a population of 22 million as compared to the $5^1/_2$ million non-slave population in the South (E); twice the railroad mileage as in the South, and much better organized and equipped (C); and 81 percent of the manufacturing capacity of the nation (A). In addition, the navy belonged to the Union, and most of the officer corps remained loyal to the Union and formed the nucleus of the powerful naval force which eventually helped strangle the Confederacy (D).

14. **(A)** Ottmar Mergenthaler invented the linotype machine in 1886 (A). It cut printing costs so dramatically that, combined with the invention of the Bullock press and the manufacture of paper from wood pulp instead of wastepaper and rags, it made it possible to sell newspapers and magazines at a price low enough to be afforded by mass audiences. Elisha Otis invented the mechanical elevator. Thomas Edison, who took out more than a thousand patents, is associated with such products as the incandescent light bulb, the phonograph, the microphone, and the motion picture camera, among others. Arthur Little invented plastics, while Leo Baekeland invented rayon. The X-ray tube was developed by William Coolidge.

15. **(D)** The main migration of Americans from farms to cities took place during the Industrial Revolution of the late nineteenth century and the first two decades of the twentieth century (A). Americans moved northward primarily during and after World War I (B) and westward primarily during the 1800s (E). People moved from cities to suburbs rather than the other way round (C). During the 1960s and 1970s, Americans moved to the Sunbelt for two main reasons (D). One was the job opportunities that resulted from the development of electronics, insurance, and banking industries in the South. The other was the region's mild climate and numerous recreational activities. Most of the migrants were either educated young people or retired senior citizens.

16. **(C)** The French abandoned their attempt to build "a path between the seas" in 1889 (B). When Great Britain and Germany tried to collect their debts in Latin America by force, President Theodore Roosevelt convinced the parties to arbitrate the dispute, and arrangements were made for payment of the debts (E). However, Roosevelt wanted to prevent any future European interference in the Western Hemisphere, so he declared that only the United States had the right to interfere in Latin America's internal affairs (C). The issue of friendship among

Latin American nations did not arise (D), nor was there any attempt on the part of the United States to provide massive aid to Latin American governments (A).

17.   **(C)**   Many women became active in the settlement-house movement (A) well before World War I. During the war, women were not barred from working in defense industries (B) but rather were encouraged to take the place of male workers who had been drafted. Women have not yet achieved pay equality (D). Women did not begin organizing to oppose the cult of domesticity (E) until the 1960s. In 1918, Congress approved the so-called Anthony amendment giving women the right to vote (C). The change became part of the Constitution in 1920 when the last of the necessary states ratified the Nineteenth Amendment.

18.   **(E)**   All were complaints of the colonists against the British. Parliamentary taxation was used to support Britain's forces in North America. The colonists claimed the right to tax themselves through their own colonial assemblies. At odds over the issue of the sovereignty of Britain's Parliament, the colonies did reconcile with Britain on a number of occasions. When a Tea Act was imposed on the colonies, the Americans rebelled against an even more oppressive tax and took violent measures. Revolutionary governments were formed in the colonies against the arbitrary power of England. The next step was all-out war.

19.   **(A)**   Massachusetts Bay was the colony established by the Puritans in 1630. Maryland (B) was set up as a refuge for Catholics. The Carolinas (C) were settled by proprietors. New York (D) and New Jersey (E) were gifts to the relatives and friends of the English monarch. Both remained royal colonies.

20.   **(C)**   Automobile manufacturing stimulated supporting industries (B) and helped turn the United States into a nation of paved roads (A). Mobility enabled people to live in a suburb and commute to work in the central city (D). Mobility, combined with the privacy the automobile afforded, also contributed to sexual license (E). Although fewer commuters used railroads once the automobile was mass produced, railroads are still widely used for shipping freight. Thus, the correct answer is (C).

21.   **(B)**   The CCC had several immediate results. About 2.7 million single young men were employed by the CCC (A) for a monthly paycheck of $30 (C). The workers were sent to rural rather than urban areas (D), where they planted some 200 million trees on the Great Plains. The long-term result was the prevention of a second "Dust Bowl." The first "Dust Bowl" was created in the 1930s, after a severe drought on the Great Plains turned up to one foot of topsoil into dust and winds blew the dust eastward in such great quantities that houses were literally buried beneath it. The creation of the "Dust Bowl" set off an exodus of farmers from Oklahoma, Kansas, and Texas to California. The plight of the migrants, who were known mostly as "Okies," was vividly described by John Steinbeck in his book *The Grapes of Wrath*.

22.   **(D)**   Lewis and Clark were sent by President Jefferson to explore the Louisiana Purchase. Their exploration took over two years during which time they found a land route to the Pacific, strengthened U.S. claims to the Oregon Territory, and gathered information about the country and the Native Americans who lived there. They did build a fort, Fort Clatsop, on the Pacific Coast where they wintered before returning east. Florida was occupied and governed by Spain in 1804, and President Jefferson would have hesitated a long time before provoking the Spanish by sending in a team of explorers (A). Jefferson had, upon hearing that France has secretly reacquired Louisiana, initiated negotiations to purchase the city of New Orleans to insure free access to the Gulf of Mexico for the produce of Ohio Valley farmers (B). The Mississippi River (C) had belonged to the United States since the 1783 Treaty of Paris that ended the American Revolution. Only the port of New Orleans was owned by a foreign power. Since the Pacific Coast was not claimed by the United States, the establishment of permanent forts there (E) would have been out of the question. Fort Clatsop was meant only to provide shelter until the departure of the party in the spring.

23.   **(D)**   Mass spectator interest in sports developed in the late 1800s (A). Television did not become popular until after World War II (C). Many Americans flocked to plays or participated in amateur theatrics (E), and radio was popular because, after the initial cost of the instrument, it was free (B). However, the correct answer is (D). Movies were the great means of escape from the misery of the depression. They enabled people to transport themselves in imagination to places where excitement thrived, justice triumphed, and life was both amusing and secure.

24.   **(E)**   The United States established an embargo on the export of oil and other vital products to Japan several months before the Japanese attack on Pearl Harbor (A). The opening of a second front (D) was the decisive strategy employed in the European theater, when Allied forces invaded German-held territory from the west to balance the Soviet invasion of German-held territory from the east. Although the United States dropped atomic bombs on Japan, the action took place during the last week of World War II and involved only two bombs, one of which was dropped on Hiroshima and the other on Nagasaki (B). The use of kamikaze or suicide pilots, who crashed their planes onto the decks of enemy ships, was a strategy employed by the Japanese, not the Allies (C). The correct answer is (E). The Allies attacked only selected islands in the Pacific, bypassing others which they attacked later on after the supply lines to those islands had been cut.

25.   **(C)**   The Bill of Rights, the first ten amendments to the Constitution, protects individual liberties. The Bill of Rights became part of the Constitution in 1791 and has never been amended. The Supremacy Clause (A), found in Article VI of the Constitution, establishes the primary position of the Constitution and all laws of the United States. The Preamble is the introduction to the Constitution,

and sets out the purposes for it creation (B). The "Great Compromise" (D) was the agreement to combine the interests of the large and small states by setting up a bicameral legislature, one house based on representation according to state population, the other on equal delegations from each state. The "Three-Fifths Compromise" (E) was the agreement to count, for purposes of representation in the House of Representatives, only three-fifths of a state's slave population, but to use the same basis for levying direct taxes upon the states.

MINI TEST 2

1. Ⓐ Ⓑ Ⓒ Ⓓ Ⓔ
2. Ⓐ Ⓑ Ⓒ Ⓓ Ⓔ
3. Ⓐ Ⓑ Ⓒ Ⓓ Ⓔ
4. Ⓐ Ⓑ Ⓒ Ⓓ Ⓔ
5. Ⓐ Ⓑ Ⓒ Ⓓ Ⓔ
6. Ⓐ Ⓑ Ⓒ Ⓓ Ⓔ
7. Ⓐ Ⓑ Ⓒ Ⓓ Ⓔ
8. Ⓐ Ⓑ Ⓒ Ⓓ Ⓔ
9. Ⓐ Ⓑ Ⓒ Ⓓ Ⓔ
10. Ⓐ Ⓑ Ⓒ Ⓓ Ⓔ
11. Ⓐ Ⓑ Ⓒ Ⓓ Ⓔ
12. Ⓐ Ⓑ Ⓒ Ⓓ Ⓔ
13. Ⓐ Ⓑ Ⓒ Ⓓ Ⓔ
14. Ⓐ Ⓑ Ⓒ Ⓓ Ⓔ
15. Ⓐ Ⓑ Ⓒ Ⓓ Ⓔ
16. Ⓐ Ⓑ Ⓒ Ⓓ Ⓔ
17. Ⓐ Ⓑ Ⓒ Ⓓ Ⓔ
18. Ⓐ Ⓑ Ⓒ Ⓓ Ⓔ
19. Ⓐ Ⓑ Ⓒ Ⓓ Ⓔ
20. Ⓐ Ⓑ Ⓒ Ⓓ Ⓔ
21. Ⓐ Ⓑ Ⓒ Ⓓ Ⓔ
22. Ⓐ Ⓑ Ⓒ Ⓓ Ⓔ
23. Ⓐ Ⓑ Ⓒ Ⓓ Ⓔ
24. Ⓐ Ⓑ Ⓒ Ⓓ Ⓔ
25. Ⓐ Ⓑ Ⓒ Ⓓ Ⓔ

MINI TEST 2

DIRECTIONS: Choose the correct answer for each of the 25 questions below.

1. The American victory at Saratoga in 1777 was the turning point of the War for Independence because it

   (A) forced Loyalists to side with the Continentals.

   (B) broke the spirit of the British forces.

   (C) convinced the French to join the war against England.

   (D) drove the British out of New York.

   (E) confirmed General Washington's dominance over the British.

2. Which of the following describes the position of the "doves" in the Vietnam War?

   (A) The United States should not support anti-democratic governments like those of South Vietnam.

   (B) Instead of spending money on the war, the United States should spend it on domestic needs.

   (C) The domino theory was not valid.

   (D) The conflict in Vietnam was a civil war in which the United States should not interfere.

   (E) All of the above.

3. The United States adopted the Open Door policy with China in 1899 and 1900 in order to

   (A) protect America's share in the China trade.

   (B) encourage Chinese workers to migrate to the United States.

   (C) obtain a naval base in the Pacific.

   (D) encourage the colonization of China by industrial powers.

   (E) bring about an end to China's war with Japan.

4.   The Supreme Court case of *Korematsu v. United States* (1944) was significant because it

   (A)   prohibited prayer in public schools on the grounds of separation of church and state.

   (B)   upheld the doctrine of "separate but equal" educational facilities for blacks and whites.

   (C)   declared that President Roosevelt's wartime order relocating Japanese-Americans to concentration camps was unconstitutional.

   (D)   upheld President Roosevelt's wartime order relocating Japanese-Americans to concentration camps.

   (E)   ordered the desegregation of public schools.

5.   The issue of the admission of new states to the Union as either free states or slave states was temporarily settled in 1820 by the

   (A)   Kansas-Nebraska Act.

   (B)   Missouri Compromise.

   (C)   Adams-Onis Treaty.

   (D)   Hartford Convention.

   (E)   *Marbury v. Madison* Supreme Court case.

6.   French interest in North America centered on the trade with Native Americans for

   (A)   gold.   (B)   furs.

   (C)   tobacco.   (D)   fish.

   (E)   (B) and (D).

7.   The indenture system established by the Virginia Company of London would have most likely appealed to which of the following?

   (A)   Gentleman-explorers

   (B)   Poor workers in England

   (C)   Tobacco planters in Virginia

   (D)   Native Americans

   (E)   (B) and (C).

8.   The leading scandal of Warren Harding's administration was

   (A)   Watergate.   (B)   Teapot Dome.

(C)   Iran-Contra.   (D)   the Chambers-Hiss case.

(E)   the Black Sox scandal.

9.   Each of the following events was important in the early development of the Cold War between the United States and the Soviet Union EXCEPT

(A)   President Ronald Reagan called for extensive funding of "Star Wars."

(B)   Winston Churchill described the Iron Curtain in a speech.

(C)   President Harry S. Truman announced the "Truman Doctrine."

(D)   the United States airlifted supplies to Berlin.

(E)   George F. Kennan wrote an anonymous article for the magazine *Foreign Affairs.*

10.   The near failure of the Jamestown settlement in its early years was attributed to

(A)   often hostile relations between settlers and Native Americans.

(B)   the belief of some settlers that they were above physical labor.

(C)   the settlers' desire to search for gold instead of planting crops.

(D)   a low, swampy location prone to disease.

(E)   All of the above.

11.   The first Africans were brought to Virginia in

(A)   1622.   (B)   1619.

(C)   1612.   (D)   1607.

(E)   1590.

12.   Robert E. Lee's planned invasion of Pennsylvania and the North's territory was foiled at the three-day battle of

(A)   Bull Run.   (B)   Cold Harbor.

(C)   Vicksburg.   (D)   Gettysburg.

(E)   Petersburg.

13.   The United States annexed Hawaii in 1898 for all of the following reasons EXCEPT

(A)   a political debt to Hawaii's sugar growers.

(B)   the strategic importance of Pearl Harbor as a Pacific naval base.

(C)   a general increase in American interests overseas.

(D)   the activities of American Christian missionaries.

(E)   a desire for land to relieve the overcrowding of American cities.

14.   The Constitutional Convention of 1787 was called together with the initial purpose of

(A)   establishing a new government.

(B)   proclaiming George Washington president.

(C)   establishing an American monarchy.

(D)   revising the Articles of Confederation.

(E)   finding a better way to tax the new states.

15.   English and French explorers of the late 1400s and 1500s explored North America in the hope of finding

(A)   gold and silver.

(B)   the "Seven Cities of Cibola."

(C)   a fabled fountain of youth.

(D)   new lands to colonize.

(E)   a Northwest passage to the Orient.

16.   All of the following inventions aided industrial development in the United States in the late 1800s and early 1900s EXCEPT

(A)   the telephone.   (B)   the electric light.

(C)   rayon.   (D)   the automobile.

(E)   the computer.

17.   The Religious Right supports all of the following EXCEPT

(A)   prayer in the public schools.

(B)   the banning of abortion.

(C)   the teaching of creationism.

(D)   a strong national defense.

(E)   the Equal Rights Amendment.

18.   Passage of the Eighteenth Amendment led to all of the following EXCEPT

(A)   a tremendous increase in organized crime.

(B)   a decline in drunkenness and alcoholism.

(C) an increase in public drinking by women.

(D) an increase in public respect for law enforcement.

(E) a sharp political split on the issue of prohibition.

19. The first attempt at establishing an English settlement in North America was in 1587 at

(A) Newfoundland.   (B) Montreal.

(C) Roanoke Island.   (D) Nova Albion.

(E) St. Augustine.

20. The Immigration Act of 1965

I.   adopted the national origin system.

II.   discontinued the national origin system.

III. based immigration on such things as skills and the need for political asylum.

IV. was deeply resented by such groups as Italian-Americans and Polish-Americans.

(A) I only.   (B) II only.

(C) I and IV.   (D) II and III.

(E) I and III.

21. The intention of President James Monroe in issuing the Monroe Doctrine was to

(A) drive Britain from Canada.

(B) establish American control in Mexico.

(C) warn European nations not to attempt further colonization in the Americas.

(D) declare war on France.

(E) drive Native Americans from the East Coast to lands west of the Mississippi River.

22. French exploration and settlement of North America was helped by the establishment in 1608 of a trading post on the St. Lawrence River called

(A) Plymouth.   (B) Montreal.

(C) Fort Orange.   (D) Quebec.

(E) New Amsterdam.

23. Which of the following authors is correctly paired with a work that he wrote?

    (A) Upton Sinclair: *The Red Badge of Courage*

    (B) Mark Twain: *The Gilded Age*

    (C) Henry James: *The Jungle*

    (D) Jack London: *The Adventures of Huckleberry Finn*

    (E) Stephen Crane: *The Call of the Wild*

24. President Franklin D. Roosevelt established the Fair Employment Practices Committee in 1941 to ensure consideration for minorities in defense employment largely because

    (A) the southern wing of the Democratic party strongly supported the idea.

    (B) the northern wing of the Democratic party strongly supported the idea.

    (C) A. Philip Randolph, the president of the Brotherhood of Sleeping Car Porters, proposed a black march on Washington.

    (D) he believed it would help insure his reelection in 1944 because blacks and other minorities would vote for him.

    (E) his wife, Eleanor, nagged him to do so.

25. The Dutch colony of New Netherlands was centered on large estates worked by tenant farmers who were transported to the New World by wealthy landowners called

    (A) freemen.   (B) patroons.

    (C) governors.   (D) burgesses.

    (E) monarchs.

MINI TEST 2

ANSWER KEY

1. (C)	6. (E)	11. (B)	16. (E)	21. (C)
2. (E)	7. (E)	12. (D)	17. (E)	22. (D)
3. (A)	8. (B)	13. (E)	18. (D)	23. (B)
4. (D)	9. (A)	14. (D)	19. (C)	24. (C)
5. (B)	10. (E)	15. (E)	20. (D)	25. (B)

DETAILED EXPLANATIONS
OF ANSWERS

1.   **(C)**   The Battle of Saratoga was the first time an entire British army surrendered. France, observing the abilities of the Americans, openly recognized American independence and sent aid. The Loyalists, those American colonists who remained loyal to the King, continued to fight the independence movement, and were involved in the fight at King's Mountain in 1780, as well as other battles (A). Certainly the British forces continued the struggle and won major victories at Charleston and Camden, South Carolina, just before their final defeat at Yorktown (B). Generals John Stark and Horatio Gates led the Continental armies at Saratoga, not George Washington (E). The British armies did leave New York following the Saratoga surrender, but primarily because they undertook a different strategy—an invasion of the South (D). The French alliance proved to be the significant turning point of the war.

2.   **(E)**   The position of the "doves" in the Vietnam War combined a belief that the United States should focus on its domestic problems and a belief that elements of American foreign policy exaggerated the direct dangers of communism to the United States. Many "doves" supported Lyndon Johnson's War on Poverty and felt that the United States could not pay for both "guns and butter" (B). Many "doves" argued that just because one nation turned Communist, that did not automatically mean that every other nearby nation would likewise become Communist (C). There were other factors to be considered, such as the strength of the local economy and the devotion of the people to democracy. Many "doves" opposed supporting authoritarian regimes just because they were anti-Communist (A). Most important of all, perhaps, was the belief on the part of the "doves" that the war in Vietnam was basically a civil war and it was not possible for the United States to police the world (D). Thus, the correct answer is (E).

3.   **(A)**   The United States first suspended Chinese immigration in 1882 (B). The United States already had naval bases in the Pacific (C), since it had obtained Pearl Harbor in 1886 and had annexed the Philippines in 1898. One of the reasons for the Open Door policy was to prevent the colonization of China by industrial powers (D). The Sino-Japanese War had ended in 1895 (E) with an overwhelming victory for Japan. Thus, the correct answer is (A).

4.   **(D)**   After the bombing of Pearl Harbor in December of 1941, many people in California, Oregon, and Washington became convinced that the bombing could not have taken place unless the enemy planes were aided by people of Japanese descent in the United States. There was also a great deal of jealousy of Japanese-Americans because of their economic success as farmers and small-businesspeople. As a result of political pressure, President Franklin D. Roosevelt

issued an executive order relocating about 120,000 Japanese-Americans from western states to ten concentration camps in California, Arizona, and Arkansas. The president justified his order on the grounds of national security. The internees were not released until almost the end of World War II. However, Americans of German or Italian descent were not interned, which indicated that a major reason for the relocation of Japanese-Americans was unabashed racism rather than national security. After the war ended, the federal government paid the former internees $35 million as compensation for their lost homes, farms, and businesses, although the actual value of the lost property was estimated to have been $400 million. In 1988, Congress apologized to Japanese-Americans for the internment order and ordered a tax-free payment of $20,000 to each former internee who was still living.

5.   **(B)**   The Missouri Compromise temporarily settled the issue of slavery in the states that were being carved out of the Louisiana Territory. Missouri was admitted as a slave state, Maine was admitted as a free state, and slavery was prohibited north of the 36 degrees, 30 minutes line of latitude. The Kansas-Nebraska Act (A), passed in 1854, gave the inhabitants of those two new territories the option of legalizing slavery or not. The effect of this bill was to effectively nullify the Missouri Compromise (B). The Adams-Onis Treaty (C) was the agreement between the United States and Spain, signed in 1819, by which all of Florida was ceded to the United States, and we in turn gave up our claims to Texas. The Hartford Convention (D) met in 1814 and consisted of delegates from the New England states who were unhappy with President Madison's handling of the war with England. They discussed secession from the Union, but cooler heads prevailed, and nothing came of it. The case of *Marbury v. Madison* (E), decided in 1803, involved the claim of a Federalist appointee against the new Republican secretary of state, James Madison, for non-delivery of his commission as justice of the peace. Chief Justice John Marshall, himself a Federalist, used this case to establish for the Supreme Court the power to rule on the constitutional validity of federal laws.

6.   **(E)**   The French traded with Native Americans for furs (B) and fish (D), both of which existed in bounty in North America. Gold (A) was not available in eastern North America in colonial times, and tobacco (C) was raised in quantity only by the English in the Chesapeake colonies.

7.   **(E)**   Both poor English workers (C) and tobacco planters (B) would have supported the indenture system. The system provided a way for the poor of England to find work and a new life in the New World. Planters benefited because they could be assured of a steady work force for a specific period of time. Gentlemen-explorers would not have been looking for a labor supply, since they usually operated alone or in small groups (A). Native Americans were unaffected by the indenture system except insofar as they were further displaced from their land by the ever-spreading communities of European settlers (D).

8. **(B)** The Watergate scandal led to the resignation of President Richard Nixon (A). The Iran-Contra scandal—which involved using money from the illegal sale of arms to Iran to help equip the Nicaraguan *contras*—took place during Ronald Reagan's second term (C). The Whittaker Chambers-Alger Hiss case, in which Chambers accused Hiss of being a Communist agent and Hiss was convicted of perjury for denying the accusation, took place when Harry S. Truman was president (D). The Black Sox scandal, which affected the integrity of major league baseball when it was revealed that members of the Chicago White Sox team had accepted bribes to throw ball games, occurred in 1919, during the administration of Woodrow Wilson (E). The correct answer is (B). Harding's Secretary of the Interior, Albert Fall, secretly leased naval oil reserves at Teapot Dome to several oil company executives in exchange for money and other gifts. Fall was later convicted, fined, and imprisoned for bribery.

9. **(A)** Winston Churchill's speech at Fulton, Missouri, in March of 1946 was the first graphic description of the post World War II situation in Europe (B). Churchill used the term "Iron Curtain" to refer to the barrier of secrecy and censorship that separated the democratic nations of Europe, with their free elections and freedom of speech and press, from the authoritarian nations now controlled by the Soviet Union. That same year, career diplomat George F. Kennan, in an anonymous article for the magazine *Foreign Affairs* (E), called for "containment" of communism, that is, for steady pressure to keep the Soviets from extending their power. In 1947, President Harry S. Truman stated that the United States must support free peoples who were resisting Communist domination (C). As a consequence of the Truman Doctrine, the United States sent missions in economic and military aid to Greece and Turkey, and the danger of Communist governments being set up in those two countries more or less disappeared. In 1948, the Soviet Union instituted a blockade of Berlin to protest the decision by the United States, France, and Great Britain to unify their zones of Western Germany (D). The airlift lasted for almost a year, until the Soviet Union realized that it was beaten and lifted the blockade. President Ronald Reagan's call for spending trillions of dollars on a computer-controlled strategic defense initiative, popularly known as "Star Wars," did not take place until 1983. Thus, the correct answer is (A).

10. **(E)** Jamestown was nearly undone by a combination of factors: a poor location, often inhospitable Native Americans, and the lack of a skilled work force dedicated to planting crops. Relations with the Indians in Virginia deteriorated until 1622, when an Indian uprising almost destroyed the colony and forced its bankruptcy and takeover by the Crown. John Smith's dictatorial rule was necessitated by the refusal of some English "gentlemen" to stoop to physical labor (B), and the early infatuation with the desire to search for gold rather than work the gardens (C). The eventual removal of the settlement inland to the site of Williamsburg in the 1690s was necessitated by the perennial outbreaks of malarial fevers from the swampy location on the river (D).

11. **(B)** The first Africans were brought to Virginia in 1619 as indentured workers and not as slaves. Blacks became enslaved later as colonial codes were set up to control their movements, prohibit intermarriage with whites, and tie them to the plantations of the South. The Roanoke colony disappeared in 1590 (E), and there were no blacks in that settlement. The Jamestown colony was established in 1607 (D), but no black workers were imported there. John Rolfe began to experiment in 1612 with tobacco culture in Virginia (C), and in 1622 (A) a massive Indian uprising against the Virginia settlement came close to destroying the colony.

12. **(D)** Gettysburg was the climatic battle of the Civil War. Lee lost more than 20,000 men and was unable to succeed in a large-scale invasion of the North. Bull Run is the name given to two battles at Manassas, Virginia, in 1861 and 1862, both of which were resounding Confederate victories (A). Cold Harbor (B) was fought in northern Virginia in the summer of 1864 as Grant was driving on Richmond, and was also a repulse of the Union army. Petersburg (E) was a result of that drive, and turned into a winter-long siege of that city by Grant's army. Vicksburg (C) was the last Confederate stronghold on the Mississippi River, and it fell the same day, July 4, 1863, that Lee's defeated army left the field at Gettysburg.

13. **(E)** Hawaii's sugar planters had played a major role in overthrowing the native Hawaiian government in 1893 and establishing a new government friendly to the United States (A). The United States could more easily protect its naval base at Pearl Harbor if it owned Hawaii (B). The United States gradually became involved in the "new imperialism" of the late 1800s, which was geared to finding markets for surplus industrial production, access to needed raw materials, and opportunities for overseas investment (C). American Christian missionaries were extremely active in Hawaii and supported American rule there (D). The United States never considered sending its "surplus" population to other places. Thus, the correct answer is (E).

14. **(D)** The delegates to the Constitutional Convention wanted to reform the existing Articles of Confederation which, in the view of many, was too weak to solve the problems of the young nation. The convention ended up discarding the Articles, and framed an entirely new government. The idea of drafting a completely new Constitution would have been unacceptable to the voters who elected them to go to Philadelphia, and their instructions specified revision, not replacement, of the Articles (A). George Washington went to Philadelphia as a delegate, but the executive office of President did not exist before the new Constitution was drafted (B). There was some sentiment for the creation of a monarchy, but it was a minority view (C). One of the failures of the Articles government was in the collection of taxes (E), but regulation of trade and internal order were much more pressing issues in the minds of delegates particularly as news of Shays's Rebellion reached Philadelphia.

15.   **(E)**   The English and French hoped to find a large river or series of waterways through the North American continent to the Orient. Their primary concern in exploring North America was access to the riches of Asia via a Northwest Passage. Although precious metals (A) would have been a welcome find for the English and French explorers, like John Cabot and Jacques Cartier, their motives were more commercial. Until after 1600, no serious attempts were made to establish permanent colonies in the New World (D). The Seven Cities of Cibola was the objective of the Spaniard Coronado's venture into the North American southwest in the 1540s (B), while Spain's Ponce de Leon searched unsuccessfully for the fountain of youth in Florida (C).

16.   **(E)**   The telephone (A) speeded up communication; the electric light (B) enabled business to be carried out in the absence of direct sunlight; and the automobile (D) improved transportation and spawned a variety of new industries, while the invention of rayon (C) and other synthetic fibers helped the textile industry expand. Although the computer (E) increased the speed at which businesses transactions are completed, it was not developed until the 1940s.

17.   **(E)**   Many members of the Religious Right are fundamentalists who interpret the Bible literally. As a result, they reject scientific hypotheses about the creation of the universe and support the teaching of creationism (C), which asserts that God created the world in six days and that the different species that inhabit the world have not evolved. Members of the Religious Right are disturbed about what they see as a decline in traditional values, especially those having to do with the family. Accordingly, they oppose abortion (B) and believe that a woman's place is in the home (E). They also believe that prayer in public schools (A) would encourage a return to traditional values, which include keeping the United States militarily powerful (D).

18.   **(D)**   The passage of the Eighteenth Amendment meant that people had to spend more to obtain liquor illegally. This led to somewhat lower consumption, which in turn brought about a decline in drunkenness and alcoholism (B). At the same time, it made the smuggling of liquor into the United States from Canada a highly lucrative endeavor, and the trade soon came under the control of organized crime (A). To market the smuggled liquor, criminals opened speakeasies, which attracted women customers as well as men (C). Although federal agents made numerous attempts to close down the speakeasies, most local policemen turned a blind eye to them, often in exchange for bribes. This corruption of law enforcement officials, combined with a widespread absence of popular support for prohibition, led to a sharp division among voters as to whether or not the Eighteenth Amendment was a good idea (E). Thus, the correct answer is (D).

19.   **(C)**   Roanoke Island was an unsuccessful attempt at establishing an English colony in North America. Its inhabitants disappeared without a trace in 1590. Newfoundland had been visited seasonally for years by English fishermen,

but no attempts to settle permanently were made before 1600 (A). Nova Albion means "New England," and the cod fisheries there attracted only seasonal fishermen until 1620, when the Plymouth Company sent out the *Mayflower* (D). Montreal (B) was established by the French in 1642; St. Augustine by the Spanish in 1565 (E).

20.   **(D)**   The Immigration Act of 1965 dropped the national origin system that had been adopted by the Immigration Act of 1924 and that discriminated against immigrants from southern and eastern Europe. Instead, the 1965 act based immigration quotas on such things as skills and the need for political asylum.

21.   **(C)**   The Monroe Doctrine placed the Americas outside of further European colonization and intervention. The doctrine became a cornerstone of American foreign policy. The idea arose from the political realignments taking place in Europe following the defeat of Napoleon in 1815. The Latin American nations has just established their independence during the upheavals of the Napoleonic years, and the newly reestablished monarchies, particularly in Spain and Portugal, were moving to reassert their claims to their rebellious American colonies. Monroe's statement was not meant as a claim on Mexico (B) or any other neighbor, nor as a threat of war (D), but to declare the Western Hemisphere closed to European expansion. Since he was depending on the British navy to enforce this declaration, he certainly had no intentions of threatening British colonial possessions (A). Andrew Jackson was the president who drove the Native Americans from their homes in the East, across the Mississippi River to the newly designated Indian Territory, in 1830 (E).

22.   **(D)**   Quebec was established as a trading post in 1608 by Samuel de Champlain. New France eventually spread out from this gateway on the St. Lawrence River. Plymouth (A) was established by English dissenters we call Pilgrims, in 1620. Montreal (B) was founded by the French as a fur trade exchange post in 1642. New Amsterdam (E) was founded by the Dutch in 1624 as a trading post to service the Hudson River Valley. Fort Orange (C) was a Dutch settlement on the present site of Albany, New York, established in 1617.

23.   **(B)**   *The Gilded Age* (1873), which Mark Twain wrote in collaboration with Charles Dudley Warner, satirized the materialism and corruption of the 1870s so effectively that most historians have since applied the term to that particular period in American history. Twain's *The Adventures of Huckleberry Finn* (1884) not only evokes the author's boyhood in Hannibal, Missouri, but is also a slashing attack against racial prejudice. The correct matches for the other answer choices are: Upton Sinclair—*The Jungle*; Jack London—*The Call of the Wild*; Stephen Crane—*The Red Badge of Courage;* Henry James—no work cited.

24.   **(C)**   Neither the northern wing (B) nor the southern wing (A) of the Democratic party was especially concerned about equalizing job opportunities for African-Americans in the 1940s. Roosevelt's action in setting up the FEPC

would not have garnered him many votes in 1944 (D), especially since blacks in many southern states were prevented from voting by restrictive requirements—including poll taxes and unfair literacy tests—for voter registration. Although Eleanor Roosevelt was a strong supporter of civil rights for African-Americans and urged her husband to take more positive steps in that area, F.D.R. issued his executive order in 1941 only after A. Philip Randolph threatened to lead a march of tens of thousands of blacks to Washington if the president did not do so (C).

25.　**(B)**　The colony of New Netherlands was organized around the patroon system. The few patroon families came to dominate life in the Dutch colony of present-day New York. The term "freemen" (A) would apply more appropriately to the English settlers in Virginia and Massachusetts Bay. The Dutch patroons were landowners and were subject themselves to the governor in New Amsterdam (C). Burgesses (D) were representatives to the colonial legislature in Virginia. Monarchs (E) were the kings of the European mother countries, who never visited their American possessions.

The ESSENTIALS®
of HISTORY

REA's **Essentials of History** series offers a new approach to the study of history that is different from what has been available previously. Compared with conventional history outlines, the **Essentials of History** offer far more detail, with fuller explanations and interpretations of historical events and developments. Compared with voluminous historical tomes and textbooks, the **Essentials of History** offer a far more concise, less ponderous overview of each of the periods they cover.

The **Essentials of History** provide quick access to needed information, and will serve as handy reference sources at all times. The **Essentials of History** are prepared with REA's customary concern for high professional quality and student needs.

UNITED STATES HISTORY
1500 to 1789 From Colony to Republic
1789 to 1841 The Developing Nation
1841 to 1877 Westward Expansion & the Civil War
1877 to 1912 Industrialism, Foreign Expansion & the Progressive Era
1912 to 1941 World War I, the Depression & the New Deal
America since 1941: Emergence as a World Power

WORLD HISTORY
Ancient History (4500 BCE to 500 CE)
The Emergence of Western Civilization
Medieval History (500 to 1450 CE)
The Middle Ages

EUROPEAN HISTORY
1450 to 1648 The Renaissance, Reformation & Wars of Religion
1648 to 1789 Bourbon, Baroque & the Enlightenment
1789 to 1848 Revolution & the New European Order
1848 to 1914 Realism & Materialism
1914 to 1935 World War I & Europe in Crisis
Europe since 1935: From World War II to the Demise of Communism

CANADIAN HISTORY
Pre-Colonization to 1867
The Beginning of a Nation
1867 to Present
The Post-Confederate Nation

*If you would like more information about any of these books,
complete the coupon below and return it to us or visit your local bookstore.*

Research & Education Association
61 Ethel Road W., Piscataway, NJ 08854
Phone: (732) 819-8880   **website: www.rea.com**

Please send me more information about your History Essentials® books.

Name _____

Address _____

City _____ State _____ Zip _____

Research & Education Association

VERBAL BUILDER:

An Excellent Review *for* Standardized Tests

Specifically designed to prepare you for all tests requiring verbal ability, including

SAT • ACT • GRE • GMAT
LSAT • MCAT • CBEST
PRAXIS • PPST • PSAT
CLEP • CLAST

Available at your local bookstore or order directly from us by sending in coupon below.

Research & Education Association
61 Ethel Road W., Piscataway, NJ 08854
Phone: (732) 819-8880   **website: www.rea.com**

VISA   MasterCard

☐ Payment Enclosed
☐ Visa   ☐ MasterCard

Charge Card Number

| | | | | | | | | | | | | | | | |

Expiration Date: _____ / _____
Mo.   Yr.

Please ship REA's **"Verbal Builder"** @ $16.95 plus $4.00 for shipping.

Name _____

Address _____

City _____ State _____ Zip _____

Available at your local bookstore or order directly from us by sending in coupon below.

Research & Education Association
61 Ethel Road W., Piscataway, NJ 08854
Phone: (732) 819-8880   **website: www.rea.com**

VISA   **MasterCard**

☐ Payment Enclosed
☐ Visa   ☐ MasterCard

Charge Card Number

Expiration Date: _____ / _____
Mo.   Yr.

Please ship REA's **"GRE General w/ Software"** @ $35.95 plus $4.00 for shipping.

Name _____

Address _____

City _____ State _____ Zip _____

REA'S
PROBLEM SOLVERS®

PROBLEM SOLVERS

Physics

The Perfect Resource for:
- any class
- any exam
- any problem

A Reference for Life

The PROBLEM SOLVERS® are comprehensive supplemental textbooks designed to save time in finding solutions to problems. Each PROBLEM SOLVER® is the first of its kind ever produced in its field. It is the product of a massive effort to illustrate almost any imaginable problem in exceptional depth, detail, and clarity. Each problem is worked out in detail with a step-by-step solution, and the problems are arranged in order of complexity from elementary to advanced. Each book is fully indexed for locating problems rapidly.

Accounting	Genetics
Advanced Calculus	Geometry
Algebra & Trigonometry	Linear Algebra
Automatic Control Systems/Robotics	Mechanics
Biology	Numerical Analysis
Business, Accounting & Finance	Operations Research
Calculus	Organic Chemistry
Chemistry	Physics
Differential Equations	Pre-Calculus
Economics	Probability
Electrical Machines	Psychology
Electric Circuits	Statistics
Electromagnetics	Technical Design Graphics
Electronics	Thermodynamics
Finite & Discrete Math	Topology
Fluid Mechanics/Dynamics	Transport Phenomena

If you would like more information about any of these books,
complete the coupon below and return it to us or visit your local bookstore.

Research & Education Association
61 Ethel Road W., Piscataway, NJ 08854
Phone: (732) 819-8880   **website: www.rea.com**

Please send me more information about your Problem Solver® books.

Name _____

Address _____

City _____ State _____ Zip _____

REA's Test Preps
The Best in Test Preparation

- REA "Test Preps" are **far more** comprehensive than any other test preparation series
- Each book contains up to **eight** full-length practice tests based on the most recent exams
- **Every** type of question likely to be given on the exams is included
- Answers are accompanied by **full** and **detailed** explanations

REA publishes over 70 Test Preparation volumes in several series. They include:

Advanced Placement Exams (APs)
Biology
Calculus AB & Calculus BC
Chemistry
Economics
English Language & Composition
English Literature & Composition
European History
French
Government & Politics
Physics B & C
Psychology
Spanish Language
Statistics
United States History
World History

College-Level Examination Program (CLEP)
Analyzing and Interpreting Literature
College Algebra
Freshman College Composition
General Examinations
General Examinations Review
History of the United States I
History of the United States II
Human Growth and Development
Introductory Sociology
Principles of Marketing
Spanish

SAT Subject Tests
Biology E/M
Chemistry
English Language Proficiency Test
French
German

SAT Subject Tests (cont'd)
Literature
Mathematics Level 1, 2
Physics
Spanish
United States History

Graduate Record Exams (GREs)
Biology
Chemistry
Computer Science
General
Literature in English
Mathematics
Physics
Psychology

ACT - ACT Assessment

ASVAB - Armed Services Vocational Aptitude Battery

CBEST - California Basic Educational Skills Test

CDL - Commercial Driver License Exam

CLAST - College Level Academic Skills Test

COOP & HSPT - Catholic High School Admission Tests

ELM - California State University Entry Level Mathematics Exam

FE (EIT) - Fundamentals of Engineering Exams - For both AM & PM Exams

FTCE - Florida Teacher Certification Exam

GED - High School Equivalency Diploma Exam (U.S. & Canadian editions)

GMAT - Graduate Management Admission Test

LSAT - Law School Admission Test

MAT - Miller Analogies Test

MCAT - Medical College Admission Test

MTEL - Massachusetts Tests for Educator Licensure

NJ HSPA - New Jersey High School Proficiency Assessment

NYSTCE: LAST & ATS-W - New York State Teacher Certification

PLT - Principles of Learning & Teaching Tests

PPST - Pre-Professional Skills Tests

PSAT / NMSQT

SAT

TExES - Texas Examinations of Educator Standards

THEA - Texas Higher Education Assessment

TOEFL - Test of English as a Foreign Language

TOEIC - Test of English for International Communication

USMLE Steps 1,2,3 - U.S. Medical Licensing Exams

U.S. Postal Exams 460 & 470

Research & Education Association
61 Ethel Road W., Piscataway, NJ 08854
Phone: (732) 819-8880   **website: www.rea.com**

Please send me more information about your Test Prep books.

Name _____

Address _____

City _____ State _____ Zip _____

REA's Test Prep Books Are The Best!

(a sample of the <u>hundreds of letters</u> REA receives each year)

" I am writing to congratulate you on preparing an exceptional study guide. In five years of teaching this course I have never encountered a more thorough, comprehensive, concise and realistic preparation for this examination. "
Teacher, Davie, FL

" I have found your publications, *The Best Test Preparation...*, to be exactly that. "
Teacher, Aptos, CA

" I used your *CLEP Introductory Sociology* book and rank it 99% — thank you! "
Student, Jerusalem, Israel

" Your *GMAT* book greatly helped me on the test. Thank you. "
Student, Oxford, OH

" I recently got the *French SAT II* Exam book from REA. I congratulate you on first-rate French practice tests. "
Instructor, Los Angeles, CA

" Your *AP English Literature and Composition* book is most impressive. "
Student, Montgomery, AL

" The REA *LSAT* Test Preparation guide is a winner! "
Instructor, Spartanburg, SC

(more on front page)